SCOTT FORESMAN

Reading STREET

FLORIDA

Grade **5** Unit **4**

Adapting

PEARSON
Scott Foresman

scottforesman.com

Editorial Offices: Glenview, Illinois • Parsippany, New Jersey • New York, New York
Sales Offices: Boston, Massachusetts • Duluth, Georgia • Glenview, Illinois
Coppell, Texas • Sacramento, California • Mesa, Arizona

We dedicate Reading Street to
Peter Jovanovich.

His wisdom, courage,
and passion for education
are an inspiration to us all.

Cover Greg Newbold

About the Cover Artist

Award-winning artist Greg Newbold began drawing and painting at age three—and never stopped. His illustrated books for children include *Spring Song* and *Winter Lullaby*. Mr. Newbold also does illustrations for magazines, motion pictures, and food products, such as catsup and jelly. He creates his illustrations in a studio next to his house, snuggled in the Rocky Mountains of Utah.

ISBN-13: 978-0-328-24447-8

ISBN-10:   0-328-24447-3

Copyright © 2009 Pearson Education, Inc.

1 2 3 4 5 6 7 8 9 10 V064 16 15 14 13 12 11 10 09 08 07

Reading STREET

Where the Love of Reading Begins

Florida

Adapting

How do people and animals adapt to different situations?

Weslandia

A boy changes the world around him.

FICTION

connect to **SOCIAL STUDIES**

Stretching Ourselves

Young people make the most of their lives.

EXPOSITORY NONFICTION

connect to **SCIENCE**

Exploding Ants

Insects adapt to their environment.

EXPOSITORY NONFICTION

connect to **SCIENCE**

The Stormi Giovanni Club

A girl adapts to a new school.

PLAY

connect to **SOCIAL STUDIES**

The Gymnast

A boy tries to turn himself into an athlete.

AUTOBIOGRAPHY

connect to **SOCIAL STUDIES**

Unit 4
Skills Overview

 **FCAT Tested Skill**

		WEEK 1	**WEEK 2**
		396–411 **Weslandia/ Under the Back Porch/ Keziah** *How do people adapt to difficult situations?* **FICTION**	416–435 **Stretching Ourselves/ Helpful Tools** *How do people adapt to living with physical limitations?* **EXPOSITORY NONFICTION**
Reading	**Comprehension**	**T** Skill Draw Conclusions Strategy Answer Questions **T** REVIEW Skill Main Idea	**T** Skill Generalize Strategy Predict **T** REVIEW Skill Graphic Sources
	Vocabulary	**T** Strategy Word Structure	**T** Strategy Context Clues
	Fluency	Punctuation Clues/Accuracy	Emotion/Accuracy
Word Work	**Spelling and Phonics**	Words From Many Cultures	Prefixes *over-, under-, sub-, super-, out-*
Oral Language	**Speaking/Listening/ Viewing**	Demonstration Analyze Illustrations	Oral Presentation Listen to Oral Presentations
Language Arts	**Grammar, Usage, and Mechanics**	**T** Subject and Object Pronouns	**T** Pronouns and Antecedents
	Weekly Writing	E-Mail Writing Trait: Conventions	Journal Entry Writing Trait: Focus/Ideas
	Unit Process Writing	Story	Story
	Research and Study Skills	Instruction Manual	Technology: Telephone Directory
	Integrate Science and Social Studies Standards	Society, Culture, Government	Human Body Systems, Physical Limitations, Disease

FCAT READING TEST PREPARATION
Writing in Response to Literature

Practice for short response
See Reader Response pages:
Weeks 1, 3, 4, 5

Practice for extended response
See Reader Response page:
Week 2

How do people and animals adapt to different situations?

WEEK 3	**WEEK 4**	**WEEK 5**

440–457
Exploding Ants/The Creature from the Adapting Lagoon

EXPOSITORY NONFICTION

How do animals adapt to survive?

462–483
The Stormi Giovanni Club/Think Dress Codes Are a Drag?

PLAY

How do people adapt to a new school?

488–503
The Gymnast/All About Gymnastics

AUTOBIOGRAPHY

Why do people try to change themselves?

T ◎ **Skill** Graphic Sources ◎ **Strategy** Monitor and Fix Up T REVIEW **Skill** Author's Purpose	T ◎ **Skill** Generalize ◎ **Strategy** Story Structure T REVIEW **Skill** Draw Conclusions	T ◎ **Skill** Draw Conclusions ◎ **Strategy** Visualize T REVIEW **Skill** Generalize
T ◎ **Strategy** Context Clues	T ◎ **Strategy** Context Clues	T ◎ **Strategy** Word Structure
Tempo and Rate/Accuracy	Tone of Voice/Accuracy	Punctuation Clues/Accuracy
Homophones	Suffixes *-ible, -able*	Negative Prefixes
Description Listen to Poetry	Advice Listen to Advice	Informational Speech Analyze Media
T Possessive Pronouns	T Indefinite and Reflexive Pronouns	T Using *Who* and *Whom*
Tell a Story About an Animal Writing Trait: Support/Word Choice	Advice Writing Trait: Support/Voice	Tell How You Achieved a Goal Writing Trait: Support/Word Choice
Story	Story	Story
Magazine/Periodical	Thesaurus	Graphs

Animals, Environments-Biomes, Adaptations	Individual Development, Interactions, Groups, Communication	Individual Development and Identity, Sports

FCAT WRITING+ TEST PREPARATION

Trait of the Week

Week 1 Conventions
Week 2 Focus/Ideas
Week 3 Support/Word Choice

Week 4 Support/Voice
Week 5 Support/Word Choice

◎ **Target Skill**
T **Tested Skill**

Skills Overview   390d

Unit 4
Monitor Progress

 **FCAT Tested Skill**

Predictors of Reading Success		WEEK 1	WEEK 2	WEEK 3	WEEK 4
WCPM	**Fluency**	Punctuation Clues 120–128 WCPM	Emotion 120–128 WCPM	Tempo and Rate 120–128 WCPM	Tone of Voice 120–128 WCPM
Vocabulary	**Vocabulary/ Concept Development** (assessed informally)	barren edible island livestock	dedication leg brace polio triumphant	African black mambas constrictors reptiles	count on settle in
	Lesson Vocabulary	**Strategy** Word Structure blunders civilization complex envy fleeing inspired rustling strategy	**Strategy** Context Clues abdomen artificial gait handicapped therapist wheelchair	**Strategy** Context Clues critical enables mucus scarce specialize sterile	**Strategy** Context Clues cavities combination demonstrates episode profile strict
Retelling	**Text Comprehension**	**Skill** Draw Conclusions **Strategy** Answer Questions	**Skill** Generalize **Strategy** Predict	**Skill** Graphic Sources **Strategy** Monitor and Fix Up	**Skill** Generalize **Strategy** Story Structure

🔵 **Target Skill**   ⚙️ **SuccessTracker/Unit 4 Benchmark Tested Skills**

Make Data–Driven Decisions

Data Management	Classroom Management
• Assess	• Monitor Progress
• Diagnose	• Group
• Prescribe	• Differentiate Instruction
• Disaggregate	• Inform Parents

WEEK 5

Punctuation Clues

120–128 WCPM

champion
competitive
develop
perfected

Strategy Word
Structure

bluish
cartwheels
gymnastics
hesitation
limelight
skidded
somersault
throbbing
wincing

Skill Draw
Conclusions

Strategy
Visualize

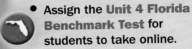

ONLINE CLASSROOM

Manage Data

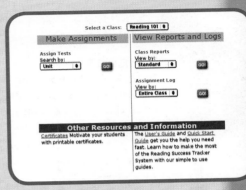

- Assign the **Unit 4 Florida Benchmark Test** for students to take online.

- SuccessTracker records results and generates reports by school, grade, classroom, or student.

- Use reports to disaggregate and aggregate Unit 4 skills and standards data to monitor progress.

- Based on class lists created to support the categories important for AYP (gender, ethnicity, migrant education, English proficiency, disabilities, economic status), reports let you track adequate yearly progress every six weeks.

Group

- Use results from **Unit 4 Florida Benchmark Tests** taken online through SuccessTracker to regroup students.

- Reports in SuccessTracker suggest appropriate groups for students based on test results.

Individualize Instruction

- Tests are correlated to Unit 4 tested skills and standards so that prescriptions for individual teaching and learning plans can be created.

- Individualized prescriptions target instruction and accelerate student progress toward learning outcome goals.

- Prescriptions include resources to reteach Unit 4 skills and standards.

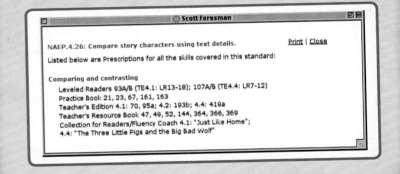

NAEP.4.26: Compare story characters using text details.   Print | Close

Listed below are Prescriptions for all the skills covered in this standard:

Comparing and contrasting
Leveled Readers 93A/B (TE4.1: LR13-18); 107A/B (TE4.4: LR7-12)
Practice Book: 21, 23, 67, 161, 163
Teacher's Edition 4.1: 70, 95a; 4.2: 193b; 4.4: 419a
Teacher's Resource Book 47, 49, 52, 144, 364, 366, 369
Collection for Readers/Fluency Coach 4.1: "Just Like Home";
4.4: "The Three Little Pigs and the Big Bad Wolf"

Grouping for AYP

STEP 1

Diagnose and Differentiate

Diagnose

To make initial grouping decisions, use the Baseline Group Test or another initial placement test. Depending on students' ability levels, you may have more than one of each group.

Differentiate

If... student performance is **Below-Level** **then**... use the regular instruction and the daily Strategic Intervention lessons, pp. DI•2–DI•50.

If... student performance is **On-Level** **then**... use the regular instruction for On-Level learners throughout each selection.

If... student performance is **Advanced** **then**... use the regular instruction and the daily instruction for Advanced learners, pp. DI•3–DI•51.

Group Time

On-Level

- Explicit instructional routines teach core skills and strategies.
- Independent activities provide practice for core skills and extension and enrichment options.
- Leveled readers (LR1–45) provide additional reading and practice with core skills and vocabulary.

Strategic Intervention

- Daily Strategic Intervention lessons provide more intensive instruction, more scaffolding, more practice with critical skills, and more opportunities to respond.
- Reteach lessons (DI•52–DI•56) provide additional instructional opportunities with target skills.
- Leveled readers instruction (LR1–45) builds background for the main selection and provides practice with target skills and vocabulary.

Advanced

- Daily Advanced Lessons provide compacted instruction for accelerated learning, options for investigative work, and challenging reading content.
- Leveled readers (LR1–45) provide additional reading tied to lesson concepts.

Additional opportunities to differentiate instruction:
- Reteach Lessons, pp. DI•52–DI•516
- Leveled Reader Instruction and Leveled Practice, LR1–45
- My Sidewalks on Scott Foresman Reading Street Intensive Reading Intervention Program

MY SiDEWALKS ON
SCOTT FORESMAN
READING STREET
Intensive Reading Intervention

4–Step Plan for Assessment

1. **Diagnose and Differentiate**
2. **Monitor Progress**
3. **Assess and Regroup**
4. **Summative Assessment**

Monitor Progress

STEP 2

- **Guiding comprehension questions** and skill and strategy instruction during reading
- **Monitor Progress boxes** to check comprehension and vocabulary
- **Weekly Assessments** on Day 3 for comprehension, Day 4 for fluency, and Day 5 for vocabulary
- **Practice Book** pages at point of use
- **Weekly Selection Tests** or **Fresh Reads for Differentiated Test Practice**

Assess and Regroup

STEP 3

- **Days 3, 4, and 5 Assessments** Record results of weekly Days 3, 4, and 5 assessments in retelling, fluency, and vocabulary (WA16–WA17) to track student progress.
- **Unit 4 Florida Benchmark Test** Administer this test to check mastery of unit skills.
- Use weekly assessment information, Florida Unit Benchmark Test performance, and the Unit 4 Assess and Regroup (p. WA18) to make regrouping decisions. See the time line below.

YOU ARE HERE
Begin Unit 4

SCOTT FORESMAN ASSESSMENT

Group Baseline Group Test → Assess → Regroup Units 1 and 2 → Regroup Unit 3 → Regroup Unit 4 (p. WA18) → Regroup Unit 5 → Assess

END OF YEAR

Week | 1 | 5 | 10 | 15 | 20 | 25 | 30

OUTSIDE ASSESSMENT

Initial placement → Outside assessment for regrouping → Outside assessment for regrouping

Outside assessments (e.g., DIBELS) may recommend regrouping at other times during the year.

Summative Assessment

STEP 4

- **Florida Benchmark Assessment** Use to measure a student's mastery of each unit's skills.
- **Florida End-of-Year Benchmark Assessment** Use to measure a student's mastery of program skills covered in all six units.

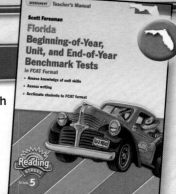

Theme Launch

Discuss the Big Idea

As a class, discuss the Big Idea question, *How do people and animals adapt to different situations?*

Explain that people and animals sometimes have to adapt to new situations or surroundings. Sometimes animals adapt to better protect themselves. Humans adapt to overcome physical limitations, or improve their lives.

Ask students to give examples of how people or animals might react to a new situation, such as a change in their environment.

One example of people and animals adapting to new situations is how they react to the changing of the seasons. When the weather gets colder, people wear different clothes and spend time doing different activities. Some animals might grow more fur or hibernate.

Theme and Concept Connections

Weekly lesson concepts help students connect the reading selections and the unit theme. Theme-related activities throughout the week provide opportunities to explore the relationships among the selections, the lesson concepts, and the unit theme.

UNIT 4

Read Onlin
PearsonSuccess

Adapting

How do people and animals adapt to different situations?

390

CONNECTING CULTURES

Use the following selections to explore the ways young people respond when they feel different from others or have to adapt to a new place.

Weslandia Have students discuss the reasons Wesley creates Weslandia and how others react to it. They can share their own experiences of feeling different from others and what they did in these situations.

The Stormi Giovanni Club Have students discuss how Stormi deals with moving to a new school. They can also share their ideas about adapting to new places.

Weslandia
A boy changes the world around him.
FICTION

connect to **SOCIAL STUDIES**

Paired Selection
"Under the Back Porch" and "Keziah"
POETRY

Stretching Ourselves
Young people make the most of their lives.
EXPOSITORY NONFICTION

connect to **SCIENCE**

Paired Selection
Helpful Tools
EXPOSITORY NONFICTION

Exploding Ants
Insects adapt to their environment.
EXPOSITORY NONFICTION

connect to **SCIENCE**

Paired Selection
The Creature from the Adapting Lagoon
EXPERIMENT

The Stormi Giovanni Club
A girl adapts to a new school.
PLAY

connect to **SOCIAL STUDIES**

Paired Selection
Think Dress Codes Are a Drag?
NEWSPAPER ARTICLE

The Gymnast
A boy tries to turn himself into an athlete.
AUTOBIOGRAPHY

connect to **SOCIAL STUDIES**

Paired Selection
All About Gymnastics
ONLINE REFERENCE SOURCES

391

Unit Inquiry Project

Adaptations

In the unit inquiry project, students each choose a group of people or animals and research how they have adapted to different situations. Students may use print or online resources as available.

The project assessment rubric can be found on p. 504a. Discuss the rubric's expectations before students begin the project. **Rubric 4 3 2 1**

PROJECT TIMETABLE

WEEK	ACTIVITY/SKILL CONNECTION
1	**IDENTIFY QUESTIONS** Discuss groups and situations students could research, such as how immigrants or refugees adapt to new locations or how bears adapt to humans moving into their habitats. Each student chooses a group and situation and browses a few Web sites or print reference materials to develop an inquiry question about it.
2	**NAVIGATE/SEARCH** Students conduct effective information searches and look for text and images that can help them answer their questions.
3	**ANALYZE** Students explore Web sites or print materials. They analyze the information they have found to determine whether or not it will be useful to them. Students print or take notes on valid information.
4	**SYNTHESIZE** Students combine relevant information they've collected from different sources to develop answers to their inquiry questions from Week 1.
5	**ASSESSMENT OPTIONS** **COMMUNICATE** Each student creates a graphic organizer that shows how a group of people or animals have adapted to a specific situation. Students may also give oral presentations based on their research notes.

Pages 390–391

LA.5.6.1.1 Read and interpret informational text and organize information (e.g., use graphic organizers) from multiple sources

LA.5.6.2.1 Select a topic for inquiry, formulate a search plan, and apply evaluative criteria to select and use resources

LA.5.6.2.2 Read and record information systematically, evaluating the validity and reliability of information by examining several source

LA.5.6.3.2 Use a variety of reliable media sources to gather information effectively

CONCEPT DEVELOPMENT

Unit 4
Adapting

CONCEPT QUESTION

How do people and animals adapt to different situations?

Week 1

Expand the Concept
How do people adapt to difficult situations?

Connect the Concept

Literature

Time for SOCIAL STUDIES

Develop Language
barren, edible, island, livestock

Social Studies Content
Declaration of Independence
Amish Culture
African American Authors

Writing
E-mail

Internet Inquiry
Explore Civilizations

Week 2

Expand the Concept
How do people adapt to living with physical limitations?

Connect the Concept

Literature

TIME FOR Science

Develop Language
dedication, leg brace, polio, triumphant

Science Content
Animal Characteristics
Animal Survival
Food Web
Habitat

Writing
Journal Entry

Internet Inquiry
Adapting to Physical Limitations

Week 3

Expand the Concept
How do animals adapt to survive?

Connect the Concept

Literature

TIME FOR Science

Develop Language
African black mambas, constrictors, reptiles

Science Content
Biomes
Human Adaptations
Animal Experiments

Writing
Story About an Animal

Internet Inquiry
Animal Adaptations

Week 4

Expand the Concept
How do people adapt to a new school?

Connect the Concept

Literature

Time for SOCIAL STUDIES

Develop Language
count on, settle in

Social Studies Content
Moving
E-mail
Friendship

Writing
Advice

Internet Inquiry
E-mail

Week 5

Expand the Concept
Why do people try to change themselves?

Connect the Concept

Literature

Time for SOCIAL STUDIES

Develop Language
champion, competitive, develop, perfected

Social Studies Content
Gymnastics
Nadia Comaneci

Writing
Describe How You Achieved a Goal

Internet Inquiry
Gymnastics

Florida

Planning Guide for Sunshine State Standards

Weslandia

Reading

Word Work Words from Many Cultures: 411i–411j

Comprehension Draw Conclusions: 392–393, 396–407, 410–411, 411b
Answer Questions: 392–393, 396–407, 410–411

Vocabulary Lesson Vocabulary: 394b, 403, 407
Word Structure: 394–395, 403, 411c

Fluency Model Punctuation Clues: 392l–392m, 411a

Self-Selected Reading: LR1–9, TR16–17

Literature Genre—Fiction: 396
Reader Response: 408

Writing

Four-Elements Writing Conventions: 409, 411g–411h

Writing E-Mail: 411g–411h

Grammar, Usage, and Mechanics Subject and Object Pronouns: 411e–411f

Research/Study Instruction Manual: 411l

Communication and Media

Speaking/Listening Build Concept Vocabulary: 392l, 403, 407, 411c
Read Aloud: 392m

Viewing Analyze Illustrations: 411d

Technology New Literacies: 411k

Unit Skills

Writing Story: WA2–9

Poetry: 504–507

Project/Wrap-Up: 508–509

Grade 5 Benchmarks for Language Arts

The student will:

LA.5.1.4.1 Understand spelling patterns.

LA.5.1.4.2 Recognize structural analysis.

LA.5.1.5.2 Adjust reading rate based on purpose, text difficulty, form, and style.

LA.5.1.6.1 Use new vocabulary that is introduced and taught directly.

LA.5.1.6.2 Listen to, read, and discuss familiar and conceptually challenging text.

LA.5.1.6.7 Use meaning of familiar base words and affixes to determine meanings of unfamiliar complex words.

LA.5.1.7.3 Determine the main idea or essential message in grade-level text through inferring.

LA.5.2.1.5 Demonstrate an understanding of a literary selection, and depending on the selection, include evidence from the text and personal experience.

The student will:

LA.5.2.2.4 Identify the characteristics of a variety of types of text (e.g., practical/functional texts).

LA.5.3.4.4 Edit writing for grammar and language conventions, including the correct use of subjective and objective pronouns.

LA.5.4.2.4 Write a variety of communications (e.g., letters, messages).

The student will:

LA.5.1.6.1 Use new vocabulary that is introduced and taught directly.

LA.5.6.2.1 Select a topic for inquiry, formulate a search plan, and apply evaluative criteria to select and use appropriate resources.

LA.5.6.2.4 Record basic bibliographic data and present quotes using ethical practices (e.g., avoids plagiarism).

The student will:

LA.5.2.1.3 Demonstrate how descriptive and figurative language help to communicate meaning in a poem.

LA.5.4.1.1 Write narratives that establish a situation and plot with rising action, conflict, and resolution.

LA.5.4.2.2 Record information (e.g., charts) related to a topic.

This Week's Leveled Readers

Intervention

My Sidewalks on Reading Street provides collaborative, parallel, intensive intervention when used with *Reading Street*.

Below-Level

Fiction

The student will:

LA.5.1.7.3 Determine the main idea or essential message in grade-level text through inferring.

LA.5.2.1.4 Identify an author's theme, and use details from the text to explain how the author developed that theme.

On-Level

Fiction

The student will:

LA.5.1.7.3 Determine the main idea or essential message in grade-level text through inferring.

LA.5.2.1.5 Demonstrate an understanding of a literary selection, and depending on the selection, include evidence from the text and personal experience.

Advanced

Nonfiction

The student will:

LA.5.1.7.3 Determine the main idea or essential message in grade-level text through inferring.

LA.5.2.2.2 Use information from the text to answer questions related to explicitly stated main ideas or relevant details.

Correlation to Robert Marzano's Instructional Strategies

- Reinforcing effort and providing recognition: pp. 408–409
- Homework and practice: pp. 392f–392g, 393, 395, 408
- Nonlinguistic representations: p. 411d
- Cooperative learning: pp. 392j–392k

- Setting objectives and providing feedback: p. 392m
- Generating and testing hypotheses: p. 396
- Cues, questions, and advance organizers: pp. 394a, 394b, 411c

Florida Assessment for FCAT Success

Selection Tests, pp. 61–64

Fresh Reads for Differentiated Test Practice, pp. 91–96

Unit 4 Benchmark Test in FCAT Format, pp. 1–21

Success Tracker™ Online Test to Monitor Benchmarks

Content-Area Standards Taught During the Reading Lesson

Science

The student:

SC.F.1.2.2. Knows how all animals depend on plants

SC.F.1.2.3. Knows that living things are different but share similar structures

SC.F.1.2.4.5.1. Uses magnifying tools to identify similar and different kinds of structures

SC.G.1.2.7. Knows that variations in light, water, temperature, and soil content are largely responsible for the existence of different kinds of organisms and population densities in an ecosystem

SC.G.2.2.1.5.1. Knows that adaptations to their environment may increase the survival of a species

Social Studies

The student:

SS.A.5.2.7.5.1. Knows social transformations that have taken place in United States

SS.B.1.2.5.5.1. Understands varying perceptions of regions in the United States

SS.B.2.2.2.5.1. Understands ways the physical environment supports human activities in the United States

SS.C.2.2.2.5.1. Extends and refines understanding of ways personal responsibility is important

CONNECT TO SF SOCIAL STUDIES

TIME SAVERS FOR FLORIDA TEACHERS

 Comprehension Skill: Draw Conclusions

Unit 4: *Adapting*

Question of the Week: How do people adapt to difficult situations?

Social Studies Concepts:
- Society
- Culture
- Government
- Declaration of Independence
- Ways of Life

 Reading Skill: **Draw Conclusions, Unit 5, pp. 334–335**

These lessons in *Scott Foresman Social Studies* support the concepts taught in this week's lesson of *Reading Street.*

Unit 1, Chapter 1, Lesson 1, "Migration to the Americas," pp. 54–57

Unit 4, Chapter 9, Lesson 1, "Declaring Independence," pp. 296–300

Unit 4, Chapter 9, Issues and Viewpoints, "Seeking Freedom," pp. 310–311

Unit 4
Adapting

CONCEPT QUESTION
How do people and animals adapt to different situations?

Week 1

EXPAND THE CONCEPT
How do people adapt to difficult situations?

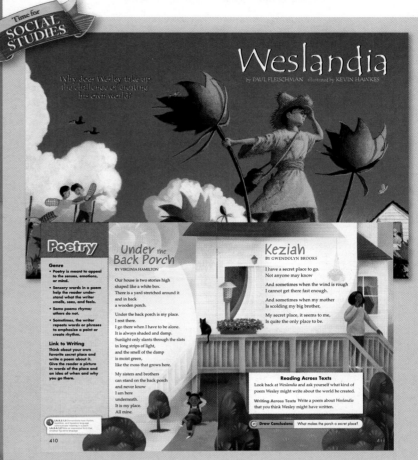

CONNECT THE CONCEPT

▶ **Develop Language**
barren, edible, island, livestock

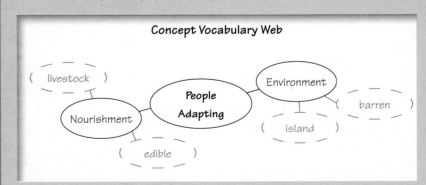

Concept Vocabulary Web

▶ **Social Studies Content**
Declaration of Independence, Amish Culture, African American Authors

▶ **Writing**
E-mail

▶ **Internet Inquiry**
Explore Civilizations

Preview Your Week

How do people adapt to difficult situations?

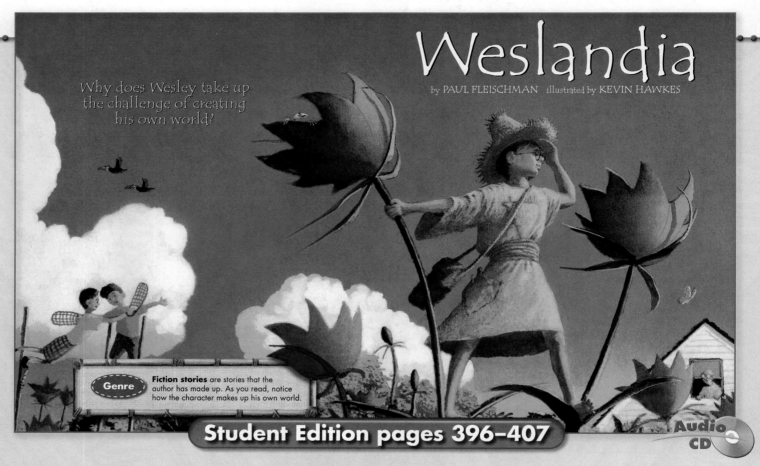

Why does Wesley take up the challenge of creating his own world?

Weslandia
by PAUL FLEISCHMAN illustrated by KEVIN HAWKES

Genre **Fiction stories** are stories that the author has made up. As you read, notice how the character makes up his own world.

Student Edition pages 396–407

Audio CD

ONLINE
PearsonSuccessNet.com

- **Student Edition**
- **Leveled Readers**

Genre Fiction
Vocabulary Strategy Word Structure
Comprehension Skill Draw Conclusions
Comprehension Strategy Answer Questions

Paired Selection

Reading Across Texts
Think About Poetry a Fictional Character Might Write

Genre
Poetry

Poetry

Under the Back Porch
BY VIRGINIA HAMILTON

...is meant to appeal ...enses, emotions, ...d.

- **Sensory words in a poem help the reader understand what the writer smells, sees, and feels.**
- **Some poems rhyme; others do not.**
- **Sometimes, the writer repeats words or phrases to emphasize a point or create rhythm.**

Link to Writing
Think about your own favorite secret place and write a poem about it. Give the reader a picture in words of the place and an idea of when and why you go there.

Our house is two stories high
shaped like a white box.
There is a yard stretched around it
and in back
a wooden porch.

Under the back porch is my place.
I rest there.
I go there when I have to be alone.
It is always shaded and damp.
Sunlight only slants through the slats
in long strips of light,
and the smell of the damp
is moist green,
like the moss that grows here.

My sisters and brothers
can stand on the back porch
and never know
I am here
underneath.
It is my place.
All mine.

Keziah
BY GWENDOLYN BROOKS

I have a secret place to go.
Not anyone may know

And sometimes when the wind is rough
I cannot get there fast enough.

And sometimes when my mother
Is scolding my big brother,

My secret place, it seems to me,
Is quite the only place to be.

Reading Across Texts
Look back at *Weslandia* and ask yourself what kind of poem Wesley might write about the world he created.

Writing Across Texts Write a poem about *Weslandia* that you think Wesley might have written.

Draw Conclusions What makes the porch a secret place?

410

Student Edition pages 410–411

Audio CD

Florida Social Studies Standards This Week

SS.A.4.2.2.5.2 Understands everyday life in Colonial America

SS.A.5.2.7.5.1 Knows social transformations that have taken place in United States

SS.B.1.2.5.5.1 Understands varying perceptions of regions in the United States

Time for
SOCIAL STUDIES

Leveled Readers

◉ **Skill** Draw Conclusions

◉ **Strategy** Answer Questions

Lesson Vocabulary

Below-Level

On-Level

Advanced

ELL Reader

· Concept Vocabulary
· Text Support
· Language Enrichment

The Anasazi:
The Ancient Builders

Time for
SOCIAL STUDIES

Integrate Social Studies Standards

• **Society**
• **Culture**
• **Government**

✓ **Read**

Weslandia,
pp. 396–407

"Under the Back Porch" and "Keziah,"
pp. 410–411

Leveled Readers

Below-Level   **On-Level**   **Advanced**

• Support Concepts   • Develop Concepts   • Extend Concepts
                                          • Social Studies Extension Activity

ELL Reader

✓ **Build Concept Vocabulary**
People Adapting,
pp. 392l–392m

✓ **Teach Social Studies Concepts**
Declaration of Independence,
p. 399
Amish Culture, p. 405
African American Authors,
p. 411

✓ **Explore Social Studies Center**
Plan a Society, p. 392k

Florida Weekly Plan

READING

45–90 minutes

TARGET SKILLS OF THE WEEK

- **Comprehension Skill**
  Draw Conclusions
- **Comprehension Strategy**
  Answer Questions
- **Vocabulary Strategy**
  Word Structure

LANGUAGE ARTS

30–60 minutes

Trait of the Week

Conventions

DAY 1 — PAGES 392l–394b, 411a, 411e–411k

Oral Language

QUESTION OF THE WEEK *How do people adapt to difficult situations?*

Read Aloud: "The Black Stallion" 392m
Build Concepts, 392l

Comprehension/Vocabulary

Comprehension Skill/Strategy Lesson, 392–393
- Draw Conclusions **T**
- Answer Questions
Build Background, 394a

Introduce Lesson Vocabulary, 394b
blunders, civilization, complex, envy, fleeing, inspired, rustling, strategy **T**

Read Leveled Readers

Grouping Options 392f–392g

Fluency

Model Punctuation Clues, 392l–392m, 411a

Grammar, 411e
Introduce Subject and Object Pronouns **T**

Writing Workshop, 411g
Introduce E-mail
Model the Trait of the Week: Conventions

Spelling, 411i
Pretest for Words from Many Cultures

Internet Inquiry, 411k
Identify Questions

DAY 2 — PAGES 394–403, 411a, 411e–411k

Oral Language

QUESTION OF THE DAY *Why do you think Wesley was such an outcast at school?*

Comprehension/Vocabulary

Vocabulary Strategy Lesson, 394–395
- Word Structure **T**

Read *Weslandia,* 396–403

Grouping Options 392f–392g

- Draw Conclusions **T**
- Word Structure
- **REVIEW** Main Idea **T**
Develop Vocabulary

Fluency

Choral Reading, 411a

Grammar, 411e
Develop Subject and Object Pronouns **T**

Writing Workshop, 411g
Improve Writing with Refer to the Text

Spelling, 411i
Teach the Generalization

Internet Inquiry, 411k
Navigate/Search

DAILY WRITING ACTIVITIES

Day 1 Write to Read, 392

Day 2 Words to Write, 395
Strategy Response Log, 396, 403

DAILY SOCIAL STUDIES CONNECTIONS

Day 1 People Adapting Concept Web, 392l

Day 2 Time for Social Studies: Declaration of Independence, 399
Revisit the People Adapting Concept Web, 403

DAILY SUCCESS PREDICTORS
for Adequate Yearly Progress

Monitor Progress and Corrective Feedback

Vocabulary   Check Vocabulary, *392l*

RESOURCES FOR THE WEEK

- Practice Book, *pp. 151–160*
- Word Study and Spelling Practice Book, *pp. 61–64*
- Grammar and Writing Practice Book, *pp. 61–64*

- Selection Test, *pp. 61–64*
- Fresh Reads for Differentiated Test Practice, *pp. 91–96*
- The Grammar and Writing Book, *pp. 140–145*

Grouping Options for Differentiated Instruction

Turn the page for the small group lesson plan.

DAY 3 PAGES 404–409, 411a, 411e–411k

Oral Language

QUESTION OF THE DAY *Would you like to be Wesley's friend? Why or why not?*

Comprehension/Vocabulary

Read *Weslandia*, 404–408

Grouping Options
392f–392g

Draw Conclusions **T**

Answer Questions

Develop Vocabulary

Reader Response

Selection Test

Fluency

Model Punctuation Clues, 411a

Grammar, 411f
Apply Subject and Object Pronouns in Writing **T**

Writing Workshop, 409, 411h
Write Now
Prewrite and Draft

Spelling, 411j
Connect Spelling to Writing

Internet Inquiry, 411k
Analyze Sources

Day 3 Strategy Response Log, 406
Think and Explain, 408

Day 3 Time for Social Studies: Amish Culture, 405
Revisit the People Adapting Concept
Web, 407

DAY 4 PAGES 410–411a, 411e–411k

Oral Language

QUESTION OF THE DAY *Where is a special, safe place you like to go when you want to be alone?*

Comprehension/Vocabulary

Read "Under the Back Porch," 410; "Keziah," 411

Grouping Options
392f –392g

Expository Nonfiction

Poetry

Reading Across Texts

Fluency

Partner Reading, 411a

Grammar, 411f
Practice Subject and Object Pronouns for Standardized Tests **T**

Writing Workshop, 411h
Draft, Revise, and Publish

Spelling, 411j
Provide a Strategy

Internet Inquiry, 411k
Synthesize Information

Day 4 Writing Across Texts, 411

Day 4 Time for Social Studies: African American Authors, 411

DAY 5 PAGES 411a–411l

Oral Language

QUESTION OF THE WEEK *To wrap up the week, revisit the Day 1 question.*
Build Concept Vocabulary, 411c

Fluency

Read Leveled Readers

Grouping Options 392f–392g

Assess Reading Rate, 411a

Comprehension/Vocabulary

Reteach Draw Conclusions, 411b **T**

Idiom, 411b

Review Word Structure, 411c **T**

Speaking and Viewing, 411d
Demonstration
Analyze Illustrations

Grammar, 411f
Cumulative Review

Writing Workshop, 411h
Connect to Unit Writing

Spelling, 411j
Posttest for Words from Many Cultures

Internet Inquiry, 411k
Communicate Results

Research/Study Skills, 411l
Instruction Manual

Day 5 Idiom, 411b

Day 5 Revisit the People Adapting Concept
Web, 411c

KEY ◉ Target Skill   **T** Tested Skill   **FCAT Tested Skill**

Check Retelling, *408*   Check Fluency WCPM, *411a*   Check Vocabulary, *411c*

SUCCESS PREDICTOR

Small Group Plan *for Differentiated Instruction*

Daily Plan AT A GLANCE

Reading
Whole Group
- Oral Language
- Comprehension/Vocabulary

Group Time
Differentiated Instruction

Meet with small groups to provide:
- Skill Support
- Reading Support
- Fluency Practice

Read

This week's lessons for daily group time can be found behind the Differentiated Instruction (DI) tab on pp. DI·2–DI·11.

Whole Group
- Fluency

Language Arts
- Grammar
- Writing
- Spelling
- Research/Inquiry
- Speaking/Listening/Viewing

Use *My Sidewalks on Reading Street* for Tier III intensive reading intervention.

DAY 1

On-Level
Teacher-Led
Page DI · 3
- Develop Concept Vocabulary
- **Read** On-Level Reader *Adventure to the New World*

Strategic Intervention
Teacher-Led
Page DI · 2
- Reinforce Concepts
- **Read** Below-Level Reader *Learning to Play the Game*

Advanced
Teacher-Led
Page DI · 3
- **Read** Advanced Reader *Cheaper, Faster, Better: Recent Technological Innovations*
- Independent Extension Activity

ⓘ Independent Activities
While you meet with small groups, have the rest of the class...
- Visit the Reading/Library Center, p. 392j
- Listen to the Background Building Audio
- Finish Write to Read, p. 392
- Complete Practice Book pp. 153–154
- Visit Cross-Curricular Centers

DAY 2

On-Level
Teacher-Led
Pages 398–403
- **Read** *Weslandia*

Strategic Intervention
Teacher-Led
Page DI · 4
- Practice Lesson Vocabulary
- Read Multisyllabic Words
- **Read** or Listen to *Weslandia*

Advanced
Teacher-Led
Page DI · 5
- Extend Vocabulary
- **Read** *Weslandia*

ⓘ Independent Activities
While you meet with small groups, have the rest of the class...
- Visit the Reading/Library Center, p. 392j
- Listen to the AudioText for *Weslandia*
- Finish Words to Write, p. 395
- Complete Practice Book pp. 155–156
- Write in their Strategy Response Logs, pp. 396, 403
- Visit Cross-Curricular Centers
- Work on inquiry projects

DAY 3

On-Level
Teacher-Led
Pages 404–407
- **Read** *Weslandia*

Strategic Intervention
Teacher-Led
Page DI · 6
- Practice Draw Conclusions and Answer Questions
- **Read** or Listen to *Weslandia*

Advanced
Teacher-Led
Page DI · 7
- Extend Draw Conclusions and Answer Questions
- **Read** *Weslandia*

ⓘ Independent Activities
While you meet with small groups, have the rest of the class...
- Visit the Reading/Library Center, p. 392j
- Listen to the AudioText for *Weslandia*
- Write in their Strategy Response Logs, p. 406
- Finish Think and Explain, p. 408
- Complete Practice Book p. 157
- Visit Cross-Curricular Centers
- Work on inquiry projects

① Begin with whole class skill and strategy instruction.

② Meet with small groups to provide differentiated instruction.

③ Gather the whole class back together for fluency and language arts.

On-Level

Teacher-Led
Pages 410–411

- **Read** "Under the Back Porch" and "Keziah"

Strategic Intervention

Teacher-Led
Page DI · 8

- Practice Retelling
- **Read** or Listen to "Under the Back Porch" and "Keziah"

Advanced

Teacher-Led
Page DI · 9

- **Read** "Under the Back Porch" and "Keziah"
- Genre Study

DAY 4

ⓘ Independent Activities

While you meet with small groups, have the rest of the class...

- Visit the Reading/Library Center, p. 392j
- Listen to the AudioText for "Under the Back Porch" and "Keziah"
- Visit the Writing/Vocabulary Center

- Finish Writing Across Texts, p. 411
- Visit Cross-Curricular Centers
- Work on inquiry projects

On-Level

Teacher-Led
Page DI · 11

- **Reread** Leveled Reader *Adventure to the New World*
- Retell *Adventure to the New World*

Strategic Intervention

Teacher-Led
Page DI · 10

- **Reread** Leveled Reader *Learning to Play the Game*
- Retell *Learning to Play the Game*

Advanced

Teacher-Led
Page DI · 11

- **Reread** Leveled Reader *Cheaper, Faster, Better: Recent Technological Innovations*
- Share Extension Activity

DAY 5

ⓘ Independent Activities

While you meet with small groups, have the rest of the class...

- Visit the Reading/Library Center, p. 392j
- Complete Practice Book pp. 158–160

- Visit Cross-Curricular Centers
- Work on inquiry projects

Grouping Place English language learners in the groups that correspond to their reading abilities in English.

Use the appropriate Leveled Reader or other text at students' instructional level.

TIP Send home the appropriate Multilingual Summary of the main selection on Day 1.

Take It to the NET™ ONLINE
PearsonSuccessNet.com

Jeanne Paratore
For ideas on using repeated readings, see the article "Using Repeated Readings to Promote Reading Success..." by Scott Foresman author J. Paratore and J. Turpie.

TEACHER TALK

An **Idiom** is a phrase that cannot be understood from the ordinary meaning of the words that form it, such as "hold your tongue." Idioms are especially difficult for English language learners.

Be sure to schedule time for students to work on the unit inquiry project "Adaptations." This week students develop inquiry questions about how groups of people or animals have adapted to different situations.

Looking Ahead

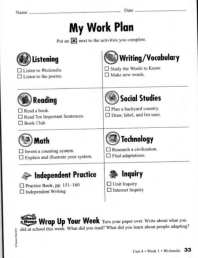

▲ **Group-Time Survival Guide**
p. 33, Weekly Contract

☑ Customize Your Plan by Stran

ORAL LANGUAGE

Concept Development

How do people adapt to difficult situations?

CONCEPT VOCABULARY
barren   edible   island   livestock

BUILD

☐ **Question of the Week** Introduce and discuss the question of the week. This week students will read a variety of texts and work on projects related to the concept *people adapting*. Post the question for students to refer to throughout the week. **DAY 1** *392d*

☐ **Read Aloud** Read aloud from "The Black Stallion." Then begin a web to build concepts and concept vocabulary related to this week's lesson and the unit theme, Adapting. Introduce the concept words *barren, edible, island,* and *livestock* and have students place them on the web. Display the web for use throughout the week. **DAY 1** *392l-392m*

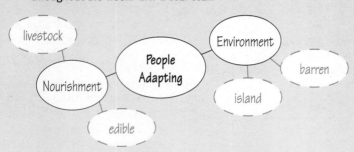

DEVELOP

☐ **Question of the Day** Use the prompts from the Weekly Plan to engage students in conversations related to this week's reading and the unit theme. **EVERY DAY** *392d-392e*

☐ **Concept Vocabulary Web** Revisit the People Adapting Concept Web and encourage students to add concept words from their reading and life experiences. **DAY 2** *403*, **DAY 3** *407*

CONNECT

☐ **Looking Back/Review/Connect** Revisit the People Adapting Concept Web and discuss how it relates to this week's lesson and the unit theme. Then make connections to next week's lesson. **DAY 5** *411c*

CHECK

☐ **Concept Vocabulary Web** Use the People Adapting Concept Web to check students' understanding of the concept vocabulary words *barren, edible, island,* and *livestock*. **DAY 1** *392l*, **DAY 5** *411c*

VOCABULARY

 **STRATEGY WORD STRUCTURE**
An inflected ending is a letter or letters added to a base word. The endings *-ed, -ing,* and *-s* may be added to verbs to change the tense. You can use inflected endings to help figure out the meaning of an unfamiliar word.

LESSON VOCABULARY
blunders   fleeing
civilization inspired
complex   rustling
envy   strategy

TEACH

☐ **Words to Know** Give students the opportunity to tell what they already know about this week's lesson vocabulary words. Then discuss word meaning. **DAY 1** *394b*

☐ **Vocabulary Strategy Lesson** Use the vocabulary strategy lesson in the Student Edition to introduce and model this week's strategy, *word structure.* **DAY 2** *394-395*

Vocabulary Strategy Lesson

PRACTICE/APPLY

☐ **Leveled Text** Read the lesson vocabulary in the context of leveled text. **DAY 1** *LR1-LR9*

☐ **Words in Context** Read the lesson vocabulary and apply *word structure* in the context of *Weslandia.* **DAY 2** *396-403,* **DAY 3** *404-408*

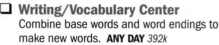
Leveled Readers

☐ **Writing/Vocabulary Center** Combine base words and word endings to make new words. **ANY DAY** *392k*

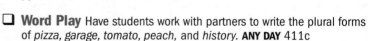
Main Selection—Fiction

☐ **Homework** Practice Book pp. 154-155. **DAY 1** *394b,* **DAY 2** *395*

☐ **Word Play** Have students work with partners to write the plural forms of *pizza, garage, tomato, peach,* and *history.* **ANY DAY** *411c*

ASSESS

☐ **Selection Test** Use the Selection Test to determine students' understanding of the lesson vocabulary words. **DAY 3**

RETEACH/REVIEW

☐ **Reteach Lesson** If necessary, use this lesson to reteach and review *word structure.* **DAY 5** *411c*

Use your school-based instructional focus calendar to determine which strands to teach.

 Target your instruction on FCAT tested skills.

 Check students' understanding of FCAT tested standards.

COMPREHENSION

 SKILL DRAW CONCLUSIONS A *conclusion* is a decision you make after thinking about the details in what you read. Often prior knowledge can help you draw, or make, a conclusion. When drawing a conclusion, you need to make sure it makes sense and is supported by what you have read.

STRATEGY ANSWER QUESTIONS Answering questions can help you understand the text. Sometimes you must draw a conclusion to answer a question asked in a book, by a teacher, or on a test. The details or answers you need may be in one place or in several places.

TEACH

❏ **Skill/Strategy Lesson** Use the skill/strategy lesson in the Student Edition to introduce and model *draw conclusions* and *answer questions*. **DAY 1** *392-393*

Skill/Strategy Lesson

❏ **Extend Skills** Teach about idioms. **ANY DAY** *411b*

PRACTICE/APPLY

❏ **Leveled Text** Apply *draw conclusions* and *answer questions* to read leveled text. **DAY 1** *LR1–LR9*

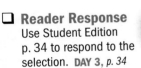

Leveled Readers

❏ **Skills and Strategies in Context** Read *Weslandia*, using the Guiding Comprehension questions to apply *draw conclusions* and *answer questions*. **DAY 2** *396–403*, **DAY 3** *404-408*

Main Selection—Fiction

❏ **Reader Response** Use Student Edition p. 34 to respond to the selection. **DAY 3, p. 34**

Paired Selection—Poetry

❏ **Skills and Strategies in Context** Read the poems. Then have students discuss and write across texts. **DAY 4** *410-411*

❏ **Homework** Practice Book pp. 153, 157, 158. **DAY 1** *393*, **DAY 3** *407*, **DAY 5** *411b*

ASSESS

❏ **Selection Test** Determine students' understanding of the selection and their use of *draw conclusions*. **DAY 3**

❏ **Retell** Have students retell *Weslandia*. **DAY 3** *408-409*

RETEACH/REVIEW

❏ **Reteach Lesson** If necessary, reteach and review *draw conclusions*. **DAY 5** *411b*

FLUENCY

SKILL PUNCTUATION CLUES Punctuation within text guides readers. Punctuation shows a reader where to pause (periods or commas), change inflection (question marks), and express emotion (exclamation marks).

TEACH

❏ **Read Aloud** Model fluent reading by rereading "The Black Stallion." Focus on this week's fluency skill, punctuation clues. **DAY 1** *392l–392m, 411a*

PRACTICE/APPLY

❏ **Choral Reading** Read aloud selected paragraphs from *Weslandia* modeling changing inflections, expressions, and pauses. Then practice as a class, doing three choral readings of the selected paragraphs. **DAY 2** *411a*, **DAY 3** *411a*

❏ **Partner Reading** Have partners practice reading aloud, following punctuation clues, and offering each other feedback. As students reread, monitor their progress toward their individual fluency goals. **DAY 4** *411a*

❏ **Listening Center** Have students follow along with the AudioText for this week's selections. **ANY DAY** *392j*

❏ **Reading/Library Center** Have students reread a selection of their choice. **ANY DAY** *392j*

❏ **Fluency Coach** Have students use Fluency Coach to listen to fluent readings or practice reading on their own. **ANY DAY**

ASSESS

❏ **Check Fluency** wcpm Do a one-minute timed reading, paying special attention to this week's skill—punctuation clues. Provide feedback for each student. **DAY 5** *411a*

GRAMMAR

SKILL SUBJECT AND OBJECT PRONOUNS When a pronoun is used as the subject of a sentence, it is called a *subject pronoun. I, you, he, she, it, we,* and *they* are subject pronouns. Pronouns that are used after action verbs or as objects of prepositions are called *object pronouns. Me, you, him, her, it, us,* and *them* are object pronouns.

TEACH

❑ **Grammar Transparency 16** Use Grammar Transparency 16 to teach subject and object pronouns. **DAY 1** *411e*

Grammar Transparency 16

PRACTICE/APPLY

❑ **Develop the Concept** Review the concept of subject and object pronouns and provide guided practice. **DAY 2** *411e*

❑ **Apply to Writing** Have students review something they have written and apply subject and object pronouns. **DAY 3** *411f*

❑ **Test Preparation** Examine common errors in subject and object pronouns to prepare for standardized tests. **DAY 4** *411f*

❑ **Homework** Grammar and Writing Practice Book pp. 61–63. **DAY 2** *411e,* **DAY 3** *411f,* **DAY 4** *411f*

ASSESS

❑ **Cumulative Review** Use Grammar and Writing Practice Book p. 64. **DAY 5** *411f*

RETEACH/REVIEW

❑ **Daily Fix-It** Have students find and correct errors using grammar, spelling, and punctuation. **EVERY DAY** *411e–411f*

❑ **The Grammar and Writing Book** Use pp. 140–143 of The Grammar and Writing Book to extend instruction for using subject and object pronouns. **ANY DAY**

The Grammar and Writing Book

WRITING

Trait of the Week

CONVENTIONS Conventions are rules for written language such as proper punctuation and capitalization. Conventions are signals that writers use to make the meaning clear to readers.

TEACH

❑ **Writing Transparency 16A** Use the model to introduce and discuss the Trait of the Week. **DAY 1** *411g*

❑ **Writing Transparency 16B** Use the transparency to show students how referring to the text can improve their writing. **DAY 2** *411g*

Writing Transparency 16A   **Writing Transparency 16B**

PRACTICE/APPLY

❑ **Write Now** Examine the model on Student Edition p. 409. Then have students write their own e-mail. **DAY 3** *409, 411h* **DAY 4** *411h*

> **Prompt** In *Weslandia,* a boy decides to remake his world rather than accept it as it is. Think about someone you know who doesn't always "follow the herd." Now write an e-mail to that person reacting to something he or she has done.

Write Now p. 409

❑ **Writing/Vocabulary Center** Combine base words and word endings to make new words. **ANY DAY** *392k*

ASSESS

❑ **Writing Trait Rubric** Use the rubric to evaluate students' writing. **DAY 4** *411h*

RETEACH/REVIEW

❑ **The Grammar and Writing Book** Use pp. 140–145 of The Grammar and Writing Book to extend instruction for using subject and object pronouns, referring to the text, and e-mails. **ANY DAY**

The Grammar and Writing Book

① Use your school-based instructional focus calendar to determine which strands to teach.

② Target your instruction on FCAT tested skills.

③ Check students' understanding of FCAT tested standards.

SPELLING

GENERALIZATION WORDS FROM MANY CULTURES Many words in English come from other languages and may have unexpected spellings: _khaki, ballet_. These words often do not follow the phonics rules students typically apply so other strategies must be applied for learning to spell them.

TEACH

☐ **Pretest** Give the pretest for words from many cultures. Guide students in self-correcting their pretests and correcting any misspellings. DAY 1 _411i_

☐ **Think and Practice** Connect spelling to the phonics generalization for words from many cultures. DAY 2 _411i_

PRACTICE/APPLY

☐ **Connect to Writing** Have students use spelling words to write an e-mail note to a friend or family member. Then review frequently misspelled words: _our, again_. DAY 3 _411j_

☐ **Homework** Word Study and Spelling Practice Book pp. 61–64. EVERY DAY

RETEACH/REVIEW

☐ **Review** Review spelling words to prepare for the posttest. Then provide students with a spelling strategy—problem parts. DAY 4 _411j_

ASSESS

☐ **Posttest** Use dictation sentences to give the posttest for words from many cultures. DAY 5 _411j_

Spelling Words

1. khaki	8. canyon	15. barbecue
2. hula	9. yogurt	16. safari
3. banana	10. banquet	17. buffet
4. ballet	11. macaroni	18. stampede
5. waltz	12. polka	19. karate
6. tomato*	13. cobra	20. kiosk
7. vanilla	14. koala	

Challenge Words

21. papaya	23. sauerkraut	25. tsunami
22. artichoke	24. succotash	

*Word from the selection

RESEARCH AND INQUIRY

☐ **Internet Inquiry** Have students conduct an Internet inquiry on civilizations. EVERY DAY _411k_

☐ **Instruction Manual** Review the features and how instruction manuals are organized, and discuss how students can use manuals to learn how to do something. DAY 5 _411l_

☐ **Unit Inquiry** Allow time for students to develop inquiry questions about how groups of people or animals have adapted to different situations. ANY DAY _391_

SPEAKING AND VIEWING

☐ **Demonstration** Have students choose one of Wes's _Weslandia_ projects and prepare a how-to demonstration for the class. DAY 5 _411d_

☐ **Analyze Illustrations** Have students study the illustrations on pp. 398-399 and p. 405 and answer questions. DAY 5 _411d_

Resources for Differentiated Instruction

LEVELED READERS

▶ **Comprehension**
- 🎯 **Skill** Draw Conclusions
- 🎯 **Strategy** Answer Questions

▶ **Lesson Vocabulary**
- 🎯 Word Structure

blunders · rustling · complex · envy · inspired · fleeing · strategy · civilization

▶ **Social Studies Standards**
- Society
- Culture
- Government

Leveled Reader Database ONLINE

PearsonSuccessNet.com

Use the Online Database of over 600 books to

- Download and print additional copies of this week's leveled readers.
- Listen to the readers being read online.
- Search for more titles focused on this week's skills, topic, and content.

On-Level

ADVENTURE TO THE NEW WORLD
BY GRETCHEN MCBRIDE
ILLUSTRATED BY PHYLLIS POLLEMA-CAHILL

On-Level Reader

On-Level Practice TE p. LR5

On-Level Practice TE p. LR6

Strategic Intervention

Social Studies
Learning to Play the Game
by Adam McClellan
illustrated by Dan Grant

Below-Level Reader

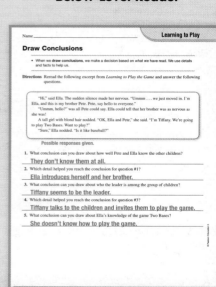

Below-Level Practice TE p. LR2

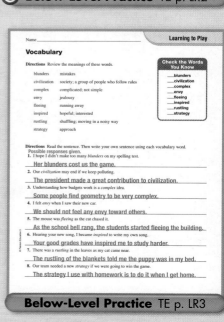

Below-Level Practice TE p. LR3

Advanced

Advanced Reader

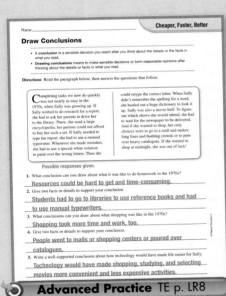

Advanced Practice TE p. LR8

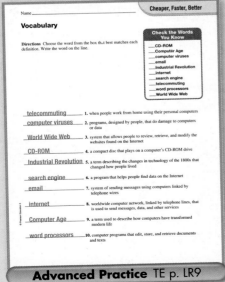

Advanced Practice TE p. LR9

ELL

ELL Reader

ELL Poster 16

Teacher's Edition Notes

ELL notes throughout this lesson support instruction and reference additional resources at point of use.

Teaching Guide pp. 106–112, 242–243

- Multilingual summaries of the main selection
- Comprehension lesson
- Vocabulary strategies and word cards
- ELL Reader 5.4.1 lesson

ELL and Transition Handbook

Ten Important Sentences

- Key ideas from every selection in the Student Edition
- Activities to build sentence power

More Reading

Readers' Theater Anthology

- Fluency practice
- Five scripts to build fluency
- Poetry for oral interpretation

Leveled Trade Books

- Extended reading tied to the unit concept
- Lessons in the Trade Book Library Teaching Guide

School + Home

Homework

- Family Times Newsletter
- ELL Multilingual Selection Summaries

Take-Home Books

- Leveled Readers

Cross-Curricular Centers

 Listening

 Reading/Library

 Math

Listen to the SELECTIONS

MATERIALS   SINGLES
CD player, headphones, AudioText CD, student book

LISTEN TO LITERATURE Listen to *Weslandia*, "Under the Back Porch," and "Keziah," as you follow or read along in your book. Listen to draw conclusions about what happens in the story and the poems.

If there is anything you don't understand, you can listen again to any section.

Read it AGAIN!

MATERIALS   SINGLES PAIRS GROUPS
Collection of books for self-selected reading, reading logs, student book

Select a book you have already read. Record the title of the book in your reading log. You may want to read with a partner.

Choose from the following:

- **Leveled Readers**
- **ELL Readers**
- **Stories Written by Classmates**
- **Books from the Library**
- *Weslandia*

TEN IMPORTANT SENTENCES Read the Ten Important Sentences for *Weslandia*. Then locate the sentences in the student book.

BOOK CLUB Look at "Meet Authors" on p. 770 of the student book. As a group, think of some questions you would like to ask the author, and write him a letter. Read other books by Paul Fleischman and get together with a group to share your favorites.

Invent a Counting System

MATERIALS   SINGLES
Writing and drawing materials

In *Weslandia*, Wesley adopts a new counting system based on the number eight. Design your own counting system, based on a number you choose.

1. Choose a number for your counting system.
2. Write a paragraph explaining your counting system. Include the reasons you chose this number.
3. Draw a picture that illustrates how to count objects using your system.

EARLY FINISHERS Divide a day into the same number of segments as the number you used for your counting system. Describe each segment of the day and decide what each is called.

My Counting System

My counting system is based on the number eight, because my birthday is on July 8th. To use my counting system, count by 8s.

8   16

Pages 392j–392k

LA.5.1.6.7 Use meaning of familiar base words to determine meanings of unfamiliar complex words

LA.5.5.2.1 Listen to gain information for a variety of purposes

LA.5.6.1.1 Read and interpret informational text

Scott Foresman Reading Street Centers Survival Kit

Use the *Weslandia* materials from the Reading Street Centers Survival Kit to organize this week's centers.

Writing/Vocabulary

Play with *Word Endings*

MATERIALS | SINGLES
Writing materials, index cards

Combine base words and word endings to make new words.

1. Write these four base words on separate index cards: *flee, blunder, inspire, rustle.* Put the cards face down in a pile. Write these word endings on separate cards: *-ing, -s,* and *-ed* and put them in a second pile, face down.
2. Choose one card from each pile. Combine the base word with the ending and use the word in a sentence that makes its meaning clear.
3. Time yourself. See how many words and sentences you can create in three minutes.

EARLY FINISHERS Combine the four base words with each of the three word endings and write them down. Remember spelling rules for adding endings to words.

> "The mouse was fleeing from the hungry cat."

Social Studies

Plan a Society

MATERIALS | SINGLES
Writing and art materials

Plan your own backyard country the way that Wesley did in *Weslandia*.

1. Draw a picture of each plant you would grow in your backyard country and label it.
2. Think about the things for which Wesley used his plants. List things for which you would use your plants next to each drawing.

EARLY FINISHERS Name your backyard country. Create rules for your new country.

Shavonda's World

Fuzzy Flower

used for: blankets, socks, mittens

Canopy Leaf Tree

tree leaves used for: fans, umbrella, roof for house

Technology

Explore *Ancient Cultures*

MATERIALS | SINGLES
Internet access, printer

Find out more about how ancient civilizations adapted to their environments.

1. Follow classroom rules to conduct an Internet search using a student-friendly search engine for information about an ancient civilization such as the Egyptians or Romans.
2. Narrow your search to focus on how the civilization adapted to its natural environment.
3. Print the information you find.

EARLY FINISHERS Underline the information you found that relates to food, clothing, and shelter.

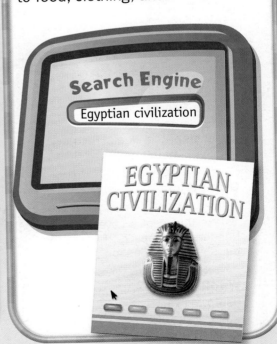

Search Engine

Egyptian civilization

EGYPTIAN CIVILIZATION

ALL CENTERS

OBJECTIVES

- ● Build vocabulary by finding words related to the lesson concept.
- ↻ Listen to draw conclusions.

Concept Vocabulary

barren not able to produce much

edible fit to eat

island body of land smaller than a continent and completely surrounded by water

livestock farm animals

Monitor Progress

Check Vocabulary

If...	then... use the
students are unable to place words on the Web,	Concept Vocabulary Routine on p. D1·1 to teach the words. Provide additional words for practice, such as *low tide* and *shellfish.*

SUCCESS PREDICTOR

DAY 1   Grouping Options

Reading

Whole Group
Introduce and discuss the Question of the Week. Then use pp. 392l–394b.

Group Time
Differentiated Instruction
Read this week's Leveled Readers. See pp. 392f–392g for the small group lesson plan.

Whole Group
Use p. 411a.

Language Arts
Use pp. 411e–411k.

Build Concepts

FLUENCY

MODEL PUNCTUATION CLUES As you read the excerpt from "The Black Stallion," model responding to punctuation while reading aloud by pausing for commas or periods or by raising your voice at the end of a question, as in the example, "Hadn't he called it carragheen?"

LISTENING COMPREHENSION

After reading an excerpt from "The Black Stallion," use the following questions to assess listening comprehension.

1. **How is Alec feeling in paragraph 1?** *(He is weak and hungry; willing to eat seaweed.)* ***Draw Conclusions***

2. **Do you think Alec will survive? Why or why not?** *(Possible response: He will survive because he was clever enough to find food, and water from a spring.)* ***Draw Conclusions***

BUILD CONCEPT VOCABULARY

Start a web to build concepts and vocabulary related to this week's lesson and the unit theme.

- Draw the People Adapting Concept Web.

- Read the sentence with *island* again. Ask students to pronounce it and discuss its meaning.

- Place *island* in an oval attached to *Environment*. Explain that an *island* is related to this concept. Read the sentences in which *barren, edible,* and *livestock* appear. Have students pronounce the words, place them on the web, and provide reasons.

- Brainstorm additional words and categories for the web. Keep the web on display and add words throughout the week.

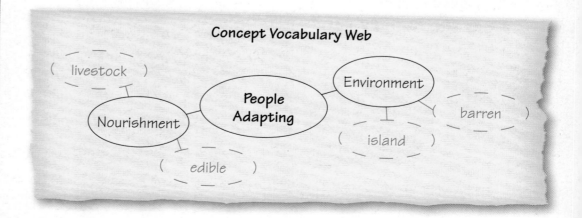

Concept Vocabulary Web

from THE BLACK STALLION

by WALTER FARLEY

On his way home from a visit with his uncle in India, Alec is shipwrecked. He is the only survivor of the accident, and he must adapt to a strange island alone.

One morning Alec made his way weakly toward the rocky side of the island. He came to the huge rocks and climbed on top of one of them. It was more barren than any other part of the island. It was low tide and Alec's eyes wandered over the stony shore, looking for any kind of shellfish he might be able to eat. He noticed the mosslike substance on all the rocks at the water's edge, and on those that extended out. What was that stuff the biology teacher had made them eat last term in one of their experiments? Hadn't he called it carragheen [KAIR ah jeen]? Yes, that was it. A sort of seaweed, he had said, that grew abundantly along the rocky parts of the Atlantic coast of Europe and North America. When washed and dried, it was edible for humans and livestock. Could the moss on the rocks below be it? Alec scarcely dared to hope.

Slowly Alec made the dangerous descent. He reached the water level and scrambled across the rocks. He took a handful of the soft greenish-yellow moss which covered them and raised it to his lips. It smelled the same. He tasted it. The moss was terribly salty from the sea, but it was the same as he had eaten that day in the classroom!

Eagerly he filled his pockets with it, then removed his shirt and filled it full. He climbed up again and hurried back to camp. There he emptied the moss onto the ground beside the spring. The next quarter of an hour he spent washing it, and then placed it out in the sun to dry. Hungrily he tasted it again. It was better—and it was food!

Activate Prior Knowledge

Before students listen to the Read Aloud, ask them what they know about people adapting to new environments.

Set Purpose

Read aloud the title and have students predict what the selection will be about.

Read the introduction aloud. Have students listen for details to help them draw conclusions about Alec.

Creative Response

Working in groups, have students create narrations that include Alec's thoughts and feelings as he makes his way down the rocks to get to the seaweed. *Drama*

Develop Concept Vocabulary

Read aloud every day from a book of your choice related to the concept and use the Concept Vocabulary Routine on p. DI·1 to develop concept vocabulary. For suggestions, see p. TR14.

Access Content Before reading, share this summary: Alec is shipwrecked all alone on a strange island. Looking for food, he sees a mosslike substance. It looks like something he ate in biology class. He examines the moss and determines that it is good to eat.

Homework Send home this week's Family Times newsletter.

Pages 392l–392m

LA.5.1.6.1 Use new vocabulary that is introduced and taught directly

LA.5.1.6.2 Listen to and discuss conceptually challenging text

LA.5.5.2.1 Listen and speak to gain and share information for a variety of purposes, including dramatic recitations

SUCCESS PREDICTOR

Vocabulary

SKILLS ⟷ STRATEGIES IN CONTEXT

Draw Conclusions
Answer Questions

OBJECTIVES

- Draw conclusions.

- Draw conclusions to answer questions.

Skills Trace	
Draw Conclusions	
Introduce/Teach	TE: 5.4 392–393, 484–485; 5.6 634–635
Practice	Practice Book: 153, 157, 158, 186, 193, 197, 198, 253, 257, 258, 276, 296
Reteach/Review	TE: 5.4 411b, 467, 503b, DI·52, DI·56; 5.6 653b, 683, 687, 735, 745, DI·52
Test	Selection Test: 61–64, 77–80, 101–104; Benchmark Test: Units 4,6

INTRODUCE

If you see clothes hanging on a line, you might conclude that someone is doing laundry. What might you conclude if you see a person leaning ladders against the house and opening paint cans? *(The person is going to paint the house.)*

Have students read the information on p. 392. Explain the following:

- To draw conclusions, or make inferences, you need to pull together and evaluate information while thinking about your prior knowledge.

- Sometimes you need to draw conclusions to answer questions posed by others.

Use Skill Transparency 16 to teach draw conclusions and answer questions.

Comprehension

Skill
Draw Conclusions

Strategy
Answer Questions

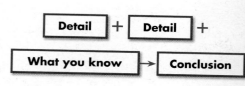 **LA.5.1.7.3** Determine main idea through inferring
LA.5.1.7.8 Use self-monitoring strategies

Draw Conclusions

- A conclusion is a decision you make after thinking about the details in what you read.

- Often your prior knowledge can help you draw, or make, a conclusion.

- When you draw a conclusion, be sure it makes sense and is supported by what you have read.

Detail	+	Detail	+

What you know	→	Conclusion

Strategy: Answer Questions

Sometimes you must draw a conclusion to answer a question asked in a book, by a teacher, or on a test. The details you need for your answer may be in one place or in several places. Use those details plus what you already know to draw a conclusion that answers the question.

Write to Read

1. Read "The Go-Cart." Make two graphic organizers like the one above to help draw conclusions about why Jeff entered the go-cart race and how he felt about himself.

2. Answer this question and explain your answer: Was Jeff's family helpful and supporting?

392

Strategic Intervention

Draw Conclusions Show students a picture of a child who is crying. Ask students what they would say about the child. *(He or she is sad.)* Students should tell how they know the child is sad. *(The child is crying, and I know that I cry when I'm sad.)* Point out that they used details in the picture and their own knowledge to draw a conclusion about the child in the picture.

ELL

Access Content

Beginning/Intermediate For a Picture It! lesson on draw conclusions, see ELL Teaching Guide, pp. 106–107.

Advanced Before students read "The Go-Cart," ask them to share what they know about a go-cart. Have them study the picture carefully and name the characteristics they see. If necessary, provide them with additional information. Ask students how a ride in a go-cart would feel.

The Go-Cart

The summer had been downright boring. Nothing extraordinary had occurred. Then one day Jeff read the announcement in the local newspaper: "Go-Cart Race Next Month! First Prize $1,000!" He decided that he had to enter that race.

"But Jeff, you don't own a go-cart," his father said.

The newspaper noted that the go-cart had to be homemade, not factory-manufactured and bought. Jeff had been saving his allowance for what seemed like an eternity, and he had enough money to buy the plans and parts for a go-cart.

"But Jeff, you've never built anything," his mother said.

Jeff set about his building task. He read the instructions that came with his go-cart kit carefully. If something was confusing or hard to understand, he called the hardware store and asked for a clerk to explain. Every day he toiled on his go-cart, and every night it was that much closer to being finished.

Finally, the day of the race arrived. Jeff put on his helmet and revved his engine. The announcer roared, "On your mark! Get set! Go!" And Jeff, who had never raced a go-cart before, was off!

> **1 Skill** Why do you think Jeff *had* to enter the go-cart race?

> **2 Strategy** To answer that question, you need to draw a conclusion. The details in the paragraph can help you.

> **3 Skill** How do you think Jeff felt about himself as he revved his engine, waiting for the race to begin?

> **4 Strategy** To answer that question, think of details from throughout the story. Also think how *you* would feel if you were in Jeff's place.

393

---

raw Conclusions

- A **conclusion** is a decision you make after thinking about the details in what you read.
- Often your prior knowledge can help you draw, or make, a conclusion.
- When you draw a conclusion, be sure it makes sense and is supported by what you have read.

Directions Read the following passage. Then complete the diagram.

Several factors led to the formation of cities. First, small agricultural groups grew larger when farmers and hunters were able to provide a steady supply of food for more people. Also, settlers started keeping herds of animals for food and other purposes. Because of these developments there was enough food for everyone, so settlers had time to learn new skills. They started making better tools and finding new uses for them. Better tools led to improvements in living conditions. Workers built structures to protect the community and to store food. They traded with other groups for items they needed. As more people lived together, members of the community started having different responsibilities and social relationships changed. Eventually, these communities developed a system to govern themselves. They also created a written language.

Possible answers given.

Detail:	Detail:	Detail:	What you know:
1. Farmers and hunters provided food for more people.	2. Settlers learned new skills.	3. Settlers made better tools and found new uses for them.	4. Good tools make tough jobs easier.

Conclusion
5. More food and better tools led to formation of cities.

Home Activity Your child drew a conclusion from facts or details found in a reading passage. Tell him or her a short story about an event that happened in your life. Have your child single out two or three details from the story and form a conclusion about it.

Practice Book p. 153.

CORRECTIVE FEEDBACK

LA.5.1.7.3 Determine main idea or essential message through inferring

- **Question** Use the question below to address this FCAT tested standard. Have students write their answers on a sheet of paper.
- **Check** Scan students' responses by having them hold up their papers.
- **Correct** If necessary, provide corrective feedback.
- **Adjust** Pair students who correctly answered the question with students who did not for peer tutoring. Have them complete Practice Book p. 153 together.

Did Jeff do a careful job of building his go-cart? What details in the story help you answer the question?

TEACH

1 SKILL Use paragraph 1 to model how to draw a conclusion.

> **Think Aloud** **MODEL** The first paragraph tells me that Jeff is bored. Then it tells about a go-cart race with a big prize. I think Jeff wants to enter the race because he is bored and because he wants to win the prize money.

2 STRATEGY Discuss how to draw a conclusion to answer a question.

> **Think Aloud** **MODEL** To answer the question, I needed to draw a conclusion. I used details in the paragraph and what I already knew to figure out why Jeff wanted to enter the go-cart race. I used inference to draw my conclusions.

PRACTICE AND ASSESS

3 SKILL Possible responses: nervous, excited

4 STRATEGY The story says that Jeff works hard to build a go-cart, so he must want to race. I know how I would feel, and I think Jeff would feel the same way.

WRITE Have students complete steps 1 and 2 of the Write to Read activity. You might consider using this as a whole-class activity.

Monitor Progress

Draw Conclusions

If... students are unable to complete **Write to Read** on p. 392,	**then...** use Practice Book p. 153 to provide additional practice.

Practice Book p. 153.

ELL

Build Background Use ELL Poster 16 to build background and vocabulary for the lesson concept of how plants adapt.

▲ **ELL Poster** 16

Build Background

ACTIVATE PRIOR KNOWLEDGE

BEGIN A SEMANTIC WEB about plant parts.

- Write "plant parts" on the chalkboard and draw an oval around it. Challenge students to name as many plant parts as they can think of. Record student answers on the semantic web. Add additional ovals if necessary.

- If students don't suggest these words, add them to the web: *seeds, seedlings, oil, flowers, bark, roots, stalk, tubers.* Discuss the meaning of each word, using a dictionary or a science book.

- Tell students to look for how Wes uses plant parts as they read this week's selection.

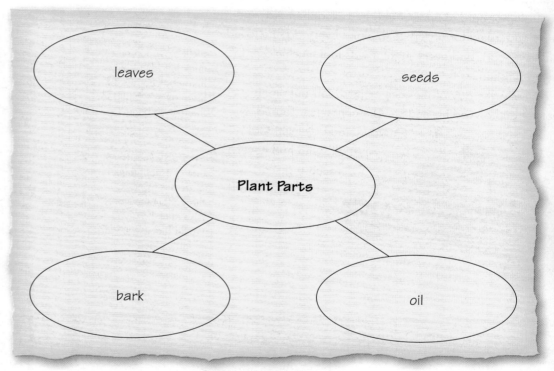

▲ **Graphic Organizer** 15

BACKGROUND BUILDING AUDIO This week's audio explores gardening with children. After students listen, discuss what challenges and rewards gardening with children might bring. Ask students what they found most surprising.

Background Building Audio

Page 394a

LA.5.1.6.4 Categorize key vocabulary

LA.5.1.6.10 Determine meanings of words by using a dictionary

LA.5.1.7.1 Use prior knowledge

LA.5.3.1.3 Organize ideas using strategies and tools (graphic organizer)

Introduce Vocabulary

WORD MEANING CHART

Create a word meaning chart using the categories *Word*, *Meaning*, and *Sentence* for the *Words to Know*. Using a three-column chart, students will put a check in the *Meaning* column if they know the definition of the word, and a check in the *Sentence* column if they can use the word correctly in a sentence. Students may add checks or more words to the chart during the week. **Activate Prior Knowledge**

Word	Meaning	Sentence
blunder		✓
civilization		
complex	✓	
envy		
fleeing		✓
inspired		
rustling	✓	
strategy	✓	

▲ **Graphic Organizer** 26

Tell students that the word *complex* is a homograph. Homographs are words that are spelled the same but have different meanings. *Complex* can be a noun or an adjective and has two pronunciations. Have them practice pronouncing it both ways. Ask students to look up *complex* in a dictionary, write a meaning for each part of speech, and then use each of the meanings in a sentence. Then ask students to predict which meaning will be used in the selection. **Homographs**

Have students share when they may have used or heard some of these words. Ask them to find synonyms *(fleeing/running, rustling/moving, blunders/mistakes)* or antonyms *(inspired/bored, fleeing/arriving)* for some of the words. **Synonyms • Antonyms**

Use the Multisyllabic Word Routine on p. DI·1 to help students read multisyllabic words.

Lesson Vocabulary

WORDS TO KNOW

T blunders stupid mistakes

T civilization the ways of living of a people or nation

T complex made up of a number of parts; hard to understand

T envy feeling of discontent, dislike, or desire because another person has what you want

T fleeing running away

T inspired filled with a thought or feeling; influenced

T rustling causing a light, soft sound of things gently rubbing together

T strategy the skillful planning and management of anything

MORE WORDS TO KNOW

breakfasting eating the first meal of the day

innovations changes made in the established way of doing things

seedlings young plants grown from seeds

T = Tested Word

Vocabulary

Directions Choose the word from the box that best matches each definition below. Write the word on the line.

civilization _____ 1. the ways of living of a people or nation

strategy _____ 2. the skillful planning and management of anything

rustling _____ 3. causing a light, soft sound of things gently rubbing together

blunders _____ 4. stupid mistakes

Check the Words You Know

___ blunders
___ civilization
___ complex
___ envy
___ fleeing
___ inspired
___ rustling
___ strategy

Directions Choose the word from the box that best fits in the sentence. Write the word on the line shown to the left.

fleeing _____ 5. In his dreams, dragons were after him and he was _____

complex _____ 6. Cities are more _____ than tiny villages.

inspired _____ 7. The people who created the earliest forms of writing were _____ by a need to communicate ideas.

Envy _____ 8. _____ arises when someone else gets something we wanted.

strategy _____ 9. To play a game or sport well, you need to form a _____

rustling _____ 10. As they hiked through the woods, they could hear the fallen leaves _____

Write a Description

On a separate sheet of paper, describe a sport you like to play, like soccer or chess. What are the rules? What are the best strategies?

Descriptions should include words from the vocabulary list and details such as the best strategies to use to win the game.

Home Activity Your child identified and used vocabulary words from *Weslandia*. Read a short story with your child. Have him or her point out unfamiliar words. Work together to figure out the meaning of each word by using words that appear near it.

▲ **Practice Book** p. 154

Page 394b

LA.5.1.6.8 Use knowledge of antonyms, synonyms, and homographs to determine meanings of words

Weslandia   **394b**

Vocabulary Strategy

Use word structure and word endings to determine meaning.

INTRODUCE

Discuss the strategy for word structure using the steps on p. 394.

TEACH

- Have students read "Long-Ago Lives," using word structure to find meanings of words.
- Model using word structure to determine the meaning of *rustling*.

Think Aloud

MODEL I don't recognize a base word in *rustling*, but I do see an *-ing* ending. I remember that sometimes a base word drops the final *-e*. If I drop the *-ing* and add an *-e*, the base word is *rustle*, which is what leaves do in the wind. So *rustling* must mean "making a light, soft sound."

Words to Know

envy
fleeing
civilization
complex
strategy
blunders
inspired
rustling

Remember
Try the strategy. Then, if you need more help, use your glossary or dictionary.

Vocabulary Strategy
for Endings

Word Structure The endings *-ed*, *-ing*, and *-s* may be added to verbs to change the tense. You can use endings to help you figure out the meaning of an unfamiliar word.

1. Examine the unfamiliar word to see if it has a base word you know.

2. Check to see if the ending *-s*, *-ed*, or *-ing* has been added to a base word. Remember that some base words drop the final *-e* before adding an ending. For example, *rustle* becomes *rustling*.

3. Reread the sentence and make sure the word shows action. (The ending *-s* may be added to nouns too.)

4. Decide how the ending changes the meaning of the base word.

5. Try the meaning in the sentence.

As you read "Long-Ago Lives," look for words that end with *-ed*, *-ing*, or *-s*. Use the endings to help figure out their meanings.

LA.5.1.6.2 Develop vocabulary by reading and discussing text
LA.5.1.6.4 Categorize key vocabulary

DAY 2 Grouping Options

Reading
Whole Group Discuss the Question of the Day. Then use pp. 394–397.

Group Time Differentiated Instruction
Read *Weslandia*. See pp. 392f–392g for the small group lesson plan.

Whole Group Use p. 411a.

Language Arts
Use pp. 411e–411k.

Strategic Intervention

Word Structure Have students circle the word endings for *fleeing*, *blunders*, and *inspired*.

ELL

Access Content Use ELL Poster 16 to preteach vocabulary. Choose from the following to meet language proficiency levels.

Beginning Use the Multilingual Lesson Vocabulary list that begins on p. 272 of the ELL Teaching Guide, as well as other home-language resources, to provide translations of the tested words.

Intermediate Ask students to share what they know about the words *civilization* and *complex*, based on home language cognates. (For example; Spanish: *Civilización*)

Advanced Teach the lesson on pp. 394–395. Have students select other vocabulary words and add them to their word meaning charts.

Resources for home-language words may include parents, bilingual staff members, bilingual dictionaries, or online translation sources.

Long-Ago Lives

We do not tend to think with envy about the lives of people who lived thousands of years ago. We are likely to imagine them fleeing for their lives from enemies or wild beasts. Any civilization without excellent shopping, television, and computers seems far too primitive for us.

However, we have learned much about early cultures. What we have learned shows us that their world was often complex, not simple. They were not all that different from us. For example, two thousand years ago the Mayan people played a ball game. The game was played by teams on stone courts with special goals. Players needed great strength and skill. The strategy was to send a heavy ball through a high stone ring using only hips, knees, elbows, and buttocks. Kings might play this game, for which the stakes were very high. No one wanted to make any blunders because the loser might lose his head!

This game may have inspired our modern game of soccer. Stand on one of these ancient ball courts and you can almost hear the rustling of a feather headdress and the yelling of the crowd.

Words to Write

Look at the pictures in *Weslandia*. Choose one to write about. Use as many words from the Words to Know list as you can.

395

Connect to Phonics

Word Study/Decoding Point out that the spelling of the base word often changes before adding an inflected ending. Model identifying the inflected ending and base word using *inspired* from p. 395, paragraph 3. Have students suggest other words they know with the inflected endings *-ed*, *-ing* and *-s*. Have them identify the inflected ending and base in each word. Then have them identify the meaning of each word with and without the inflected ending.

Pages 394–395

LA.5.1.4.2 Recognize structural analysis

LA.5.1.4.3 Use language structure to read multi-syllabic words in text

LA.5.1.6.2 Develop vocabulary by reading and discussing text

LA.5.1.6.4 Categorize key vocabulary

LA.5.1.6.7 Use meaning of familiar base words and affixes to determine meanings of unfamiliar complex words

PRACTICE AND ASSESS

- Have students determine the meanings of the remaining words and explain the strategy they used.

- Point out that a base word sometimes is changed before an ending is added, such as dropping a final *e* or doubling the final consonant.

- If students made a word meaning chart on p. 394b, have them add a column for word endings.

- Have students complete Practice Book p. 155.

WRITE Students should use words from the list and other words with endings to describe their picture.

Monitor Progress

Word Structure

If... students need more practice with the lesson vocabulary,	**then...** use Tested Vocabulary Cards.

Vocabulary · Word Structure

- An **ending** is a letter or letters added to the end of a base word.
- Recognizing an ending will help you figure out the word's meaning.
- The endings *–s* and *–es* can be added to singular nouns to make them plural. The endings *–s*, *–ed*, and *–ing* can be added to verbs to change the tense. The endings *–er* and *–est* can be added to adjectives to use them to compare.

Directions Read the following passage. Then answer the questions below.

Lisa enjoyed camping with her brother and parents every autumn. In a way she felt they were fleeing civilization and their complex city life. She had noticed that life in the city often makes people anxious. She always felt happier while hiking through the woods and sleeping under the stars. There was no one to envy because the beauty of nature surrounded them. Even the blunders they made turned into games to play. Once they hiked down the wrong trail and got lost. Instead of worrying, they worked together to find the quickest way back. When she returned to the city, Lisa felt inspired by the beauty she had enjoyed.

Possible answers given.

1. In the word *fleeing*, how does the *–ing* change the meaning of the root word?
   It changes the tense of the verb.

2. What is the difference between the *–s* in *blunders* and the *–s* in *makes*?
   The first *–s* makes a noun plural, while the second *–s* puts a verb in the present tense.

3. How does the *–er* change the meaning of the root in *happier*?
   It makes a comparison.

4. What does the *–ed* in *hiked* do to the meaning of the root word?
   It puts the verb into the past tense.

5. Change some of the endings in this sentence to put the verbs in the past tense: "Lisa calls out to her family, and then walks down the trail to meet them."
   Lisa called out to her family, and then walked down the trail to meet them.

School + Home Home Activity Your child identified and used endings added to base words, such as *–s*, *–ed*, *–ing*, and *–est*. Read a newspaper or magazine article with your child. Change the endings of some of the words and discuss with him or her how the sentences' meanings change.

▲ **Practice Book** p. 155

WORD AWARENESS Post this week's lesson vocabulary on a Word Wall or have students write the words and meanings in their Writing Logs for ready access during writing.

Prereading Strategies

- Draw conclusions to improve comprehension.
- Answer questions to help draw conclusions.

GENRE STUDY

Fiction

Weslandia is a fiction story. Explain that in fiction, characters and events may be realistic, even though they might be unusual or even unlikely in some way. *Weslandia* might also be called a modern-day fable, for the reader can infer a message at its conclusion.

PREVIEW AND PREDICT

Have students preview the title and illustrations and make predictions about the main character. Students should use lesson vocabulary words as they talk about what they expect to read.

Strategy Response Log

Ask Questions Have students make a list of questions they have about the selection based on the pictures. Students will answer these questions and ask others in the Strategy Response Log activity on p. 403.

Use Strategies Have students record in their strategy response logs reading strategies they use during reading and tell why they use them.

Why does Wesley take up the challenge of creating his own world?

Genre — **Fiction stories** are stories that the author has made up. As you read, notice how the character makes up his own world.

396

ELL

Activate Prior Knowledge Have students talk about plants they know and ways different parts of the plants can be used. Provide vocabulary for the different plant parts, such as *leaves*, *stems*, *flowers*, *fruit*, *roots*, and *stalks*.

Consider having students read the selection summary in English or in students' home languages. See the Multilingual Summaries in the ELL Teaching Guide, pp. 110–112.

Weslandia

by PAUL FLEISCHMAN   illustrated by KEVIN HAWKES

397

SET PURPOSE

Discuss the picture on pages 396–397. Ask students where they think the boy is and what he is doing. Have them tell what they hope to find out as they read the story.

Remind students to draw conclusions and answer questions as they read.

STRATEGY RECALL

Students have now used these before-reading strategies:

- preview the selection to be aware of its genre, features, and possible content;
- activate prior knowledge about that content and what to expect of that genre;
- make predictions;
- set a purpose for reading.

Remind students to be aware of and flexibly use the during-reading strategies they have learned:

- link prior knowledge to new information;
- summarize text they have read so far;
- ask clarifying questions;
- answer questions they or others pose;
- check their predictions and either refine them or make new predictions;
- recognize the text structure the author is using, and use that knowledge to make predictions and increase comprehension;
- visualize what the author is describing;
- monitor their comprehension and use fix-up strategies.

After reading, students will use these strategies:

- summarize or retell the text;
- answer questions they or others pose;
- reflect to make new information become part of their prior knowledge.

 **AudioText**

 Pages 396–397

LA.5.1.7.1 Use prior knowledge to make predictions, and establish a purpose for reading

LA.5.1.7.8 Use strategies to repair comprehension when self-monitoring, including questioning

LA.5.2.1.1 Demonstrate knowledge of the characteristics of various genres (fiction)

Guiding Comprehension

1 🔁 **Draw Conclusions • Critical**

On p. 398, Wesley's mother says, "He sticks out." What does this sentence tell you about Wesley?

Possible response: Wesley is different from other boys his age.

Monitor Progress

🔁 **Draw Conclusions**

If... students are unable to draw a conclusion,	**then...** use the skill and strategy instruction on p. 399.

2 Setting • Inferential

What do you think is the setting of this story? Why?

A neighborhood in a town. I think it is a town and not a city because the illustrations show yards, fences, and trees.

EXTEND SKILLS

Repetition

Point out that one literary device that authors use to enhance language or emphasize ideas is repetition of sounds, words, thoughts, or sentences. Ask students to reread p. 399 and look for a phrase that is repeated. *("...he answered on Wednesday, ...he answered on Thursday, ...he answered on Friday.")*

Page 398

LA.5.1.7.3 Determine the essential message through inferring

LA.5.2.1.2 Locate and analyze character development, plot structure, and setting

LA.5.2.1.3 Demonstrate how repetition helps to communicate meaning

"*O*f course he's miserable," moaned Wesley's mother. "He sticks out."

"Like a nose," snapped his father.

Listening through the heating vent, Wesley knew they were right. He was an outcast from the civilization around him.

He alone in his town disliked pizza and soda, alarming his mother and the school nurse. He found professional football stupid. He'd refused to shave half his head, the hairstyle worn by all the other boys, despite his father's bribe of five dollars.

Passing his neighborhood's two styles of housing—garage on the

398

Access Content Explain the idiom *sticks out* is the opposite of *fits in*. It means that a person is different and that people around him notice it. Ask students to name the ways in which Wesley sticks out.

left and garage on the right—Wesley alone dreamed of more exciting forms of shelter. He had no friends, but plenty of tormentors.

Fleeing them was the only sport he was good at.

Each afternoon his mother asked him what he'd learned in school that day.

"That seeds are carried great distances by the wind," he answered on Wednesday.

"That each civilization has its staple food crop," he answered on Thursday.

"That school's over and I should find a good summer project," he answered on Friday.

399

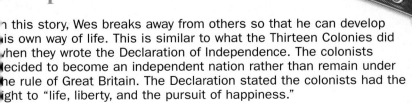

Declaration of Independence

In this story, Wes breaks away from others so that he can develop his own way of life. This is similar to what the Thirteen Colonies did when they wrote the Declaration of Independence. The colonists decided to become an independent nation rather than remain under the rule of Great Britain. The Declaration stated the colonists had the right to "life, liberty, and the pursuit of happiness."

SKILLS ↔ STRATEGIES IN CONTEXT

Draw Conclusions

FCAT TESTED SKILL

TEACH

- Tell students that a conclusion is a decision you make after thinking about details in a story. Prior knowledge can help them draw conclusions. Any conclusion must make sense and be supported by details.

- Model drawing a conclusion about Wes.

Think Aloud **MODEL** The details on page 398 tells a lot about Wes. His mother says he sticks out, and Wes doesn't mind that he does. He doesn't like pizza, soda, or football. He refuses to wear his hair like the other boys. My conclusion about Wes is that he is not like the other boys.

PRACTICE AND ASSESS

Have students reread p. 399. Ask which conclusion is best supported by information on p. 399. *(Choice a)*

a) Wes is smart.

b) Wes likes to run.

c) Wes hates school.

EYE ON FCAT

CORRECTIVE FEEDBACK

LA.5.1.7.3 Determine main idea or essential message through inferring

- **Question** Use Whiteboard or Transparency 16a, items 1–3, to ask questions that address this standard in FCAT format. Have students write their answers on a sheet of paper.
- **Check** Scan students' responses by having them hold up their papers.
- **Correct** If necessary, provide corrective feedback and review pp. 392–393.

> 1 Which of the following statements from the story BEST supports the conclusion that Wesley is different from the other boys his age?
>
> (A) School is over and Wesley wants to find a summer project.
> (B) Wesley makes up sports that could be played by one player.
> (C) Wesley does not like pizza, soda, or the haircut worn by other boys.
> (D) Wesley's fellow gardeners grow very traditional vegetables in their gardens.

▲ **FCAT Whiteboard Activity** 16a/ **FCAT Transparency** 16a

Guiding Comprehension

③ Figurative Language • Critical

What does it mean when the author says that "Wesley's thoughts shot sparks" in paragraph 2 on p. 400?

Possible response: It means that Wes was thinking and had come up with a good idea.

④ Main Idea • Inferential

Find a main idea and one supporting detail from pp. 400–401.

Main Idea: Wesley decides to grow his own staple food crop and begin his own civilization for his summer project. Detail: He turned over a plot of ground in his yard.

Monitor Progress

REVIEW Main Idea

If... students have difficulty finding a main idea and a supporting detail,	**then...** use the skill and strategy instruction on p. 401.

---

⑤ Characters • Critical

Text to Self **Think of a time when you felt like you were different from everyone else. How did it feel and what did you do about it?**

Answers will vary. Responses should include students' recollections of a time they've felt like they didn't belong and how they dealt with it.

As always, his father mumbled, "I'm sure you'll use that knowledge often."

③ Suddenly, Wesley's thoughts shot sparks. His eyes blazed. His father was right! He could actually *use* what he'd learned that week for a summer project that would top all others. He would

④ grow his own staple food crop—and found his own civilization!

The next morning he turned over a plot of ground in his yard. That night a wind blew in from the west. It raced through the trees and set his curtains snapping. Wesley lay awake, listening. His land was being planted.

400

Extend Language Reread aloud the phrase "and found his own civilization." Explain that in this example, *found* is a present tense verb that means to set up something. Tell students that *found* can also be a past tense verb that means something that is come upon by chance, as in the sentence, "I found a nickel on the sidewalk."

Page 400

LA.5.1.7.3 Determine the main idea through identifying relevant details

LA.5.2.1.5 Demonstrate understanding of a literary selection and include evidence from personal experience

LA.5.2.1.7 Identify and explain an author's use of figurative language and examine how it is used to describe people

Five days later the first seedlings appeared.

"You'll have almighty bedlam on your hands if you don't get those weeds out," warned his neighbor.

"Actually, that's my crop," replied Wesley. "In this type of garden there are no weeds."

Following ancient tradition, Wesley's fellow gardeners grew tomatoes, beans, Brussels sprouts, and nothing else. Wesley found it thrilling to open his land to chance, to invite the new and unknown.

The plants shot up past his knees, then his waist. They seemed **5** to be all of the same sort. Wesley couldn't find them in any plant book.

401

Main Idea REVIEW

TEACH

- Remind students that the main idea is the most important idea about the topic.
- Details are pieces of information that support or tell more about the main idea.
- Model finding a main idea and a supporting detail from pp. 400–401:

Think Aloud **MODEL** These pages discuss how Wesley decides to grow his own staple food crop and founded a new civilization for his summer project. This is the main idea. One detail that supports this idea is that "he turned over a plot of ground in his backyard."

PRACTICE AND ASSESS

- Have students find another detail on p. 401 that supports the main idea. *(seedlings appeared)*
- To assess, use Practice Book p. 156.

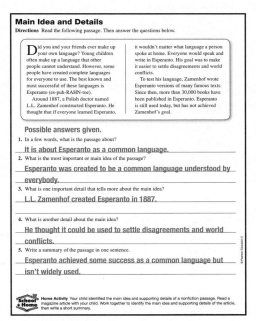

▲ **Practice Book** p. 156

Page 401

LA.5.1.7.3 Determine the main idea through inferring, paraphrasing, summarizing, and identifying relevant details

Guiding Comprehension

6  **Vocabulary • Word Structure**

What is the base word of *blushing*? How does the ending *-ing* change the meaning of the base word?

The base word is *blush*, which means "to turn red." Adding *-ing* makes it mean "the act of turning red."

Monitor Progress

 Word Structure

If... students have difficulty recognizing how the ending *-ing* changes the base word,	then... use vocabulary strategy instruction on p. 403.

---

7 Main Idea • Inferential

Besides growing a food crop, what else did Wesley do as part of his summer project?

He ate fruit from his plants, made a cup from half a rind, built his own squeezing device so he could make fruit juice, prepared tubers from his plants on the family barbecue, and wove a hat and a robe.

Tech Files
ONLINE

Have students type the keywords *backyard garden fruit* in a student-friendly search engine to learn about other types of fruit Wes could have grown in his garden. Be sure to follow classroom rules for Internet use.

"Are those tomatoes, beans, or Brussels sprouts?" asked Wesley's neighbor.

"None of the above," replied Wesley.

6 Fruit appeared, yellow at first, then blushing to magenta. Wesley picked one and sliced through the rind to the juicy purple center. He took a bite and found the taste an entrancing blend of peach, strawberry, pumpkin pie, and flavors he had no name for.

Ignoring the shelf of cereals in the kitchen, Wesley took to breakfasting on the fruit. He dried half a rind to serve as a cup, built his own squeezing device, and drank the fruit's juice throughout the day.

402

ELL

Extend Language Read aloud the phrase "and found the taste an entrancing blend of..." Pronounce the word *entrancing* clearly, putting stress on the second syllable. Explain that *entrancing* means delightful.

Page 402

LA.5.1.4.2 Recognize structural analysis

LA.5.1.6.7 Use meaning of familiar base words and affixes to determine meanings of unfamiliar complex words

LA.5.1.7.3 Determine the main idea through inferring

Pulling up a plant, he found large tubers on the roots. These he boiled, fried, or roasted on the family barbecue, seasoning them with a pinch of the plant's highly aromatic leaves.

It was hot work tending to his crop. To keep off the sun, Wesley wove himself a hat from strips of the plant's woody bark. His success with the hat inspired him to devise a spinning wheel and loom on which he wove a loose-fitting robe from the stalks' soft inner fibers.

Unlike jeans, which he found scratchy and heavy, the robe was comfortable, reflected the sun, and offered myriad opportunities for pockets.

403

Word Structure

TEACH

- Tell students that the endings *-ed*, *-ing*, and *-s* may be added to verbs to change the tense and the meaning of the word.

- Model using word structure to determine the meaning of *blushing*.

Think Aloud **MODEL** The word *blushing* has an *-ing* ending, and the base word is *blush*. I've heard of *blush* before. It means "to turn red." So, in this sentence *blushing* must mean the fruit was turning a shade of red.

PRACTICE AND ASSESS

Have students use word structure to determine the meaning of other verbs on pp. 402–403 that end in *-ed* or *-ing*. Ask them to identify verbs in which a final *e* is dropped (*squeezing, ignoring*) or a *y* is changed to *i* (*replied, dried, fried*) before adding the ending.

Answer Questions Have students review the questions they asked about the story earlier and answer any of those they can. (See p. 396.) Have them add any new questions they may have about the story.

Develop Vocabulary

PRACTICE LESSON VOCABULARY

Have students give a brief oral response to each question.

1. What kind of *blunders* might a baseball player make? *(A baseball player might drop the ball or strike out.)*

2. What kinds of things are painters *inspired* by? *(They are filled with feelings or influenced by the beauty around them.)*

3. What is a good *strategy* for passing a test? *(Studying is a good plan for doing well on a test.)*

BUILD CONCEPT VOCABULARY

Review previous concept words with students. Ask if students have found any words today in their reading or elsewhere that they would like to add to the People Adapting Concept Web, such as *outcast* and *alarming*.

Page 403

LA.5.1.4.2 Recognize structural analysis

LA.5.1.6.1 Use new vocabulary that is introduced and taught directly

LA.5.1.6.7 Use meaning of familiar base words and affixes to determine meanings of unfamiliar complex words

LA.5.1.7.8 Use strategies to repair comprehension when self-monitoring, including questioning

If you want to teach this story in two sessions, stop here.

Guiding Comprehension

If you are teaching this story in two days, discuss any conclusions students may have drawn so far and review the vocabulary.

8 **Graphic Sources • Inferential**

What does the picture on p. 404 show about Wesley's method of telling time?

Possible response: It shows the sundial he created with a stalk and how he divided it into eight segments.

9 **Draw Conclusions • Inferential**

Why do you think Wesley's schoolmates went from being scornful to curious about his summer project?

Possible response: They probably saw that Wesley was doing some interesting things that they wanted to do too.

Monitor Progress

Draw Conclusions

If... students have difficulty drawing conclusions to answer questions,	then... use the skill and strategy instruction on p. 405.

DAY 3 Grouping Options

Reading
Whole Group Discuss the Question of the Day.

Group Time Differentiated Instruction
Read *Weslandia*. See pp. 392f–392g for the small group lesson plan.

Whole Group Discuss the Reader Response questions on p. 408. Then use p. 411a.

Language Arts
Use pp. 411e–411k.

His schoolmates were scornful, then curious. Grudgingly, Wesley allowed them ten minutes apiece at his mortar, crushing the plant's seeds to collect the oil.

This oil had a tangy scent and served him both as suntan lotion and mosquito repellent. He rubbed it on his face each morning and sold small amounts to his former tormentors at the price of ten dollars per bottle.

"What's happened to your watch?" asked his mother one day.

Wesley admitted that he no longer wore it. He told time by

404

ELL

Access Content Read aloud the phrase "and had divided the day into eight segments." Explain that *segments* are sections, or parts, into which a whole can be divided. Point out that in our civilization, days are divided into 24 segments, or hours.

Page 404

LA.5.1.7.3 Determine the main idea or essential message through inferring
LA.5.2.2.1 Locate, explain, and use information from text features (illustrations)

the stalk that he used as a sundial and had divided the day into eight segments—the number of petals on the plant's flowers.

He'd adopted a new counting system as well, based likewise upon the number eight. His domain, home to many such innovations, he named "Weslandia."

Uninterested in traditional sports, Wesley made up his own. These were designed for a single player and used many different parts of the plant. His spectators looked on with envy.

Realizing that more players would offer him more scope, Wesley invented other games that would include his schoolmates,

405

Amish Culture

Time for SOCIAL STUDIES

Traditionally, the Amish people live a self-sufficient life that is different from much of American society. They make their own clothing and live off their own land. They travel by horse and buggy and do not use electricity in their homes. They are a very religious people who respect tradition.

Page 405

LA.5.1.7.3 Determine the main idea or essential message through inferring

LA.5.2.1.5 Demonstrate understanding of a literary selection, and include evidence from the text and personal experience

LA.5.2.2.2 Use information from the text to answer questions related to relevant details

Draw Conclusions Answer Questions

TEACH

Have students reread pp. 404–405. Model drawing a conclusion about why Wes's school-mates changed their minds, using both prior knowledge and answers to questions raised throughout the story.

Think Aloud **MODEL** Kids who are different are often teased by others so that probably explains why Wes's schoolmates were scornful at first. But once they saw the interesting things he was doing, they became curious. I think they changed their minds because they wanted to have fun too.

PRACTICE AND ASSESS

Have students work in pairs to answer the questions below to help them draw conclusions about the story.

1) Why didn't Wes wear his watch anymore? *(He used his sundial to tell time instead.)*

2) Why did he name his civilization "Weslandia?" *(He named it after himself because he created it.)*

3) Why did Wesley design sports for a single player? *(He didn't have teammates when he created them.)*

EXTEND SKILLS

Stereotype

A stereotype is an oversimplified idea about a person or a group of people. *Nerd* and *dweeb* are just two of the many words people find to insult others who are unpopular or don't fit in. In *Weslandia*, Wes's schoolmates torment him at first because he is not interested in fitting into their world (Wes may consider *them* stereotypes), but later they are curious and finally even envious of his individuality. Have students identify other examples of stereotypes that they know about.

Guiding Comprehension

10 **Draw Conclusions • Inferential**

How do Wes's parents feel about his summer project?

Possible response: They are pleased with it because it makes Wes happy.

11 Author's Purpose • Critical

How do you think the author feels about independent thinking and creative kids like Wes?

Possible response: He probably thinks that it's a good idea for kids to be creative and not always follow what the crowd does.

12 **Draw Conclusions • Critical**

Text to World **What would our world be like if no one was like Wes and everyone lived the same way?**

Possible response: Our world would be pretty boring and no one would come up with new ideas.

Strategy Response Log

Summarize When students finish reading the selection, provide this prompt: Recall all of the things Wesley does to create his own civilization in *Weslandia*. Then write down only the most important points.

Use Strategies Meet with students to review their list of the reading strategies they realized they were using as they read.

games rich with strategy and complex scoring systems. He tried to be patient with the other players' blunders.

August was unusually hot. Wesley built himself a platform and took to sleeping in the middle of Weslandia. He passed the evenings playing a flute he'd fashioned from a stalk or gazing up at the sky, renaming the constellations.

His parents noted Wesley's improved morale. "It's the first
10 time in years he's looked happy," said his mother.

Wesley gave them a tour of Weslandia.

"What do you call this plant?" asked his father. Not knowing

406

Page 406

LA.5.1.7.2 Identify author's purpose

LA.5.1.7.3 Determine the main idea or essential message through inferring

LA.5.1.7.8 Use strategies to repair comprehension when self-monitoring, including summarizing

its name, Wesley had begun calling it "swist," from the sound of its leaves rustling in the breeze.

In like manner, he'd named his new fabrics, games, and foods, until he'd created an entire language.

Mixing the plant's oil with soot, Wesley made a passable ink. As the finale to his summer project, he used the ink and his own eighty-letter alphabet to record the history of his civilization's founding.

In September, Wesley returned to school . . . **11**
He had no shortage of friends. **12**

407

Develop Vocabulary

PRACTICE LESSON VOCABULARY

Students orally respond *yes* or *no* to each question and provide a reason.

1. Could you build a *complex* model without the directions? *(No; I could not build a very difficult model without directions.)*

2. Would a modern *civilization* include a government? *(Yes; a modern civilization needs leadership and rules.)*

3. Can a snake make a *rustling* sound? *(Yes; snakes can move with quick, small, rubbing sounds.)*

BUILD CONCEPT VOCABULARY

Review previous concept words with students. Ask if students have come across any words today in their reading or elsewhere that they would like to add to the People Adapting Concept Web, such as *patient* and *morale*.

 STRATEGY SELF-CHECK

Answer Questions

Have students answer these questions: Why did Wesley feel miserable at the beginning of the story? Why did Wesley feel happy at the end of the story? What conclusions can you draw about Wes at the end of the story? Use Practice Book p. 157.

SELF-CHECK

Students can ask themselves these questions to assess their ability to use the skill and strategy.

- Did I use my own experiences to draw conclusions about the story?
- Did I use the answers to questions to help me draw conclusions about the story?

Monitor Progress

Draw Conclusions

If... students have difficulty drawing conclusions,	then... use the Reteach lesson on p. 411b.

Page 407

LA.5.1.6.1 Use new vocabulary
LA.5.1.7.3 Determine the essential message through inferring

Draw Conclusions

- A **conclusion** is a decision you make after thinking about the details in what you read.
- Often your prior knowledge can help you draw, or make, a conclusion.
- When you draw a conclusion, be sure it makes sense and is supported by what you have read.

Directions Read the following passage. Then answer the questions below.

When Kyoung first arrived in the United States, he saw all the tall buildings and cars and people. It looked just like he'd seen in the movies. Everyone and everything moved very quickly. There also was so much more of everything than in his village in his old country. It wasn't until he got to his new home in Maryville that time seemed to slow down.

At school, the other students didn't talk to him much because they had trouble pronouncing his name. His teacher suggested they call him "Bill." So Bill became his nickname. The other students talked to him more, asking questions about his country or what had gone through before he came to the United States. He tried to explain, but it was not always easy. The cultures were very different and he was still learning English. Nevertheless, he told them a little each time they asked.

Possible answers given.

1. How do you think Kyoung felt when he first reached the U.S.?
   He may have felt excited, and a little frightened and homesick.
2. What parts of the text helped you reach the conclusion you described above?
   The passage describes how the U.S. seems like a movie, and how everything is big and fast-moving.
3. What things that you already knew helped you reach the conclusion you described above?
   Big cities are often amazing to people from the countryside.
4. Do you think Kyoung using the nickname "Bill" was a good idea? Why or why not?
   Yes; It made students more willing to try talking with him.
5. How do you think Kyoung felt when other students asked him about his past? Is your conclusion based on the passage, on your own experience, or both?
   Happy to be asked; I based my answer on the text and on how I would feel if I were Kyoung.

School Home Home Activity Your child drew conclusions from the details of a brief story. Read an article or story with your child about a faraway place. Ask him or her questions about how someone from there of your child's age might adapt to life in the United States.

▲ **Practice Book** p. 157

Reader Response

Open for Discussion Personal Response

MODEL I would love to visit a place like Weslandia, but not live there. I think it would be lonely there without friends and family to share it.

Comprehension Check Critical Response

1. Possible response: He must have had fun describing new fruit and thinking about how to make a flute from a stalk. *Author's Purpose*

2. Responses will vary, but should include that the illustrations show the boy is curious and imaginative. *Draw Conclusions*

3. Possible response: I would admire anyone with that much creativity and courage to be different. *Answer Questions*

4. Possible response: Wesley's *strategy* to change things was to invent his own *civilization*; this made others feel *envy* and *inspired* them. *Vocabulary*

THINK AND EXPLAIN For test practice, assign a 5 minute time limit. For assessment, see the Scoring Rubric at the right.

Retell

Have students retell *Weslandia*.

Monitor Progress

Check Retelling 4 3 2 1 Rubric

If... students have difficulty retelling the story,	then... use the Retelling Cards and the Scoring Rubric for Retelling on p. 409 to assist fluent retelling.

SUCCESS PREDICTOR

Check Retelling Have students use the story illustrations to guide their retellings. Be sure to focus on comprehension and overlook any mistakes in English. For more ideas on assessing students' retellings, see the ELL and Transition Handbook.

Reader Response

Open for Discussion Would you like to live in Weslandia or a land of your own making? What is your opinion about making a new civilization? Use *Weslandia* as support for your opinion.

1. *Weslandia* shows that you can find a fun idea for a fantasy tale just beyond your own back door. How can you tell that Paul Fleischman had fun inventing this story? Use examples from the text. **Think Like an Author**

2. Pretend you have never read *Weslandia*. Look only at the illustrations, from start to finish. Then draw conclusions about the plot and characters. Use examples from the art to support those conclusions. **Draw Conclusions**

3. Would you say that Wesley is a person you could admire? Support your answer with details from the story. **Answer Questions**

4. Wesley sees himself as an outcast from civilization. What do you think he meant? What did he do to change his situation? Answer using words from the Words to Know list. **Vocabulary**

READ THINK EXPLAIN

Think and Explain Look at the picture on pages 404–405 and read the story's final sentence. Explain how they make a surprise ending to *Weslandia*.

Meet author **Paul Fleischman on page 770.**

LA.5.1.7.1 Explain text features, illustrations
LA.5.1.7.2 Identify author's purpose

408

READ THINK EXPLAIN

THINK AND EXPLAIN TWO-POINT SCORING RUBRIC

Top-Score Response A top-score response uses the picture on pp. 404–405 and the final sentence to conclude that schoolmates who once made fun of Wesley want to play his games and be friends.

Example of a Top-Score Response In the picture, the students who used to make fun of Wesley are playing the games he has invented. Now they admire Wesley for all his inventions. It is surprising that he has become popular over the summer. Wesley has not changed, but his classmates have come to appreciate him.

For additional rubrics, see p. WA10.

Write Now

e-mail

More FCAT WRITING+
See *The Grammar and Writing Book*, pages 140–145.

Prompt

In *Weslandia*, a boy decides to remake his world rather than accept it as it is.

Think about someone you know who doesn't always "follow the herd."

Now write an e-mail to that person reacting to something he or she has done.

Writing Trait

In e-mail, use **conventions**, such as proper punctuation and capitalization, so that your message will be clearly understood.

Student Model

E-mail heading contains important information.

Subject: Explain, please
Date: 3/31/07
From: Jimmy Tuff
To: Wesley
cc: Biff, Travis, Kirk

E-mail can use informal language and tone.

Hey, Wesley, what are you doing in that weed patch? Mom says the seeds might blow into our garden plot. Then we'd have weeds too!

Conventions of capitalization and punctuation help make writer's meaning clear.

That straw hat and robe thing you wear make me laugh. But I wouldn't mind trying that tasty-looking fruit. How about sharing some?

We kids can't figure out what you're up to. Please meet us in the park this afternoon and tell us what's going on.

Jimmy

Use the model to help you with your own e-mail writing.

LA.5.3.1.2 Determine intended audience
LA.5.3.4.2 Use capitalization correctly

409

Write Now

Look at the Prompt Explain that each sentence in the prompt has a purpose.

- Sentence 1 presents a topic.
- Sentence 2 suggests students think about the topic.
- Sentence 3 tells what to write.

Strategies to Develop Conventions

Have students

- write complete sentences with correct end punctuation.
- use apostrophes in contractions correctly.
- use capital letters for the pronoun *I* and to begin proper nouns and sentences.

NO: here's what i think, wesley.
YES: Here's what I think, Wesley.

For additional suggestions and rubric, see pp. 411g–411h.

Writer's Checklist

☑ **Focus** Does the subject line name the topic?
☑ **Organization** Does the e-mail have a clear beginning and ending?
☑ **Support** Do details support the main idea?
☑ **Conventions** Are pronoun forms correct?

Page 409
LA.5.3.1.2 Determine intended audience
LA.5.3.4.2 Use capitalization correctly
LA.5.3.4.3 Use punctuation correctly

Scoring Rubric | Narrative Retelling

Rubric 4 3 2 1	4	3	2	1
Connections	Makes connections and generalizes beyond the text	Makes connections to other events, stories, or experiences	Makes a limited connection to another event, story, or experience	Makes no connection to another event, story, or experience
Author's Purpose	Elaborates on author's purpose	Tells author's purpose with some clarity	Makes some connection to author's purpose	Makes no connection to author's purpose
Characters	Describes the main character(s) and any character development	Identifies the main character(s) and gives some information about them	Inaccurately identifies some characters or gives little information about them	Inaccurately identifies the characters or gives no information about them
Setting	Describes the time and location	Identifies the time and location	Omits details of time or location	Is unable to identify time or location
Plot	Describes the problem, goal, events, and ending using rich detail	Tells the problem, goal, events, and ending with some errors that do not affect meaning	Tells parts of the problem, goal, events, and ending with gaps that affect meaning	Retelling has no sense of story

Retelling Plan

☑ **Week 1** This week assess Strategic Intervention students.
☐ **Week 2** Assess Advanced students.
☐ **Week 3** Assess Strategic Intervention students.
☐ **Week 4** Assess On-Level students.
☐ **Week 5** Assess any students you have not yet checked during this unit.

Use the Retelling Chart on p. TR16 to record retelling.

Selection Test To assess with *Weslandia*, use Selection Tests, pp. 61–64.

Fresh Reads for Differentiated Test Practice For weekly leveled practice, use pp. 91–69.

Retelling

SUCCESS PREDICTOR

Poetry

- Examine features of poetry.
- Practice a test-taking strategy.
- Compare and contrast across texts.

PREVIEW

Ask students to preview the poems by looking at the pictures and reading the title and first few lines of each poem. After they preview ask:

- **What do you think these two poems will be about?** (Possible response: Places around the house that kids use to play or hide in.)

Link to Writing

Before students begin to write, have partners describe their secret places. Encourage them to ask each other questions about how the place looks, sounds, smells, and feels.

 **AudioText**

DAY 4 Grouping Options

Reading

Whole Group Discuss the Question of the Day.

Group Time Differentiated Instruction
Read "Under the Back Porch" and "Keziah." See pp. 392f–392g for the small group lesson plan.

Whole Group Use p. 411a.

Language Arts
Use pp. 411e–411k.

Poetry

Genre

- Poetry is meant to appeal to the senses, emotions, or mind.

- Sensory words in a poem help the reader understand what the writer smells, sees, and feels.

- Some poems rhyme; others do not.

- Sometimes, the writer repeats words or phrases to emphasize a point or create rhythm.

Link to Writing

Think about your own favorite secret place and write a poem about it. Give the reader a picture in words of the place and an idea of when and why you go there.

LA.5.2.1.3 Demonstrate how rhythm, repetition, and figurative language communicate meaning in a poem
LA.5.4.1.2 Write an expressive form that employs figurative language

410

Under the Back Porch

BY VIRGINIA HAMILTON

Our house is two stories high
shaped like a white box.
There is a yard stretched around it
and in back
a wooden porch.

Under the back porch is my place.
I rest there.
I go there when I have to be alone.
It is always shaded and damp.
Sunlight only slants through the slats
in long strips of light,
and the smell of the damp
is moist green,
like the moss that grows here.

My sisters and brothers
can stand on the back porch
and never know
I am here
underneath.
It is my place.
All mine.

Page 410

LA.5.1.7.1 Use prior knowledge to make predictions
LA.5.2.1.3 Demonstrate how rhythm, repetition, and figurative language communicate meaning in a poem
LA.5.4.1.2 Write a variety of expressive forms (poetry)

Keziah

BY GWENDOLYN BROOKS

I have a secret place to go.
Not anyone may know

And sometimes when the wind is rough
I cannot get there fast enough.

And sometimes when my mother
Is scolding my big brother,

My secret place, it seems to me,
Is quite the only place to be.

Reading Across Texts

Look back at *Weslandia* and ask yourself what kind of poem Wesley might write about the world he created.

Writing Across Texts Write a poem about *Weslandia* that you think Wesley might have written.

Draw Conclusions What makes the porch a secret place?

411

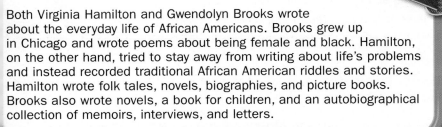

African American Authors

Both Virginia Hamilton and Gwendolyn Brooks wrote about the everyday life of African Americans. Brooks grew up in Chicago and wrote poems about being female and black. Hamilton, on the other hand, tried to stay away from writing about life's problems and instead recorded traditional African American riddles and stories. Hamilton wrote folk tales, novels, biographies, and picture books. Brooks also wrote novels, a book for children, and an autobiographical collection of memoirs, interviews, and letters.

POETRY

Use the sidebar on p. 410 to guide discussion.

- Explain to students that poetry is the arrangement of words in lines having rhythm or a regularly repeated accent, and, often, rhyme.
- Ask students to tell how they know these are poems by looking at them.

Draw Conclusions

Possible response: No one knows about it.

> **Page 411**
>
> **LA.5.1.7.3** Determine the essential message through inferring
> **LA.5.1.7.7** Compare and contrast elements in multiple texts
> **LA.5.2.1.1** Demonstrate knowledge of characteristics of genres (poetry)
> **LA.5.4.1.2** Write a variety of expressive forms

CONNECT TEXT TO TEXT

Reading Across Texts

Have students find words and details about Weslandia. Then discuss how the details could be used to write a poem.

Writing Across Texts Students can describe all of Weslandia or concentrate on one feature of it. Their poems may rhyme or not.

Fluency Assessment Plan

☑ **This week assess Advanced students.**
☐ **Week 2** Assess Strategic Intervention students.
☐ **Week 3** Assess On-Level students.
☐ **Week 4** Assess Strategic Intervention students.
☐ **Week 5** Assess any students you have not yet checked during this unit.

Set individual goals for students to enable them to reach the year-end goal.
• Current Goal: 120–128 wcpm
• Year-End Goal: 140 wcpm

Oral fluency depends not only on reading without halting but also on word recognition. After students read passages aloud for assessment, help them recognize unfamiliar English words and their meanings. Focus on each student's progress.

To develop fluent readers, use Fluency Coach.

 Page 411a
LA.5.1.5.1 Demonstrate the ability to read grade level text
LA.5.1.5.2 Adjust reading rate based on form and style

 Grouping Options

Reading
Whole Group
Revisit the Question of the Week.

Group Time
Differentiated Instruction
Reread this week's Leveled Readers. See pp. 392f–392g for the small group lesson plan.

Whole Group
Use p. 411b–411c.

Language Arts
Use pp. 411d–411l.

PUNCTUATION CLUES
Fluency

DAY 1

Model Reread "The Black Stallion" on p. 392m. Explain that as you read, you will use punctuation as a guide, for instance pausing at commas and raising your voice slightly to indicate a question. Model for students as you read.

DAY 2

Choral Reading Read aloud p. 400. Have students notice how you use an excited tone of voice when reading sentences that end with exclamation points and pause at the dash. Have students practice as a class doing three choral readings.

DAY 3

Model Read aloud p. 402. Have students notice pauses for commas and periods, and how your voice changes when reading the question. Practice as a class by doing three choral readings.

DAY 4

Partner Reading Partners practice reading p. 402, three times. Encourage them to read with pauses and expression, using punctuation as a guide. Have them offer each other feedback.

Monitor Progress | Check Fluency WCPM

As students reread, monitor their progress toward their individual fluency goals. Current Goal: 120–128 words correct per minute. End-of-Year Goal: 140 WCPM. Have library books or other texts available at a variety of reading levels for students to use to practice fluency. See pp. DI·57–DI·58.

If... students cannot read fluently at a rate of 120–128 words correct per minute,
then... make sure students practice with text at their independent level. Provide additional fluency practice, pairing nonfluent readers with fluent readers.

If... students already read at 140 words correct per minute,
then... they do not need to reread three to four times.

SUCCESS PREDICTOR

DAY 5

Assessment
Individual Reading Rate Use the Fluency Assessment Plan and do a one-minute timed reading of either selection from this week to assess students in Week 1. Pay special attention to this week's skill, punctuation clues. Provide corrective feedback for each student.

RETEACH

Draw Conclusions

TEACH

Review the definition for *conclusion* on p. 392. Complete Practice Book p. 158 as a class. Point out that students need to complete sentences 1–3, and explain what they know about playing games, before drawing a conclusion in sentence 5.

ASSESS

Have students reread "Keziah" on p. 411 in their books and draw conclusions about why the speaker likes his secret place. *(Possible response: He likes to be away from problems, in a quiet place sometimes.)*

For additional instruction on drawing conclusions, see DI•52.

EXTEND SKILLS

Idiom

TEACH

An idiom is a group of words that cannot be understood by the ordinary meaning of the words. Examples include "pulling your leg" or "bury the hatchet."

- In idioms, words take on non-literal meanings.
- Often the meaning of idioms can be understood by figuring out what makes sense in context.

Reread p. 400, paragraph 3 together as a class and point out the idiom: "(the wind) set his curtains snapping." Explain that Wesley's curtains don't actually snap, but they make a noise that sounds like snapping when the wind blows them hard.

ASSESS

Have students brainstorm and write down other idioms they know as well as their meaning.

OBJECTIVES

- Draw conclusions to improve comprehension.
- Recognize and interpret idioms.

Skills Trace
Draw Conclusions

Introduce/Teach	TE: 5.4 392–393, 484–485; 5.6 634–635
Practice	Practice Book: 153, 157, 158, 186, 193, 197, 198, 253, 257, 258, 276, 296
Reteach/Review	TE: 5.4 411b, 467, 503b, DI•52, DI•56; 5.6 653b, 683, 687, 735, 745, DI•52
Test	Selection Test: 61–64, 77–80, 101–104; Benchmark Test: Units 4, 6

ELL

Access Content Reteach the skill by reviewing the Picture It! lesson on draw conclusions in the ELL Teaching Guide, pp. 106–107.

Draw Conclusions

- A **conclusion** is a decision you make after thinking about the details of what you read.
- Often your prior knowledge can help you draw, or make, a conclusion.
- When you draw a conclusion, be sure it makes sense and is supported by what you have read.

Directions Read the following passage. Then complete the diagram.

People have played games throughout history. There are all kinds of games—card games, board games, sports games, children's games, and problem-solving games. People have invented games that can be played by one person, a few people, or by whole teams. Games give people a chance to challenge their minds and bodies. They also give people the thrill of winning. Best of all, games are fun.

Possible answers given.

Detail:	Detail:	Detail:	What you know:
1. People have played games **throughout** **recorded** **history.**	2. There are many different **kinds of** **games.**	3. Games challenge people's **minds** **and bodies.**	4. I like **playing** **games.**

Conclusion
5. People everywhere **love to play games.**

School + Home **Home Activity** Your child drew conclusions from facts or details found in a reading passage about games. Read a story or an article with your child. Work with him or her to draw conclusions from the details in it.

▲ **Practice Book** p. 158

Page 411b

LA.5.1.7.3 Determine the essential message through inferring
LA.5.2.1.7 Identify and explain an author's use of idiomatic language

Vocabulary and Word Study

VOCABULARY STRATEGY
Word Structure

ENDINGS Remind students that -*ed*, -*ing*, and -*s* may be added to verbs to change the tense. The endings can also be used to help determine the meaning of an unfamiliar word. Have students examine words with these endings from *Weslandia*. Ask students to identify base words and meanings and then see if they can make new words with the other two endings.

Word	Base Word	Meaning	New Words
moaned	moan	made a long, low sound of pain	moaning, moans
listening			
replied			
adopted			

Plural Nouns

The ending -*s* can also be added to nouns to make them plural. Some plural nouns require an -*es* ending. Nouns ending in a consonant and *y* change the *y* to *i* before adding -*es*. Have students work with partners to write the plural forms of these five nouns from *Weslandia*.

1. pizza: pizzas
2. garage
3. tomato
4. peach
5. history

BUILD CONCEPT VOCABULARY
People Adapting

LOOKING BACK Remind students of the question of the week: *How do people adapt to difficult situations?* Discuss how this week's Concept Web of vocabulary words relates to the theme of adapting. Ask students if they have any words or categories to add. Discuss whether the words and categories are appropriately related to the concept.

REVIEW/CONNECT Preview the title of the next selection, *Stretching Ourselves.* Ask students which Concept Web words might apply to the new selection based on the title alone.

Put a star next to these words on the web.

Display the Concept Web and revisit the vocabulary words as you read the next selection to check predictions.

Monitor Progress
Check Vocabulary

If... students suggest words or categories that are not related to the concept,	then... review the words and categories on the Concept Web and discuss how they relate to the lesson concept.

SUCCESS PREDICTOR

Speaking and Viewing

SPEAKING

Demonstration

SET-UP Have students choose one of Wes's Weslandia projects and prepare a how-to demonstration for the class.

TOPICS Students can choose to demonstrate weaving cloth, crushing seeds to make oil, creating a sundial, adopting a new counting system, devising an 80-letter alphabet, building a flute, or making up sports and games. Encourage them to choose something that they are comfortable with and can get the materials they need. Students may work in pairs.

PLANNING Provide these planning tips for students:

- Make sure you have all of the materials you need before you begin your demonstration. Plan how to lay them out and in what order.
- Try out your project to see if it works.
- Practice your demonstration to make sure you can do it in the time allotted.

ADAPTATION Advise students to think of ways they will handle any problems that may come up during their demonstrations, such as running out of materials or dropping something. Encourage them to allow extra time in case they need to correct any errors or redo a step.

VIEWING

Analyze Illustrations

Have students study the illustrations on pp. 398–399 and p. 405 then answer these questions orally or in writing.

1. **What is happening in the illustrations on pp. 398–399? Describe Wes's surroundings.** *(Possible responses: He's being chased by bullies. His surroundings are messy, disorganized.)*

2. **What do you think the illustrator wants to convey about Wes based on the illustrations on pp. 398–399?** *(Possible responses: He's awkward, unhappy, a misfit, unpopular.)*

3. **Look at the illustration on p. 405. Compare Wes in that illustration to Wes in the illustrations on pp. 398–399.** *(Responses will vary but may include how Wes became happier and more confident, and his surroundings appear more orderly.)*

the stalk that he used as a sundial and had divided the day into eight segments—the number of petals on the plant's flowers.

He'd adopted a new counting system as well, based likewise upon the number eight. His domain, home to many such innovations, he named "Weslandia."

Uninterested in traditional sports, Wesley made up his own. These were designed for a single player and used many different parts of the plant. His spectators looked on with envy.

Realizing that more players would offer him more scope, Wesley invented other games that would include his schoolmates,

9

405

Pages 411c–411d

LA.5.1.4.3 Use language structure to read multi-syllabic words

LA.5.1.6.4 Categorize key vocabulary

LA.5.1.7.1 Explain the purpose of text features (illustrations)

LA.5.5.2.1 Listen and speak to gain and share information (presentations)

LA.5.5.2.2 Make formal oral presentations

Vocabulary

SUCCE PREDICT

Grammar Subject and Object Pronouns

OBJECTIVES

- Define and identify subject and object pronouns.
- Use subject and object pronouns in writing.
- Become familiar with pronoun assessment on high-stakes tests.

Monitor Progress

Grammar

If... students have difficulty identifying subject and object pronouns,	then... provide additional instruction and practice in The Grammar and Writing Book pp. 140–143.

DAILY FIX-IT

This week use Daily Fix-It Transparency 16.

Spiral REVIEW

Support Grammar See the Grammar Transition lessons in the ELL and Transition Handbook.

▲ **The Grammar and Writing Book**
For more instruction and practice, use pp. 140–143.

DAY 1 Teach and Model

DAILY FIX-IT

1. Caleb told we about a book he red. *(us; read)*

2. It were about islands with natives and bannana trees. *(was; banana)*

READING-GRAMMAR CONNECTION

Write this sentence on the board:

He was an outcast from the civilization around him.

Explain that *he* is a subject pronoun, and *him* is an object pronoun. *He* is the subject of the sentence, and *him* is the object of the preposition *around.*

Display Grammar Transparency 16. Read aloud the definitions and sample sentences. Work through the items.

Subject and Object Pronouns

A **subject pronoun** is used in the subject of a sentence. Singular subject pronouns are *I, you, he, she,* and *it.* Plural subject pronouns are *we, you,* and *they.* When you use a person's name and a pronoun in a compound subject, be sure to use a subject pronoun.
    We invented an imaginary country. It is far away. She and I planned a trip there.
An **object pronoun** is used in the predicate of a sentence after an action verb or with a preposition, such as *for, at, into, with,* or *to.* Singular object pronouns are *me, you, him, her,* and *it.* Plural object pronouns are *us, you,* and *them.* When you use a person's name and a pronoun in a compound object, be sure to use an object pronoun.
    That story reminds me of him. Leon told them. He helped Jenny and me.

Directions Write *S* if the underlined word is a subject pronoun. Write *O* if the word is an object pronoun.

1. I would like a treehouse. — S
2. Will you help me with the project? — O
3. Dad and we can get lumber and nails. — S
4. Use this rope to lift materials to Dad and him. — O
5. You and I have done a fine job. — S
6. They'll climb up the ladder with us. — S
7. It will make a great clubhouse. — S
8. Let's invite Danny and her to join. — O
9. She and Jamahl brought sandwiches. — S
10. This lunch in the branches tasted great to them. — O

Directions Underline the correct pronoun in ( ) to complete each sentence.

11. Sometimes (us, we) pretend the treehouse is a fort.
12. Both Brian and (I, me) want to be in charge.
13. Larry and (them, they) will be the troops.
14. Janmarie made a cool flag for (us, we).
15. We made (her, she) an honorary member of our club.
16. Because Dad helped us, we made (he, him) an honorary member too.

Unit 4 Weslandia   **Grammar 16**

▲ **Grammar Transparency** 16

DAY 2 Develop the Concept

DAILY FIX-IT

3. The natives had lived on the iland for centurys. *(island; centuries)*

4. Them ate the roots, leaves, and fruits of a plant that growed there. *(They; grew)*

GUIDED PRACTICE

Review the concept of subject and object pronouns.

- When a pronoun is used as the subject of a sentence, it is called a **subject pronoun.** *I, you, he, she, it, we,* and *they* are subject pronouns.

- Pronouns that are used after action verbs or as objects of prepositions are called **object pronouns.** *Me, you, him, her, it, us* and *them* are object pronouns.

HOMEWORK Grammar and Writing Practice Book p. 61. Work through the first two items with the class.

Subject and Object Pronouns

A **subject pronoun** is used in the subject of a sentence. Singular subject pronouns are *I, you, he, she,* and *it.* Plural subject pronouns are *we, you,* and *they.* When you use a person's name and a pronoun in a compound subject, be sure to use a subject pronoun.
    He has many original ideas. They are exciting and unusual.
    Mom and I made bird feeders.
An **object pronoun** is used in the predicate of a sentence after an action verb or with a preposition, such as *for, at, into, with,* or *to.* Singular object pronouns are *me, you, him, her,* and *it.* Plural object pronouns are *us, you,* and *them.* When you use a person's name and a pronoun in a compound object, be sure to use an object pronoun.
    The teacher asked him about his project. It seemed brilliant to me.
    This project was fun for James and me.

Directions Write *S* if the underlined word is a subject pronoun. Write *O* if the word is an object pronoun.

1. Some kids don't know what to think about him. — O
2. They can't understand someone who is different from them. — O
3. She praised his project for its originality. — S
4. Rainelle and I invited him to sit with us. — S
5. We were fascinated by his ideas. — S
6. He has become a valued friend to her and me. — O

Directions Underline the correct pronoun in ( ) to complete each sentence.

7. Most people choose friends who are like (them, they).
8. (Them, They) feel comfortable with people who agree with them.
9. You and (I, me) have different points of view.
10. A friend with original ideas always surprises (I, me).
11. (Us, We) need to think about what we do and say.
12. (I, Me) prefer independent thinkers.
13. Jose and (him, she) agree with me.
14. We have many exciting conversations with (he, him) and (she, her).

Home Activity Your child learned about subject and object pronouns. Read a magazine article with your child. Ask him or her to identify several subject pronouns and object pronouns in the article.

▲ **Grammar and Writing Practice Book** p. 61

CORRECTIVE FEEDBACK

LA.5.3.4.4 Use subjective and objective pronouns

- **Question** Use Whiteboard or Transparency 16b, items 1–3, to ask questions that address this standard in FCAT format. Have students write their answers on a sheet of paper.
- **Check** Scan students' responses by having them hold up their papers.
- **Correct** If necessary, provide corrective feedback and review pp. 140–145 in *The Grammar and Writing Book*.

1 Which pronoun completes the sentence?

Paul and _____ went fishing last week.

(A) he
(B) him
(C) her

◄ **FCAT Whiteboard Activity** 16b/**FCAT Transparency** 16b

DAY 3 Apply to Writing

DAILY FIX-IT

5. If I went to a jungle I would take a safarie. *(jungle,; safari)*

6. Help! There's a crockodile in the pool. *(crocodile; pool!)*

AVOID REPETITION

Subject and object pronouns allow writers to avoid repeating nouns.

Repetitive: The twins said that the twins would help in the garden.

Better: The twins said they would help in the garden.

- Have students review something they have written. They may be able to improve it by replacing nouns with subject and object pronouns.

HOMEWORK Grammar and Writing Practice Book p. 62.

Subject and Object Pronouns

Directions Use a pronoun from the box to complete each sentence. Write the sentence.

| they | he | I | us |
| them | she | me | you |

1. My mom and ___I___ plant a garden every summer.
2. ___She___ lets me pick out the seeds we will plant.
3. Some new flowers surprised ___us___ both this season.
4. ___They___ looked very strange among the roses and daisies.
5. As we watched ___them___ grow, we became more and more amazed.
6. Their enormous leaves and huge white flowers puzzled ___me___ and Mom.
7. Finally, Dad confessed. ___He___ had planted moonflower seeds to surprise us!
8. Would ___you___ have fallen for his joke?

Directions Write a paragraph about a unique person you know. Use subject and object pronouns correctly.

Possible answer: My friend Carrie is one-of-a-kind. She leaves me funny phone messages in rhyme. They always make me laugh. One time she convinced a group of us to try to make the world's biggest doughnut. It was a doughy disaster! Carrie also competes in the race-walk. For her, an Olympic gold medal in this sport is a serious goal.

School-Home CONNECTION Home Activity Your child learned how to use subject and object pronouns in writing. Ask your child to write a description of something he or she did with a friend or a group. Remind your child to use subject and object pronouns correctly.

▲ **Grammar and Writing Practice Book** p. 62

DAY 4 Test Preparation

DAILY FIX-IT

7. Paul and him wrote a book on finding food in the wild! *(he; wild.)*

8. The section on edible Flowers are interesting. *(flowers is)*

STANDARDIZED TEST PREP

Test Tip

You may be asked to identify the correct pronoun in a phrase such as *Jane and I* or *Terry and her*. Decide whether the subject pronoun or object pronoun is correct by saying the sentence with just the pronoun and not the rest of the phrase. *Example:* <u>I</u> climbed the mountain. <u>Jane and I</u> climbed the mountain. Jane showed <u>her</u> our pictures. Jane showed <u>Terry and her</u> our pictures.

HOMEWORK Grammar and Writing Practice Book p. 63.

Subject and Object Pronouns

Directions Mark the letter of the pronoun that correctly completes each sentence.

1. ___ like to find wild foods.
   A Them
   (B) I
   C Me
   D She

2. You can make a meal of ___.
   A we
   B they
   (C) them
   D he

3. Dana and ___ found wild strawberries.
   (A) he
   B him
   C us
   D them

4. In the fall ___ harvest cattails.
   A me
   B her
   C us
   (D) they

5. ___ can grind the roots to make flour.
   A Him
   (B) We
   C Them
   D Her

6. Papa and ___ hunt for mushrooms in the woods.
   A her
   B me
   (C) she
   D us

7. Have ___ ever picked wild asparagus?
   (A) you
   B it
   C them
   D him

8. Uncle Dick and ___ found hickory nuts.
   A us
   B her
   C them
   (D) they

9. Dad asked Phil and ___ to shell the nuts.
   A she
   B he
   (C) me
   D I

10. He and ___ agreed it is a messy job.
    A them
    (B) I
    C it
    D her

School-Home CONNECTION Home Activity Your child prepared for taking tests on subject and object pronouns. Have your child write subject pronouns and object pronouns on index cards. Then mix the cards and sort them into subject pronoun and object pronoun piles.

▲ **Grammar and Writing Practice Book** p. 63

DAY 5 Cumulative Review

DAILY FIX-IT

9. The tamato was an early food of South american natives. *(tomato; American)*

10. Chocolate also comed to us, from Native Americans. *(came; us from)*

ADDITIONAL PRACTICE

Assign pp. 140–143 in The Grammar and Writing Book.

EXTRA PRACTICE Grammar and Writing Practice Book p. 137.

TEST PREPARATION Grammar and Writing Practice Book pp. 155–156.

ASSESSMENT

CUMULATIVE REVIEW Grammar and Writing Practice Book p. 64.

Subject and Object Pronouns

Directions Write the letter of each pronoun next to the correct category.

___B___ 1. Singular subject pronoun
___E___ 2. Plural object pronoun
___C___ 3. Singular object pronoun
___A___ 4. Plural subject pronoun
___D___ 5. Singular and plural, subject and object pronoun

A we
B she
C me
D you
E them

Directions Write *S* if the underlined word is a subject pronoun. Write *O* if the word is an object pronoun.

6. <u>We</u> learned about the Anasazi people. ___S___
7. <u>They</u> built a civilization in the Southwest. ___S___
8. Like many civilizations, <u>it</u> depended on crops. ___S___
9. Maize and pumpkins provided the staple foods for <u>them</u>. ___O___
10. Little rain fell, but the Anasazi hoarded <u>it</u> to water crops. ___O___
11. The teacher asked Lia and <u>me</u> to report on cliff dwellings. ___O___

Directions Underline the correct pronoun in ( ) to complete each sentence.

12. My family and (I, me) visited Chaco Canyon.
13. (Us, We) learned about the pueblos the Anasazi built there.
14. Their skill in building with adobe amazed Sara and (I, me).
15. The people who lived here disappeared 800 years ago and took little with (them, they).
16. Why they left is a mystery to (us, we).
17. Scientists and (they, them) agree that drought may have forced them to migrate.

School-Home CONNECTION Home Activity Your child reviewed subject and object pronouns. Challenge your child to write sentences using you, he, she, it, him, her, and them correctly.

▲ **Grammar and Writing Practice Book** p. 64

Writing Workshop E-mail

OBJECTIVES

- Identify the characteristics of an e-mail.
- Write an e-mail that refers to a text.
- Focus on conventions.
- Use a rubric.

Genre E-mail
Writer's Craft Refer to the Text
Writing Trait Conventions

ELL

Conventions In assessing the writing of language learners, remember that a consistent grammatical error may reflect the writing conventions of the home language. Address the skill by using the appropriate Grammar Transition lessons in the ELL and Transition Handbook.

Writing Traits

FOCUS/IDEAS All details are focused on ideas about the story.

ORGANIZATION/PARAGRAPHS The e-mail contains several paragraphs, each developing its own topic.

SUPPORT/VOICE The writer's personality and interest come through. The language brings the topic to life.

SUPPORT/WORD CHOICE The writer engages the reader with precise, colorful words.

SUPPORT/SENTENCES The writer uses questions and exclamations for interest.

CONVENTIONS Spelling, punctuation, capitalization, and grammar (including subject and object pronouns) are accurate.

DAY 1 Model the Trait

READING-WRITING CONNECTION

- *Weslandia* tells about an unusual, inventive character.
- Students can refer to the text for examples of Wesley's creativity and a model of conventions.
- Students will write an **e-mail** using details from the text and correct spelling, punctuation, capitalization, and grammar.

MODEL CONVENTIONS Discuss Writing Transparency 16A. Then discuss the model and the writing trait of conventions.

 Think Aloud I see that the writer has filled in the subject and names of the sender and receiver. These headings are a convention of e-mail messages. The writer uses complete sentences with correct capitalization and punctuation.

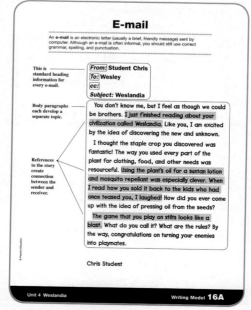

▲ **Writing Transparency 16A**

DAY 2 Improve Writing

WRITER'S CRAFT
Refer to the Text

Display Writing Transparency 16B. Read the directions and work together to use the text to locate supporting details.

Think Aloud **REFER TO THE TEXT FOR DETAILS** Wesley is a unique character. Tomorrow we will write about someone we know who is unique. Who can I use as my subject? I have a friend who likes to mix all sorts of foods together to make new recipes. He is unique. I can think about my friend and recall examples that show his creativity and unusual approach.

GUIDED WRITING Some students may need more help shaping text references. Have them page through *Weslandia* and point out details they enjoyed. Help them state these details in sentences that could be added to the writing model.

▲ **Writing Transparency 16B**

Pages 411g–411h

LA.5.3.1.3 Organize ideas using strategies and tools (graphic organizer)

LA.5.3.4.4 Edit writing for parts of speech, and subjective and objective pronouns

LA.5.4.2.4 Write a variety of communications (messages)

DAY 3 Prewrite and Draft

READ THE WRITING PROMPT

on page 409 in the Student Edition.

In Weslandia, a boy decides to remake his world rather than accept it as it is.

Think about someone you know who doesn't always "follow the herd."

Now write an e-mail to that person about something he or she has done.

FCAT Writing+ Test Tips

- Make direct references to the story to create a connection between you and the recipient of your e-mail.
- Don't stray—focus on two or three interesting actions of the character.
- Remember to use correct spelling—even in an e-mail.

GETTING STARTED Students can do any of the following:

- Review personal experiences to recall the character's actions.
- Write ideas and details they might want to include in a word web that has the character's name in the center.
- Think about the character's personality and write to the person with that in mind.

DAY 4 Draft and Revise

EDITING/REVISING CHECKLIST

☑ Did I refer to the text of a story in the e-mail?

☑ Have I used subject and object pronouns correctly?

☑ Have I spelled words from other cultures correctly?

See *The Grammar and Writing Book,* pp. 140–145.

Revising Tips

Conventions

- As you read each sentence, identify its subject and predicate to be sure it is complete.
- Check that each sentence begins with a capital letter and ends with an end mark.
- In order to focus on spelling, read each sentence in the e-mail backwards.

PUBLISHING Students can read their e-mails in small groups and then ask others to tell what they would like to ask each character. Some students may wish to revise their work later.

ASSESSMENT Use the scoring rubric to evaluate students' work.

DAY 5 Connect to Unit Writing

	Story
Week 1	E-mail 411g–411h
Week 2	Journal Entry 435g–435h
Week 3	Story About an Animal 457g–457h
Week 4	Advice 483g–483h
Week 5	Describe How You Achieved a Goal 503g–503h

PREVIEW THE UNIT PROMPT

Tell a story about a character who succeeds by adapting to a new situation. Focus on an event that shows this person's resourcefulness and ingenuity. Your story may be real or imagined.

APPLY

- Refer to the text of a familiar story with a similar character to build understanding of personality traits.

Writing Trait Rubric

	6	5	4	3	2	1
Conventions	Excellent control of spelling, grammar, and punctuation	Very good control of spelling, grammar, and punctuation	Good control of spelling, grammar, and punctuation	Adequate control of spelling, grammar, and punctuation	Limited control of spelling, grammar, and punctuation	Poor control of spelling, grammar, and punctuation
	No errors or only minor errors in e-mail	Few errors in e-mail	No serious errors that affect understanding in e-mail	Few distracting errors in e-mail	Several distracting errors in e-mail	Many errors that affect understanding in e-mail

Spelling & Phonics Words From Many Cultures

Generalization

Connect to Phonics Many words in English come from other languages and may have unexpected spellings: *khaki, ballet*. These words often do not follow the phonics rules students typically apply so other strategies must be applied for learning to spell them.

Spelling Words

1. khaki	11. macaroni
2. hula	12. polka
3. banana	13. cobra
4. ballet	14. koala
5. waltz	15. barbecue
6. tomato*	16. safari
7. vanilla	17. buffet
8. canyon	18. stampede
9. yogurt	19. karate
10. banquet	20. kiosk

Challenge Words

21. papaya	24. succotash
22. artichoke	25. tsunami
23. sauerkraut	

* Word from the selection

ELL

Spelling/Phonics Support See the ELL and Transition Handbook for spelling support.

DAY 1 — Pretest and Sort

PRETEST

Use the Dictation Sentences from Day 5 to administer the pretest. Read the word, read the sentence, and then read the word again. Guide students in self-correcting their pretests and correcting any misspellings.

Monitor Progress

Spelling

If...	then...
If... students misspell more than 5 pretest words,	then... use words 1–10 for Strategic Intervention.
If... students misspell 1–5 pretest words,	then... use words 1–20 for On-Level practice.
If... students correctly spell all pretest words,	then... use words 1–25 for Advanced Learners.

HOMEWORK Spelling Practice Book, p. 61.

▲ **Spelling Practice Book** p. 61

DAY 2 — Think and Practice

TEACH

Words from different cultures may have unusual spellings for some sounds. Write *ballet* and *buffet* on the board. Underline the final *-et* in each word. Explain that this is pronounced as long *a*. Explain that in French, *et* at the end of the word is always pronounced as long *a*. Explain that *banquet* in French is pronounced like "bankay" with a long *a*, but in English it is pronounced "bankwet".

> *ay*
> *ballet*

FIND THE PATTERN Ask students to identify words that end in the short *a* sound. Have them group words with the short *a* sound together.

HOMEWORK Spelling Practice Book, p. 62.

▲ **Spelling Practice Book** p. 62

DAY 3 — Connect to Writing

WRITE AN E-MAIL

Ask students to write an e-mail using at least four spelling words. The e-mail can be a note to a friend or family member.

Frequently Misspelled Words

our   again

These words may seem easy to spell, but they are often misspelled by fifth-graders. Alert students to the unique spelling of these words.

HOMEWORK Spelling Practice Book, p. 63.

Words from Many Cultures

Proofread a Poster Circle the seven spelling errors in the school poster. Write the words correctly. Write the last sentence, using correct punctuation.

Our New After-School Programs

Learn to Dance
- poka and Texas two-step
- ballet (with tutus, and toe shoes)
- walts and other ballroom dances
- hula and dances of the Pacific

Learn Martial Arts
- karatie • Judo • kung fu

Learn How to Cook
- barbecue sauces
- tomatoe salads
- homemade yogurt
- macaronie and cheese and other pastas
- banananna cream pie and other desserts

Sign up at the kyosk outside the office.
Bring a permission form from your parents?

1. polka   2. waltz
3. karate   4. macaroni
5. tomato   6. banana
7. kiosk
8. Bring a permission form from your parents.

Spelling Words
khaki
hula
banana
ballet
waltz
tomato
vanilla
canyon
yogurt
banquet
macaroni
polka
cobra
koala
barbecue
safari
buffet
stampede
karate
kiosk

Frequently Misspelled Words
our
again

Proofread Words Circle the correct spelling of the list word. Write the word.

9. The frightened cattle started to ____.
stamped   stampede   stamped   9. stampede

10. I love the assortment of foods on the restaurant ____.
buffet   buffay   buffee   10. buffet

School + Home Home Activity Your child identified misspelled list words. Say a list word and spell it incorrectly. Ask your child to spell the word correctly.

▲ **Spelling Practice Book** p. 63

DAY 4 — Review

REVIEW WORDS FROM OTHER CULTURES

Have partners play games of "Hangman" to review spelling words.

Spelling Strategy
Problem Parts

We all have words that are hard for us to spell.

Step 1: Ask yourself: Which part of the word gives me a problem?

Step 2: Underline the problem part.

Step 3: Picture the word. Focus on the problem part.

For example: khaki, banquet, waltz

HOMEWORK Spelling Practice Book, p. 64.

Words from Many Cultures

Spelling Words				
khaki	hula	banana	ballet	waltz
tomato	vanilla	canyon	yogurt	banquet
macaroni	polka	cobra	koala	barbecue
safari	buffet	stampede	karate	kiosk

Words in Context Write list words to complete the menu.

1. Welcome to the 5th Grade ____.
2. Eat all you want at the ____!
1st Course Appetizer
3. green salad from the ____
4. cucumber with ____ dressing
2nd Course Entrée
5. chicken served fresh from the ____
6. ____ and cheese
3rd Course Dessert
7. ____ split sundae
Your choice of
8. ____, chocolate, or strawberry ice cream

1. banquet
2. buffet
3. tomato
4. yogurt
5. barbecue
6. macaroni
7. banana
8. vanilla

Word Search Find ten list words hidden in the puzzle. Words are down, across, and diagonal. Write the words on the line.

S S C S S F S J K D A L
T T J Ö K L S Y O M T K
K A I B Q S Y A N J H H
X A M E R W R L H H A
L H S R P S A F A R I K
L N U U A E W A L T Z I
E B D L P T D K I O S K
T V H L A T E E L J U H

9. ballet
10. hula
11. khaki
12. koala
13. stampede
14. cobra
15. karate
16. kiosk
17. safari
18. waltz

School + Home Home Activity Your child has learned to read, write, and spell words from other cultures. Take turns spelling the list words.

▲ **Spelling Practice Book** p. 64

DAY 5 — Posttest

DICTATION SENTENCES

1. He bought new khaki pants.
2. The hula dancers swayed.
3. A yellow banana is ripe.
4. The ballet started at three o'clock.
5. I would like to know how to waltz.
6. The tomato was delicious.
7. Add a teaspoon of vanilla.
8. The canyon was deep.
9. I like frozen yogurt.
10. Thanksgiving dinner was a banquet.
11. I love macaroni and cheese.
12. The polka is a lively dance.
13. The cobra is a hooded snake.
14. The koala lives in the trees.
15. We cooked on the barbecue pit.
16. They went on an African photo safari.
17. The buffet had many foods.
18. The cattle raced down the street in a stampede.
19. I take karate lessons.
20. I bought the newspaper at the kiosk.

CHALLENGE

21. I love the taste of papaya juice.
22. It's fun to peel and eat artichoke leaves.
23. Some like to have sauerkraut and mustard on their hotdogs.
24. Succotash is a dish of lima beans and corn.
25. The earthquake under the ocean caused a huge tsunami.

OBJECTIVES

- Formulate an inquiry question that is connected to this week's lesson focus.
- Effectively and efficiently find, evaluate, and communicate information related to an inquiry question using electronic sources.

New Literacies

Day 1	Identify Questions
Day 2	Navigate/Search
Day 3	Analyze
Day 4	Synthesize
Day 5	Communicate

Page 411k

LA.5.6.2.1 Select a topic for inquiry, formulate a search plan, and apply evaluative criteria (validity)

LA.5.6.2.2 Read and record information systematically, evaluating validity and reliability

LA.5.6.2.3 Write an informational report

LA.5.6.2.4 Record basic bibliographic data and present quotes using ethical practices (avoids plagiarism)

LA.5.6.3.2 Use a variety of reliable media sources to gather and transmit information effectively

LA.5.6.4.2 Use appropriate digital tools (word processing)

NEW LITERACIES
Internet Inquiry Activity
EXPLORE CIVILIZATIONS

Use the following 5-day plan to help students conduct this week's Internet inquiry activity on civilizations. Remind students to follow classroom rules when using the Internet.

DAY 1

Identify Questions Discuss the lesson focus question: *How do people adapt to difficult situations?* Then, remind students of the civilization Wes creates for himself in *Weslandia* and why he creates it. Have students research other types of civilizations. For example, students might consider exploring the Mayan civilization or the Ancient Greek civilization.

DAY 2

Navigate/Search Explain that keywords or phrases for search engines should be as specific as possible. A keyword like *civilization* is too broad and will likely yield too many results. Suggest that they streamline their searches by using keywords such as *Mayan Civilization* or *Ancient Greece* to find Web sites that will answer their questions.

DAY 3

Analyze Have students skim and scan the Web sites they identified on Day 2 and analyze their credibility. Remind them to revise their inquiry questions as needed based on the information they find.

DAY 4

Synthesize Have students synthesize information by combining relevant ideas from different sources to develop answers to their inquiry questions. Remind students to avoid plagiarism by documenting their sources in an annotated bibliography and restating information in their own words or providing quotation marks around direct quotes. If they have to insert their own words into a direct quote, they would put them between brackets. Have students think about methods for communicating their results.

DAY 5

Communicate Have students use a word processing program to create summaries of the information they found about ancient civilizations. Encourage them to illustrate their reports with drawing tools or clip art.

Instruction Manual

TEACH

Ask students how they can find out how to bake a cake, or how to program a new cell phone. Students should mention a cookbook and an instruction manual. Make sure they understand that a cookbook is a kind of instruction manual. Explain:

- A **manual** is a book that contains instructions on how to do something.
- **Instructions** tell how to do something, usually in the form of a numbered list. Instructions also tell how to follow a **procedure**, or method of doing something.
- The instructions should be read completely before you begin.
- To follow the instructions, read the first step, do what it says, then go on to the next step. Try to visualize each step as you go.
- Manuals often contain warnings about a procedure, explaining any danger involved. These are marked with an exclamation mark, or the word WARNING or CAUTION.

Have students work in pairs, and give each partner an instruction manual. They should identify the parts that are defined above and read them carefully. Then, discuss these questions:

1. **What instructions does the manual contain?** (Possible response: How to put a table together.)

2. **What should you do after you read the instructions?** (Students should identify the first step.)

3. **What warnings might you need to know before attempting to complete the procedure?** (Students should note any warnings included in their instruction manuals.)

Fone-It M-235

Answering Machine

RECORDING AN OUTGOING MESSAGE
1. Make sure the answering machine is on.
2. Press the MENU button on the answering machine two times. You will hear "Set outgoing message." Press the SELECT button to confirm your choice.
3. Listen to the prompt. After you hear the beep, record your outgoing message. Remember to speak loudly and clearly.
4. When you have finished your message, press the SELECT button again to end the recording.

ASSESS

As students work with the manual, check that they can read and understand the instructions. Have students locate transition words that move them from one step to another as they read.

For more practice or to assess students, use Practice Book pp. 159–160.

Page 411l

LA.5.2.2.1 Locate and use text features (transition words/phrases)

LA.5.2.2.4 Identify characteristics of a variety of types of text (practical/functional texts)

LA.5.6.1.1 Read and interpret informational text (multi-step directions and performing a task)

OBJECTIVES

- Review the terms *manual* and *instructions*.
- Understand how instruction manuals are organized.

▲ **Practice Book** p. 159

▲ **Practice Book** p. 160

Weslandia

Assessment Checkpoints *for the Week*

Selection Assessment

Use pp. 61–64 of Selection Tests to check:

☑ **Selection Understanding**

☑ **Comprehension Skill** *Draw Conclusions*

☑ **Selection Vocabulary**

blunders	fleeing
civilization	inspired
complex	rustling
envy	strategy

Leveled Assessment

Use pp. 91–96 of Fresh Reads for Differentiated Test Practice to check:

☑ **Comprehension Skill** *Draw Conclusions*

☑ **REVIEW Comprehension Skill** *Main Idea*

☑ **Fluency** *Words Correct Per Minute*

On-Level

Strategic Intervention

Advanced

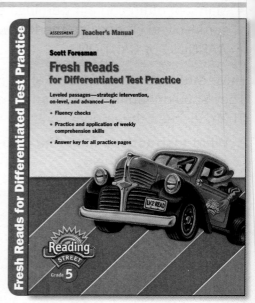

Managing Assessment

Use Assessment Handbook for:

☑ **Observation Checklists**

☑ **Record-Keeping Forms**

☑ **Portfolio Assessment**

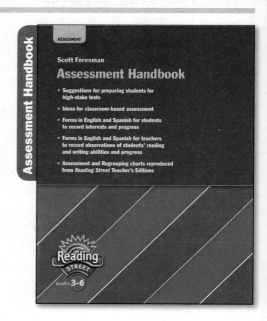

Florida

Planning Guide for Sunshine State Standards

Stretching Ourselves

Reading Street Teacher's Edition pages	Grade 5 Benchmarks for Language Arts

Reading

Word Work Prefixes *over-, under-, sub-, super-, out-:* 435i–435j

Comprehension Generalize: 412–413, 416–431, 434–435, 435b
Predict: 412–413, 416–431, 434–435

Vocabulary Lesson Vocabulary: 414b, 423, 431, 434
Context Clues: 414–415, 425, 435c

Fluency Model Emotion: 412l–412m, 435a

Self-Selected Reading: LR10–18, TR16–17

Literature Genre—Expository Nonfiction: 416
Reader Response: 432

The student will:

LA.5.1.4.1 Understand spelling patterns.

LA.5.1.4.2 Recognize structural analysis.

LA.5.1.5.2 Adjust reading rate based on purpose, text difficulty, form, and style.

LA.5.1.6.1 Use new vocabulary that is introduced and taught directly.

LA.5.1.6.2 Listen to, read, and discuss familiar and conceptually challenging text.

LA.5.1.6.3 Use context clues to determine meanings of unfamiliar words.

LA.5.1.7.1 Make and confirm predictions.

LA.5.1.7.3 Determine the main idea or essential message in grade-level text through inferring.

LA.5.3.4.1 Edit writing for grammar and language conventions, including the correct use of spelling, using spelling rules and knowledge of prefixes.

Writing

Four-Elements Writing Focus/Ideas: 433, 435g–435h

Writing Journal Entry: 435g–435h

Grammar, Usage, and Mechanics Pronouns and Antecedents: 435e–435f

Research/Study Technology—Telephone Directory: 435l

The student will:

LA.5.2.2.4 Identify the characteristics of a variety of types of text (e.g., practical/functional texts).

LA.5.3.3.1 Revise by evaluating the draft for development of ideas and content.

LA.5.3.4.4 Edit writing for grammar and language conventions, including the correct use of pronouns.

LA.5.4.1.2 Write a variety of expressive forms.

Communication and Media

Speaking/Listening Build Concept Vocabulary: 412l, 423, 431, 435c
Read Aloud: 412m

Technology New Literacies: 435k

The student will:

LA.5.1.6.1 Use new vocabulary that is introduced and taught directly.

LA.5.1.6.2 Listen to, read, and discuss familiar and conceptually challenging text.

LA.5.6.2.2 Read and record information systematically, evaluating the reliability of information in text by examining several sources of information.

Unit Skills

Writing Story: WA2–9

Poetry: 504–507

Project/Wrap-Up: 508–509

The student will:

LA.5.2.1.3 Demonstrate how descriptive and figurative language help to communicate meaning in a poem.

LA.5.4.1.1 Write narratives that establish a situation and plot with rising action, conflict, and resolution.

LA.5.4.2.2 Record information (e.g., charts) related to a topic.

Intervention

My Sidewalks on Reading Street provides collaborative, parallel, intensive intervention when used with *Reading Street*.

This Week's Leveled Readers

Below-Level

Fiction

The student will:

LA.5.1.7.3 Determine the main idea or essential message in grade-level text through inferring.

LA.5.2.1.4 Identify an author's theme, and use details from the text to explain how the author developed that theme.

On-Level

Nonfiction

The student will:

LA.5.1.7.1 Make and confirm predictions.

LA.5.1.7.3 Determine the main idea or essential message in grade-level text through inferring.

Advanced

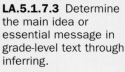

Nonfiction

The student will:

LA.5.1.7.3 Determine the main idea or essential message in grade-level text through inferring.

LA.5.2.2.2 Use information from the text to answer questions related to explicitly stated main ideas or relevant details.

Correlation to Robert Marzano's Instructional Strategies

- Reinforcing effort and providing recognition: pp. 432–433
- Homework and practice: pp. 412f–412g, 413, 415, 432
- Cooperative learning: pp. 412j–412k
- Setting objectives and providing feedback: p. 412m
- Generating and testing hypotheses: p. 416
- Cues, questions, and advance organizers: pp. 414a, 435c

Florida Assessment for FCAT Success

Selection Tests, pp. 65–68

Fresh Reads for Differentiated Test Practice, pp. 97–102

Unit 4 Benchmark Test in FCAT Format, pp. 1–21

Success Tracker™ Online Test to Monitor Benchmarks

Content-Area Standards Taught During the Reading Lesson

Science	Social Studies
The student:	**The student:**
SC.F.1.2.1.5.1. Understands how body systems interact	**SS.C.2.2.2.5.1.** Extends and refines understanding of ways personal and civic responsibility are important
SC.F.2.2.1.5.1. Knows that many characteristics of an organism are inherited from the genetic ancestors of the organism	
SC.H.3.2.1.5.1. Knows how technology has improved human lives	
SC.H.3.2.1.5.2. Knows how new inventions lead to other inventions	

CONNECT TO SF SCIENCE

TIME SAVERS FOR FLORIDA TEACHERS

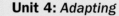

Unit 4: *Adapting*

Question of the Week: How do people adapt to living with physical limitations?

Science Concepts:
- **Human Body Systems**
- **Physical Limitations**
- **Disease**

These lessons in *Scott Foresman Science* support the concepts taught in this week's lesson of *Reading Street.*

Unit A, Chapter 2, Lesson 2, "How do cells work together?" pp. 42–45

Unit A, Chapter 2, Lesson 3, "How do organs work together?" pp. 46–49

Unit A, Chapter 3, Career, "Physical Therapist," p. 56

Unit 4
Adapting

CONCEPT QUESTION
How do people and animals adapt to different situations?

Week 1

How do people adapt to difficult situations?

Week 2

How do people adapt to living with physical limitations?

Week 3

How do animals adapt to survive?

Week 4

How do people adapt to a new school?

Week 5

Why do people try to change themselves?

Week 2

TIME FOR Science

EXPAND THE CONCEPT
How do people adapt to living with physical limitations?

CONNECT THE CONCEPT

▶ Develop Language
dedication, leg brace, polio, triumphant

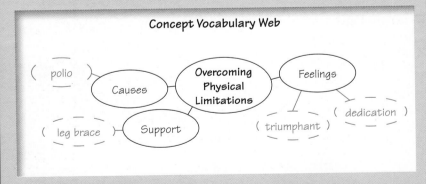

Concept Vocabulary Web

▶ Science Content
Animal Characteristics, Animal Survival, Food Web, Habitat

▶ Writing
Journal Entry

▶ Internet Inquiry
Adapting to Physical Limitations

Stretching Ourselves   **412a**

Preview Your Week

How do people adapt to living with physical limitations?

BY ALDEN R. CARTER   PHOTOGRAPHS BY CAROL S. CARTER

Stretching Ourselves
Kids with *Cerebral Palsy*

Genre
Expository nonfiction gives information about the real world. What special kind of information is the author giving you here?

How do Emily, Nic, and Tanner adapt to cerebral palsy?

416

Student Edition pages 416–431

Audio CD

Read It ONLINE
PearsonSuccessNet.com

- Student Edition
- Leveled Readers

Genre Expository Nonfiction
Vocabulary Strategy Context Clues
Comprehension Skill Generalize
Comprehension Strategy Predict

Paired Selection

Reading Across Texts
Think About How Helpful Technological Devices are Used

Genre
Expository Nonfiction

Text Features
Headings
Photos

Science in Reading

Expository Nonfiction

Genre
- Expository nonfiction can explain helpful technological devices.
- The author explains how these devices work, who uses them, and why.

Text Features
- Headings name the devices, and photos help explain them.
- Look over the headings and photos to see what the selection will explain.

Link to Science
Selections that deal with new technologies are important in a world like ours, with so many new inventions designed to help people. Research other helpful new technologies. Find a device that seems especially helpful and report on it to the class.

helpful tools
by Sally Hobart Alexander

Slowly, between the ages of twenty-four and twenty-six, Sally Hobart Alexander lost her sight. She went on to become an award-winning author of books for young people. In one of these books she describes tools that helped her adapt to blindness. One of these tools is Braille, a writing system that uses raised dots to stand for letters and numbers.

BRAILLE CLOTHING TAG
About the size of a fingernail, these metal tags have holes at either end for pinning or sewing onto labels. They tell me colors: "YW" for yellow, "PK" for pink, and "PP" for purple. When clothes are multicolored, I pin several tags onto the labels at once.

TALKING CLOCK
These clocks come in many varieties. The most common is pocket-sized, but I've had talking clocks inside ballpoint pens and key chains. You simply push a button, and a robot voice calls out the time.

A Braille watch saved me. It looks like a regular wristwatch, except that the crystal pops up when you push a button, usually the winder. You can feel that the hour hand is shorter and sits below the minute hand. All the numbers have raised dots beside them. The

the exact time so often I memorized it. I'd always taken telling time for granted, and I felt lost. I developed a good sense of how long it took to do things, but my estimates could be off by ten minutes. Without a watch, I could miss a bus or an appointment. I could arrive at work late.

BRAILLE WATCH
Imagine a life without clocks or watches, and you'll have an idea of my life when I first became blind. I dialed the phone number for

numbers 3, 6, and 9 have two raised dots, and the 12 has three.

BRAILLE TIMER
Usually three inches high and two inches wide, this device has raised dots by each number and works just like any other timer. I also use Braille labels on spices and cans. My microwave has a Braille pad.

Reading Across Texts
What helpful technological devices are mentioned in *Stretching Ourselves* and "Helpful Tools," and what are they used for?

Writing Across Texts Display your answers in a two-column chart.

Generalize Why have these devices been invented?

434

Student Edition pages 434–435

Audio CD

Florida Science Standards This Week

SC.F.1.2.1.5.1 Understands how body systems interact
SC.H.3.2.1.5.1 Knows how technology has improved human lives
SC.H.3.2.1.5.2 Knows how new inventions lead to other inventions

TIME FOR Science

Leveled Readers

🎯 **Skill** Generalize
🎯 **Strategy** Predict
Lesson Vocabulary

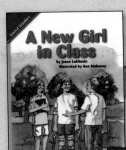

Below-Level

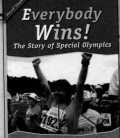

On-Level

Advanced

ELL Reader

· Concept Vocabulary
· Text Support
· Language Enrichment

Integrate Science Standards

• **Human Body Systems**
• **Physical Limitations**
• **Disease**

✓ **Read**

Stretching Ourselves,
pp. 416–431

"Helpful Tools,"
pp. 434–435

Leveled Readers

Below-Level **On-Level** **Advanced**

• Support Concepts • Develop Concepts • Extend Concepts

ELL Reader

✓ **Build Concept Vocabulary**
Overcoming Physical
Limitations, pp. 412l–412m

✓ **Teach Science Concepts**
Polio, p. 419
Nervous System, p. 421
Assistive Technology, p. 425
The Human Eye, p. 435

✓ **Explore Science Center**
Design a Tool, p. 412k

Florida Weekly Plan

READING

45–90 minutes

TARGET SKILLS OF THE WEEK

- **Comprehension Skill**
  Generalize
- **Comprehension Strategy**
  Predict
- **Vocabulary Strategy**
  Context Clues

DAY 1
PAGES 412l–414b, 435a, 435e–435k

Oral Language

QUESTION OF THE WEEK *How do people adapt to living with physical limitations?*

Read Aloud: "Wilma Unlimited," 412m
Build Concepts, 412l

Comprehension/Vocabulary

Comprehension Skill/Strategy Lesson, 412–413
- Generalize **T**
- Predict **T**

Build Background, 414a

Introduce Lesson Vocabulary, 414b
abdomen, artificial, gait, handicapped, therapist, wheelchair **T**

Read Leveled Readers

Grouping Options 412f–412g

Fluency

Model Emotion, 412l–412m, 435a

DAY 2
PAGES 414–423, 435a, 435e–435k

Oral Language

QUESTION OF THE DAY *How do specialists and others help Emily and Nic overcome their physical limitations?*

Comprehension/Vocabulary

Vocabulary Strategy Lesson, 414–415
- Context Clues **T**

Read *Stretching Ourselves,* 416–423

Grouping Options 412f–412g

- Generalize **T**
- Predict **T**
- **REVIEW** Graphic Sources **T**

Develop Vocabulary

Fluency

Choral Reading, 435a

LANGUAGE ARTS

30–60 minutes

Trait of the Week

Focus/Ideas

Grammar, 435e
Introduce Pronouns and Antecedents **T**

Writing Workshop, 435g
Introduce Journal Entry
Model the Trait of the Week: Focus/Ideas

Spelling, 435i
Pretest for Prefixes *over-, under-, sub-, super-, out-*

Internet Inquiry, 435k
Identify Questions

Grammar, 435e
Develop Pronouns and Antecedents **T**

Writing Workshop, 435g
Improve Writing with Elaboration

Spelling, 435i
Teach the Generalization

Internet Inquiry, 435k
Navigate/Search

DAILY WRITING ACTIVITIES

Day 1 Write to Read, 412

Day 2 Words to Write, 415
Strategy Response Log, 416, 423

DAILY SCIENCE CONNECTIONS

Day 1 Overcoming Physical Limitations Concept Web, 412l

Day 2 Time for Science: Nervous System, 421
Revisit the Overcoming Physical Limitations Concept Web, 423

DAILY SUCCESS PREDICTORS
for Adequate Yearly Progress

Monitor Progress and Corrective Feedback

Vocabulary — Check Vocabulary, *412l*

RESOURCES FOR THE WEEK

- Practice Book, *pp. 161–170*
- Word Study and Spelling Practice Book, *pp. 65–68*
- Grammar and Writing Practice Book, *pp. 65–68*

- Selection Test, *pp. 65–68*
- Fresh Reads for Differentiated Test Practice, *pp. 97–102*
- The Grammar and Writing Book, *pp. 146–151*

Grouping Options for Differentiated Instruction

Turn the page for the small group lesson plan.

DAY 3
PAGES 424–433, 435a, 435e–435k

Oral Language

QUESTION OF THE DAY *How are the kids in the selection the same as and different than kids in your class?*

Comprehension/Vocabulary

Read *Stretching Ourselves, 424–432*

Grouping Options 412f–412g

- 🎯 Generalize **T**
- 🎯 Predict
- 🎯 Context Clues **T**
- Develop Vocabulary

Reader Response

Selection Test

Fluency

Model Emotion, 435a

Grammar, 435f
Apply Pronouns and Antecedents in Writing **T**

Writing Workshop, 433, 435h
Write Now
Prewrite and Draft

Spelling, 435j
Connect Spelling to Writing

Internet Inquiry, 435k
Analyze Sources

Day 3 Strategy Response Log, 430
Think and Explain, 432

Day 3 Time for Science: Assistive Technology, 425
Revisit the Overcoming Physical Limitations
Concept Web, 431

DAY 4
PAGES 434–435a, 435e–435k

Oral Language

QUESTION OF THE DAY *What inner traits can physically challenged people draw on to help them overcome the daily limitations confronting them?*

Comprehension/Vocabulary

Read "Helpful Tools," 434–435

Grouping Options 412f –412g

Expository Nonfiction
Reading Across Texts
Content-Area Vocabulary

Fluency

Partner Reading, 435a

Grammar, 435f
Practice Pronouns and Antecedents for
Standardized Tests **T**

Writing Workshop, 435h
Draft, Revise, and Publish

Spelling, 435j
Provide a Strategy

Internet Inquiry, 435k
Synthesize Information

Day 4 Writing Across Texts, 435

Day 4 Time for Science: The Human Eye, 435

DAY 5
PAGES 435a–435l

Oral Language

QUESTION OF THE WEEK *To wrap up the week, revisit the Day 1 question.*
Build Concept Vocabulary, 435c

Fluency

Read Leveled Readers

Grouping Options 412f–412g

Assess Reading Rate, 435a

Comprehension/Vocabulary

- 🎯 Reteach Generalize, 435b **T**
- Simile, 435b
- 🎯 Review Context Clues, 435c **T**

Speaking and Listening, 435d
Oral Presentation
Listen to Oral Presentations

Grammar, 435f
Cumulative Review

Writing Workshop, 435h
Connect to Unit Writing

Spelling, 435j
Posttest for Prefixes *over-, under-, sub-, super-, out-*

Internet Inquiry, 435k
Communicate Results

Research/Study Skills, 435l
Telephone Directory

Day 5 Simile, 435b

Day 5 Revisit the Overcoming Physical Limitations
Concept Web, 435c

KEY 🎯 Target Skill   **T** Tested Skill   **FCAT Tested Skill**

Comprehension   Check Retelling, *432*

Fluency   Check Fluency WCPM, *435a*

Vocabulary   Check Vocabulary, *435c*

SUCCE
PREDICT

Small Group Plan *for Differentiated Instruction*

Daily Plan AT A GLANCE

Reading
Whole Group
- Oral Language
- Comprehension/Vocabulary

Group Time
Differentiated Instruction
Meet with small groups to provide:
- Skill Support
- Reading Support
- Fluency Practice

Read

This week's lessons for daily group time can be found behind the Differentiated Instruction (DI) tab on pp. DI·12–DI·21.

Whole Group
- Fluency

Language Arts
- Grammar
- Writing
- Spelling
- Research/Inquiry
- Speaking/Listening/Viewing

Use *My Sidewalks on Reading Street* for Tier III intensive reading intervention.

DAY 1

On-Level	Strategic Intervention	Advanced
Teacher-Led *Page DI·13*	**Teacher-Led** *Page DI·12*	**Teacher-Led** *Page DI·13*
• Develop Concept Vocabulary	• Reinforce Concepts	• Read Advanced Reader *Feel, Think, Move*
• Read On-Level Reader *Everybody Wins! The Story of Special Olympics*	• Read Below-Level Reader *A New Girl in Class*	• Independent Extension Activity

i Independent Activities
While you meet with small groups, have the rest of the class...

- Visit the Reading/Library Center, p. 412j
- Listen to the Background Building Audio
- Finish Write to Read, p. 412
- Complete Practice Book pp. 163–164
- Visit Cross-Curricular Centers

DAY 2

On-Level	Strategic Intervention	Advanced
Teacher-Led *Pages 418–423*	**Teacher-Led** *Page DI·14*	**Teacher-Led** *Page DI·15*
• Read *Stretching Ourselves*	• Practice Lesson Vocabulary	• Extend Vocabulary
	• Read Multisyllabic Words	• Read *Stretching Ourselves*
	• Read or Listen to *Stretching Ourselves*	

i Independent Activities
While you meet with small groups, have the rest of the class...

- Visit the Reading/Library Center, p. 412j
- Listen to the AudioText for *Stretching Ourselves*
- Finish Words to Write, p. 415
- Complete Practice Book pp. 165–166
- Write in their Strategy Response Logs, pp. 416, 423
- Visit Cross-Curricular Centers
- Work on inquiry projects

DAY 3

On-Level	Strategic Intervention	Advanced
Teacher-Led *Pages 424–431*	**Teacher-Led** *Page DI·16*	**Teacher-Led** *Page DI·17*
• Read *Stretching Ourselves*	• Practice Generalize and Predict	• Extend Generalize and Predict
	• Read or Listen to *Stretching Ourselves*	• Read *Stretching Ourselves*

i Independent Activities
While you meet with small groups, have the rest of the class...

- Visit the Reading/Library Center, p. 412j
- Listen to the AudioText for *Stretching Ourselves: Kids with Cerebral Palsy*
- Write in their Strategy Response Logs, p. 430
- Finish Think and Explain, p. 432
- Complete Practice Book p. 167
- Visit Cross-Curricular Centers
- Work on inquiry projects

① Begin with whole class skill and strategy instruction.

② Meet with small groups to provide differentiated instruction.

③ Gather the whole class back together for fluency and language arts.

On-Level

Teacher-Led
Pages 434–435

- **Read** "Helpful Tools"

Strategic Intervention

Teacher-Led
Page DI · 18

- Practice Retelling
- **Read** or Listen to "Helpful Tools"

Advanced

Teacher-Led
Page DI · 19

- **Read** "Helpful Tools"
- Genre Study

DAY 4

(i) Independent Activities

While you meet with small groups, have the rest of the class...

- Visit the Reading/Library Center, p. 412j
- Listen to the AudioText for "Helpful Tools"
- Visit the Writing/Vocabulary Center
- Finish Writing Across Texts, p. 435
- Visit Cross-Curricular Centers
- Work on inquiry projects

On-Level

Teacher-Led
Page DI · 21

- **Reread** Leveled Reader *Everybody Wins! The Story of Special Olympics*
- Retell *Everybody Wins! The Story of Special Olympics*

Strategic Intervention

Teacher-Led
Page DI · 20

- **Reread** Leveled Reader *A New Girl in Class*
- Retell *A New Girl in Class*

Advanced

Teacher-Led
Page DI · 21

- **Reread** Leveled Reader *Feel, Think, Move*
- Share Extension Activity

DAY 5

(i) Independent Activities

While you meet with small groups, have the rest of the class...

- Visit the Reading/Library Center, p. 412j
- Complete Practice Book pp. 168–170
- Visit Cross-Curricular Centers
- Work on inquiry projects

Grouping Place English language learners in the groups that correspond to their reading abilities in English.

Use the appropriate Leveled Reader or other text at students' instructional level.

TIP Send home the appropriate Multilingual Summary of the main selection on Day 1.

Take It to the NET
ONLINE
PearsonSuccessNet.com

Sharon Vaughn
For research on intervention, see the article "Group Size and Time Allotted to Intervention" by Scott Foresman author S. Vaughn and S. Linan-Thompson.

TEACHER TALK

Differentiated Instruction is instruction tailored to the needs of groups of students, such as struggling students, gifted students, or English language learners.

Be sure to schedule time for students to work on the unit inquiry project "Adaptations." This week students conduct searches to find information about groups of people or animals who have adapted to different situations.

Looking Ahead

Name _____ Date _____

My Work Plan

Put an ☒ next to the activities you complete.

Listening
- ☐ Listen to *Stretching Ourselves.*
- ☐ Listen to "Helpful Tools."

Writing/Vocabulary
- ☐ Study the Words to Know.
- ☐ Write a biography.

Reading
- ☐ Read a book.
- ☐ Read Ten Important Sentences.
- ☐ Book Club

Science
- ☐ Brainstorm tool ideas.
- ☐ Draw and label a tool.

Health
- ☐ Research CP therapy.
- ☐ List three methods.

Technology
- ☐ Find information about CP.
- ☐ Evaluate Web site reliability.

Independent Practice
- ☐ Practice Book, pp. 161–170
- ☐ Independent Writing

Inquiry
- ☐ Unit Inquiry
- ☐ Internet Inquiry

Wrap Up Your Week Turn your paper over. Write about what you did at school this week. What did you read? What did you learn about overcoming physical limitations?

34 Unit 4 • Week 2 • *Stretching Ourselves*

▲ **Group-Time Survival Guide**
p. 34, Weekly Contract

☑ Customize Your Plan *by Strand*

ORAL LANGUAGE

Concept Development

How do people adapt to living with physical limitations?

CONCEPT VOCABULARY

dedication   leg brace   polio   triumphant

BUILD

☐ **Question of the Week** Introduce and discuss the question of the week. This week students will read a variety of texts and work on projects related to the concept *overcoming physical limitations.* Post the question for students to refer to throughout the week. **DAY 1** *412d*

☐ **Read Aloud** Read aloud "Wilma Unlimited." Then begin a web to build concepts and concept vocabulary related to this week's lesson and the unit theme, Adapting. Introduce the concept words *dedication, leg brace, polio,* and *triumphant* and have students place them on the web. Display the web for use throughout the week. **DAY 1** *412l–412m*

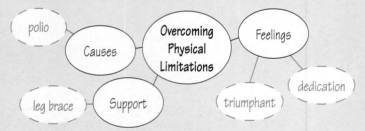

DEVELOP

☐ **Question of the Day** Use the prompts from the Weekly Plan to engage students in conversations related to this week's reading and the unit theme. **EVERY DAY** *412d–412e*

☐ **Concept Vocabulary Web** Revisit the Overcoming Physical Limitations Concept Web and encourage students to add concept words from their reading and life experiences. **DAY 2** *423*, **DAY 3** *431*

CONNECT

☐ **Looking Back/Review/Connect** Revisit the Overcoming Physical Limitations Concept Web and discuss how it relates to this week's lesson and the unit theme. Then make connections to next week's lesson. **DAY 5** *435c*

CHECK

☐ **Concept Vocabulary Web** Use the Overcoming Physical Limitations Concept Web to check students' understanding of the concept vocabulary words *dedication, leg brace, polio,* and *triumphant.* **DAY 1** *412l,* **DAY 5** *435c*

VOCABULARY

STRATEGY

CONTEXT CLUES When you find a word you do not know in a text, look for clues to its meaning. You can find context clues among the words around the unfamiliar word. The situation the author is describing or the words of a character may suggest the unknown word's meaning.

LESSON VOCABULARY

abdomen   handicapped
artificial   therapist
gait   wheelchair

TEACH

☐ **Words to Know** Give students the opportunity to tell what they already know about this week's lesson vocabulary words. Then discuss word meaning. **DAY 1** *414b*

☐ **Vocabulary Strategy Lesson** Use the vocabulary strategy lesson in the Student Edition to introduce and model this week's strategy, *context clues.* **DAY 2** *414–415*

Vocabulary Strategy Lesson

PRACTICE/APPLY

☐ **Leveled Text** Read the lesson vocabulary in the context of leveled text. **DAY 1** *LR10–LR18*

☐ **Words in Context** Read the lesson vocabulary and apply *context clues* in the context of *Stretching Ourselves.* **DAY 2** *416–423,* **DAY 3** *424–432*

Leveled Readers

☐ **Writing/Vocabulary Center** Write a brief biography of a person you know or have heard of who lives with a physical challenge. **ANY DAY** *412k*

Main Selection—Nonfiction

☐ **Homework** Practice Book pp. 164–165. **DAY 1** *414b,* **DAY 2** *415*

☐ **Word Play** Have students list words from *Stretching Ourselves* that are homophones and write sentences using both words. **ANY DAY** *435c*

ASSESS

☐ **Selection Test** Use the Selection Test to determine students' understanding of the lesson vocabulary words. **DAY 3**

RETEACH/REVIEW

☐ **Reteach Lesson** If necessary, use this lesson to reteach and review *context clues.* **DAY 5** *435c*

1 Use your school-based instructional focus calendar to determine which strands to teach.

2 Target your instruction on FCAT tested skills.

3 Check students' understanding of FCAT tested standards.

COMPREHENSION

🎯 **SKILL GENERALIZE**   A generalization is made after thinking about a number of examples or facts and identifying what they have in common. A valid generalization can be supported by facts or details and a faulty generalization cannot.

🎯 **STRATEGY PREDICT**   To predict means to tell what you think will happen next and why it will happen. Good readers look for clues and combine those clues with what they already know to tell what is going to happen next.

TEACH

☐ **Skill/Strategy Lesson** Use the skill/strategy lesson in the Student Edition to introduce and model *generalize* and *predict*. DAY 1 *412-413*

Skill/Strategy Lesson

☐ **Extend Skills** Teach similes. **ANY DAY** *435b*

PRACTICE/APPLY

☐ **Leveled Text** Apply *generalize* and *predict* to read leveled text. DAY 1 *LR10–LR18*

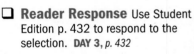
Leveled Readers

☐ **Skills and Strategies in Context** Read *Stretching Ourselves,* using the Guiding Comprehension questions to apply *generalize* and *predict*. DAY 2 *416-423,* DAY 3 *424-432*

Main Selection—Nonfiction

☐ **Reader Response** Use Student Edition p. 432 to respond to the selection. DAY 3, *p. 432*

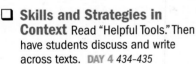

☐ **Skills and Strategies in Context** Read "Helpful Tools." Then have students discuss and write across texts. DAY 4 *434-435*

Paired Selection—Nonfiction

☐ **Homework** Practice Book pp. 163, 167, 168. DAY 1 *413* DAY 3 *431,* DAY 5 *435b*

ASSESS

☐ **Selection Test** Determine students' understanding of the selection and their use of *generalize*. **DAY 3**

☐ **Retell** Have students retell *Stretching Ourselves*. DAY 3 *432-433*

RETEACH/REVIEW

☐ **Reteach Lesson** If necessary, reteach and review *generalize*. DAY 5 *435b*

FLUENCY

SKILL EMOTION   Reading with emotion means reading words as if you were the character. Changing the intonation makes the reading more expressive and lively to the listeners.

TEACH

☐ **Read Aloud** Model fluent reading by rereading "Wilma Unlimited." Focus on this week's fluency skill, emotion. DAY 1 *412l-412m, 435a*

PRACTICE/APPLY

☐ **Choral Reading** Read aloud selected paragraphs from *Stretching Ourselves,* emphasizing the intonations in your voice. Then practice as a class, doing three choral readings of the paragraphs. DAY 2 *435a,* DAY 3 *435a*

☐ **Partner Reading** Have partners practice reading with emotion and offering each other feedback. As students reread, monitor their progress toward their individual goals. DAY 4 *435a*

☐ **Listening Center** Have students follow along with the AudioText for this week's selections. **ANY DAY** *412j*

☐ **Reading/Library Center** Have students reread a selection of their choice. **ANY DAY** *412j*

☐ **Fluency Coach** Have students use Fluency Coach to listen to fluent readings or practice reading on their own. **ANY DAY**

ASSESS

☐ **Check Fluency** WCPM Do a one-minute timed reading, paying special attention to this week's skill—emotion. Provide feedback for each student. DAY 5 *412l-412m, 435a*

☑ Customize Your Plan *by Stran*

GRAMMAR

SKILL PRONOUNS AND ANTECEDENTS A pronoun takes the place of a noun or nouns. An antecedent, or referent, is the noun or nouns to which the pronoun refers. A pronoun and its antecedent must agree in number and gender.

TEACH

☐ **Grammar Transparency 17** Use Grammar Transparency 17 to teach pronouns and antecedents. **DAY 1** *435e*

Grammar Transparency 17

PRACTICE/APPLY

☐ **Develop the Concept** Review the concept of pronouns and antecedents and provide guided practice. **DAY 2** *435e*

☐ **Apply to Writing** Have students review something they have written and apply pronouns and antecedents. **DAY 3** *435f*

☐ **Test Preparation** Examine common errors in using pronouns and antecedents to prepare for standardized tests. **DAY 4** *435f*

☐ **Homework** Grammar and Writing Practice Book pp. 65–67. **DAY 2** *435e*, **DAY 3** *435f*, **DAY 4** *435f*

ASSESS

☐ **Cumulative Review** Use Grammar and Writing Practice Book p. 68. **DAY 5** *435f*

RETEACH/REVIEW

☐ **Daily Fix-It** Have students find and correct errors in grammar, spelling, and punctuation. **EVERY DAY** *435e–435f*

☐ **The Grammar and Writing Book** Use pp. 146–149 of The Grammar and Writing Book to extend instruction for pronouns and antecedents. **ANY DAY**

The Grammar and Writing Book

WRITING

Trait of the Week

FOCUS/IDEAS Good writers focus on a main idea and develop this idea with strong supporting details. Having a purpose—whether it is to inform, to persuade, or to entertain—helps keep focus on the main idea.

TEACH

☐ **Writing Transparency 17A** Use the model to introduce and discuss the Trait of the Week. **DAY 1** *435g*

☐ **Writing Transparency 17B** Use the transparency to show students how elaboration can improve their writing. **DAY 2** *435g*

Writing Transparency 17A   **Writing Transparency 17B**

PRACTICE/APPLY

☐ **Write Now** Examine the model on Student Edition p. 433. Then have students write their own journal entry. **DAY 3** *435h*, **DAY 4** *435h*

   Prompt Kids with special challenges are featured in *Stretching Ourselves*. Think about someone you know who has special mental or physical challenges. Now write a journal entry describing your observations and feelings about that person.

Write Now p. 433

☐ **Writing/Vocabulary Center** Write a brief biography of a person you know or have heard of who lives with a physical challenge. **ANY DAY** *412k*

ASSESS

☐ **Writing Trait Rubric** Use the rubric to evaluate students' writing. **DAY 4** *435h*

RETEACH/REVIEW

☐ **The Grammar and Writing Book** Use pp. 146–151 of The Grammar and Writing Book to extend instruction for pronouns and antecedents, elaboration, and journal entry. **ANY DAY**

The Grammar and Writing Book

1 Use your school-based instructional focus calendar to determine which strands to teach.

2 Target your instruction on FCAT tested skills.

3 Check students' understanding of FCAT tested standards.

SPELLING

GENERALIZATION PREFIXES _OVER-_, _UNDER-_, _SUB-_, _SUPER-_, _OUT-_
When prefixes _over-_, _under-_, _sub-_, _super-_, and _out-_ are added to words, the base word stays the same: <u>over</u>look, <u>under</u>line, <u>sub</u>way, <u>super</u>market, <u>out</u>let. The base word is also pronounced the same as it was before the prefix was added.

TEACH

❑ **Pretest** Give the pretest for words with prefixes _over-_, _under-_, _sub-_, _super-_, _out-_. Guide students in self-correcting their pretests and correcting any misspellings. **DAY 1** _435i_

❑ **Think and Practice** Connect spelling to the phonics generalization for prefixes _over-_, _under-_, _sub-_, _super-_, _out-_. **DAY 2** _435i_

PRACTICE/APPLY

❑ **Connect to Writing** Have students use spelling words to write a journal entry. Then review frequently misspelled words: _outside, because_. **DAY 3** _435j_

❑ **Homework** Word Study and Spelling Practice Book pp. 65–68. **EVERY DAY**

RETEACH/REVIEW

❑ **Review** Review spelling words to prepare for the posttest. Then provide students with a spelling strategy—divide and conquer. **DAY 4** _435j_

ASSESS

❑ **Posttest** Use dictation sentences to give the posttest for words with prefixes _over-_, _under-_, _sub-_, _super-_, _out-_. **DAY 5** _435j_

Spelling Words

1. overlook
2. underline
3. subway
4. subset
5. supermarket
6. outlet
7. underground
8. overboard
9. undercurrent
10. superstar
11. overtime
12. supersonic
13. submarine
14. undercover
15. overcast
16. outfield
17. output
18. supernatural
19. subdivision
20. subhead

Challenge Words

21. overwhelm
22. superimpose
23. underestimate
24. underprivileged
25. subcommittee

RESEARCH AND INQUIRY

❑ **Internet Inquiry** Have students conduct an Internet inquiry on Adapting to physical limitations. **EVERY DAY** _435k_

❑ **Telephone Directory** Review with students the features of a telephone directory and have students conduct an online search in an online telephone directory to find phone numbers of people and businesses. **DAY 5** _435l_

❑ **Unit Inquiry** Allow time for students to find information about groups of people or animals that have adapted to different situations. **ANY DAY** _391_

SPEAKING AND LISTENING

❑ **Oral Presentation.** Have students prepare an oral presentation on some of the tools and adaptive technology available to help handicapped people. **DAY 5** _435d_

❑ **Listen to Oral Presentations** Have students listen to and evaluate the oral presentations given by their classmates. **DAY 5** _435d_

Resources for
Differentiated Instruction

LEVELED READERS

▶ **Comprehension**
- ◉ **Skill** Generalize
- ◉ **Strategy** Predict

▶ **Lesson Vocabulary**
- ◉ Context Clues

▶ **Science Standards**
- **Human Body Systems**
- **Physical Limitations**
- **Disease**

Leveled Reader Database ONLINE
PearsonSuccessNet.com

Use the Online Database of over 600 books to
- Download and print additional copies of this week's leveled readers.
- Listen to the readers being read online.
- Search for more titles focused on this week's skills, topic, and content.

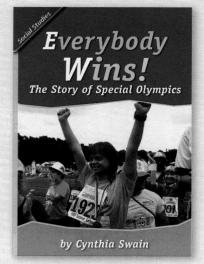

On-Level Reader

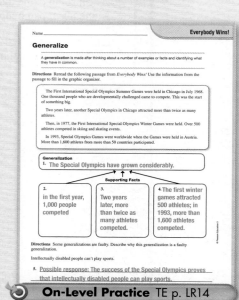

◉ **On-Level Practice** TE p. LR14

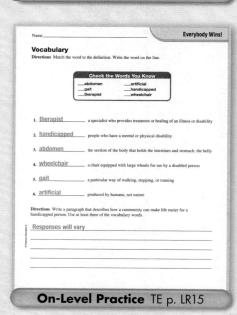

On-Level Practice TE p. LR15

Below-Level Reader

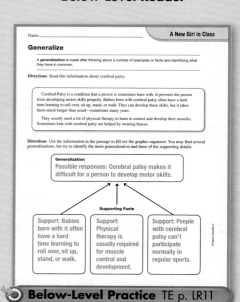

◉ **Below-Level Practice** TE p. LR11

Below-Level Practice TE p. LR12

Advanced

Advanced Reader

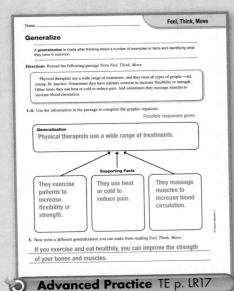

Advanced Practice TE p. LR17

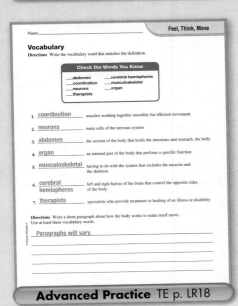

Advanced Practice TE p. LR18

ELL Reader

ELL Poster 17

Teacher's Edition Notes

ELL notes throughout this lesson support instruction and reference additional resources at point of use.

**Teaching Guide
pp. 113–119, 244–245**

- Multilingual summaries of the main selection
- Comprehension lesson
- Vocabulary strategies and word cards
- ELL Reader 5.4.2 lesson

ELL and Transition Handbook

Ten Important Sentences

- Key ideas from every selection in the Student Edition
- Activities to build sentence power

More Reading

Readers' Theater Anthology
- Fluency practice
- Five scripts to build fluency
- Poetry for oral interpretation

Leveled Trade Books

Advanced

Below-Level

On-Level

- Extended reading tied to the unit concept
- Lessons in the Trade Book Library Teaching Guide

Homework
- Family Times Newsletter
- ELL Multilingual Selection Summaries

Take-Home Books
- Leveled Readers

Cross-Curricular Centers

Listening

Listen to the Selections

MATERIALS `SINGLES`
CD player, headphones, AudioText CD, student book

LISTEN TO LITERATURE Listen to *Stretching Ourselves* and "Helpful Tools" as you follow or read along in your book. Listen for generalizations in the story.

If there is anything you don't understand, you can listen again to any section.

Reading/Library

Read it AGAIN!

MATERIALS `SINGLES` `PAIRS` `GROUPS`
Collection of books for self-selected reading, reading logs, student book

Select a book you have already read. Record the title of the book in your reading log. You may want to read with a partner.

Choose from the following:

- Leveled Readers
- ELL Readers
- Stories Written by Classmates
- Books from the Library
- *Stretching Ourselves*

TEN IMPORTANT SENTENCES Read the Ten Important Sentences for *Stretching Ourselves*. Then locate the sentences in the student book.

BOOK CLUB What can you learn from reading about people with physical challenges? Read other stories about coping with physical challenge and discuss with the group.

Classroom Library

Health

Find Out More

MATERIALS `SINGLES` `PAIRS`
Writing materials, Internet access, books on cerebral palsy, e-mail program

Use resources to find out more about the treatment of cerebral palsy (CP).

1. Follow classroom rules for searching the Internet. Use a student-friendly search engine to find information about types of medical and physical therapy for people with CP.
2. List three methods with a brief description of each.

EARLY FINISHERS Write an e-mail to a friend or family member to share what you learned about cerebral palsy.

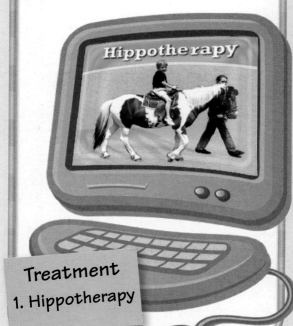

Treatment
1. Hippotherapy

Scott Foresman Reading Street Centers Survival Kit

Use the *Stretching Ourselves* materials from the Reading Street Centers Survival Kit to organize this week's centers.

Writing/Vocabulary

Write a Biography

MATERIALS [SINGLES]
Writing materials, journals

Write a brief biography of a person you know or have heard of who lives with a physical challenge.

1. Make some notes about the person's life based on what you already know or by using Internet or library resources.
2. Write a journal entry describing what he or she has taught you about living with a physical challenge.

EARLY FINISHERS Write a paragraph based on your notes. Include details about how the person copes with his or her physical challenge.

Dear Journal,
   I have a neighbor who uses a wheelchair…

Science

Design a TOOL

MATERIALS [SINGLES] [PAIRS] [GROUPS]
Writing and art materials

Design a helpful tool that could be used by a student with physical challenges in your school.

1. Think about a physical challenge that someone might face in your school and brainstorm ideas for tools that could help him or her.
2. Draw and label the tool and its parts.
3. Then survey 3–5 classmates on the usefulness of this tool.

EARLY FINISHERS Write a caption describing the tool and explaining why it would be helpful.

Automatic Door Opener

open
close
button to open door
button to close door

Technology

Verify Sources

MATERIALS [SINGLES]
Internet access

Identify reliable sites with information about cerebral palsy.

1. Follow classroom rules for searching the Internet for information about cerebral palsy. Use a student-friendly search engine.
2. Scan through the first five sites your search engine lists.
3. Evaluate the reliability of a site by finding out who published it, when it was published, and if it is clear, well–written, and informative.

EARLY FINISHERS Choose the site you find most reliable and explain your reasons for choosing it.

when it was published
who published it

Cerebral Palsy
by Dr. Wehmeyer
10/5/06

ALL CENTERS

OBJECTIVES

- Build vocabulary by finding words related to the lesson concept.
- Listen for generalizations.

Concept Vocabulary

dedication devotion

leg brace a device used to support a leg

polio a severe, infectious, viral disease that destroys nervous tissue in the spinal cord causing paralysis and wasting away of muscles

triumphant victorious or successful

Monitor Progress

Check Vocabulary

If...	then...
students are unable to place words on the Web,	...use the Concept Vocabulary Routine on p. DI·1 to teach the words. Provide additional words for practice, such as *paralyzed* and *scholarship*.

SUCCESS PREDICTOR

DAY 1 Grouping Options

Reading
Whole Group
Introduce and discuss the Question of the Week. Then use pp. 412l–414b.

Group Time
Differentiated Instruction
 this week's Leveled Readers. See pp. 412f–412g for the small group lesson plan.

Whole Group
Use p. 435a.

Language Arts
Use pp. 435e–435k.

Build Concepts

FLUENCY

MODEL EMOTION As you read "Wilma Unlimited," use your voice to model reading with emotion. You can speak softly and slowly when reading the introduction and first paragraph which talk about her physical limitations and with energy and building enthusiasm as you read the rest about how Wilma overcomes her limitations to become a great athletic success.

LISTENING COMPREHENSION

After reading "Wilma Unlimited," use the following questions to assess listening comprehension.

1. **What generalization can you make about Wilma Rudolph and others who overcome physical limitations?** *(Possible response: People who overcome physical limitations are courageous and determined.)* **Generalize**

2. **What caused Wilma Rudolph to switch from basketball to track?** *(A college coach liked the way she ran when she played basketball and helped her get a track-and-field scholarship.)* **Cause and Effect**

BUILD CONCEPT VOCABULARY

Start a web to build concepts and vocabulary related to this week's lesson and the unit theme.

- Draw the Overcoming Physical Limitations Concept Web.

- Read the sentence with the word *polio* again. Ask students to pronounce *polio* and discuss its meaning.

- Place *polio* in an oval attached to *Causes*. Explain that *polio* is related to this concept. Read the sentences in which *leg brace, dedication* and *triumphant* appear. Have students pronounce the words, place them on the web, and provide reasons.

- Brainstorm additional words and categories for the web. Keep the web on display and add words throughout the week.

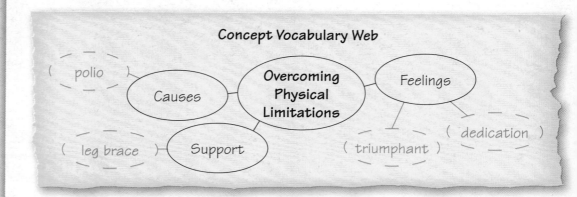
Concept Vocabulary Web

Wilma Unlimited

by Kathleen Krull

Olympic runner Wilma Rudolph contracted polio as a child, resulting in a paralyzed left leg. She survived, but it was assumed that she would never walk without the aid of a leg brace, much less run. In this passage, Wilma overcomes her physical limitation with hard work and dedication.

Whispers rippled throughout the gathering. Wilma Rudolph was walking. Row by row, heads turned toward her as she walked alone down the aisle. Her large family, all her family's friends, everyone from school—each person stared wide-eyed. The singing never stopped; it seemed to burst right through the walls and into the trees. Finally, Wilma reached a seat in the front and began singing too, her smile triumphant.

Wilma practiced walking as often as she could after that, and when she was twelve years old, she was able to take off the brace for good. She and her mother realized she could get along without it, so one memorable day they wrapped the hated brace in a box and mailed it back to the hospital.

As soon as Wilma sent that box away, she knew her life was beginning all over again.

After years of sitting on the sidelines, Wilma couldn't wait to throw herself into basketball, the game she most liked to watch. She was skinny, but no longer tiny. Her long, long legs would propel her across the court and through the air, and she knew all the rules and all the moves.

In high school, she led her basketball team to one victory after another. Eventually, she took the team all the way to the Tennessee state championships. There, to everyone's astonishment, her team lost.

Wilma had become accustomed to winning. Now she slumped on the bench, all the liveliness knocked out of her.

But at the game that day was a college coach. He admired Wilma's basketball playing but was especially impressed by the way she ran. He wanted her for his track-and-field team.

With his help, Wilma won a full athletic scholarship to Tennessee State University. She was the first member of her family to go to college.

Eight years after she mailed her brace away, Wilma's long legs and years of hard work carried her thousands of miles from Clarksville, Tennessee. The summer of 1960 she arrived in Rome, Italy, to represent the United Stated at the Olympic Games—as a runner.

Activate Prior Knowledge

Before students listen to the Read Aloud, ask them what they know about physical limitations and how they affect people.

Set Purpose

Read aloud the title and have students predict what the selection will be about.

Read the introduction aloud. Have students listen for generalizations and details that can be used to prove or disprove their validity.

Creative Response

Have students work in groups to reenact the scene in which Wilma first walks in front of her family and friends. Remind students to use facial expressions to convey emotions. *Drama*

Develop Concept Vocabulary

Read aloud every day from a book of your choice related to the concept and use the Concept Vocabulary Routine on p. DI·1 to develop concept vocabulary. For suggestions, see p. TR14.

Access Content Before reading, share this summary: As a child, Wilma had polio. Her left leg was paralyzed and she wore a brace. She worked hard to walk again. She returned her brace to the hospital and began to play basketball. She won an athletic scholarship to college and later represented the U.S. at the Olympics as a sprinter.

 Homework Send home this week's Family Times newsletter.

Pages 412m

LA.5.1.6.2 Listen to and discuss conceptually challenging text

LA.5.1.6.4 Categorize key vocabulary

LA.5.1.7.3 Determine the main idea or essential message through inferring

LA.5.1.7.4 Identify cause-and-effect relationships

LA.5.5.2.1 Listen and speak to gain and share information (dramatic recitations)

SKILLS ⟷ STRATEGIES IN CONTEXT

Generalize
Predict

OBJECTIVES

- Identify and make generalizations.
- Use generalizations to predict.

Skills Trace

Generalize

Introduce/Teach	TE: 5.4 412–413, 458–459; 5.5 604–605
Practice	Practice Book: 163, 167, 168, 183, 187, 188, 243, 247, 248
Reteach/Review	TE: 5.4 435b, 483b, 493, DI·53, DI·55; 5.5 625b, DI·56
Test	Selection Test: 65–68, 73–76, 97–100; Benchmark Test: Unit 4

INTRODUCE

Read or write the following on the board: *Many students in our school have disabilities. Several students wear glasses that help them see better. Some have hearing aids that help them to hear. Still others have wheelchairs that help them get around the building and their classrooms.* Ask students to identify the generalization. (*Many students in our school have disabilities.*)

Have students read the information on p. 412. Explain the following:

- Some authors use broad statements, or generalizations, in their writing.
- Not all generalizations are valid. So, before accepting the validity of a generalization, be sure to look for details that support it.
- Recognizing generalizations can help you predict other points the author will make.

Use Skill Transparency 17 to teach generalizing and predicting.

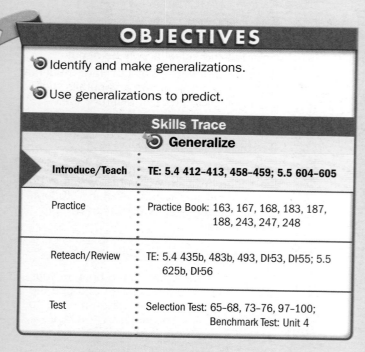

Comprehension

Skill
Generalize

Strategy
Predict

 LA.5.1.7.8 Use self-monitoring strategy, predicting

 ## Generalize

- An author may write similar details about different things or people. You can use these similar details to make a general statement that covers all the things or people. This statement is called a generalization.

- A valid generalization can be supported by facts or details. A faulty generalization cannot.

- Sometimes an author makes a generalization and uses a clue word such as *all, many,* or *in general* to signal it.

General Statement—Clue word?		
Detail	Detail	Detail

 ## Strategy: Predict

Active readers try to predict what will happen next. When you read a generalization, be on the lookout for similar details that fit it. You can also use a generalization to predict other details that fit it.

Write to Read

1. Read *CP.* Using a graphic organizer like the one above, write the generalization that the author makes about cerebral palsy.

2. Write a generalization of your own about people you know. Give three details that support your generalization.

412

 Strategic Intervention

Generalize Remind students that generalizations are broad statements that often include clue words such as *in general, many,* or *all.* Ask students to identify other words that may signal generalizations. (*always, never, most*) Reread the sentence, *Many students in our school have handicaps.* Then have students identify the clue word (*many*) that helps them know the statement is a generalization.

ELL

Access Content

Beginning/Intermediate For a Picture It! lesson on generalize, see ELL Teaching Guide, pp. 113–114.

Advanced Before students read "CP," have them read the first sentence in the third paragraph. Ask them to identify the key word that signals that the author is making a generalization. Then ask them to look for the facts that support the generalization.

CP

You might see a person in a wheelchair and think, "That person must have hurt his legs." But that is not always the case. He may have cerebral palsy (CP).

CP is a disorder that happens when the brain is damaged before or during birth. It might also happen when a child is very young. This brain damage leads to problems with moving, and sometimes with speaking, seeing, hearing, or learning.

In general, people with CP do not have full control of their muscles. In some cases, muscles may move when the person does not want them to. Some people with CP have quick, jerky body movements. Others have smaller, slower movements of the face, neck, arms, and legs. In some cases, muscles may not move at all. That's why some people with CP must use wheelchairs.

We don't have a cure for cerebral palsy. However, there are treatments that can help. Many children and adults with this disorder live full, complete, and happy lives.

1. **Skill** Look for clue words in this next paragraph that signal the author is making a generalization.

2. **Strategy** What kinds of details do you predict you will read about next?

3. **Strategy** What other problems can you predict for people without full control of their muscles?

4. **Skill** In the final paragraph, what generalization does the author make about people with CP?

413

TEACH

1. **SKILL** Use paragraph 3 to model how to use clue words to identify a generalization.

Think Aloud **MODEL** The third paragraph begins with the words "In general." I know that these words often signal a generalization. As I keep reading, I find that the words *in general* precede a broad statement that applies to many people: "People with CP do not have full control of their muscles." This is a generalization.

2. **STRATEGY** Use a generalization to predict.

Think Aloud **MODEL** Since the first sentence in the paragraph expresses a generalization about the muscles of people with CP, I predict that the author will provide details to support the generalization. I think the following sentences will tell how CP affects a person's muscles.

PRACTICE AND ASSESS

3. **STRATEGY** Answers will vary but may include issues related to learning or sports.

4. **SKILL** Generalization: Many children and adults with CP live full, complete, and happy lives.

WRITE Have students complete steps 1 and 2 of the Write to Read activity. You might consider using this as a whole-class activity.

Monitor Progress

Generalize

If... students are unable to complete **Write to Read** on p. 412,	then... use Practice Book p. 163 to provide additional practice.

Pages 412–413

LA.5.1.7.1 Use prior knowledge to make predictions

LA.5.1.7.3 Determine the main idea through inferring and identifying relevant details

LA.5.1.7.8 Use strategies to repair comprehension when self-monitoring, including predicting

Generalize

- An author may write similar details about different things or people. You can use these similar details to make a general statement that covers all the things or people. This statement is called a **generalization**.
- A **valid** generalization can be supported by facts or details. A **faulty** generalization cannot.
- Sometimes an author makes a generalization and uses a clue word such as *all*, *many*, or *generally* to signal it.

Directions Read the following passage. Then complete the diagram below.

> John heard a program on the radio about diabetes. One woman described how she found out she had the disease. She always felt thirsty even though she drank a lot of water. She was also really hungry all the time, even though she ate a lot. She went to see her doctor, who said that she should be tested for diabetes because unusual thirst and hunger are generally symptoms. The test showed that she had diabetes.
>
> A young boy spoke next. He too was always thirsty and hungry. He thought he was just growing, but one day he passed out at school. As the boy finished speaking, John realized that he was really hungry and thirsty. He was pouring some juice when he remembered he had eaten just a half-hour ago. He thought about the program, and he asked his mom to make a doctor's appointment.

Possible answers given.

General Statement
1. Unusual thirst and hunger are generally symptoms of diabetes. 2. Clue word: **generally**

Supporting Details
3. A woman with the symptoms had diabetes. 4. A young boy with the symptoms had diabetes. 5. John thought he had the symptoms of diabetes.

School + Home **Home Activity** Your child read a short passage and recognized a generalization. Read a newspaper or magazine article together and ask your child to find a generalization along with details that support it.

Practice Book p. 163

Stretching Ourselves 413

Tech Files ONLINE

Students can use a student-friendly search engine and the key words *nervous system disorders* or *muscular diseases* to look for more information about other diseases that affect muscle coordination and use. Be sure to follow classroom guidelines for Internet use.

ELL

Build Background Use ELL Poster 17 to build background and vocabulary for the lesson concept of overcoming physical limitations.

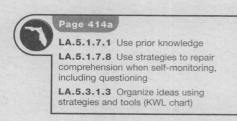

▲ **ELL Poster** 17

Build Background

ACTIVATE PRIOR KNOWLEDGE

BEGIN A KWL CHART about cerebral palsy.

• Give students two to three minutes to write as many things as they know about cerebral palsy. Prompt them with categories from the Concept Web from p. 412l. Record what students know in the first column of the KWL chart.

• Give students two minutes to write three questions they would like to ask about cerebral palsy. Record questions in the second column of the KWL chart. Add a question of your own.

• Tell students that, as they read, they should look for the answers to their questions and note any new information to add to the chart.

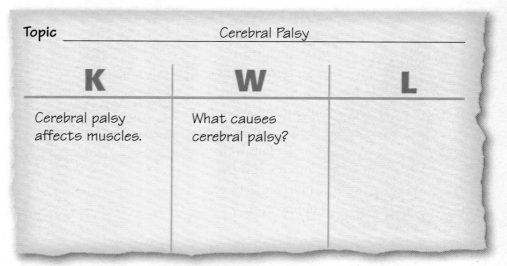

Topic		Cerebral Palsy
K	**W**	**L**
Cerebral palsy affects muscles.	What causes cerebral palsy?	

▲ **Graphic Organizer** 4

BACKGROUND BUILDING AUDIO This week's audio explores the challenges of cerebral palsy. After students listen, discuss what they found most surprising about the disease.

 **Background Building Audio**

Introduce Vocabulary

DEFINITION CARDS

Write each of the Words to Know on an index card. On separate cards, write the definition of each word. Read each word aloud to the students and then read the definitions. Have students think about where they may have seen or heard some of these words. *Activate Prior Knowledge*

Distribute the definition and word cards to the students. Have one student hold up and read a definition card. The student with the correct word match stands up and says the word. Repeat with reading the word first and then the matching definition.

Point out that one of this week's words is a homophone *(gait)* and another is a multiple-meaning word *(stroke)*. Make students aware that they may learn new definitions for these words. (For additional practice with multiple meaning words, see p. 435c.) *Homophones • Multiple-Meaning Words*

Also, have students use these steps for reading multisyllabic words. (See the Multisyllabic Word Routine on p. DI·1.)

1. **Look for Meaningful Word Parts** (base words, endings, prefixes, suffixes, roots) Think about the meaning of each part. Use the parts to read the word. Model: I see the suffix *-ist* at the end of *therapist*. The word *therapist* comes from the root word *therapy* which means "treatment of diseases, injuries, or disorders," and *-ist* means "an expert in a particular field." Therefore, *therapist* means "a person who specializes in the treatment of diseases, injuries, or disorders."

2. **Chunk Words with No Recognizable Parts** Say each chunk slowly. Then say the chunks fast to make a word. Model: *ar, ti, fi, cial—artificial.*

Lesson Vocabulary

WORDS TO KNOW

T abdomen the part of the body containing the stomach, intestines, and other important organs

T artificial made by human skill or labor; not natural

T gait a manner of walking or running

T handicapped having a physical or mental disability

T therapist a person who specializes in treatment of diseases, injuries, or disorders

T wheelchair a chair on wheels, used by people who are sick or who are unable to walk

MORE WORDS TO KNOW

blender an electric kitchen appliance for grinding, mixing, or beating

cerebral palsy paralysis caused by damage to the brain before or at birth

stroke a sudden attack of illness, especially one caused by a blood clot or bleeding in the brain

T = Tested Word

Vocabulary

Directions Choose the word from the box that best matches each definition. Write the word on the line.

artificial _____ 1. made by human skill or labor; not natural

Check the Words You Know
___abdomen
___artificial
___gait
___handicapped
___therapist
___wheelchair

gait _____ 2. manner of walking or running

handicapped _____ 3. having a physical or mental disability

abdomen _____ 4. the part of the body containing the stomach, the intestines, and other important organs

therapist _____ 5. person who specializes in the treatment of diseases, or injuries

Directions Complete each sentence with the correct word from the box. Write the word on the line shown to the left.

wheelchair _____ 6. Malik used a _____ because the muscles in his legs were not strong.

therapist _____ 7. Every week, he went to an appointment with his physical _____, who helped him do exercises to strengthen his legs.

gait _____ 8. He could walk on his own, but his _____ was still awkward.

abdomen _____ 9. They also worked on the muscles in his _____ and chest so he would not get a sore back.

handicapped _____ 10. Malik never thought of himself as _____ because he worked so hard and could tell he was making progress.

Write a Newspaper Article
On a separate sheet of paper, write a newspaper article about a person who has a disability or chronic illness. Write about the difficulties this person deals with every day. Use as many vocabulary words as you can.
Newspaper articles should include words from the vocabulary list and details about a disability or chronic illness.

 Home Activity Your child identified and used vocabulary words from *Stretching Ourselves*. Read a story or nonfiction article with your child about someone who has a disability or a chronic illness. Discuss any unfamiliar terms that appear in the article.

▲ **Practice Book** p. 164

Page 414b

LA.5.1.4.3 Use language structure to read multi-syllabic words

LA.5.1.6.1 Use new vocabulary that is introduced and taught directly

LA.5.1.6.8 Use knowledge of homophones to determine meanings of words

Vocabulary Strategy

OBJECTIVE

🎯 Use context clues to determine word meaning.

INTRODUCE

Discuss the strategy for context clues using the steps on p. 414 .

TEACH

- Have students read "Physical Therapists," paying attention to how vocabulary is used.
- Model using context clues to determine the meaning of *handicapped*.

Think Aloud **MODEL** As I read the first paragraph, it talks about therapists who work with people who are hurt or have trouble moving. *Handicapped* must mean "having a physical disability."

Words to Know

therapist
handicapped
gait
artificial
wheelchair
abdomen

Remember
Try the strategy. Then, if you need more help, use your glossary or dictionary.

Vocabulary Strategy
for Unfamiliar Words

Context Clues When you find a word you do not know in a text, look for clues to its meaning. The situation the author is describing or the words of a character may suggest the unknown word's meaning.

1. Read the words around the unknown word. Do they suggest a meaning for this word?
2. If not, then read the sentences around the word. Look for examples, comparisons, or contrasts that suggest the meaning of the word.
3. Think of a meaning and test it. Does this meaning make sense?
4. If you cannot find the meaning quickly, look it up in a dictionary or talk with a friend about it.

As you read "Physical Therapists," look for clues to the meaning of each unknown word in the words and sentences around it.

LA.5.1.6.2 Develop vocabulary by reading and discussing text
LA.5.1.6.3 Use context clues

414

DAY 2 Grouping Options

Reading
Whole Group Discuss the Question of the Day. Then use pp. 414–417.

Group Time Differentiated Instruction
Read *Stretching Ourselves.* See pp. 412f–412g for the small group lesson plan.

Whole Group Use p. 435a.

Language Arts
Use pp. 435e–435k.

Strategic Intervention

🎯 **Context Clues** Have students work with partners to determine the meaning of *gait* by following the steps on p. 414.

ELL

Access Content Use ELL Poster 17 to preteach vocabulary. Choose from the following to meet language proficiency levels.

Beginning Point out clues on p. 415, paragraph 3, that show what a *therapist* does.

Intermediate Before reading, have students choose a vocabulary word and use it to complete a vocabulary frame. After reading, have students verify the definition.

Advanced Teach the lesson on pp. 414–415. Have students determine whether any of the tested words have cognates in their home languages.

Resources for home-language words may include parents, bilingual staff members, bilingual dictionaries, or online translation sources.

Physical Therapists

The work of a physical therapist can be very rewarding. This person works with people who are hurt or have problems moving because of a physical condition. Sports players with hurt muscles or bones may visit a therapist. People who suffer from diseases that make it hard to move also see a therapist regularly. They may be handicapped by sickness, but exercise and training can help them move more easily.

A person who has had a broken leg needs to use it as it heals. The body learns how to move again after resting a long time. The muscles have become shorter. They need to be stretched and trained. This can mean the difference between walking with a limp or with a smooth gait.

Watch a therapist at work. You may see him or her helping a person with an artificial leg learn how to walk again. It is a very different job from walking on two whole legs. The therapist may be massaging and stretching the muscles of someone who must use a wheelchair. A person who cannot move much needs to work the muscles of arms, legs, abdomen, and back. Otherwise, they become very weak and small. Everyone wants to be able to move well!

Words to Write

Write a journal entry telling what you think it would be like to have a disorder such as cerebral palsy. Use as many words from the Words to Know list as you can.

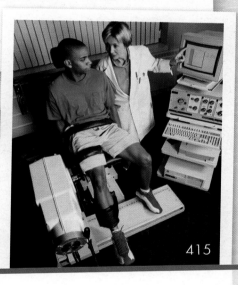

415

CORRECTIVE FEEDBACK

LA.5.1.6.3 Use context clues to determine meanings of unfamiliar words

- **Question** Use the question below to address this FCAT tested standard. Have students write their answers on a sheet of paper.
- **Check** Scan students' responses by having them hold up their papers.
- **Correct** If necessary, provide corrective feedback.
- **Adjust** Pair students who have correctly identified the correct answer with students who did not for peer tutoring. Have them complete Practice Book p. 165 together.

Which words in this sentence help you understand the word *limber*? *No longer stiff, his legs were limber from the exercises and he could easily bend his knees.*

PRACTICE AND ASSESS

- Have students determine the meanings of the remaining words and explain the context clues they used.
- Point out that context clues aren't always available. Students may have to use the glossary or a dictionary to find the exact meaning of some words.
- If you made definition cards on p. 414, have students review the word meanings.
- Have students complete Practice Book p. 165.

WRITE Writing should include lesson vocabulary words that describe what it is like to have a disability.

Monitor Progress

↻ Context Clues

If... students need more practice with the lesson vocabulary,	then... use Tested Vocabulary Cards.

Vocabulary · Context Clues

- When you find a word you do not know in a text, look for clues to its meaning.
- You can find **context clues** among the words around the unfamiliar word.

Directions Read the following passage about disabilities. Then answer the questions below.

Anita's friend Jessica asked her a hard question. "Anita, how come some people at school say you are handicapped? You walk like everyone else and don't have to use a wheelchair."

Anita thought carefully about how she would answer. "My disability is hard for people to see. I am autistic. It is hard for me to understand what other people are telling me or if they are happy or sad. Sometimes my voice sounds artificial like a robot's."

Jessica said, "You do have your ways, but you and I talk just fine."

"You are used to me," said Anita. "I also go to a speech therapist every week to help me learn how to talk with other people."

Possible answers given.

1. What does *wheelchair* mean? What context clues helped you to determine the meaning?
   A *wheelchair* is used by people who can't walk. Because Anita can walk, she doesn't have to use a wheelchair.

2. What does *disability* mean? What context clues helped you to determine the meaning?
   a handicap; Jessica asks why people think Anita is handicapped.

3. What does *artificial* mean? What clues help you to determine the meaning?
   not natural; Anita says her voice is like a robot's.

4. How would using context clues help you determine the meaning of *speech therapist*?
   A *speech therapist* helps people learn how to speak. Anita says the speech therapist helps her learn to talk.

5. What context clues helped you understand what *autistic* means?
   disability; hard to understand other people; voice sounds artificial

 Home Activity Your child identified and used context clues to understand new words of a passage. Have a discussion with your child in which you use context clues to give clues to the meaning of new words.

▲ **Practice Book** p. 165

WORD AWARENESS Post this week's lesson vocabulary on a Word Wall or have students write the words and meanings in their Writing Logs for ready access during writing.

Prereading Strategies

OBJECTIVES

- Recognize and make generalizations to improve comprehension.
- Use generalizations to predict.

GENRE STUDY

Expository Nonfiction

Stretching Ourselves is expository nonfiction. Explain that expository nonfiction contains factual materials and communicates information about the real world.

PREVIEW AND PREDICT

Have students preview the selection title and illustration and identify the topic of this selection. Students should use lesson vocabulary words as they talk about what they expect to learn.

Strategy Response Log

Ask Questions Have students ask two questions about the ways children with cerebral palsy adapt to their condition. Students will answer their questions in the Strategy Response Log activity on p. 423.

Use Strategies Have students record in their strategy response logs reading strategies they use during reading and tell why they use them.

> **Genre** Expository nonfiction gives information about the real world. What special kind of information is the author giving you here?

416

ELL

Access Content Use the pictures and quotations to help students preview the selection. Point to each child and provide students with language to talk about his or her physical limitations.

Consider having students read the selection summary in English or in students' home languages. See the Multilingual Summaries in the ELL Teaching Guide, pp. 117–119.

Pages 416–417

LA.5.1.7.1 Use prior knowledge to make predictions, and establish a purpose for reading

LA.5.1.7.8 Use strategies to repair comprehension when self-monitoring, including questioning

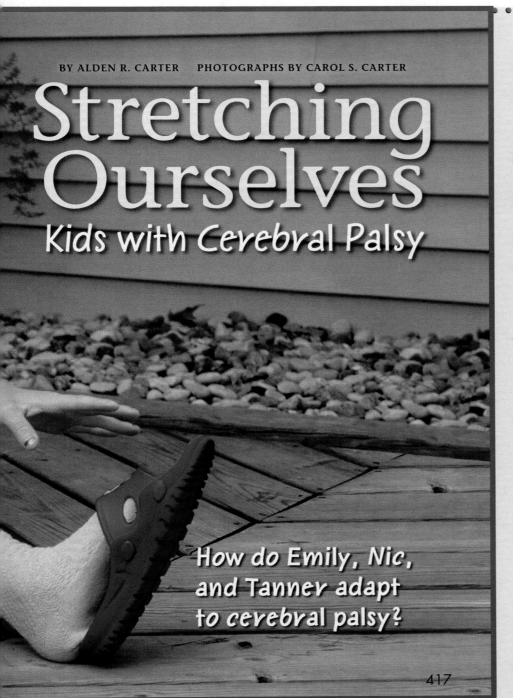

BY ALDEN R. CARTER   PHOTOGRAPHS BY CAROL S. CARTER

Stretching Ourselves
Kids with *Cerebral Palsy*

How do Emily, Nic, and Tanner adapt to cerebral palsy?

417

SET PURPOSE

Read the first page of the selection aloud to students. Have them consider their preview discussion and tell what they hope to find out as they read.

Remind students to look for details to make generalizations as they read.

STRATEGY RECALL

Students have now used these before-reading strategies:

- preview the selection to be aware of its genre, features, and possible content;
- activate prior knowledge about that content and what to expect of that genre;
- make predictions;
- set a purpose for reading.

Remind students that, as they read, they should monitor their own comprehension. If they realize something does not make sense, they can regain their comprehension by using fix-up strategies they have learned, such as:

- use phonics and word structure to decode new words;
- use context clues or a dictionary to figure out meanings of new words;
- adjust their reading rate—slow down for difficult text, speed up for easy or familiar text, or skim and scan just for specific information;
- reread parts of the text;
- read on (continue to read for clarification);
- use text features such as headings, subheadings, charts, illustrations, and so on as visual aids to comprehension;
- make a graphic organizer or a semantic organizer to aid comprehension;
- use reference sources, such as an encyclopedia, dictionary, thesaurus, or synonym finder;
- use another person, such as a teacher, a peer, a librarian, or an outside expert, as a resource.

After reading, students will use these strategies:

- summarize or retell the text;
- answer questions they or others pose;
- reflect to make new information become part of their prior knowledge.

Audio CD   **AudioText**

Guiding Comprehension

①  Generalize • Inferential

Find the generalization about people with cerebral palsy on p. 418, paragraph 4. Is it valid? Why?

The generalization is that most people with cerebral palsy have tight muscles and tendons. It is a valid generalization because the rest of the information in the paragraph supports it.

Monitor Progress
 **Generalize**

If... students are unable to recognize the generalization,	**then...** use the skill and strategy instruction on p. 419.

② **Cause and Effect • Literal**

What caused Emily's cerebral palsy?

Her brain did not receive enough oxygen while she was in her mother's womb.

Tech Files
ONLINE

Students can learn more about cerebral palsy on the Internet by typing the keywords *cerebral palsy* into a student-friendly search engine. Be sure to follow classroom rules for Internet use.

Page 418

LA.5.1.7.3 Determine the essential message through inferring and identifying relevant details

LA.5.1.7.4 Identify cause-and-effect relationships

LA.5.6.2.2 Read information, evaluating the validity of information in text

---

Bedtime always comes too soon at Emily's house. After snack and medicine, her dad helps her stretch her arms, hands, and legs.

"Sassafras!" she growls. "Rhubarb!"

"You okay, Emmers?" he asks.

"Yep," Emily says, because even if stretching hurts, it helps her to move better.

① Emily has cerebral palsy (CP). Most people with CP have tight muscles and tendons. Tendons are the thin, stretchy cords that connect muscles to bones. Our bodies move when muscles contract and relax, pulling or releasing tendons that move the bones of our arms, legs, hands, or spines. Stretching helps the muscles and tendons to work more freely.

② Emily has CP because her brain did not receive enough oxygen while she was in her mother's womb. The brain

419

Generalize

TEACH

- Tell students that generalizations are broad statements that apply to many examples. Some generalizations use clue words such as *always, most, all* or *usually.*

- Generalizations are valid if they can be supported by the text.

- Model recognizing and determining the validity of generalizations on p. 418.

Think Aloud **MODEL** I read the sentence "Most people with CP have tight muscles and tendons" and noticed the word *most.* This is a clue that the sentence probably is a generalization. The generalization is valid because I can find details to support it in the rest of the paragraph.

PRACTICE AND ASSESS

Ask if the sentence "Bedtime always comes too soon at Emily's house" states a generalization and if so, why. *(Yes, it is a generalization. "Always" is a clue word and the sentence is a broad statement.)*

Page 419

LA.5.1.7.3 Determine the mail idea or essential message through inferring and identifying relevant details

LA.5.2.2.1 Explain information from text features (illustrations)

LA.5.6.2.2 Read information, evaluating the validity of information in text

EXTEND SKILLS

Photo Essay

Point out that this selection is a photo essay. Photo essays are a collection of photographs and text around a specific topic that are written to entertain or inform. The photos are meant to make the information more real. In this case, the photo essay was written to inform readers about living with cerebral palsy.

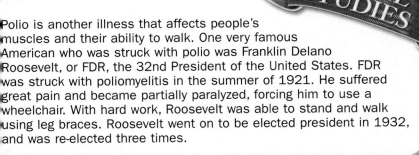

Polio

Polio is another illness that affects people's muscles and their ability to walk. One very famous American who was struck with polio was Franklin Delano Roosevelt, or FDR, the 32nd President of the United States. FDR was struck with poliomyelitis in the summer of 1921. He suffered great pain and became partially paralyzed, forcing him to use a wheelchair. With hard work, Roosevelt was able to stand and walk using leg braces. Roosevelt went on to be elected president in 1932, and was re-elected three times.

Stretching Ourselves **419**

Guiding Comprehension

3 Graphic Sources • Inferential
Question the Author **Why do you think the author chose to use photographs to illustrate this selection?**

Possible response: He wanted to make the subject more real and understandable.

Monitor Progress
REVIEW Graphic Sources

If... students have difficulty interpreting graphic resources,	then... use the skill and strategy instruction on p. 421.

4 Draw Conclusions • Critical
Text To Self **Does Emily remind you of someone you know or have heard of who lives with a disability? Explain.**

Possible response: Yes, she reminds me of an aunt I have who is blind. She can read Braille and has a seeing-eye dog to help her get around.

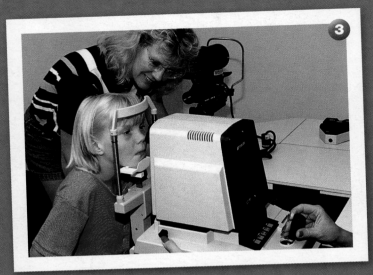

"I'm not 'sweetie,' I'm *souvy*," Emily says, but she has to grin.

420

ELL

Extend Language Write the word *affect* on the board. Tell students that *affect* means to make something happen. Write *effect* on the board. Explain that an *effect* is a result. Use each word in a sentence. Then challenge pairs of students to make a sentence with each word.

Page 420

LA.5.1.7.1 Explain purpose of text features (illustrations)

LA.5.2.1.5 Demonstrate an understanding of a literary selection, and include evidence from the text and personal experience

LA.5.2.2.1 Locate, explain, and use information from text features (illustrations)

controls how we move, speak, see, smell, hear, and learn. People with CP can have trouble with any or all of these things. There is no cure for CP, and they must work hard to learn things that come easily to others. Emily practiced a whole summer with her mom and her brother Andrew, learning how to skate.

Because the muscles and tendons in her legs are tight, Emily's movements are stiff, and she walks slightly bent forward. Twice a week, Emily's mom takes her to see a physical therapist.

"I'm real bossy with my legs," she tells the therapist.

"That's good!" Ms. Park says. "But this morning, just relax. We're going to do a gait test to see how your legs are working with each other. Then we'll know the best exercises for you."

Emily's had operations on the muscles of her feet, bladder, and eyes. They've helped, but she's impatient. "Radishes!" she mutters, when she has to have another test to see how well her eyes are working together.

Emily's mom says, "Try again, sweetie."

"I'm not 'sweetie,' I'm *soury*," Emily says, but she has to grin.

Having CP is tough. Emily used to get upset a lot. But she practices staying calm by mothering her dolls and caring for her dogs. Bole and Zuko don't always do what she wants, but she's learned to talk firmly instead of yelling. **4**

Cerebral palsy can affect how much and how fast a person can learn. Tasks that are simple for most people can be big challenges for people with CP. At school, Emily attends a special class for kids who need extra help. Today Mrs. Bauer

421

Nervous System

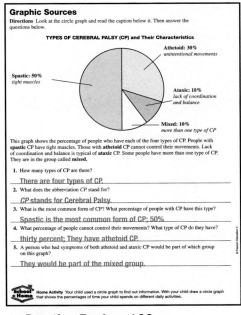

TIME FOR Science

The human nervous system consists of the central nervous system (the brain and the spinal cord) and the nerves. The nervous system carries signals through the nerves to the spinal cord and on to the brain. The brain processes that information and sends messages to the muscles, which in turn respond and enable us to walk, talk, feel, taste, smell, and so on. Cerebral palsy and multiple sclerosis are two conditions that affect the nervous system's ability to function properly.

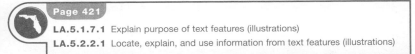

Page 421

LA.5.1.7.1 Explain purpose of text features (illustrations)
LA.5.2.2.1 Locate, explain, and use information from text features (illustrations)

SKILLS ⟷ STRATEGIES IN CONTEXT

Graphic Sources REVIEW

TEACH

- Explain to students that photographs are one form of graphic sources, but others include charts, graphs, maps, or other illustrations.
- Tell students that authors use graphic sources to enhance the text.
- Model why the author chose photographs for graphic sources in this selection.

Think Aloud **MODEL** When I look at the photographs in this selection I see pictures of real people, like Emily, who live with cerebral palsy. I think the author used photographs on purpose to make cerebral palsy seem more real.

PRACTICE AND ASSESS

- Have students look at the bottom photograph on p. 420 and tell what it says about Emily. (*It shows that even though she has a disability, she is just like other kids who like to play with their dogs.*)
- To assess, use Practice Book 166.

▲ **Practice Book** p. 166

Guiding Comprehension

5 **Figurative Language • Inferential**

What does Emily mean when she says she is "like flowers and a rainbow"?

She is covered with all different colors of paint.

6 **Compare and Contrast • Inferential**

How does Nic's case of CP compare to Emily's?

Nic has a more severe case of CP—he spends most of his time in a wheelchair and can only speak a few words. Emily has greater mobility and can speak well.

7 **Draw Conclusions • Inferential**

How would you describe Nic?

Possible answers: brave, hard-working, positive, funny.

---

is teaching them how to take better care of their hair, teeth, and skin. Emily grumbles about a snarl in Lizzy's hair.

"Celery!" Lizzy yelps.

"No vegetables!" Mrs. Bauer says. "Just keep at it. And, Emily be gentle."

Emily also gets extra help for reading and math and then goes to regular classes for art, social studies, and music. She's especially good at art, and never minds getting paint all over herself. "I'm like flowers and a rainbow!" she says.

Emily and Nic are friends at Grant School. Nic has CP because his brain was badly damaged during birth. He spends most of his time in a wheelchair and can speak only a few words. But no one likes playing ball, making jokes, or teasing the teachers more than Nic.

Every day Nic practices simple words with Ms. Larson, a speech therapist. She also helps him learn the buttons on his computer, which has an artificial voice. Nic's favorite button is "Give me a big bear hug!"

A lot of the other kids think his computer is pretty cool. At recess, Nic shows them how to use it. He makes it say "Let's play ball" and "Let's swing."

At the end of the school day, Nic rides the handicapped bus home. When Gale, his bus driver, starts the elevator, Nic likes to make crashing sounds. "Oh, my gosh, you're breaking the elevator again!" Gale yells.

While his mom gets supper ready, Nic reads books with his cousin Shylo. Turning the pages is pretty good practice for his hands. He particularly likes books about bulldozers, farms, and football.

422

Access Content Nic likes books about bulldozers. Tell students that a *bulldozer* is a powerful tractor used for clearing land by moving earth and rocks. Ask students if they have ever seen a bulldozer at a construction site.

Page 422

LA.5.1.7.3 Determine the main idea or essential message through inferring

LA.5.1.7.7 Compare and contrast

LA.5.2.1.7 Identify and explain author's use of figurative language (similes)

"I'm like flowers and a rainbow!" she says.

423

STRATEGY SELF-CHECK

Predict

Ask students to go back to the predictions they made about the selection prior to reading. Were their predictions accurate? *(Responses will vary.)* Remind them that as they read, they should check to see if their predictions were accurate and keep making, refining, and confirming new ones. Remind them that it can be helpful to use the generalizations they make as they read to make predictions.

SELF-CHECK

Students can ask themselves these questions to assess their ability to use the skill and strategy.

- Was I able to make predictions based on the selection title, photographs, and what I know about cerebral palsy?
- Did I justify, refine, and confirm my predictions as I read?
- Did I use generalizations to help me make predictions?

Monitor Progress
Generalize

If... students have difficulty making generalizations or predictions,	then... revisit the skill lesson on pp. 412–413. Reteach as necessary.

 Strategy Response Log

Answer Questions Provide the following prompt: Have you answered the questions you wrote before reading? (See p. 416.) Write another question you would like to ask about CP. Continue reading to answer your question.

Page 423
LA.5.1.6.1 Use new vocabulary
LA.5.1.7.1 Make and confirm predictions
LA.5.1.7.8 Use strategies to repair comprehension when self-monitoring, including predicting and questioning

If you want to teach this selection in two sessions, stop here.

Develop Vocabulary

PRACTICE LESSON VOCABULARY

Students respond orally as to whether each statement is *true* or *false* and explain their answer if it is false.

1. A *therapist* provides treatment to people with disabilities. *(True)*

2. A person's *gait* is best seen when he or she walks. *(True)*

3. *Handicapped* children with CP always are confined to wheelchairs. *(False. Some children with less severe cases of CP don't need one.)*

BUILD CONCEPT VOCABULARY

Review previous concept words with students. Ask if students have come across any words today in their reading or elsewhere that they would like to add to the Overcoming Physical Limitations Concept Web, such as *challenges*.

Guiding Comprehension

If you are teaching the selection in two days, discuss any generalizations and review the vocabulary.

8 ◉ **Vocabulary • Context Clues**

Use context clues to figure out the meaning of *pump* on p. 425, paragraph 4.

Clues: takes medicine, in his abdomen, delivers medicine. Meaning: a machine for forcing liquids in and out of things.

Monitor Progress
◉ **Context Clues**

If... students have difficulty using context clues to determine the meaning of *pump*,	**then...** use the vocabulary strategy instruction on p. 425.

9 ◉ **Predict • Inferential**

Predict what you will learn about CP by reading about Tanner's experiences.

Possible response: How CP affects people with milder cases.

DAY 3 \ **Grouping Options**

Reading
Whole Group Discuss the Question of the Day.

Group Time Differentiated Instruction
Read *Stretching Ourselves.* See pp. 412f–412g for the small group lesson plan.

Whole Group Discuss the Reader Response questions on p. 432. Then use p. 435a.

Language Arts
Use pp. 435e–435k.

"Way to go, Nic!" And Nic's grin says everything he needs to say.

424

ⒺⓁⓁ

Build Background Nic and his family go bowling. Explain that bowling is a game you play by rolling a heavy ball down a wooden lane in a bowling alley. The object of the game is to knock down wooden pins located at the far end of the lane. Choose a volunteer to act out bowling a ball.

Page 424

LA.5.1.6.3 Use context clues to determine meanings of unfamiliar words
LA.5.1.7.1 Make predictions
LA.5.1.7.8 Use strategies to repair comprehension when self-monitoring, including checking context clues

Nic, his mom, and his cousins go bowling some Friday nights. It's not easy for Nic because his hands won't always do what he wants them to do. When he gets a good roll, his mom yells, "Way to go, Nic!" And Nic's grin says everything he needs to say.

Just like at Emily's, bedtime always comes too soon at Nic's house. Nic and his mom add a few sentences to a letter for his dad, who is way across the ocean in the army. "Is there anything more you want to say?" his mom asks. Nic hugs himself, sending his dad a very big bear hug.

Saturdays are great days. At swimming class, Nic can kick, splash, and go under the water as much as he wants. (His mom yells if he does too much kicking, splashing, or diving in the bathtub.)

"Lie back and relax, Tiger," Mr. Scheuer says. "We're going to practice floating."

Like Emily, Nic takes medicine for his CP. Last year, the doctors put a tiny pump in his abdomen. All day and all night, the pump delivers a small amount of medicine to help his muscles work better. Along with exercise and practice, the medicine may someday make it possible for Nic to walk on his own. **8**

Nic feels loose after swimming. He practices with his walker. It's hard and frustrating. "Need some help, Nicky?" his mom calls. Nic shakes his head, growls "Self," and takes another step.

Tanner, too, would rather do things himself—even when they take longer. Tanner has milder CP than Nic or Emily, and many people don't notice his limp or his weak left arm. **9**

425

Assistive Technology

Nic's computer with an artificial voice is an example of an assistive technology that helps people with physical disabilities live and work independently. Assistive technology may take the shape of simple tools, such as a pencil grip or sophisticated devices like a computer that can be operated with a switch for people who cannot use a keyboard. Other examples are screen readers for visually impaired people and close-captioning for the hearing-impaired.

VOCABULARY STRATEGY

Context Clues

TEACH

Read the fourth paragraph on p. 425. Model using context clues to determine the meaning of *pump*.

Think Aloud **MODEL** The paragraph says that doctors put a tiny *pump* in Nic's abdomen to deliver medicine to help his muscles work better. I've heard of the word *pump* before, as in a pump at the gas station that puts gas into a car, so I imagine it works like that. This pump puts medicine directly into his body.

PRACTICE AND ASSESS

Have students use context clues to determine the meaning of *frustrating* on p. 425 paragraph 5. (Clues: *hard, shakes his head and growls*. Meaning: *causing a feeling of anger or helplessness*)

CORRECTIVE FEEDBACK

LA.5.1.6.3 Use context clues to determine meanings of unfamiliar words

- **Question** Use Whiteboard or Transparency 17a, items 1–3, to ask questions that address this standard in FCAT format. Have students write their answers on a sheet of paper.
- **Check** Scan students' responses by having them hold up their papers.
- **Correct** If necessary, provide corrective feedback and review pp. 414–415.

> **1** Read this sentence from the story.
>
> **We're going to do a gait test to see how your legs are working with each other.**
>
> The word *gait* relates to
>
> Ⓐ the opening in a fence.
> Ⓑ the tests doctors perform.
> Ⓒ the speed at which an injury heals.
> Ⓓ how a person walks or moves on foot.

▲ **FCAT Whiteboard Activity** 17a/ **FCAT Transparency** 17a

Stretching Ourselves **425**

Guiding Comprehension

10 **Generalize • Inferential**

What is a generalization you can make about children with CP based on what you've read about Emily, Nic, and Tanner?

They have to work harder and be extremely brave, but they can enjoy many of the same things other kids do.

Monitor Progress	
Generalize	
If... students have difficulty making generalizations,	**then...** use the skill and strategy instruction on p. 427.

11 **Draw Conclusions • Inferential**

Does Tanner's CP prevent him from being a good older brother to Cole? Explain.

No, while his mom is busy, Tanner plays with his brother just as any other kid would.

Tanner had bleeding in the brain—what's called a stroke—before he was born. Every day he practices to make his arm stronger and his fingers more nimble.

Tanner loves to play ball, especially football. "I'm going to be a fullback someday," he tells his brother, Anthony.

10 "You bet!" Anthony says. "Just keep practicing."

Tanner is looking forward to having an operation to help his left arm. But first he must train it to move more freely. The doctors have given him a special brace to exercise his arm. "How does that feel?" his stepdad asks.

"Heavy, but I can handle it," Tanner says.

While his mom is busy, Tanner takes care of his new

11 brother, Cole. "Slide the rings, Cole!" he tells him. Tanner could show him better using his right arm, but he practices using his left instead.

Tanner has a lot on his mind, and sometimes he falls behind in school. But he asks questions and gets help from friends. Pretty soon he's caught up again.

"Arithmetic takes practice, practice, practice," Ms. Johnson tells the class.

"You bet!" Tanner says. After all, he knows lots about practicing.

No one in class—except maybe Ms. Johnson—reads stories better than Tanner. He does lots of different voices and can always make kids laugh. Next year maybe he'll try out for the football team *and* the school play.

426

ELL

Extend Language Read aloud the phrase, "a special brace to exercise his arm." Explain that *brace* is a multiple-meaning word. Here it means something that holds parts together or holds something steady. To brace something means to support it or hold it steady.

"I'm going to be a fullback someday," he tells his brother, Anthony.

427

SKILLS ←→ STRATEGIES IN CONTEXT

Generalize Predict

TEACH

Reread the information about Tanner in the last paragraph on p. 426. Ask students to briefly tell what new information they learned about Tanner. *(Tanner is great at reading stories; he might try out for the school play.)* Tell them that they can use this information to help make a prediction about children with CP.

Think Aloud **MODEL** Now that I know that children with CP can do many of the same things that other children can do, I can predict that as they grow older, they will be able to do many of the same things that other adults can do.

PRACTICE AND ASSESS

Have students predict what other generalizations they will be able to make based on the facts the author provides about Tanner on p. 426, paragraph 3. *(Surgery sometimes helps people with CP.)*

Page 427

LA.5.1.7.1 Make predictions

LA.5.1.7.3 Determine the main idea or essential message through inferring and summarizing

LA.5.1.7.8 Use strategies to repair comprehension when self-monitoring, including rereading and predicting

Guiding Comprehension

12 **Author's Purpose • Inferential**

Why do you think the author tells you Tanner sometimes feels sad and mad when friends try to rush him?

Regardless of our physical state, internally we all experience the same emotions.

13 **Generalize • Inferential**

Paragraph 4 on p. 429 states that "Almost every Sunday, Leslie rides her horse." Is this a generalization? Explain your answer.

Yes. The word *almost* is used as a clue word. The sentence is a broad statement.

428

ELL

Access Content Read aloud the question "Ready to trot, Em?" Explain that horses trot. *Trot* means to move more quickly than a walk but not as fast as a gallop. Ask volunteers to trot or gallop. Challenge classmates to tell which they are doing.

Page 428

LA.5.1.7.2 Identify author's purpose

LA.5.1.7.3 Determine the main idea or essential message through inferring

Tanner loves recess. But sometimes friends shout "Hurry up, Tanner!" when he's already hurrying as fast as he can. And that makes him sad and a little mad.

But he remembers what his mom says: "You're way ahead on learning to be brave, Tanner."

People with CP *are* brave. Leslie Martin has had four operations for her CP.

"Last time they sort of tossed me in a blender and poured a new kid out the other side," she likes telling people.

Almost every Sunday, Leslie rides her horse, Annie. This summer she's going to teach Emily to ride.

"Ready to trot, Em?" she asks.

"You bet your broccoli!" Emily says.

429

Generalize

TEACH

- Generalizations are broad statements that apply to many examples.
- Some generalizations include clue words; others do not.
- Valid generalizations are able to be supported with details in text or from our general knowledge.
- Model recognizing a generalization on p. 429.

Think Aloud **MODEL** In paragraph 4, I read the sentence "Almost every Sunday, Leslie rides her horse." I think that *almost* is a clue word for a generalization. It makes a broad statement about something Leslie does frequently.

PRACTICE AND ASSESS

Ask students to tell how they could prove or disprove the validity of the generalization about Leslie riding her horse "almost every Sunday." *(You could ask Leslie how often she rides on Sundays or you can assume that she might have other things to do on some Sundays.)*

Page 429

LA.5.1.7.3 Determine the main idea or essential message through inferring

LA.5.6.2.2 Read information, evaluating the validity of information in text

Guiding Comprehension

14 **Draw Conclusions • Critical**

The selection gives two examples of jobs that adults with CP might have. What other jobs might adults with CP have?

Answers will vary, but with the exception of jobs that require physical prowess, students should include jobs that other adults have.

15 **Predict • Critical**

Were the predictions you made about CP accurate? If not, revise your predictions.

Answers will vary.

16 **Summarize • Critical**

Text To World **What did you learn about people with CP?**

Summaries will vary but should include the idea that people with CP have to work harder to do certain things, but otherwise are like you and me.

Strategy Response Log

Summarize When students finish reading the selection, provide this prompt: How would you summarize what you learned about CP in the selection *Stretching Ourselves*? Write four or five sentences to explain the important points of the selection.

Use Strategies Meet with students to review their list of the reading strategies they realized they were using as they read.

Pages 430–431

LA.5.1.6.1 Use new vocabulary

LA.5.1.7.1 Make and confirm predictions

LA.5.1.7.3 Determine the main idea or essential message through summarizing

LA.5.1.7.8 Use strategies to repair comprehension when self-monitoring, including summarizing

LA.5.4.2.1 Write in a variety of forms (summaries)

---

14 Adults with CP work at many different jobs. Greg Kucjek, a friend of Tanner and his stepdad, schedules routes for a big fleet of trucks.

"Let me take it for a cruise, Greg," Tanner says.

Greg laughs. "In a few years, Tan my man."

Tom Hilber, who works as a welcomer and guide at the Marshfield Clinic, is a special friend to Nic and a lot of kids who come to the clinic for help.

"Give a five and you'll get a ten back every time," he often says.

Like many people with CP, Tom is married. He and his wife, Jenny, have two grown children and two grandchildren.

Having CP means working hard at simple things. Tanner explains it this way: "Kids with CP are always trying. It can be tough when our bodies don't do what we want them to do. Some of us can't even talk to ask for something or to tell how we feel. But we keep working to do as much as we can."

Emily says, "Sometimes people are scared or shy because we move or talk funny. But you don't have to be. We like the same things you like. So, as Nic says—

15
16
"Give us a bear hug!"

430

Access Content Explain that the phrase "take it for a cruise" means to take something out for a ride, or to drive something. Ask students what Tanner wanted to take for a cruise.

"Let me take it for a cruise, Greg," Tanner says.

431

STRATEGY SELF-CHECK

Confirm Predictions

Have students review their pre-reading predictions. Ask them to confirm or revise those predictions based on the generalizations and details in the selection.

SELF-CHECK

Students can ask themselves these questions to assess understanding of the selection.

- Did I recognize generalizations and the details given to support them as I read *Stretching Ourselves*?
- Did I use generalizations to make predictions?
- Did I refine and confirm predictions as I read?

Monitor Progress

Generalize

If... students have difficulty making generalizations and making, confirming, justifying, and refining predictions,	then... use the Reteach lesson on pp. 435b.

Generalize

- An author may write similar details about different things or people. You can use these similar details to make a general statement that covers all the things or people. This statement is called a **generalization**.
- A **valid** generalization can be supported by facts or details. A **faulty** generalization cannot.

Directions Read the first paragraph of the passage and make a prediction about what the rest of the passage will be about. Finish reading the passage. Then answer the questions below.

In July, 1968, Eunice Kennedy Shriver opened the first Special Olympics Games. She knew many athletes would win, but she also knew many would not. She wanted to encourage all of the athletes to do their best. So she told them that the gladiators in Rome said, "Let me win, but if I cannot win, let me be brave in the attempt." This became the Special Olympics Athlete Oath.

Through Special Olympics, many people with intellectual disabilities realize their full potential and become productive members of society. They train all year and compete in a variety of sports. In the process, they develop physical fitness, demonstrate courage, and experience joy. Special Olympics also creates an environment of acceptance for people with intellectual disabilities.

Possible answers given.
1. Write a generalization from this passage about how the Special Olympics affects its participants.
   Many people with intellectual disabilities realize their full
   potential and become productive members of society.
2. How did you know this was a generalization?
   The clue word *many.*
3. What detail supports the generalization?
   They train all year and compete in a variety of sports.
4. What other detail supports the generalization?
   They develop physical fitness, by training and competing.
5. After you read the first paragraph, what did you predict the rest of the article would be about? Was your prediction accurate?
   I predicted the rest of the passage would be about Special
   Olympics athletes. My prediction was correct.

Home Activity Your child read a short passage and recognized a generalization using clue words. Read an article together and challenge your child to find generalizations.

 **Practice Book** p. 167

Develop Vocabulary

PRACTICE LESSON VOCABULARY

Have students answer *yes* or *no* to each question and provide a reason.

1. Are computer-generated voices *artificial*? *(Yes; they are not real.)*

2. Does everyone who has CP need a *wheelchair*? *(No; many people with CP can walk on their own.)*

3. Is your *abdomen* in your head? *(No; your abdomen is between your chest and legs.)*

BUILD CONCEPT VOCABULARY

Review previous concept words with students. Ask if students have met any words today in their reading or elsewhere that they would like to add to the Overcoming Physical Limitations Concept Web such as *brave*.

Stretching Ourselves **431**

Reader Response

Open for Discussion Personal Response

MODEL I'd think about what we have in common. Then I'd think about things that we could possibly do together.

Comprehension Check Critical Response

1. Responses will vary but should describe how a photo makes the text seem clearer. ***Author's Purpose***

2. Possible response: Kids with CP have physical challenges, but otherwise they are just like other kids their age. Details will vary. 🔾 ***Generalize***

3. Responses will vary but should provide details such as: They probably enjoy playing the same games kids our age do. 🔾 ***Predict***

4. Possible response: Someone with CP who uses a *wheelchair* needs to travel in a *handicapped* accessible vehicle. 🔾 ***Vocabulary***

THINK AND EXPLAIN For test practice, assign a 10–15 minute time limit. For assessment, see the Scoring Rubric at the right.

Retell

Have students retell *Stretching Ourselves*.

Monitor Progress

Check Retelling Rubric 4 3 2 1

| **If...** students have difficulty retelling the selection, | **then...** use the Retelling Cards and the Scoring Rubric for Retelling on p. 433 to assist fluent retelling. |

SUCCESS PREDICTOR

Check Retelling Students should use photos of Emily, Nic, and Tanner to guide their retellings. For more ideas, see the ELL and Transition Handbook.

Reader Response

Open for Discussion Imagine that Emily, Nic, and Tanner were part of your life. How would you interact with them?

1. The photos and words in *Stretching Ourselves* work together to give you facts, ideas, and feelings. Choose one photo and the text that goes with it. Explain how they work together. **Think Like an Author**

2. Make a generalization about the daily lives of the kids in *Stretching Ourselves*. Support it with details from the text. **Generalize**

3. Extend the generalization you made in #2. Predict other details that are not in the text that you think would fit your generalization. **Predict**

4. *Stretching Ourselves* shows that dealing with CP can be a difficult task. Use words from the Words to Know list to explain why. **Vocabulary**

Think and Explain *Stretching Ourselves* is about more than just stretching arms and legs. Use details and information from the selection to explain how the title applies to the selection.

Meet author Alden Carter on page 766 and illustrator Carol Carter on page 772.

LA.5.2.2.1 Use text features
LA.5.2.2.2 Use text to answer questions

432

THINK AND EXPLAIN FOUR-POINT SCORING RUBRIC

Top-Score Response A top-score response will use details from the selection to show how children with CP must extend themselves, to work hard to do the things that come easily to others.

Example of a Top-Score Response "Stretching Ourselves" refers to the way kids with CP have to work extra hard to do things that are easy for most people. For example, Emily practiced all summer with help from her brother and mother to learn how to skate. Nic practices hard every day to be able to say simple words. Kids with CP also stretch themselves by bravely facing painful operations and therapy.

For additional rubrics, see p. WA10.

Write Now
Journal Entry

More FCAT WRITING+
See *The Grammar and Writing Book*, pages 146–151.

Prompt

Kids with special challenges are featured in *Stretching Ourselves.*

Think about someone you know who has special mental or physical challenges.

Now write a journal entry describing your observations and feelings about that person.

Writing Trait

In a journal entry, **focus** on an **idea** and elaborate with facts, details, and examples.

Student Model

> **Writer focuses on main idea:** experiences with a hearing-impaired friend.

July 10

This week I made friends with Nell, a hearing-impaired girl who communicates using sign language. When we arrived at summer camp, I felt sorry for Nell. I didn't think we'd be able to talk at all. But she taught me how to sign phrases such as "What's your name?" and "That's really cool!"

> **Writer tells about different feelings and explains change.**

Nell has a great imagination, and she's really fun to play with. She's patient too when she's teaching others how to sign. The next time I meet a hearing-impaired person, I'll be able to start a conversation right away!

> **Positive statement provides strong ending.**

Use the model to help you write your own journal entry.

LA.5.3.2.1 Focus on main idea with development of details
LA.5.4.1.2 Write an expressive form that employs appropriate format

433

Write Now

Look at the Prompt Have students identify and discuss key words and phrases in the prompt. *(special mental or physical challenges, journal entry, observations and feelings)*

Strategies to Develop Focus/Ideas

Have students

- think about someone with special mental or physical challenges among their friends, classmates, relatives, or people they have read about or seen on television.
- visualize how they would feel if they were that person and think about what they might do to overcome their challenges.
- state the main idea at the beginning of their journal entry and elaborate on it in the rest of the entry.

For additional suggestions and rubric, see pp. 435g–435h.

Hints for Better Writing

- Carefully read the prompt.
- Use a graphic organizer to plan your writing.
- Support your ideas with information and details.
- Use words that help readers understand.
- Proofread and edit your work.

Page 433

LA.5.3.2.1 Focus on main idea with development of details
LA.5.4.1.2 Write an expressive form that employs appropriate format

Scoring Rubric — Expository Retelling

Rubric 4 3 2 1	4	3	2	1
Connections	Makes connections and generalizes beyond the text	Makes connections to other events, texts, or experiences	Makes a limited connection to another event, text, or experience	Makes no connection to another event, text, or experience
Author's Purpose	Elaborates on author's purpose	Tells author's purpose with some clarity	Makes some connection to author's purpose	Makes no connection to author's purpose
Topic	Describes the main topic	Identifies the main topic with some details early in retelling	Identifies the main topic	Retelling has no sense of topic
Important Ideas	Gives accurate information about events, steps, and ideas using details and key vocabulary	Gives accurate information about events, steps, and ideas with some detail and key vocabulary	Gives limited or inaccurate information about events, steps, and ideas	Gives no information about events, steps, and ideas
Conclusions	Draws conclusions and makes inferences to generalize beyond the text	Draws conclusions about the text	Is able to draw few conclusions about the text	Is unable to draw conclusions or make inferences about the text

Retelling Plan

☑ **Week 1** Assess Strategic Intervention students.

☑ **This week assess Advanced students.**

☐ **Week 3** Assess Strategic Intervention students.

☐ **Week 4** Assess On-Level students.

☐ **Week 5** Assess any students you have not yet checked during this unit.

Use the Retelling Chart on p. TR17 to record retelling.

Selection Test To assess with *Stretching Ourselves*, use Selection Tests, pp. 65-68–000.

Fresh Reads for Differentiated Test Practice For weekly leveled practice, use pp. 97–102.

Retelling

SUCCESS PREDICTOR

Science in Reading

OBJECTIVES

- Examine features of expository nonfiction.
- Practice a test-taking strategy.
- Compare and contrast across texts.

PREVIEW/USE TEXT FEATURES

As students preview "Helpful Tools," have them look at the headings and photos. Ask:

- **How do the headings help you know what the text is about?** *(They identify the helpful tools.)*

Link to Science

Students can use the key words *disability* or *assistive technology* on a student-friendly search engine to research other helpful technologies on the Internet.

Page 434

LA.5.1.6.1 Use new vocabulary
LA.5.2.2.1 Use text features (headings and illustrations)

DAY 4 Grouping Options

Reading
Whole Group Discuss the Question of the Day.

Group Time Differentiated Instruction
Read "Helpful Tools." See pp. 412f–412g for the small group lesson plan.

Whole Group Use p. 435a.

Language Arts
Use pp. 435e–435k.

Science in Reading

Expository Nonfiction

Genre

- **Expository nonfiction can explain helpful technological devices.**

- **The author explains how these devices work, who uses them, and why.**

Text Features

- **Headings name the devices, and photos help explain them.**

- **Look over the headings and photos to see what the selection will explain.**

Link to Science

Selections that deal with new technologies are important in a world like ours, with so many new inventions designed to help people. Research other helpful new technologies. Find a device that seems especially helpful and report on it to the class.

SC.H.3.2.4.1 Extend knowledge of ways that people can solve problems

434

helpful tools

by Sally Hobart Alexander

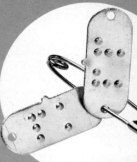

Slowly, between the ages of twenty-four and twenty-six, Sally Hobart Alexander lost her sight. She went on to become an award-winning author of books for young people. In one of these books she describes tools that helped her adapt to blindness. One of these tools is Braille, a writing system that uses raised dots to stand for letters and numbers.

BRAILLE CLOTHING TAG
About the size of a fingernail, these metal tags have holes at either end for pinning or sewing onto labels. They tell me colors: "YW" for yellow, "PK" for pink, and "PP" for purple. When clothes are multicolored, I pin several tags onto the labels at once.

Content-Area Vocabulary	Science
adapt	to change to fit different conditions; adjust
device	something invented or made for a particular purpose or special purpose

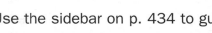

TALKING CLOCK
These clocks come in many varieties. The most common is pocket-sized, but I've had talking clocks inside ballpoint pens and key chains. You simply push a button, and a robot voice calls out the time.

BRAILLE WATCH
Imagine a life without clocks or watches, and you'll have an idea of my life when I first became blind. I dialed the phone number for

the exact time so often I memorized it. I'd always taken telling time for granted, and I felt lost. I developed a good sense of how long it took to do things, but my estimates could be off by ten minutes. Without a watch, I could miss a bus or an appointment. I could arrive at work late.

A Braille watch saved me. It looks like a regular wristwatch, except that the crystal pops up when you push a button, usually the winder. You can feel that the hour hand is shorter and sits below the minute hand. All the numbers have raised dots beside them. The

numbers 3, 6, and 9 have two raised dots, and the 12 has three.

BRAILLE TIMER
Usually three inches high and two inches wide, this device has raised dots by each number and works just like any other timer. I also use Braille labels on spices and cans. My microwave has a Braille pad.

Reading Across Texts

What helpful technological devices are mentioned in *Stretching Ourselves* and "Helpful Tools," and what are they used for?

Writing Across Texts Display your answers in a two-column chart.

Generalize Why have these devices been invented?

435

The Human Eye

Although small—only about one inch in diameter—the human eye is a very complex and important organ. When you look at something you are seeing the reflection of light rays from that object. Light rays pass through the cornea, which sits in front of the colored part of the eye called the iris, and then through the lens. The cornea and lens focus the light into a clear upside-down image on the retina at the back of the eye. The retina then sends these signals to the brain and we see the images right side up.

EXPOSITORY NONFICTION

Use the sidebar on p. 434 to guide discussion.

- Point out that expository nonfiction explains what something is like.
- Explain that the reader can use headings to help find important information.
- Discuss with students the types of objects that will be explained in this selection.

Audio CD AudioText

Generalize

The devices rely on touch and hearing.

CONNECT TEXT TO TEXT

Reading Across Texts

Have students scan both selections for the names or photos of technological tools that can aid people with disabilities.

Writing Across Texts Have students list the names of the helpful technological devices in one column and their functions in another.

Page 435
LA.5.1.7.7 Compare and contrast elements in multiple texts
LA.5.2.2.3 Organize information (charting)

Stretching Ourselves **435**

Fluency Assessment Plan

- ☑ **Week 1** Assess Advanced students.
- ☑ **This week assess Strategic Intervention students.**
- ☐ **Week 3** Assess On-Level students.
- ☐ **Week 4** Assess Strategic Intervention students.
- ☐ **Week 5** Assess any students you have not yet checked during this unit.

Set individual goals for students to enable them to reach the year-end goal.
- Current Goal: 120–128 wcpm
- Year-End Goal: 140 wcpm

Fluency, particularly for English learners reading texts in English, develops gradually and through much practice. Focus on each student's improvement rather than solely monitoring the number of words correct per minute.

 To develop fluent readers, use Fluency Coach.

Page 435a

LA.5.1.5.1 Demonstrate the ability to read grade level text

LA.5.1.5.2 Adjust reading rate based on purpose and style

DAY 5 Grouping Options

Reading
Whole Group
Revisit the Question of the Week.

Group Time
Differentiated Instruction
Reread this week's Leveled Readers. See pp. 412f–412g for the small group lesson plan.

Whole Group
Use p. 435b–435c.

Language Arts
Use pp. 435d–435l.

EMOTION
Fluency

DAY 1

Model Reread "Wilma Unlimited" on p. 412m. Explain that you will use your voice to show surprise, happiness, and excitement as you read. Model for students as you read.

DAY 2

Choral Reading Read aloud paragraphs 3–6 on p. 421. Have students notice how you use your voice to show Emily's impatience and Emily's mom's encouragement. Have students practice as a class doing three choral readings of the paragraphs on p. 421.

DAY 3

Model Read aloud paragraphs 3–5 on p. 425. Have students notice how you read about Nic's swim class with excitement and growl the word "Self" as Nic does to show his determination. Practice as a class by doing three choral readings.

DAY 4

Partner Reading Partners practice reading aloud paragraphs 3–5 on p. 425, three times. Students should read with emotion and offer each other feedback.

Monitor Progress Check Fluency WCPM

As students reread, monitor their progress toward their individual fluency goals. Current Goal: 120–128 words correct per minute. End-of-Year Goal: 140 WCPM. Have library books or other texts available at a variety of reading levels for students to use to practice fluency. See pp. DI·57–DI·58.

If... students cannot read fluently at a rate of 120–128 words correct per minute,
then... make sure students practice with text at their independent level. Provide additional fluency practice, pairing nonfluent readers with fluent readers.

If... students already read at 140 words correct per minute,
then... they do not need to reread three to four times.

SUCCESS PREDICTOR

DAY 5

Assessment
Individual Reading Rate Use the Fluency Assessment Plan and do a one-minute timed reading of either selection from this week to assess students in Week 2. Pay special attention to this week's skill, emotion. Provide corrective feedback for each student.

RETEACH

Generalize

TEACH

Review the definition of *generalization* on p. 412. Students can complete Practice Book p. 168 on their own, or you can complete it as a class. Point out that students will need to complete the sentences in each box of the chart. For example, in the box labeled "General Statement—Clue Word?" students need to complete the generalization and write the clue words that signal it.

ASSESS

Have students read the last paragraph on p. 421. Have them identify the generalization and the clue word that signals it. *(Generalization: Tasks that are simple for most people can be big challenges for people with CP; Clue word: most.)*

For additional instruction on generalize, see DI·53.

EXTEND SKILLS

Simile

TEACH

Similes are a type of figurative language. They usually compare two unlike things that are alike in at least one way.

• Similes may include the words *like* or *as.*

• Similes can be used to call attention to a quality that is the same in the two things being compared.

Remind students about the simile on p. 422, paragraph 2: "I'm like flowers and a rainbow."

ASSESS

Have students reread p. 425, paragraph 3. Ask them to write a simile using the word *like* or *as,* that describes Nic when he is in the water. *(Possible response: Nic is like a dolphin in the water.)*

LA.5.1.7.3 Determine the main idea or essential message through inferring
LA.5.4.1.2 Write expressive forms that employ figurative language (simile)

OBJECTIVES

• Make a generalization.

• Recognize and use similes.

Skills Trace
Generalize

Introduce/Teach	TE: 5.4 412–413, 458–459; 5.5 604–605
Practice	Practice Book: 163, 167, 168, 183, 187, 188, 196, 243, 247, 248
Reteach/Review	**TE: 5.4 435b, 483b, 493, DI•53, DI•55; 5.5 625b, DI•56**
Test	Selection Test: 65–68, 73–76, 97–100; Benchmark Test: Unit 4

Access Content Reteach the skill by reviewing the Picture It! lesson on generalizing in the ELL Teaching Guide, pp. 113–114.

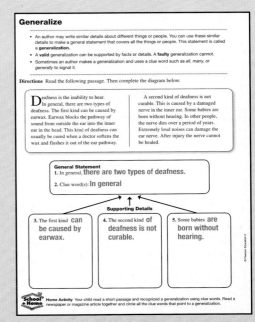

▲ **Practice Book** p. 168

Vocabulary and Word Study

VOCABULARY STRATEGY
Context Clues

UNFAMILIAR WORDS Remind students they can use context clues to determine the meanings of unfamiliar words. Have students locate context clues and identify the meanings of these words from *Stretching Ourselves*. Have students confirm word meanings using a dictionary.

Word	Context Clues	Meaning
contract	muscles, move	become shorter or smaller; shrink
tendons		
nimble		

Homophones

Homophones are words that are pronounced the same but have different meanings and spellings. Have students list words from *Stretching Ourselves* and "Helpful Tools" that are homophones and write sentences using both words.

Homophones	Sentences
gait/gate	Her *gait* is very slow. Close the *gate* on your way out.
way/weigh	
weak/week	

BUILD CONCEPT VOCABULARY
Overcoming Challenges

LOOKING BACK Remind students of the question of the week: *How do people adapt to living with physical limitations?* Discuss how this week's Concept Web of vocabulary words relates to the theme of overcoming physical limitations. Ask students if they have any words or categories to add. Discuss whether the words and categories are appropriately related to the concept.

REVIEW/CONNECT Preview the title of the next selection, *Exploding Ants: Amazing Facts About How Animals Adapt.* Ask students which Concept Web words might apply to the new selection based on the title alone.

Put a star next to these words on the web.

Display the Concept Web and revisit the vocabulary words as you read the next selection to check predictions.

Monitor Progress

Check Vocabulary

If... students suggest words or categories that are not related to the concept,	then... review the words and categories on the Concept Web and discuss how they relate to the lesson concept.

SUCCESS PREDICTOR

Speaking and Listening

SPEAKING

Oral Presentation

SET-UP Have students prepare an oral presentation on some of the tools and adaptive technology available to help handicapped people.

PLANNING Have students determine which tools or technology they will include in their presentations. They may choose from the tools and technology described in *Stretching Ourselves* or "Helpful Tools," or they may talk about other tools with which they are familiar.

VISUAL AIDS Suggest that students copy or obtain pictures of the tools or technology they plan to speak about. If the item itself is readily available, they may also want to show it so as to increase audience interest and understanding. Tell students to be sure to practice with any tools beforehand so that they can demonstrate them smoothly.

Delivery Tips

- Be familiar enough with your material so that you don't have to read your whole presentation from your notes.
- Make eye contact with your audience.
- Use correct grammar and avoid slang.
- Allow time for and encourage questions.

LISTENING

Listen to Oral Presentations

Have students listen to and evaluate the oral presentations given by their classmates. Have them answer these questions orally or in writing.

1. **What topics did the speaker cover in his or her presentation?**
2. **Did the speaker support his or her main idea or topic with details and examples?**
3. **Did the speaker include mostly facts or opinions in his or her presentation? Give examples.**

Support Vocabulary Use the following to review and extend vocabulary and to explore lesson concepts further:
- ELL Poster 17, Days 3–5 instruction
- Vocabulary Activities and Word Cards in ELL Teaching Guide, pp. 115–116

Assessment For information on assessing students' speaking and listening, see the ELL and Transition Handbook.

Pages 435c–435d

LA.5.1.6.3 Use context clues to determine meanings of unfamiliar words

LA.5.1.6.4 Categorize key vocabulary

LA.5.1.6.8 Use knowledge of homophones to determine meanings of words

LA.5.5.2.1 Listen and speak to gain and share information for a variety of purposes, including formal presentations

LA.5.5.2.2 Make formal oral presentations, demonstrating appropriate use of supporting graphics (illustrations, images, and props)

Vocabulary

SUCCES PREDICTO

Grammar   Pronouns and Antecedents

OBJECTIVES

- Define and identify pronouns and antecedents.
- Use pronouns that agree with their antecedents.
- Use pronouns and antecedents in writing.
- Become familiar with pronoun assessment on high-stakes tests.

Monitor Progress

Grammar

If... students have difficulty identifying pronouns and antecedents,	then... provide additional instruction and practice in The Grammar and Writing Book pp. 146–149.

DAILY FIX-IT

This week use Daily Fix-It Transparency 17.

Spiral REVIEW

Support Grammar See the Grammar Transition lessons in the ELL and Transition Handbook.

▲ **The Grammar and Writing Book**
For more instruction and practice, use pp. 146–149.

DAY 1   Teach and Model

DAILY FIX-IT

1. Handicapped children need a outllet for their energy too. *(an outlet)*

2. Perry has cerebral palzy and they has difficulty walking and talking. *(palsy, and he has)*

READING-GRAMMAR CONNECTION

Write this sentence on the board:

It's not easy for Nic because his hands won't always do what he wants them to do.

Explain that the underlined **pronouns** *his* and *he* refer to Nic. *Nic* is the **antecedent** of *his* and *he.*

Display Grammar Transparency 17. Read aloud the definitions and sample sentences. Work through the items.

Pronouns and Antecedents

A **pronoun** takes the place of a noun or nouns. An **antecedent**, or referent, is the noun or nouns to which the pronoun refers. A pronoun and its antecedent must agree in number and gender.

Before you use a pronoun, ask yourself whether the antecedent is singular or plural. If the antecedent is singular, decide whether it is masculine, feminine, or neuter. Then choose a pronoun that agrees. In the following sentences, the antecedents are underlined once; the pronouns are underlined twice.

When Emily exercises, she stretches muscles and tendons. They are tight and sore.

Directions Underline the antecedent once and the pronoun twice in each sentence.

1. Sam is happy because he can jump and run.
2. Because Janelle enjoys swimming, she swims on the YMCA team.
3. Janelle and Sam are lucky because they have healthy bodies.
4. Some children have cerebral palsy, and it causes problems with body movement and control.
5. These children need therapy to help them move freely.
6. Nolan uses a wheelchair, and a computer allows him to communicate.
7. The computer has an artificial voice, so it produces spoken words.
8. Megan remains cheerful although therapy can be painful for her.
9. Fred and I think that we will study medicine.
10. Doctors and scientists believe that they will be able to prevent cerebral palsy some day.

Directions Write a pronoun to replace each underlined noun or noun phrase.

11. Our class learned about muscles and bones when our class studied the human body.
we or it
12. Bones form the skeleton, and the skeleton supports the body.
it
13. Two bones meet at a joint, where the two bones are connected by ligaments.
they
14. Muscles have tendons that connect muscles to bones.
them

Unit 4 Stretching Ourselves   Grammar **17**

▲ **Grammar Transparency** 17

DAY 2   Develop the Concept

DAILY FIX-IT

3. Beryl has CP. Can her swim. *(she swim?)*

4. She loves swimming it are fun to splash and kick in the water. *(swimming. It is)*

GUIDED PRACTICE

Review the concept of pronouns and antecedents.

- A **pronoun** takes the place of a noun or nouns.

- An **antecedent,** or referent, is the noun or nouns to which the pronoun refers.

- Each pronoun must agree with its antecedent in number and gender.

HOMEWORK Grammar and Writing Practice Book p. 65. Work through the first two items with the class.

Pronouns and Antecedents

A **pronoun** takes the place of a noun or nouns. An **antecedent**, or referent, is the noun or nouns to which the pronoun refers. A pronoun and its antecedent must agree in number and gender.

Before you use a pronoun, ask yourself whether the antecedent is singular or plural. If the antecedent is singular, decide whether it is masculine, feminine, or neuter. Then choose a pronoun that agrees. In the following sentences, the antecedents are underlined once; the pronouns are underlined twice.

Charlie participates in tennis and track for exercise. They keep him in shape.

Directions Circle the correct pronoun or pronouns in ( ) to complete each sentence. The antecedent of each pronoun is underlined to help you.

1. Will loves tennis because (it, he) takes strength and speed.
2. Iris practices figure skating, and (they, she) is good at it.
3. The twins play baseball, but bowling interests (them, they) too.
4. Exercise makes people feel good because (it, they) keeps (she, them) fit.
5. José lost strength when (he, him) broke his leg.
6. The physical therapist showed José exercises that helped (he, him).

Directions Underline the antecedent once and the pronoun twice in each sentence.

7. An English doctor wrote about a disorder he observed in many children.
8. The children had stiff muscles, so moving was difficult for them.
9. As these children grew up, the condition did not grow worse, nor did it grow better.
10. Dr. William Little made the discovery, and he named the disorder Little's disease.
11. Several disorders are called cerebral palsy, and Little's disease is one of them.
12. A girl with cerebral palsy will have difficulty when she tries to move about.

Home Activity Your child learned about pronouns and antecedents. Read a magazine article together and have your child find pronouns that have antecedents and identify both.

▲ **Grammar and Writing Practice Book** p. 65

CORRECTIVE FEEDBACK

LA.5.3.4.5 Use noun/pronoun agreement

- **Question** Use Whiteboard or Transparency 17b, items 1–3, to ask questions that address this standard in FCAT format. Have students write their answers on a sheet of paper.
- **Check** Scan students' responses by having them hold up their papers.
- **Correct** If necessary, provide corrective feedback and review pp. 146–151 in *The Grammar and Writing Book*.

① In which item do the **pronouns and antecedents** not agree?

Ⓐ If David teaches soccer, he will need uniforms and equipment. They are ruined from last year.

Ⓑ If David teaches soccer, he will need new uniforms and equipment because they are ruined from last year.

◀ **FCAT Whiteboard Activity** 17b/**FCAT Transparency** 17b

DAY 3 — Apply to Writing

DAILY FIX-IT

5. Eric and Sally helps their sister. She help her stretch and exercise. *(help; They)*

6. Dont ovorlook the handicapped. They have a great deal to offer. *(Don't; overlook)*

WRITE CLEAR ANTECEDENTS

Explain that if a pronoun's antecedent is unclear, the sentence should be rewritten.

Unclear: Dad and Amir exercise daily in his room.

Clear: Dad and Amir exercise daily in Amir's room.

- Have students review something they have written to see if they can improve it by clarifying pronoun references.

HOMEWORK Grammar and Writing Practice Book p. 66.

Pronouns and Antecedents

Directions Write a sentence or a pair of sentences using the noun or noun phrase and pronoun. Use each noun as an antecedent of each pronoun. **Possible answers:**

1. Kids with CP/they
   Kids with CP want to do everything normal kids do, but they must work harder at it.

2. exercise/it
   You should get plenty of exercise because it makes your body healthy.

3. strong muscles/them
   This body builder has strong muscles. She worked hard to get them.

4. physical therapist/he
   A physical therapist talked to me. He said my muscles need to be stretched.

5. girl with CP/her
   I watched a girl with CP work out. A therapist helped her stretch.

Directions Write a paragraph about someone who works hard to overcome a physical handicap. Use at least four pronouns with their antecedents. Underline the antecedent for each pronoun.
   Possible answer: Hal has scoliosis. It is a curvature of the spine. He has to wear a brace at night. Every evening, Hal does exercises to strengthen the muscles attached to his spine. They tend to be weaker on one side.

 Home Activity Your child learned how to use pronouns and antecedents in writing. With your child, write a paragraph about a hard worker you admire. Have your child point out pronouns and underline their antecedents.

▲ **Grammar and Writing Practice Book** p. 66

DAY 4 — Test Preparation

DAILY FIX-IT

7. The girls exercise after school, and them get a snack at the supermarkit. *(they; supermarket)*

8. On friday after practice the coach buys they ice cream. *(Friday; them)*

STANDARDIZED TEST PREP

Test Tip

When the antecedent of a pronoun is the pronoun *everyone*, *everybody*, or *everything*, use a singular pronoun to agree with the referent.

No: Everyone did their best.

Yes: Everyone did his best. (*or* Everyone did her best.)

HOMEWORK Grammar and Writing Practice Book p. 67.

Pronouns and Antecedents

Directions Read the following paragraph. Mark the letter of the pronoun that correctly completes each sentence.

(1) Carlie is my newest cousin; _____ was born in June. (2) Mom, Dad, and I drove to the hospital so _____ could see her. (3) There were six babies in the nursery; _____ were all sleeping. (4) When a baby is born, _____ is checked carefully. (5) If there is any problem, doctors want to catch _____ right away. (6) For example, heart and lungs are checked to make sure _____ are functioning normally. (7) Carlie's doctor examined _____ and reported that everything is fine. (8) When my cousin Jimmy was born, _____ had a heart murmur. (9) Doctors operated on _____ and corrected the problem. (10) Parents always say that for _____, the main thing is having a happy, healthy baby.

1. Ⓐ she
   B her
   C they
   D him

2. A he
   B they
   C us
   Ⓓ we

3. A them
   Ⓑ they
   C she
   D he

4. A him
   B her
   Ⓒ it
   D them

5. A they
   Ⓑ it
   C she
   D her

6. Ⓐ they
   B it
   C them
   D we

7. A she
   Ⓑ her
   C them
   D they

8. A him
   Ⓑ he
   C it
   D them

9. Ⓐ him
   B he
   C she
   D her

10. A she
   B he
   C they
   Ⓓ them

 Home Activity Your child prepared for taking tests on pronouns and antecedents. Have your child rewrite a paragraph from a story, replacing each pronoun with its antecedent. Ask him or her to explain why pronouns make the story sound better.

▲ **Grammar and Writing Practice Book** p. 67

DAY 5 — Cumulative Review

DAILY FIX-IT

9. Can your ride the sub-way in a wheel chair? *(you; subway)*

10. Marias operation lasted four ours. *(Maria's; hours)*

ADDITIONAL PRACTICE

Assign pp. 146–149 in The Grammar and Writing Book.

EXTRA PRACTICE Grammar and Writing Practice Book p. 138.

TEST PREPARATION Grammar and Writing Practice Book pp. 155–156.

ASSESSMENT

CUMULATIVE REVIEW Grammar and Writing Practice Book p. 68.

Pronouns and Antecedents

Directions Match the pronoun with the noun or noun phrase that could be its antecedent. Write the letter of the correct antecedent next to the pronoun.

E 1. she   A boys and girls
A 2. them   B Mr. Zimmerman
D 3. it   C Grandpa and I
C 4. we   D the prize
B 5. he   E Susan

Directions Circle the antecedent of the underlined pronoun in each sentence.

6. When muscles contract, they shorten.

7. A voluntary muscle contracts when you want it to.

8. Involuntary muscles are controlled by your brain. You do not tell them what to do.

9. The heart is an involuntary muscle, so it works automatically.

10. Leila explained how she slows her heart rate by relaxing.

Directions Write a pronoun to replace each underlined noun or noun phrase.

11. When people think of movement, people think of muscle power.
   they

12. A muscle is vital to moving the body, but a muscle is only part of the story.
   it

13. The bones are the other part. Bones move the body when muscles contract and pull on bones.
   They; them

14. Carole flexed her arm, and Carole felt her bicep muscle contract.
   she

15. Sean exclaimed, "Sean can see the muscles working in pairs! One contracts and the other relaxes."
   I

 Home Activity Your child reviewed pronouns and antecedents. Have your child dictate sentences about how he or she used muscles today. Ask your child to underline pronouns and circle any antecedents in the sentences.

▲ **Grammar and Writing Practice Book** p. 68

Writing Workshop

Journal Entry

OBJECTIVES

- Identify the characteristics of a journal entry.
- Write a journal entry that elaborates on a topic.
- Focus on focus/ideas.
- Use a rubric.

Genre Journal Entry
Writer's Craft Elaboration
Writing Trait Focus/Ideas

ELL

Focus/Ideas Talk with English learners about what they plan to write. Record ideas and help them generate language for support. Help them tighten their focus by eliminating unrelated details. See more writing support in the ELL and Transition Handbook.

Writing Traits

FOCUS/IDEAS The writer explores each idea in detail, expressing thoughts on the concept clearly. (*I wonder if I would be cheerful and strong. . . .*)

ORGANIZATION/PARAGRAPHS The journal entry flows naturally with the writer's thoughts and emotions.

SUPPORT/VOICE The writer's emotions are clear and show involvement with the subject.

SUPPORT/WORD CHOICE Words are specific and lively and suggest natural speech. (*it nearly drove me crazy!*)

SUPPORT/SENTENCES Varied sentences give the text an easy flow and rhythm.

CONVENTIONS There is excellent control and accuracy.

DAY 1 — Model the Trait

READING-WRITING CONNECTION

- *Stretching Ourselves* focuses on what life is like for children with cerebral palsy.
- The selection explores this main idea by describing the struggles and focusing on the positive attitudes of kids with CP.
- Students will write a **journal entry** focusing on an idea and elaborating with details and examples.

MODEL FOCUS/IDEAS Discuss Writing Transparency 17A. Then discuss the model and the writing trait of focus/ideas.

Think Aloud The writer focuses on what he feels about kids with CP. In the first paragraph, he states that he feels sorry for them because of the difficulties they have. Every detail in the paragraph focuses on why he feels sorry for them.

Journal Entry

A journal is a place to "think out loud" on paper. In a **journal entry** you can describe what happened during your day, examine your feelings, or explore an idea. Journal writing can help you make discoveries about yourself and the world.

March 6, 2008

Today I read about children with cerebral palsy (CP). At first, I felt sorry for Emily, Nic, and Tanner. Imagine not being able to walk and run like other kids do! The stretching exercises they must do to help them move are painful. Any physical activity takes longer than normal and is more difficult for them than it is for me. They may also need operations and special medicines.

I wonder if I would be cheerful and strong like these three kids are if I had their problems. What if, like Nic, I could not talk to people unless I had a computer with a voice? Dad says that I am such a chatterbox, and I was born talking. I tried not talking for thirty minutes today, and it nearly drove me crazy! I think if it was hard for me to communicate, I would say the most important things first—like "thank you" and "I love you."

The more I think about the CP kids, the more I admire them. They work so hard. They endure pain and face the challenge of being different. They will never have the ease and freedom of movement I have. Yet they look so happy in the pictures! They have that "You bet I can handle it" attitude that gets things done.

Writer examines feelings about kids with CP.

Details elaborate by giving reasons for feeling sorry.

Writer makes discovery about self through elaboration.

Writer's viewpoint has changed.

Unit 4 Stretching Ourselves Writing Model **17A**

▲ **Writing Transparency 17A**

DAY 2 — Improve Writing

WRITER'S CRAFT
Elaboration

Display Writing Transparency 17B. Work together to use the text to locate supporting details.

Think Aloud **ELABORATE ON AN IDEA** Tomorrow we will write about our feelings for someone who faces physical or mental challenges. If I chose a blind person what details and examples could I use to elaborate on my feelings about this person? I might describe how the person has adapted when getting dressed or telling time. I might explain how I admire the person for doing everyday activities I need my sight to do.

GUIDED WRITING Some students may need more help elaborating ideas. Have them reread parts of *Stretching Ourselves* and work with them to identify details and explanations that support ideas.

Elaboration

Elaboration means expanding and developing ideas with details, explanations, and descriptions. When you pinpoint a central idea to write about, ask yourself, "How can I develop this idea? What details can I add to help readers understand it better?"

Directions For each sentence, choose the phrase or clause from the box that helps explain or clarify the idea.

adults like Tom Hilber have a job and family | brain damage causes lack of muscle control
he can move more easily | deal with the pain and frustration of operations and exercises

1. Nic feels free when he's swimming because __Nic feels free when he's swimming because he can move more easily.__

2. Kids with CP must have great courage to __Kids with CP must have great courage to deal with the pain and frustration of operations and exercises.__

3. CP is not a disease but a disorder in which __CP is not a disease but a disorder in which brain damage causes lack of muscle control.__

4. CP does not prevent people from living a normal life; for example __CP does not prevent people from living a normal life; for example, adults like Tom Hilber have a job and family.__

Directions Provide elaboration for the underlined phrase or clause to make the ideas clear. Rewrite the sentence. Possible answer:

5. Swimming is excellent exercise for people with CP because the water lets them do stuff. __Swimming is excellent exercise for people with CP because the water supports the body and allows for freedom of movement not possible on land.__

Unit 4 Stretching Ourselves Writer's Craft **17B**

▲ **Writing Transparency 17B**

Pages 435g–435h

LA.5.3.2.1 Use a pre-writing plan to focus on main idea with development of supporting details, elaborating using supporting details
LA.5.3.3.1 Evaluate draft for development of ideas and point of view
LA.5.3.3.2 Create clarity by deleting extraneous or repetitious information
LA.5.4.1.2 Write in expressive forms

DAY 3 — Prewrite and Draft

READ THE WRITING PROMPT

on page 433 in the Student Edition.

Kids with special challenges are featured in Stretching Ourselves.

Think about someone you know who has special mental or physical challenges.

Now write a journal entry describing your observations and feelings about that person.

FCAT Writing+ Test Tips

- Include details you know about people who face physical or mental challenges.
- Choose words that communicate clearly what it is like to have a physical or mental challenge from your point of view or how you feel about it.
- Use questions and exclamations as well as statements to help convey your emotions and thought processes.

GETTING STARTED Students can do any of the following:

- Collect details related to the main idea in a graphic organizer.
- Brainstorm words and phrases that express feelings about the challenge.
- Choose details about their subjects that help explain why students feel as they do.

DAY 4 — Draft and Revise

EDITING/REVISING CHECKLIST

☑ Did I elaborate main ideas with enough details?

☑ Are pronouns and antecedents used correctly?

☑ Are words with prefixes *over-*, *under-*, *sub-*, *super-*, and *out-* spelled correctly?

See *The Grammar and Writing Book,* pp. 146–151.

Revising Tips

Focus/Ideas

- Elaborate, if necessary, by providing more information or details.
- Delete words and sentences that distract from your main idea.
- Describe something you learned from the contact.

PUBLISHING Students can add a drawing to illustrate their feelings or conclusions about the topic. Some students may wish to revise their work later.

ASSESSMENT Use the scoring rubric to evaluate students' work.

DAY 5 — Connect to Unit Writing

	Story
Week 1	E-mail 411g–411h
Week 2	Journal Entry 435g–435h
Week 3	Story About an Animal 457g–457h
Week 4	Advice 483g–483h
Week 5	Describe How You Achieved a Goal 503g–503h

PREVIEW THE UNIT PROMPT

Tell a story about a character who succeeds by adapting to a new situation. Focus on an event that shows this person's resourcefulness. Your story may be real or imagined.

APPLY

- A story has a beginning, middle, and end and focuses on one incident or event.
- Use elaboration, such as adding precise, vivid words or additional details, to flesh out the plot of a story.

Writing Trait Rubric

	6	5	4	3	2	1
	Excellent focus with many vivid supporting details; nothing superfluous	Strong focus with many supporting details; nothing superfluous	Clear focus with some details; all details on topic	Adequate focus; few supporting details and some unrelated details	Lacking focus; few supporting details and some unrelated details	Unfocused with little support and many unrelated details
Focus/Ideas	Excellent journal entry with interesting, well-supported main idea	Interesting journal entry with well-supported main idea	Journal entry with adequately supported main idea	Sharper focus on main idea needed in journal entry	Journal entry with unclear and/or unsupported main idea	Journal entry with no clear focus or main idea

Spelling & Phonics

Prefixes *over-, under-, sub-, super-, out-*

Generalization

Connect to Phonics When prefixes *over-, under-, sub-, super-,* and *out-* are added to words, the base word stays the same: <u>over</u>look, <u>under</u>line, <u>sub</u>way, <u>super</u>market, <u>out</u>let. The base word is also pronounced the same as it was before the prefix was added.

Spelling Words

1. overlook	11. overtime
2. underline	12. supersonic
3. subway	13. submarine
4. subset	14. undercover
5. supermarket	15. overcast
6. outlet	16. outfield
7. underground	17. output
8. overboard	18. supernatural
9. undercurrent	19. subdivision
10. superstar	20. subhead

Challenge Words

21. overwhelm	24. underprivileged
22. superimpose	25. subcommittee
23. underestimate	

ELL

Spelling/Phonics Support See the ELL and Transition Handbook for spelling support.

DAY 1 Pretest and Sort

PRETEST

Use the Dictation Sentences from Day 5 to administer the pretest. Read the word, read the sentence, and then read the word again. Guide students in self-correcting their pretests and correcting any misspellings.

Monitor Progress

Spelling

If… students misspell more than 5 pretest words,	**then…** use words 1–10 for Strategic Intervention.
If… students misspell 1–5 pretest words,	**then…** use words 1–20 for On-Level practice.
If… students correctly spell all pretest words,	**then…** use words 1–25 for Advanced Learners.

HOMEWORK Spelling Practice Book, p. 65.

▲ **Spelling Practice Book** p. 65

DAY 2 Think and Practice

TEACH

Write *submarine* on the board. Have a volunteer draw a line dividing the prefix from the base word. Say the prefix and then the word. Have the class repeat. Explain that these prefixes do not change the spelling of the base word.

sub|marine

FIND THE PATTERN Ask students to identify the prefixes that have one syllable and the prefixes that have two syllables.

HOMEWORK Spelling Practice Book, p. 66.

▲ **Spelling Practice Book** p. 66

Pages 435i–435j
LA.5.1.4.1 Understand spelling patterns
LA.5.1.4.2 Recognize structural analysis
LA.5.4.1.2 Write in expressive forms

DAY 3 Connect to Writing

WRITE A JOURNAL ENTRY

Review the concept of a journal or diary with students. Have them write a journal entry about something they have done or would like to do. Have them use at least three list words in their writing.

Frequently Misspelled Words

outside   *because*

These words may seem easy to spell, but they are often misspelled by fifth-graders. Alert students that the base word side does not change when the prefix is added. Tell them that because is a word by itself, not a word with a prefix.

HOMEWORK Spelling Practice Book, p. 67.

Prefixes *over-, under-, sub-, super-, out-*

Proofread a Paragraph Circle six spelling errors. Write the words correctly. Find one punctuation error and write the sentence using the correct punctuation.

If you had a choice, would you want to break the sound barrier in a *super sonic* jet? Is cruising beneath the surface of the sea in a *sub marine* more your style? What about riding underground on a large *sub way* system? Would you rather stay all night in a deserted house waiting for something *super natural* to happen? Do you like sports. Perhaps you'd really rather be playing ball in the *out field*? Fortunately, one doesn't have to be a *super star* to do any of these things.

Spelling Words
overlook
underline
subway
subset
supermarket
outlet
underground
overboard
undercurrent
superstar
overtime
supersonic
submarine
undercover
overcast
outfield
output
supernatural
subdivision
subhead

1. supersonic 2. submarine
3. subway 4. supernatural
5. outfield 6. superstar
7. Do you like sports?

Proofread Words Circle the word that is spelled correctly.

8. submarine / submareen / submarein
9. subdivion / subdivison / subdivision
10. subsonic / supersonic / supresonic
11. underline / undeline / undrline
12. outfield / outfeld / outfield
13. overcast / overcas / ovrcast
14. overlok / overlook / ovarlock
15. suparmarkit / suprmarkat / supermarket
16. overboard / overbored / ovarboard

Frequently Misspelled Words
outside
because

Home Activity Your child identified misspelled list words. Ask your child to tell you which three words are most difficult and then have your child spell them with you.

▲ **Spelling Practice Book** p. 67

DAY 4 Review

REVIEW WORDS WITH PREFIXES
over-, under-, sub-, super-, out-

Have partners write each list word on a small piece of paper. Have them fold the papers and mix them up. Partners then take turns picking and asking each other to spell the words. A correct spelling means the speller keeps the paper. For an incorrect spelling, the paper goes to the partner. The partner with more papers is the winner.

Spelling Strategy
Divide and Conquer

Use syllables to make long words easier to study. Draw a line between the base word and the prefix. Then study the word one part at a time.

For example: sub/division, over/board, under/ground

HOMEWORK Spelling Practice Book, p. 68.

Prefixes *over-, under-, sub-, super-, out-*

Spelling Words

overlook	underline	subway	subset	supermarket
outlet	underground	overboard	undercurrent	superstar
overtime	supersonic	submarine	undercover	overcast
outfield	output	supernatural	subdivision	subhead

Complete the Word Add a prefix to each word to make a list word. Write the complete word on the line.

1. ___way   1. subway
2. ___put   2. output
3. ___natural   3. supernatural
4. ___market   4. supermarket
5. ___line   5. underline
6. ___head   6. subhead
7. ___division   7. subdivision
8. ___current   8. undercurrent

Word Search Find and circle ten list words hidden in the puzzle. Words are down, across, and diagonal. Write the words on the lines.

```
U S D L T J J I G O S S
R N J D Z D F F H V U U
T O D S X O W Y O E B B
G O V E R L O O K R M H
S U P E R S T A R B A E
B T Q A R C P C T O R A
B P K D N C O L K A I D
S U B S E T A V W R N H
L T X E A J Y S E D Y
S U B W A Y B P T R O L
```

9. output
10. overcast
11. subhead
12. subset
13. superstar
14. overboard
15. overlook
16. submarine
17. subway
18. undercover

Home Activity Your child has learned to read, write, and spell words with prefixes. See if you can recombine prefixes and list words to make other words such as outline.

▲ **Spelling Practice Book** p. 68

DAY 5 Posttest

DICTATION SENTENCES

1. Some details are easy to overlook.
2. Underline the verb in each sentence.
3. The subway train goes fast.
4. A subset is a part of a larger set.
5. Our supermarket is huge.
6. The new store is a shoe outlet.
7. Underground tunnels are dark.
8. We threw crumbs overboard.
9. The ocean's undercurrent is strong.
10. Fans ran after the superstar.
11. I worked overtime last week.
12. The supersonic jet is loud.
13. The submarine finally surfaced.
14. The police work undercover to solve crimes.
15. The overcast day turned sunny.
16. The ball was caught in the outfield.
17. The printer's output is 60 pages per minute.
18. Some things seem supernatural.
19. A subdivision is being built near our apartment.
20. Outlines have subheads.

CHALLENGE

21. Beautiful scenery can overwhelm my senses.
22. To make purple, superimpose clear red plastic over blue plastic.
23. Never underestimate the goodness of people.
24. We collected clothing for underprivileged children.
25. A subcommittee was created to make new school rules.

OBJECTIVES

- Formulate an inquiry question that is connected to this week's lesson focus.

- Effectively and efficiently find, evaluate, and communicate information related to an inquiry question using electronic sources.

New Literacies	
Day 1	**Identify Questions**
Day 2	**Navigate/Search**
Day 3	**Analyze**
Day 4	**Synthesize**
Day 5	**Communicate**

Page 435k

LA.5.4.2.1 Write in a variety of informational/expository forms

LA.5.6.2.1 Select a topic for inquiry, formulate a search plan, and apply evaluative criteria

LA.5.6.2.2 Read and record information systematically, evaluating validity and reliability of imformation

LA.5.6.4.2 Determine and use appropriate digital tools (word processing and web tools)

NEW LITERACIES

Internet Inquiry Activity

EXPLORE ADAPTING TO PHYSICAL LIMITATIONS

Use the following 5-day plan to help students conduct this week's Internet inquiry activity on adapting to physical limitations. Remind students to follow classroom rules when using the Internet.

DAY 1

Identify Questions Discuss the lesson focus question: *How do people adapt to living with physical limitations?* Brainstorm ideas for specific inquiry questions. For example, students might want to find out what technology is available to help people who are hearing-impaired. Have students work individually, in pairs, or in small groups to write inquiry questions.

DAY 2

Navigate/Search Have students begin Internet searches using a student-friendly search engine and keywords related to their inquiry topics. Explain that it helps to know if a Web site has a particular slant. Tell students that the ending of a URL tells you something about who published it. For example, Web site URLs ending with *.com* are commercial web sites that may be trying to sell something; those ending with *.org* are sponsored by organizations dedicated to sharing information about a specific topic; those ending in *.edu* are from colleges, universities, or other educational institutions; and those ending in *.gov* are sponsored by the government.

DAY 3

Analyze Have students skim and scan the Web sites they identified on Day 2. Note that they may choose to follow some of the links provided on the Web sites. Remind students that they should analyze links before clicking on them to determine if they are likely to lead to reliable sources.

DAY 4

Synthesize Have students synthesize information from Day 3. Remind them that when they synthesize, they combine relevant ideas and information from different sources to develop answers to their inquiry questions. Encourage students to think about the best methods for communicating what they've learned to the class.

DAY 5

Communicate Have students share their inquiry results. They can use a word processing program to create informational articles for a newsletter about what they learned.

RESEARCH/STUDY SKILLS

Telephone Directory

TEACH

Ask students where they can look to find the phone number for a classmate or for a local pet store. Lead them to suggest using telephone directories. Show a print telephone directory to point out the following features, but emphasize that all of the same information is available in online directories.

- A **telephone directory** lists names, phone numbers, and addresses for people and businesses.

- The **white pages** list phone numbers for people and businesses in alphabetical order. When searching online you need to provide a city and state for the search.

- The **yellow pages** list phone numbers and ads for businesses. Entries are grouped alphabetically by type of business. When searching online you need to provide a city and state for the search.

Have students work in groups to use computers to search an online telephone directory. If computers are not available, have students look at a sample picture of an online directory search page. Then, discuss these questions.

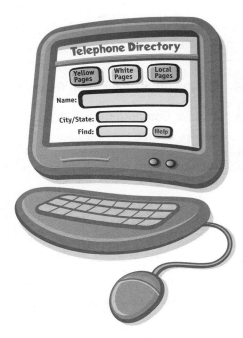

1. **When searching an online directory, what information do you need to find someone's telephone number?** (A person's last name. For better results, last name, first name, city, and state.)

2. **Will you get good search results if you only know someone's first name and the city where he or she lives? Explain.** (No; there could be many people in the city with the same first name.)

ASSESS

As students become familiar with online directories, be sure they can identify the information necessary for a successful search and are able to distinguish between searching the white pages and searching the yellow pages. If computers are available, you may provide students with time to conduct at least one search.

For more practice or to assess students, use Practice Book pp. 169–170.

Telephone Directory

A **telephone directory** is an alphabetical index of names and telephone numbers for a selected geographical area. The **white pages** list entries for individual people and businesses. The **yellow pages** list entries and ads for businesses. Entries are grouped by category or type of business, such as restaurants. This information is available in reference books or on the Internet. You can search online to find phone numbers for people and businesses in other cities, states, and even countries.

Directions The computer screen shows you how to search a directory of online white pages. Use the computer screen to answer the questions that follow.

> **Enter the first and last name of the person and click *Find!***
> For better results, enter the city and state also.
>
> Last Name (required)
> First Name
> City   State
> Country
>   **Find!**   If you need help, click here.

1. What entries will you get if you type "Reyes" in the field for Last Name, "Philadelphia" in the City field, and "PA" (for Pennsylvania) in the State field?
   The results would feature telephone numbers for all the people with the last name Reyes in Philadelphia, PA.
2. You know Sue Costello lives in Florida. Tell how to find her phone number and address.
   Type "Costello" in the Last Name field, "Sue" in the First Name field, and "FL" in the State field.
3. Would typing "Julia" in the First Name field and "Texas" in the State field give you good search results? Explain.
   Possible answer: No; There are probably many people named Julia in Texas, and it would be hard to locate the person you wanted.
4. How does using an online telephone directory rather than a telephone book increase the information you can get?
   Possible answer: You can get information about regions for which you do not have a telephone book.

▲ **Practice Book** p. 169

Directions The computer screen shows you how to search a directory of online yellow pages. Use the computer screen to answer the questions that follow.
Possible answers given for 6–10.

> **Enter a business category or name. Then click *Find!***
>
> City   State
>   **Find!**   If you need help, click here.

5. What will you get if you enter the category "state park" and "FL" for State?
   You would be given the names and telephone numbers of state parks in Florida.
6. If you want information about Nancy & Beth's Catering Services in St. Louis, Missouri, what should you enter?
   Enter "catering" in the Category field, "St. Louis" in the City field, and "Missouri" in the State field.
7. If you want to find a bike rental in Phoenix, Arizona, what should you enter?
   Enter "bicycle rental" in the Category field, "Phoenix" in the City field, and "Arizona" in the State field.
8. If you enter "toy store" in the category field, will this produce good search results? Explain.
   No; the State field has to have something in it for the search to work.
9. Which of the three fields could you leave blank? Explain how filling in this field would narrow your search.
   the City field; Putting information in the City field would restrict your results to companies in a certain city only.
10. Can you use an online telephone directory if you don't know how to spell the name of a business? Explain.
    Yes; If you know what kind of business it is, and the city and state it is in, you could look for it in the results of a category search.

School + Home **Home Activity** Your child learned about using telephone directories. Look at an online telephone directory together. Ask your child to locate emergency phone numbers, maps, and phone numbers of local businesses and residences.

▲ **Practice Book** p. 170

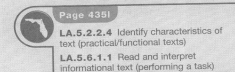

Page 435l

LA.5.2.2.4 Identify characteristics of text (practical/functional texts)

LA.5.6.1.1 Read and interpret informational text (performing a task)

Assessment Checkpoints *for the Week*

Selection Assessment

Use pp. 65–68 of Selection Tests to check:

- ☑ **Selection Understanding**
- ☑ **Comprehension Skill** *Generalize*
- ☑ **Selection Vocabulary**
  abdomen
  artificial
  gait
  handicapped
  therapist
  wheelchair

ASSESSMENT

Scott Foresman
Selection Tests
Teacher's Manual

- Assess comprehension of weekly selections
- Assess understanding of weekly comprehension skills
- Assess knowledge of selection vocabulary

Selection Tests

Reading STREET Grade 5

Leveled Assessment

On-Level
Strategic Intervention
Advanced

Use pp. 97–102 of Fresh Reads for Differentiated Test Practice to check:

- ☑ **Comprehension Skill** *Generalize*
- ☑ **REVIEW** **Comprehension Skill** *Graphic Sources*
- ☑ **Fluency** *Words Correct Per Minute*

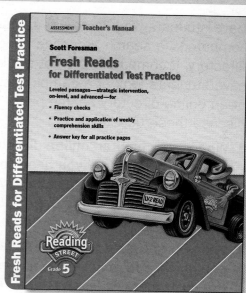

ASSESSMENT   Teacher's Manual

Scott Foresman
Fresh Reads
for Differentiated Test Practice

Leveled passages—strategic intervention, on-level, and advanced—for
- Fluency checks
- Practice and application of weekly comprehension skills
- Answer key for all practice pages

Fresh Reads for Differentiated Test Practice

Reading STREET Grade 5

Managing Assessment

Use Assessment Handbook for:

- ☑ **Observation Checklists**
- ☑ **Record-Keeping Forms**
- ☑ **Portfolio Assessment**

ASSESSMENT

Scott Foresman
Assessment Handbook

- Suggestions for preparing students for high-stake tests
- Ideas for classroom-based assessment
- Forms in English and Spanish for students to record interests and progress
- Forms in English and Spanish for teachers to record observations of students' reading and writing abilities and progress
- Assessment and Regrouping charts reproduced from *Reading Street* Teacher's Editions

Assessment Handbook

Reading STREET Grades 3–6

Florida

Planning Guide for Sunshine State Standards

Exploding Ants

Reading Street Teacher's Edition pages	Grade 5 Benchmarks for Language Arts
Reading	

Reading

Word Work Homophones: 457i–457j

Comprehension Graphic Sources: 436–437, 440–451, 454–457, 457b
Monitor and Fix Up: 436–437, 440–451, 454–457

Vocabulary Lesson Vocabulary: 438b, 447, 451, 454
Context Clues: 438–439, 447, 457c

Fluency Model Tempo and Rate: 436l–436m, 457a

Self-Selected Reading: LR19–27, TR16–17

Literature Genre—Expository Nonfiction: 440
Reader Response: 452

The student will:

LA.5.1.4.1 Understand spelling patterns.

LA.5.1.4.2 Recognize structural analysis.

LA.5.1.5.2 Adjust reading rate based on purpose, text difficulty, form, and style.

LA.5.1.6.1 Use new vocabulary that is introduced and taught directly.

LA.5.1.6.2 Listen to, read, and discuss familiar and conceptually challenging text.

LA.5.1.6.3 Use context clues to determine meanings of unfamiliar words.

LA.5.1.6.8 Use knowledge of synonyms and homophones to determine meanings of words.

LA.5.1.7.1 Explain the purpose of text features (e.g., diagrams, illustrations, charts) and use prior knowledge to make and confirm predictions.

LA.5.1.7.8 Use strategies to repair comprehension of grade-appropriate text when self-monitoring indicates confusion, including clarifying by checking other sources.

Writing

Four-Elements Writing Support/Word Choice: 453, 457g–457h

Writing Tell a Story About an Animal: 457g–457h

Grammar, Usage, and Mechanics Possessive Pronouns: 457e–457f

Research/Study Magazine/Periodical: 457l

The student will:

LA.5.2.2.4 Identify the characteristics of a variety of types of text (e.g., reference).

LA.5.3.3.1 Revise by evaluating the draft for word choice.

LA.5.3.4.4 Edit writing for grammar and language conventions, including the correct use of pronouns.

LA.5.4.1.2 Write a variety of expressive forms (e.g., short story).

Communication and Media

Speaking/Listening Build Concept Vocabulary: 436l, 447, 451, 457c
Read Aloud: 436m

Technology New Literacies: 457k

The student will:

LA.5.1.6.1 Use new vocabulary that is introduced and taught directly.

LA.5.1.6.2 Listen to, read, and discuss familiar and conceptually challenging text.

LA.5.6.2.4 Record basic bibliographic data and present quotes using ethical practices (e.g., avoids plagiarism).

Unit Skills

Writing Story: WA2–9

Poetry: 504–507

Project/Wrap-Up: 508–509

The student will:

LA.5.2.1.3 Demonstrate how descriptive and figurative language help to communicate meaning in a poem.

LA.5.4.1.1 Write narratives that establish a situation and plot with rising action, conflict, and resolution.

LA.5.4.2.2 Record information (e.g., charts) related to a topic.

Intervention

MY SIDEWALKS ON
SCOTT FORESMAN
READING STREET
Intensive Reading Intervention

My Sidewalks on Reading Street provides collaborative, parallel, intensive intervention when used with *Reading Street*.

This Week's Leveled Readers

Below-Level

Nonfiction

The student will:

LA.5.1.7.1 Explain the purpose of text features and use prior knowledge to make and confirm predictions.

LA.5.2.2.2 Use information from the text to answer questions related to explicitly stated main ideas or relevant details.

On-Level

Nonfiction

The student will:

LA.5.1.7.1 Explain the purpose of text features and use prior knowledge to make and confirm predictions.

LA.5.1.7.8 Use strategies to repair comprehension of grade-appropriate text when self-monitoring indicates confusion, including clarifying by checking other sources.

Advanced

Nonfiction

The student will:

LA.5.1.7.1 Explain the purpose of text features and use prior knowledge to make and confirm predictions.

LA.5.2.2.3 Organize information to show understanding.

- Reinforcing effort and providing recognition: pp. 452–453
- Homework and practice: pp. 436f–436g, 437, 439, 452
- Cooperative learning: pp. 436j–436k

- Setting objectives and providing feedback: p. 436m
- Generating and testing hypotheses: p. 440
- Cues, questions, and advance organizers: pp. 438a, 457c

Florida Assessment for FCAT Success

Selection Tests, pp. 69–72

Fresh Reads for Differentiated Test Practice, pp. 103–108

Unit 4 Benchmark Test in FCAT Format, pp. 1–21

Success Tracker™ Online Test to Monitor Benchmarks

Content-Area Standards Taught During the Reading Lesson

Science

The student:

SC.F.1.2.2. Understands the ways animals depend on plants

SC.F.1.2.3. Knows that living things are different but share similar structures

SC.G.1.2.2.5.1. Understands how the environment affects organisms

SC.G.1.2.5. Knows that animals eat plants to acquire energy

SC.G.2.2.1.5.1. Knows that adaptations to their environment may increase the survival of a species

SC.H.1.2.2.5.1. Understands that scientists use different kinds of investigation

CONNECT TO SF SCIENCE

TIME SAVERS FOR FLORIDA TEACHERS

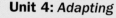

Unit 4: *Adapting*

Question of the Week: How do animals adapt to survive?

Science Concepts:
- **Animals**
- **Environments/Biomes**
- **Adaptations**

These lessons in *Scott Foresman Science* **support the concepts taught in this week's lesson of** *Reading Street.*

Unit A, Chapter 1, Lesson 2, "How do we classify vertebrates?" pp. 10–17

Unit A, Chapter 1, Lesson 3, "How do we classify invertebrates?" pp. 18–21

Unit A, Chapter 5, Lesson 2, "What are land biomes?" pp. 130–135

Unit A, Chapter 5, Lesson 6, "What cycles occur in ecosystems?" pp. 148–153

Unit A, Chapter 6, Lesson 2, "How do species change?" pp. 170–173

Unit 4
Adapting

EXPAND THE CONCEPT
How do animals adapt to survive?

CONCEPT QUESTION
How do people and animals adapt to different situations?

Week 1

How do people adapt to difficult situations?

Week 2

How do people adapt to living with physical limitations?

Week 3

How do animals adapt to survive?

Week 4

How do people adapt to a new school?

Week 5

Why do people try to change themselves?

CONNECT THE CONCEPT

▶ **Develop Language**
African black mambas, constrictors, reptiles

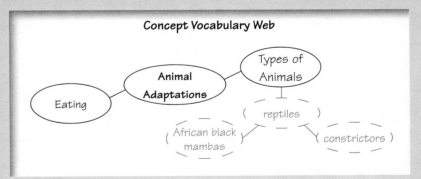

Concept Vocabulary Web

▶ **Science Content**
Biomes, Human Adaptations, Animal Experiments

▶ **Writing**
Story About an Animal

▶ **Internet Inquiry**
Animal Adaptations

Preview Your Week

How do animals adapt to survive?

exploding ants

by Joanne Settel, Ph.D.

Amazing **Facts** About
How Animals Adapt

How do insects
adapt to find food,
shelter, and safety?

Genre **Expository nonfiction** explains what certain things are and how they came to be or behave. As you read, notice how the author explains insect behavior.

440

Student Edition pages 440–451

Audio CD

Read It

ONLINE

PearsonSuccessNet.com

- **Student Edition**
- **Leveled Readers**

Genre Expository Nonfiction
Vocabulary Strategy Context Clues
Comprehension Skill Graphic Sources
Comprehension Strategy Monitor and Fix Up

Paired Selection

Reading Across Texts
Make a List About a Creature

Genre
Experiment

Text Features
Purpose
Materials
Step-by-Step Instructions

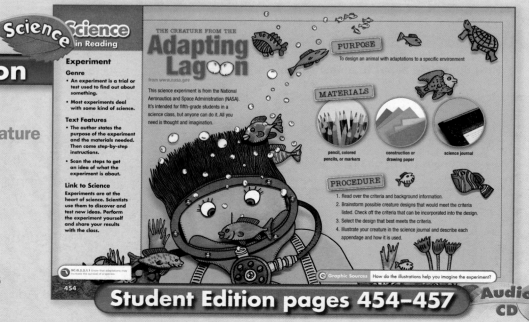

Science in Reading

Experiment

Genre
- An experiment is a trial or test used to find out about something.
- Most experiments deal with some kind of science.

Text Features
- The author states the purpose of the experiment and the materials needed. Then come step-by-step instructions.
- Scan the steps to get an idea of what the experiment is about.

Link to Science
Experiments are at the heart of science. Scientists use them to discover and test new ideas. Perform the experiment yourself and share your results with the class.

THE CREATURE FROM THE
Adapting Lagoon

from www.nasa.gov

This science experiment is from the National Aeronautics and Space Administration (NASA). It's intended for fifth-grade students in a science class, but anyone can do it. All you need is thought and imagination.

PURPOSE
To design an animal with adaptations to a specific environment

MATERIALS

pencil, colored pencils, or markers

construction or drawing paper

science journal

PROCEDURE
1. Read over the criteria and background information.
2. Brainstorm possible creature designs that would meet the criteria listed. Check off the criteria that can be incorporated into the design.
3. Select the design that best meets the criteria.
4. Illustrate your creature in the science journal and describe each appendage and how it is used.

454

Graphic Sources How do the illustrations help you imagine the experiment?

Student Edition pages 454–457

Audio CD

Florida Science Standards This Week

SC.C.2.2.4.5.1 Knows how motion is different in space and on Earth
SC.F.1.2.2 Understands the ways animals depend on plants
SC.G.1.2.2.5.1 Understands how the environment affects organisms
SC.G.1.2.5 Knows that animals eat plants to acquire energy
SC.H.1.2.2.5.1 Understands that scientists use different kinds of investigation

Leveled Readers

⊚ **Skill** Graphic Sources
⊚ **Strategy** Monitor and Fix Up
Lesson Vocabulary

Below-Level

On-Level

Advanced

ELL Reader
· Concept Vocabulary
· Text Support
· Language Enrichment

Integrate Science Standards

- **Animals**
- **Environments/Biomes**
- **Adaptations**

✓ Read

Exploding Ants,
pp. 440–451

"The Creature from the Adapting Lagoon,"
pp. 454–457

Leveled Readers

Below-Level   **On-Level**   **Advanced**

· Support Concepts   · Develop Concepts   · Extend Concepts

ELL Reader

 Build Concept Vocabulary
Animal Adaptations,
pp. 436l–436m

 Teach Science Concepts
Biomes, p. 445
Human Adaptations, p. 449
Animal Experiments, p. 455

 Explore Science Center
Explore Animals, p. 436k

Florida Weekly Plan

READING

45–90 minutes

TARGET SKILLS OF THE WEEK

🔗 **Comprehension Skill**
Graphic Sources

🔗 **Comprehension Strategy**
Monitor and Fix Up

🔗 **Vocabulary Strategy**
Context Clues

DAY 1
PAGES 436l–438b, 457a, 457e–457k

Oral Language

QUESTION OF THE WEEK *How do animals adapt to survive?*

Read Aloud: "Snake Scientist," 436m
Build Concepts, 436l

Comprehension/Vocabulary

Comprehension Skill/Strategy Lesson, 436–437
🔗 Graphic Sources **T**
🔗 Monitor and Fix Up
Build Background, 438a
Introduce Lesson Vocabulary, 438b
critical, enables, mucus, scarce, specialize, sterile **T**

Read Leveled Readers

Grouping Options 436f–436g

Fluency

Model Tempo and Rate, 436l–436m, 457a

DAY 2
PAGES 438–447, 457a, 457e–457k

Oral Language

QUESTION OF THE DAY *What animal ways of eating and finding shelter seem especially gross?*

Comprehension/Vocabulary

Vocabulary Strategy Lesson, 438–439
🔗 Context Clues **T**

Read *Exploding Ants,* 440–447

Grouping Options
436f–436g

🔗 Graphic Sources **T**
🔗 Context Clues
REVIEW Author's Purpose **T**
Develop Vocabulary

Fluency

Echo Reading, 457a

LANGUAGE ARTS

30–60 minutes

Trait of the Week

Support/Word Choice

Grammar, 457e
Introduce Possessive Pronouns **T**

Writing Workshop, 457g
Introduce Telling a Story About an Animal
Model the Trait of the Week: Support/Word Choice

Spelling, 457i
Pretest for Homophones

Internet Inquiry, 457k
Identify Questions

Grammar, 457e
Develop Possessive Pronouns **T**

Writing Workshop, 457g
Improve Writing with Mood

Spelling, 457i
Teach the Generalization

Internet Inquiry, 457k
Navigate/Search

DAILY WRITING ACTIVITIES

Day 1 Write to Read, 436

Day 2 Words to Write, 439
Strategy Response Log, 440, 447

DAILY SCIENCE CONNECTIONS

Day 1 Animal Adaptations Concept Web, 436l

Day 2 Time for Science: Biomes, 445
Revisit the Animal Adaptations Concept Web, 447

DAILY SUCCESS PREDICTORS
for Adequate Yearly Progress

Monitor Progress and Corrective Feedback

Vocabulary — Check Vocabulary, *436l*

Grouping Options for Differentiated Instruction

Turn the page for the small group lesson plan.

DAY 3 PAGES 448–453, 457a, 457e–457k

Oral Language

QUESTION OF THE DAY *How does the ability of a snake to gulp down prey larger than itself help it survive?*

Comprehension/Vocabulary

Read *Exploding Ants,* 448–452

Grouping Options 436f–436g

- 🎯 Graphic Sources **T**
- 🎯 Monitor and Fix Up
- Develop Vocabulary

Reader Response
Selection Test

Fluency

Model Tempo and Rate, 457a

Grammar, 457f
Apply Possessive Pronouns in Writing **T**

Writing Workshop, 453, 457h
Write Now
Prewrite and Draft

Spelling, 457j
Connect Spelling to Writing

Internet Inquiry, 457k
Analyze Sources

Day 3 Strategy Response Log, 450
Think and Explain, 452

Day 3 Time for Science: Human Adaptations, 449
Revisit the Animal Adaptations Concept Web, 451

DAY 4 PAGES 454–457a, 457e–457k

Oral Language

QUESTION OF THE DAY *What adaptations do you think humans would have to undergo if they lived like fish in an underwater environment?*

Comprehension/Vocabulary

Read "The Creature from the Adapting Lagoon," 454–457

Grouping Options 436f –436g

Experiment
Reading Across Texts
Content-Area Vocabulary

Fluency

Partner Reading, 457a

Grammar, 457f
Practice Possessive Pronouns for Standardized Tests **T**

Writing Workshop, 457h
Draft, Revise, and Publish

Spelling, 457j
Provide a Strategy

Internet Inquiry, 457k
Synthesize Information

Day 4 Writing Across Texts, 457

Day 4 Time for Science: Animal Experiments, 455

DAY 5 PAGES 457a–457l

Oral Language

QUESTION OF THE WEEK *To wrap up the week, revisit the Day 1 question.*
Build Concept Vocabulary, 457c

Fluency

Read Leveled Readers

Grouping Options 436f–436g

Assess Reading Rate, 457a

Comprehension/Vocabulary

- 🎯 Reteach Graphic Sources, 457b **T**
- Metaphor, 457b
- 🎯 Review Context Clues, 457c **T**

Speaking and Listening, 457d
Description
Listen to Poetry

Grammar, 457f
Cumulative Review

Writing Workshop, 457h
Connect to Unit Writing

Spelling, 457j
Posttest for Homophones

Internet Inquiry, 457k
Communicate Results

Research/Study Skills, 457l
Magazine/Periodical

Day 5 Metaphor, 457b

Day 5 Revisit the Animal Adaptations Concept Web, 457c

KEY 🎯 Target Skill   **T** Tested Skill   **FCAT Tested Skill**

Comprehension Check Retelling, *452*

Fluency Check Fluency WCPM, *457a*

Vocabulary Check Vocabulary, *457c*

SUCCE
PREDICT

Small Group Plan for Differentiated Instruction

Daily Plan AT A GLANCE

Reading
Whole Group
- Oral Language
- Comprehension/Vocabulary

Group Time
Differentiated Instruction

Meet with small groups to provide:
- Skill Support
- Reading Support
- Fluency Practice

Read

This week's lessons for daily group time can be found behind the Differentiated Instruction (DI) tab on pp. DI·22–DI·31.

Whole Group
- Fluency

Language Arts
- Grammar
- Writing
- Spelling
- Research/Inquiry
- Speaking/Listening/Viewing

Use *My Sidewalks on Reading Street* for Tier III intensive reading intervention.

DAY 1

On-Level
Teacher-Led
Page DI · 23
- Develop Concept Vocabulary
- **Read** On-Level Reader *Changing to Survive: Bird Adaptations*

Strategic Intervention
Teacher-Led
Page DI · 22
- Reinforce Concepts
- **Read** Below-Level Reader *Surviving the Weather: Animals in Their Environments*

Advanced
Teacher-Led
Page DI · 23
- **Read** Advanced Reader *A Home for Humans in Outer Space: Is It Possible?*
- Independent Extension Activity

(i) Independent Activities
While you meet with small groups, have the rest of the class...
- Visit the Reading/Library Center, p. 436j
- Listen to the Background Building Audio
- Finish Write to Read, p. 436
- Complete Practice Book pp. 173–174
- Visit Cross-Curricular Centers

DAY 2

On-Level
Teacher-Led
Pages 442–447
- **Read** *Exploding Ants*

Strategic Intervention
Teacher-Led
Page DI · 24
- Practice Lesson Vocabulary
- Read Multisyllabic Words
- **Read** or Listen to *Exploding Ants*

Advanced
Teacher-Led
Page DI · 25
- Extend Vocabulary
- **Read** *Exploding Ants*

(i) Independent Activities
While you meet with small groups, have the rest of the class...
- Visit the Reading/Library Center, p. 436j
- Listen to the AudioText for *Exploding Ants*
- Finish Words to Write, p. 439
- Complete Practice Book pp. 175–176
- Write in their Strategy Response Logs, pp. 440, 447
- Visit Cross-Curricular Centers
- Work on inquiry projects

DAY 3

On-Level
Teacher-Led
Pages 448–451
- **Read** *Exploding Ants*

Strategic Intervention
Teacher-Led
Page DI · 26
- Practice Graphic Sources and Monitor and Fix Up
- **Read** or Listen to *Exploding Ants*

Advanced
Teacher-Led
Page DI · 27
- Extend Graphic Sources and Monitor and Fix Up
- **Read** *Exploding Ants*

(i) Independent Activities
While you meet with small groups, have the rest of the class...
- Visit the Reading/Library Center, p. 436j
- Listen to the AudioText for *Exploding Ants*
- Write in their Strategy Response Logs, p. 450
- Finish Think and Explain, p. 452
- Complete Practice Book p. 177
- Visit Cross-Curricular Centers
- Work on inquiry projects

① Begin with whole class skill and strategy instruction.

② Meet with small groups to provide differentiated instruction.

③ Gather the whole class back together for fluency and language arts.

DAY 4

On-Level
Teacher-Led
Pages 454–457

- **Read** "The Creature from the Adapting Lagoon"

Strategic Intervention
Teacher-Led
Page DI · 28

- Practice Retelling
- **Read** or Listen to "The Creature from the Adapting Lagoon"

Advanced
Teacher-Led
Page DI · 29

- **Read** "The Creature from the Adapting Lagoon"
- Genre Study

ⓘ Independent Activities

While you meet with small groups, have the rest of the class...

- Visit the Reading/Library Center, p. 436j
- Listen to the AudioText for "The Creature from the Adapting Lagoon"
- Visit the Writing/Vocabulary Center

- Finish Writing Across Texts, p. 457
- Visit Cross-Curricular Centers
- Work on inquiry projects

DAY 5

On-Level
Teacher-Led
Page DI · 31

- **Reread** Leveled Reader *Changing to Survive: Bird Adaptations*
- Retell *Changing to Survive: Bird Adaptations*

Strategic Intervention
Teacher-Led
Page DI · 30

- **Reread** Leveled Reader *Surviving the Weather: Animals in Their Environments*
- Retell *Surviving the Weather: Animals in Their Environments*

Advanced
Teacher-Led
Page DI · 31

- **Reread** Leveled Reader *A Home for Humans in Outer Space: Is It Possible?*
- Share Extension Activity

ⓘ Independent Activities

While you meet with small groups, have the rest of the class...

- Visit the Reading/Library Center, p. 436j
- Complete Practice Book pp. 178–180

- Visit Cross-Curricular Centers
- Work on inquiry projects

Grouping Place English language learners in the groups that correspond to their reading abilities in English.

Use the appropriate Leveled Reader or other text at students' instructional level.

TIP Send home the appropriate Multilingual Summary of the main selection on Day 1.

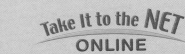

Take It to the NET ONLINE
PearsonSuccessNet.com

P. David Pearson
For ideas on teaching comprehension strategies, see the article "Developing Expertise in Reading Comprehension" by Scott Foresman author P. David Pearson and others.

TEACHER TALK

Fix-up strategies are strategies readers use when they realize they do not understand something. Adjusting reading rate, rereading, and using a reference source are a few fix-up strategies.

Looking Ahead

Be sure to schedule time for students to work on the unit inquiry project "Adaptations." This week students analyze information they have gathered about groups of people or animals who have adapted to different situations.

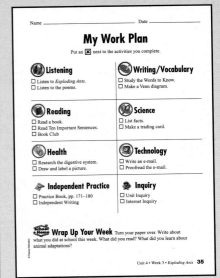

▲ **Group-Time Survival Guide**
p. 35, Weekly Contract

Exploding Ants **436g**

Customize Your Plan *by Strand*

ORAL LANGUAGE

Concept Development

How do animals adapt to survive?

CONCEPT VOCABULARY

African black mambas   *constrictors*   *reptiles*

BUILD

❑ **Question of the Week** Introduce and discuss the question of the week. This week students will read a variety of texts and work on projects related to the concept *animal adaptations*. Post the question for students to refer to throughout the week. **DAY 1** *436d*

❑ **Read Aloud** Read aloud "Snake Scientist." Then begin a web to build concepts and concept vocabulary related to this week's lesson and the unit theme, Adapting. Introduce the concept words *African black mambas, constrictors,* and *reptiles* and have students place them on the web. Display the web for use throughout the week. **DAY 1** *436l–436m*

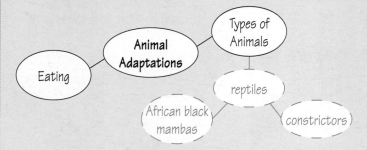

DEVELOP

❑ **Question of the Day** Use the prompts from the Weekly Plan to engage students in conversations related to this week's reading and the unit theme. **EVERY DAY** *436d–436e*

❑ **Concept Vocabulary Web** Revisit the Animal Adaptations Concept Web and encourage students to add concept words from their reading and life experiences. **DAY 2** *447,* **DAY 3** *451*

CONNECT

❑ **Looking Back/Review/Connect** Revisit the Animal Adaptations Concept Web and discuss how it relates to this week's lesson and the unit theme. Then make connections to next week's lesson. **DAY 5** *457c*

CHECK

❑ **Concept Vocabulary Web** Use the Animal Adaptions Concept Web to check students' understanding of the concept vocabulary words *African black mambas, constrictors,* and *reptiles.* **DAY 1** *436l,* **DAY 5** *457c*

VOCABULARY

CONTEXT CLUES
When you are reading, you may come across a difficult or unfamiliar word. Sometimes an author writes a synonym, a different word that almost means the same thing, to help you understand the difficult or unfamiliar word.

LESSON VOCABULARY

critical	scarce
enables	specialize
mucus	sterile

TEACH

❑ **Words to Know** Give students the opportunity to tell what they already know about this week's lesson vocabulary words. Then discuss word meaning. **DAY 1** *438b*

❑ **Vocabulary Strategy Lesson** Use the vocabulary strategy lesson in the Student Edition to introduce and model this week's strategy, *context clues.* **DAY 2** *438–439*

Vocabulary Strategy Lesson

PRACTICE/APPLY

❑ **Leveled Text** Read the lesson vocabulary in the context of leveled text. **DAY 1** *LR19–LR27*

❑ **Words in Context** Read the lesson vocabulary and apply *context clues* in the context of *Exploding Ants.* **DAY 2** *440–447,* **DAY 3** *448–452*

Leveled Readers

❑ **Writing/Vocabulary Center** Use a Venn diagram to show similarities and differences in the ways that owls and snakes digest their food. **ANY DAY** *436k*

Main Selection—Nonfiction

❑ **Homework** Practice Book pp. 174–175. **DAY 1** *438b,* **DAY 2** *439*

❑ **Word Play** Have students find related words from the following verbs and identify their parts of speech: *adapt, survive,* and *defend.* **ANY DAY** *457c*

ASSESS

❑ **Selection Test** Use the Selection Test to determine students' understanding of the lesson vocabulary words. **DAY 3**

RETEACH/REVIEW

❑ **Reteach Lesson** If necessary, use this lesson to reteach and review *context clues.* **DAY 5** *457c*

① Use your school-based instructional focus calendar to determine which strands to teach.

② Target your instruction on FCAT tested skills.

③ Check students' understanding of FCAT tested standards.

COMPREHENSION

SKILL GRAPHIC SOURCES Graphic sources are graphs, maps, pictures, photographs, and diagrams that organize information and help strengthen understanding of the text.

STRATEGY MONITOR AND FIX UP To monitor means to stop reading occasionally and check to be sure you understand what you are reading. Fix up means to do something to regain understanding when you do not understand or are confused.

TEACH

- ☐ **Skill/Strategy Lesson** Use the skill/strategy lesson in the Student Edition to introduce and model *graphic sources* and *monitor and fix up.* **DAY 1** 436-437

  Skill/Strategy Lesson

- ☐ **Extend Skills** Teach metaphors. **ANY DAY** 457b

PRACTICE/APPLY

- ☐ **Leveled Text** Apply *graphic sources* and *monitor and fix up* to read leveled text. **DAY 1** LR19–LR27

- ☐ **Skills and Strategies in Context** Read *Exploding Ants,* using the Guiding Comprehension questions to apply *graphic sources* and *monitor and fix up.* **DAY 2** 440–447, **DAY 3** 448–452

  Leveled Readers

- ☐ **Reader Response** Use Student Edition p. 452 to respond to the selection. **DAY 3,** p. 452

  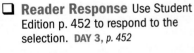

  Main Selection—Nonfiction

- ☐ **Skills and Strategies in Context** Read "The Creature from the Adapting Lagoon." Then have students discuss and write across texts. **DAY 4** 454–457

  Paired Selection—Nonfiction

- ☐ **Homework** Practice Book pp. 173, 177, 178 **DAY 1** 437, **DAY 3** 451, **DAY 5** 457b

ASSESS

- ☐ **Selection Test** Determine students' understanding of the selection and their use of *graphic sources.* **DAY 3**

- ☐ **Retell** Have students retell *Exploding Ants.* **DAY 3** 452–453

RETEACH/REVIEW

- ☐ **Reteach Lesson** If necessary, reteach and review *graphic sources.* **DAY 5** 457b

FLUENCY

SKILL TEMPO AND RATE. Reading with appropriate tempo means that you take breaths at appropriate times and pause at punctuation. Reading with an appropriate rate means that you do not read too fast or too slow.

TEACH

- ☐ **Read Aloud** Model fluent reading by rereading "Snake Scientist." Focus on this week's fluency skill, tempo and rate. **DAY 1** 436l–436m, 457a

PRACTICE/APPLY

- ☐ **Echo Reading** Read aloud selected paragraphs from *Exploding Ants,* modeling appropriate reading rate and tempo. Have students practice, doing three echo readings of the selected paragraphs. **DAY 2** 457a, **DAY 3** 457a

- ☐ **Partner Reading** Have partners practice reading aloud, reading with appropriate rate and tempo and offering each other feedback. As students reread, monitor their progress toward their individual fluency goals. **DAY 4** 457a

- ☐ **Listening Center** Have students follow along with the AudioText for this week's selections. **ANY DAY** 436j

- ☐ **Reading/Library Center** Have students reread a selection of their choice. **ANY DAY** 436j

- ☐ **Fluency Coach** Have students use Fluency Coach to listen to fluent readings or practice reading on their own. **ANY DAY**

ASSESS

- ☐ **Check Fluency** WCPM Do a one-minute timed reading, paying special attention to this week's skill—tempo and rate. Provide feedback for each student. **DAY 5** 457a

☑ Customize Your Plan by Strand

GRAMMAR

SKILL POSSESSIVE PRONOUNS Possessive pronouns show who or what owns something. Some examples of possessive pronouns are *my, your, mine, her, hers, his, its,* and *ours.* Possessive pronouns do no use an apostrophe.

TEACH

☐ **Grammar Transparency 18** Use Grammar Transparency 18 to teach possessive pronouns. **DAY 1** *457e*

Grammar Transparency 18

PRACTICE/APPLY

☐ **Develop the Concept** Review the concept of possessive pronouns and provide guided practice. **DAY 2** *457e*

☐ **Apply to Writing** Have students review something they have written and apply possessive pronouns. **DAY 3** *457f*

☐ **Test Preparation** Examine common errors in possessive pronouns to prepare for standardized tests. **DAY 4** *457f*

☐ **Homework** Grammar and Writing Practice Book pp. 69–71. **DAY 2** *457e,* **DAY 3** *457f,* **DAY 4** *457f*

ASSESS

☐ **Cumulative Review** Use Grammar and Writing Practice Book p. 72. **DAY 5** *457f*

RETEACH/REVIEW

☐ **Daily Fix-It** Have students find and correct errors in grammar, spelling, and punctuation. **EVERY DAY** *457e–457f*

☐ **The Grammar and Writing Book** Use pp. 152–155 of The Grammar and Writing Book to extend instruction for possessive pronouns. **ANY DAY**

The Grammar and Writing Book

WRITING

Trait of the Week

WORD CHOICE Good writers choose their words carefully. Strong verbs, specific nouns, and vivid adjectives help writers elaborate on their ideas. Well-chosen words make writing clear and lively.

TEACH

☐ **Writing Transparency 18A** Use the model to introduce and discuss the Trait of the Week. **DAY 1** *457g*

☐ **Writing Transparency 18B** Use the transparency to show students how mood can improve their writing. **DAY 2** *457g*

Writing Transparency 18A   **Writing Transparency 18B**

PRACTICE/APPLY

☐ **Write Now** Examine the model on Student Edition p. 453. Then have students write their own story about an animal. **DAY 3** *453, 457h,* **DAY 4** *457h*

> **Prompt** The author of *Exploding Ants* describes unusual or unexpected animal behaviors. Think about your own experiences observing animals. Now write a story about an animal whose behavior surprised you.

Write Now p. 453

☐ **Writing/Vocabulary Center** Use a Venn diagram to show similarities and differences in the ways that owls and snakes digest their food. **ANY DAY** *436k*

ASSESS

☐ **Writing Trait Rubric** Use the rubric to evaluate students' writing. **DAY 4** *457h*

RETEACH/REVIEW

☐ **The Grammar and Writing Book** Use pp. 152–157 of The Grammar and Writing Book to extend instruction for possessive pronouns, mood, and animal stories. **ANY DAY**

The Grammar and Writing Book

① Use your school-based instructional focus calendar to determine which strands to teach.

② Target your instruction on FCAT tested skills. FCAT TESTED SKILL

③ Check students' understanding of FCAT tested standards. EYE ON FCAT

SPELLING

GENERALIZATION HOMOPHONES A homophone is a word that sounds exactly like another word but has a different spelling and meaning: *cent, sent.* Homophones occur because many letters and letter combinations make more than one sound.

TEACH

❑ **Pretest** Give the pretest for homophones. Guide students in self-correcting their pretests and correcting any misspellings. **DAY 1** *457i*

❑ **Think and Practice** Connect spelling to the phonics generalization for homophones. **DAY 2** *457i*

PRACTICE/APPLY

❑ **Connect to Writing** Have students use spelling words to write a description. Then review frequently misspelled words: *when, then, went.* **DAY 3** *457j*

❑ **Homework** Word Study and Spelling Practice Book pp. 69–72. **EVERY DAY**

RETEACH/REVIEW

❑ **Review** Review spelling words to prepare for the posttest. Then provide students with a spelling strategy—rhyming helpers. **DAY 4** *457j*

ASSESS

❑ **Posttest** Use dictation sentences to give the posttest for words with homophones. **DAY 5** *457j*

Spelling Words

1. cent	8. their*	15. pale
2. sent	9. there*	16. pail
3. scent	10. they're*	17. aloud
4. threw	11. chili	18. allowed
5. through*	12. chilly	19. course
6. weather	13. tide	20. coarse
7. whether	14. tied	

Challenge Words

21. counsel	23. bizarre	25. patients
22. council	24. bazaar	26. patience

*Word from the selection

RESEARCH AND INQUIRY

❑ **Internet Inquiry** Have students conduct an Internet inquiry on animal adaptations. **EVERY DAY** *457k*

❑ **Magazine/Periodical** Review and analyze the features and format of a magazine article and then discuss how students can use these resources to find information. **DAY 5** *457l*

❑ **Unit Inquiry** Allow time for students to analyze information they have gathered about groups of people or animals who have adapted to different situations. **ANY DAY** *391*

SPEAKING AND LISTENING

❑ **Description** Have students brainstorm a list of descriptive words to describe animals and then use some of those words to present a description of an animal and its features. **DAY 5** *457d*

❑ **Listen to Poetry** Have students listen to a poem about an animal and answer questions. **DAY 5** *457d*

Resources for Differentiated Instruction

LEVELED READERS

▶ **Comprehension**
- 🎯 **Skill** Graphic Sources
- 🎯 **Strategy** Monitor and Fix Up

▶ **Lesson Vocabulary**
- 🎯 Context Clues

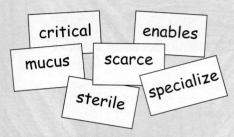

critical   enables   mucus   scarce   specialize   sterile

▶ **Science Standards**
- • Animals
- • Environments/Biomes
- • Adaptations

Leveled Reader Database

ONLINE

PearsonSuccessNet.com

Use the Online Database of over 600 books to
- Download and print additional copies of this week's leveled readers.
- Listen to the readers being read online.
- Search for more titles focused on this week's skills, topic, and content.

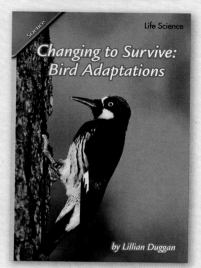

Life Science

Changing to Survive: Bird Adaptations

by Lillian Duggan

On-Level Reader

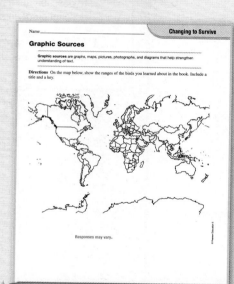

🎯 **On-Level Practice** TE p. LR23

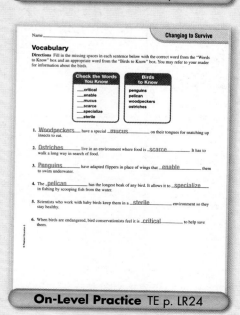

On-Level Practice TE p. LR24

Life Science

Surviving the Weather: Animals in Their Environments

by Joe Adair

Below-Level Reader

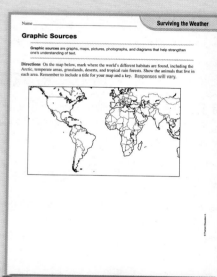

🎯 **Below-Level Practice** TE p. LR20

Below-Level Practice TE p. LR21

Advanced

Advanced Reader

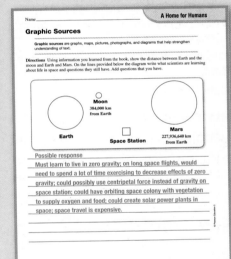

Name_____   A Home for Humans

Graphic Sources

Graphic sources are graphs, maps, pictures, photographs, and diagrams that help strengthen understanding of text.

Directions Using information you learned from the book, show the distance between Earth and the moon and Earth and Mars. On the lines provided below the diagram write what scientists are learning about life in space and questions they still have. Add questions that you have.

Moon
384,000 km from Earth

Earth   Space Station   Mars
227,936,640 km from Earth

Possible response
Must learn to live in zero gravity; on long space flights, would need to spend a lot of time exercising to decrease effects of zero gravity; could possibly use centripetal force instead of gravity on space station; could have orbiting space colony with vegetation to supply oxygen and food; could create solar power plants in space; space travel is expensive.

Advanced Practice TE p. LR26

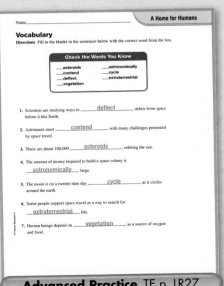

Name_____   A Home for Humans

Vocabulary
Directions Fill in the blanks in the sentences below with the correct word from the box.

Check the Words You Know
___asteroids   ___astronomically
___contend   ___cycle
___deflect   ___extraterrestrial
___vegetation

1. Scientists are studying ways to _____deflect_____ debris from space before it hits Earth.

2. Astronauts must _____contend_____ with many challenges presented by space travel.

3. There are about 100,000 _____asteroids_____ orbiting the sun.

4. The amount of money required to build a space colony is _____astronomically_____ large.

5. The moon is on a twenty-nine day _____cycle_____ as it circles around the earth.

6. Some people support space travel as a way to search for _____extraterrestrial_____ life.

7. Human beings depend on _____vegetation_____ as a source of oxygen and food.

Advanced Practice TE p. LR27

ELL

ELL Reader

ELL Poster 18

Teacher's Edition Notes

ELL notes throughout this lesson support instruction and reference additional resources at point of use.

Teaching Guide pp. 120–126, 246–247

- Multilingual summaries of the main selection
- Comprehension lesson
- Vocabulary strategies and word cards
- ELL Reader 5.4.3 lesson

ELL and Transition Handbook

Ten Important Sentences

- Key ideas from every selection in the Student Edition
- Activities to build sentence power

More Reading

Readers' Theater Anthology
- Fluency practice
- Five scripts to build fluency
- Poetry for oral interpretation

Leveled Trade Books

Advanced
Below-Level
On-Level

- Extended reading tied to the unit concept
- Lessons in the Trade Book Library Teaching Guide

School + Home

Homework
- Family Times Newsletter
- ELL Multilingual Selection Summaries

Take-Home Books
- Leveled Readers

Family Times

Cross-Curricular Centers

Listen to the Selections

MATERIALS
CD player, headphones, AudioText CD, student book

`SINGLES`

LISTEN TO LITERATURE Listen to *Exploding Ants* and "The Creature from the Adapting Lagoon" as you follow or read along in your book.

If there is anything you don't understand, you can listen again to any section.

Read It Again!

MATERIALS
Collection of books for self-selected reading, reading logs, student book

`SINGLES`
`PAIRS`
`GROUPS`

Select a book you have already read. Record the title of the book in your reading log. You may want to read with a partner.

Choose from the following:

- **Leveled Readers**
- **ELL Readers**
- **Stories Written by Classmates**
- **Books from the Library**
- *Exploding Ants*

TEN IMPORTANT SENTENCES Read the Ten Important Sentences for *Exploding Ants*. Then locate the sentences in the student book.

BOOK CLUB Gather as a group to discuss the illustrations in *Exploding Ants*. How do the illustrations help you better understand the information in the story? Find other nonfiction books with interesting illustrations and share your favorites with the group.

Understand Digestion

MATERIALS
Writing and art materials, reference sources

`SINGLES`

Animals have different ways of digesting and using food. Research information on the human digestive system.

1. **Locate information about the human digestive system.**
2. **Draw a picture of the digestive system.**
3. **Label its parts.**

EARLY FINISHERS Make a list describing the important steps in the human digestive process.

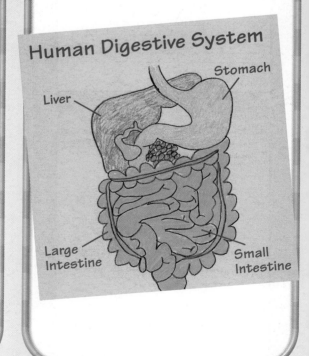

Human Digestive System

Liver

Stomach

Large Intestine

Small Intestine

Scott Foresman Reading Street Centers Survival Kit

Use the *Exploding Ants* materials from the Reading Street Centers Survival Kit to organize this week's centers.

Writing/Vocabulary

Compare *Digestion*

MATERIALS
Writing materials, Venn diagram

`SINGLES`

Use a Venn diagram to show similarities and differences in the ways that owls and snakes digest their food.

1. List the eating habits of owls in the left circle.
2. List the eating habits of snakes in the right circle.
3. List the eating habits that are similar to both animals in the middle circle.

EARLY FINISHERS Write a short paragraph summarizing your findings.

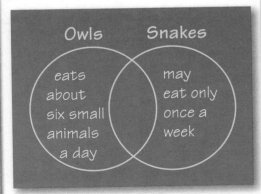

Science

Explore Animals

MATERIALS
Writing and art materials, student book

`SINGLES`

Explore the ways that animals are adapted to their environments.

1. Choose an animal from *Exploding Ants.*
2. Find and list 2 to 3 interesting facts about that animal.
3. Make a trading card with a picture of the animal on the front and the facts you found on the back.

EARLY FINISHERS Design an information poster about your animal. Illustrate it with pictures. Display your poster in your classroom.

Technology

Compose an *E-mail*

MATERIALS
E-mail program

`SINGLES`
`PAIRS`

Share some fun animal facts with a friend or family member.

1. Follow classroom rules for composing and sending an e-mail to someone you know.
2. Write a list of the five strangest animal facts you learned and send it to a friend or family member who you think would find it interesting.
3. Include a subject line and proofread your message before sending it.

EARLY FINISHERS Add a fact to your list that you make up and challenge a friend to guess which fact is false.

ALL CENTERS

OBJECTIVES

- Build vocabulary by finding words related to the lesson concept.
- Listen to identify author's purpose.

Concept Vocabulary

African black mambas poisonous snakes from Africa that are related to cobras

constrictors snakes that kill prey by crushing it in their coils

reptiles cold-blooded animals with backbones and lungs, usually covered with horny plates or scales

Monitor Progress

Check Vocabulary

If...	then...
students are unable to place words on the Web,	use the Concept Vocabulary Routine on p.D1·1 to teach the words. Provide additional words for practice, such as *dinosaurs* and *prey*.

SUCCESS PREDICTOR

DAY 1 Grouping Options

Reading
Whole Group
Introduce and discuss the Question of the Week. Then use pp. 436l–438b.

Group Time
Differentiated Instruction
Read this week's Leveled Readers. See pp. 436f–436g for the small group lesson plan.

Whole Group
Use p. 457a.

Language Arts
Use pp. 457e–457k.

Build Concepts

FLUENCY

MODEL TEMPO AND RATE As you read "Snake Scientist," keep your pace slow and steady. Be sure to enunciate words that convey scientific information, such as *extinct, scale-covered,* and *cold-blooded.*

LISTENING COMPREHENSION

After reading "Snake Scientist," use the following questions to assess listening comprehension.

1. **What is the author's purpose for writing "Snake Scientist"? Explain your answer.** *(He is writing to inform readers about snakes.)* **Author's Purpose**

2. **How are snakes like and unlike dinosaurs?** *(They are both reptiles; dinosaurs are extinct but snakes are not.)* **Compare and Contrast**

BUILD CONCEPT VOCABULARY

Start a web to build concepts and vocabulary related to this week's lesson and the unit theme.

- Draw the Animal Adaptations Concept Web.

- Read the sentence with the word *reptiles* again. Ask students to pronounce *reptiles* and discuss its meaning.

- Place *reptiles* in an oval attached to *Types of Animals*. Explain that students can list different kinds of reptiles in ovals attached to this category. Read the sentences in which *African black mambas* and *constrictors* appear. Have students pronounce the words, place them on the web, and provide reasons.

- Brainstorm additional words and categories for the web. Keep the web on display and add words throughout the week.

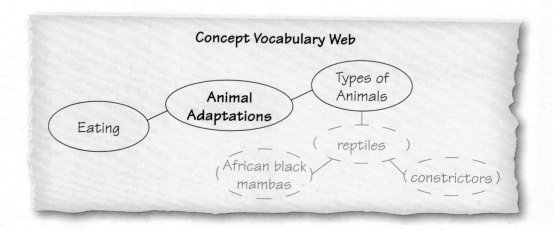

Concept Vocabulary Web

SNAKE SCIENTIST

by Sy Montgomery

Many people are afraid of snakes. But don't be afraid! You'll miss out on some amazing and mysterious animals. Some people claim snakes are more interesting than dinosaurs—and they aren't extinct.

Both snakes and dinosaurs are reptiles—scale-covered, cold-blooded animals. Lizards, crocodiles, and turtles are reptiles, too. But snakes are perhaps the most unusual and fascinating members of the family: long, thin tubes without legs, eye-lids, or ears. And yet snakes are the superheroes of the reptile world, with abilities that other reptiles don't have.

Snakes are agile and quick. African black mambas can slither five miles per hour. Snakes flow across land, climb high into trees, burrow deep into the ground, and swim across marshes, lakes, and even oceans. Some kinds, like the sea snakes that have paddle-shaped tails, swim so well they never come out on land at all. And the so-called flying snakes of Southeast Asia and the East Indies hurl themselves from treetops and glide through the air.

Though snakes have no ears, they sense vibrations with the bones of their jaws that we, with our ears, perceive as sound. With forked tongues, they "taste" odors, picking up chemical information that leads them along an invisible trail to a frog or a rat or another snake. When a snake flicks its tongue in and out, it is collecting chemical particles and transferring them to a special organ in the roof of their mouth called the Jacobson's organ. If one tip of the forked tongue picks up more particles than the other, the snake knows which direction to follow.

Snakes abilities seem almost magical. They can swallow prey bigger than their own heads by the incredible feat of unhinging their jaws from their skulls. Some snakes, such as vipers, have evolved poisonous saliva—venom—to kill their prey; other constrictors like boas and anacondas, literally hug their food to death. Snakes can go for weeks or months without a meal. They can "see" heat with special heat receptors in their heads called pit organs.

And snakes can shed their skin—even the "skin" over their eyeballs. Shedding begins at the lips, and as the snake crawls out of the old skin it turns inside out, sort of like a person peeling off a sweater. If you find a shed skin, the tail points in the direction in which the snake was moving.

No wonder people around the world regard snakes with amazement.

Activate Prior Knowledge

Before students listen to the Read Aloud, ask them what they know about snakes and how they feel about snakes.

Set Purpose

Read aloud the title and have students predict what the selection will be about.

Have students listen to determine the author's purpose.

Creative Response

Have students present charades showing the ways in which snakes move in their habitats and sense the world around them. **Drama**

Develop Concept Vocabulary

Read aloud every day from a book of your choice related to the concept and use the Concept Vocabulary Routine on p. DI·1 to develop concept vocabulary. For suggestions, see p. TR14.

Access Content Before reading, review the meanings of the following words: *burrow*, *hurl*, *unhinge*, and *shed*. Explain how and why the snake performs each of these actions.

Homework Send home this week's Family Times newsletter.

Pages 436l–436m

LA.5.1.6.2 Listen to and discuss conceptually challenging text

LA.5.1.6.4 Categorize key vocabulary

LA.5.1.7.2 Identify author's purpose

LA.5.1.7.7 Compare and contrast

LA.5.5.2.1 Listen and speak to gain and share information (dramatic recitations)

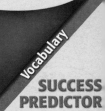

Vocabulary

SUCCESS PREDICTOR

BEFORE READING

 SKILLS ⟷ STRATEGIES IN CONTEXT

Graphic Sources
Monitor/Fix Up

FCAT TESTED SKILL

OBJECTIVES

- Use graphic sources to aid comprehension.
- Monitor comprehension by using graphic sources.

Skills Trace
Graphic Sources

Introduce/Teach	TE: 5.3 364–365; 5.4 436–437; 5.5 536–537
Practice	Practice Book: 143, 147, 148, 166, 173, 177, 178, 213, 217, 218, 226, 246
Reteach/Review	TE: 5.3 383b, DI·56; 5.4 421, 457b, DI·54; 5.5 559b, 569, 613, DI·53
Test	Selection Test: 57–60, 69–72, 85–88; Benchmark Test: Unit 5

INTRODUCE

Show students a map of the United States. Ask them what information this graphic source gives. Discuss what written information the graphic source could clarify. *(Possible responses: The map shows the geographic features of North Carolina. It could clarify information about where cities grew up.)*

Have students read the information on p. 436. Explain the following:

- Graphic sources can help you understand information in a text.
- You can use graphic sources and other references to monitor and fix up problems in understanding what you read.

Use Skill Transparency 18 to teach graphic sources and monitor and fix up.

exploding ants

Comprehension

Skill
Graphic Sources

Strategy
Monitor and Fix Up

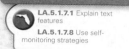

LA.5.1.7.1 Explain text features
LA.5.1.7.8 Use self-monitoring strategies

 # Graphic Sources

- A graphic source, such as a picture, diagram, or chart, organizes information and makes it easy to see.
- Preview the graphic sources in a selection to help you predict what you will be reading about.
- As you read, compare the information in the text with the graphic source.

Strategy: Monitor and Fix Up

Good readers make sure they understand what they read. If a graphic source is part of a text, you can use it to help you understand. You can also use other references to help you. If you do not understand a word, you can look it up in a dictionary. If you need more information about a subject, you can check an encyclopedia.

 Write to Read

1. Read "Ant Facts." Use both the text and the diagram to write a paragraph about an ant's antennae. Tell what they look like and what they are for. Include how to pronounce the word.

2. Use the diagram to write a description of the legs of an ant.

436

Strategic Intervention

Graphic Sources Explain that there are many kinds of graphic sources. In "Ant Facts," there is a diagram. To help students use the diagram, have them examine it before they begin reading. Have students point to these parts of the ant as you say them aloud: *head, abdomen, hind leg, foreleg, thorax, antennae, middle leg,* and *mandible.*

ELL

Access Content

Beginning/Intermediate For a Picture It! lesson on graphic sources, see ELL Teaching Guide, pp. 120–121.

Advanced Before students read "Ant Facts," have them look at the diagram and talk about the parts of an ant. Discuss the number of legs, antennae, body sections, and mandibles ants have.

Ant Facts

Skill Preview the title and the diagram. What do you think you will be reading about ants?

Have you ever observed an ant crawling across a sidewalk lugging food back to its colony? To you, the food is the tiniest scrap. But to the ant, its size and weight are tremendous. Ants can carry objects that weigh several times more than they do. That is only one of the amazing facts about ants.

There are thousands of different species of ants. Some harvest their own food. Some wage war. Some take slaves. Yet all ants share certain characteristics.

Strategy What are antennae? If you don't know, look at the diagram. If you want to find out how to pronounce the word *antennae*, in which reference source would you look?

An ant's body is divided into three sections: the head, the thorax, and the abdomen. An ant's head is large with two antennae, which are used for smelling and feeling. Its mouth has two sets of mandibles. One set is for carrying. The other is for chewing. The thorax is the middle part of the ant. It's connected to the abdomen by a small, waistlike section. The abdomen is large and oval-shaped.

Strategy What is a mandible? If you don't know, where could you look to find out?

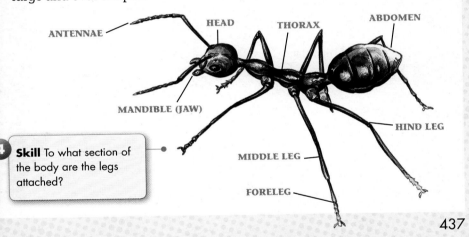

ANTENNAE   HEAD   THORAX   ABDOMEN
MANDIBLE (JAW)
HIND LEG
MIDDLE LEG
FORELEG

Skill To what section of the body are the legs attached?

437

Graphic Sources

- A **graphic source**, such as a picture, diagram, or chart, organizes information visually.
- Preview the graphic sources to help you predict what you will be reading about.

Directions Study the following diagram. Then answer the questions below.

antennae   head   thorax   abdomen
compound eyes
jaws
wings
walking legs   jumping legs

GRASSHOPPER

1. What is the purpose of this diagram?
   Possible answer: The diagram shows the different parts of a grasshopper's body.
2. What are the three parts of the grasshopper's body?
   The three parts are the abdomen, thorax, and head.
3. What do grasshoppers use to hop, walk, and fly?
   Grasshoppers use their jumping legs for hopping, walking legs for walking, and wings for flying.
4. How many legs does the grasshopper have? How does the diagram show you this?
   six; The diagram uses arrows and labels to show the legs.
5. What is the location of the grasshopper's two front legs? What other job might the front legs perform in addition to walking?
   close to the grasshopper's jaws; Possible answer: Grasshoppers might use the front legs to hold food while they eat.

Home Activity Your child used a graphic source to answer questions. Together, read a newspaper or magazine article that includes a graphic source. Ask your child to answer questions about the article based on the information shown in the graphic source.

▲ **Practice Book** p. 173

TEACH

1 SKILL Preview the article.

Think Aloud **MODEL** The title of the article tells me that it's about ants. The diagram gives me more specific information. It suggests that I'll be reading about the different parts of an ant's body.

2 STRATEGY Use graphic sources and other references to help understand the text.

Think Aloud **MODEL** From the text I know that an ant uses its antennae for smelling and feeling. However, I'm not sure what antennae are, so I will look at the diagram. Now I know what antennae are. I also know that I could look in a dictionary to find out how to pronounce the word.

PRACTICE AND ASSESS

3 STRATEGY A *mandible* is a jaw. I could look at the diagram or in a dictionary to find out what a *mandible* is.

4 SKILL thorax

WRITE Have students complete steps 1 and 2 of the Write to Read activity. Call on volunteers to read aloud their paragraphs and descriptions. Discuss how students used the diagram to help them.

Monitor Progress

⟳ Graphic Sources

If... students are unable to complete **Write to Read** on p. 436,	**then...** use Practice Book p. 173 to provide additional practice.

To learn more about these animals, students can use the keywords *ants*, *owls*, and *snakes* in a student-friendly search engine. Be sure to follow classroom rules for using the Internet.

ELL

Build Background Use ELL Poster 18 to build background and vocabulary for the lesson concept of adaptations.

▲ **ELL Poster** 18

Page 438a

LA.5.1.7.1 Use prior knowledge
LA.5.1.7.8 Use strategies to repair comprehension when self-monitoring, including using semantic organizers

438a   Adapting • Week 3

Build Background

ACTIVATE PRIOR KNOWLEDGE

HAVE STUDENTS BEGIN A SEMANTIC WEB about ants, owls, and snakes.

- Use a semantic web and write the word "Animals" in a large oval in the center. Write "Ants," "Owls," and "Snakes" in three medium-sized ovals.

- Invite students to brainstorm things they know about each animal. Record answers in small ovals. Add more ovals if necessary.

- Tell students that, as they read, they should look for other information to add to the web.

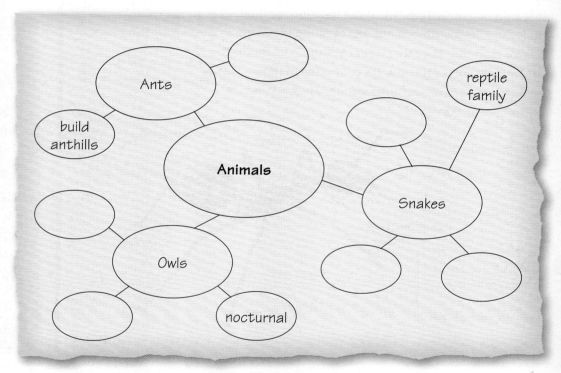

▲ **Graphic Organizer** 16

BACKGROUND BUILDING AUDIO This week's audio explores familiar animal adaptations. After students listen, discuss what students found most surprising.

Background Building Audio

Introduce Vocabulary

PREDICT DEFINITIONS

Read aloud the lesson vocabulary with students. Have students predict a definition for each word and write a sentence. Have students verify their predictions by looking up the word in a dictionary. If their sentences are incorrect, have them write other ones.

My mom *enables* my grandma to go grocery shopping by driving her to the store.

Doctors *specialize* in different areas of medical practice.

Water is *scarce* in the desert, so you should carry plenty of water if you go hiking.

My parents feel it is *critical* that I do my best in school.

When you have a cold, your nose can become full of *mucus*.

You should use *sterile* jars and lids if you can your own food.

At the end of the week, have students review their sentences and improve upon them based on what they learned.

Use the Multisyllabic Word Routine on p. DI·1 to help students read multisyllabic words.

Lesson Vocabulary

WORDS TO KNOW

T critical being important to the outcome of a situation

T enables gives ability, power, or means to; makes able

T mucus a slimy substance produced in the nose and throat to moisten and protect them

T scarce hard to get; rare

T specialize to develop in a special way

T sterile free from germs

MORE WORDS TO KNOW

aborigines the earliest known inhabitants of Australia

nauseating sickening; causing nausea

predator animal or person that lives by killing and eating other animals

T = Tested Word

Vocabulary

Directions Choose the word from the box that best matches each definition. Write the word on the line.

mucus — 1. a slimy substance produced in the nose and throat to moisten and protect them

sterile — 2. free from germs

enables — 3. gives ability, power, or means to; makes able

specialize — 4. to develop in a special way

critical — 5. being important to the outcome of a situation

Check the Words You Know
___critical
___enables
___mucus
___scarce
___specialize
___sterile

Directions Circle the word or group of words that has the same or nearly the same meaning as the first word.

Example: **melody**	words	(tune)	ringing
6. scarce	plenty	many	(rare)
7. critical	(important)	useful	relaxed
8. sterile	dirty	(germ-free)	bacteria
9. enables	teaches	makes empty	(allows)
10. specialize	stretch	(adapt)	organize

Write a Description
On a separate sheet of paper, write a description of a grasshopper or another insect with which you are familiar. Your description should include as many details as possible. Use as many vocabulary words as you can.

Descriptions should include words from the vocabulary list as well as details about a grasshopper or another familiar insect.

Home Activity Your child identified and used vocabulary words from *Exploding Ants*. Pretend each of you is a research scientist. Use the vocabulary words to discuss a new species of insect you have discovered together.

▲ **Practice Book** p. 174

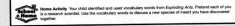

Page 438b

LA.5.1.6.1 Use new vocabulary that is introduced and taught directly

Vocabulary Strategy

OBJECTIVE

⊙ Use context clues and synonyms to determine word meaning.

INTRODUCE

Discuss the strategy for context clues using the steps on p. 438.

TEACH

- Have students read "Small But Mighty," paying attention to how context clues including synonyms and definitions within the text, are used to identify word meanings.

- Model using context clues to determine the meaning of *scarce*.

Think Aloud **MODEL** I see the clue word *or* immediately after *scarce*, which makes me think that the next word, *rare*, might be a synonym. It makes sense in the place of *scarce*—which must mean "rare."

DAY 2 Grouping Options

Reading

Whole Group Discuss the Question of the Day. Then use pp. 438–441.

Group Time Differentiated Instruction
Read *Exploding Ants.* See pp. 436f–436g for the small group lesson plan.

Whole Group Use p. 457a.

Language Arts
Use pp. 457e–457k.

Words to Know

- enables
- scarce
- specialize
- critical
- mucus
- sterile

Remember

Try the strategy. Then, if you need more help, use your glossary or dictionary.

Vocabulary Strategy
for Synonyms

Context Clues Synonyms are different words that mean almost the same thing. Sometimes an author writes a synonym near a difficult word to help readers understand the word.

1. Read the words and sentences around the unknown word. Is there a synonym?

2. To help find synonyms, look for *or* or *like*, or look for a word set off by commas.

3. Try using the synonym in place of the unknown word. Does this meaning make sense?

4. If these tips do not help, look up the unknown word in the dictionary or talk with a friend about it.

As you read "Small But Mighty," check the context of words you don't know. See if a nearby synonym gives a clue to a word's meaning.

LA.5.1.6.6 Identify "shades of meaning"
LA.5.1.6.8 Use knowledge of synonyms

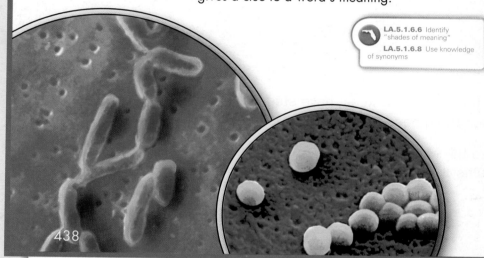

438

Strategic Intervention

⊙ **Context Clues** Have students find the synonym for *critical* (important) by first locating the clue word *(or)* in paragraph 2.

ELL

Access Content Use ELL Poster 18 to preteach vocabulary. Choose from the following to meet language proficiency levels.

Beginning Use the Multilingual Lesson Vocabulary list that begins on p. 272 of the ELL Teaching Guide, as well as other home-language resources to provide translations of the tested words.

Intermediate Before reading, have students use the vocabulary words to complete a word rating chart. After reading, ask them to revisit their charts and make the appropriate changes to their ratings.

Advanced Teach the lesson on pp. 438–439. Have students determine whether any of the tested words have cognates in their home languages.

Resources for home-language words may include parents, bilingual staff members, bilingual dictionaries, or online translation sources.

Small But M/GHTY

Bacteria are made up of just one cell. However, they adapt just like all living things. In fact, their size enables them to do this more quickly than larger animals. We have medicines to kill harmful bacteria. However, bacteria have changed so that they can stand up to many medicines. Medicines that still work against them are becoming scarce, or rare. Doctors use these medicines less often so bacteria will not "learn" how to live with them.

Different bacteria specialize in different ways. Some live in your gut and help you digest your food. Some change milk into cheese or sour cream. Still others are critical, or important, to the making of soil. They break down dead plant and animal matter.

Most bacteria are helpful, but a few kinds can harm us. One kind causes the disease called pneumonia. The bacteria get inside the body and reproduce quickly. They give off poisons, or wastes, in the body. The body fights back. It raises its temperature. It produces more mucus to protect the lining of organs. It is best to keep surfaces as sterile as possible so you do not touch harmful bacteria.

Words to Write

Choose an animal in the photographs or artwork from *Exploding Ants*. Write about what seems to make the animal special. Use as many words from the Words to Know list as you can.

439

CORRECTIVE FEEDBACK

LA.5.1.6.8 Use knowledge of synonyms to determine meanings of words

- **Question** Use the question below to address this FCAT tested standard. Have students write their answers on a sheet of paper.
- **Check** Scan students' responses by having them hold up their papers.
- **Correct** If necessary, provide corrective feedback.
- **Adjust** Pair students who have correctly identified the correct answer with students who did not for peer tutoring. Have them complete Practice Book p.175 together.

What words in paragraph 3 of "Small But Mighty" help you understand the word *pneumonia*?

PRACTICE AND ASSESS

- Have students determine the meanings of the remaining words and explain the context clues they used.
- Remind students that context doesn't work with every word. Students may have to use the glossary or a dictionary to help them.
- Return to the Predict Definitions activity on p. 438b and have students revise their predictions.
- Have students complete Practice Book p. 175.

WRITE Students should add a clue word and synonym for at least one of the list words related to the animal they chose.

Monitor Progress

Context Clues

If... students need more practice with the lesson vocabulary,	then... use Tested Vocabulary Cards.

Vocabulary · Context Clues

- **Context clues** include definitions, explanations, and **synonyms**.
- Synonyms are different words that mean the same or almost the same thing.
- Sometimes an author writes a synonym near a difficult word to help readers understand the word. To find synonyms, look for the words or, such as, and like, or for a phrase set off by commas.

Directions Read the following passage about insects. Then answer the questions below.

To some people, insects such as mosquitoes are simply pests. But many insects are useful. Honeybees, for example, make honey. They also pollinate plants by carrying pollen from one plant to another. This enables, or allows, the plant to grow and develop. Pollination is essential, or critical, for many things we eat. Growers use honeybees in apple orchards, for example. Beekeepers raise colonies, or communities, of bees.

Some insects eat garbage. Others specialize in or focus on eating harmful insects. Many types of butterflies are abundant, though some species are becoming scarce.

1. What word in the passage is a synonym for *enables*? How do you know it is a synonym?
   allows; The phrase "or allows" is set off by commas.

2. What suggests that *essential* and *critical* are synonyms?
   The phrase "or critical" is set off by commas and appears near the word essential.

3. The word *mosquitoes* follows the words *such as*. How do you know it is not a synonym for *insects*?
   Possible answer: Mosquitoes is an example of an insect, not a synonym for the word insect.

4. What is another word for *colonies*? What context clue helps you to identify the synonym?
   communities; The phrase "or communities" is set off by commas.

5. Rewrite the last sentence to provide a synonym for the word *scarce*.
   Possible answers: Many types of butterflies are abundant, though some are becoming scarce, or rare.

School Home Home Activity Your child identified and used synonyms to help him or her understand other words. Together, read an article about a scientific subject in a newspaper or magazine, noting any challenging vocabulary. Try to use synonyms and other context clues to clarify the meanings of these words.

▲ **Practice Book** p. 175

WORD AWARENESS Post this week's lesson vocabulary on a Word Wall or have students write the words and meanings in their Writing Logs for ready access during writing.

Prereading Strategies

GENRE STUDY

Expository Nonfiction

Exploding Ants is expository nonfiction, which gives information about the real world.

PREVIEW AND PREDICT

Have students preview the graphic sources and discuss the topics they think this selection will cover. Students should use lesson vocabulary words as they talk about what they expect to learn.

Strategy Response Log

Activate Prior Knowledge Have students record at least three things they know about animal adaptation. Students will check and, if needed, fix up their understanding in the Strategy Response Log activity on p. 447.

Use Strategies Have students record in their strategy response logs reading strategies they use during reading and tell why they use them.

exploding ants

by Joanne Settel, Ph.D.

Amazing **Facts** About How Animals Adapt

Genre — **Expository nonfiction** explains what certain things are and how they came to be or behave. As you read, notice how the author explains insect behavior.

440

Access Content Read aloud the subheads in the selection. (The words in leaves are also subheads.) Point to the pictures and help students name the animals and insects.

Consider having students read the selection summary in English or in students' home languages. See the Multilingual Summaries in the ELL Teaching Guide, pp. 124–126.

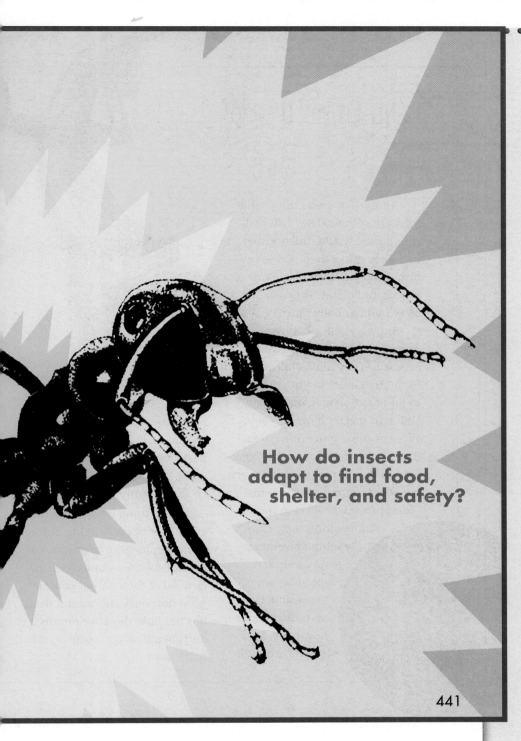

How do insects adapt to find food, shelter, and safety?

441

SET PURPOSE

Discuss the picture on p. 441. Point out the physical characteristics of the ant and discuss how they might help it survive. Have students tell what they hope to learn as they read the selection.

Remind students to use graphic sources as they read to help them understand the text.

STRATEGY RECALL

Students have now used these before-reading strategies:

- preview the selection to be aware of its genre, features, and possible content;
- activate prior knowledge about that content and what to expect of that genre;
- make predictions;
- set a purpose for reading.

Remind students to be aware of and flexibly use the during-reading strategies they have learned:

- link prior knowledge to new information;
- summarize text they have read so far;
- ask clarifying questions;
- answer questions they or others pose;
- check their predictions and either refine them or make new predictions;
- recognize the text structure the author is using, and use that knowledge to make predictions and increase comprehension;
- visualize what the author is describing;
- monitor their comprehension and use fix-up strategies.

After reading, students will use these strategies:

- summarize or retell the text;
- answer questions they or others pose;
- reflect to make new information become part of their prior knowledge.

 **AudioText**

 Pages 440–441

LA.5.1.7.1 Use prior knowledge to make predictions, and establish a purpose for reading

LA.5.2.2.1 Use information from text features (illustrations)

Guiding Comprehension

1 🔄 **Graphic Sources • Inferential**

Look at the photo of the lizard and snake on p. 442. What information does it provide?

It shows how a predator (the snake) captures its prey (the lizard).

Monitor Progress

🔄 Graphic Sources

If... students have difficulty interpreting graphic sources,	**then...** use the skill and strategy instruction on p. 443.

---

2 **Draw Conclusions • Inferential**

Why is it important for species to specialize in where they live or what they eat?

Possible response: It allows them to survive. If they all ate the same thing, or lived in the same place, some species wouldn't be able to survive.

Why animals do gross things

1

Animals often do things that seem gross to us. They eat foods that people would find nauseating. They make their homes in disgusting places and feed on mucus and blood. They swell or blow up their body parts.

But while these behaviors are nasty to us, they are critical to life on earth. They make it possible for many kinds of living things to find food, shelter, and safety. Different species make use of every possible space and gobble down every nutritious crumb of food in the natural world. If every species of animal ate the same kind of food, or lived in the same place, there simply wouldn't be enough to go around. It would become impossible for all of the species to survive. So instead, animals

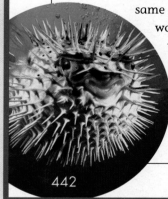

442

specialize. One predator eats flesh, while another feeds on blood.

As a result, when it comes to eating, nothing is wasted. Almost every part of every living animal, from skin to dung to mucus, can provide food for some other species. All of these things contain good nutrients. An animal that has the right digestive organs and chemicals can easily break them down.

E L L

Context Clues Point out the word *gross* in the first sentence on p. 442 and explain that it is an example of slang. Help them reread the rest of the paragraph and use context to guess what *gross* means. *(vulgar or disgusting)*

Page 442

LA.5.1.7.3 Determine the main idea or essential message through inferring

LA.5.2.2.1 Use information from text features (e.g., illustrations)

Similarly, when it comes to finding shelter, animals make use of any hole or space or building material that they can find. For example, the smelly, slimy holes and organs inside the body of a bigger animal can often provide a warm, protective home for small animals like insects.

Finally, animals often put their body parts to good use. Animals don't have bags to carry things around, tools to open things, knives to cut things, or weapons to defend themselves. Instead, they use their own bodies in ways that seem gross to us. By stretching, swelling, and bursting open, they can trick predators, store food, swallow big gulps, and defend their nests.

443

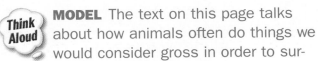

Graphic Sources

FCAT TESTED SKILL

DURING READING

TEACH

- Explain to students that graphic sources such as the photos on this page, can help strengthen their understanding of the text.
- Model using graphic sources alongside text on p. 442.

Think Aloud **MODEL** The text on this page talks about how animals often do things we would consider gross in order to survive. The photo shows how a snake uses its body to capture a lizard by wrapping its body around it. It is gross, but it shows an example of what animals need to do to capture prey.

PRACTICE AND ASSESS

Have students explain how another graphic source on pp. 442–443 helps clarify or add to information given in the text. *(Possible response: The photo of the frog, which can stick out its tongue a very long way, shows me that animals put their body parts to good use not only to scare off predators but to capture prey.)*

EYE ON FCAT

CORRECTIVE FEEDBACK

LA.5.1.7.1 Explain purpose of text features (illustrations)

- **Question** Use Whiteboard or Transparency 18a, items 1–3, to ask questions that address this standard in FCAT format. Have students write their answers on a sheet of paper.
- **Check** Scan students' responses by having them hold up their papers.
- **Correct** If necessary, provide corrective feedback and review pp. 436–437.

> **1** Why does the author include images of honey ant repletes in this selection?
>
> Ⓐ to persuade the reader to dislike repletes
> Ⓑ to show how strong the repletes' claws are
> Ⓒ to help readers understand how the repletes look
> Ⓓ to demonstrate how people can use the repletes for food

▲ **FCAT Whiteboard Activity** 18a/
FCAT Transparency 18a

Exploding Ants

443

off off

Guiding Comprehension

3 **Author's Purpose • Inferential**

What is the author's purpose on p. 444, paragraphs 1–3?

The author's purpose is to explain what repletes are and to tell how they use their bodies to store food.

Monitor Progress

REVIEW Author's Purpose

If... students have difficulty identifying the author's purpose,	then... use the skill and strategy instruction on p. 445.

4 **Graphic Sources • Inferential**

What does the picture at the top of pp. 444–445 illustrate?

It illustrates how repletes feed, swell, hang from the roof of the nest, and feed other ants.

Tech Files ONLINE

Students can type the keywords *honey ants* in a student-friendly search engine to learn more about these fascinating insects. Be sure to follow classroom guidelines for Internet use.

Swelling, expanding and exploding Bodies

Living honey jars

The swollen sacs of nectar that hang from the roof of a honey ant nest are actually alive. They're the fat bodies of ants that have turned themselves into living honey jars.

The "honey jars" are worker ants that store food and are known as *repletes*. Repletes spend their lives hanging upside-down from the roof of their nest waiting to feed or be fed. Their bodies provide sterile, airtight food containers.

It is when the colony has lots of extra food that the repletes get fed. Each replete receives regurgitated, or spit-up, food from hundreds of ordinary worker ants. The food consists of a golden liquid filled with a predigested mix of termite parts and plant nectar.

As they take in more and more food, the repletes swell. Soon their rear ends or abdomens are as large

444

ELL

Access Content Explain that *nectar* is a sweet liquid made by flowers. It is gathered by bees and honey ants to make honey. Ask students what the nectar is mixed with to make the golden liquid the ants eat. *(termite parts)*

Page 444

LA.5.1.7.1 Explain purpose of text features (illustrations)
LA.5.1.7.2 Identify author's purpose
LA.5.2.2.1 Locate, explain, and use information from text features (illustrations)

as small grapes. The swollen ants then climb to the roof of the nest and continue to eat. They remain on the roof for months, hanging by their claws, barely able to move. If for some reason a replete falls down, other workers must help drag its large, balloonlike body back up to the ceiling.

When food supplies outside the nest run low, the repletes become the feeders. Hungry nest mates now gather round for food. They touch the repletes' antennae with their own. The repletes then regurgitate big drops of golden honey.

The extra food provided by the repletes is important to the colony survival. Honey ants live in large colonies in dry desert regions of North America, Africa, and Australia, where food is often scarce. Storing food in their living honey jars

enables the colony to make it through the hottest, driest desert seasons.

The sweet "honey" of the honey ant repletes is not only food for other ants, but also for some people. The aborigines in Australia consider the swollen honey ants to be sweet treats and pop them into their mouths like candy.

445

Biomes

TIME FOR Science

A *biome* is an ecological system with its own kind of climate, plants, animals, and other living things. There are two types of aquatic biomes, freshwater and marine. The forest biome is tremendously important to humans, but is constantly threatened by pollution and deforestation. The desert biome covers areas of the Earth's surface that get less than 50 cm of precipitation per year. The grasslands biome is characterized by grasses as opposed to large shrubs or trees. Tundra, the coldest biome, consists of treeless plains in the arctic regions of the world.

SKILLS ←→ STRATEGIES IN CONTEXT

Author's Purpose REVIEW

FCAT TESTED SKILL

TEACH

- Remind students that authors write for one or more reasons.
- Explain that an author's purpose can affect the way you read and comprehend text.

Think Aloud **MODEL** The descriptions of honey ant nests and repletes on p. 444, paragraphs 1–3, contain many facts that I need to read carefully to understand. This tells me that the author is writing to inform.

PRACTICE AND ASSESS

- Have students identify text features that indicate that the author is writing to inform. *(Possible response: The selection has a lot of pictures. They work with the words to give information about animal adaptations.)*
- To assess, use Practice Book p. 176.

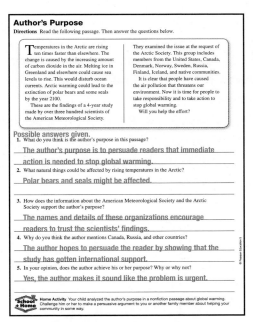

▲ **Practice Book** p. 176

Page 445
LA.5.1.7.1 Explain purpose of text features (illustrations)
LA.5.1.7.2 Identify author's purpose

Guiding Comprehension

5 👁 **Vocabulary • Context Clues**

What is a synonym for the word *mandibles* on p. 446? How do you know?

Jaws. The clue word *or* signals another meaning for *mandibles*.

Monitor Progress

👁 **Context Clues**

If... students have difficulty finding a synonym for *mandibles*,	**then...** use vocabulary strategy instruction on p. 447.

---

6 **Compare and Contrast • Inferential**

What do *Camponotus* ants and *Globitermes sulfureus* termites have in common?

When threatened, both animals burst open and spray a harmful liquid on their opponents.

7 **Draw Conclusions • Inferential**

Text to World **Explain why adaptation is important for all animal species, not just insects.**

Possible response: Adaptation is important to all animals' survival. Specialized features help animals avoid predators, find food, and build shelters.

Exploding ants

Soldier ants of the species *Camponotus saundersi* are designed to explode. These ants make themselves burst to defend their colony from other invading insects. When ants explode, they spray out a sticky chemical that kills or glues their opponents in place.

Camponotus ants manufacture their deadly chemicals inside their own bodies. The chemicals are stored in two big sacs called *mandibular glands*. These glands take up most of the ant's body opening, just under the mandibles, or jaws.

446

ELL

Access Content Tell students that an *intruder* is a person or animal that forces its way into a place where it was not invited.

Page 446

LA.5.1.6.3 Use context clues to determine meanings of unfamiliar words

LA.5.1.7.3 Determine the main idea or essential message through inferring

LA.5.1.7.7 Compare and contrast

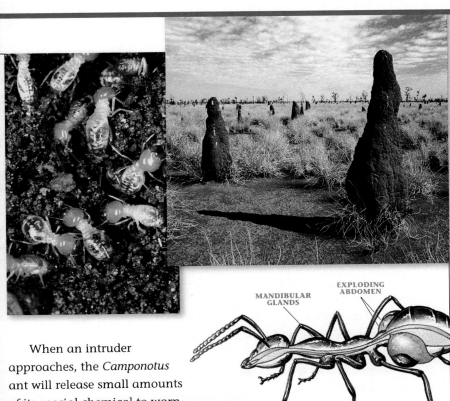

MANDIBULAR GLANDS

EXPLODING ABDOMEN

When an intruder approaches, the *Camponotus* ant will release small amounts of its special chemical to warn away the invader. If the intruder actually attacks, however, the *Camponotus* ant takes the next step. It violently contracts, or

tightens, its muscles, bursting open and spewing out its deadly chemicals.

Camponotus ants aren't the only insect with this unusual behavior. It turns out that soldiers of the termite species *Globitermes sulfureus* are also exploders, bursting open when threatened and spraying a sticky yellow liquid all over their opponents.

6

7

447

Develop Vocabulary

PRACTICE LESSON VOCABULARY

Students orally respond to each question.

1. Can *mucus* be found in the antennae or the mouth? *(mouth)*

2. Is a *sterile* bandage clean or filthy? *(clean)*

3. Are water and food *critical* to adaptation or to survival? *(survival)*

BUILD CONCEPT VOCABULARY

Review previous concept words with students. Ask if students have come across any words today in their reading or elsewhere that they would like to add to the Animal Adaptations Concept Web, such as *spewing* and *threatened*.

FCAT TESTED SKILL

VOCABULARY STRATEGY

Context Clues

TEACH

Model finding a synonym for the word *mandibles* on p. 446.

Think Aloud

MODEL Some sentences contain a synonym near a difficult word to help readers understand that word. Within the same sentence that *mandibles* appears, I see the clue word *or* which tells me that *jaws* is a synonym for *mandibles*, or another word that means the same. Sometimes the context gives an example of the unknown word or an action of the unknown word, which helps me figure out its meaning.

PRACTICE AND ASSESS

Have students find a synonym for *intruder* on p. 447, paragraph 1. *(invader)* Then have students find an example of the context giving an example that defines the word. *(exploders)*

Strategy Response Log

Monitor Comprehension Have students check the three things they wrote about animal adaptation. (See p. 440.) Then have students record two new pieces of information about ants in their semantic.

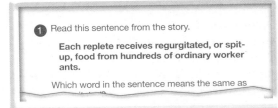
EYE ON FCAT

CORRECTIVE FEEDBACK

LA.5.1.6.8 Use knowledge of synonyms to determine meanings of words

• **Question** Use Whiteboard or Transparency 18b, items 1–3, to ask questions that address this standard in FCAT format. Have students write their answers on a sheet of paper.

• **Check** Scan students' responses by having them hold up their papers.

• **Correct** If necessary, provide corrective feedback and review pp. 414–415.

1 Read this sentence from the story.

Each replete receives regurgitated, or spit-up, food from hundreds of ordinary worker ants.

Which word in the sentence means the same as

▲ **FCAT Whiteboard Activity** 18b/ **FCAT Transparency** 18b

If you want to teach this selection in two sessions, stop here.

Guiding Comprehension

If you are teaching this selection in two days, discuss the graphic sources so far and review the vocabulary.

8 🎯 **Graphic Sources • Critical**

What do the illustrations on p. 448 show you about owls that the text does not?

They show how an owl looks, its habitat, and its young.

Monitor Progress

🎯 **Graphic Sources**

If... students have difficulty using graphic sources to improve their understanding,	**then...** use the skill and strategy instruction on p. 449.

---

9 **Cause and Effect • Literal**

What causes owls to spit up pellets?

The owl swallows its prey whole. It digests the soft, nutritious parts and it spits up the rest as waste, in the form of pellets.

Page 448

LA.5.1.7.1 Explain purpose of text features (illustrations)
LA.5.1.7.4 Identify cause-and-effect relationships
LA.5.2.2.1 Explain and use information from text features (illustrations)

DAY 3 Grouping Options

Reading
Whole Group Discuss the Question of the Day.

Group Time Differentiated Instruction
Read *Exploding Ants.* See pp. 436f–436g for the small group lesson plan.

Whole Group Discuss the Reader Response questions on p. 452. Then use p. 457a.

Language Arts
Use pp. 457e–457k.

Getting it down
A ball of bones

Every evening before it goes off to hunt, an owl spits up a few balls of fur and bones. The balls, or pellets, are what's left of the owl's last meal. An owl preys on small animals, such as mice, moles, shrews, birds, and insects. When the feathered predator captures its prey, it doesn't take the time to kill its victim and then pick out the fleshy, nutritious parts. It simply swallows the animal whole. Then the owl digests all the soft stuff, the muscles and organs. The

rest, the fur, feathers, teeth, and bones, are wastes. The owl gets rid of these by regurgitating a pellet.

Owls normally spit up two pellets a day. Over time the pellets pile up and form large heaps under the owl's roosting, or resting, site. By examining these

448

ELL

Extend Language Explain that *prey* is an animal that is hunted by another animal for food. "To prey" means to hunt for food.

OWL PELLETS

pellets, scientists can learn all about an owl's diet. A pellet of a barn owl, for example, usually contains entire skeletons of two or three mammals, lots of fur, and insect parts. That means that a barn owl gulps down around six small mammals a day.

Six small mammals at two to six ounces each seems like a lot of meat for a bird that weighs less than one pound. The twelve-ounce owl, however, doesn't get fat on this feast. Most of its food is just the fur and bones that get chucked up as round pellets.

449

Human Adaptations

TIME FOR Science

The human body adapts to a wide range of environmental conditions. This enables us to survive in most regions of the world, despite climate and humidity. When in high altitudes, our bodies adapt so that we are able to receive the oxygen we need. The human body has also developed behaviors to help us survive in extreme temperatures such as staying in motion to ward off cold, and sweating to survive in extreme heat.

SKILLS ↔ STRATEGIES IN CONTEXT

Graphic Sources Monitor/Fix Up

FCAT TESTED SKILL

TEACH

Have students use the illustrations on p. 448 to go beyond the text to improve their understanding about owls.

Think Aloud

MODEL The text mostly talks about how owls hunt and digest their prey. The illustrations add to my understanding by showing what young owls look like and where they live. At first, I a pictured a pellet as a small smooth ball but the picture shows that they are, like the author says, hunks of fur and bones.

PRACTICE AND ASSESS

Have students work in pairs to analyze the illustration on p. 449 and discuss what it shows. *(what owl pellets look like)*

Page 449

LA.5.1.6.1 Use new vocabulary
LA.5.1.7.1 Explain purpose of text features (illustrations)
LA.5.2.2.1 Explain and use information from text features (illustrations)

EXTEND SKILLS

Jargon

Remind students that jargon is the language of a special group. Scientists have their own unique jargon. For example, *repletes* is a scientific term that refers to honey ants. Have students find examples of other scientific jargon in *Exploding Ants*.

Guiding Comprehension

10 **Author's Purpose • Inferential**

The author's main purpose with this selection is to inform. What additional purpose does she have? Explain.

Possible response: To entertain. You can tell from the informal tone she sometimes uses, like "Gulping down a whole pig or chicken... [is] no big deal."

11 **Cause and Effect • Inferential**

Why can a snake eat large prey whole?

A snake's jaw can open very wide.

12 **Compare and Contrast • Inferential**

Text to World **What animal adaptations have you observed or heard about in the world around you?**

Possible response: I've noticed birds using bits of paper or cloth in their nests. I think birds adapted to living in cities by using materials that were available to them.

Strategy Response Log

Summarize When students finish reading the selection, provide this prompt: What kinds of amazing facts are discussed in *Exploding Ants*? Write your response as a brief summary of the selection.

Use Strategies Meet with students to review their list of the reading strategies they realized they were using as they read.

Pages 450–451

LA.5.1.6.1 Use new vocabulary

LA.5.1.7.2 Identify author's purpose

LA.5.1.7.4 Identify cause-and-effect relationships

LA.5.1.7.7 Compare and contrast

LA.5.1.7.8 Use strategies to repair comprehension when self-monitoring, including summarizing and questioning, and clarifying by checking sources

Big, big gulps

10 Gulping down a whole pig or chicken may sound like an impossible task for a snake. But it's no big deal for a twenty-foot python. In fact, many snakes often swallow food much bigger than their own heads. Even very small snakes may feast on mice, rats, birds, frogs, and whole eggs.

The snake's ability to swallow big prey results from the special design of its jaw. The bones of its mouth are loosely joined to its skull. A stretchy strip of tissue called a *ligament* holds together the two halves of the lower jaw. When the snake swallows its dinner, its mouth can stretch wide open. The lower jawbones spread apart and each bone moves separately to pull the prey into the mouth.

Snakes generally try to gulp down their food headfirst. This causes the prey's legs to fold back as the snake swallows. In addition, the snake's sharp teeth are curved

450

E L L

Understanding Idioms Explain that the phrase *grab a meal* means "to have something to eat." Ask students how often most snakes "grab a meal." *(once a week)*

backward, preventing the squirming prey from wiggling back out. As the snake works its food down its throat, it pushes its windpipe out of its mouth. This means that it doesn't have to stop breathing as it swallows.

Because snakes eat such big meals, they don't need to eat every day. Most snakes only have to grab a meal once a week, and some only eat once every month. Large pythons hold the record, however. After feasting on a pig or chicken, these huge snakes can go for more than a year without any other food!

451

STRATEGY SELF-CHECK

Monitor and Fix-Up

Have students review the graphic sources to clarify any questions or misunderstandings they may have about the selection. Use Practice Book p. 177.

SELF-CHECK

Students can ask themselves these questions to assess their ability to use the skill and strategy.

- Did I use the illustrations to help me understand the text as I read?
- Did I make sure I understood the selection as I read it?
- Did I use the illustrations to help me clarify any questions or misunderstandings?

Monitor Progress
 **Graphic Sources**

| **If...** students have difficulty using graphic sources to monitor and fix-up comprehension, | **then...** use the Reteach Lesson on p. 457b. |

Develop Vocabulary

PRACTICE LESSON VOCABULARY

Have students orally respond *yes* or *no* to each question and provide a reason for each answer.

1. **Is water *scarce* in the desert?** *(Yes; water is hard to find.)*

2. **Does an animal *specialize* in order to digest its food?** *(No; an animal will specialize in order to survive in its environment.)*

3. **Is a frog's slimy skin the main thing that *enables* it to catch insects?** *(No; a frog's long, sticky tongue helps him catch insects.)*

BUILD CONCEPT VOCABULARY

Review previous concept words with students. Ask if students have come across any words today in their reading or elsewhere that they would like to add to the Animal Adaptations concept web, such as *prey* and *design*.

Graphic Sources

- A **graphic source,** such as a picture, diagram, or chart, organizes information visually.
- Preview the graphic sources to help you predict what you will be reading about.

Directions Study the following map. Then answer the questions below.

The Fall Migration of Monarch Butterflies (September – November)

Possible answers given for 1, 2, 5.

1. What does the map show you?
   The map shows the migration patterns of monarch butterflies.

2. In what kind of article might you see this graphic source?
   It might appear in an encyclopedia entry about butterflies.

3. In what main direction do the butterflies migrate?
   They travel towards the south.

4. How many months does the process of migration take? How do you know?
   three; The map's title tells the timetable for migration.

5. Good readers make sure they understand what they read, including graphic sources. If you were confused by something in this graphic source, what could you do?
   I could check an encyclopedia entry about butterflies or monarchs.

Home Activity Your child used a graphic source to find information, and he or she also suggested how to respond to confusion about some part of the graphic source. Read a nonfiction article about animals with your child. Discuss what steps he or she could take to clear up confusion about some aspect of the article.

▲ **Practice Book** p. 177

Reader Response

Open for Discussion Personal Response

MODEL I'd call it gross, but I'm not a scientist. A scientist may have a different opinion than I do.

Comprehension Check Critical Response

1. Possible response: I might organize it by showing a picture of each animal with a caption describing what it is doing. **Author's Purpose**

2. Possible response: The illustrations show animal adaptations, such as the "living honey jars." **Graphic Sources**

3. Barn owls eat so much because most of their food is indigestible fur and bones. **Monitor and Fix Up**

4. Possible response: If animals did not *specialize* and all ate the same things, then food would become very *scarce*. **Vocabulary**

THINK AND EXPLAIN For test practice, assign a 5 minute time limit. For assessment, see the Scoring Rubric at the right.

Retell

Have students retell *Exploding Ants*.

Monitor Progress

Check Retelling Rubric 4 3 2 1

If... students have difficulty retelling the selection,	then... use the Retelling Cards and the Scoring Rubric for Retelling on p. 453 to assist fluent retelling.

SUCCESS PREDICTOR

Check Retelling Have students use the selection illustrations to guide their retellings. For more ideas on assessing students' retellings, see the ELL and Transition Handbook.

Reader Response

Open for Discussion This selection may not be appropriate for dinner table conversation. But would a true scientist call it gross? What is your opinion?

1. *Exploding Ants* begins with a general idea: "Why animals do gross things." Then the author gives specific examples that show why. Is this the way you would organize a selection like this, or do you have other ideas? **Think Like an Author**

2. The title includes the words "Amazing Facts About How Animals Adapt." Look at the illustrations and discuss how they help explain the title. **Graphic Sources**

3. Why do barn owls eat about six small mammals a day, and how can they accomplish this amazing feat? Reread pages 448–449 and discuss the details. **Monitor and Fix Up**

4. The author states that animals *specialize* in what they eat. How does this specialization help them? What would happen if they did not specialize? Use words from the Words to Know list to answer these questions. **Vocabulary**

Think and Explain How do soldier ants operate? Use details and information on pages 446–447 to write a task list for a loyal soldier ant.

Meet author Joanne Settel on page 767.

LA.5.1.7.5 Explain text structure
LA.5.2.2.1 Use text features

452

THINK AND EXPLAIN TWO-POINT SCORING RUBRIC
Top-Score Response A top-score response will use details from pp. 446–447 of the selection to list steps a soldier ant takes to defend the colony from invaders.

Example of a Top-Score Response (1) Watch closely for intruders. (2) Release chemicals as a warning to stay away. (3) If attacked, tighten muscles to explode abdomen and spray attacker.

For additional rubrics, see p. WA10.

Page 452
LA.5.1.7.5 Explain text structure
LA.5.2.2.1 Use text features (illustrations)

Write Now

Animal Story

More FCAT WRITING+
See *The Grammar and Writing Book*, pages 152–157.

Prompt

The author of *Exploding Ants* describes unusual or unexpected animal behaviors. Think about your own experiences observing animals. Now write a story about an animal whose behavior surprised you.

Writing Trait

Effective **word choice** means using exact nouns, strong verbs, and vivid adjectives for your story.

Student Model

Strong, precise nouns, verbs, and adjectives show effective <u>word choice</u>.

> One summer, we had a family of barred owls living in the leafy tops of the maple trees in our yard. We watched the drama unfold as Mama Owl taught her young owlets to fly and hunt.

Events are told in order shown with time-order phrases.

> Over time, the hungry hunters picked our neighborhood clean of mice, snakes, and other small animals. Now the alley cats were lean and hungry.

> One day, an owl spied a tasty treat in the grass—a long, slithery snake. The owl swooped down, gripped the snake in its talons, and flew off in triumph.

Conclusion reveals surprise asked for in prompt.

> Imagine its disappointment when the owl discovered that its prize was, in fact, a piece of garden hose!

Use the model to help you write your own animal story.

LA.5.3.3.3 Create interest by modifying word choices
LA.5.4.1.2 Write an expressive form

453

Write Now

Look at the Prompt Explain that each sentence in the prompt has a purpose.

- Sentence 1 presents a topic.
- Sentence 2 suggests students think about the topic.
- Sentence 3 tells what to write—a story.

Strategies to Develop Word Choice

Have students

- draw a picture of or visualize their animal and list details.
- use vivid words to describe the animal and its actions.

NO: funny skin
YES: wrinkled, grey hide
NO: got the snake.
YES: swooped down on the snake.

For additional suggestions and rubric, see pp. 457g–457h.

Writer's Checklist

☑ **Focus** Do all sentences help develop the story?

☑ **Organization** Are events told in logical sequence?

☑ **Support** Do details help readers visualize things?

☑ **Conventions** Are verb tenses consistent?

Page 453
LA.5.3.3.3 Create interest by modifying word choices
LA.5.4.1.2 Write an expressive form (short story)

Scoring Rubric | Expository Retelling

Rubric 4 3 2 1	4	3	2	1
Connections	Makes connections and generalizes beyond the text	Makes connections to other events, texts, or experiences	Makes a limited connection to another event, text, or experience	Makes no connection to another event, text, or experience
Author's Purpose	Elaborates on author's purpose	Tells author's purpose with some clarity	Makes some connection to author's purpose	Makes no connection to author's purpose
Topic	Describes the main topic	Identifies the main topic with some details early in retelling	Identifies the main topic	Retelling has no sense of topic
Important Ideas	Gives accurate information about events, steps, and ideas using details and key vocabulary	Gives accurate information about events, steps, and ideas with some detail and key vocabulary	Gives limited or inaccurate information about events, steps, and ideas	Gives no information about events, steps, and ideas
Conclusions	Draws conclusions and makes inferences to generalize beyond the text	Draws conclusions about the text	Is able to draw few conclusions about the text	Is unable to draw conclusions or make inferences about the text

Retelling Plan

☑ **Week 1** Assess Strategic Intervention students.

☑ **Week 2** Assess Advanced students.

☑ **This week assess Strategic Intervention students.**

☐ **Week 4** Assess On-Level students.

☐ **Week 5** Assess any students you have not yet checked during this unit.

Use the Retelling Chart on p. TR17 to record retelling.

Selection Test To assess with *Exploding Ants*, use Selection Tests, pp. 69–72.

Fresh Reads for Differentiated Test Practice For weekly leveled practice, use pp. 103–108.

SUCCESS PREDICTOR

Science in Reading

PREVIEW/USE TEXT FEATURES

As students preview "The Creature from the Adapting Lagoon," have them look at the introduction, subheads, and illustrations. After they preview ask:

● **How can you tell that this is a serious scientific experiment?** *(Possible response: It was created by NASA for use in fifth-grade science classes.)*

● **How do the step-by-step instructions help you understand the experiment?** *(Possible response: The steps break the procedure into parts, which makes it easier to understand.)*

Link to Science

Set out the needed materials. Then read the purpose aloud and make sure students understand the task before they begin.

DAY 4   Grouping Options

Reading
Whole Group Discuss the Question of the Day.

Group Time Differentiated Instruction
Read "The Creature from the Adapting Lagoon." See pp. 436f–436g for the small group lesson plan.

Whole Group Use p. 457a.

Language Arts
Use pp. 457e–457k.

Science in Reading

Experiment

Genre

● An experiment is a trial or test used to find out about something.

● Most experiments deal with some kind of science.

Text Features

● The author states the purpose of the experiment and the materials needed. Then come step-by-step instructions.

● Scan the steps to get an idea of what the experiment is about.

Link to Science

Experiments are at the heart of science. Scientists use them to discover and test new ideas. Perform the experiment yourself and share your results with the class.

THE CREATURE FROM THE
Adapting Lagoon

from www.nasa.gov

This science experiment is from the National Aeronautics and Space Administration (NASA). It's intended for fifth-grade students in a science class, but anyone can do it. All you need is thought and imagination.

SC.G.2.2.1.1 Know that adaptations may increase the survival of a species

454

Content-Area Vocabulary	Science
adaptations	changes in structure, form, or habits to suit conditions Adaptations may be inherited within a species to increase rates of reproduction and survival.
criteria	rules or standards for making a judgment
predators	animals that live by killing and eating other animals

Page 454

LA.5.1.7.1 Explain purpose of text features
LA.5.2.2.1 Locate, explain, and use information from text features (subheadings and illustrations)
LA.5.6.1.1 Read and interpret informational text for a variety of purposes (multi-step directions)

PURPOSE

To design an animal with adaptations to a specific environment

MATERIALS

pencil, colored pencils, or markers

construction or drawing paper

science journal

PROCEDURE

1. Read over the criteria and background information.
2. Brainstorm possible creature designs that would meet the criteria listed. Check off the criteria that can be incorporated into the design.
3. Select the design that best meets the criteria.
4. Illustrate your creature in the science journal and describe each appendage and how it is used.

Graphic Sources How do the illustrations help you imagine the experiment?

455

Animal Experiments

TIME FOR Science

By experimenting with animals, scientists have gained data that show how humans will react to traveling and living in space. In 1948, in White Sands, New Mexico, a rhesus macaque monkey named Albert was launched into space in a V2 rocket. At that time, no one knew whether humans could survive space travel. Experimenting with animals helped scientists find the answer. Today, scientists take animals into space to find answers to questions concerning diverse topics such as genetics and microgravity.

EXPERIMENT

Use the sidebar on p. 454 to guide discussion.

- Explain to students that an experiment gives step-by-step instructions for performing a test or investigation.
- Point out that the steps are usually numbered, but they could be presented with clue words such as *first*, *next*, *then*, and *finally*.
- Discuss with students the importance of following the steps in order and adjusting reading rate when trying to solve problems or as in doing experiments.

Audio CD AudioText

Graphic Sources

Possible response: The illustrations show some of the criteria that the design should meet.

Page 455

LA.5.1.7.1 Explain the purpose of text features (graphics)
LA.5.6.1.1 Read and interpret informational text for a variety of purposes (multi-step directions and performing a task)

ELL

Access Content Preview the selection by reading aloud the title and the Introduction. Point out that students will be reading a science experiment. Have them take turns reading the subheads aloud. Identify the meanings of *procedure* ("way of doing something") and *criteria* ("rules for making a judgment"). Ask students to use the pictures to help them predict what the experiment will be about.

Strategies for Nonfiction

USE SUBHEADS Explain to students that a subhead lets the reader know what information he or she will be reading. When a selection has subheads, such as the boxed subheads in "The Creature from the Adapting Lagoon," we can use them to locate information to answer test questions. Provide the following strategy.

Use the Strategy

1. Read the test question and locate a keyword or phrase.
2. Scan the subheads in the experiment, looking for matches to your keyword or phrase.
3. When you find a match, read the information to find an answer to the test question.

GUIDED PRACTICE Have students discuss how they would use the strategy to answer the following question.

What is the goal of "The Creature from the Adapting Lagoon" experiment?

INDEPENDENT PRACTICE After students answer the following test question, discuss the process they used to find information.

Which criteria will you focus on when designing your animal's eating adaptation?

CRITERIA

- Animal lives in water.
- It can move quickly away from its predators.
- It tests its food before eating it.
- It can break apart hard bits of food.
- It loves to eat shelled animals.
- It has appendages to hold its young.
- It can defend itself easily against predators.
- It can create water currents to bring food to its mouth.
- It has a very large body.
- It can walk on the seafloor for kilometers without stopping.
- It breathes air.

 Monitor & Fix Up How can you organize the criteria?

456

ELL

Test Practice Write the Independent Practice test question on the board. Work with students to identify a keyword *(criteria)* that they could use for their answer search. Have students scan the subheads, looking for the keyword. Ask students to answer the test question in a complete sentence.

Page 456
LA.5.1.7.8 Use strategies to repair comprehension when self-monitoring
LA.5.2.2.1 Locate and use information from text features (subheadings)
LA.5.2.2.2 Use information from the text to answer questions

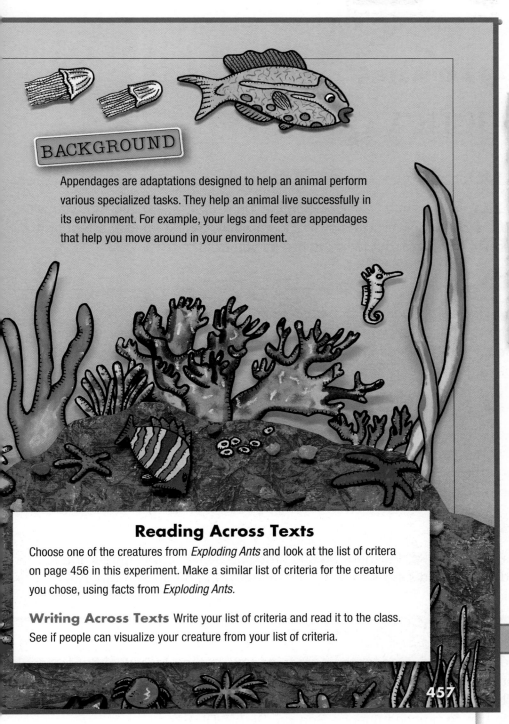

BACKGROUND

Appendages are adaptations designed to help an animal perform various specialized tasks. They help an animal live successfully in its environment. For example, your legs and feet are appendages that help you move around in your environment.

Reading Across Texts

Choose one of the creatures from *Exploding Ants* and look at the list of criteria on page 456 in this experiment. Make a similar list of criteria for the creature you chose, using facts from *Exploding Ants*.

Writing Across Texts Write your list of criteria and read it to the class. See if people can visualize your creature from your list of criteria.

457

CONNECT TEXT TO TEXT

Reading Across Texts

Read the criteria list on p. 456 aloud. Discuss with students the focus of each criterion *(animal's habitat, defense mechanism, eating habits, mobility)*. Have students use this information to help them develop criteria lists for their creatures from *Exploding Ants*.

Writing Across Texts Have students take turns reading aloud their criteria lists. Encourage students to listen to the complete list before trying to guess the creature.

Monitor and Fix Up

Possible response: I would definitely reread the criteria before I begin the experiment. I would organize the criteria by categories such as physical needs or special skills.

Page 457

LA.5.1.7.7 Compare and contrast elements in multiple texts
LA.5.4.2.1 Write in a variety of informational/expository forms
LA.5.4.2.2 Record information (lists) related to a topic

Fluency Assessment Plan

- ☑ **Week 1** Assess Advanced students.
- ☑ **Week 2** Assess Strategic Intervention students.
- ☑ **This week assess On-Level students.**
- ☐ **Week 4** Assess Strategic Intervention students.
- ☐ **Week 5** Assess any students you have not yet checked during this unit.

Set individual goals for students to enable them to reach the year-end goal.

- Current Goal: 120–128 wcpm
- Year-End Goal: 140 wcpm

English language learners may be able to decode some English words but still not know the meanings. Help students recognize that they will understand sentences better and read more fluently as they learn more English words.

 Fluency Coach CD To develop fluent readers, use Fluency Coach.

Page 457a
LA.5.1.5.1 Demonstrate the ability to read grade level text
LA.5.1.5.2 Adjust reading rate based on purpose and text difficulty

DAY 5 Grouping Options

Reading
Whole Group
Revisit the Question of the Week.

Group Time
Differentiated Instruction
Reread this week's Leveled Readers. See pp. 436f–436g for the small group lesson plan.

Whole Group
Use p. 457b–457c.

Language Arts
Use pp. 457d–457l.

TEMPO AND RATE
Fluency

DAY 1

Model Reread aloud "Snake Scientist" on p. 436m. Explain that you will read the nonfiction article slowly and carefully, paying special attention to scientific words. Model for students as you read.

DAY 2

Echo Reading Read aloud paragraphs 2 and 3 on p. 444. Have students notice how you adjust your rate for scientific words, such as *repletes* and *regurgitated.* Then lead students in three echo readings of paragraphs 2 and 3, p. 444.

DAY 3

Model Read aloud p. 446. Have students notice how you enunciate the words *mandibular glands* and *mandibles* that convey scientific information. Have students practice as a class by leading them in three echo readings.

DAY 4

Partner Reading Partners practice reading aloud p. 446 three times. Students should read slowly and confidently and offer each other feedback.

Monitor Progress | Check Fluency WCPM

As students reread, monitor their progress toward their individual fluency goals. Current Goal: 120–128 words correct per minute. End-of-Year Goal: 140 WCPM. Have library books or other texts available at a variety of reading levels for students to use to practice fluency. See pp. DI·57–DI·58.

If... students cannot read fluently at a rate of 120–128 words correct per minute,
then... make sure students practice with text at their independent level. Provide additional fluency practice, pairing nonfluent readers with fluent readers.

If... students already read at 140 words correct per minute,
then... they do not need to reread three to four times.

SUCCESS PREDICTOR

DAY 5

Assessment
Individual Reading Rate Use the Fluency Assessment Plan and do a one-minute timed reading of either selection from this week to assess students in Week 3. Pay special attention to this week's skill, tempo and rate. Provide corrective feedback for each student.

RETEACH

Graphic Sources

FCAT TESTED SKILLS

TEACH

Review the definition of *graphic sources* on p. 436. Students can complete Practice Book p. 178 on their own, or you can complete it as a class. Tell them to read the diagram showing the stages of a butterfly's life counter-clockwise, following the numbered pictures in order, from 1–4.

ASSESS

Have partners discuss what the illustration at the top of p. 451 shows and find the text that it supports. *(Possible response: The picture shows a snake swallowing its prey whole. It supports the text on pp. 450–451).*

For additional instruction on graphic sources, see DI·54.

EXTEND SKILLS

Metaphor

TEACH

A metaphor is a comparison between two unlike things that are alike in at least one way.

- In a metaphor, the similarity is implied—not stated using words of comparison.
- A metaphor calls attention to certain qualities of one or both things being compared.

Have students reread pp. 444–445. Discuss the metaphor comparing repletes to "living honey jars".

ASSESS

Working in small groups, have students write their own metaphors compar-ing an animal in the selection to something else. *(Possible response: The Camponotus ant is a bomb.)*

LA.5.1.7.1 Explain the purpose of text features (diagrams and illustrations)
LA.5.2.2.1 Locate, explain, and use information from text features (illustrations)
LA.5.4.1.2 Write expressive forms that employ figurative language (metaphor)

OBJECTIVES

- Recognize and use graphic sourc-es visually to gain information quickly.
- Write a metaphor.

Skills Trace	
Graphic Sources	
Introduce/Teach	TE: 5.3 364–365; 5.4 436–437; 5.5 536–537
Practice	Practice Book: 143, 147, 148, 166, 173, 177, 178, 213, 217, 218, 226, 246
Reteach/Review	**TE: 5.3 383b, DI•56; 5.4 421, 457b, DI•54; 5.5 559b, 569, 613, DI•53**
Test	Selection Test: 57–60, 69–72, 85–88; Benchmark Test: Unit 5

ELL

Access Content Reteach the skill by reviewing the Picture It! lesson on graphic sources in the ELL Teaching Guide, pp. 121–122.

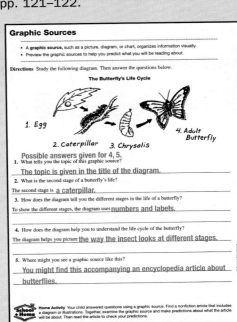

▲ **Practice Book** p. 178

Vocabulary and Word Study

VOCABULARY STRATEGY
Context Clues

UNFAMILIAR WORDS Remind students to use context clues to determine the meanings of unfamiliar words. Have each student choose an unfamiliar word from *Exploding Ants* and complete a word frame for it. Students should base their predicted definitions on context clues from the selection and write sentences using the word in similar contexts. They should use a dictionary for the verified definitions and write other sentences using the exact definitions.

opponents

Word

➡️ ⬅️

Association or Symbol

Predicted definition: _____

One good sentence: _____

_____

Verified definition:

_____

Another good sentence:

_____

Related Words

From the verb *specialize* you can find other related parts of speech such as *special* (adjective) or *specialty* (noun). Have students find related words from these verbs and identify their parts of speech.

Verb	Related Words
adapt	adaptation (n.); adaptable (adj.)
survive	
defend	

BUILD CONCEPT VOCABULARY
Animal Adaptations

LOOKING BACK Remind students of the question of the week: *How do animals adapt to survive?* Discuss how this week's Concept Web of vocabulary words relates to the theme of adaptation. Ask students if they have any words or categories to add. Discuss whether the words and categories are appropriately related to the concept.

REVIEW/CONNECT Preview the title of the next selection, *The Stormi Giovanni Club*. Ask students which Concept Web words might apply to the new selection based on the title alone.

Put a star next to these words on the web.

Display the Concept Web and revisit the vocabulary words as you read the next selection to check predictions.

Monitor Progress
Check Vocabulary

If... students suggest words or categories that are not related to the concept,	then... review the words and categories on the Concept Web and discuss how they relate to the lesson concept.

SUCCESS PREDICTOR

Speaking and Listening

SPEAKING

Description

SET-UP Have students give a description of the animal they wrote about in Writing Workshop. They may choose to describe another animal instead.

PLANNING Students should begin by brainstorming a list of descriptive words to describe their animals. Suggest that they focus on sensory words, such as words that describe what the animal looks like, what it sounds like, and what it feels like. Encourage them to study photos of their animals as they brainstorm. In addition to their animals' basic physical features, students may want to describe other aspects, such as interesting habits or adaptive features.

VISUAL AIDS Encourage students to include visual aids in their presentations to show their animals and their animals' interesting features. Students can bring in photos from books or the Internet.

Organization Tips
• First tell what the animal is and where it is found. Then tell what you're going to describe about it.
• Describe everything about one feature, such as your animals' claws, before going on to another feature, such as its nest or diet.
• Keep in mind the time line for completion of your report.

LISTENING

Listen to Poetry

Have students listen to a poem about an animal. If available, you can play a recording of a poem, or read one aloud. After students listen, have them discuss these questions as a class.

1. **How does the speaker feel about the animal described in the poem? Use details from the poem to support your answer.** *(Guide students to note the speaker's tone and language.)*
2. **What is the purpose of the poem? How do you know?**
3. **How is the poem different from an informational article about animals?**

Support Vocabulary Use the following to review and extend vocabulary and to explore lesson concepts further:
• ELL Poster 18, Days 3–5 instruction
• Vocabulary Activities and Word Cards in ELL Teaching Guide, pp. 122–123

Assessment For information on assessing students' speaking and listening, see the ELL and Transition Handbook.

Pages 457c–457d

LA.5.1.6.3 Use context clues to determine meanings of unfamiliar words
LA.5.1.6.4 Categorize key vocabulary
LA.5.5.2.1 Listen for a variety of purposes, including poetic recitations
LA.5.5.2.2 Make formal oral presentations, demonstrating appropriate language choices and use of supporting graphics (illustrations and images)

SUCCES PREDICTO

Grammar Possessive Pronouns

Monitor Progress

Grammar

If... students have difficulty identifying possessive pronouns,	then... provide additional instruction and practice in The Grammar and Writing Book pp. 152–155.

DAILY FIX-IT

This week use Daily Fix-It Transparency 18. *Spiral REVIEW*

Support Grammar See the Grammar Transition lessons in the ELL and Transition Handbook.

▲ **The Grammar and Writing Book** For more instruction and practice, use pp. 152–155.

DAY 1 Teach and Model

DAILY FIX-IT

1. A skunk sprays a bad-smelling sent to keep enemys away. *(scent; enemies)*

2. That serves as there protection? *(their protection.)*

READING-GRAMMAR CONNECTION

Write this sentence on the board:

Animals often put <u>their</u> body parts to good use.

Explain that *their* is a possessive pronoun. It is used in the place of the possessive noun, *animals'*, to show that the animals own, or possess, the body parts.

Display Grammar Transparency 18. Read aloud the definitions and sample sentences. Work through the items.

Possessive Pronouns

Possessive pronouns show who or what owns, or possesses, something. *My, mine, your, yours, her, hers, his, its, our, ours, their,* and *theirs* are possessive pronouns.
- Use *my, your, her, our,* and *their* before nouns.
  This is <u>my</u> cat. It was <u>her</u> dog. They fed <u>their</u> fish.
- Use *mine, yours, hers, ours,* and *theirs* alone.
  The cat is <u>mine</u>. The dog was <u>hers</u>. The fish are <u>theirs</u>.
- *His* and *its* can be used both before nouns and alone.
  He found <u>his</u> dog. The dog is <u>his</u>.
  The dog hurt <u>its</u> paw. The paw is <u>its</u>.
- Do not use an apostrophe with a possessive pronoun.

Directions Underline the pronoun that correctly completes each sentence.
1. Ants use (theirs, <u>their</u>) antennae for touch and smell.
2. That nest under the tree is (their, <u>theirs</u>).
3. An ant has two stomachs in (<u>its</u>, our) abdomen.
4. One stomach stores food for other ants to share, and another stomach holds (it's, <u>its</u>) own food.
5. The queen is larger than the other ants, and (her, <u>hers</u>) body is an egg factory.
6. All the worker ants are sterile, so the egg-laying task is all (her, <u>hers</u>).
7. A male ant lives apart from the colony and plays (<u>his</u>, theirs) part by mating with the queen.
8. I sometimes get ants in (<u>my</u>, hers) house.
9. The house with purple trim is (my, <u>mine</u>).
10. Don't have (<u>your</u>, theirs) picnic next to an ant colony!

Directions Write the possessive pronoun that can replace the underlined word or words.
11. Steven brought <u>Steven's</u> ant farm to class.
    his
12. The class and I spent <u>the class's and my</u> time watching them work.
    our
13. Ms. Pearce told us about <u>Ms. Pearce's</u> trip to South America.
    her
14. She saw army ants marching to and from <u>the army ants'</u> colony.
    their

Unit 4 Exploding Ants   Grammar **18**

▲ **Grammar Transparency** 18

DAY 2 Develop the Concept

DAILY FIX-IT

3. Because clear scales cover the eyes of a snake. It's eyes are always open. *(snake, Its)*

4. Snakes raises their body temperature by laying in the sun. *(raise; lying)*

GUIDED PRACTICE

Review the concept of possessive pronouns.

- **Possessive pronouns** show who or what owns something.
- *My, your, her, our,* and *their* are used before nouns.
- *Mine, yours, hers, ours,* and *theirs* are used alone.
- *His* and *its* can be used both before nouns and alone.
- No possessive pronoun uses an apostrophe.

HOMEWORK Grammar and Writing Practice Book p. 69.

Possessive Pronouns

Possessive pronouns show who or what owns, or possesses, something. *My, mine, your, yours, her, hers, his, its, our, ours, their,* and *theirs* are possessive pronouns.
- Use *my, your, her, our,* and *their* before nouns.
  Is that <u>your</u> cat? It was <u>her</u> gerbil. They pet <u>our</u> dog.
- Use *mine, yours, hers, ours,* and *theirs* alone.
  The cat is <u>yours</u>. That gerbil is <u>hers</u>. The dog is <u>ours</u>.
- *His* and *its* can be used both before nouns and alone.
  He lost <u>his</u> ferret. The ferret is <u>his</u>.
  The dog lost <u>its</u> collar. The collar is <u>its</u>.
- Do not use an apostrophe with a possessive pronoun.

Directions Replace the underlined words or phrases with possessive pronouns. Rewrite the sentences.
1. An ant colony relies on the ant colony's queen.
   <u>An ant colony relies on its queen.</u>
2. Both males and females have wings on <u>the males' and females'</u> bodies.
   <u>Both males and females have wings on their bodies.</u>
3. The queen ant flies to a new location to start a colony, then sheds the queen's wings.
   <u>The queen ant flies to a new location to start a colony, then sheds her wings.</u>
4. Ants are very strong for <u>ants'</u> size and can carry 25 times <u>ants'</u> weight.
   <u>Ants are very strong for their size and can carry 25 times their weight.</u>
5. Most of us think that ants are pests to be swept out of <u>most of us's</u> way.
   <u>Most of us think that ants are pests to be swept out of our way.</u>

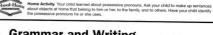
Home Activity Your child learned about possessive pronouns. Ask your child to make up sentences about objects at home that belong to him or her, to the family, and to others. Have your child identify the possessive pronouns he or she uses.

▲ **Grammar and Writing Practice Book** p. 69

CORRECTIVE FEEDBACK

Preview LA.6.3.4.4 Use parts of speech/pronouns

- **Question** Use Whiteboard or Transparency 18c, items 1–3, to ask questions that address this standard in FCAT format. Have students write their answers on a sheet of paper.
- **Check** Scan students' responses by having them hold up their papers.
- **Correct** If necessary, provide corrective feedback and review pp. 152–157 in *The Grammar and Writing Book*.

---

1 Mark the letter of the correctly spelled **possessive pronoun** that completes the sentence.

The painting is _____.

- Ⓐ theirs'
- Ⓑ theirs
- Ⓒ their's

◀ **FCAT Whiteboard Activity** 18c/**FCAT Transparency** 18c

DAY 3 · Apply to Writing

DAILY FIX-IT

5. They're are a snake under that chair! *(There is)*

6. That is mine snake named sue. *(my; Sue)*

WATCH FOR ITS AND IT'S

Explain that the contraction *it's* stands for the words *it is* and is never used to show possession. No possessive pronoun uses an apostrophe.

No: Its a shame that owl broke it's wing.

Yes: It's a shame that owl broke its wing.

- Have students review something they have written to see if they can improve it by correcting mistakes in their use of possessive pronouns.

HOMEWORK Grammar and Writing Practice Book p. 70.

Possessive Pronouns

Directions Underline the error in each sentence. Write the correct possessive pronoun in the space above the error.

its
(1) Each animal is adapted to it's environment. (2) For example, snakes have temperature **their** **their**
sensing organs on they're heads. (3) They can use these organs to locate there prey in the dark. **her**
(4) My corn snake Lolamae can take a whole mouse or egg in hers mouth. (5) She can unhinge **her** **hers**
her's bottom jaw to fit in a big meal. (6) The aquarium in the corner is her. (7) Lolamae will be **your** **my**
happy to slither up yours arm. (8) It took mine mom a long time to get used to Lolamae too.

Directions Write a paragraph about pets you and your friends have owned. Describe some unique features of the pets. Use at least five possessive pronouns. Underline the possessive pronouns in your paragraph.

Possible answer: My family and I have ordinary pets. Tigger is my orange cat, and Wolfus is a hound that belongs to our family. However, my friend Van is another matter! Most people have fish in their aquariums. Van has tarantulas in his. He says spiders make great pets. That is one person's opinion. What is yours?

Home Activity Your child learned how to use possessive pronouns in writing. Have your child write interview questions to ask you about a prized possession and then write your answers below the questions.

▲ **Grammar and Writing Practice Book** p. 70

DAY 4 · Test Preparation

DAILY FIX-IT

7. On saturday morning you can bring you dog for training. *(Saturday; your)*

8. Dogs are allways aloud in the pet store. *(always allowed)*

STANDARDIZED TEST PREP

Test Tip

Although possessive nouns use an apostrophe (*Jean's dog*), possessive pronouns never do (*her dog*).

No: A dog loves it's owner.

Yes: A dog loves its owner.

No: That dog is her's.

Yes: That dog is hers.

HOMEWORK Grammar and Writing Practice Book p. 71.

Possessive Pronouns

Directions Write the letter of the possessive pronoun that correctly completes each sentence in the paragraph.

(1) Last night I heard a haunting sound outside _____ window. (2) My brother and I ran into _____ yard to find out what it was. (3) He shined _____ flashlight up into a tree. (4) We saw two big eyes, and _____ unblinking stare unnerved me. (5) It was only a screech owl, but _____ hoot sounded eerie. (6) Since that night, owls have become a hobby of _____. (7) Mom loaned me some of _____ biology books. (8) Did you know that owls can turn _____ heads almost completely around? (9) This is an adaptation of _____ that allows them to turn their heads to follow a moving object. (10) Now Mom and I spend _____ free time on weekends bird watching.

1. A mine
   Ⓑ my
   C theirs
   D hers

2. A her
   B hers
   Ⓒ our
   D theirs

3. A mine
   Ⓑ his
   C its
   D their

4. A your
   Ⓑ its
   C their
   D theirs

5. A theirs
   Ⓑ its
   C hers
   D her

6. Ⓐ mine
   B our
   C their
   D it's

7. A hers
   Ⓑ her
   C their
   D theirs

8. A our
   Ⓑ her
   Ⓒ their
   D my

9. A hers
   B his
   C their
   Ⓓ theirs

10. A mine
    B my
    Ⓒ ours
    Ⓓ our

Home Activity Your child prepared for taking tests on possessive pronouns. Have your child choose a magazine article and find possessive pronouns in it. Ask him or her to name the person or thing each possessive pronoun stands for.

▲ **Grammar and Writing Practice Book** p. 71

DAY 5 · Cumulative Review

DAILY FIX-IT

9. That fish is pail so it will blend in with the sandy ocean botem. *(pale; bottom)*

10. Animals bodies and behaviors are adapted to its environments. *(Animals'; their)*

ADDITIONAL PRACTICE

Assign pp. 152–155 in The Grammar and Writing Book.

EXTRA PRACTICE Grammar and Writing Practice Book p. 139.

TEST PREPARATION Grammar and Writing Practice Book pp. 155–156.

ASSESSMENT

CUMULATIVE REVIEW Grammar and Writing Practice Book p. 72.

Possessive Pronouns

Directions Write the letter of the possessive pronoun that can replace the underlined word or words in each phrase.

B 1. Aaron's and Mike's question A her
E 2. Mr. Shaefer's lesson B their
D 3. the book's index C our
C 4. Sam's and my interest D its
A 5. Mom's degree E his

Directions Underline the pronoun that correctly completes each sentence.

6. We will catch fireflies in (theirs, our) hands.
7. Which of these jars is (your, yours)?
8. Be sure to punch air holes in (it's, its) top.
9. Dusk is (their, theirs) time to glow and flash.
10. I have ten fireflies in (my, mine) jar.
11. The light flashes from (their, it's) abdomen.
12. We let the fireflies go. Our friends released (their, theirs) later.

Directions Write the possessive pronoun that can replace the underlined word or words.

13. A snake sheds a snake's skin when it outgrows it.
    its

14. This bleached-out turtle shell is the one belonging to me.
    mine

15. Zara and Ted explained that the rat was Zara's and the hamster was Ted's.
    hers; his

Home Activity Your child reviewed possessive pronouns. Ask your child to list the possessive pronouns on this page, use each one in an example sentence, and tell you what possessive noun the possessive pronoun replaces.

▲ **Grammar and Writing Practice Book** p. 72

Writing Workshop Tell a Story About an Animal

OBJECTIVES

- Identify the characteristics of a story.
- Write a story about an animal, using words, style, and tone to create a mood.
- Focus on word choice.
- Use a rubric.

Genre Story
Writer's Craft Mood
Writing Trait Support/Word Choice

ELL

Support/Word Choice Work with students to use vivid words that appeal to readers' senses. A bilingual dictionary, picture dictionary, or thesaurus, as well as other home-language speakers, may help provide words that create pictures for readers.

Writing Traits

FOCUS/IDEAS The details build and develop the plot.

ORGANIZATION/PARAGRAPHS The story flows from beginning to middle to end with logical paragraph breaks.

SUPPORT/VOICE The writing conveys personality and feeling.

SUPPORT/WORD CHOICE Lively verbs, precise nouns, and vivid modifiers engage readers.

SUPPORT/SENTENCES The dialogue sounds natural. Sentences are varied and interesting.

CONVENTIONS There is excellent control and accuracy. Quotation marks are used accurately with commas and end marks.

DAY 1 Model the Trait

READING-WRITING CONNECTION

- *Exploding Ants* gives facts about remarkable animal adaptations.
- Vivid and specific concrete language helps readers to picture animals in action and creates admiration for them.
- Students will write a **story about an animal** using lively and vivid language to create a mood.

MODEL SUPPORT/WORD CHOICE

Discuss Writing Support Transparency 18A. Then discuss the model and the writing trait of word choice.

 Think Aloud I see that the writer uses the word *saunter,* rather than walk, to more specifically describe the cat's relaxed, unconcerned attitude, despite the fact that its owners have been frantically calling for it. The writer also uses specific describing words such as *yawning blissfully* to help readers visualize the scene.

Story About an Animal

A **story** tells about an event or how characters solve a problem. It has a beginning, middle, and end. Dialogue, style, and tone are tools that a writer uses to give a story a certain feeling, or mood. For example, the mood might be humorous or suspenseful.

The Missing Cat

"I can't find Bear!" cried June. Bear was June's half-grown kitten. His name came from his habit of disappearing into boxes and bags and under beds. He would sleep peacefully in the dark while the whole family called and searched. Finally, he would saunter out, yawning blissfully. June decided that the cat was in fact hibernating. These hidey holes were as close to a cave as he could get.

Mom asked, "Have you looked in his favorite caves?"

"Of course, Mom!" June groaned. "Where can he be?"

They sat at the kitchen table and thought. Then they heard a tiny scratching sound. It was coming from one of the drawers! Somehow, Bear had squeezed his way into a kitchen drawer. Now he was happily wedged into the tiniest cave yet.

Finally, June and Mom got Bear unstuck. He walked away, tail in the air, as if he'd just checked out of a deluxe hotel!

Descriptive details create a humorous picture.

Dialogue sounds natural.

Ending creates a memorable, humorous image.

Unit 4 Exploding Ants   **Writing Model 18A**

▲ **Writing Transparency** 18A

DAY 2 Improve Writing

WRITER'S CRAFT
Mood

Display Writing Transparency 18B. Read the directions and work together to identify the mood of each paragraph.

 Think Aloud **ESTABLISH A MOOD** Tomorrow we will write stories about animals that surprised us. What details could be used to capture a mood of surprise? I could say, "The bug suddenly soared about ten feet backwards, all the while facing me." This describes a surprising action exactly. I could say, "I stopped dead in my tracks and rubbed my eyes." This statement has a tone of astonishment.

GUIDED WRITING Some students may need more help identifying mood. Have them read parts of different stories aloud and talk about the feelings these words elicit.

Mood

The **mood** of a story is the overall feeling it creates for the reader. For example, the mood may be humorous, serious, or suspenseful. Descriptive details, the things characters say, and the tone with which they speak are some things that help create the mood.

Directions Match each passage with the mood it creates.

suspenseful   admiring

1. I had to give that housefly credit. I had swatted at it dozens of times. It neatly avoided my swatter every time. How did it always manage to take off just before the swatter hit? It could see in any direction. I knew, with its compound eyes. It could fly in any direction instantly, without runway or fuel. It could land on the ceiling, out of reach, because its legs were fitted with barbs for hanging on.

admiring

2. I held my breath. "All right," I said to myself, "The bear has seen you. Now what?" Should I run for it? Would it attack? What did it want? I stood frozen to the ground. It was like one of those awful dreams where you can't move. The bear snuffled noisily at the air and stood on its hind legs, eyeing me carefully. I could only hope it would go for the food in my tent. I began mentally measuring the distance from the bear to me and from me to the car. If it turned toward the tent, I just might be able to make it to the car.

suspenseful

Directions On a separate sheet of paper, write a passage about an animal in which you build a specific mood. Write the mood you hope to create on the first line. Then write your passage.

Possible answer: Mood: frightened. The spider sat right in front of my nose. I had run under the tree to hide from my brother and came within two inches of the biggest, blackest spider I had ever seen! Its long pointed legs raised one by one, reminding me of daggers. My whole body began to quake, and chills ran up my spine. "Please," I prayed, "don't let it be a jumping spider!"

Unit 4 Exploding Ants   **Writer's Craft 18B**

▲ **Writing Transparency** 18B

Pages 457g–457h

LA.5.3.2.1 Use a pre-writing plan, elaborating using descriptive language and word choices appropriate to selected tone and mood
LA.5.3.3.1 Evaluate draft for word choice
LA.5.4.1.2 Write expressive forms that employ dialogue, characterization, and plot

Trait of the Week

Support/ Word Choice

DAY 3 Prewrite and Draft

READ THE WRITING PROMPT

on page 453 in the Student Edition.

The author of Exploding Ants describes unusual and unexpected animal behaviors.

Think about your own experiences observing animals.

Now write a story about an animal whose behavior surprised you.

FCAT Writing+ Test Tips

- State the problem or event you will describe. What events make up the beginning, middle, and end?
- Choose a mood and list words that go with that mood.
- Write dialogue that sounds like natural speech.

GETTING STARTED Students can do any of the following:

- Make a story plan listing the animal, any characters, and plot events.
- Brainstorm vivid verbs, precise nouns, and describing words to create an image of the animal.
- Experiment with dialogue: what characters will say and how they will say it.

DAY 4 Draft and Revise

EDITING/REVISING CHECKLIST

☑ Did I create a mood with my choice of details?

☑ Have I used possessive pronouns correctly?

☑ Did I use the correct homophone for the context?

See *The Grammar and Writing Book*, pp. 152-157.

Revising Tips

Support/ Word Choice

- Choose words that communicate a specific mood or tone.
- Refer to dictionaries and thesauruses for word choice and correct spelling.
- Avoid wording that sounds stiff and unnatural.
- Use a precise noun or verb to convey your meaning.

PUBLISHING Suggest that students illustrate their stories with animal pictures that enhance the mood. Some students may wish to revise their work later.

ASSESSMENT Use the scoring rubric to evaluate students' work.

DAY 5 Connect to Unit Writing

	Story
Week 1	E-mail 411g–411h
Week 2	Journal Entry 435g–435h
Week 3	Story About an Animal 457g–457h
Week 4	Advice 483g–483h
Week 5	Describe How You Achieved a Goal 503g–503h

PREVIEW THE UNIT PROMPT

Tell a story about a character who succeeds by adapting to a new situation. Focus on an event that shows this person's resourcefulness. Your story may be real or imagined.

APPLY

- A story has a beginning, middle, and end and focuses on one incident or event.
- Develop your story using plot elements such as exposition, conflict, rising action, climax, falling action, and resolution.
- Use words, details, style, and tone to create mood in a story.

Writing Trait Rubric

	6	5	4	3	2	1
Support/ Word Choice	Vivid style created by use of exact nouns, strong verbs, exciting adjectives, and clear figurative language	Style created by use of exact nouns, strong verbs, adjectives, and figurative language	Some style created by strong and precise words	Little style created by strong, precise words; some lack of clarity	No style created by word choice; unclear	Word choice vague or incorrect
	Uses strong, specific words that make story unusually clear and lively	Uses strong, specific words that make story clear and lively	Uses some specific words that make story clear	Needs more precise word choice to create style and clarity in story	Story uninteresting due to dull word choice	Story made dull or unclear by poor word choice

Spelling & Phonics Homophones

DAY 1 Pretest and Sort

DAY 2 Think and Practice

OBJECTIVE

● Spell homophones.

Generalization

Connect to Phonics A homophone is a word that sounds exactly like another word but has a different spelling and meaning: *cent, sent.* Homophones occur because many letters and letter combinations make more than one sound.

Spelling Words

1. cent
2. sent
3. scent
4. threw
5. through*
6. weather
7. whether
8. their*
9. there*
10. they're*

11. chili
12. chilly
13. tide
14. tied
15. pale
16. pail
17. aloud
18. allowed
19. course
20. coarse

Challenge Words

21. counsel
22. council
23. bizarre

24. bazaar
25. patients
26. patience

* Words from the selection

ELL

Spelling/Phonics Support See the ELL and Transition Handbook for spelling support.

PRETEST

Use the Dictation Sentences from Day 5 to administer the pretest. Read the word, read the sentence, and then read the word again. Guide students in self-correcting their pretests and correcting any misspellings.

Monitor Progress

Spelling

If...	then...
If... students misspell more than 5 pretest words,	then... use words 1–10 for Strategic Intervention.
If... students misspell 1–5 pretest words,	then... use words 1–20 for On-Level practice.
If... students correctly spell all pretest words,	then... use words 1–26 for Advanced Learners.

HOMEWORK Spelling Practice Book, p. 69.

▲ **Spelling Practice Book** p. 69

TEACH

Explain that homonyms are words with the same sound but different spelling and meaning. Write *threw* and *through* on the board. Point and say each word. Underline the /oo/ sound in each word and say it aloud. Cross out and write *oo.* Then point to each word and use it in a sentence. Repeat with other homonyms.

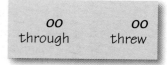

oo	oo
through	threw

FIND THE PATTERN Ask students to circle the word parts in each homophone pair or group that are spelled differently.

HOMEWORK Spelling Practice Book, p. 70.

▲ **Spelling Practice Book** p. 70

Pages 457i–457j

LA.5.1.4.1 Understand spelling patterns
LA.5.1.6.8 Use knowledge of homophones to determine meanings of words
LA.5.4.1.2 Write expressive forms

DAY 3 — Connect to Writing

WRITE A DESCRIPTION

Have students write a description of a favorite pet, game, sport, or trip. Have students use at least four list words in their description.

Frequently Misspelled Words

when   then
went

These words may seem easy to spell, but they are often misspelled by fifth-graders because they are easy to confuse with other words. Alert students to these frequently misspelled words.

HOMEWORK Spelling Practice Book, p. 71.

Homophones

Proofread an Ad Circle six spelling errors. Write the words correctly. Find one capitalization error. Write the sentence correctly.

On a chilly day, shout (allowed) for our delicious (chilly!) It will warm you (threw) and threw! Ask about our 99 (sent) special. If the (whether) is bad, call us. We (Deliver) for free! Of course, (their) is no finer taste treat!

1. aloud   2. chili
3. through   4. cent
5. weather   6. there
7. We deliver for free!

Spelling Words
cent
sent
scent
threw
through
weather
whether
their
there
they're
chili
chilly
tide
tied
pale
pail
aloud
allowed
course
coarse

Proofread Words Circle the correct spelling of the list words. Write the word.

8. Burlap is a ____ fabric.
   corse   coarse   (coarse)   8. coarse
9. I think ____ going on a class trip tomorrow.
   (they're)   their   they'ar   9. they're
10. Sky blue is a ____ color.
    pail   (pale)   paile   10. pale
11. Your perfume has a lovely ____.
    (scent)   cent   sent   11. scent
12. I am not sure ____ I can go.
    wheather   (whether)   weather   12. whether
13. The sailor ____ down the ship's hatch.
    tide   teid   (tied)   13. tied
14. The candy cost one ____.
    scent   (cent)   sent   14. cent
15. The score was even and the game was ____.
    tide   teid   (tied)   15. tied

Frequently Misspelled Words
their
there
they're

Home Activity Your child identified misspelled and misused homophones. Say a homophone in a sentence and have your child spell it.

▲ **Spelling Practice Book** p. 71

DAY 4 — Review

REVIEW HOMOPHONES

Have partners write each list word on small index cards. Cards are shuffled and each player gets three cards. Players ask each other if they have a matching homophone for a card they have in their hand. If the partner has a card, it is handed over, if not, the player picks a card. Homophone pairs and groups are placed on the table. Play continues until all of the cards are paired/grouped.

Spelling Strategy
Rhyming Helpers

It is sometimes hard to remember which homophone spelling to use. Rhymes can help. For example:

pail/hail
I used a pail to catch the hail.

coarse/hoarse
My voice was coarse because I was hoarse.

HOMEWORK Spelling Practice Book, p. 72.

Homophones

Spelling Words
cent   sent   scent   threw   through
weather   whether   their   there   they're
chili   chilly   tide   tied   pale
pail   aloud   allowed   course   coarse

Word Search Circle eight list words that are hidden in the puzzle. Write each word you find.

T T W F A H Z C D Z Q
B W H E T H E R O E Y P
D Q R R I E H T U I J Q
S U G U O G S B R T F U
U U O H Y U K F S O S Q
Z W B L A T G F E N G I
U E M L A E U H O C Q W
L T Z C Z R W V H E J E
X W R L U L I I Y S E E
W W Z B R I K S A L C
X A W A A L Z L Y B E E
I K P T Y T Q I S Z B I

1. aloud
2. chilly
3. course
4. pail
5. their
6. through
7. tied
8. whether

Words in Context Write a list word to complete each sentence.

9. Ninety-nine plus one ____ more equals one dollar.
10. The pitcher ____ the ball over the plate.
11. We had ____ with our hot dog.
12. The ____ was perfect for the beach.
13. The boy needs sunscreen on his ____ skin.
14. Swimming is not ____ when the lifeguard is off-duty.
15. She ____ her classmate a party invitation.
16. The rose had a wonderful ____.
17. We looked for seashells when the ____ was out.
18. The ____ fabric was itchy.

9. cent
10. threw
11. chili
12. weather
13. pale
14. allowed
15. sent
16. scent
17. tide
18. coarse

Home Activity Your child has learned to read, write, and spell homophones. Say a homophone and spell it. Ask your child to say and spell the other homophone.

▲ **Spelling Practice Book** p. 72

DAY 5 — Posttest

DICTATION SENTENCES

1. A penny is one cent.
2. I sent a letter to my pen pal.
3. The flower had a sweet scent.
4. The pitcher threw a curve ball.
5. I cut through the fabric.
6. I hope the weather is nice today.
7. Did you decide whether to have carrots or corn?
8. Their cage door was open.
9. The popcorn stand is over there.
10. They're coming home tomorrow.
11. Chili peppers are hot and spicy.
12. It's damp and chilly outside today.
13. At low tide, the beach is wide.
14. I tied my laces three times.
15. Lilac is a pale purple color.
16. The farmer carried a pail of milk.
17. I like to read poetry aloud.
18. Pets are not allowed in the zoo.
19. I took a pottery course.
20. The sandpaper feels coarse.

CHALLENGE

21. A lawyer offers legal counsel.
22. The city council voted to install a stop light.
23. Some things are meant to be strange and bizarre.
24. The open-air bazaar had food, clothing, and crafts for sale.
25. The patients read magazines in the doctor's waiting room.
26. I don't have enough patience to solve that puzzle.

OBJECTIVES

- Formulate an inquiry question that is connected to this week's lesson focus.

- Effectively and efficiently find, evaluate, and communicate information related to an inquiry question using electronic sources.

New Literacies	
Day 1	**Identify Questions**
Day 2	**Navigate/Search**
Day 3	**Analyze**
Day 4	**Synthesize**
Day 5	**Communicate**

Page 457k

LA.5.5.2.2 Make formal oral presentations, demonstrating use of supporting graphics (charts, illustrations, and images)

LA.5.6.2.1 Select a topic for inquiry, formulate a search plan, and apply evaluative criteria

LA.5.6.2.2 Read and record information systematically

LA.5.6.2.4 Record basic bibliographic data using ethical practices (avoids plagiarism)

NEW LITERACIES

Internet Inquiry Activity

EXPLORE ANIMAL ADAPTATIONS

Use the following 5-day plan to help students conduct this week's Internet inquiry activity on animal adaptations. Remind students to follow classroom rules when using the Internet.

DAY 1

Identify Questions Discuss the lesson focus question: *How do animals adapt to survive?* Brainstorm ideas for specific inquiry questions about animal adaptations and survival. For example, students might want to learn about chameleons and how they adapt by changing color. Have students work individually, in pairs, or in small groups to write inquiry questions they want to answer. Students should formulate hypotheses to guide their inquiries.

DAY 2

Navigate/Search Have students write a brief description of the adaptations they want to find. Have them choose keywords and enter them into a student-friendly search engine. Students should scan the descriptions from the search before proceeding to the sites.

DAY 3

Analyze Have students skim and scan the Web sites they identified on Day 2. Circulate around the classroom to verify that the Web sites they've found answer their basic questions, and suggest that they narrow their searches or revise their inquiry questions if necessary.

DAY 4

Synthesize Have students synthesize information from Day 3 by combining the most important pieces of information from each Web site they used. Remind them to document their sources and avoid plagiarism by restating information in their own words. Encourage them to think about adding some form of visual element to their final products.

DAY 5

Communicate Have students share their inquiry results in the form of oral reports with posters featuring drawings, clip art, or some form of graphic organizers.

RESEARCH/STUDY SKILLS
Magazine/Periodical

TEACH

Ask students to name reference sources where they might locate new research about animals. Students may need prompting before they mention science or nature magazines. Explain these features of a magazine article.

- A **periodical** is a **magazine** that contains current information in the form of articles, opinion columns, letters, reports, advertisements, and reviews.

- The **headline** or **title** expresses the topic of the article.

- Most magazines include a **Table of Contents** which tells the reader what information is in the magazine and where to find it.

- Most magazines follow the **5 Ws and How** format. The article will tell you *Who? What? When? Where? Why?* and *How?*

Give students photocopies of an article from a children's science or nature magazine. Have students read the article. Then, discuss these questions as a class:

1. **Identify the 5 Ws and How the article answers.** (*Responses will vary. Call on volunteers to read aloud the relevant text.*)

2. **What does the title tell you about the article? Based on the title, did the article cover what you expected?** (*Responses will vary but may suggest the title tells the article's main idea.*)

ASSESS

Make sure students can identify the 5 Ws and How and understand the function of the article's title.

For more practice or to assess students, use Practice Book pp. 179–180.

Magazine/Periodical

- **Magazines** and **periodicals** are excellent sources of current information. They contain news articles, opinion columns, reports, reviews, letters, cartoons, advertisements, and other features.
- A table of contents helps readers locate particular stories and other information.
- Many magazine and periodical articles follow the "5 Ws and H" format. That is, they tell you *Who? What? When? Where? Why?* and *How?* in the first few paragraphs.

Directions Read this table of contents for an issue of a magazine. Then answer the questions that follow.

December Issue Volume 237 Number 4	World News
CONTENTS	72 Monarchs winter in Mexico in record numbers
Year in Review	80 Alaskan dinosaurs and the Bering Strait
24 Annual salute to the people who made discoveries that have changed our lives	**Columns**
39 Year-end updates on works-in-progress	12 Letters to the editor
Features	18 Ask the experts
44 The longest-living lungfish	93 Calendar
51 New vaccine for a dangerous disease	128 Book reviews
67 Discovery of a new species of grasshopper	

1. How would you describe the subject of this magazine?
   Possible answer: a magazine about science and scientific discoveries

2. On what page could you find information about lungfish?
   page 44

3. Where could you read what people think about a new book?
   book reviews on page 128

4. Do you think this is a new magazine or one that has been published for some time? How do you know?
   It has been published for some time; The high volume number indicates the magazine's long history.

5. If you wrote to the magazine, where might you find your comments published in the next issue?
   They would appear under Letters to the Editor.

▲ **Practice Book** p. 179

Directions Read this passage from a magazine and answer the questions below.

Who's Got the Longest-living Lungfish?
Two cities are competing for the honor of possessing the nation's longest-living lungfish. On Monday, the city of Will announced that its aquarium is celebrating the 67th birthday of its Australian lungfish on April 9. On Tuesday, one day later and fifty miles east, the city of Franklyn declared its plans to celebrate the 70th birthday of its lungfish on April 9. However, neither aquarium can prove the exact age of its lungfish.

Why the interest in elderly lungfish? Perhaps because it is a most unusual creature. It has both gills and lungs, leading scientists to believe that it is the missing link between fish and amphibians. The lungfish has the ability to be, as the saying goes, "a fish out of water." In other words, it can survive on land as well as in water. This adaptation is a big reason why the lungfish has survived for ages. Fossils show that it existed some 400 million years ago. Today the lungfish is an endangered species.

Possible answers given for 2, 5.

6. What part of the passage gives you a first impression of the article's subject?
   The title gives readers the first idea of the subject.

7. What would you identify as the *Who* of this article?
   The *who* is the aquarium in Will and the aquarium in Franklyn.

8. What would you say is the *What* of the article?
   The *what* is the nation's longest-living lungfish.

9. What is the *When* of the article?
   The *when* is April 9 (the date of the two parties) and Monday and Tuesday (when the aquariums made their announcements).

10. When might you use the information in this article?
    I might use this information while writing a report about recent events in science.

 School Home Home Activity Your child learned about reading tables of contents and articles in magazines. Look at a current issue of a magazine together and discuss the *Who, What, When, Where, Why,* and *How* of one of the articles.

▲ **Practice Book** p. 180

Page 457l

LA.5.2.2.1 Locate, explain, and use information from text features (table of contents and headings)

LA.5.2.2.4 Identify characteristics of types of text (practical/functional texts)

Assessment Checkpoints *for the Week*

Selection Assessment

Use pp. 69–72 of Selection Tests to check:

☑ **Selection Understanding**

☑ **Comprehension Skill** *Graphic Sources*

☑ **Selection Vocabulary**
critical
enables
mucus
scarce
specialize
sterile

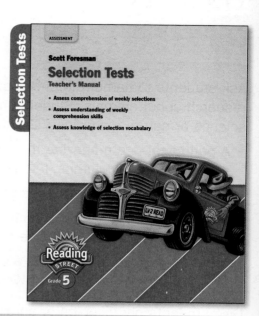

Leveled Assessment

On-Level
Strategic Intervention
Advanced

Use pp. 103–108 of Fresh Reads for Differentiated Test Practice to check:

☑ **Comprehension Skill** *Graphic Sources*

☑ **REVIEW Comprehension Skill**
Author's Purpose

☑ **Fluency** *Words Correct Per Minute*

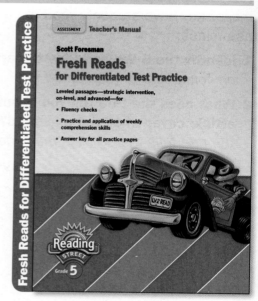

Managing Assessment

Use Assessment Handbook for:

☑ **Observation Checklists**

☑ **Record-Keeping Forms**

☑ **Portfolio Assessment**

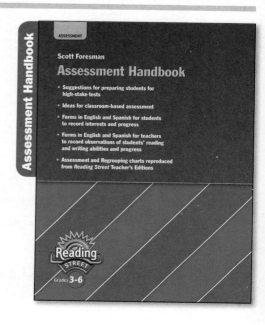

Florida

Planning Guide for Sunshine State Standards

The Stormi Giovanni Club

Reading Street Teacher's Edition pages	Grade 5 Benchmarks for Language Arts
Reading	The student will:
Word Work Suffixes *-ible, -able:* 483i–483j	**LA.5.1.4.1** Understand spelling patterns.
Comprehension Generalize: 458–459, 462–477, 480–483, 483b	**LA.5.1.4.2** Recognize structural analysis.
Story Structure: 458–459, 462–477, 480–483	**LA.5.1.5.2** Adjust reading rate based on purpose, text difficulty, form, and style.
Vocabulary Lesson Vocabulary: 460b, 469, 477, 480	**LA.5.1.6.1** Use new vocabulary that is introduced and taught directly.
Context Clues: 460–461, 473, 483c	**LA.5.1.6.2** Listen to, read, and discuss familiar and conceptually challenging text.
Fluency Model Tone of Voice: 458l–458m, 483a	**LA.5.1.6.3** Use context clues to determine meanings of unfamiliar words.
Self-Selected Reading: LR28–36, TR16–17	**LA.5.1.7.3** Determine the main idea or essential message in grade-level text through inferring.
Literature Genre—Play: 462	**LA.5.2.1.2** Locate and analyze the elements of plot structure, including exposition, rising/falling action, and problem/resolution in a variety of fiction.
Reader Response: 478	
Writing	The student will:
Four-Elements Writing Support/Voice: 479, 483g–483h	**LA.5.1.6.10** Determine alternate word choices by using a thesaurus and digital tools.
Writing Letter of Advice: 483g–483h	**LA.5.3.3.1** Revise by evaluating the draft for voice.
Grammar, Usage, and Mechanics Indefinite and Reflexive Pronouns: 483e–483f	**LA.5.3.4.4** Edit writing for grammar and language conventions, including the correct use of pronouns.
Research/Study Thesaurus: 483l	**LA.5.4.2.4** Write a variety of communications (e.g., letters) that have a clearly stated purpose and that include the proper salutation, body, closing and signature.
Communication and Media	The student will:
Speaking/Listening Build Concept Vocabulary: 458l, 469, 477, 483c	**LA.5.1.6.1** Use new vocabulary that is introduced and taught directly.
Read Aloud: 458m	**LA.5.6.2.1** Select a topic for inquiry, formulate a search plan, and apply evaluative criteria to select and use appropriate resources.
Technology New Literacies: 483k	**LA.5.6.2.2** Read and record information systematically, evaluating the reliability of information in text by examining several sources of information.
Unit Skills	The student will:
Writing Story: WA2–9	**LA.5.2.1.3** Demonstrate how descriptive and figurative language help to communicate meaning in a poem.
Poetry: 504–507	**LA.5.4.1.1** Write narratives that establish a situation and plot with rising action, conflict, and resolution.
Project/Wrap-Up: 508–509	**LA.5.4.2.2** Record information (e.g., charts) related to a topic.

Intervention

My Sidewalks on Reading Street provides collaborative, parallel, intensive intervention when used with *Reading Street*.

This Week's Leveled Readers

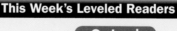

Below-Level

Fiction

The student will:

LA.5.1.7.3 Determine the main idea or essential message in grade-level text through inferring.

LA.5.2.1.2 Locate and analyze the elements of plot structure, including exposition, rising/falling action, and problem/resolution in a variety of fiction.

On-Level

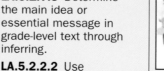

Nonfiction

The student will:

LA.5.1.7.3 Determine the main idea or essential message in grade-level text through inferring.

LA.5.2.2.2 Use information from the text to answer questions related to explicitly stated main ideas or relevant details.

Advanced

Fiction

The student will:

LA.5.1.7.3 Determine the main idea or essential message in grade-level text through inferring.

LA.5.2.1.4 Identify an author's theme, and use details from the text to explain how the author developed that theme.

- Reinforcing effort and providing recognition: pp. 478–479
- Homework and practice: pp. 458f–458g, 459, 461, 478
- Cooperative learning: pp. 458j–458k

- Setting objectives and providing feedback: p. 458m
- Generating and testing hypotheses: p. 462
- Cues, questions, and advance organizers: pp. 460a, 460b, 483c

Florida Assessment for FCAT Success

Selection Tests, pp. 73–76

Fresh Reads for Differentiated Test Practice, pp. 109–114

Unit 4 Benchmark Test in FCAT Format, pp. 1–21

Success Tracker™ Online Test to Monitor Benchmarks

Content-Area Standards Taught During the Reading Lesson

Social Studies

The student:

SS.B.1.2.5.5.1. Understands varying perceptions in the United States

SS.C.2.2.2.5.1. Extends and refines understanding of ways personal responsibility is important

CONNECT TO SF SOCIAL STUDIES

TIME SAVERS FOR FLORIDA TEACHERS

Unit 4: *Adapting*

Question of the Week: **How do people adapt to a new school?**

Social Studies Concepts:
- **Individual Development**
- **Interactions**
- **Groups**
- **Communication**

These lessons in *Scott Foresman Social Studies* support the concepts taught in this week's lesson of *Reading Street*.

Overview, Lesson 1, "The American People," pp. 6–11

Overview, Lesson 4, "Land and Regions," pp. 24–30

Unit 9, Chapter 19, Lesson 4, "Looking Toward the Future," pp. 658–667

Unit 4
Adapting

CONCEPT QUESTION
How do people and animals adapt to different situations?

EXPAND THE CONCEPT
How do people adapt to a new school?

Time for SOCIAL STUDIES

Week 1

How do people adapt to difficult situations?

Week 2

How do people adapt to living with physical limitations?

Week 3

How do animals adapt to survive?

Week 4

How do people adapt to a new school?

Week 5

Why do people try to change themselves?

CONNECT THE CONCEPT

▶ **Develop Language**
count on, settle in

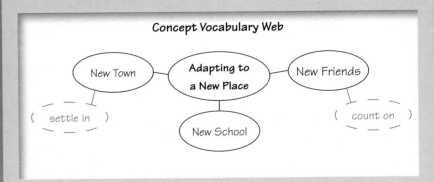

Concept Vocabulary Web

New Town — Adapting to a New Place — New Friends

(settle in)

New School

(count on)

▶ **Social Studies Content**
Moving, E-mail, Friendship

▶ **Writing**
Advice

▶ **Internet Inquiry**
E-mail

Preview Your Week

How do people adapt to a new school?

The Stormi Giovanni Club

by Lydia R. Diamond
illustrated by R. Gregory Christie

Genre A **play** is a story written to be acted out for an audience. As you read, imagine the actors speaking the lines and acting out the action.

462

How will Stormi do in her new school?

Student Edition pages 462–477

Audio CD

Read It
ONLINE
PearsonSuccessNet.com

- Student Edition
- Leveled Readers

Genre Play
Vocabulary Strategy Context Clues
Comprehension Skill Generalize
Comprehension Strategy Story Structure

SOCIAL STUDIES

Paired Selection

Reading Across Texts
Make a List of Problems Students Face at School

Genre
Newspaper Article

Text Features
Headlines, Datelines, and Illustrations

Social Studies in Reading

Newspaper Article

Genre
- A newspaper article tells readers about current events, issues, people, and places of interest.
- News articles report facts—actual events—and people's opinions.

Text Features
- A headline gives readers an idea of what the article is about.
- News articles often start with a brief story that sets the scene for the discussion that follows.
- The writer includes quotations that show differing opinions.

Link to Social Studies
Find out about dress codes in your school and other schools in your area. Are there differences? Why?

LA.5.2.2.4 Identify characteristics of nonfiction poetry.

480

FASHION

504 City & Suburbs: 754 Elsewhere

TUESDAY APRIL 15, 2003

Think

Dress codes

are a drag?

by Emilie Ostrander
Special to the *Tribune*

While shopping for new clothes, Elyse B., 13, of Mt. Prospect, Illinois, also is scouting for hot trends. Dressed in a bright pink tank top and denim capris, Elyse says she's found an outfit she likes. The catch? Her school dress code bans tank tops—and the penalty is anything but stylish. "If they catch you, you have to change into your gym uniform," she says.

For Elyse, shopping for new clothes is all about looking good without getting in trouble. "We

Savvy Shoppers Can Still Look Cool for School

can't wear spaghetti straps, halter tops, or tube tops," she explains. "Tank top straps must be the width of two fingers, and shorts and skirts have to be longer than 5 inches above the knee."

As we get into spring, many kids are ready to take their warm-weather clothes to school. But some school districts say certain styles are banned from the classroom, and there are consequences for kids who disobey.

Author's Purpose What is the author's purpose or purposes?

Student Edition pages 480–483

Audio CD

Florida Social Studies Standards This Week

SS.B.1.2.5.5.1 Understands varying perceptions in the United States

SS.B.2.2.2.5.1 Understands how the physical environment constrains and supports human activity

SS.B.2.2.3.5.1 Understands how human activity affects the physical environment

Time for
SOCIAL STUDIES

Leveled Readers

◉ **Skill** Generalize

◉ **Strategy** Story Structure

Lesson Vocabulary

Below-Level

On-Level

Advanced

ELL Reader
· Concept Vocabulary
· Text Support
· Language Enrichment

In This New Place Poems
by Linda Marino

Integrate Social Studies Standards

- **Individual Development**
- **Interactions**
- **Groups**
- **Communication**

✓ **Read**

The Stormi Giovanni Club, pp. 462–477

"Think Dress Codes Are a Drag?" pp. 480–483

Leveled Readers

Below-Level   **On-Level**   **Advanced**

· Support Concepts   · Develop Concepts   · Extend Concepts

ELL Reader

✓ **Build Concept Vocabulary**
Adapting to a New Place, pp. 458l–458m

✓ **Teach Social Studies Concepts**
Moving, p. 467
E-Mail, p. 471
Friendship, p. 473

✓ **Explore Social Studies Center**
Share Helpful Hints, p. 458k

Florida Weekly Plan

READING

45–90 minutes

TARGET SKILLS OF THE WEEK

- **Comprehension Skill**
  Generalize
- **Comprehension Strategy**
  Story Structure
- **Vocabulary Strategy**
  Context Clues

LANGUAGE ARTS

30–60 minutes

Trait of the Week

Support/Voice

DAY 1
PAGES 458l–460b, 483a, 483e–483k

Oral Language

QUESTION OF THE WEEK *How do people adapt to a new school?*

Read Aloud: "Only Fiona," 458m
Build Concepts, 458l

Comprehension/Vocabulary

Comprehension Skill/Strategy Lesson, 458–459
- Generalize **T**
- Story Structure

Build Background, 460a

Introduce Lesson Vocabulary, 460b
cavities, combination, demonstrates, episode, profile, strict **T**

Read Leveled Readers

Grouping Options 458f–458g

Fluency

Model Tone of Voice, 458l–458m, 483a

Grammar, 483e
Introduce Indefinite and Reflexive Pronouns **T**

Writing Workshop, 483g
Introduce Letter of Advice
Model the Trait of the Week: Support/Voice

Spelling, 483i
Pretest for Suffixes *-ible, -able*

Internet Inquiry, 483k
Identify Questions

DAY 2
PAGES 460–469, 483a, 483e–483k

Oral Language

QUESTION OF THE DAY *What challenges does Stormi face as a new student?*

Comprehension/Vocabulary

Vocabulary Strategy Lesson, 460
- Context Clues **T**

Read *The Stormi Giovanni Club,* 462–469

Grouping Options 458f–458g

- Generalize **T**
- Story Structure
- **REVIEW** Draw Conclusions **T**

Develop Vocabulary

Fluency

Choral Reading, 483a

Grammar, 483e
Develop Indefinite and Reflexive Pronouns **T**

Writing Workshop, 483g
Improve Writing with Good Conclusions

Spelling, 483i
Teach the Generalization

Internet Inquiry, 483k
Navigate/Search

DAILY WRITING ACTIVITIES

Day 1 Write to Read, 458

Day 2 Words to Write, 461
Strategy Response Log, 462, 469

DAILY SOCIAL STUDIES CONNECTIONS

Day 1 Adapting to a New Place Concept Web, 458l

Day 2 Time for Social Studies: Moving, 467
Revisit the Adapting to a New Place Concept Web, 469

DAILY SUCCESS PREDICTORS
for Adequate Yearly Progress

Monitor Progress and Corrective Feedback

Vocabulary   Check Vocabulary, *458l*

Grouping Options for Differentiated Instruction
Turn the page for the small group lesson plan.

DAY 3 PAGES 470–479, 483a, 483e–483k

Oral Language

QUESTION OF THE DAY *What do Stormi's experiences teach her about making friends?*

Comprehension/Vocabulary

Read *The Stormi Giovanni Club*, 470–478

Grouping Options
458f–458g

- 🔄 Generalize **T**
- 🔄 Story Structure
- 🔄 Context Clues **T**
- Develop Vocabulary

Reader Response

Selection Test

Fluency

Model Tone of Voice, 483a

Grammar, 483f
Apply Indefinite and Reflexive Pronouns in Writing **T**

Writing Workshop, 479, 483h
Write Now
Prewrite and Draft

Spelling, 483j
Connect Spelling to Writing

Internet Inquiry, 483k
Analyze Sources

Day 3 Strategy Response Log, 476
Think and Explain, 478

Day 3 Time for Social Studies: E-mail, 471
Friendship, 473; Revisit the Adapting to a New Place Concept Web, 477

DAY 4 PAGES 480–483a, 483e–483k

Oral Language

QUESTION OF THE DAY *What do you think is the significance of having a school dress code?*

Comprehension/Vocabulary

Read "Think Dress Codes Are a Drag?" 480–483

Grouping Options
458f –458g

Newspaper Article

Reading Across Texts

Content-Area Vocabulary

Fluency

Partner Reading, 483a

Grammar, 483f
Practice Indefinite and Reflexive Pronouns for Standardized Tests **T**

Writing Workshop, 483h
Draft, Revise, and Publish

Spelling, 483j
Provide a Strategy

Internet Inquiry, 483k
Synthesize Information

Day 4 Writing Across Texts, 483

Day 4 Social Studies Center: Share Helpful Hints, 458k

DAY 5 PAGES 483a–483l

Oral Language

QUESTION OF THE WEEK *To wrap up the week, revisit the Day 1 question.*
Build Concept Vocabulary, 483c

Fluency

Read Leveled Readers

Grouping Options 458f–458g

Assess Reading Rate, 483a

Comprehension/Vocabulary

- 🔄 Reteach Generalize, 483b **T**
- Mood, 483b
- 🔄 Review Context Clues, 483c **T**

Speaking and Listening, 483d
Advice
Listen to Advice

Grammar, 483f
Cumulative Review

Writing Workshop, 483h
Connect to Unit Writing

Spelling, 483j
Posttest for Suffixes *-ible, -able*

Internet Inquiry, 483k
Communicate Results

Research/Study Skills, 483l
Thesaurus

Day 5 Mood, 483b

Day 5 Revisit the Adapting to a New Place Concept Web, 483c

KEY 🔄 Target Skill   **T** Tested Skill   **FCAT Tested Skill**

Comprehension — Check Retelling, *478*

Fluency — Check Fluency WCPM, *483a*

Vocabulary — Check Vocabulary, *483c*

SUCCESS PREDICTOR

Small Group Plan for Differentiated Instruction

Daily Plan AT A GLANCE

Reading
Whole Group
- Oral Language
- Comprehension/Vocabulary

Group Time
Differentiated Instruction

Meet with small groups to provide:
- Skill Support
- Reading Support
- Fluency Practice

Read

This week's lessons for daily group time can be found behind the Differentiated Instruction (DI) tab on pp. DI·32–DI·41.

Whole Group
- Fluency

Language Arts
- Grammar
- Writing
- Spelling
- Research/Inquiry
- Speaking/Listening/Viewing

Use *My Sidewalks on Reading Street* for Tier III intensive reading intervention.

DAY 1

On-Level	Strategic Intervention	Advanced
Teacher-Led *Page DI·33*	Teacher-Led *Page DI·32*	Teacher-Led *Page DI·33*
• Develop Concept Vocabulary • **Read** On-Level Reader *The New Kid at School*	• Reinforce Concepts • **Read** Below-Level Reader *Moving*	• **Read** Advanced Reader *Nathaniel Comes to Town* • Independent Extension Activity

ⓘ Independent Activities
While you meet with small groups, have the rest of the class...

- Visit the Reading/Library Center, p. 458j
- Listen to the Background Building Audio
- Finish Write to Read, p. 458
- Complete Practice Book pp. 183–184
- Visit Cross-Curricular Centers

DAY 2

On-Level	Strategic Intervention	Advanced
Teacher-Led *Pages 464–469*	Teacher-Led *Page DI·34*	Teacher-Led *Page DI·35*
• **Read** *The Stormi Giovanni Club*	• Practice Lesson Vocabulary • Read Multisyllabic Words • **Read** or Listen to *The Stormi Giovanni Club*	• Extend Vocabulary • **Read** *The Stormi Giovanni Club*

ⓘ Independent Activities
While you meet with small groups, have the rest of the class...

- Visit the Reading/Library Center, p. 458j
- Listen to the AudioText for *The Stormi Giovanni Club*
- Finish Words to Write, p. 461
- Complete Practice Book pp. 185–186
- Write in their Strategy Response Logs, pp. 462, 469
- Visit Cross-Curricular Centers
- Work on inquiry projects

DAY 3

On-Level	Strategic Intervention	Advanced
Teacher-Led *Pages 470–477*	Teacher-Led *Page DI·36*	Teacher-Led *Page DI·37*
• **Read** *The Stormi Giovanni Club*	• Practice Generalize and Story Structure • **Read** or Listen to *The Stormi Giovanni Club*	• Extend Generalize and Story Structure • **Read** *The Stormi Giovanni Club*

ⓘ Independent Activities
While you meet with small groups, have the rest of the class...

- Visit the Reading/Library Center, p. 458j
- Listen to the AudioText for *The Stormi Giovanni Club*
- Write in their Strategy Response Logs, p. 476
- Finish Think and Explain, p. 478
- Complete Practice Book p. 187
- Visit Cross-Curricular Centers
- Work on inquiry projects

① Begin with whole class skill and strategy instruction.

② Meet with small groups to provide differentiated instruction.

③ Gather the whole class back together for fluency and language arts.

DAY 4

On-Level
Teacher-Led
Pages 480–483

- **Read** "Think Dress Codes Are a Drag?"

Strategic Intervention
Teacher-Led
Page DI · 38

- Practice Retelling
- **Read** or Listen to "Think Dress Codes Are a Drag?"

Advanced
Teacher-Led
Page DI · 39

- **Read** "Think Dress Codes Are a Drag?"
- Genre Study

i Independent Activities

While you meet with small groups, have the rest of the class...

- Visit the Reading/Library Center, p. 458j
- Listen to the AudioText for "Think Dress Codes Are a Drag?"
- Visit the Writing/Vocabulary Center

- Finish Writing Across Texts, p. 483
- Visit Cross-Curricular Centers
- Work on inquiry projects

DAY 5

On-Level
Teacher-Led
Page DI · 41

- **Reread** Leveled Reader *The New Kid at School*
- Retell *The New Kid at School*

Strategic Intervention
Teacher-Led
Page DI · 40

- **Reread** Leveled Reader *Moving*
- Retell *Moving*

Advanced
Teacher-Led
Page DI · 41

- **Reread** Leveled Reader *Nathaniel Comes to Town*
- Share Extension Activity

i Independent Activities

While you meet with small groups, have the rest of the class...

- Visit the Reading/Library Center, p. 458j
- Complete Practice Book pp. 188–190

- Visit Cross-Curricular Centers
- Work on inquiry projects

Grouping Place English language learners in the groups that correspond to their reading abilities in English.

Use the appropriate Leveled Reader or other text at students' instructional level.

TIP Send home the appropriate Multilingual Summary of the main selection on Day 1.

Take It to the NET™ ONLINE
PearsonSuccessNet.com

Peter Afflerbach
For ideas on assessing engagement, see the article "Engaged Assessment of Engaged Readers" by Scott Foresman author Peter Afflerbach.

TEACHER TALK

Curriculum compacting is a technique for content acceleration. Students skip work they already have mastered and complete more challenging content.

Be sure to schedule time for students to work on the unit inquiry project "Adaptations." This week students synthesize information about groups of people or animals who have adapted to different situations.

Looking Ahead

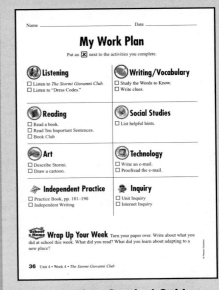

Name _____ Date _____

My Work Plan
Put an ☒ next to the activities you complete.

🎧 Listening
☐ Listen to *The Stormi Giovanni Club*.
☐ Listen to "Dress Codes."

✏️ Writing/Vocabulary
☐ Study the Words to Know.
☐ Write clues.

📖 Reading
☐ Read a book.
☐ Read Ten Important Sentences.
☐ Book Club

🌐 Social Studies
☐ List helpful hints.

🎨 Art
☐ Describe Stormi.
☐ Draw a cartoon.

💻 Technology
☐ Write an e-mail.
☐ Proofread the e-mail.

✍️ Independent Practice
☐ Practice Book, pp. 181–190
☐ Independent Writing

🔍 Inquiry
☐ Unit Inquiry
☐ Internet Inquiry

Wrap Up Your Week Turn your paper over. Write about what you did at school this week. What did you read? What did you learn about adapting to a new place?

36 Unit 4 • Week 4 • *The Stormi Giovanni Club*

▲ **Group-Time Survival Guide**
p. 36, Weekly Contract

The Stormi Giovanni Club   **458g**

☑ Customize Your Plan *by Strand*

ORAL LANGUAGE

Concept Development

How do people adapt to a new school?

CONCEPT VOCABULARY
count on   settle in

BUILD

❑ **Question of the Week** Introduce and discuss the question of the week. This week students will read a variety of texts and work on projects related to the concept *adapting to a new place*. Post the question for students to refer to throughout the week. **DAY 1** *458d*

❑ **Read Aloud** Read aloud "Only Fiona." Then begin a web to build concepts and concept vocabulary related to this week's lesson and the unit theme, Adapting. Introduce the concept words *count on* and *settle in* and have students place them on the web. Display the web for use throughout the week. **DAY 1** *458l–458m*

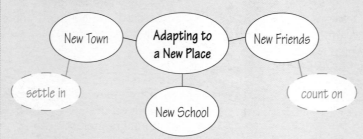

DEVELOP

❑ **Question of the Day** Use the prompts from the Weekly Plan to engage students in conversations related to this week's reading and the unit theme. **EVERY DAY** *458d–458e*

❑ **Concept Vocabulary Web** Revisit the Adapting to a New Place Concept Web and encourage students to add concept words from their reading and life experiences. **DAY 2** *469*, **DAY 3** *477*

CONNECT

❑ **Looking Back/Review/Connect** Revisit the Adapting to a New Place Concept Web and discuss how it relates to this week's lesson and the unit theme. Then make connections to next week's lesson. **DAY 5** *483c*

CHECK

❑ **Concept Vocabulary Web** Use the Adapting to a New Place Concept Web to check students' understanding of the concept vocabulary words *count on* and *settle in*. **DAY 1** *458l*, **DAY 5** *483c*

VOCABULARY

🔁 **STRATEGY**
CONTEXT CLUES
Sometimes when you are reading, you come across a word you do not know. You can use the context, the words and sentences around the word, to find clues to help figure out the meaning.

LESSON VOCABULARY
cavities   episode
combination   profile
demonstrates   strict

TEACH

❑ **Words to Know** Give students the opportunity to tell what they already know about this week's lesson vocabulary words. Then discuss word meaning. **DAY 1** *460b*

❑ **Vocabulary Strategy Lesson** Use the vocabulary strategy lesson in the Student Edition to introduce and model this week's strategy, *context clues*. **DAY 2** *460–461*

Vocabulary Strategy Lesson

PRACTICE/APPLY

❑ **Leveled Text** Read the lesson vocabulary in the context of leveled text. **DAY 1** *LR28–LR36*

❑ **Words in Context** Read the lesson vocabulary and apply *context clues* in the context of *The Stormi Giovanni Club*. **DAY 2** *462–469*, **DAY 3** *470–478*

Leveled Readers

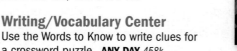

❑ **Writing/Vocabulary Center** Use the Words to Know to write clues for a crossword puzzle. **ANY DAY** *458k*

Main Selection—Drama

❑ **Homework** Practice Book pp. 184–185. **DAY 1** *460b*, **DAY 2** *461*

❑ **Word Play** Have small groups of students brainstorm a list of city nicknames they have heard of or make up some of their own. Have groups quiz each other to see if they can identify cities by their nicknames. **ANY DAY** *483c*

ASSESS

❑ **Selection Test** Use the Selection Test to determine students' understanding of the lesson vocabulary words. **DAY 3**

RETEACH/REVIEW

❑ **Reteach Lesson** If necessary, use this lesson to reteach and review *context clues*. **DAY 5** *483c*

① Use your school-based instructional focus calendar to determine which strands to teach.

② Target your instruction on FCAT tested skills.

③ Check students' understanding of FCAT tested standards.

COMPREHENSION

SKILL GENERALIZE To generalize is to make a broad statement or rule that applies to several examples.

STRATEGY STORY STRUCTURE Story structure is how a fictional story or article is put together. The structure of a story includes how the story begins (the problem), how it builds through the middle (rising action and climax), and how it ends (resolution).

TEACH

☐ **Skill/Strategy Lesson** Use the skill/strategy lesson in the Student Edition to introduce and model *generalize* and *story structure*. **DAY 1** *458–459*

☐ **Extend Skills** Teach mood. **ANY DAY** *483b*

Skill/Strategy Lesson

PRACTICE/APPLY

☐ **Leveled Text** Apply *generalize* and *story structure* to read leveled text. **DAY 1** *LR28–LR36*

☐ **Skills and Strategies in Context** Read *The Stormi Giovanni Club,* using the Guiding Comprehension questions to apply *generalize* and *story structure.* **DAY 2** *462–469,* **DAY 3** *470–478*

Leveled Readers

☐ **Reader Response** Use Student Edition p. 478 to respond to the selection. **DAY 3**, *p. 478*

READ THINK EXPLAIN

Main Selection—Drama

☐ **Skills and Strategies in Context** Read "Think Dress Codes Are a Drag?" Then have students discuss and write across texts. **DAY 4** *480–483*

☐ **Homework** Practice Book pp. 183, 187, 188. **DAY 1** *459,* **DAY 3** *477,* **DAY 5** *483b*

Paired Selection—Nonfiction

ASSESS

☐ **Selection Test** Determine students' understanding of the selection and their use of *generalize* **DAY 3**

☐ **Retell** Have students retell *The Stormi Giovanni Club.* **DAY 3** *478–479*

RETEACH/REVIEW

☐ **Reteach Lesson** If necessary, reteach and review *generalize.* **DAY 5** *483b*

FLUENCY

SKILL TONE OF VOICE Adjusting your tone of voice allows you to show different emotions as you read. Thinking about what is happening or how a character feels can help you know how to use your voice while reading. Emotions such as desperation or suspense are easily conveyed through a changing tone of voice.

TEACH

☐ **Read Aloud** Model fluent reading by rereading "Only Fiona." Focus on this week's fluency skill, tone of voice. **DAY 1** *458l–458m, 483a*

PRACTICE/APPLY

☐ **Choral Reading** Read aloud selected paragraphs from *The Stormi Giovanni Club,* emphasizing the changing inflections in your voice. Then practice as a class, doing three choral readings of the selected paragraphs. **DAY 2** *483a,* **DAY 3** *483a*

☐ **Partner Reading** Have partners practice reading aloud, reading with changing inflections to reflect different characters' emotions, and offering each other feedback. As students reread, monitor their progress toward their individual fluency goals. **DAY 4** *483a*

☐ **Listening Center** Have students follow along with the AudioText for this week's selections. **ANY DAY** *458j*

☐ **Reading/Library Center** Have students reread a selection of their choice. **ANY DAY** *458j*

☐ **Fluency Coach** Have students use Fluency Coach to listen to fluent readings or practice reading on their own. **ANY DAY**

ASSESS

☐ **Check Fluency** WCPM Do a one-minute timed reading, paying special attention to this week's skill— tone of voice. Provide feedback for each student. **DAY 5** *483a*

☑ Customize Your Plan *by Strand*

GRAMMAR

SKILL INDEFINITE AND REFLEXIVE

PRONOUNS *Indefinite pronouns* such as *somebody* or *no one,* may not refer to specific words. They do not always have definite antecedents. *Reflexive pronouns* reflect the action of the verb back on the subject. Reflexive pronouns end in *-self* or *-selves.*

TEACH

❑ **Grammar Transparency 19** Use Grammar Transparency 19 to teach indefinite and reflexive pronouns. **DAY 1** *483e*

Grammar Transparency 19

PRACTICE/APPLY

❑ **Develop the Concept** Review the concept of indefinite and reflexive pronouns and provide guided practice. **DAY 2** *483e*

❑ **Apply to Writing** Have students review something they have written and apply indefinite and reflexive pronouns. **DAY 3** *483f*

❑ **Test Preparation** Examine common errors in indefinite and reflexive pronouns to prepare for standardized tests. **DAY 4** *483f*

❑ **Homework** Grammar and Writing Practice Book pp. 73–75. **DAY 2** *483e,* **DAY 3** *483f,* **DAY 4** *483f*

ASSESS

❑ **Cumulative Review** Use Grammar and Writing Practice Book p. 76. **DAY 5** *483f*

RETEACH/REVIEW

❑ **Daily Fix-It** Have students find and correct errors in grammar, spelling, and punctuation. **EVERY DAY** *483e–483f*

❑ **The Grammar and Writing Book** Use pp. 158–161 of The Grammar and Writing Book to extend instruction for indefinite and reflexive pronouns. **ANY DAY**

The Grammar and Writing Book

WRITING

Trait of the Week

SUPPORT/VOICE Good writers have a strong voice—a personality that comes through in the tone and style of their writing. Voice shows that a writer knows and cares about a topic. A strong voice speaks directly to readers and keeps their attention.

TEACH

❑ **Writing Transparency 19A** Use the model to introduce and discuss the Trait of the Week. **DAY 1** *483g*

❑ **Writing Transparency 19B** Use the transparency to show students how good conclusions can improve their writing. **DAY 2** *483g*

Writing Transparency 19A   **Writing Transparency 19B**

PRACTICE/APPLY

❑ **Write Now** Examine the model on Student Edition p. 479. Then have students write their own letter of advice. **DAY 3** *479, 483h,* **DAY 4** *483h*

> **Prompt** In *The Stormi Giovanni Club,* other people help Stormi adjust to a new school. Think about a situation in which you could offer help or advice. Now write a letter of advice to someone in that situation.

Write Now p. 479

❑ **Writing/Vocabulary Center** Use the Words to Know to write clues for a crossword puzzle. **ANY DAY** *458k*

ASSESS

❑ **Writing Trait Rubric** Use the rubric to evaluate students' writing. **DAY 4** *483h*

RETEACH/REVIEW

❑ **The Grammar and Writing Book** Use pp. 158–163 of The Grammar and Writing Book to extend instruction for indefinite and reflexive pronouns, good conclusions, and letters of advice. **ANY DAY**

The Grammar and Writing Book

① Use your school-based instructional focus calendar to determine which strands to teach.

② Target your instruction on FCAT tested skills.

③ Check students' understanding of FCAT tested standards.

SPELLING

GENERALIZATION SUFFIXES -IBLE, -ABLE When adding the suffix *-ible* or *-able*, there are no sound clues to help you decide which form to use: *agreeable, flexible*. The vowel sound spelled by the letters *ib* and *ab* is the /ə/ and can be spelled many different ways.

TEACH

☐ **Pretest** Give the pretest for words with suffixes *-ible, -able*. Guide students in self-correcting their pretests and correcting any misspellings. DAY 1 483i

☐ **Think and Practice** Connect spelling to the phonics generalization for suffixes *-ible, -able*. DAY 2 483i

PRACTICE/APPLY

☐ **Connect to Writing** Have students use spelling words to make a poster. Then review frequently misspelled words: *when, then, went*. DAY 3 483j

☐ **Homework** Word Study and Spelling Practice Book pp. 73–76. **EVERY DAY**

RETEACH/REVIEW

☐ **Review** Review spelling words to prepare for the posttest. Then provide students with a spelling strategy—divide and conquer. DAY 4 483j

ASSESS

☐ **Posttest** Use dictation sentences to give the posttest for words with suffixes *-ible, -able*. DAY 5 483j

Spelling Words

1. sensible
2. washable
3. available
4. agreeable
5. fashionable
6. valuable
7. flexible
8. reasonable
9. favorable
10. breakable
11. convertible
12. forgettable
13. laughable
14. sociable
15. allowable
16. divisible
17. hospitable*
18. reversible
19. responsible
20. tolerable

Challenge Words

21. noticeable
22. conceivable
23. disposable
24. biodegradable
25. collapsible

*Word from the selection

RESEARCH AND INQUIRY

☐ **Internet Inquiry** Have students conduct an Internet inquiry on e-mail. **EVERY DAY** 483k

☐ **Thesaurus** Review the features associated with a thesaurus and discuss how students can use a thesaurus to locate synonyms. DAY 5 483l

☐ **Unit Inquiry** Allow time for students to synthesize the information they gathered about groups of people or animals who have adapted to different situations. **ANY DAY** 391

SPEAKING AND LISTENING

☐ **Advice** Have students write and present a speech on giving advice to a group of new students adapting to their new school. DAY 5 483d

☐ **Listen to Advice** Have students reflect on the advice they were given by classmates and answer questions. DAY 5 483d

Resources for Differentiated Instruction

LEVELED READERS

▶ **Comprehension**
- ↻ **Skill** Generalize
- ↻ **Strategy** Story Structure

▶ **Lesson Vocabulary**
- ↻ **Context Clues**

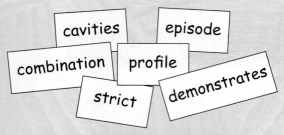

cavities · episode · combination · profile · strict · demonstrates

▶ **Social Studies Standards**
- **Individual Development**
- **Interactions**
- **Groups**
- **Communication**

On-Level

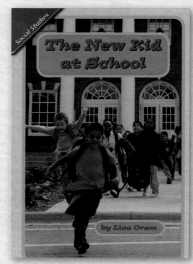

On-Level Reader

The New Kid at School

On-Level Practice TE p. LR32

On-Level Practice TE p. LR33

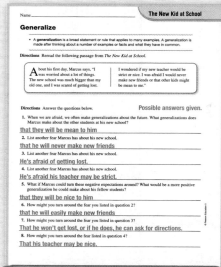

Strategic Intervention

Below-Level Reader

Moving by Vena Douglas

Below-Level Practice TE p. LR29

Below-Level Practice TE p. LR30

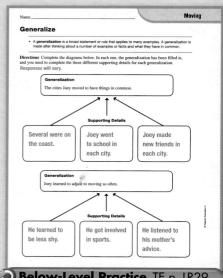

Advanced

Advanced Reader

Name_____   **Nathaniel Comes to Town**

Generalize

• A **generalization** is a broad statement or rule that applies to many examples. A generalization is made after thinking about a number of examples or facts and what they have in common.

Directions What are some of the difficulties faced by Nathaniel as a new student? What can you generalize about the difficulties that all new students face?

1-5.
Nathaniel needs to make new friends, needs to find his way in his
new class, and he needs to make Drew be his best friend.
In general, all new students have to make new friends at a new
school and fit in with the other students.

Directions Based on Drew's experiences, what can you generalize about how difficult it is to help a new student find his way?

6-10.
Drew has trouble because Nathaniel is younger than him and he's
afraid that other students will make fun of him for having a younger
friend. He gets jealous when Nathaniel sits down with one of his
friends for lunch, and later that day he snaps at him.
In general, it's very hard to fit a new person into an existing group of
friends at school. But many of Drew's problems were overcome by
the end of the story.

Advanced Practice TE p. LR35

Name_____   **Nathaniel Comes to Town**

Vocabulary
Directions Fill in the blank with the word from the box that fits best.

Check the Words You Know
___ annoyingly   ___ foreboding
___ gallantly   ___ humiliation
___ jostling   ___ skeptically

1. Drew viewed going to school with ___foreboding___ and dread.
2. Nathaniel ___gallantly___ tried to make friends at his new school.
3. The color of Drew's basketball caused him ___humiliation___.
4. In gym class, Nathaniel tried ___jostling___ for the ball.
5. Drew's sister liked to tease him ___annoyingly___.
6. Drew reacted ___skeptically___ to his teacher's cheerful greeting.

Directions Write a brief paragraph discussing Nathaniel's first day at school, using as many vocabulary words as possible.

___Possible responses will vary.___

Advanced Practice TE p. LR36

ELL

ELL Reader

ELL Poster 19

Teacher's Edition Notes

ELL notes throughout this lesson support instruction and reference additional resources at point of use.

Teaching Guide pp. 127–133, 248–249

• Multilingual summaries of the main selection

• Comprehension lesson

• Vocabulary strategies and word cards

• ELL Reader 5.4.4 lesson

ELL and Transition Handbook

Ten Important Sentences

• Key ideas from every selection in the Student Edition

• Activities to build sentence power

More Reading

Readers' Theater Anthology

• Fluency practice

• Five scripts to build fluency

• Poetry for oral interpretation

Leveled Trade Books

• Extended reading tied to the unit concept

• Lessons in the Trade Book Library Teaching Guide

Homework

• Family Times Newsletter

• ELL Multilingual Selection Summaries

Take-Home Books

• Leveled Readers

Cross-Curricular Centers

Listening

Listen to the Selections

MATERIALS [SINGLES]
CD player, headphones, AudioText CD, student book

LISTEN TO LITERATURE Listen to *The Stormi Giovanni Club* and "Think Dress Codes Are a Drag?" as you follow or read along in your book. Listen for the generalizations in each selection.

If there is anything you don't understand, you can listen again to any section.

Reading/Library

Read It Again!

MATERIALS [SINGLES] [PAIRS] [GROUPS]
Collection of books for self-selected reading, reading logs, student book

Select a book you have already read. Record the title of the book in your reading log. You may want to read with a partner.

Choose from the following:

- Leveled Readers
- ELL Readers
- Stories Written by Classmates
- Books from the Library
- *The Stormi Giovanni Club*

TEN IMPORTANT SENTENCES Read the Ten Important Sentences for *The Stormi Giovanni Club*. Then locate the sentences in the student book.

BOOK CLUB Meet as a group to read aloud. How does speaking the lines help you to understand the story and the characters? Read other short plays and get together with a group to share your favorites.

Art

Create a Cartoon

MATERIALS [SINGLES]
Writing and drawing materials

Create a cartoon sketch of Stormi Giovanni.

1. Make a list of five adjectives or phrases you would use to describe Stormi Giovanni.
3. Draw a cartoon of Stormi that shows what kind of character she is.

EARLY FINISHERS Write a caption or thought bubble to go with the cartoon.

Stormi Giovanni
1. Loyal friend
2. Funny
3. Likes her privacy
4.
5.

Scott Foresman Reading Street Centers Survival Kit
Use the *The Stormi Giovanni Club* materials from the Reading Street Centers Survival Kit to organize this week's centers.

Writing/Vocabulary

Write Clues

MATERIALS
Writing materials

GROUPS

Write clues for a crossword puzzle.

1. **Think about the meaning for each lesson vocabulary word for this week. If you're not sure, use context clues or a dictionary to help.**
2. **Write across and down clues for each word you would use in a puzzle.**

EARLY FINISHERS Find some unfamiliar words from *The Stormi Giovanni Club* and add them to your crossword puzzle list.

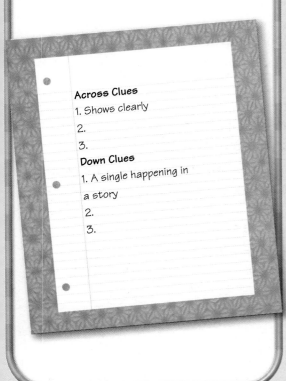

Across Clues
1. Shows clearly
2.
3.
Down Clues
1. A single happening in a story
2.
3.

Social Studies

Share Helpful Hints

MATERIALS
Writing and art materials

SINGLES
PAIRS
GROUPS

Make a list of helpful hints for a new student coming to your school for the first time.

1. **Think about the things a new student would need to know such as the rules, the schedule, and how to get around your school.**
2. **List at least five helpful hints.**

EARLY FINISHERS Design a cover for a "Welcome to Our School" packet.

Welcome to Our School: Helpful Hints for the New Student

1. Gather outside in the schoolyard before the bell rings in the morning.

2. Write your locker combination down somewhere and don't lose it!

3. Play outside or read in the library at recess time.

4. Bring money for lunch on Fridays because Friday is pizza day.

Technology

Compose an E-MAIL

MATERIALS
E-mail program

SINGLES

Write an e-mail to someone you know, just like Stormi.

1. **Follow classroom rules for composing and sending an e-mail message to someone you know.**
2. **Choose a friend or family member who goes to a different school or who lives far away and describe how things are going for you in school this year.**
3. **Include a subject line and proofread your message before sending it.**

EARLY FINISHERS Write a similar note to another friend or family member, but this time write it by hand and mail it. How is the experience different?

To: Lisa
From: Melanie
Subject: What's up?

Hi Lisa,
How are you? I can't believe we are almost done with fifth grade. My hardest subject this year is

ALL CENTERS

Concept Vocabulary

count on to expect; to rely on

settle in to take up residence in a new place; to become adjusted to

Monitor Progress

Check Vocabulary

If...	then... use the
students are unable to place words on the Web,	Concept Vocabulary Routine on p. DI·1 to teach the words. Provide additional words for practice, such as *handsomer* and *get used to*.

SUCCESS PREDICTOR

DAY 1 Grouping Options

Reading
Whole Group
Introduce and discuss the Question of the Week. Then use pp. 458l–460b.

Group Time
Differentiated Instruction
Read this week's Leveled Readers. See pp. 458f–458g for the small group lesson plan.

Whole Group
Use p. 483a.

Language Arts
Use pp. 483e–483k.

Build Concepts

FLUENCY

MODEL TONE OF VOICE Use the excerpt from "Only Fiona" as an opportunity to model tone of voice. Remind students that thinking about what is happening or how a character feels can help them know how to use their voice while they read. For example, as you read the sentence, "The only thing wrong with Elvern, Fiona thought, is that it feels like a new town, too," use a slow, quiet voice to reflect her sad mood.

LISTENING COMPREHENSION

After reading the excerpt from "Only Fiona," use the following questions to assess listening comprehension.

1. **What generalization does Fiona make about her new town?** *(Possible responses: She thinks it is nice; it's too new; she doesn't think she'll make friends she can count on.)* **Generalize**

2. **What generalization can you make about Fiona's parents?** *(Possible response: They care about her; they are good listeners.)* **Generalize**

BUILD CONCEPT VOCABULARY

Start a web to build concepts and vocabulary related to this week's lesson and the unit theme.

- Draw the Adapting to a New Place Concept Web.
- Read the sentence with the phrase *count on* again. Ask students to pronounce it and discuss its meaning.
- Place *count on* in an oval attached to *New Friends*. Explain that *count on* is related to this concept. Read the sentence in which *settle in* appears. Have students add this phrase to the web, and provide reasons.
- Brainstorm additional words and categories for the web. Keep the web on display and add words throughout the week.

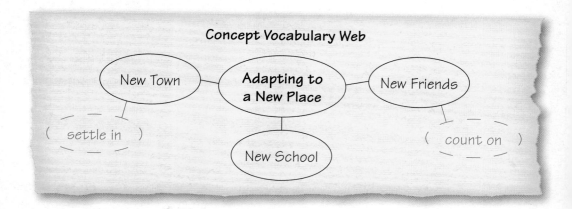

Concept Vocabulary Web

New Town — Adapting to a New Place — New Friends — (count on) — New School — (settle in)

Only Fiona

from

by Beverly Keller

When her father gets a great new job as the manager of the optical department at Molberry's Department Store, Fiona Foster and her parents move away from the small town where they have always lived. Although the new town is nice enough, without fame, siblings, pets, or real friends to count on, Fiona is having a hard time getting used to living there.

In the six weeks they'd lived in Elvern, Fiona had seen enough of it to realize that it was a much handsomer town than Kelsey. Just a few blocks from Fiona's new house was a huge park. Its trees were so tall and leafy, they seemed to be whispering even when there was no breeze. There were acres of fine, close-trimmed grass, with gentle mounds you could roll down if you took a notion.

Molberry's Department Store was the biggest store Fiona had ever seen, set in the middle of a shopping mall that was nearly as dazzling as Disneyland. Molberry's Optical Department had brand-new carpeting and chairs and *four* glass-topped tables with mirrors where customers could sit and try on frames.

The only thing wrong with Elvern, Fiona thought, is that it feels like a new town, too.

"The hardest thing about leaving a place," she told her mother now, "is giving up your friends. I knew most of those kids in Kelsey so long, I couldn't even remember how I met them. The neat thing about friends like that is that you can just count on them. You know. Not for anything special. Just to be around. You don't even care about being famous when you have friends to count on."

"You've made new friends since we moved here," her mother reminded her gently.

"Not to count on. Besides, they all live blocks away...To learn to live in a new place, you have to have a brother or a sister or a dog or a cat going through it with you, or friends you can count on."

No sooner had she gotten the last word out than Fiona realized she hadn't included parents among the things she could count on. Not only that, the things she *had* mentioned, like brothers and sisters, were mostly things parents provide. In one sentence, she thought, I insulted my mother and father in at least two different ways.

Mrs. Foster put her arms around Fiona..."You're having a bad day, aren't you, love?"

"It's only morning," Fiona pointed out.

"Things are bound to get better," her father assured her. "It takes a while to settle in, but once you get used to Elvern, you'll be glad we moved here."

Activate Prior Knowledge

Before students listen to the Read Aloud, ask them to talk about what it feels like to move to a new town or country.

Set Purpose

Read aloud the title and have students predict what the selection will be about.

Read the introduction aloud. Encourage students to listen for Fiona's generalizations about her new town.

Creative Response

Ask groups of students to work on a Readers' Theater presentation of the story. Assign roles, and have "actors" read aloud the story, using their voices to bring characters to life. **Drama**

Develop Concept Vocabulary

Read aloud every day from a book of your choice related to the concept and use the Concept Vocabulary Routine on p. DI·1 to develop concept vocabulary. For suggestions, see p. TR14.

Access Content Before reading, share this summary: Fiona's father gets a new job in a large department store in a new town. Fiona and her parents move there. Fiona knows her new town is nicer than her old town but she misses having friends she can count on. Her father reassures her saying that once she gets settled in, she will be glad they moved there.

Homework Send home this week's Family Times newsletter.

Pages 458l–458m

LA.5.1.6.2 Listen to and discuss conceptually challenging text

LA.5.1.6.4 Categorize key vocabulary

LA.5.1.7.3 Determine the main idea or essential message through inferring

LA.5.5.2.1 Listen and speak to gain and share information (dramatic recitations)

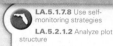 SKILLS ⬄ STRATEGIES IN CONTEXT

Generalize
Story Structure

OBJECTIVES

- Identify and make generalizations.
- Generalize to understand story structure.

Skills Trace
Generalize	
Introduce/Teach	TE: 5.4 412–413, 458–459; 5.5 604–605
Practice	Practice Book: 163, 167, 168, 183, 187, 188, 196, 243, 247, 248
Reteach/Review	TE: 5.4 435b, 483b, 493, DI·53, DI·55; 5.5 625b, DI·56
Test	Selection Test: 65–68, 73–76, 97–100; Benchmark Test: Unit 4

INTRODUCE

Write a sentence starter on the board: *Most of the students in the class are....* Have volunteers look around the room and use what they see to complete the sentences. *(For example: Most of the students in the class are ready for lunch.)* Point out that the completed sentences are generalizations about the students in the class.

Have students read the information on p. 458. Explain the following:

- A generalization is a statement about what several people or things have in common.
- Knowing how stories are generally structured can help you identify, understand, and remember key ideas.

Use Skill Transparency 19 to teach generalize and story structure.

Comprehension

Skill
Generalize

Strategy
Story Structure

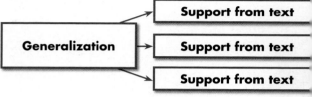
LA.5.1.7.8 Use self-monitoring strategies
LA.5.2.1.2 Analyze plot structure

 ## Generalize

- To generalize is to make a broad statement or rule that applies to several examples.
- Active readers pay close attention to what authors tell them about story characters and make generalizations about those characters as they read.

Generalization	→	**Support from text**
	→	**Support from text**
	→	**Support from text**

 ## Strategy: Story Structure

Active readers notice story structure. They note the problem characters must deal with and the rising action, climax, and outcome. Generally, authors identify the problem at the start. They work through the problem as the action rises in the middle, and then solve it with the climax and outcome.

Write to Read

1. Read "Thirty Pounds of Trouble." Make a graphic organizer similar to the one above about the story's main character, Tag.

2. Use your graphic organizer to decide whether you would like a dog like Tag and tell why.

458

Strategic Intervention

Generalize To help students understand how to generalize, work with them to create a three-column chart. In the first column, list names of popular TV shows. In the second column, list main characters in each show. In the third column, help students create generalizations about the characters using the following sentence starter: *Most of the characters in this show are....* Later, discuss students' generalizations.

ELL

Access Content

Beginning/Intermediate For a Picture It! lesson on generalize, see ELL Teaching Guide, pp. 127–128.

Advanced Before students read "Thirty Pounds of Trouble," have a volunteer read the first sentence aloud. This statement is a generalization. Students can make up two or three statements that support this generalization.

Thirty Pounds of Trouble

A new canine member in the family can bring joy. It can also bring trouble. Tag was our new dog, a mutt with the silliest grin. He weighed thirty pounds—thirty pounds of genuine trouble.

Tag commenced to wailing like a wolf whenever the moon came up, which kept us up all night. When he was inside, he whined to be let outside. When he was outside, he whimpered to get back in. He would crouch behind the couch and come hurtling out at Mother, and when Father was on the phone, Tag would seize the cord and yank the receiver away.

Finally, Mother and Father had absolutely no patience left. "Tag has got to go," they said.

"No," I cried. I adored that canine rascal, even if he did make munchies of my homework and conceal my socks in the rose bushes. I just had to find a way to keep Tag!

I know it sounds incredible, but six weeks later Tag graduated Obedience School at the head of his class. I think Tag was as surprised as we were. Now he is quiet and polite pretty much all the time. He still has that silly grin though, and he still hides my socks in the rose bushes.

1 Strategy Generally, the story's problem is told at the start. What is the problem here?

2 Skill Which generalization can you make?
a) Tag likes people.
b) Tag upsets people.
c) Tag is expensive.

3 Strategy Generally, the action rises in the middle. What is the high point of the story so far?

4 Skill What generalization can you make about the narrator's feelings for Tag? How does the text support it?

459

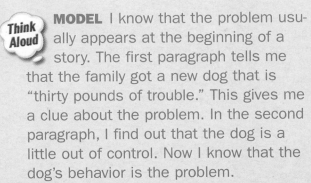

TEACH

1 STRATEGY Model locating a problem in a story.

Think Aloud **MODEL** I know that the problem usually appears at the beginning of a story. The first paragraph tells me that the family got a new dog that is "thirty pounds of trouble." This gives me a clue about the problem. In the second paragraph, I find out that the dog is a little out of control. Now I know that the dog's behavior is the problem.

2 SKILL Model how to make a generalization.

Think Aloud **MODEL** I know that a generalization tells what several people or things have in common. From paragraph 2, I know that Tag's bad behavior is bothering several people in the house. Therefore, the correct generalization is *b*.

PRACTICE AND ASSESS

3 STRATEGY Possible response: The high point occurs when the parents say, "Tag has got to go."

4 SKILL Possible response: Generalization: The narrator is generally pleased with how Tag has improved. Support: Tag graduated Obedience School at the head of his class. Now he is quiet and polite most of the time.

WRITE Have students complete steps 1 and 2 of the Write to Read activity. You might consider using this as a whole-class activity.

Monitor Progress

Generalize

If... students are unable to complete **Write to Read** on p. 458,	then... use Practice Book p. 183 to provide additional practice.

Pages 458–459

LA.5.1.7.3 Determine the main idea or essential message through inferring

LA.5.2.1.2 Locate and analyze character development, plot structure, including rising/falling action and problem/resolution

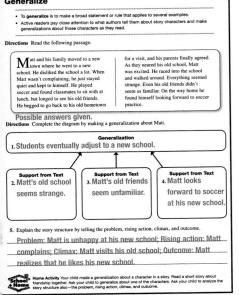

Generalize

- To **generalize** is to make a broad statement or rule that applies to several examples.
- Active readers pay close attention to what authors tell them about story characters and make generalizations about those characters as they read.

Directions Read the following passage.

Matt and his family moved to a new town where he went to a new school. He disliked the school a lot. When Matt wasn't complaining, he just stayed quiet and kept to himself. He played soccer and found classmates to sit with at lunch, but longed to see his old friends. He begged to go back to his old hometown for a visit, and his parents finally agreed. As they neared his old school, Matt was excited. He raced into the school and walked around. Everything seemed strange. Even his old friends didn't seem as familiar. On the way home he found himself looking forward to soccer practice.

Possible answers given.

Directions Complete the diagram by making a generalization about Matt.

Generalization
1. Students eventually adjust to a new school.

Support from Text
2. Matt's old school seems strange.

Support from Text
3. Matt's old friends seem unfamiliar.

Support from Text
4. Matt looks forward to soccer at his new school.

5. Explain the story structure by telling the problem, rising action, climax, and outcome.
Problem: Matt is unhappy at his new school; Rising action: Matt complains; Climax: Matt visits his old school; Outcome: Matt realizes that he likes his new school.

Home Activity Your child made a generalization about a character in a story. Read a short story about friendship together. Ask your child to generalize about one of the characters. Ask your child to analyze the story structure also—the problem, rising action, climax, and outcome.

Practice Book p. 183

The Stormi Giovanni Club **459**

ONLINE

Students can find out more about making new friends by using the keywords *making friends* or *going back to school* on a student-friendly search engine. Be sure to follow classroom rules for Internet use.

ELL

Build Background Use ELL Poster 19 to build background and vocabulary for the lesson concept of adapting to a new school.

▲ **ELL Poster** 19

Build Background

ACTIVATE PRIOR KNOWLEDGE

MAKE A CONCEPT WEB about making new friends.

• Give students two to three minutes to brainstorm ideas about making new friends.

• Have them use a concept web to record their ideas.

• Tell students that, as they read, they should look for more ideas to add to their concept web.

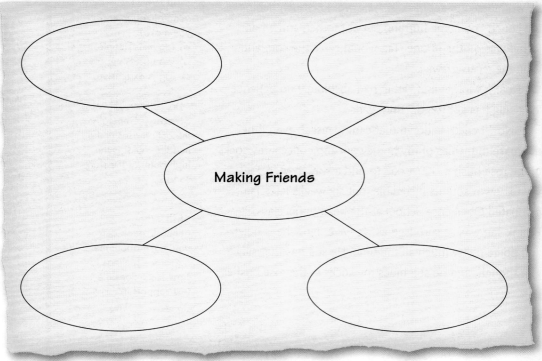

Making Friends

▲ **Graphic Organizer** 15

BACKGROUND BUILDING AUDIO This week's audio explores adapting to a new school. After students listen, discuss what they found out and what surprised them most about going to a new school.

 **Background Building Audio**

Introduce Vocabulary

WORD RATING CHART

Create word rating charts using the categories *Know, Have Seen,* and *Don't Know.*

Word Rating Chart

Word	Know	Have Seen	Don't Know
cavities	✓		
combination		✓	
demonstrates		✓	
episode			✓
profile			✓
strict	✓		

▲ **Graphic Organizer** 5

Read each word to students and have them check one of the three columns: *Know* (know and can use); *Have Seen* (have seen or heard the word; don't know meaning); *Don't Know* (don't know the word). ***Activate Prior Knowledge***

Have students share where they may have seen some of these words. Point out that some of this week's words have multiple meanings *(profile)* and students may learn new definitions for these words. ***Multiple-Meaning Words***

Check charts with students at the end of the week and have them make changes to their ratings.

Use the Multisyllabic Word Routine on p. DI·1 to help students read multisyllabic words.

Lesson Vocabulary

WORDS TO KNOW

T cavities hollow places; holes in teeth caused by decay

T combination a series of numbers or letters dialed in opening a certain kind of lock

T demonstrates shows how a thing is done

T episode one part of a story that is published or broadcast in several parts, one at a time

T profile *low profile,* moderate attitude or position, deliberately chosen in order to avoid notice

T strict very careful in following a rule or making others follow it

MORE WORDS TO KNOW

audacious rudely bold

digressed turned aside from the main subject in talking or writing

scintillating sparkling; flashing

T = Tested Word

Vocabulary

Directions Choose the word from the box that best matches each definition below. Write the word on the line.

cavities _____ 1. hollow places in teeth caused by decay

demonstrates _____ 2. shows how a thing is done

strict _____ 3. very careful in following a rule or making others follow it

episode _____ 4. one part of a story that is published or broadcast in several parts

profile _____ 5. attitude or position

Check the Words You Know
___cavities
___combination
___demonstrates
___episode
___profile
___strict

Directions Choose the word from the box that best matches each clue below. Write the word on the line.

episode _____ 6. This is one in a series.

combination _____ 7. This opens some locks.

strict _____ 8. Some teachers act this way.

profile _____ 9. A movie star would have a high one of these.

cavities _____ 10. If you don't brush your teeth, you might get these.

Write a Friendly Letter

On a separate sheet of paper, write a friendly letter that you might send to a relative telling about the beginning of a new school year. Use as many vocabulary words as you can.

Letters should include words from the vocabulary list as well as information typical to a new school year.

Home Activity Your child identified and used vocabulary words from *The Stormi Giovanni Club.* Read a story or nonfiction article with your child. Have him or her point out unfamiliar words. Together try to figure out the meaning of each word by using the words that appear near it.

▲ **Practice Book** p. 184

Page 460b

LA.5.1.6.1 Use new vocabulary that is introduced and taught directly

LA.5.1.6.9 Determine the correct meanings of words with multiple meanings

LA.5.1.7.1 Use prior knowledge

Vocabulary Strategy

FCAT TESTED SKILL

OBJECTIVE

Use context clues to determine word meaning.

INTRODUCE

Discuss the strategy for context clues using the steps on p. 460.

TEACH

- Have students read "Trouble in TV Land," paying attention to any unknown words as they read.
- Model using context clues to determine the meaning of *cavities*.

Think Aloud **MODEL** As I read the sentences around *cavities* I understand that they are talking about taking care of teeth and preventing tooth decay. I think *cavities* must mean "holes in your teeth caused by decay."

DAY 2 Grouping Options

Reading
Whole Group Discuss the Question of the Day. Then use pp. 460–463.

Group Time Differentiated Instruction
Read *The Stormi Giovanni Club.* See pp. 458f–458g for the small group lesson plan.

Whole Group Use p. 483a.

Language Arts
Use pp. 483e–483k.

Words to Know

- episode
- demonstrates
- profile
- cavities
- strict
- combination

Remember
Try the strategy. Then, if you need more help, use your glossary or dictionary.

Vocabulary Strategy
for Unfamiliar Words

Context Clues Sometimes when you are reading, you come across a word you do not know. You can use the context—the words and sentences around the word—to find clues to its meaning.

1. Reread the sentence in which the unknown word appears. Does the author give you a clue, such as a synonym?

2. If not, read the sentences around the sentence with the unknown word. Does the author give you clues, such as examples or explanations?

3. Put the clues together and decide what you think the word means.

4. Try the meaning in the sentence. Does it make sense?

As you read "Trouble in TV Land," look for context clues that help you figure out the meanings of the vocabulary words.

LA.5.1.6.2 Develop vocabulary by reading and discussing text
LA.5.1.6.3 Use context clues

460

Strategic Intervention

Context Clues Have students work with partners to follow the steps on p. 460 for other Words to Know.

ELL

Access Content Use ELL Poster 19 to preteach vocabulary. Choose from the following to meet language proficiency levels.

Beginning/Intermediate Ask students to share what they know about the words *profile, strict,* and *combination* in their home languages. For example, the Spanish cognates are: *perfil, estricto,* and *combinación.*

Advanced Teach the lesson on pp. 460–461. Have students return to the word rating chart and make appropriate changes to their ratings.

Resources for home-language words may include parents, bilingual staff members, bilingual dictionaries, or online translation sources.

TROUBLE IN TV LAND

Can a TV show teach you how to win friends in the real world? Most sitcoms solve problems in thirty minutes flat, minus about eight minutes of commercials. They present an extremely simple and reassuring view of the world. A single episode demonstrates how to teach a bully the value of kindness or how to overcome your worst fears. Nice-looking young people have a high profile in these shows, and they almost always solve their problems by the end. Plus, the commercials tell you things like how to prevent cavities and whiten your teeth. These commercial messages claim they can save you from tooth decay and so much more. If you will only buy the right clothes and choose the right cell phone, everyone will love you and you will be happy.

In the real world, problems aren't so easily solved. Things you don't enjoy, like having a strict teacher or parent, may actually be good for you. Everyone has problems. Some are as simple as forgetting a locker combination, but others are tough. You can't just make a wish and watch a failing grade go away, for example. To solve problems in the real world, you must be honest and willing to try hard, sometimes for a long time.

Words to Write

Write a letter to your favorite fictional TV character about the way he or she solves problems. Are that character's shows realistic? State your opinion and give reasons to support it. Use words in the Words to Know list if you can.

461

CORRECTIVE FEEDBACK

LA.5.1.6.3 Use context clues to determine meanings of unfamiliar words

- **Question** Use the question below to address this FCAT tested standard. Have students write their answers on a sheet of paper.
- **Check** Scan students' responses by having them hold up their papers.
- **Correct** If necessary, provide corrective feedback.
- **Adjust** Pair students who have correctly identified the correct answer with students who did not for peer tutoring. Have them complete Practice Book p. 185 together.

What clues in the first paragraph of "Trouble in TV Land" help you understand the word *sitcom*?

PRACTICE AND ASSESS

- Have students define the remaining Words to Know and explain the context clues they used.
- Review how to use the glossary or dictionary for words that students can't define in context.
- If you began a word rating chart on p. 460b, have students reassess their ratings.
- Have students complete Practice Book p. 185.

WRITE Have students follow the form of a friendly letter and use two or more Words to Know to help them express their opinions.

Monitor Progress

Context Clues

If... students need more practice with the lesson vocabulary,	**then...** use Tested Vocabulary Cards.

Vocabulary · Context Clues

- Sometimes when you are reading, you see an unfamiliar word. Use the **context**, or words around the unfamiliar word, to find clues to its meaning.
- Context clues include synonyms, examples, and explanations.

Directions Read the following passage. Then answer the questions below.

In class, Meg's teacher demonstrated, or showed, how to open the new lockers. "Dial the combination and then pull the handle," she said. Instead of paying attention, however, Meg talked to her friend about an episode of her favorite TV show, the last one of the series. "Meg, you are not supposed to talk while I am talking. I am very strict about following this rule. Please stay in class during recess," her teacher said sternly. Meg was very embarrassed, but she was glad she didn't have to stay after school. She had to go to the dentist to have her cavities filled after school.

1. What does *demonstrated* mean? What clue helps you to determine the meaning?
   Demonstrated means "showed." The clue is the synonym *showed.*

2. What does *combination* mean? How does the context help you to determine the meaning?
   Combination means "a series of numbers used in opening a lock." The clue is the word *dial.*

3. What is an *episode*? What clue helps you to determine this?
   Episode means "a story that is one in a series." The phrase "last one in the series" helps to define *episode.*

4. How do context clues help you determine the meaning of *strict*?
   Strict means "careful in following the rules." The phrases "following this rule" and "sternly" are context clues.

5. What does *cavities* mean? How can you use context clues to determine the meaning?
   Cavities means "holes or hollow places." The word "filled" is a context clue.

Home Activity Your child read a short passage and used context clues to understand new words. Work with your child to identify unfamiliar words in an article. Ask your child to find context clues to help with the understanding of the new words. Confirm the meanings with your child.

▲ **Practice Book** p. 185

WORD AWARENESS Post this week's lesson vocabulary on a Word Wall or have students write the words and meanings in their Writing Logs for ready access during writing.

Prereading Strategies

GENRE STUDY

Play

The Stormi Giovanni Club is a play. Explain that a play is a story written to be performed by actors for an audience. It is written in the form of a script.

PREVIEW AND PREDICT

Have students preview the selection title and illustrations and predict what they think the title means. Students should use lesson vocabulary words during the discussion.

Strategy Response Log

Predict Have students write their predictions in their Strategy Response Logs. Students will check their predictions in the Strategy Response Log activity on p. 469.

Use Strategies Have students record in their strategy response logs reading strategies they use during reading and tell why they use them.

The Stormi Giovanni Club

by Lydia R. Diamond
illustrated by R. Gregory Christie

Genre A **play** is a story written to be acted out for an audience. As you read, imagine the actors speaking the lines and acting out the action.

462

ELL

Activate Prior Knowledge ELL students may share the experiences of being new in a school or country. Encourage students to talk about why it is important to make new friends.

Consider having students read the selection summary in English or in students' home languages. See the Multilingual Summaries in the ELL Teaching Guide, pp. 131–133.

Pages 462–463

LA.5.1.7.1 Make predictions, and establish a purpose for reading

LA.5.1.7.8 Use strategies to repair comprehension when self-monitoring, including predicting

LA.5.2.2.1 Use information from text features (illustrations)

How will Stormi do in her new school?

463

SET PURPOSE

Read the first page of the selection aloud to students. Have them consider their preview discussion and tell what they hope to understand as they read the selection.

Remind students to make generalizations about Stormi as they read.

STRATEGY RECALL

Students have now used these before-reading strategies:

- preview the selection to be aware of its genre, features, and possible content;
- activate prior knowledge about that content and what to expect of that genre;
- make predictions;
- set a purpose for reading.

Remind students that, as they read, they should monitor their own comprehension. If they realize something does not make sense, they can regain their comprehension by using fix-up strategies they have learned, such as:

- use phonics and word structure to decode new words;
- use context clues or a dictionary to figure out meanings of new words;
- adjust their reading rate—slow down for difficult text, speed up for easy or familiar text, or skim and scan just for specific information;
- reread parts of the text;
- read on (continue to read for clarification);
- use text features such as headings, subheadings, charts, illustrations, and so on as visual aids to comprehension;
- make a graphic organizer or a semantic organizer to aid comprehension;
- use reference sources, such as an encyclopedia, dictionary, thesaurus, or synonym finder;
- use another person, such as a teacher, a peer, a librarian, or an outside expert, as a resource.

After reading, students will use these strategies:

- summarize or retell the text;
- answer questions they or others pose;
- reflect to make new information become part of their prior knowledge.

Audio CD **AudioText**

Guiding Comprehension

1 Character • Inferential

What have you learned so far about Stormi?

Possible response: She's going to a new school. She's not looking forward to it. She has a sense of humor.

2  Generalize • Inferential

What generalization can you make about how Stormi feels about starting a new school?

Possible response: She's not happy about having to start yet another new school.

Monitor Progress	
 Generalize	
If... students are unable to make a generalization,	then... use the skill and strategy instruction on p. 465.

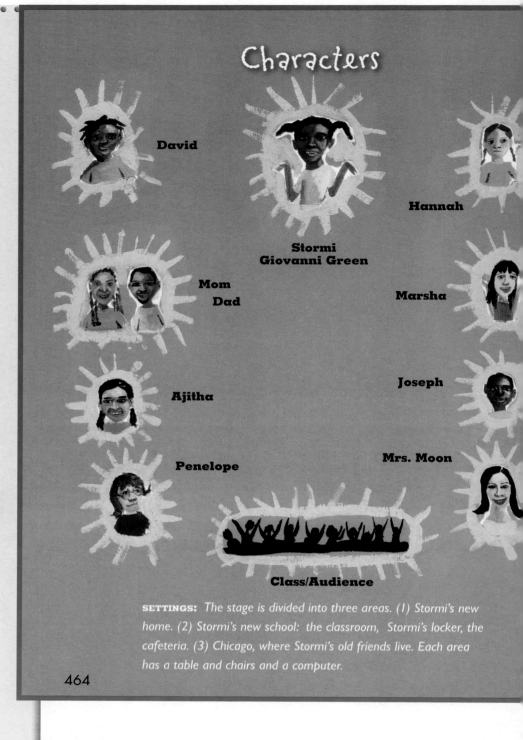

Characters

David

Stormi
Giovanni Green

Hannah

Mom
Dad

Marsha

Ajitha

Joseph

Penelope

Mrs. Moon

Class/Audience

SETTINGS: *The stage is divided into three areas. (1) Stormi's new home. (2) Stormi's new school: the classroom, Stormi's locker, the cafeteria. (3) Chicago, where Stormi's old friends live. Each area has a table and chairs and a computer.*

464

ELL

Access Content Point to the list of characters on p. 464. Explain that the audience is a group of people gathered to see or hear a performance. Tell students that throughout this play, Stormi speaks to the audience, or the class.

Page 464

LA.5.1.7.3 Determine the main idea or essential message through inferring

LA.5.2.1.2 Analyze character development

SCENE I

SETTING: *Stormi's new home. There are unpacked boxes everywhere.* MOM *holds Stormi's backpack.*

MOM: Stormi, hurry up.

STORMI *(off stage):* Coming, Mom.

MOM: You don't want to be late on your first day.

STORMI *(entering):* No. Wouldn't want that. *(to AUDIENCE)* I would rather not go at all.

MOM: Honey, don't frown. You've started at a new school before. It'll be OK.

STORMI: Yeah. *(to AUDIENCE)* OK like a book report due and you haven't read the book. OK like a trip to the dentist with five cavities. OK like walking over hot coals with bare feet.

(MOM hands STORMI her backpack and exits.)

465

Generalize

TEACH

- Tell students that a generalization is a broad statement or rule that applies to many examples.
- Authors sometimes make generalizations in the text, and readers sometimes make generalizations based on what they have read.

Think Aloud **MODEL** In the first scene between Stormi and her mother I can tell that Stormi is unhappy about starting at a new school. She says going to a new school is like going to the dentist with five cavities.

PRACTICE AND ASSESS

To assess students, ask which statement below is a generalization. *(Choice b)*

a) Stormi and her family have moved before.

b) Moving to a new place is usually difficult for people.

c) Stormi has a backpack.

Page 465

LA.5.1.7.3 Determine the main idea or essential message through inferring

Guiding Comprehension

③ Draw Conclusions • Inferential

What conclusion can you draw about the relationship between Stormi and her friends in Chicago?

They were close friends.

Monitor Progress

REVIEW Draw Conclusions

If... students have difficulty drawing conclusions,	then... use the skill and strategy instruction on p. 467.

---

④ Author's Purpose • Critical
Question the Author **In Scene II, why do you think the author includes the scenes with Stormi's friends in Chicago?**

To show Stormi's close friends and how they feel about her moving away.

⑤ Predict • Critical
Do you think Stormi will like her new school and make new friends? Why?

Possible response: Eventually she will, but at first it will be hard.

Tech Files
ONLINE

Students can learn more about the life and work of the famous poet Stormi is named after by typing *Nikki Giovanni* into a student-friendly search engine. Be sure to follow classroom guidelines for Internet use.

Page 466
LA.5.1.7.1 Use prior knowledge to make predictions
LA.5.1.7.2 Identify author's purpose
LA.5.1.7.3 Determine the main idea or essential message through inferring

---

SCENE II

SETTINGS: *In Stormi's new school,* STORMI *is in the classroom.* MOM *stands near her. In Chicago,* DAVID, PENELOPE, *and* MARSHA *stand around table.*

STORMI *(to* AUDIENCE*):* Hi. I'm Stormi Giovanni Green. I'm named after Nikki Giovanni, the famous poet. I am not a happy camper! See, Mom and Dad move around a lot with their jobs, and since I'm the kid, I go too. They're college professors. Dad teaches philosophy. Philosophers try to figure out how you know what's true and what's not true, and why some things are right and some things are wrong. I only kind of understand. Mom teaches teachers how to teach. Oops, lost my train of thought. Mom says I'm distressed. . . .

MOM: No, Stormi, you've **digressed.**

*(*MOM *exits.)*

STORMI: Digressed, right. Got off the topic. OK. I just moved here from Chicago where I had great friends, played basketball, and was on the speech team. Moving is for the birds. So this time, no new friends. In fact, no anything that I'll just have to say goodbye to. From now on it's the Stormi Giovanni Club, and I'm the only member. When I told Marsha and Penelope I was moving they said:

MARSHA & PENELOPE: NOOO!!!!

STORMI: And I said, "Yes." And they said:

MARSHA & PENELOPE: NOOO!!!!

STORMI: And I said, "Yes." And they said:

MARSHA & PENELOPE: NOOO!!!

STORMI: And David said:

466

Understanding Idioms Explain that "for the birds" is an idiom that means worthless or ridiculous. So, Stormi thinks moving is ridiculous.

DAVID: Stop! Don't say "no" again. It'll be OK.

MARSHA: Sure, we can e-mail.

PENELOPE: And telephone.

DAVID: And send letters.

PENELOPE: But it won't be the same! ③

STORMI (*to* AUDIENCE): That didn't make me feel better.

(*In Chicago,* DAVID *and* MARSHA *exit. In classroom,* MRS. MOON *enters.*) ④

STORMI: So, here I am, in homeroom, on the first day of school, keeping a low profile.

MRS. MOON: Welcome, Stormi. Please tell us about yourself.

STORMI (*to* CLASS): I'm Stormi Giovanni. From Chicago.

MRS. MOON: Please tell us about Chicago.

STORMI: It's called the Windy City (*pause*) because it's windy.

MRS. MOON: All right. Let's welcome Stormi Giovanni, class. On the count of three. One, two, three . . .

(MRS. MOON *gestures for the class to speak.*)

CLASS: WELCOME, STORMI GIOVANNI! ⑤

(MRS. MOON *exits classroom.* STORMI *sits at classroom computer.*)

467

Moving

Time for SOCIAL STUDIES

The United States is a mobile society. A recent U.S. Bureau of the Census report showed that between March 2003, and March 2004, 39 million, or 14% of the population, moved within the United States. Students in military families move three times more often than children from civilian families.

Draw Conclusions REVIEW

TEACH

- Remind students that drawing conclusions means forming reasonable opinions after thinking about the facts and details of what they have read.
- Model drawing a conclusion about Stormi's relationship with her Chicago friends.

Think Aloud **MODEL** The dialogue between Stormi and her friends shows that they didn't want her to move away and promised to keep in touch. I can draw the conclusion that Stormi and her friends were very close and that they will miss each other a lot.

PRACTICE AND ASSESS

- Have students draw a conclusion about how Stormi feels when she's introduced to the class.
- To assess, use Practice Book p. 186.

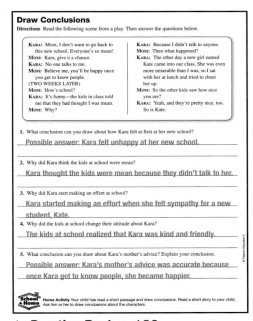

▲ **Practice Book** p. 186

Page 467
LA.5.1.7.3 Determine the main idea or essential message through inferring

The Stormi Giovanni Club **467**

Guiding Comprehension

6 **Cause and Effect • Inferential**

What happens when Hannah tries to find out more about Stormi? Why does Stormi respond that way?

Stormi is rude to her and tells her she doesn't want to talk. She does this because she doesn't want to make new friends.

7 **Character • Inferential**

Describe Hannah based on what you learn about her on pp. 468–469.

Possible answer: She's friendly and outgoing. She's trying to get to know Stormi.

8 **Compare and Contrast • Critical**

Text to Text **Think about the main character and her problem. Does this play remind you of any other stories you've read?**

Answers will vary, but students should tell about another story they've read about someone who was uncomfortable in a new situation.

STORMI: Well, I lived through homeroom. Things were OK until study hall, when I went online to check my e-mail.

(In Chicago, PENELOPE sits at computer and types.)

PENELOPE: Dear Stormi, I miss you so much. Fifth grade is definitely better than fourth. Everyone says hi. Write to me about your new friends. Love, Penelope.

(In Chicago, PENELOPE exits. In classroom, HANNAH enters and stands behind STORMI. Pens stick out of Hannah's hair, from behind her ears, and hang on a string around her neck.)

STORMI *(typing):* Dear Penelope, FYI, I won't be making friends. Love, Stormi G.

HANNAH *(tapping STORMI on the shoulder):* Do you have a pen? Maybe a roller ball or a ballpoint? Black or blue is best. I don't really go in for the funky colors, you know, the greens and pinks.

STORMI: Oh, I'll look.

(STORMI searches through her backpack.)

468

Access Content Tell students that *FYI* is an abbreviation for "for your information." Explain that it is an expression people use when they want to call attention to something, especially in business.

HANNAH: We aren't allowed to use school computers for e-mail. Mr. Morgan is very strict about that. *(pause)* A mechanical pencil might be all right.

STORMI: I have a yellow #2 pencil.

HANNAH *(examining Stormi's pencil and frowning):* No, thanks. *(handing pencil back)* So, you're the new girl?

STORMI: I guess so.

HANNAH: What brings you here?

STORMI: I don't want to talk about it.

HANNAH: OK. *(pause)* My friends Ajitha and Joseph and I sit together at lunch. If you want, tomorrow you can—

STORMI: I always bring a book.

HANNAH: Oh. Don't let Mr. Morgan see you on e-mail— it's a guaranteed detention.

STORMI: Thanks. Gotta go.

SCENE III

SETTINGS: STORMI *is in her new home. In Chicago,* MARSHA *is at the computer with* DAVID *looking over her shoulder.*

STORMI *(to audience):* Well, I made it through my first day. There's never much homework on the first day so I read a story in my creative writing class and made book covers. Marsha taught me this really cool way to make covers out of the funny papers. I finished and decided to check e-mail. I can go online for an hour after homework as long as Mom checks it first.

469

STRATEGY SELF-CHECK

Story Structure

Remind students that story structure is how a story, or play, is organized. Most stories include four parts: conflict, rising action, climax, and resolution. Explain that at this point in the play they have not reached the climax or resolution.

SELF-CHECK

Students can ask themselves these questions to assess their ability to use the skill and strategy.

- Was I able to identify the conflict and rising action in the play so far?
- Was I able to make generalizations about the play based on the conflict?

Monitor Progress
Generalize

If... students have difficulty using story structure to make a generalization,	then... revisit the skill lesson on p. 458.

Strategy Response Log

Confirm Predictions Were the predictions you made accurate? (See p. 462.) Revise your old predictions. Then make new ones about the rest of the selection.

Develop Vocabulary

PRACTICE LESSON VOCABULARY

Students orally respond *yes* or *no* to each question and provide a reason for each answer.

1. Are *cavities* found in your mouth? *(Yes; cavities are holes in teeth.)*

2. If a teacher *demonstrates* an experiment, is it assigned? *(No; it's clearly shown how it works.)*

3. Is Mr. Morgan *strict* about writing e-mail messages in school? *(Yes; He is firm about the rules.)*

BUILD CONCEPT VOCABULARY

Review previous concept words with students. Ask if students have met any words today in their reading or elsewhere that they would like to add to the Adapting to a New School concept web, such as *distressed*.

Page 469

LA.5.1.6.1 Use new vocabulary that is introduced

LA.5.1.7.1 Use prior knowledge to make and confirm predictions

LA.5.1.7.8 Use strategies to repair comprehension when self-monitoring, including predicting and questioning

LA.5.2.1.2 Locate and analyze plot structure

If you want to teach this play in two sessions, stop here.

The Stormi Giovanni Club   **469**

Guiding Comprehension

If you are teaching the play in two days, discuss any generalizations and review the vocabulary.

9 Summarize • Inferential

Summarize what happened to Stormi since she started her new school.

Mrs. Moon welcomed her to the class, she met Hannah, she e-mailed David and Marsha, and her dad asked her to try to make friends.

10 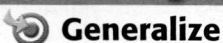 Generalize • Inferential

What generalization can you make about Stormi's friends from their e-mails?

They are thinking about her and miss her.

Monitor Progress

 Generalize

If... students have difficulty identifying generalizations,	then... use the skill and strategy instruction on p. 471.

Page 470

LA.5.1.7.3 Determine the main idea or essential message through summarizing

---

DAY 3 Grouping Options

Reading
Whole Group Discuss the Question of the Day.

Group Time Differentiated Instruction
Read *The Stormi Giovanni Club.* See pp. 458f–458g for the small group lesson plan.

Whole Group Discuss the Reader Response questions on p. 478. Then use p. 483a.

Language Arts
Use pp. 483e–483k.

9

MARSHA *(typing):* Dear Stormi, Lunch was a drag without you. But David told us a stupid joke and before we knew it we were laughing anyway. Oh, wait, David wants to say hi.

DAVID *(typing):* Hey, what do you call a cross between a television and a pizza? A really bad idea. You can do it with any two things. Funny, huh? Get it? *(MARSHA pokes DAVID's shoulder.)*

MARSHA *(typing):* Me again. Isn't that the silliest thing? I bet you're making lots of new friends. OK. Later, Alligator.

(MARSHA and DAVID exit.)

STORMI *(typing):* Hey guys. I miss you. School is OK. *(to AUDIENCE)* OK like you forget your permission slip and miss the field trip. OK like your Dad's playoff game's on TV the same night as the "to be continued" episode of your favorite show. OK like vegetarian meatloaf. *(typing)* Not much to write about. Bye.

10

(STORMI shuts off computer and sits on the floor, legs crossed, looking sad and lonely.)

STORMI: In my old house there was this little room under the stairs. Probably a closet, but it sloped down so there really wasn't enough room in it for anything. I hung a flashlight in there, and put a rug on the floor and made some pillows. I would go there anytime I was sad, or even just needed to think. Here I just have my room.

(DAD enters.)

DAD: How was school?

STORMI: OK I guess, Dad. *(to AUDIENCE)* OK like . . . never mind . . . you get it. It was not OK.

470

Understanding Idioms Restate the sentence "Lunch was a drag without you." Explain that *a drag* means "boring."

DAD: Make any new friends?

STORMI: No.

DAD: Could you try to make just one new friend? For me?

STORMI: You should make your own friends, Dad.

DAD *(laughs):* Could you try to make just one friend for *you*, then?

STORMI: I make no promises. Could you try to raise my allowance?

DAD: I make no promises, Pumpkin.

(DAD starts to leave.)

DAD: Take a look at the bay window in the living room. I thought we could hang a curtain from the ceiling and let that be your own private space.

STORMI: Thanks, Dad. I'll look at it.

(DAD exits.)

471

E-mail

Time for **SOCIAL STUDIES**

Stormi and her friends depend on e-mail to stay in touch. The first e-mail was sent in 1971. In the beginning, it was mainly used by scientists and researchers as a way to share information. It could only be sent to computers that were all connected to the same host computer. In recent years, e-mail has become the most popular application.

Generalize Story Structure

TEACH

- Remind students that when they make a generalization they need details from the text to support it.
- Model using story structure to support a generalization about Stormi's friends.

> **Think Aloud** **MODEL** On p. 470, I can generalize that Stormi's friends miss her because Marsha's e-mail says, "Lunch was a drag without you."

PRACTICE AND ASSESS

Ask students to make a generalization about Stormi's dad and support it with details from the story. *(He is supportive and wishes she would make friends. He asks her to try for his sake.)*

Page 471

LA.5.1.6.6 Identify "shades of meaning"

LA.5.1.7.3 Determine the main idea or essential message through inferring, summarizing, and identifying relevant details

LA.5.2.1.2 Locate and analyze plot structure

LA.5.2.1.7 Identify and explain author's use of idiomatic and figurative language

EXTEND SKILLS

Slang

Authors often use slang, or informal language, to make characters seem authentic. For example, Marsha writes "Later, Alligator" at the end of her e-mail, which is an expression friends might say to each other. Find other examples of slang in this play.

Guiding Comprehension

11 **Cause and Effect • Inferential**

What caused Stormi to say her second day at school was worse than the first?

She lost the paper with her locker number on it. Then she had to find the other paper with the combination on it.

12  **Vocabulary • Context Clues**

Use context clues to determine the meaning of *passion* on p. 473.

Clues: Hannah collects pens; something cool. Meaning: very strong liking for something

---

Monitor Progress

 Context Clues

If... students have difficulty using context clues to determine the meaning of *passion*,	then... use the vocabulary strategy instruction on p. 473.

SCENE IV

SETTINGS: *STORMI's locker in the hallway of her new school. Later, the school cafeteria.*

STORMI *(to AUDIENCE while removing things from her backpack):* The second day was worse than the first. I lost the little piece of paper that had my locker number on it, and I had to go to the office to get a new one. Then I had to dump everything out of my backpack to find the other little piece of paper that had the combination on it. **11** Then I had to figure out how to make the combination lock work.

(HANNAH, JOSEPH, and AJITHA enter.)

HANNAH: Do you always talk to yourself?

472

Access Content Explain that *unicorns* are imaginary animals that look like horses, but have one long horn in the middle of their foreheads.

Page 472

LA.5.1.6.3 Use context clues to determine meanings of unfamiliar words

LA.5.1.7.4 Identify cause-and-effect relationships

LA.5.1.7.8 Use strategies to repair comprehension when self-monitoring, including checking context clues

STORMI: I wasn't. I was just—

HANNAH: Whatever. I wanted you to meet Joseph. He talks to himself too.

STORMI: Hi.

JOSEPH: Hi. This is Ajitha. Ajitha, Stormi Giovanni.

AJITHA: After the poet?

STORMI (surprised): Yeah.

AJITHA: Are you having a hard time with your locker?

STORMI: We didn't have locks at my old school.

AJITHA: You don't have to lock it. I put tape on the side of mine to keep it open. Like this.

(AJITHA shows STORMI.)

STORMI: Cool. Hannah, did you find a pen?

HANNAH: I got a couple of interesting ones.

JOSEPH: Hannah collects pens.

HANNAH: I'm looking for the perfect pen.

STORMI: Why?

HANNAH: When I was little my grandpa gave me this old silver fountain pen. I wasn't supposed to take it out of the house, but I did, and I lost it. I keep thinking I'll find something almost as cool. It's my passion. **12**

STORMI: That's cool. I have a friend who collects unicorns.

JOSEPH: Next period is lunch if you want. . . .

STORMI: I have a book.

(STORMI exits.)

473

Friendship

Time for SOCIAL STUDIES

Friendships are very important for physical and emotional health. Research shows that making and having a circle of friends helps with learning and intellectual development in children. Other studies have shown that friendships can help strengthen the immune system. People who have friendships have a longer life expectancy.

VOCABULARY STRATEGY

Context Clues

TEACH

Model using context clues to figure out the meaning of *passion* on p. 473.

Think Aloud **MODEL** On p. 473 Hannah is talking about collecting pens and looking for the perfect one. From this I can tell she really likes pens, so *passion* must mean to have a strong liking for something.

PRACTICE AND ASSESS

Have students use context clues to determine the meaning of *period* on p. 473. *(Clues: lunch. Meaning: one of the parts of a school day)*

EYE ON FCAT

CORRECTIVE FEEDBACK

LA.5.1.6.3 Use context clues to determine meanings of unfamiliar words

- **Question** Use Whiteboard or Transparency 19a, items 1–3, to ask questions that address this standard in FCAT format. Have students write their answers on a sheet of paper.
- **Check** Scan students' responses by having them hold up their papers.
- **Correct** If necessary, provide corrective feedback and review pp. 460–461.

> **1** Read these sentences from the play *The Stormi Gioranni Club*.
>
> **Then I had to dump everything out of my backpack to find the other little piece of paper that had the combination on it. Then I had to figure out how to make the combination lock work.**
>
> What does the word *combination* mean in these sentences?
>
> Ⓐ a large set
> Ⓑ two or more objects
> Ⓒ a series of numbers
> Ⓓ a mixture of different things

▲ **FCAT Whiteboard Activity** 19a/
FCAT Transparency 19a

Guiding Comprehension

13 🔍 Vocabulary • Context Clues

Use context clues to determine the meaning of *hospitable* on p. 474.

Clues: no reason to be rude; just trying to be nice. Meaning: giving friendly treatment to friends or strangers.

14 Character • Critical

Why do you think Hannah continues to be friendly to Stormi even after Stormi is rude to her and her friends?

Possible response: Hannah likes Stormi and understands that she is having a hard time being new in school.

15 🔍 Generalize • Inferential

Make a generalization about Hannah and her friends. Support it with details from the play.

Hannah and her friends are friendly and understanding because they keep trying to be nice to Stormi. They invite her to sit with them at lunch.

Monitor Progress
🔄 **Generalize**
If... students have difficulty generalizing,	**then...** use the skill and strategy instruction on p. 475.

Page 474

LA.5.1.6.3 Use context clues to determine meanings of unfamiliar words

LA.5.1.7.3 Determine the main idea or essential message through identifying relevant details

LA.5.2.1.2 Analyze character development

AJITHA: That was audacious. *(pause)* Rude and bold.

HANNAH: She's OK.

JOSEPH: It would be hard to start a new school.

13 **AJITHA:** That's no reason to be rude. We were only trying to be hospitable and gregarious.

JOSEPH: I was just trying to be nice.

(They sit at a table in the school cafeteria and begin eating lunch. STORMI enters.)

STORMI *(to AUDIENCE):* Lunch at a new school is the worst. There's this awful time when you have your tray and you have to figure out where to sit. A book can really help. I sit alone and act like I'm reading. I have to act because it's hard to read in all of that noise. But today my plan didn't work. The cafeteria was packed.

AJITHA: Stormi, you can sit with us.

474

Activate Prior Knowledge Discuss the reasons why Stormi might have behaved rudely to Hannah and her friends. *(She was feeling insecure, nervous and didn't want them to know that.)*

JOSEPH: What are you reading?

STORMI: *A Wrinkle in Time.*

AJITHA: That book is quite scintillating.

HANNAH: Don't mind her. She likes to use big words. She's not trying to make you feel stupid.

STORMI *(to AJITHA):* Do you write stories?

(AJITHA pulls out a dictionary.)

AJITHA: I try to learn a new word every day. *(reading from dictionary)* Scintillate: to sparkle, gleam.

JOSEPH: *A Wrinkle in Time* is sparkly?

HANNAH: You can sit here and read if you want to.

(STORMI sits.)

JOSEPH: I thought I would try out for the play.

HANNAH: If you do, I will too.

(STORMI tries to look like she's reading but is drawn into the conversation.)

HANNAH: It's *The Wizard of Oz*, right?

STORMI: We did that at my old school. I wanted to be the Lion so badly, but I was too small for the suit. I ended up designing the set.

AJITHA: I could enjoy that.

JOSEPH: I want to be the scarecrow.

(JOSEPH does a funny scarecrow imitation, with limp knees and wobbly head movements.)

475

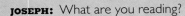 SKILLS ⬌ STRATEGIES IN CONTEXT

Generalize

TEACH

- Remind students that a generalization is a broad statement that applies to many examples.
- Model making a generalization about Hannah and her friends on p. 474.

Think Aloud **MODEL** First, I know that Hannah and her friends have tried to talk to Stormi and have invited her to sit with them at lunch, but she said no to their invitation. When Stormi can't find a place to sit in the cafeteria, they invite her to sit with them again, even though she was rude the first time. This tells me that Hannah and her friends are friendly and understanding towards Stormi.

PRACTICE AND ASSESS

- Have students state a generalization about Stormi's feelings towards Hannah and her friends at the end of p. 475. *(She begins to take an interest in them.)*
- Remind them to back up their generalization with details. *(Stormi begins talking to them and the stage directions say Stormi is "drawn into the conversation.")*

Page 475

LA.5.1.7.3 Determine the main idea or essential message through inferring and identifying relevant details

LA.5.2.1.2 Analyze character development

Guiding Comprehension

16 **Compare and Contrast • Critical**

Compare and contrast Stormi's friends in Chicago with her new friends.

Possible responses: Compare: David and Joseph both have a funny sense of humor. Hannah and Penelope both like to collect things. They like to sit together at lunch. Contrast: Joseph acts in plays. Hannah collects pens, but Penelope collects unicorns.

17 **Main Idea • Critical**

Text to Self **Describe an experience you had with being the new person in a group. How did it feel? What did you do?**

Answers will vary but should include descriptions of personal experiences where students had to adapt to new groups of people.

Strategy Response Log

Summarize When students finish reading the selection, provide this prompt: In four or five sentences, explain the most important things that happen in *The Stormi Giovanni Club*.

Use Strategies Meet with students to review their list of the reading strategies they realized they were using as they read.

Pages 476–477

LA.5.1.6.1 Use new vocabulary

LA.5.1.7.3 Determine the main idea or essential message through summarizing

LA.5.1.7.7 Compare and contrast

LA.5.1.7.8 Use strategies to repair comprehension when self-monitoring, including summarizing

LA.5.2.1.2 Locate and analyze character development and plot structure

LA.5.2.1.5 Demonstrate an understanding of a literary selection, and include evidence from personal experience

---

STORMI *(to AUDIENCE):* Lunch was almost as much fun as listening to David's lame jokes would have been. So, I've been thinking. You know how it is when you hurt your finger? Like maybe the pointing finger on the hand you write with. *(STORMI holds up finger and demonstrates.)* All of a sudden you notice all of these things you do with that finger. It hurts to put on a glove. It hurts to sharpen your pencil. It hurts to tie your shoe. And you think, I sure will be happy when this finger is better. Then one day you notice that it's better. You almost can't remember when it stopped hurting. You just didn't notice. It's the same with moving. You can't know when you will stop missing the last place so much it hurts, but you can't stop tying your shoes either. Hey, that sounds a little philosophical. My father would be proud.

(HANNAH steps forward.)

HANNAH: Look at this.

STORMI *(pointing to AUDIENCE):* I'm talking.

(HANNAH notices AUDIENCE for the first time.)

HANNAH: Oh. Hi.

AUDIENCE: Hi.

HANNAH: Look. *(She holds up a pen.)* A limited edition, 2001 four color, ball point gel ink pen, a rare and beautiful thing. . . .

(STORMI sits at the school computer.)

476

Extend Language Tell students that a person who is *stuck up* has too high an opinion of himself or herself or of what he or she can do.

STORMI *(typing):* Hey, guys. I'm sorry I haven't had much to tell you. It's silly, but I thought I would feel better if I didn't make friends. I felt worse and I think people thought I was mean. Anyway, I've met some pretty interesting people. David, you'd like Joseph. He has this funny sense of humor and likes to act in plays. There's this really odd girl who I think is my favorite. She collects pens. Like your unicorns, Penelope.... And Ajitha uses all of these big words, but she isn't stuck up or anything. *(to AUDIENCE)* So, I've decided to let other members into the Stormi Giovanni Club. Really, it's better that way I think. 17

The End

477

Develop Vocabulary

PRACTICE LESSON VOCABULARY

Students orally respond *true* or *false* to each statement and provide a reason if the answer is *false*.

1. A *combination* helps you find your locker. *(False; a combination helps you open the locker door.)*

2. A television *episode* is one show from a season. *(True)*

3. Keeping a low *profile* means you want people to notice you. *(False; a low profile means you don't want people to notice you.)*

BUILD CONCEPT VOCABULARY

Review previous concept words with students. Ask if students have come across any words that they would like to add to the Adapting to a New School Concept Web, such as *missing* and *hurting.*

Story Structure

Have students complete a story sequence chart. *(Conflict: Stormi moves to a new school; Rising Action: She resists making friends; Climax: Stormi sits with Hannah and the others at lunch and begins to like them; Resolution: Stormi decides to be friends.)* Ask students to make a new generalization about Stormi based on how she solves her problem. *(She is willing to change her mind about her new school.)*

SELF-CHECK

Students can ask themselves these questions to assess their ability to use the skill and strategy.

- Was I able to identify main elements of the story structure?
- Was I able to make generalizations?
- Did understanding the story structure help me better understand the play?

Monitor Progress

Generalize

If... students have trouble generalizing,	then... use the Reteach lesson on p. 483b.

Generalize

- To **generalize** is to make a broad statement or rule that applies to several examples.
- Active readers pay close attention to what authors tell them about story characters and make generalizations about those characters as they read.

Directions Read the following scene from a play. Then answer the questions below.

> **PRINCIPAL:** We're welcoming a student who's new to Harper School. Everyone, meet Dylan. Dylan, do you have any questions for the other students?
> **DYLAN:** What do I need to know?
> **KAMALI:** Most kids wear jeans.
> **KIM:** And T-shirts. But if you have bad words on your T-shirt, you'll be in the principal's office.
> **DAVID:** Also, there's lunch.
> **DYLAN** (sounding stressed): I guess every school is different...
> **KAMALI:** You have to get your tray a
>
> certain way.
> **KIM:** And only teachers sit by the door.
> **DAVID:** And there are Harper terms. The "field" is the blacktop, and "breakfast club" is detention.
> **DYLAN:** Wait, wait! I'm getting the feeling it's hard to fit in here.
> **DAVID:** Don't worry, we'll take you through it.
> **KIM:** Yes, we'll show you the ropes. You'll like it here.
> **DYLAN:** Thanks a lot!

1. What is the purpose of the meeting with the new student?
   The purpose is to help Dylan adjust to Harper School.
2. What generalization can you make about the attitude of Harper students at the meeting?
   The Harper students are trying to be helpful.
3. How can you generalize about the kind of advice the students give?
   The students give practical information about the school.
4. How does the advice make Dylan feel at first? How do you think Dylan's feelings change?
   He seems worried; He seems happy for the help.
5. Explain the structure of this scene. How does a problem grow during the rising action and come to a climax? What is the outcome?
   Problem: Dylan is a new student; Rising action: Harper students give advice and Dylan gets worried; Climax: students reassure Dylan; Outcome: Dylan feels better

Home Activity Your child read a short passage and made generalization about the characters. Read a story about school with your child. Work together to make generalizations about the main character.

▲ **Practice Book** p. 187

Reader Response

Open for Discussion **Personal Response**

 MODEL I would think about how Stormi felt about being new in school and how the kids tried to be friendly to her. I would think how the cast would say their lines to express their feelings.

Comprehension Check **Critical Response**

1. Responses will vary but should include specific references to the character and dialogue. **Author's Purpose**

2. Possible response: Newcomers often feel lonely. Stormi misses her school and friends in Chicago, so much that she says she won't make new friends again. **Generalize**

3. Possible response: She eventually makes friends. It makes her feel worse, not better, to keep to herself. **Story Structure**

4. Possible response: "OK like five cavities"; "OK like a diet of prunes." **Vocabulary**

 THINK AND EXPLAIN For test practice, assign a 5 minute time limit. For assessment, see the Scoring Rubric at the right.

Retell

Have students retell *The Stormi Giovanni Club.*

Monitor Progress

Check Retelling Rubric 4 3 2 1

If... students have difficulty retelling the play,	then... use the Retelling Cards and the Scoring Rubric for Retelling on p. 479 to assist fluent retelling.

SUCCESS PREDICTOR

 **ELL**

Check Retelling Before students do their retellings, go through the illustrations with them, verifying that they know the characters' names. For more ideas on assessing retellings, see the ELL and Transition Handbook.

Reader Response

Open for Discussion What is this play saying about being a newcomer and about helping one? How will you perform this play so that the audience gets the message?

1. Choose a scene and imagine yourself playing a character. Decide whether the playwright's dialogue makes it easy for you to "become" the character you're playing. **Think Like an Author**

2. Make a generalization about newcomers suggested by the play. Then look for details in the text that support this generalization. **Generalize**

3. Stormi acts differently at the start of the play than at the end. Discuss how she changes along the way and why. **Story Structure**

4. Stormi tells the audience humorous examples of what she really means when she or her mom says that school is "OK." Write one of these examples. Then write one of your own. Use words from the Words to Know list. **Vocabulary**

 Think and Explain In this play, each character is a unique individual. What is Hannah's passion and why? Use details on page 473 to explain your answer.

Meet author Lydia R. Diamond on page 771 and illustrator R. Gregory Christie on page 772.

THINK AND EXPLAIN TWO-POINT SCORING RUBRIC

Top-Score Response A top-score response will use details from p. 473 to explain that Hannah's passion for pens makes her unique.

Example of a Top-Score Response Hannah is a unique individual because her passion is to find the perfect pen in order to replace a silver fountain pen of her grandfather's that she lost. This information shows that Hannah is a character who values family possessions. It also reveals that she wants to make up for her irresponsible act and that she has determination.

For additional rubrics, see p. WA10.

 Page 478
LA.5.1.6.1 Use introduced vocabulary
LA.5.2.1.2 Analyze character development

Write Now

Letter of Advice

More FCAT WRITING+
See *The Grammar and Writing
Book*, pages 158–163.

Prompt

In *The Stormi Giovanni Club*, other people help Stormi adjust to a new school. Think about a situation in which you could offer help or advice. Now write a letter of advice to someone in that situation.

Writing Trait

Voice reveals a writer's attitude and feelings toward the subject and audience.

Student Model

Writer explains what she is offering advice about and why.

Dear Nate,

    I heard you say you didn't know how to tackle your history project. Since I'm your study partner, I thought I'd share some tips with you.

Contractions and exclamations help create informal, friendly voice.

    The main thing is to <u>not</u> put off the project! First I start by making a checklist of things to do. I put a date on the list. Each day, I check off the items on the list as I finish them. Then I make a new checklist. By the time the deadline arrives, I'm almost done and panic-free! I hope this helps.

Advice is offered in steps in separate paragraph.

               Your friend,

               Nayla

Writer uses correct letter format.

Use the model to help you write your own letter of advice.

LA.5.3.3.1 Evaluate draft for development of voice
LA.5.4.2.4 Write communications/friendly letter

479

DURING READING

Write Now

Look at the Prompt Have students identify and discuss key words and phrases in the prompt. *(situation in which you could offer help or advice, letter of advice)*

Strategies to Develop Voice

Have students

- identify their audience and purpose and decide on a voice that matches both.
- use language that conveys honesty and sincerity to the reader.

NO: Listen to me because I'm an expert on the subject.
YES: I'd like to help you because I've been in your place and I know what you're feeling.

- use language that sets an appropriate tone for their audience.

For additional suggestions and rubric, see pp. 483g–483h.

Hints for Better Writing

- Carefully read the prompt.
- Support your ideas with information and details.
- Use words that help readers understand.
- Proofread and edit your work.

 Page 479

LA.5.3.3.1 Evaluate draft for development of voice
LA.5.4.2.4 Write communications (friendly letter)

Scoring Rubric | Narrative Retelling

Rubric 4 3 2 1	4	3	2	1
Connections	Makes connections and generalizes beyond the text	Makes connections to other events, stories, or experiences	Makes a limited connection to another event, story, or experience	Makes no connection to another event, story, or experience
Author's Purpose	Elaborates on author's purpose	Tells author's purpose with some clarity	Makes some connection to author's purpose	Makes no connection to author's purpose
Characters	Describes the main character(s) and any character development	Identifies the main character(s) and gives some information about them	Inaccurately identifies some characters or gives little information about them	Inaccurately identifies the characters or gives no information about them
Setting	Describes the time and location	Identifies the time and location	Omits details of time or location	Is unable to identify time or location
Plot	Describes the problem, goal, events, and ending using rich detail	Tells the problem, goal, events, and ending with some errors that do not affect meaning	Tells parts of the problem, goal, events, and ending with gaps that affect meaning	Retelling has no sense of story

Retelling Plan

- ☑ **Week 1** Assess Strategic Intervention students.
- ☑ **Week 2** Assess Advanced students.
- ☑ **Week 3** Assess Strategic Intervention students.
- ☑ **This week assess On-Level students.**
- ☐ **Week 5** Assess any students you have not yet checked during this unit.

Use the Retelling Chart on p. TR16 to record retelling.

Selection Test To assess with The *Stormi Giovanni Club*, use Selection Tests, pp. 73–76.

Fresh Reads for Differentiated Test Practice For weekly leveled practice, use pp. 109–114.

Retelling

SUCCESS PREDICTOR

Social Studies in Reading

OBJECTIVES

- Examine features of newspaper articles.
- Practice a test-taking strategy.
- Compare and contrast across texts.

PREVIEW/USE TEXT FEATURES

As students preview "Think Dress Codes Are a Drag?" have them look at the article's headline and illustrations. After they preview ask:

- **What can you learn about the article from the headline?** *(The article is about a dress code or set of rules.)*

- **What can you learn about the article from the illustrations?** *(The article is about clothes to wear to school. Since the illustrations are amusing, perhaps the article itself will be light in tone.)*

Link to Social Studies

Have students brainstorm to identify ways to find out about dress codes in other schools. Write students' ideas on the board.

DAY 4 Grouping Options

Reading
Whole Group Discuss the Question of the Day.

Group Time Differentiated Instruction
Read "Think Dress Codes Are a Drag?" See pp. 458f–458g for the small group lesson plan.

Whole Group Use p. 483a.

Language Arts
Use pp. 483e–483k.

Social Studies in Reading

50¢ City & Suburbs: 75¢ Elsewhere

Newspaper Article

Genre
- A newspaper article tells readers about current events, issues, people, and places of interest.
- News articles report facts—actual events—and people's opinions.

Text Features
- A headline gives readers an idea of what the article is about.
- News articles often start with a brief story that sets the scene for the discussion that follows.
- The writer includes quotations that show differing opinions.

Link to Social Studies
Find out about dress codes in your school and other schools in your area. Are there differences? Why?

 LA.5.2.2.4 Identify characteristics of text/newspapers

480

Content-Area Vocabulary — Social Studies

bans	forbids; prohibits
codes	sets of rules
penalty	punishment

 ELL

Access Content Lead a picture walk to reinforce vocabulary, such as *capris, spaghetti straps* (p. 481), *midriff* (p. 482), and *sagging* (p. 483). Ask students to talk about the kinds of clothes they like to wear.

 Page 480
LA.5.1.7.1 Explain purpose of text features
LA.5.2.2.1 Locate, explain, and use information from text features (headings and illustrations)
LA.5.2.2.4 Identify the characteristics of types of text (newspapers)

TUESDAY
APRIL 15, 2003

Think Dress codes are a drag?

by Emilie Ostrander
Special to the *Tribune*

While shopping for new clothes, Elyse B., 13, of Mt. Prospect, Illinois, also is scouting for hot trends. Dressed in a bright pink tank top and denim capris, Elyse says she's found an outfit she likes. The catch? Her school dress code bans tank tops—and the penalty is anything but stylish. "If they catch you, you have to change into your gym uniform," she says.

For Elyse, shopping for new clothes is all about looking good without getting in trouble. "We

Savvy Shoppers Can Still Look Cool for School

can't wear spaghetti straps, halter tops, or tube tops," she explains. "Tank top straps must be the width of two fingers, and shorts and skirts have to be longer than 5 inches above the knee."

As we get into spring, many kids are ready to take their warm-weather clothes to school. But some school districts say certain styles are banned from the classroom, and there are consequences for kids who disobey.

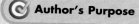

Author's Purpose What is the author's purpose or purposes?

481

NEWSPAPER ARTICLE

Use the sidebar on p. 480 to guide discussion.

- Point out that a newspaper article is a source of information. It contains facts, not opinions.
- Explain to students that a news article usually includes a dateline, headline, byline, lead paragraph, and body.
- Have students identify the lead in "Think Dress Codes Are a Drag?" Discuss with students what purpose or purposes the lead serves.

 **AudioText**

Author's Purpose

The author is writing mainly to inform.

Page 481
LA.5.1.7.2 Identify the author's purpose
LA.5.2.2.4 Identify the characteristics of types of text (newspapers)

TEST PRACTICE

Strategies for Nonfiction

USE LEADS Explain that a lead paragraph in a newspaper article contains the most important information. It answers the questions *Who? What? When? Where? Why?* and *How?* Students can use the lead to help answer test questions. Provide the following strategy.

Use the Strategy

1. Read the test question.
2. If the question is asking *Who? What? When? Where?* or *Why?* look for the information in the lead paragraph.

GUIDED PRACTICE Have students discuss how they would use the strategy to answer the following question.

> What is Elyse B. doing?

INDEPENDENT PRACTICE After students answer the following test question, discuss the process they used to find information.

> Why can't Elyse B. purchase whatever she likes?

APRIL 15, 2003

Paula J. Hlavacek is the principal of Elm Middle School in Elmwood Park. At her school, parents are contacted the first time a student breaks the code. A second offense means a trip to detention.

It may not seem like a lot of fun, but Hlavacek says the dress code is there for good reason. "When you come to school, you must be dressed for a work day in school," she says. "Clothes that are cut very short or expose the midriff are beachwear. School is a very different place."

While dress codes may seem unfair, Hlavacek says students can expect the same restrictions for their teachers. "Whatever rules we hold for them, we hold for ourselves," she says. So while students can't wear tank tops in scorching weather, neither can their teachers.

Ryan M., 16, of Lincolnwood says he doesn't dress like his dean [principal of a private school]. "I like to wear my pants low," he says, something his dean can't

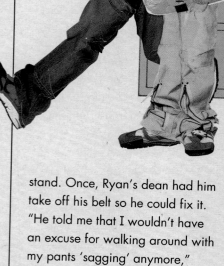

stand. Once, Ryan's dean had him take off his belt so he could fix it. "He told me that I wouldn't have an excuse for walking around with my pants 'sagging' anymore," Ryan says.

While Ryan and Elyse wish their school dress codes were less

 Generalize How is a rule a kind of generalization?

482

 ELL

Independent Practice Before students do the Independent Practice test question, verify that they understand what *dress code* means. Explain that Elyse would dress differently were it not for the dress code. Point out the unacceptable tank top in the illustration on p. 480.

Page 482

LA.5.2.2.2 Use information from the text to answer questions related to explicitly stated main ideas or relevant details
LA.5.3.2.3 Study the leads of authors

strict, Kyah K., 8, of Aurora says she thinks dress codes are a good idea. "Sometimes everyone wants to be cool, so they wear really tacky clothes," she says. "I think they should obey the rules and wear those clothes at home."

Being creative is key to still being in style and not breaking the school dress code, says Gregg Andrews, fashion director for [a department store]. "It's about creating personal style," he says.

Kyah says she has an eye for style, and thinks clothes can say a lot about a person. "My clothes say that I'm a creative person," she says. "I try to put on some mis-matchy things or things that will go together very well."

Reading Across Texts

Look back at *The Stormi Giovanni Club* and this newspaper article. Make a list of problems that the students in these selections face during a typical day at school.

Writing Across Texts Write some advice on how to successfully deal with each of these problems. Combine your results with classmates' advice. Assemble a book of advice on how to get along in school.

483

CONNECT TEXT TO TEXT

Reading Across Texts

Have students list the problems on the left side of a T-chart.

Writing Across Texts Students can record their advice for each problem on the right side of the T-chart. When students are finished, work with them to create one master chart. Then have students work in small groups to assemble the book of advice, each group having responsibility for one task, such as book cover, table of contents, illustrations, and text.

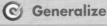 Generalize

Possible response: Like a generalization, a rule can be applied to many examples.

 Page 483

LA.5.1.7.7 Compare and contrast elements in multiple texts (characters and problems)

LA.5.4.2.1 Write in a variety of informational/expository forms

LA.5.4.2.2 Record information (lists) related to a topic

Fluency Assessment Plan

☑ **Week 1** Assess Advanced students.

☑ **Week 2** Assess Strategic Intervention students.

☑ **Week 3** Assess On-Level students.

☑ **This week assess Strategic Intervention students.**

☐ **Week 5** Assess any students you have not yet checked during this unit.

Set individual goals for students to enable them to reach the year-end goal.

• Current Goal: 120–128 wcpm

• Year-End Goal: 140 wcpm

Provide opportunities for students to read one-on-one with an aide or parent volunteer, if possible. The adult models by reading first, and the child reads and rereads the same text, with adult guidance. Allow extra repetitions for English language learners, to improve fluency.

 To develop fluent readers, use Fluency Coach.

Page 483a

LA.5.1.5.1 Demonstrate the ability to read grade level text

LA.5.1.5.2 Adjust reading rate based on purpose and style

DAY 5 Grouping Options

Reading
Whole Group
Revisit the Question of the Week.

Group Time
Differentiated Instruction
Reread this week's Leveled Readers. See pp. 458f–458g for the small group lesson plan.

Whole Group
Use p. 483b–483c.

Language Arts
Use pp. 483d–483l.

TONE OF VOICE
Fluency

DAY 1

Model Reread the excerpt from "Only Fiona" on p. 458m. Explain that you will use tone of voice to show Fiona's sadness at being in a new place and missing her old friends. Model for students as you read.

DAY 2

Choral Reading Read aloud the first fifteen lines (up to the end of Scene II) on p. 469. Have students notice how you change your tone when speaking as Hannah and when speaking as Stormi to reflect each girl's feelings or mood. Ask students to practice as a class, doing three choral readings of p. 469.

DAY 3

Model Read aloud p. 475. Ask students to pay attention to how your voice changes to reflect each character's feelings and personality, and the change in your voice when you read questions. Practice as a class by doing three choral readings.

DAY 4

Partner Reading Partners practice reading aloud p. 475 three times. Students should read with proper emotion and tones of voice.

Monitor Progress | Check Fluency WCPM

As students reread, monitor their progress toward their individual fluency goals. Current Goal: 120–128 words correct per minute. End-of-Year Goal: 140 WCPM. Have library books or other texts available at a variety of reading levels for students to use to practice fluency. See pp. DI·57–DI·58.

If... students cannot read fluently at a rate of 120–128 words correct per minute,
then... make sure students practice with text at their independent level. Provide additional fluency practice, pairing nonfluent readers with fluent readers.

If... students already read at 140 words correct per minute,
then... they do not need to reread three to four times.

SUCCESS PREDICTOR

DAY 5

Assessment
Individual Reading Rate Use the Fluency Assessment Plan and do a one-minute timed reading of either selection from this week to assess students in Week 4. Pay special attention to this week's skill, tone of voice. Provide corrective feedback for each student.

RETEACH

Generalize

TEACH

Review the definition of *generalize* on p. 458. Have students use the information to complete Practice Book p. 188. Remind students that each of Dan's friends has unique qualities, so, each supporting detail should be different.

ASSESS

Have students use pp. 465–466 in their books to make a generalization about the relationship between Stormi and her mother. Tell students to support their generalization with details from the text. *(Possible response: Stormi and her mom have a typical mother-daughter relationship. Her mom urges her to move along so she won't be late and corrects her when she frowns and digresses.)*

For additional instruction on generalize, see DI·55.

EXTEND SKILLS

Mood

TEACH

The atmosphere or feeling of a story is its *mood.*

- The mood of a story may be hilarious, thoughtful, sad, eerie, dreamlike, and so on. The possibilities include every emotional state.
- An author creates mood through characters, setting, descriptive details, and word choice.

Work with students to describe the mood of Scene II on pp. 466–469 of *The Stormi Giovanni Club.* Students can discuss Stormi's state of mind and identify details that the author gives about her old friends in Chicago before agreeing on the mood of the scene.

ASSESS

Have students write about the mood of Scene IV. Ask the following questions to prompt students' responses:

1. **What change in the main character helps you identify the mood?**
2. **What descriptive details are clues to the mood?**

Page 483b

LA.5.1.7.3 Determine the main idea or essential message inferring and identifying relevant details

LA.5.2.1.7 Identify and explain an author's use of descriptive and figurative language

OBJECTIVES

- Use details from a text to make a generalization.
- Describe the mood of a scene.

Skills Trace

Generalize

Introduce/Teach	TE: 5.4 412–413, 458–459; 5.5 604–605
Practice	Practice Book: 163, 167, 168, 183, 187, 188, 196, 243, 247, 248
Reteach/Review	TE: 5.4 435b, 483b, 493, DI•53, DI•55; 5.5 625b, DI•56
Test	Selection Test: 65–68, 73–76, 97–100; Benchmark Test: Unit 4

ELL

Access Content Reteach the skill by reviewing the Picture It! lesson on generalize in the ELL Teaching Guide, pp. 127–128.

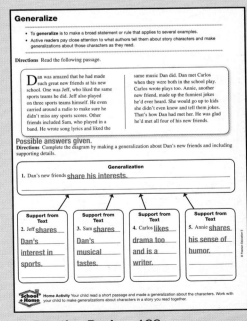

▲ **Practice Book** p. 188

Vocabulary and Word Study

Context Clues

UNFAMILIAR WORDS Remind students that they can use context clues to determine the meanings of unfamiliar words. Have students work with partners to use context clues to find the meanings of these words from *The Stormi Giovanni Club*. Then, encourage students to verify if their definitions are correct by looking the words up in a dictionary.

Word	Context Clues	Meaning	Correct?
philosophy	college professors; what is true; right or wrong	the science of teaching about life	yes
funky			
limited			

City Nicknames

In *The Stormi Giovanni Club*, Stormi tells the class she is from "The Windy City." Have groups of students brainstorm a list of city nicknames they've heard of or make up some of their own. Have groups quiz each other to see if they can identify cities by their nicknames.

City	Nickname
New York City	The Big Apple

Adapting to a New Place

LOOKING BACK Remind students of the question of the week: How do people adapt to a new school? Discuss how this week's Concept Web of vocabulary words relates to the theme of adapting. Ask students if they have any words or categories to add. Discuss if words and categories are appropriately related to the concept.

REVIEW/CONNECT Preview the title of the next selection, "The Gymnast." Ask students which Concept Web words might apply to the new selection based on the title alone.

Put a star next to these words on the web.

Display the Concept Web and revisit the vocabulary words as you read the next selection to check predictions.

<table>
<tr><td colspan="2">Monitor Progress</td></tr>
<tr><td colspan="2">Check Vocabulary</td></tr>
<tr><td>If... students suggest words or categories that are not related to the concept,</td><td>then... review the words and categories on the Concept Web and discuss how they relate to the lesson concept.</td></tr>
</table>

SUCCESS PREDICTOR

Speaking and Listening

SPEAKING

Advice

SET-UP During Writing Workshop, students wrote advice to a new student. Here, they can use that advice and any other ideas they have to plan a speech in which they give advice to a group of new students about how to adapt to their new school.

ORGANIZATION Encourage students to open with anecdotes or bits of personal experience that show what it is like to be a new student. Then they each should offer at least three pieces of advice and explain the importance of them.

AUDIENCE As they plan their speeches, remind students that their audience will be a group of new students, and the occasion will be a kind of orientation day. Suggest that they think about the best ways to get their points across. To make their points memorable for their audience, students might consider recasting their points into three easy-to-remember words or phrases, or they might plan simple handouts with their points on them.

LISTENING

Listen to Advice

Have students reflect on the advice they were given. Then, working alone or with a partner, they can answer the following questions.

1. **What is the best piece of advice you heard? Why?**
2. **Do you think the advice you heard will change the way you interact with a new student in the future?**
3. **How do you think Stormi Giovanni would react to some of the advice your classmates gave in their speeches?**

Support Vocabulary Use the following to review and extend vocabulary and to explore lesson concepts further:
- ELL Poster 19, Days 3–5 instruction
- Vocabulary Activities and Word Cards in ELL Teaching Guide, pp. 129–130

Assessment For information on assessing students' speaking and listening, see the ELL and Transition Handbook.

Pages 483c–483d

LA.5.1.6.3 Use context clues to determine meanings of unfamiliar words
LA.5.1.6.4 Categorize key vocabulary
LA.5.5.2.1 Listen and speak to gain and share information for a variety of purposes
LA.5.5.2.2 Make formal oral presentations

Vocabulary

SUCCES PREDICTO

Grammar Indefinite and Reflexive Pronouns

OBJECTIVES

- Define and identify indefinite and reflexive pronouns.
- Use indefinite and reflexive pronouns in writing.
- Become familiar with indefinite and reflexive pronouns on high-stakes tests.

Monitor Progress

Grammar

If... students have difficulty identifying indefinite and reflexive pronouns,	then... provide additional instruction and practice in The Grammar and Writing Book pp. 158–161.

DAILY FIX-IT

This week use Daily Fix-It Transparency 19.

Spiral REVIEW

Support Grammar See the Grammar Transition lessons in the ELL and Transition Handbook.

▲ **The Grammar and Writing Book**
For more instruction and practice, use pp. 158–161.

DAY 1 Teach and Model

DAILY FIX-IT

1. A knew house seem strange at first. *(new; seems)*

2. The movers unloaded the van, by theirselves. *(van by themselves)*

READING-GRAMMAR CONNECTION

Write this sentence on the board:

Stormi introduces <u>herself</u>, and <u>everyone</u> says hello.

Explain that the reflexive pronoun *herself* reflects the action of the verb *introduces* back upon the subject *Stormi*. The indefinite pronoun *everyone* is singular.

Display Grammar Transparency 19. Read aloud the definitions and sample sentences. Work through the items.

Indefinite and Reflexive Pronouns

Indefinite pronouns may not refer to specific words. They do not always have definite antecedents: Has <u>anyone</u> met the new kid?
Some common indefinite pronouns are listed below.

Singular Indefinite Pronouns	Plural Indefinite Pronouns
someone, somebody, anyone, anybody, everyone, everybody, something, no one, either, each	few, several, both, others, many, all, some

- Use singular verb forms with singular indefinite pronouns and plural verb forms with plural indefinite pronouns: <u>Everyone</u> gets a cookie. <u>Few</u> turn it down.

Reflexive pronouns reflect the action of the verb back on the subject.
Reflexive pronouns end in *-self* or *-selves*: We introduced <u>ourselves</u> to her.

Singular Reflexive Pronouns	Plural Reflexive Pronouns
myself, himself, herself, itself, yourself	ourselves, yourselves, themselves

- There are no such words as *hisself, theirself, theirselves,* or *ourself.*

Directions Underline the pronoun in each sentence. Write *indefinite* or *reflexive* to identify the kind of pronoun it is. Then write *singular* or *plural* to show its number.

1. <u>Everyone</u> is really thirsty. — indefinite singular
2. Has <u>anyone</u> seen the glasses? — indefinite singular
3. The boys help <u>themselves</u> to milk. — reflexive plural
4. <u>Others</u> want cider or lemonade. — indefinite plural
5. Ileana brought <u>herself</u> a soda. — reflexive singular

Directions Underline the correct pronoun in ( ) to complete each sentence.

6. (<u>Someone</u>, Several) welcomes the new students to school.
7. Often that person is the principal (<u>himself</u>, hisself).
8. (<u>Few</u>, No one) want to move to a new school.
9. (<u>Everyone</u>, Many) looks at a new kid curiously.
10. I always introduce (<u>myself</u>, myselves) with a smile.
11. (Everybody, <u>Several</u>) were friendly to the new boy.
12. Omar and Jai introduced (theirself, <u>themselves</u>).

Unit 4 The Stormi Giovanni Club   Grammar **19**

▲ **Grammar Transparency** 19

DAY 2 Develop the Concept

DAILY FIX-IT

3. Ryan is hospitible to both freinds and strangers. *(hospitable; friends)*

4. Michigan avenue stores are fashionable. And we often shop there. *(Avenue; fashionable, and)*

GUIDED PRACTICE

Review the concept of indefinite and reflexive pronouns.

- **Indefinite pronouns,** such as *somebody* and *no one,* do not always have definite antecedents.

- **Reflexive pronouns** reflect the action of the verb back upon the subject. Reflexive pronouns end in *-self* or *-selves.*

- There are no such words as *hisself, theirself, theirselves,* or *ourself.*

HOMEWORK Grammar and Writing Practice Book p. 73. Work through the first two items with the class.

Indefinite and Reflexive Pronouns

Indefinite pronouns may not refer to specific words. They do not have definite antecedents.
<u>Someone</u> called and left a message.
Some common indefinite pronouns are listed below.

Singular Indefinite Pronouns	Plural Indefinite Pronouns
someone, somebody, anyone, anybody, everyone, everybody, something, no one, either, each	few, several, both, others, many, all, some

- Use singular verb forms with singular indefinite pronouns and plural verb forms with plural indefinite pronouns: <u>Everyone</u> feels lonely at times. <u>Others</u> offer them friendship.

Reflexive pronouns reflect the action of the verb back on the subject. Reflexive pronouns end in *-self* or *-selves:* Vic wrote a note to <u>himself</u>.

Singular Reflexive Pronouns	Plural Reflexive Pronouns
himself, herself, myself, itself, yourself	ourselves, yourselves, themselves

- There are no such words as *hisself, theirself, theirselves,* or *ourself.*

Directions Underline the correct pronoun in ( ) to complete each sentence.

1. (<u>Anyone</u>, Many) benefits by making new friends.
2. (Many, <u>Anyone</u>) treasure old friends too.
3. My friends and I taught (ourself, <u>ourselves</u>) chess.
4. We play in the cafeteria, but (<u>few</u>, no one) know this.
5. (<u>Everyone</u>, Others) is welcome to join us.
6. A new student introduced (<u>himself</u>, hisself).
7. (Some, <u>Someone</u>) calls him Dylan.
8. (<u>Something</u>, Many) tells me Dylan has learned chess from a master.
9. We know the moves, but he knows the game (<u>itself</u>, themselves).
10. (Someone, <u>Others</u>) tell me I'm good at chess, but Dylan beat me.
11. I hope Dylan enjoyed (herself, <u>himself</u>) today.
12. You should learn chess (ourself, <u>yourself</u>).

Home Activity Your child learned about indefinite and reflexive pronouns. Ask your child to make up several statements about making friends using pronouns such as everybody, no one, many, few, and myself.

▲ **Grammar and Writing Practice Book** p. 73

483e   Adapting • Week 4

EYE ON FCAT

CORRECTIVE FEEDBACK

Preview LA.6.3.4.4 Use parts of speech/pronouns

- **Question** Use Whiteboard or Transparency 19b, items 1–3, to ask questions that address this standard in FCAT format. Have students write their answers on a sheet of paper.
- **Check** Scan students' responses by having them hold up their papers.
- **Correct** If necessary, provide corrective feedback and review pp. 158–163 in *The Grammar and Writing Book*.

---

1 Which sentence has a **reflexive pronoun**?

- Ⓐ I taught myself checkers.
- Ⓑ Everyone should know the game.
- Ⓒ Do you want to play checkers with me?

◀ **FCAT Whiteboard Activity** 19b/**FCAT Transparency** 19b

DAY 3 — Apply to Writing

DAILY FIX-IT

5. Ever girl in the scout troop made a birdhouse by hisself. *(Every; herself)*

6. They learned how to hamer nails into would safely. *(hammer; wood)*

PRONOUN ANTECEDENTS

Singular indefinite pronouns such as *everyone, anybody,* and *someone* may be used as pronoun antecedents. Use a singular pronoun with these words.

No: Everybody loves their present.

Yes: Everybody loves his present.

Yes: Everybody loves her present.

- Have students review something they have written to see if they can improve it by correcting mistakes in pronoun number agreement.

HOMEWORK Grammar and Writing Practice Book p. 74.

Indefinite and Reflexive Pronouns

| ourselves | everyone | yourself | few |
| myself | anyone | herself | both |

Directions Choose a pronoun from the box to complete each sentence correctly. Be sure indefinite pronouns used as subjects agree in number with their verbs.

1. "Tell us about ___**yourself**___, Tonya," says the teacher.
2. I think to ___**myself**___, "This is going to be good!"
3. ___**Everyone**___ leans forward to listen.
4. Tonya is a cowgirl who taught ___**herself**___ to ride.
5. ___**Few**___ of us know anything at all about horses.
6. Tonya says that ___**anyone**___ can ride her gentle horse Bluebonnet.
7. All of us think to ___**ourselves**___, "I might not be able to!"
8. My friend Tonya has two horses, and ___**both**___ are beautiful.

Directions Write several sentences about a time you made a new friend. Use some indefinite and reflexive pronouns. Underline the indefinite and reflexive pronouns you use.

___Possible answer: I felt sorry for myself when I had to move. The first day of school, kids were talking among themselves. Someone walked up and introduced herself to me, and Margaret and I became friends. The other kids were nice too, and that day I met several of them.___

Home Activity Your child learned how to write indefinite and reflexive pronouns. Have your child write these pronouns on cards. Choose several cards at a time and ask him or her to write sentences using the pronouns.

▲ **Grammar and Writing Practice Book** p. 74

DAY 4 — Test Preparation

DAILY FIX-IT

7. This locker is more harder to open than last years locker. *(is harder; year's)*

8. Do you carry all yur books to every class. *(your; class?)*

STANDARDIZED TEST PREP

Test Tip

Plural reflexive pronouns end with *-selves.* Singular reflexive pronouns end with *-self.*

No: themself, itselves, myselves

Yes: themselves, itself, myself

HOMEWORK Grammar and Writing Practice Book p. 75.

Indefinite and Reflexive Pronouns

Directions Mark the letter of the pronoun that correctly completes each sentence.

1. This alarm clock turns ___ off.
   A themself
   B itself
   C herself
   D yourself

2. ___ lets the dog out at 3.
   Ⓐ Someone
   B Many
   C Something
   D Few

3. ___ is welcome to try out.
   A Themselves
   B Others
   Ⓒ Anyone
   D Many

4. Marla taught ___ to sing.
   A itself
   B themselves
   C himself
   Ⓓ herself

5. ___ sends us a mystery package every year.
   A Himself
   Ⓑ Somebody
   C Both
   D Several

6. ___ likes getting a shot.
   A Myself
   B Few
   Ⓒ No one
   D Many

7. Sam bought ___ a watch.
   A itself
   B themself
   Ⓒ himself
   D hisself

8. ___ is wrong.
   A Myself
   Ⓑ Something
   C Itself
   D Others

9. May we help ___?
   A ourself
   B themself
   C hisself
   Ⓓ ourselves

10. ___ volunteer for safety patrol duty.
    Ⓐ Many
    B No one
    C Everyone
    D Someone

Home Activity Your child prepared for taking tests on indefinite and reflexive pronouns. Have your child write each indefinite and reflexive pronoun on an index card. Mix the cards and have your child sort them by type and number.

▲ **Grammar and Writing Practice Book** p. 75

DAY 5 — Cumulative Review

DAILY FIX-IT

9. Ms. Roman told Jeff to help yourself to the pizza he ate three slices. *(himself; pizza. He)*

10. Because Jordan is responsable, he can use the computor. *(responsible; computer)*

ADDITIONAL PRACTICE

Assign pp. 158–161 in The Grammar and Writing Book.

EXTRA PRACTICE Grammar and Writing Practice Book p. 140.

TEST PREPARATION Grammar and Writing Practice Book pp. 155–156.

ASSESSMENT

CUMULATIVE REVIEW Grammar and Writing Practice Book p. 76.

Indefinite and Reflexive Pronouns

Directions Underline the pronoun in each sentence. Write *indefinite* or *reflexive* to identify the kind of pronoun it is. Then write *singular* or *plural* to show its number.

1. <u>Everyone</u> wants friends. ___indefinite___ ___singular___
2. Anna told <u>herself</u> to smile. ___reflexive___ ___singular___
3. A smile multiplies <u>itself</u>. ___reflexive___ ___singular___
4. <u>Many</u> begin to smile at Anna. ___indefinite___ ___plural___
5. <u>Anybody</u> can give a smile. ___indefinite___ ___singular___

Directions Underline the correct pronoun in ( ) to complete each sentence.

6. (Someone, <u>Both</u>) are friendly.
7. (<u>Everyone</u>, Many) agrees they are good friends.
8. (No one, <u>Others</u>) are welcome in our club.
9. (<u>Several</u>, Anybody) have inquired about joining.
10. The boys signed (himself, <u>themselves</u>) up for bowling class.
11. (<u>Anybody</u>, Yourself) can try out for the class play.
12. Marcus and I practiced our parts by (himself, <u>ourselves</u>).

Directions Choose a pronoun from the box to complete each sentence correctly. Be sure indefinite pronouns used as subjects agree in number with their verbs.

| ourselves | everybody | themselves | few |

13. ___**Everybody**___ in class was to choose an after-school activity.
14. A ___**few**___ of us are signing up for poetry.
15. Ms. Lonway will let us choose a poet for ___**ourselves**___.
16. Humorous poets don't take ___**themselves**___ too seriously.

Home Activity Your child reviewed indefinite and reflexive pronouns. Have your child reread a favorite story and identify the indefinite and reflexive pronouns in it as singular or plural.

▲ **Grammar and Writing Practice Book** p. 76

The Stormi Giovanni Club   **483f**

Writing Workshop
Letter of Advice

OBJECTIVES

- Identify the characteristics of a letter of advice.
- Write advice to a student at a new school.
- Focus on voice.
- Use a rubric.

Genre Letter of Advice
Writer's Craft Good Conclusions
Writing Trait Support/Voice

ELL

Support/Voice Encourage English learners to use a bilingual dictionary if available to find powerful verbs to express feelings. For example, *delighted* or *cheerful* could express happiness. See more writing support in the ELL and Transition Handbook.

Writing Traits

FOCUS/IDEAS The letter is focused on suggestions to help a new student fit in.

ORGANIZATION/PARAGRAPHS The letter has a greeting, body, closing, and signature. The body is divided into logical paragraphs.

SUPPORT/VOICE The writer is caring and sincere and speaks to the individual.

SUPPORT/WORD CHOICE Words are specific and accurate (*meets after school on Tuesdays*), and they sound natural.

SUPPORT/SENTENCES Sentences are well constructed and varied.

CONVENTIONS There is excellent control and accuracy.

DAY 1 — Model the Trait

READING-WRITING CONNECTION

- *The Stormi Giovanni Club* explores a girl's difficulties adjusting to a new school; each character has a unique voice.

- The story addresses the trauma of starting over with honesty and humor; the main character draws realistic conclusions.

- Students will write a **letter of advice,** drawing good conclusions in a sincere voice.

MODEL SUPPORT/VOICE Discuss Writing Transparency 19A. Then discuss the model and the writing trait of voice.

Think Aloud The writer establishes a friendly and welcoming voice by beginning with the exclamation, "Welcome to Wilshire Elementary School!" She sounds sincerely happy that Terry has come to Wilshire. Her advice is clear and helpful.

Advice

You may be asked to give **advice,** or specific suggestions for solving a problem. Advice columnists give advice every day as they respond to people's letters. They use logic and what they know about a situation to draw conclusions and suggest a plan of action. Use similar strategies when you give advice.

Advice from Alison

Dear Terry,

Welcome to Wilshire Elementary School! You say in your letter that you are interested in plants and computers. Wilshire has an active Plant Club that meets after school on Tuesdays in the greenhouse. Kids in this club learn about growing and caring for plants. Twice a year, they take plants they have grown to nursing homes around town.

As a fifth grader, you'll have six weeks of computer class in the spring. You'll learn about software and the Internet. Ms. Punti tells some funny jokes too!

As for making friends, kids at Wilshire are friendly. Just be sure you wear a smile to school. Also, ask people for help in learning new routines. Once you start talking, you'll soon find friends who fit you like a glove!

Good luck!

Alison

It is logical to conclude that Plant Club will interest someone who is interested in plants.

Details give a new student information about Plant Club.

Suggestions give specific actions to help make friends.

Unit 4 The Stormi Giovanni Club — Writing Model **19A**

▲ **Writing Transparency** 19A

DAY 2 — Improve Writing

WRITER'S CRAFT
Good Conclusions

Display Writing Transparency 19B. Read the directions and work together to draw logical conclusions based on given information.

Think Aloud

DRAW GOOD CONCLUSIONS Tomorrow we will write letters of advice. That will require drawing conclusions about how to solve a problem. Suppose a friend wants permission to go to an overnight party. I could conclude that she should give her parents lots of information about how safe the situation will be. I will need to draw conclusions based on my experiences with sleepovers and the facts about this party.

GUIDED WRITING Some students may need more help drawing conclusions. Work with them as they offer conclusions about the selection and explain why their conclusions are logical.

Good Conclusions

To draw **good conclusions,** think about the facts and details you have learned from reading. Also, think about what you already know. Make a general statement based on these clues.

Directions Choose the best conclusion for the paragraph. Write the letter on the line. Then write a sentence telling why your choice is best.

Fifth graders have many heavy textbooks. I can't even fit all my books into my backpack, and it is a big one! We also have to move to different classrooms several times a day. Sometimes we have to go upstairs or downstairs carrying that heavy load. I know several kids who have sore backs because of this. My best friend even had to see a doctor about muscle pain.

D

A   Fifth graders should not have textbooks!
B   Fifth graders should be given weight training for stronger muscles.
C   Fifth graders should study only one subject for two weeks.
D   Fifth graders should have lockers to store textbooks they aren't using.

Possible answer: D. Lockers will solve the problem. No other conclusion is logical or reasonable for an elementary school.

Directions Write a good conclusion for the paragraph below.

When kids get to fifth grade, they often begin middle school. This means they attend school at a new building. For the first time, they have a whole team of teachers. This means kids travel to different classrooms for reading, math, science, and so on. The time allowed to pass between classes is four minutes. A sticky locker can make a kid late for class.

Possible answer: These are only a few of the stresses that fifth graders must cope with in their new environment.

Unit 4 The Stormi Giovanni Club — Writer's Craft **19B**

▲ **Writing Transparency** 19B

Pages 483g–483h

LA.5.3.1.1 Prewrite by generating ideas from multiple sources (text and brainstorming)
LA.5.3.3.1 Evaluate draft for voice
LA.5.4.2.4 Write communications (friendly letter)

Trait of the Week

Support/ Voice

DAY 3 — Prewrite and Draft

READ THE WRITING PROMPT

on page 479 in the Student Edition.

In The Stormi Giovanni Club, *other people help Stormi adjust to a new school.*

Think about a situation in which you could offer help or advice.

Now write a letter of advice to someone in that situation.

FCAT Writing+ Test Tips

- Include specific information about the situation and the advice you can offer.
- Draw conclusions based on facts about the situation and what you know from personal experience.
- Include all the parts of a friendly letter.

GETTING STARTED Students can do any of the following.

- Summarize the facts or knowledge they have gained about this kind of situation.
- List suggestions for solving the problem that make sense based on the facts.
- Brainstorm supporting details for the advice to be given.

DAY 4 — Draft and Revise

EDITING/REVISING CHECKLIST

☑ Are the conclusions in my letter logical?

☑ Have I used indefinite and reflexive pronouns correctly?

☑ Did I spell words that end with -ible and -able correctly?

See *The Grammar and Writing Book,* pp. 158–163.

Revising Tips

Support/Voice

- Write sentences that sound like natural speech.
- Deal honestly but sincerely with the writer's problem.
- Let your feelings show in your choice of words.

PUBLISHING Students can use their letters to create an advice column on a bulletin board. Some students may wish to revise their work later.

ASSESSMENT Use the scoring rubric to evaluate students' work.

DAY 5 — Connect to Unit Writing

Story	
Week 1	E-mail 411g–411h
Week 2	Journal Entry 435g–435h
Week 3	Story About an Animal 457g–457h
Week 4	Advice 483g–483h
Week 5	Describe How You Achieved a Goal 503g–503h

PREVIEW THE UNIT PROMPT

Tell a story about a character who succeeds by adapting to a new situation. Focus on an event that shows this person's resourcefulness. Your story may be real or imagined.

APPLY

- A story has a beginning, middle, and end and focuses on one incident or event.
- The end of a story should be a logical conclusion to the action.

Writing Trait Rubric

	6	5	4	3	2	1
Support/ Voice	Excellent sense of writer's attitude toward topic; strongly engages audience and speaks directly to them	Strong sense of how writer feels and thinks about topic; engages audience and speaks directly to them	Clear sense of how writer feels and thinks; engages audience	Some sense of how writer feels and thinks; writer somewhat involved with audience	Little sense of how writer feels and thinks; weak attempt to engage audience	No sense of how writer feels and thinks about topic; no attempt to engage audience
	Uses well-chosen words in letter to clearly show feelings toward topic	Uses words in letter that clearly show feelings about topic	Uses words in letter that show some feelings about topic	Needs to use more words in letter that show feelings about topic	Few words in letter that show feelings about topic	Uses no words in letter that show feelings about topic

Spelling & Phonics   Suffixes *-ible, -able*

DAY 1 Pretest and Sort

DAY 2 Think and Practice

OBJECTIVE

● Identify and spell suffixes *-ible* and *-able.*

Generalization

Connect to Phonics When adding the suffix *-ible* or *-able,* there are no sound clues to help you decide which form to use: *agreeable, flexible.* The vowel sound spelled by the letters *ib* and *ab* is the /ə/ and can be spelled many different ways.

Spelling Words

1. sensible	11. convertible
2. washable	12. forgettable
3. available	13. laughable
4. agreeable	14. sociable
5. fashionable	15. allowable
6. valuable	16. divisible
7. flexible	17. hospitable*
8. reasonable	18. reversible
9. favorable	19. responsible
10. breakable	20. tolerable

Challenge Words

21. noticeable	24. biodegradable
22. conceivable	25. collapsible
23. disposable	

* Word from the selection

Spelling/Phonics Support See the ELL and Transition Handbook for spelling support.

PRETEST

Use the Dictation Sentences from Day 5 to administer the pretest. Read the word, read the sentence, and then read the word again. Guide students in self-correcting their pretests and correcting any misspellings.

Monitor Progress

Spelling

If...	then...
If... students misspell more than 5 pretest words,	**then...** use words 1–10 for Strategic Intervention.
If... students misspell 1–5 pretest words,	**then...** use words 1–20 for On-Level practice.
If... students correctly spell all pretest words,	**then...** use words 1–25 for Advanced Learners.

HOMEWORK Spelling Practice Book, p. 73.

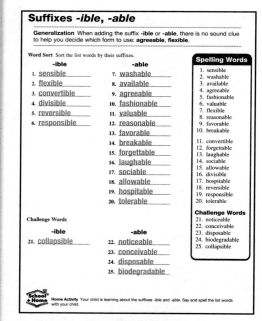

▲ **Spelling Practice Book** p. 73

TEACH

Draw columns on the board. Label the left column *-able,* and the right column *-ible.* Say a list word and ask students in which column the word should be written. Do not correct. Do this with all the list words. Then have students compare the words on the board to their word lists. Have volunteers come to the board and write the words in the correct column where applicable.

reversible

FIND THE PATTERN Ask students to draw a line between the word and the suffix. Have them identify which words have changed when a suffix has been added and which have not.

HOMEWORK Spelling Practice Book, p. 74.

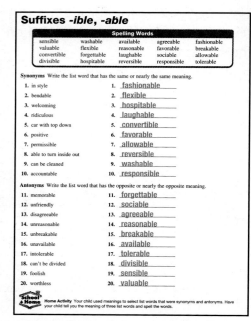

▲ **Spelling Practice Book** p. 74

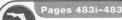

Pages 483i–483j

LA.5.1.4.1 Understand spelling patterns

LA.5.3.4.1 Use spelling rules, knowledge of root words, and suffixes

LA.5.4.3.2 Write persuasive text that includes persuasive techniques (word choice and emotional appeal)

DAY 3 Connect to Writing

MAKE A POSTER

Have students make a poster that advertises an item, event, movie, book, or similar item. Encourage them to use as many list words as they can in the poster to grab attention and provide information.

Frequently Misspelled Words

when   then   went

These words may seem easy to spell, but they are often misspelled by fifth-graders. Alert students to these frequently misspelled words.

HOMEWORK Spelling Practice Book, p. 75.

Suffixes -ible, -able

Proofread an Article Find five spelling errors and one capitalization error in the article. Circle the errors and write the corrections on the line.

Fashion Sense
Store buyers are responsible for ordering fashionible clothing customers will like. Last year, mrs. Clark, the store buyer, ordered dozens of reversible sweaters. The sweaters were washable, avalible in a variety of colors, and at a reasonible price. When the sweaters sold out quickly, the buyer knew she had made a sensible choice.

Spelling Words
sensible
washable
available
agreeable
fashionable
valuable
flexible
reasonable
favorable
breakable
convertible
forgettable
laughable
sociable
allowable
divisible
hospitable
reversible
responsible
tolerable

Frequently Misspelled Words
when
then
went

1. fashionable   2. washable
3. available   4. reasonable
5. sensible   6. Mrs.

Proofread Words Circle the correct spelling of the list word.

7. The gymnast is as _____ as a rubber band.
   flexable   flexibel   (flexible)

8. Porcelain china is delicate and _____.
   (breakable)   breakabel   breakible

9. Be _____ to your guests when they visit.
   hospital   (hospitable)   hospitible

10. I'd love to have a car with a _____ top.
    (convertible)   convertable   convertibel

11. Sixty-three is _____ by seven.
    dividable   divisable   (divisible)

12. Eat three _____ and balanced meals every day.
    (sensible)   sensable   senseable

Home Activity Your child identified misspelled list words. Ask your child to spell three list words that end in -ible and three list words that end in -able.

▲ **Spelling Practice Book** p. 75

DAY 4 Review

REVIEW SUFFIXES

Have partners take turns saying the base word of each list word to a partner. The partner responds by adding the suffix and then spelling the word. Partners should say and spell each of the list words.

Spelling Strategy
Divide and Conquer

It's easier to remember how to spell words if you break them into parts first. Draw a line between the word and its suffix. Study the word one part at a time.

HOMEWORK Spelling Practice Book, p. 76.

Suffixes -ible, -able

Spelling Words				
sensible	washable	available	agreeable	fashionable
valuable	flexible	reasonable	favorable	breakable
convertible	forgettable	laughable	sociable	allowable
divisible	hospitable	reversible	responsible	tolerable

Crossword Puzzle Use clues to find the list words. Write each letter in a box.

Across
6. friendly
7. levelheaded
8. silly

9. welcoming
10. positive

Down
1. stylish
2. bearable
3. unmemorable
4. precious
5. bendable

Definitions Write the list word that fits the definition.
11. anything that can be cleaned with soap and water
12. separable into equal parts
13. able to obtain
14. fragile and delicate

11. washable
12. divisible
13. available
14. breakable

Home Activity Your child has learned to read, write, and spell words with suffixes. Have your child pick out the five hardest words to review with you.

▲ **Spelling Practice Book** p. 76

DAY 5 Posttest

DICTATION SENTENCES

1. Those are sensible shoes.
2. Cotton fabrics are washable.
3. Good seats were still available.
4. The terms were agreeable.
5. People like fashionable clothing.
6. Gold is valuable.
7. The flexible straw bent slightly.
8. That store has reasonable prices.
9. The play got a favorable review.
10. The plates are breakable.
11. The convertible sofa can be used as a bed for guests.
12. That boring movie is forgettable.
13. The silly dog was laughable.
14. Bees are sociable animals.
15. Staying up late is allowable on Friday.
16. One hundred is divisible by ten.
17. The host has been hospitable to all the guests.
18. My coat is reversible.
19. A lifeguard is responsible for all the swimmers.
20. Heat is tolerable with air conditioning.

CHALLENGE

21. The new paint made a noticeable difference in the room.
22. It was conceivable that the reporter misheard the information.
23. Let's use disposable dishes at the party.
24. Grass clippings are biodegradable.
25. The collapsible table was stored in the closet for later use.

OBJECTIVES

- Formulate an inquiry question that is connected to this week's lesson focus.
- Effectively and efficiently find, evaluate, and communicate information related to an inquiry question using electronic sources.

New Literacies

Day 1	Identify Questions
Day 2	Navigate/Search
Day 3	Analyze
Day 4	Synthesize
Day 5	Communicate

Page 483k

LA.5.6.2.1 Select a topic for inquiry, formulate a search plan, and apply evaluative criteria (usefulness, validity, currentness, and objectivity)

LA.5.6.2.2 Read and record information systematically

NEW LITERACIES

Internet Inquiry Activity

EXPLORE E-MAIL

Use the following 5-day plan to help students conduct this week's Internet inquiry activity about e-mail. Remind students to follow classroom rules when using the Internet.

DAY 1

Identify Questions Discuss the lesson focus question: *How do people adapt to a new school?* Then have students recall how Stormi relies on e-mail to communicate with her friends back home and how her teacher won't allow them to use school computers for e-mail. Brainstorm ideas for specific inquiry questions about using e-mail. For example, students might want to learn about rules for e-mail etiquette. Have students work individually, in pairs, or in small groups to write inquiry questions they want to answer.

DAY 2

Navigate/Search Explain the keyword *e-mail* will likely yield thousands of sites, so the choice of keyword should be specific, such as *e-mail etiquette.* Point out that keywords will appear as bold type in Web site descriptions. Students should use the words around the bold keywords as context clues to determine if a site contains relevant information.

DAY 3

Analyze Have students skim and scan the Web sites they identified on Day 2. Ask them to read each site for information that relates to their inquiry questions, taking notes as they go. Students should analyze information for credibility, reliability, and usefulness by looking at who the author is, what his or her background is on the topic, and when it was published.

DAY 4

Synthesize Have students synthesize information from Day 3 to answer their inquiry questions. Ask them to think about the best methods for sharing the information with the rest of the class.

DAY 5

Communicate Have students decide how they want to share their inquiry results. Students might want to write and print e-mails to the class that summarize the results of their inquiries.

RESEARCH/STUDY SKILLS
Thesaurus

TEACH

Ask students where they should look if they want to find a synonym for the word *digress.* Students may need prompting before they mention a thesaurus. Show a thesaurus to students and explain how to use it.

- A **thesaurus** is a book of synonyms, words that mean the same or almost the same as another word.

- Not all synonyms mean exactly the same. It is important to check in a dictionary the meaning of a synonym you find in a thesaurus to make sure that the synonym has the meaning you want.

- Most print thesauruses have an index in the back. You look up the word in the index for which you want synonyms.

- With electronic thesauruses, you type a word into a search box.

- With a word processor thesaurus, you highlight the word and use the thesaurus under TOOLS to find synonyms.

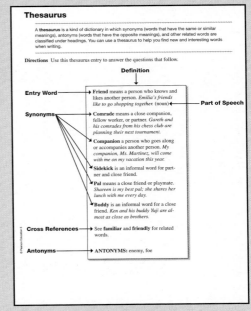

Have students work in groups to practice using a thesaurus—print, electronic, or word processing—and a dictionary. Each group should find the best synonym for a lesson vocabulary word from *The Stormi Giovanni Club.* Then, discuss these questions:

1. **How might you need to change the form of *cavities* to find a synonym?** (*From the plural to the singular, cavity*)

2. **Suppose you find these synonyms for *scintillating*: *witty, good, smart, piquant, clever.* How do you choose the best one?** (*You look up the synonyms whose meanings you do not know in a dictionary.*)

ASSESS

As students work with the thesaurus, check that they are able to locate synonyms, or alternate word choices, for words, either using the index in a print thesaurus or using the appropriate method in an electronic thesaurus. Be sure they use a dictionary to check the meanings of synonyms.

For more practice or to assess students, use Practice Book pp. 189–190.

Thesaurus

A **thesaurus** is a kind of dictionary in which synonyms (words that have the same or similar meanings), antonyms (words that have the opposite meanings), and other related words are classified under headings. You can use a thesaurus to help you find new and interesting words when writing.

Directions Use this thesaurus entry to answer the questions that follow.

Definition

Entry Word — **Friend** means a person who knows and likes another person. *Emilia's friends like to go shopping together.* (noun) — **Part of Speech**

Synonyms — **Comrade** means a close companion, fellow worker, or partner. *Gareth and his comrades from his chess club are planning their next tournament.*

Companion a person who goes along or accompanies another person. *My companion, Ms. Martinez, will come with me on my vacation this year.*

Sidekick is an informal word for partner and close friend.

Pal means a close friend or playmate. *Shareen is my best pal; she shares her lunch with me every day.*

Buddy is an informal word for a close friend. *Ken and his buddy Yuji are almost as close as brothers.*

Cross References — See **familiar** and **friendly** for related words.

Antonyms — **ANTONYMS:** enemy, foe

▲ **Practice Book** p. 189

Possible answers given for 4–6, 8–10.

1. What entry word is shown?
   Friend is the entry word.
2. Name the part of speech of the entry word.
   It is a noun.
3. What synonyms are given for the entry word?
   comrade, companion, sidekick, pal, buddy
4. Rewrite this sentence using one of the synonyms in the entry: *My friend May and I like to listen to music.*
   My pal May and I like to listen to music.
5. Rewrite this sentence by replacing the underlined words with a word from the entry: *Our cat is no friend of our neighbor's dog.*
   Our cat is the enemy of our neighbor's dog.
6. Would you use *sidekick* when introducing your friend to the school principal. Explain?
   No because *sidekick* is informal.
7. How would you find additional words that have meanings similar to the entry word?
   You would look under *familiar* and *friendly.*
8. How does the meaning of *friend* help you understand the meaning of *foe?*
   Foe is the antonym, or opposite, of *friend,* so it must mean the same as enemy.
9. If you looked up *large* in a thesaurus, what synonyms do you think you would find?
   Big, huge, and *gigantic* are possible synonyms.
10. How do you think a thesaurus could help you write a report?
    A thesaurus could help you find more varied and precise words.

Home Activity Your child answered questions about a thesaurus entry. Look at a thesaurus together. Ask your child to locate several entries using entry words you tell him or her. Discuss the synonyms for different shades of meaning.

▲ **Practice Book** p. 190

Assessment Checkpoints *for the Week*

Selection Assessment

Use pp. 73–76 of Selection Tests to check:

 Selection Understanding

 Comprehension Skill *Generalize*

 Selection Vocabulary
cavities
combination
demonstrates
episode
profile
strict

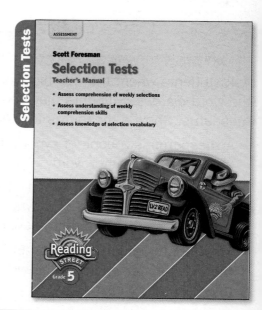

ASSESSMENT

Scott Foresman
Selection Tests
Teacher's Manual

- Assess comprehension of weekly selections
- Assess understanding of weekly comprehension skills
- Assess knowledge of selection vocabulary

Reading STREET Grade 5

Leveled Assessment

On-Level
Strategic Intervention
Advanced

Use pp. 109–114 of Fresh Reads for Differentiated Test Practice to check:

 Comprehension Skill *Generalize*

 REVIEW **Comprehension Skill**
Draw Conclusions

 Fluency *Words Correct Per Minute*

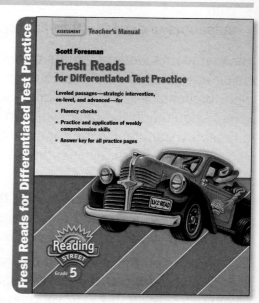

ASSESSMENT   Teacher's Manual

Scott Foresman
Fresh Reads
for Differentiated Test Practice

Leveled passages—strategic intervention, on-level, and advanced—for
- Fluency checks
- Practice and application of weekly comprehension skills
- Answer key for all practice pages

Reading STREET Grade 5

Managing Assessment

Use Assessment Handbook for:

 Observation Checklists

 Record-Keeping Forms

 Portfolio Assessment

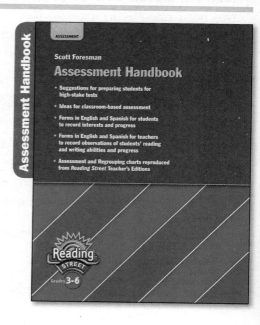

ASSESSMENT

Scott Foresman
Assessment Handbook

- Suggestions for preparing students for high-stake tests
- Ideas for classroom-based assessment
- Forms in English and Spanish for students to record interests and progress
- Forms in English and Spanish for teachers to record observations of students' reading and writing abilities and progress
- Assessment and Regrouping charts reproduced from *Reading Street* Teacher's Editions

Reading STREET Grades 3–6

Florida

Planning Guide for Sunshine State Standards

The Gymnast

Reading Street Teacher's Edition pages	Grade 5 Benchmarks for Language Arts

Reading

Word Work Negative Prefixes: 503i–503j

Comprehension Draw Conclusions: 484–485, 488–497, 500–503, 503b
Visualize: 484–485, 488–497, 500–503

Vocabulary Lesson Vocabulary: 486b, 493, 497
Word Structure: 486–487, 495, 503c

Fluency Model Punctuation Clues: 484l–484m, 503a

Self-Selected Reading: LR37–45, TR16–17

Literature Genre—Autobiography: 488
Reader Response: 498

The student will:

LA.5.1.4.1 Understand spelling patterns.

LA.5.1.4.2 Recognize structural analysis.

LA.5.1.5.2 Adjust reading rate based on purpose, text difficulty, form, and style.

LA.5.1.6.1 Use new vocabulary that is introduced and taught directly.

LA.5.1.6.2 Listen to, read, and discuss familiar and conceptually challenging text.

LA.5.1.6.7 Use meaning of familiar base words and affixes to determine meanings of unfamiliar complex words.

LA.5.1.7.3 Determine the main idea or essential message in grade-level text through inferring.

LA.5.3.4.1 Edit writing for grammar and language conventions, including the correct use of spelling, using spelling rules and knowledge of prefixes.

Writing

Four-Elements Writing Support/Word Choice: 499, 503g–503h

Writing Writing for Tests: 503g–503h

Grammar, Usage, and Mechanics Using *Who* and *Whom*: 503e–503f

Research/Study Graphs: 503l

The student will:

LA.5.2.2.1 Locate, explain, and use information from text features (e.g., graphs).

LA.5.3.3.1 Revise by evaluating the draft for word choice.

LA.5.3.4.4 Edit writing for grammar and language conventions, including the correct use of pronouns.

LA.5.4.1.2 Write a variety of expressive forms.

Communication and Media

Speaking/Listening Build Concept Vocabulary: 484l, 493, 497, 503c
Read Aloud: 484m

Viewing Analyze a Video: 503d

Technology New Literacies: 503k

The student will:

LA.5.1.6.1 Use new vocabulary that is introduced and taught directly.

LA.5.6.2.1 Select a topic for inquiry, formulate a search plan, and apply evaluative criteria to select and use appropriate resources.

LA.5.6.3.1 Examine how ideas are presented in a variety of nonprint media.

Unit Skills

Writing Story: WA2–9

Poetry: 504–507

Project/Wrap-Up: 508–509

The student will:

LA.5.2.1.3 Demonstrate how descriptive and figurative language help to communicate meaning in a poem.

LA.5.4.1.1 Write narratives that establish a situation and plot with rising action, conflict, and resolution.

LA.5.4.2.2 Record information (e.g., charts) related to a topic.

Intervention

This Week's Leveled Readers

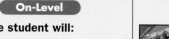

My Sidewalks on Reading Street provides collaborative, parallel, intensive intervention when used with *Reading Street*.

Below-Level

Let the Games Begin: History of the Olympics

Nonfiction

The student will:

LA.5.1.7.3 Determine the main idea or essential message in grade-level text through inferring.

LA.5.2.2.2 Use information from the text to answer questions related to explicitly stated main ideas or relevant details.

On-Level

Strange Sports with Weird Gear

Nonfiction

The student will:

LA.5.1.7.3 Determine the main idea or essential message in grade-level text through inferring.

LA.5.2.2.3 Organize information to show understanding.

Advanced

WHAT MAKES GREAT ATHLETES

Nonfiction

The student will:

LA.5.1.7.3 Determine the main idea or essential message in grade-level text through inferring.

LA.5.1.7.5 Identify the text structure an author uses and explain how it impacts meaning in text.

Correlation to Robert Marzano's Instructional Strategies

- Reinforcing effort and providing recognition: pp. 498–499
- Homework and practice: pp. 484f–484g, 485, 487, 498
- Nonlinguistic representations: p. 503d
- Cooperative learning: pp. 484j–484k

- Setting objectives and providing feedback: p. 484m
- Generating and testing hypotheses: p. 488
- Cues, questions, and advance organizers: pp. 486a, 486b, 503c

Florida Assessment for FCAT Success

 **Selection Tests, pp. 77–80**

 **Fresh Reads for Differentiated Test Practice, pp. 115–120**

 **Unit 4 Benchmark Test in FCAT Format, pp. 1–21**

 **Success Tracker™ Online Test to Monitor Benchmarks**

Content-Area Standards Taught During the Reading Lesson

Social Studies	Science
The student:	**The student:**
SS.B.2.2.2.5.1. Understands how the physical environment constrains human activity	**SC.F.1.2.1.5.1.** Understands how body systems interact
SS.B.2.2.3.5.1. Understands how human activity affects the physical environment	
SS.C.2.2.2.5.1. Extends and refines understanding of ways personal responsibility is important	

CONNECT TO SF SOCIAL STUDIES
TIME SAVERS FOR FLORIDA TEACHERS

 Comprehension Skill: **Draw Conclusions**

Unit 4: *Adapting*

Question of the Week: **Why do people try to change themselves?**

Social Studies Concepts:
- **Individual Development and Identity**
- **Sports**
- **Nadia Comaneci**

 Reading Skill: **Draw Conclusions, Unit 5, pp. 334–335**

These lessons in *Scott Foresman Social Studies* support the concepts taught in this week's lesson of *Reading Street.*

Overview, Lesson 1, "The American People," pp. 6–11

Unit 9, Chapter 19, Lesson 3, "The Cold War Continues," pp. 650–655

Unit 4
Adapting

Week 5

Why do people try to change themselves

How do people and animals adapt to different situations?

Week 1

How do people adapt to difficult situations?

Week 2

How do people adapt to living with physical limitations?

Week 3

How do animals adapt to survive?

Week 4

How do people adapt to a new school?

Week 5

Why do people try to change themselves?

▶ **Develop Language**

champion, competitive, develop, perfected

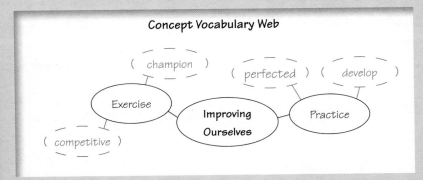

Concept Vocabulary Web

▶ **Social Studies Content**

Gymnastics, Nadia Comaneci

▶ **Writing**

Describe How You Achieved a Goal

▶ **Internet Inquiry**

Gymnastics

Preview Your Week

Why do people try to change themselves?

Will Gary succeed in becoming the person he wants to be?

The Gymnast
by Gary Soto

Genre Autobiography is the story of a person's life or of a single event in it, told by the person who lived it. As you read, notice how the author looks back at himself from a humorous point of view.

Student Edition pages 488–497

Audio CD

Read It ONLINE

PearsonSuccessNet.com

- Student Edition
- Leveled Readers

Genre	Autobiography
Vocabulary Strategy	Word Structure
Comprehension Skill	Draw Conclusions
Comprehension Strategy	Visualize

Paired Selection

SOCIAL STUDIES

Reading Across Texts

Compare Information in Two Selections

Genre

Online Reference Sources

Text Features

Organization of Electronic References

Reading Online

PearsonSuccessNet.com

All About Gymnastics

Online Reference Sources

Genre
- You can find reference sources, such as almanacs and dictionaries, on Internet Web sites.
- Some Web sites give you several different reference sources all in one place.

Text Features
- These electronic reference sources look a lot like printed sources, and they're organized the same way.
- Instead of turning pages by hand, you click through them with a mouse.

Link to Social Studies
Explore a topic you like. Use an encyclopedia, dictionary, and other reference sources. Write down facts you find.

After reading Gary Soto's "The Gymnast," Alice decides she might want to do gymnastics. So she goes to an online reference Web site.

This site has four reference sources: an atlas, almanac, dictionary, and encyclopedia. When Alice types the keyword "gymnastics" into the Search engine and clicks on "go," the site gives her a list of results that begins like this:

Search "gymnastics" GO!

Atlas
Almanac
Dictionary
Encyclopedia

Search Results: "gymnastics"

Gymnastics (Encyclopedia)
gymnastics, exercises for the balanced development of the body (see also aerobics).

Alice clicks on this gymnastics encyclopedia link and gets an entry for gymnastics that ends like this:

Encyclopedia

gymnastics
Women compete in the vault, floor exercises, balance beam, and uneven parallel bars, as well as in rhythmic gymnastics and on the trampoline.

Visualize Picture the steps Alice takes as she does her search.

Student Edition pages 500–503

Audio CD

484b   Adapting • Week 5

Florida Social Studies Standards This Week

SS.A.1.2.1.5.2 Understands the effects of individuals on historical events

SS.B.2.2.2.5.1 Understands how the physical environment constrains human activity

SS.B.2.2.3.5.1 Understands how human activity affects the physical environment

Time for
SOCIAL
STUDIES

Leveled Readers

⊚ **Skill** Draw Conclusions

⊚ **Strategy** Visualize

Lesson Vocabulary

Below-Level

On-Level

Advanced

ELL Reader

· Concept Vocabulary
· Text Support
· Language Enrichment

Fast as Lightning

Time for
SOCIAL
STUDIES

Integrate Social Studies Standards

- **Individual Development and Identity**
- **Sports**

✓ Read

"The Gymnast,"
pp. 488–497

"All About Gymnastics,"
pp. 500–503

Leveled Readers

Below-Level   **On-Level**   **Advanced**

- Support Concepts   - Develop Concepts   - Extend Concepts

ELL Reader

Fast as Lightning

✓ **Build Concept Vocabulary**
Improving Ourselves,
pp. 484l–484m

✓ **Teach Social Studies Concepts**
Gymnastics, p. 491
Nadia Comaneci, p. 495

✓ **Explore Social Studies Center**
Explore a New Interest,
p. 484k

Florida Weekly Plan

READING

45–90 minutes

TARGET SKILLS OF THE WEEK

- **Comprehension Skill**
  Draw Conclusions
- **Comprehension Strategy**
  Visualize
- **Vocabulary Strategy**
  Word Structure

LANGUAGE ARTS

30–60 minutes

Trait of the Week

Support/Word Choice

DAY 1
PAGES 484l–486b, 503a, 503e–503k

Oral Language

QUESTION OF THE WEEK *Why do people try to change themselves?*

Read Aloud: "The Winning Stroke," 484m
Build Concepts, 484l

Comprehension/Vocabulary

Comprehension Skill/Strategy Lesson, 484–485
- Draw Conclusions **T**
- Visualize

Build Background, 486a

Introduce Lesson Vocabulary, 486b
bluish, cartwheels, gymnastics, hesitation, limelight, skidded, somersault, throbbing, wincing **T**

Read Leveled Readers

Grouping Options 484f–484g

Fluency

Model Punctuation Clues, 484l–484m, 503a

Grammar, 503e
Introduce Using *Who* and *Whom* **T**

Writing Workshop, 503g
Introduce Descriptive Writing
Model the Trait of the Week: Support/Word Choice

Spelling, 503i
Pretest for Negative Prefixes

Internet Inquiry, 503k
Identify Questions

DAY 2
PAGES 486–493, 503a, 503e–503k

Oral Language

QUESTION OF THE DAY *Why does Gary want to take up gymnastics?*

Comprehension/Vocabulary

Vocabulary Strategy Lesson, 486–487
- Word Structure **T**

Read "The Gymnast," 488–493

Grouping Options 484f–484g

- Draw Conclusions **T**
- **REVIEW** Generalize **T**

Develop Vocabulary

Fluency

Echo Reading, 503a

Grammar, 503e
Develop Using *Who* and *Whom* **T**

Writing Workshop, 503g
Improve Writing with Sensory Details

Spelling, 503i
Teach the Generalization

Internet Inquiry, 503k
Navigate/Search

DAILY WRITING ACTIVITIES

Day 1 Write to Read, 484

Day 2 Words to Write, 487
Strategy Response Log, 488, 493

DAILY SOCIAL STUDIES CONNECTIONS

Day 1 Improving Ourselves Concept Web, 484l

Day 2 Time for Social Studies: Gymnastics, 490
Revisit the Improving Ourselves Concept Web, 493

DAILY SUCCESS PREDICTORS
for Adequate Yearly Progress

Monitor Progress and Corrective Feedback

Vocabulary Check Vocabulary, *484l*

RESOURCES FOR THE WEEK

- Practice Book, *pp. 191–200*
- Word Study and Spelling Practice Book, *pp. 77–80*
- Grammar and Writing Practice Book, *pp. 77–80*

- Selection Test, *pp. 77–80*
- Fresh Reads for Differentiated Test Practice, *pp. 115–120*
- The Grammar and Writing Book, *pp. 164–169*

Grouping Options for Differentiated Instruction
Turn the page for the small group lesson plan.

DAY 3 | PAGES 494–499, 503a, 503e–503k

Oral Language

QUESTION OF THE DAY *What do you think happens to Gary's dream of being a gymnast?*

Comprehension/Vocabulary

Read "The Gymnast," 494–498

Grouping Options 484f–484g

- Visualize
- Word Structure **T**
- Develop Vocabulary

Reader Response

Selection Test

Fluency

Model Punctuation Clues, 503a

Grammar, 503f
Apply Using *Who* and *Whom* in Writing **T**

Writing Workshop, 499, 503h
Write Now
Prewrite and Draft

Spelling, 503j
Connect Spelling to Writing

Internet Inquiry, 503k
Analyze Sources

Day 3 Strategy Response Log, 496
Think and Explain, 498

Day 3 Time for Social Studies: Nadia Comaneci, 495; Revisit the Improving Ourselves Concept Web, 497

DAY 4 | PAGES 500–503a, 503e–503k

Oral Language

QUESTION OF THE DAY *What is the importance of practice in perfecting any talent or skill?*

Comprehension/Vocabulary

Read "All About Gymnastics," 500–503

Grouping Options 484f –484g

Online Reference
Sources
Reading Across Texts

Fluency

Partner Reading, 503a

Grammar, 503f
Practice Using *Who* and *Whom* for Standardized Tests **T**

Writing Workshop, 503h
Draft, Revise, and Publish

Spelling, 503j
Provide a Strategy

Internet Inquiry, 503k
Synthesize Information

Day 4 Writing Across Texts, 503

Day 4 Social Studies Center: Explore a New Interest, 484k

DAY 5 | PAGES 503a–503l

Oral Language

QUESTION OF THE WEEK *To wrap up the week, revisit the Day 1 question.*
Build Concept Vocabulary, 503c

Fluency

Read Leveled Readers

Grouping Options 484f–484g

Assess Reading Rate, 503a

Comprehension/Vocabulary

- Reteach Draw Conclusions, 503b **T**

Simile, 503b

- Word Structure, 503c **T**

Speaking and Viewing, 503d
Informational Speech
Analyze a Video

Grammar, 503f
Cumulative Review

Writing Workshop, 503h
Connect to Unit Writing

Spelling, 503j
Posttest for Negative Prefixes

Internet Inquiry, 503k
Communicate Results

Research/Study Skills, 503l
Graphs

Day 5 Simile, 503b

Day 5 Revisit the Improving Ourselves Concept Web, 503c

KEY ⊙ **Target Skill** **T** **Tested Skill** **FCAT Tested Skill**

Comprehension Check Retelling, *498*

Fluency Check Fluency WCPM, *503a*

Vocabulary Check Vocabulary, *503c*

SUCCES
PREDICTO

Small Group Plan for Differentiated Instruction

Daily Plan AT A GLANCE

Reading
Whole Group
- Oral Language
- Comprehension/Vocabulary

Group Time
Differentiated Instruction

Meet with small groups to provide:
- Skill Support
- Reading Support
- Fluency Practice

Read

This week's lessons for daily group time can be found behind the Differentiated Instruction (DI) tab on pp. DI·42–DI·51.

Whole Group
- Fluency

Language Arts
- Grammar
- Writing
- Spelling
- Research/Inquiry
- Speaking/Listening/Viewing

Use *My Sidewalks on Reading Street* for Tier III intensive reading intervention.

DAY 1

On-Level
Teacher-Led
Page DI·43
- Develop Concept Vocabulary
- **Read** On-Level Reader *Strange Sports with Weird Gear*

Strategic Intervention
Teacher-Led
Page DI·42
- Reinforce Concepts
- **Read** Below-Level Reader *Let the Games Begin: History of the Olympics*

Advanced
Teacher-Led
Page DI·43
- **Read** Advanced Reader *What Makes Great Athletes*
- Independent Extension Activity

(i) Independent Activities
While you meet with small groups, have the rest of the class...
- Visit the Reading/Library Center, p. 484j
- Listen to the Background Building Audio
- Finish Write to Read, p. 484
- Complete Practice Book pp. 193–194
- Visit Cross-Curricular Centers

DAY 2

On-Level
Teacher-Led
Pages 490–493
- **Read** *The Gymnast*

Strategic Intervention
Teacher-Led
Page DI·44
- Practice Lesson Vocabulary
- Read Multisyllabic Words
- **Read** or Listen to *The Gymnast*

Advanced
Teacher-Led
Page DI·45
- Extend Vocabulary
- **Read** *The Gymnast*

(i) Independent Activities
While you meet with small groups, have the rest of the class...
- Visit the Reading/Library Center, p. 484j
- Listen to the AudioText for *The Gymnast*
- Finish Words to Write, p. 487
- Complete Practice Book pp. 195–196
- Write in their Strategy Response Logs, pp. 488, 493
- Visit Cross-Curricular Centers
- Work on inquiry projects

DAY 3

On-Level
Teacher-Led
Pages 494–497
- **Read** *The Gymnast*

Strategic Intervention
Teacher-Led
Page DI·46
- Practice Draw Conclusions and Visualize
- **Read** or Listen to *The Gymnast*

Advanced
Teacher-Led
Page DI·47
- Extend Draw Conclusions and Visualize
- **Read** *The Gymnast*

(i) Independent Activities
While you meet with small groups, have the rest of the class...
- Visit the Reading/Library Center, p. 484j
- Listen to the AudioText for *The Gymnast*
- Write in their Strategy Response Logs, p. 496
- Finish Think and Explain, p. 498
- Complete Practice Book p. 197
- Visit Cross-Curricular Centers
- Work on inquiry projects

① Begin with whole class skill and strategy instruction.

② Meet with small groups to provide differentiated instruction.

③ Gather the whole class back together for fluency and language arts.

DAY 4

On-Level
Teacher-Led
Pages 500–503

- **Read** "All About Gymnastics"

Strategic Intervention
Teacher-Led
Page DI · 48

- Practice Retelling
- **Read** or Listen to "All About Gymnastics"

Advanced
Teacher-Led
Page DI · 49

- **Read** "All About Gymnastics"
- Genre Study

 Independent Activities

While you meet with small groups, have the rest of the class...

- Visit the Reading/Library Center, p. 484j
- Listen to the AudioText for "All About Gymnastics"
- Visit the Writing/Vocabulary Center

- Finish Writing Across Texts, p. 503
- Visit Cross-Curricular Centers
- Work on inquiry projects

DAY 5

On-Level
Teacher-Led
Page DI · 51

- **Reread** Leveled Reader *Strange Sports with Weird Gear*
- Retell *Strange Sports with Weird Gear*

Strategic Intervention
Teacher-Led
Page DI · 50

- **Reread** Leveled Reader *Let the Games Begin: History of the Olympics*
- Retell *Let the Games Begin: History of the Olympics*

Advanced
Teacher-Led
Page DI · 51

- **Reread** Leveled Reader *What Makes Great Athletes*
- Share Extension Activity

 Independent Activities

While you meet with small groups, have the rest of the class...

- Visit the Reading/Library Center, p. 484j
- Complete Practice Book pp. 198–200

- Visit Cross-Curricular Centers
- Work on inquiry projects

 Grouping Place English language learners in the groups that correspond to their reading abilities in English.

Use the appropriate Leveled Reader or other text at students' instructional level.

TIP Send home the appropriate Multilingual Summary of the main selection on Day 1.

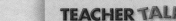 **Take It to the NET** ONLINE
PearsonSuccessNet.com

Deborah Simmons and Edward Kame'enui
For research on word recognition and diverse learners, see the article "Understanding the Primary Role of Word Recognition..." by Scott Foresman authors Deborah Simmons and Ed Kame'enui, and D. Chard.

TEACHER TALK

Structural analysis is the process of using knowledge of base words, endings, and affixes to decode words.

Be sure to schedule time for students to work on the unit inquiry project "Adaptations." This week students present graphic organizers with information about the ways people or animals adapt.

Looking Ahead

Name _____ Date _____

My Work Plan
Put an ☒ next to the activities you complete.

Listening
☐ Listen to *The Gymnast*.
☐ Listen to "All About Gymnastics."

Writing/Vocabulary
☐ Study the Words to Know.
☐ Write an autobiography.

Reading
☐ Read a book.
☐ Read Ten Important Sentences.
☐ Book Club

Social Studies
☐ Research a sport.
☐ Make a list.

Art
☐ Create a book cover.

Technology
☐ Choose a sports legend.
☐ Find an autobiography.

Independent Practice
☐ Practice Book, pp. 191–200
☐ Independent Writing

Inquiry
☐ Unit Inquiry
☐ Internet Inquiry

Wrap Up Your Week Turn your paper over. Write about what you did at school this week. What did you read? What did you learn about improving ourselves?

Unit 4 • Week 5 • *The Gymnast* **37**

▲ **Group-Time Survival Guide**
p. 37, Weekly Contract

☑ Customize Your Plan *by Strand*

ORAL LANGUAGE

 SOCIAL STUDIES

Concept Development

Why do people try to change themselves?

CONCEPT VOCABULARY
champion   competitive   develop   perfected

BUILD

☐ **Question of the Week** Introduce and discuss the question of the week. This week students will read a variety of texts and work on projects related to the concept *improving ourselves*. Post the question for students to refer to throughout the week. DAY 1 *484d*

☐ **Read Aloud** Read aloud "The Winning Stroke." Then begin a web to build concepts and concept vocabulary related to this week's lesson and the unit theme, Adapting. Introduce the concept words *champion, competitive, develop,* and *perfected* and have students place them on the web. Display the web for use throughout the week. DAY 1 *484l–484m*

DEVELOP

☐ **Question of the Day** Use the prompts from the Weekly Plan to engage students in conversations related to this week's reading and the unit theme. EVERY DAY *484d–484e*

☐ **Concept Vocabulary Web** Revisit the Improving Ourselves Concept Web and encourage students to add concept words from their reading and life experiences. DAY 2 *493*, DAY 3 *497*

CONNECT

☐ **Unit Review** Revisit the Improving Ourselves Concept Web and discuss how it relates to this week's lesson and the unit theme. DAY 5 *503c*

CHECK

☐ **Concept Vocabulary Web** Use the Improving Ourselves Concept Web to check students' understanding of the concept vocabulary words *champion, competitive, develop,* and *perfected.* DAY 1 *484l*, DAY 5 *503c*

VOCABULARY

STRATEGY WORD STRUCTURE
Recognizing a suffix can help you figure out the meaning of an unknown word. A suffix is a syllable added to the end of a base word that changes the base word's meaning.

LESSON VOCABULARY
bluish   skidded
cartwheels   somersault
gymnastics   throbbing
hesitation   wincing
limelight

TEACH

☐ **Words to Know** Give students the opportunity to tell what they already know about this week's lesson vocabulary words. Then discuss word meaning. DAY 1 *486b*

☐ **Vocabulary Strategy Lesson** Use the vocabulary strategy lesson in the Student Edition to introduce and model this week's strategy, *word structure.* DAY 2 *486–487*

Vocabulary Strategy Lesson

PRACTICE/APPLY

☐ **Leveled Text** Read the lesson vocabulary in the context of leveled text. DAY 1 *LR37–LR45*

Leveled Readers

☐ **Words in Context** Read the lesson vocabulary and apply *word structure* in the context of *The Gymnast.* DAY 2 *488–493*, DAY 3 *494–498*

☐ **Writing/Vocabulary Center** Think of a memorable event in your own life and create an autobiographical story outline for it. ANY DAY *484k*

Main Selection—Nonfiction

☐ **Homework** Practice Book pp. 194–195. DAY 1 *486b*, DAY 2 *487*

☐ **Word Play** Using the words *gymnastics* and *philosophy* invite teams of students to come up with related words. ANY DAY *503c*

ASSESS

☐ **Selection Test** Use the Selection Test to determine students' understanding of the lesson vocabulary words. DAY 3

RETEACH/REVIEW

☐ **Reteach Lesson** If necessary, use this lesson to reteach and review *word structure.* DAY 5 *503c*

❶ Use your school-based instructional focus calendar to determine which strands to teach.

❷ Target your instruction on FCAT tested skills.

❸ Check students' understanding of FCAT tested standards.

COMPREHENSION

SKILL DRAW CONCLUSIONS A conclusion is a sensible decision you make after you think about facts or details that you read. Drawing conclusions may also be known as making inferences. Often prior knowledge can help you draw, or make, a conclusion.

STRATEGY VISUALIZE Visualizing, or creating pictures of the story in your mind, can help you understand what is happening in what you are reading. It can also help you draw conclusions about what is happening and why.

TEACH

☐ **Skill/Strategy Lesson** Use the skill/strategy lesson in the Student Edition to introduce and model *draw conclusions* and *visualize*. DAY 1 *484-485*

Skill/Strategy Lesson

☐ **Extend Skills** Teach similes. ANY DAY *503b*

PRACTICE/APPLY

☐ **Leveled Text** Apply *draw conclusions* and *visualize* to read leveled text. DAY 1 *LR37-LR45*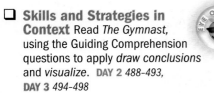

Leveled Readers

☐ **Skills and Strategies in Context** Read *The Gymnast*, using the Guiding Comprehension questions to apply *draw conclusions* and *visualize*. DAY 2 *488-493*, DAY 3 *494-498*

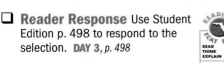

Main Selection—Nonfiction

☐ **Reader Response** Use Student Edition p. 498 to respond to the selection. DAY 3, *p. 498*

☐ **Skills and Strategies in Context** Read "All About Gymnastics." Then have students discuss and write across texts. DAY 4 *500-503*

Paired Selection–Nonfiction

☐ **Homework** Practice Book pp. 193, 197, 198. DAY 1 *485*, DAY 3 *497*, DAY 5 *503b*

ASSESS

☐ **Selection Test** Determine students' understanding of the selection and their use of *draw conclusions*. DAY 3

☐ **Retell** Have students retell *The Gymnast*. DAY 3 *498-499*

RETEACH/REVIEW

☐ **Reteach Lesson** If necessary, reteach and review *draw conclusions*. DAY 5 *503b*

FLUENCY

SKILL PUNCTUATION CLUES Punctuation within text guides readers. Punctuation shows a reader where to pause (periods or commas), change inflection (question marks), and express emotion (exclamation marks).

TEACH

☐ **Read Aloud** Model fluent reading by rereading "The Winning Stroke." Focus on this week's fluency skill, punctuation clues. DAY 1 *484l-484m, 503a*

PRACTICE/APPLY

☐ **Echo Reading** Read aloud selected paragraphs from *The Gymnast*, modeling changing inflections, expressions, and pauses. Then practice as a class, doing three echo readings of the selected paragraphs. DAY 2 *503a*, DAY 3 *503a*

☐ **Partner Reading** Have partners practice reading aloud, following punctuation clues and offering each other feedback. As students reread, monitor their progress toward their individual fluency goals. DAY 4 *503a*

☐ **Listening Center** Have students follow along with the AudioText for this week's selections. ANY DAY *484j*

☐ **Reading/Library Center** Have students reread a selection of their choice. ANY DAY *484j*

☐ **Fluency Coach** Have students use Fluency Coach to listen to fluent readings or practice reading on their own. ANY DAY

ASSESS

☐ **Check Fluency** WCPM Do a one-minute timed reading, paying special attention to this week's skill— punctuation clues. Provide feedback for each student. DAY 5 *503a*

☑ Customize Your Plan *by Strand*

GRAMMAR

SKILL USING *WHO* AND *WHOM* The pronoun *who* is used as a subject in a sentence or clause. The pronoun *whom* is used as an object (object of a preposition or direct object).

TEACH

☐ **Grammar Transparency 20** Use Grammar Transparency 20 to teach using *who* and *whom*. **DAY 1** *503e*

Grammar Transparency 20

PRACTICE/APPLY

☐ **Develop the Concept** Review the concept of using *who* and *whom* and provide guided practice. **DAY 2** *503e*

☐ **Apply to Writing** Have students review something they have written and apply using *who* and *whom*. **DAY 3** *503f*

☐ **Test Preparation** Examine common errors in using *who* and *whom* to prepare for standardized tests. **DAY 4** *503f*

☐ **Homework** Grammar and Writing Practice Book pp. 77–79. **DAY 2** *503e*, **DAY 3** *503f*, **DAY 4** *503f*

ASSESS

☐ **Cumulative Review** Use Grammar and Writing Practice Book p. 80. **DAY 5** *503f*

RETEACH/REVIEW

☐ **Daily Fix-It** Have students find and correct errors in grammar, spelling, and punctuation. **EVERY DAY** *503e–503f*

☐ **The Grammar and Writing Book** Use pp. 164–167 of The Grammar and Writing Book to extend instruction for using *who* and *whom*. **ANY DAY**

The Grammar and Writing Book

WRITING

Trait of the Week

SUPPORT WORD CHOICE Good writers choose their words carefully. Strong verbs, specific nouns, and vivid adjectives help writers elaborate on their ideas. Well-chosen and exact words make writing

TEACH

☐ **Writing Transparency 20A** Use the model to introduce and discuss the Trait of the Week. **DAY 1** *503g*

☐ **Writing Transparency 20B** Use the transparency to show students how sensory details can improve their writing. **DAY 2** *503g*

Writing Transparency 20A   **Writing Transparency 20B**

PRACTICE/APPLY

☐ **Write Now** Examine the model on Student Edition p. 499. Then have students write their own description. **DAY 3** *499, 503h*, **DAY 4** *503h*

> **Prompt** In *The Gymnast*, a boy learns that he can't be anybody but himself. Think about an important lesson you have learned. Now write a description of the lesson and how you learned it.

Write Now p. 499

☐ **Writing/Vocabulary Center** Think of a memorable event in your own life and create an autobiographical story outline for it. **ANY DAY** *484k*

ASSESS

☐ **Writing Trait Rubric** Use the rubric to evaluate students' writing. **DAY 4** *503h*

RETEACH/REVIEW

☐ **The Grammar and Writing Book** Use pp. 164–169 of The Grammar and Writing Book to extend instruction for using *who* and *whom*, sensory details, and descriptions. **ANY DAY**

The Grammar and Writing Book

❶ Use your school-based instructional focus calendar to determine which strands to teach.

❷ Target your instruction on FCAT tested skills.

❸ Check students' understanding of FCAT tested standards.

SPELLING

GENERALIZATION NEGATIVE PREFIXES When adding prefixes *il-*, *in-*, *im-*, and *ir-*, make no change in the base word: <u>*il*</u>legal, <u>*in*</u>visible, <u>*im*</u>possible, <u>*ir*</u>regular. All of the prefixes mean "not." Vowels before double consonants usually have a short sound.

TEACH

❑ **Pretest** Give the pretest for words with negative prefixes. Guide students in self-correcting their pretests and correcting any misspellings. **DAY 1** *503i*

❑ **Think and Practice** Connect spelling to the phonics generalization for negative prefixes. **DAY 2** *503i*

PRACTICE/APPLY

❑ **Connect to Writing** Have students use spelling words to write a description. Then review frequently misspelled words: *through, always.* **DAY 3** *503j*

❑ **Homework** Word Study and Spelling Practice Book pp. 77–80. **EVERY DAY**

RETEACH/REVIEW

❑ **Review** Review spelling words to prepare for the posttest. Then provide students with a spelling strategy—divide and conquer. **DAY 4** *503j*

ASSESS

❑ **Posttest** Use dictation sentences to give the posttest for words with negative prefixes. **DAY 5** *503j*

Spelling Words

1. invisible	8. impatient	15. illogical
2. illiterate	9. independent	16. indefinite
3. irregular	10. incorrect	17. inappropriate
4. irresistible	11. inactive	18. immobile
5. impossible	12. imperfect	19. irresponsible
6. informal	13. impolite	20. inexpensive
7. illegal	14. immature	

Challenge Words

21. irrelevant	23. intolerant	25. impersonal
22. irreparable	24. indisputable	

RESEARCH AND INQUIRY

❑ **Internet Inquiry** Have students conduct an Internet inquiry on gymnastics. **EVERY DAY** *503k*

❑ **Graphs** Review the terms and features associated with different types of graphs, and discuss how students can use graphs to gather and display information. **DAY 5** *503l*

❑ **Unit Inquiry** Allow time for students to present the information they gathered about the ways people or animals adapt to different situations. **ANY DAY** *391*

SPEAKING AND VIEWING

❑ **Informational Speech** Have students write and deliver an informational speech about a gymnast or gymnastics. **DAY 5** *503d*

❑ **Analyze a Video** Have students view a video that focuses on gymnastics and answer questions. **DAY 5** *503d*

Resources for Differentiated Instruction

LEVELED READERS

▶ **Comprehension**
  - **Skill** Draw Conclusions
  - **Strategy** Visualize

▶ **Lesson Vocabulary**
  - **Word Structure**

bluish skidded hesitation wincing limelight somersault gymnastics cartwheels throbbing

▶ **Social Studies Standards**
  - **Individual Development and Identity**
  - **Sports**

Leveled Reader Database ONLINE
PearsonSuccessNet.com

Use the Online Database of over 600 books to
- Download and print additional copies of this week's leveled readers.
- Listen to the readers being read online.
- Search for more titles focused on this week's skills, topic, and content.

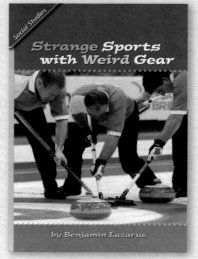

Social Studies

Strange Sports with Weird Gear

by Benjamin Lazarus

On-Level Reader

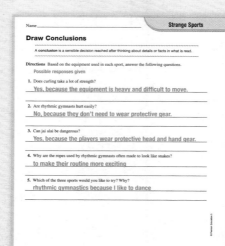

On-Level Practice TE p. LR41

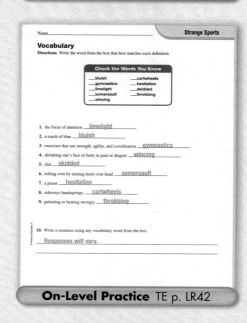

On-Level Practice TE p. LR42

Social Studies

Let the Games Begin: History of the Olympics

by Lara Bove

Below-Level Reader

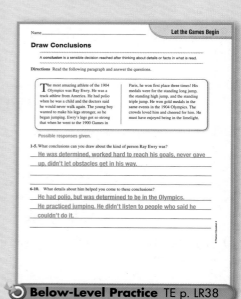

Below-Level Practice TE p. LR38

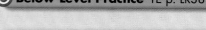

Below-Level Practice TE p. LR39

Advanced

Advanced Reader

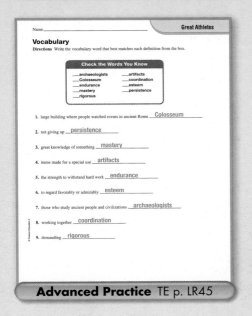

Advanced Practice TE p. LR44

Advanced Practice TE p. LR45

ELL

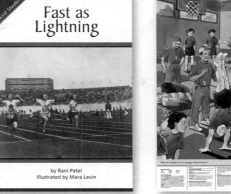

Fast as Lightning

by Rani Patel
Illustrated by Mara Levin

ELL Reader

ELL Poster 20

Teacher's Edition Notes

ELL notes throughout this lesson support instruction and reference additional resources at point of use.

Teaching Guide
pp. 134–140, 250–251

- Multilingual summaries of the main selection
- Comprehension lesson
- Vocabulary strategies and word cards
- ELL Reader 5.4.5 lesson

ELL and Transition Handbook

Ten Important Sentences

- Key ideas from every selection in the Student Edition
- Activities to build sentence power

More Reading

Readers' Theater Anthology

- Fluency practice
- Five scripts to build fluency
- Poetry for oral interpretation

Leveled Trade Books

Advanced

Below-Level

On-Level

- Extended reading tied to the unit concept
- Lessons in the Trade Book Library Teaching Guide

School + Home

Homework
- Family Times Newsletter
- ELL Multilingual Selection Summaries

Take-Home Books
- Leveled Readers

The Gymnast **484i**

Cross-Curricular Centers

Listening

Listen to the Selections

MATERIALS `SINGLES`
CD player, headphones, AudioText CD, student book

LISTEN TO LITERATURE Listen to "The Gymnast" and "All About Gymnastics" as you follow or read along in your book. Listen to draw conclusions about the characters and events in "The Gymnast".

If there is anything you don't understand, you can listen again to any section.

Reading/ Library

Read It Again!

MATERIALS `SINGLES` `PAIRS` `GROUPS`
Collection of books for self-selected reading, reading logs, student book

Select a book you have already read. Record the title of the book in your reading log. You may want to read with a partner.

Choose from the following:

- **Leveled Readers**
- **ELL Readers**
- **Stories Written by Classmates**
- **Books from the Library**
- ***The Gymnast***

TEN IMPORTANT SENTENCES Read the Ten Important Sentences for "The Gymnast". Then locate the sentences in the student book.

BOOK CLUB Look at "Meet Authors" on p. 763 of the student book to help you set up an author study of Gary Soto. What can you tell about the author based on this story? Read other books by Soto and get together with a group to share your favorites.

Art

Design a Book Cover

MATERIALS `SINGLES`
Writing and art materials

Design a book cover for your autobiography.

1. **Think about an image that will make your readers want to learn more about you.**
2. **Design and draw the cover for your book. Don't forget to add the title and author!**

EARLY FINISHERS Write a paragraph for the back of the book jacket summarizing the subject of the book.

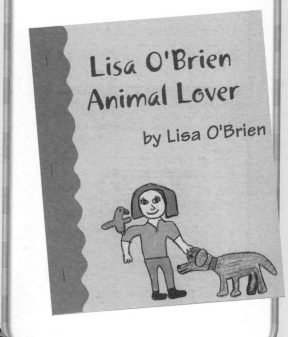

Pages 484j–484k

LA.5.1.6.2 Listen to and read familiar text
LA.5.3.1.3 Prewrite by organizing ideas
LA.5.6.3.2 Use a variety of sources to gather information effectively

Scott Foresman Reading Street Centers Survival Kit

Use *The Gymnast* materials from the Reading Street Centers Survival Kit to organize this week's centers.

Writing/Vocabulary

Write About *Your Life*

MATERIALS   SINGLES
Writing materials, outline form

In "The Gymnast", the narrator describes a single event in his childhood. Think of a memorable event in your own life and create an autobiographical story outline for it.

1. Use an outline to organize the major topics of your autobiography.
2. Below each main heading list the subtopics you will cover.
3. Below the main headings, list details you want to include.
4. Add a title.

EARLY FINISHERS Use the outline to write the first paragraph of your autobiography.

Title: Moving Day
A. Leaving our Old House
 1. A huge blue moving van came to pick up our things.
 2. Said a sad goodbye to my friends in the neighborhood.

Social Studies

Explore a New Interest

MATERIALS   SINGLES
Writing materials, library and Internet access

Find out more about a sport or hobby that interests you.

1. Think of a sport or hobby that you've always wanted to learn more about.
2. Follow classroom rules for using library or Internet resources to learn more about it.
3. Make a list of things you learned about the sport or hobby.

EARLY FINISHERS Find someone you know who already plays the sport or hobby. List 2 or 3 facts about this person.

Lacrosse

1. Lacrosse is the oldest team sport in North America.
2. Lacrosse was first played by Native Americans.

Technology

Search For Information

MATERIALS   SINGLES   PAIRS   GROUPS
Internet access

Choose a favorite sports legend. Search for an autobiography of his or her life.

1. Follow classroom rules for using the Internet to search for information. Use a student-friendly search engine.
2. For keywords, type the person's name followed by *autobiography*. You can search a library database the same way to see if you can locate a book.
3. If you are unable to find any sources. repeat the process for another sports legend.

EARLY FINISHERS Read to find out when, how, and why this person became involved in his or her sport.

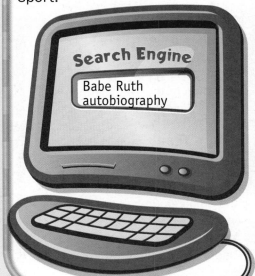

Search Engine

Babe Ruth autobiography

ALL CENTERS

OBJECTIVES

- Build vocabulary by finding words related to the lesson concept.
- Listen to draw conclusions.

Concept Vocabulary

champion person that wins first place in a game or contest

competitive involving trying to win something

develop to work to have something

perfected removed all faults from

Monitor Progress

Check Vocabulary

If...	then...
students are unable to place words on the Web,	use the Concept Vocabulary Routine on p. D1·1 to teach the words. Provide additional words for practice, such as *mastered*, *churning*, and *wake*.

SUCCESS PREDICTOR

DAY 1 Grouping Options

Reading

Whole Group

Introduce and discuss the Question of the Week. Then use pp. 484l–486b.

Group Time

Differentiated Instruction

Read this week's Leveled Readers. See pp. 484f–484g for the small group lesson plan.

Whole Group

Use p. 503a.

Language Arts

Use pp. 503e–503k.

Build Concepts

FLUENCY

MODEL PUNCTUATION CLUES As you read "The Winning Stroke," make a point of pausing after commas and periods. Change your intonation to indicate a question or exclamation—for example, "Just watch this takeoff!"

LISTENING COMPREHENSION

After reading "The Winning Stroke," use the following questions to assess listening comprehension.

1. **Do you think Jerry will turn out to be a champion swimmer? Why?** (Possible response: He will be a champion because he is enthusiastic and determined.) **Draw Conclusions**

2. **Make a generalization about the sport of competitive swimming.** (Possible response: It is very hard work and it requires a lot of practice.) **Generalize**

BUILD CONCEPT VOCABULARY

Start a web to build concepts and vocabulary related to this week's lesson and the unit theme.

- Draw the Improving Ourselves Concept Web.

- Read the sentence with the word *competitive* again. Ask students to pronounce *competitive* and discuss its meaning.

- Place *competitive* in an oval attached to *Exercise*. Explain that *competitive* is related to this concept. Read the sentences in which *champion, develop,* and *perfected* appear. Have students pronounce the words, place them on the web, and provide reasons.

- Brainstorm additional words and categories for the web. Keep the web on display and add words throughout the week.

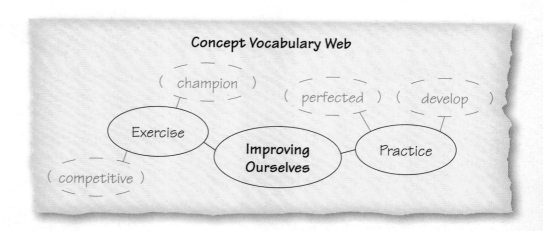

Concept Vocabulary Web

The Winning Stroke

Jerry Grayson is new to the sport of competitive swimming, and to the Boston Blues swim team. He isn't sure he has what it takes to be a champion swimmer, but he is willing to try his hardest.

by Matt Christopher

When Tony arrived at the shallow end, Coach Fulton described the way he wanted Jerry to practice his turns.

"You two guys start out with Jerry about ten feet away. Swim toward the edge, and then all three of you do your turns at the same time. I want you to develop a rhythm to it that's solid and dependable, Jerry. And when you have it down, you can practice on your own. Tanya, you're not doing anything right now," he called to her. "Come over and keep an eye on their turns. I'll be back in fifteen minutes."

The next quarter of an hour went like a breeze. Jerry could hardly believe how natural the turn had become after he got it right. How could he even have thought of racing until he knew stuff like this?

During the next week, Jerry managed to work in some extra coaching from Mr. Fulton, Tony, or Tanya—and even from some of the other members of the team once in a while.

After he perfected his flip turn, he learned how to dive perfectly.

"A long shallow dive can cut seconds from your time," Tanya explained. "The farther out you go, the less distance you have to swim. And if you don't have to come up from below, you can start swimming sooner. The same is true for the backstroke takeoff. Push yourself as far as possible from the wall."

And with each session, he got more and more comfortable. By the end of the week, he couldn't resist showing Tanya how well he had mastered one of his big problems.

"Just watch this takeoff!" he shouted. Then he demonstrated how well he had learned to start off in a backstroke race. As he pushed himself off from the side of the pool, Tanya jumped in on one side and Tony, who appeared out of nowhere, jumped in on the other. The two of them started backstroking furiously next to him, churning up a tidal wave of water in their combined wake.

But Jerry wasn't ruffled. He kept his head and continued to do exactly what he had learned. When he touched the opposite edge of the pool, Wayne Cabot shouted down to the three of them.

"The winner by a good palm and a half, Jerry Grayson!"

The winner—Jerry Grayson! It sounded great. Deep down, he knew that he would love to hear those words in a real race.

Activate Prior Knowledge

Before students listen to the Read Aloud, ask them what they know about swimming and competing in swimming matches.

Set Purpose

Read aloud the title and have students predict what the selection will be about.

Read the introduction aloud. Students should listen in order to draw conclusions about Jerry.

Creative Response

Have students perform a charade of the last scene in which Jerry is declared the winner. Remind them to use facial expressions and body movements to show Jerry's excitement. *Drama*

Develop Concept Vocabulary

Read aloud every day from a book of your choice related to the concept and use the Concept Vocabulary Routine on p. DI·1 to develop concept vocabulary. For suggestions, see p. TR14.

Access Content Before reading, share this summary: Jerry Grayson is new to competitive swimming. The coach has him practice turns. Then he shows Jerry how to take long shallow dives. Finally, Jerry learns the backstroke takeoff. Now he is ready to race.

Homework Send home this week's Family Times newsletter.

Pages 484l–484m

LA.5.1.6.2 Listen to and discuss conceptually challenging text

LA.5.1.6.4 Categorize key vocabulary

LA.5.1.7.1 Use prior knowledge

LA.5.1.7.3 Determine the main idea or essential message through inferring

 SKILLS ⟷ STRATEGIES IN CONTEXT

Draw Conclusions
Visualize

 FCAT TESTED SKILL

OBJECTIVES

⟳ Draw conclusions using information in the text and prior knowledge.

⟳ Visualize to draw conclusions.

Skills Trace

⟳ Draw Conclusions	
Introduce/Teach	TE: 5.4 392–393, 484–485; 5.6 634–635
Practice	Practice Book: 153, 157, 158, 186, 193, 197, 198, 253, 257, 258, 276, 296
Reteach/Review	TE: 5.4 411b, 467, 503b, DI·52, DI·56; 5.6 653b, 683, 687, 735, 745, DI·52
Test	Selection Test: 61–64, 77–80, 101–104; Benchmark Test: Units 4,6

INTRODUCE

Read the following aloud: *Students are lined up early at the bus stop. They are all wearing new shoes and carrying new backpacks. A clean and shiny bus can be seen heading in their direction.* Then ask, "Do you think this scene takes place at the beginning of the school year or the end?" *(the beginning)* "How do you know?" *(Everything is clean and new.)*

Have students read the information on p. 484. Explain the following:

- To draw conclusions you need to evaluate the information in the text while thinking about your own knowledge and experiences.

- Visualizing enables you to become involved with the text and draw conclusions about what is happening and why.

Use Skill Transparency 20 to teach draw conclusions and visualize.

Comprehension

Skill
Draw Conclusions

Strategy
Visualize

LA.5.1.7.3 Determine main idea through inferring
LA.5.1.7.8 Use self-monitoring strategies

⟳ Draw Conclusions

- A conclusion is a sensible decision you make after you think about facts or details that you read.

- Drawing conclusions may also be called making inferences.

- Use your prior knowledge to help you draw conclusions.

What does the text say?	→	What can I conclude?
What do I already know?		

⟳ Strategy: Visualize

Active readers visualize as they read. They make pictures in their mind. Visualizing can help you understand what is happening in what you read. It can also help you draw conclusions about what is happening and why.

Write to Read

1. Read "How to Do a Cartwheel." Use a graphic organizer like the one above to draw a conclusion about which way to start a cartwheel.

2. Describe how to do a handstand, a somersault, or some other action without naming it. Exchange papers with a classmate. Try to visualize and draw a conclusion about what your classmate is describing.

484

Strategic Intervention

⟳ **Draw Conclusions** Read "How to Do a Cartwheel" with students. Stop at several points in the article to have students draw conclusions. Use a graphic organizer like the one on p. 484 to help students record the evidence that leads to their conclusions.

ELL

Access Content

Beginning/Intermediate For a Picture It! lesson on draw conclusions, see ELL Teaching Guide, pp. 134–135.

Advanced Before students read "How to Do a Cartwheel," ask for a volunteer to model doing a cartwheel. Point out the student's starting position and where the hands are placed as the feet are lifted off the ground.

How to Do a Cartwheel

To begin a cartwheel, stand erect with one foot slightly in front of you. Use the foot of the side you feel is stronger. Let's assume you're doing a right-sided cartwheel. (To perform a left-sided cartwheel, reverse these directions. Use left for right and right for left.) ●

Raise both arms and lift your right foot. As you put it back down, reach to your right side and down toward the ground with your right arm. Begin lifting your left leg. Touch your right hand to the ground. Almost immediately, turn your upper body to touch your left hand to the ground beside your right hand. Your right leg should now be off the ground too. For a moment, you will be in a handstand—both hands down, both legs up.

Now bring your left foot down on the other side, lifting your right hand off the ground. Then bring your right foot down, lifting your left hand. You should be standing erect again.

The trick to performing a cartwheel is to keep your back and legs straight up, not out to the side. It sounds easy but it's not. Learning to cartwheel takes practice, practice, practice. ●

1 **Skill** Why do you think it's important to start out with the side you feel is stronger? (Think how you would feel starting on your weaker side.)

2 **Strategy** Visualize how you start out doing a cartwheel and what comes next.

3 **Skill** Why do you think this action is called a cartwheel?

4 **Strategy** Picture what someone looks like doing a cartwheel. Then picture the actual wheel of a cart. That can help you understand the name *cartwheel*.

485

TEACH

1 **SKILL** Model how to draw conclusions.

 MODEL I see in the text that to do a cartwheel, you have to put one arm down on the ground to support your body as you begin the cartwheel. I know that the first arm down will bear the most weight. Therefore, it makes sense that you should begin with your stronger side.

2 **STRATEGY** Visualize the action described.

 MODEL As I read the text, I make a picture in my mind of what's happening. I see that when you start a cartwheel, you raise both arms and lift one foot off the ground. You start the motion by placing the raised foot on the ground. As you place your hands on the ground one at a time, your legs go up in the air one at a time. As your legs come down one at a time, your hands come up off the ground and into the air one at a time.

PRACTICE AND ASSESS

3 **SKILL** Possible response: Your body turns like a wheel on a cart.

4 **STRATEGY** Have a volunteer draw a picture of a wheel that is found on a cart. Have students compare this picture to a person doing a cartwheel.

WRITE Have students complete steps 1 and 2 of the Write to Read activity. You might consider using this as a whole-class activity.

Monitor Progress

Draw Conclusions

If... students are unable to complete **Write to Read** on p. 484,	then... use Practice Book p. 193 to provide additional practice.

Draw Conclusions

- A **conclusion** is a sensible decision you make after you think about facts or details that you read.
- Drawing conclusions may also be called making inferences.
- Use your prior knowledge to help you draw conclusions.

Directions Read the following passage. Then complete the diagram below.

Enrique is a young gymnast who is training for the Olympics. He goes to live at the Olympic Training Center in Colorado Springs. There he trains twelve hours a day with other athletes. In addition, he regularly takes part in competitions to test his skills. Enrique sets goals for himself. He wants to improve in gymnastics skills and to learn routines that are more difficult. His training schedule is so demanding, he does not have time to go to a regular school. He studies all of his school subjects with a tutor. After more years of training, Enrique hopes to make the Olympic team.

Possible answers given.

What does the text say?	What does the text say?	What do I already know?
1.Enrique lives at a training center.	2.He trains twelve hours a day.	3.It is hard to make it into the Olympics.

What can I conclude?
4.Enrique works hard to go to the Olympics.

5. Visualize Enrique studying with his tutor. What conclusion can you draw about the advantages or disadvantages of studying with a tutor rather than studying at a regular school?
A disadvantage to having a tutor would be not having the time to socialize you would get at a school.

 Home Activity Your child read a short passage and drew a conclusion based on the details in it. Tell your child a story about an athlete you know about. Ask your child to visualize the details as you describe them. Ask your child to draw a conclusion based on the details you provide.

CORRECTIVE FEEDBACK

 LA.5.1.7.3 Determine main idea or essential message through inferring

- **Question** Use the question below to address this FCAT tested standard. Have students write their answers on a sheet of paper.
- **Check** Scan students' responses by having them hold up their papers.
- **Correct** If necessary, provide corrective feedback.
- **Adjust** Pair students who correctly answered the question with students who did not for peer tutoring. Have them complete Practice Book p. 193 together.

Why do you think it's not easy to do a cartwheel?

Tech Files
ONLINE

Have students use a student-friendly search engine and the keywords *USA Gymnastics* to find up-to-date information about gymnastics in the United States. Be sure to follow classroom guidelines for Internet use.

ELL

Build Background Use ELL Poster 20 to build background and vocabulary for the lesson concept of individual development and identity.

▲ **ELL Poster** 20

Build Background

ACTIVATE PRIOR KNOWLEDGE

BEGIN A KWL CHART about gymnastics.

• Give students a few minutes to write what they know about gymnastics. Prompt by asking students to recall a gymnastics competition they may have watched or participated in. Record what students know on a KWL chart.

• Give students two minutes to write two or three questions about the topic. Record questions on the KWL chart. Add a question of your own.

• Tell students that, as they read, they should look for the answers to their questions and note any new information to add to the chart.

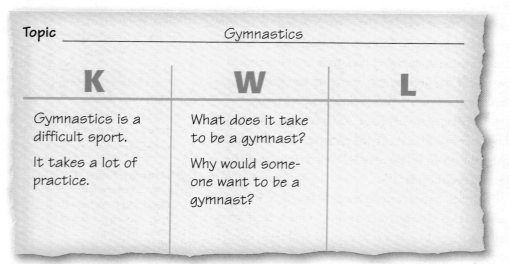

Topic	Gymnastics	
K	**W**	**L**
Gymnastics is a difficult sport.	What does it take to be a gymnast?	
It takes a lot of practice.	Why would someone want to be a gymnast?	

▲ **Graphic Organizer** 4

BACKGROUND BUILDING AUDIO This week's audio explores the topic of gymnastics. After students listen, discuss the challenges of learning the sport. Lead students to a general discussion of learning something new and working hard to meet one's goals.

Background Building Audio

Page 486a
LA.5.1.7.1 Use prior knowledge
LA.5.3.1.3 Organize ideas using strategies and tools (KWL chart)

486a Adapting • Week 5

Introduce Vocabulary

WORD RATING CHART

Create word rating charts using the categories *Know, Have Seen,* and *Don't Know.* Use the word rating chart.

Word Rating Chart

Word	Know	Have Seen	Don't Know
bluish		✓	
cartwheels	✓		
gymnastics	✓		
hesitation	✓		
limelight			✓
skidded		✓	
somersault			
throbbing			
wincing			

▲ **Graphic Organizer** 5

Read aloud the lesson vocabulary. Then have students sort the words into the three categories: *Know* (know and can use); *Have Seen* (have seen or heard the word; don't know meaning); *Don't Know* (don't know the word). ***Activate Prior Knowledge***

Invite students to share their work. Explain that two of this week's words are compound words. Have students identify the two words. *(limelight and cartwheels)* Write the words on the board. Have a volunteer point out the two smaller words in each compound word. ***Compound Words***

As a class, return to students' word rating charts after they finish reading and have students make changes to their ratings.

Use the Multisyllabic Word Routine on p. DI·1 to help students read multisyllabic words.

Lesson Vocabulary

WORDS TO KNOW

T bluish somewhat blue

T cartwheels sideways handsprings with the legs and arms kept straight

T gymnastics a sport in which very difficult exercises are performed

T hesitation act of failing to act promptly

T limelight center of public attention and interest

T skidded slipped or slid sideways while moving

T somersault to run or jump, turning the heels over the head

T throbbing beating rapidly or strongly

T wincing drawing back suddenly

MORE WORDS TO KNOW

backflips backwards somersaults performed in the air

solitary without companions

spindly very long and slender

T = Tested Word

Vocabulary

Directions Choose the word from the box that best matches each definition below. Write the word on the line.

somersault _____ 1. to run or jump, turning the heels over the head

gymnastics _____ 2. a sport in which very difficult exercises are performed

hesitation _____ 3. act of failing to act promptly

bluish _____ 4. somewhat blue

cartwheels _____ 5. sideways handsprings with the legs and arms kept straight

Check the Words You Know
___bluish
___cartwheels
___gymnastics
___hesitation
___limelight
___skidded
___somersault
___throbbing
___wincing

Directions Choose the word from the box that matches the clues and complete the crossword puzzle.

DOWN
6. the pain I felt when I broke my toe
7. the color of a pale sky
8. the place the star wants to be

ACROSS
9. what my bicycle did when I slammed on the brakes
10. what I am doing when I eat food I don't like

Write a News Report
Imagine you're a sports reporter covering a gymnastics meet. On a separate sheet of paper write a news report. Use as many vocabulary words as you can.
News reports should include words from the vocabulary list and basic facts about a gymnastics meet.

 Home Activity Your child identified and used vocabulary words from *The Gymnast.* Skim the articles about a single sport in the sports section of a newspaper. Point out and define the vocabulary that is used to describe each type of sport.

▲ **Practice Book** p. 194

Page 486b

LA.5.1.6.1 Use new vocabulary that is introduced and taught directly

LA.5.1.6.7 Use meaning of familiar base words and affixes to determine meanings of unfamiliar complex words

Vocabulary Strategy

⊙ Use word structure and suffixes to determine word meaning.

INTRODUCE

Discuss the strategy for word structure using the steps on p. 486.

TEACH

- Have students read "It's Easier in Daydreams," noting any words with suffixes.
- Model using word structure to determine the meaning of *hesitation*.

MODEL I recognize the base word *hesitate*, even though the final *e* is dropped. *Hesitate* means "to pause." I also see the suffix *-ion*. I know this suffix means "state of being," so I can guess that *hesitation* means "in a state of hesitation," or "in a state of pausing."

Words to Know

limelight
hesitation
somersault
gymnastics
cartwheels
throbbing
wincing
skidded
bluish

Remember
Try the strategy. Then, if you need more help, use your glossary or dictionary.

Vocabulary Strategy
for Suffixes

Word Structure A suffix is a syllable added to the end of a base word that changes the base word's meaning. The spelling of the base word may also change when the suffix is added. For example, when the suffix *-ion* is added to *appreciate*, the final *e* is dropped: *appreciation*. Adding this suffix adds the meaning "the act or state of being ___." The suffix *-ish* adds the meaning "somewhat" or "like," as in *brownish*. Recognizing a suffix can help you figure out the meaning of an unknown word.

1. Look at the unknown word. See if you recognize a base word in it.
2. Check to see if the suffix *-ion*, *-tion*, or *-ish* has been added to the base word.
3. Ask yourself how the suffix changes the meaning of the base word.
4. Try the new meaning in the sentence to see if it makes sense.

As you read "It's Easier in Daydreams," look for words that end with suffixes. Analyze the base words and the suffixes to figure out the meanings of words you do not know.

LA.5.1.6.4 Categorize key vocabulary
LA.5.1.6.7 Use meaning of affixes

486

DAY 2 **Grouping Options**

Reading
Whole Group Discuss the Question of the Day. Then use pp. 486–489.

Group Time Differentiated Instruction
Read *The Gymnast.* See pp. 484f–484g for the small group lesson plan.

Whole Group Use p. 503a.

Language Arts
Use pp. 503e–503k.

Strategic Intervention

⊙ **Word Structure** Review meanings for the common suffixes *-ish* ("somewhat") and *-like* ("resembling") by discussing the meanings of the words *childish* and *childlike*.

Access Content Use ELL Poster 20 to preteach vocabulary. Choose from the following to meet language proficiency levels.
Beginning Use the Multilingual Lesson Vocabulary list that begins on p. 272 of the ELL Teaching Guide, as well as other home-language resources to provide translations of the tested words.
Intermediate After reading, have students create a semantic web with words related to gymnastics.
Advanced Teach the lesson on pp. 486–487. Have students return to the word rating chart and make appropriate changes to their ratings.
Resources for home-language words may include parents, bilingual staff members, bilingual dictionaries, or online translation sources.

It's Easier in Daydreams

I love to watch Olympic gymnasts. In fact, I hope to be one myself one day. In my daydreams, I am already a star. The audience roars as I step into the limelight. Without any hesitation, I somersault across the gym. I move with terrific speed and grace. The judges smile and nod and hold up score cards with perfect 10.0's on them.

So you can understand why I was so upset after what happened. I signed up for a gymnastics class offered by the park district. The teacher showed us how to do cartwheels. "This is easy!" I thought, so

I didn't pay attention. When it was my turn, I ran to the mat, closed my eyes, and threw myself at it. The next thing I knew, I was flat on my back. My head and knees were throbbing. I couldn't help wincing in pain as I got up. On the next try, I lost my nerve and put on the brakes. I skidded several feet into a wall and thumped my shoulder. There's a nice bluish bruise there to remind me. I have a long way to go to reach the Olympics.

Words to Write

Imagine that you are a sports writer. Write an article about a gymnastics competition or some other sporting event you just watched. Use words from the Words to Know list and as many words connected with the sport as you can.

487

PRACTICE AND ASSESS

- Have students work with partners to determine the base word, suffix, and meaning of the remaining Words to Know.
- Remind students that sometimes the suffix changes the meaning of the base word.
- If you began a word rating chart on p. 486b, have students reassess their ratings.
- Have students complete Practice Book p. 195.

WRITE Students should use the Words to Know and other words with suffixes in their writing.

Monitor Progress

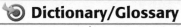

Dictionary/Glossary

If... students need more practice with the lesson vocabulary,	**then...** use Tested Vocabulary Cards for this week.
If... students need cumulative practice with tested vocabulary,	**then...** use Tested Vocabulary Cards from all previous weeks for cumulative review.

Vocabulary · Word Structure

- A **suffix** is added to the end of a base word to change its meaning or the way it is used in a sentence.
- The suffix *–ish* means "somewhat," as in *childish*. The suffix *–ion* means "the act or state of being _____," as in *determination*. The suffix *–ics* means "study or system," as in *athletics*. You can use suffixes to help you figure out the meanings of words.

Directions Read the following passage. Notice the words with suffixes as you read. Then answer the questions below.

> The gymnastics meet started with a spectacular balance beam routine by Amy's main competitor. Then Amy hopped onto the beam and started her routine with no hesitation. She did fine on her somersaults and cartwheels, but on one backflip she had a bad landing. Her ankle felt like a knife had ripped through it, and she saw bluish stars in front of her eyes. Still, she finished her routine, wincing with the pain. When the numbers came up, she scored the highest! Although her ankle was throbbing, she stepped to the judges' table and accepted her medal.

1. What is the suffix in *gymnastics*? How does the suffix change the meaning of the base word?
   –ics; Gymnastics means "the study or system of physical exercises."

2. What is the suffix in *hesitation*? How does the suffix change the meaning of the base word?
   –ion; The suffix *–ion* changes *hesitate* to a noun that means "failing to act promptly."

3. What is the suffix in *bluish*? How does the suffix change the meaning of the base word?
   –ish; Bluish means "somewhat blue."

4. Change *competitor* into a noun by adding a suffix. What is the meaning of the new word?
   competition; The meaning is "the act of being a competitor."

5. Write two other words that use the suffixes. Write a definition for each word.
   Possible answer: Subtraction: the act of subtracting; Physics: the study of the physical world.

Home Activity Your child read a short passage and identified and used suffixes to understand new words. Work with your child to identify unfamiliar words with suffixes. Then ask your child how the suffixes help him or her to understand the meaning of the new words. Confirm the meanings by looking them up in a dictionary.

▲ **Practice Book** p. 195

WORD AWARENESS Post this week's lesson vocabulary on a Word Wall or have students write the words and meanings in their Writing Logs for ready access during writing.

Pages 486–487

LA.5.1.6.1 Use new vocabulary that is introduced and taught directly
LA.5.1.6.4 Categorize key vocabulary
LA.5.1.6.7 Use meaning of affixes

Prereading Strategies

OBJECTIVES

◎ Draw conclusions using information in the text and prior knowledge.

◎ Visualize to draw conclusions about a selection.

GENRE STUDY

Autobiography

"The Gymnast" is an autobiography. Explain that an autobiography is a story about a person's life and is written by the person who lived it. An autobiography can be about the person's whole life, part of that person's life, or a single event.

PREVIEW AND PREDICT

Have students read the opening question and the title on pp. 488–489. Then ask them to do a picture walk through the selection. When they finish, have students identify the subject of the selection. Ask, "What do you think the 'The Gymnast' is about?" Students should use lesson vocabulary words in their discussion.

Strategy Response Log

Graphic Organizer Have students close their eyes and picture a gymnast performing. Then ask them to divide a page in half in their strategy response logs to make a two-column chart. On the left, have them draw what they "see" when they visualize a gymnast performing. Students will review their notes and drawings in the Strategy Response Log activity on p. 493.

Use Strategies Have students record in their strategy response logs reading strategies they use during reading and tell why they use them.

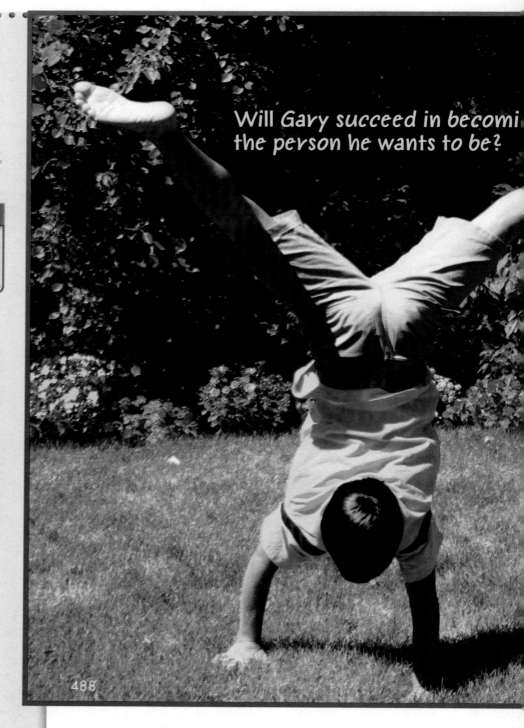

Will *Gary* succeed in becomi[ng] the *person* he wants to be?

488

ELL

Access Content Ask students to turn to the picture on p. 491 and choose a volunteer to read the words aloud. Repeat this with the words and pictures on pp. 492, 495, and 496.

Consider having students read the selection summary in English or in students' home languages. See the Multilingual Summaries in the ELL Teaching Guide, pp. 138–140.

The Gymnast

by Gary Soto

Genre

Autobiography is the story of a person's life or of a single event in it, told by the person who lived it. As you read, notice how the author looks back at himself from a humorous point of view.

489

SET PURPOSE

Read the first page of the selection aloud to students. Have them recall what they "saw" when they pictured a gymnast performing. Have them read to find out what Gary Soto has to say about gymnasts.

Remind students to visualize the people, places, and actions as they read. In addition, have them keep track of key details that they can use when drawing conclusions about the selection.

STRATEGY RECALL

Students have now used these before-reading strategies:

- preview the selection to be aware of its genre, features, and possible content;
- activate prior knowledge about that content and what to expect of that genre;
- make predictions;
- set a purpose for reading.

Remind students to be aware of and flexibly use the during-reading strategies they have learned:

- link prior knowledge to new information;
- summarize text they have read so far;
- ask clarifying questions;
- answer questions they or others pose;
- check their predictions and either refine them or make new predictions;
- recognize the text structure the author is using, and use that knowledge to make predictions and increase comprehension;
- visualize what the author is describing;
- monitor their comprehension and use fix-up strategies.

After reading, students will use these strategies:

- summarize or retell the text;
- answer questions they or others pose;
- reflect to make new information become part of their prior knowledge.

 **AudioText**

 Pages 488–489

LA.5.1.7.1 Make predictions and establish a purpose for reading

LA.5.1.7.8 Use strategies to repair comprehension when self-monitoring, including using graphic organizers

LA.5.2.2.1 Use information from text features (illustrations)

Guiding Comprehension

1  **Draw Conclusions • Inferential**

Reread p. 490, paragraph 1. What makes Gary feel jealous?

Gary's mother is proud of Gary's cousin, Isaac. She is always talking about Isaac. Gary knows that people admire gymnasts.

Monitor Progress

 **Draw Conclusions**

If... students are unable to draw conclusions about the author's feelings,	**then...** use the skill and strategy instruction on p. 491.

2 Point of View • Inferential

From whose point of view is "The Gymnast" told? How do you know?

It's told from Gary's point of view. We know this because the selection is an autobiography. Gary uses first-person narration and tells about events from his own life.

Tech Files ONLINE

Students who have access to the Internet can use a student-friendly search engine and the keywords *Olympic gymnasts* to learn about top international gymnasts who have participated in the Olympic games. Be sure to follow classroom guidelines for Internet use.

For three days of my eleventh summer I listened to my mother yap about my cousin, Isaac, who was taking gymnastics. She was proud of him, she said one evening at the stove as she pounded a round steak into carne asada and crushed a heap of beans into refritos. I was jealous because I had watched my share of *Wide World of Sports* and knew that people admired an athlete who could **somersault** without hurting himself. I pushed aside my solitary game of Chinese checkers and spent a few minutes rolling around the backyard until I was dizzy and itchy with grass.

That Saturday, I went to Isaac's house where I ate plums and sat under an aluminum arbor watching my cousin, dressed in gymnastic shorts and top, do spindly **cartwheels** and back flips in his backyard while he instructed, "This is the correct way." He breathed in the grassy air, leaped, and came up smiling the straightest teeth in the world.

I followed him to the front lawn. When a car passed he did a **back flip** and looked out the side of his eyes to see if any of the passengers were looking. Some pointed while others looked ahead dully at the road.

490

Gymnastics

Time for **SOCIAL STUDIES**

Modern gymnastics was introduced to Europe in the early 1800s and to the United States in the 1830s. Some 65 years later, the first major gymnastics competition was held at the 1896 Olympics in Athens, Greece.

ELL

Extend Language Point to the word "yap." Explain that "yap" has two meanings. Help students name the more common meaning (the sharp barking sound a dog makes). Tell them that "yap" can also mean to talk a lot. Ask students why Gary's mother was yapping about his cousin.

Page 490

LA.5.1.7.2 Identify how an author's perspective influences text
LA.5.1.7.3 Determine the main idea or essential message through inferring

490 Adapting • Week 5

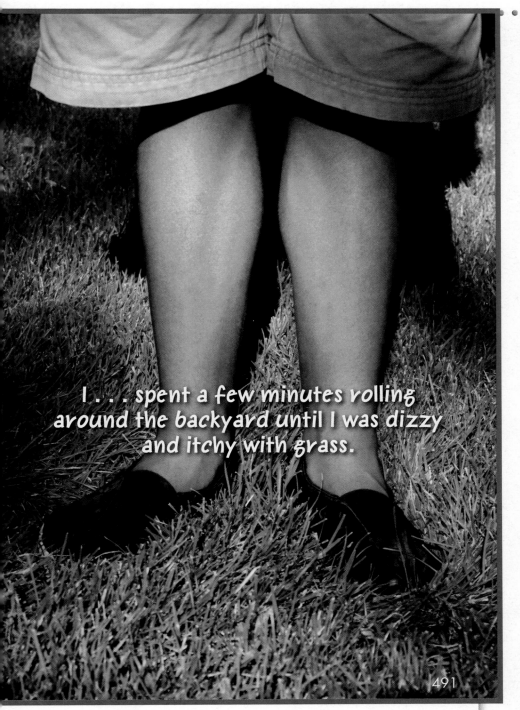

I . . . spent a few minutes rolling around the backyard until I was dizzy and itchy with grass.

491

SKILLS ↔ STRATEGIES IN CONTEXT

Draw Conclusions

TEACH

- Remind students that drawing conclusions means making a sensible decision after they think about facts or details in a selection.

- Point out that keeping track of their conclusions as they read can make it easier to understand and respond to the text.

- Explain that self-questioning will help them draw conclusions as they read. Model the process for students.

MODEL As I read the first paragraph, I ask myself, "What does Gary recall about his eleventh summer? What does Gary know from watching *Wide World of Sports?*" I use my answers to these questions to draw the conclusion that Gary's mother's comments about Isaac and Gary's knowledge that people admire gymnasts makes him jealous.

PRACTICE AND ASSESS

Have students reread the sentence, "When a car passed he did a back flip and looked out the side of his eyes to see if any of the passengers were looking." Then ask, "Which of these is a sensible conclusion to draw about Isaac?" *(Choice a)*

a) Isaac likes an audience.

b) Isaac is shy.

c) Isaac is embarrassed to be a gymnast.

CORRECTIVE FEEDBACK

LA.5.1.7.3 Determine main idea or essential message through inferring

- **Question** Use Whiteboard or Transparency 20a, items 1–3, to ask questions that address this standard in FCAT format. Have students write their answers on a sheet of paper.
- **Check** Scan students' responses by having them hold up their papers.
- **Correct** If necessary, provide corrective feedback and review pp. 484–485.

❶ Which of the following conclusions can you draw about Gary?

Ⓐ He loves doing gymnastics.
Ⓑ He is not very good at gymnastics.
Ⓒ He will probably be a professional gymnast someday.
Ⓓ He has been taking gymnastics lessons for a long time.

▲ **FCAT Whiteboard Activity** 20a/**FCAT Transparency** 20a

Guiding Comprehension

③ Generalize • Inferential

Make a generalization about gymnasts based on what you read about Issac.

Possible response: Gymnasts spend a lot of time practicing.

Monitor Progress
REVIEW Generalize

If... students have difficulty generalizing,	**then...** use the skill and strategy lesson on page 493.

④ Details and Facts • Inferential

What does Gary seem to think is most interesting about gymnastics?

Possible response: He likes the equipment—the tape, shoes, chalk.

⑤ Character • Critical

Text to Self **Does Gary remind you of anyone in your own life? Explain why.**

Answers will vary but should be supported by details from the selection.

But when I did a cartwheel, the shoes flew off, along with the tape.

492

Access Content Gary thinks his cousin is a *show-off*. Explain that a *show-off* is someone who behaves in a way that calls attention to him or herself.

Pages 492–493

LA.5.1.6.1 Use new vocabulary that is introduced and taught directly

LA.5.1.7.3 Determine the main idea or essential message through inferring and identifying relevant details

LA.5.2.1.5 Demonstrate an understanding of a literary selection, and include evidence from personal experience

My cousin was a show-off, but I figured he was allowed the limelight before one appreciative dog who had come over to look. I envied him and his cloth gymnast shoes. I liked the way they looked, slim, black, and cool. They seemed special, something I could never slip onto my feet.

I ate the plums and watched him until he was sweaty and out of breath. When he was finished, I begged him to let me wear his cloth shoes. Drops of sweat fell at his feet. He looked at me with disdain, ran a yellow towel across his face, and patted his neck dry. He tore the white tape from his wrists—I liked the tape as well and tried to paste it around my wrists. He washed off his hands. I asked him about the white powder, and he said it kept his hands dry. I asked him why he needed dry hands to do cartwheels and back flips. He said that all gymnasts kept their hands dry, then drank from a bottle of greenish water he said was filled with nutrients.

I asked him again if I could wear his shoes. He slipped them off and said, "OK, just for a while." The shoes were loose, but I liked them. I went to the front yard with my wrists dripping tape and my hands white as gloves. I smiled slyly and thought I looked neat. But when I did a cartwheel, the shoes flew off, along with the tape, and my cousin yelled and stomped the grass.

3

4

5

493

Develop Vocabulary

PRACTICE LESSON VOCABULARY

Have students respond true or false to each statement and give reasons.

1. Gymnastics is easy to learn. *(False; gymnastics requires many years of practice.)*

2. Cartwheels don't involve using your hands. *(False; cartwheels involve using your hands to turn end over end).*

3. Someone would be wincing in pain if he had fallen off his bike. *(True; someone might wince with pain if he fell off his bike).*

BUILD CONCEPT VOCABULARY

Review previous concept words with students. Ask if students have come across any words today in their reading or elsewhere that they would like to add to the Improving Ourselves Concept Web, such as *appreciative*.

SKILLS ⟷ STRATEGIES IN CONTEXT

Generalize REVIEW

TEACH

- Generalizations are broad statements or rules that apply to many examples.
- Model how to form a generalization about gymnasts.

Think Aloud **MODEL** In this story, Isaac practices a lot. I know that gymnastics is very hard. I can generalize that gymnasts spend a lot of time practicing.

PRACTICE AND ASSESS

- Have students reread the second paragraph on p. 493. What generalization does Issac make about gymnasts? *(They all keep their hands dry.)*
- To assess, use Practice Book p. 196.

Strategy Response Log

Visualize Have students review their two-column chart and drawings. (See p. 488.) Have them continue to add to the chart as they read.

Generalize

Directions Read the passage. Then answer the questions below.

Many schools require every student to play at least one sport. By playing sports, many young people say that they meet new friends. By being on a team, a young person can learn cooperation and fair play. Playing a sport can build strength, flexibility, and endurance, and improve fitness. Many experts say young people get a boost in self-confidence as they succeed with new skills they learn through playing sports. Finally, for most young athletes, playing sports is simply a lot of fun.

Possible answers given.

1. Based on the passage, what is a generalization you can make about playing sports?
   Playing sports has many advantages.

2. Which detail from the passage that supports this generalization?
   Playing sports can build friendships.

3. What other detail supports this generalization?
   Playing sports can increase fitness and strength.

4. What is a generalization that is stated in the passage?
   For most young athletes, playing sports is a lot of fun.

5. Write a generalization of your own about sports. Write at least one detail to back it up.
   Playing sports can be difficult if you are not very athletic. A slow runner has trouble keeping up during a soccer game.

School Home Home Activity Your child read a short passage and made a generalization based on the passage. Tell your child some specific details about a subject you think is important. Ask him or her to make a generalization about the subject.

▲ **Practice Book** p. 196

If you want to teach this selection in two sessions, stop here.

Guiding Comprehension

If you are teaching the selection in two days, discuss any conclusions so far and review the vocabulary.

6 Predict • Critical

How do you think the selection will end? What helped you make your prediction?

Answers will vary but should be supported with evidence from the selection.

7 🔊 Vocabulary • Word Structure

What is the base word in *hesitation*? What suffix has been added to the base word? What does the word mean?

The base word is *hesitate*. The suffix is *-ion*. *Hesitation* means "the state of failing to act promptly."

Monitor Progress

🔊 Word Structure

If... students need help understanding word structure and identifying suffixes,	**then**... use the vocabulary strategy instruction on page 495.

DAY 3 — Grouping Options

Reading
Whole Group Discuss the Question of the Day.

Group Time Differentiated Instruction
 *The Gymnast.* See pp. 484f–484g for the small group lesson plan.

Whole Group Discuss the Reader Response questions on p. 498. Then use p. 503a.

Language Arts
Use pp. 503e–503k.

I was glad to get home. I was jealous and miserable, but the next day I found a pair of old vinyl slippers in the closet that were sort of like gymnastic shoes. I pushed my feet into them, tugging and wincing because they were too small. I took a few steps, admiring my feet, which looked like bloated water balloons, and went outside to do cartwheels on the front lawn. A friend skidded to a stop on his bike, one cheek fat with sunflower seeds. His mouth churned to a stop. He asked why I was wearing slippers on a hot day. I made a face at him and said that they were gymnastic shoes, not slippers. He watched me do *cartwheels*

6 for a while, then rode away doing a wheelie.

I returned inside. I looked for tape to wrap my wrists, but could find only circle bandages in the medicine cabinet. I dipped my hands in flour to keep them dry and went back outside to do cartwheels and, finally, after much

7 hesitation, a *back flip* that nearly cost me my life when I landed on my head. I crawled to the shade, stars of pain pulsating in my shoulder and neck.

My brother glided by on his bike, smooth as a kite. He stared at me and asked why I was wearing slippers. I didn't answer him. My neck still hurt. He asked about the flour on my hands, and I told him to leave me alone. I turned on the hose and drank cool water.

494

ELL

Build Background Point to the word *wheelie*. Help students recognize the word *wheel* in *wheelie*. Explain that a wheelie is a stunt done on a bicycle by raising the front wheel up in the air while riding. Ask students why they think Gary's friend rode away doing a wheelie.

Page 494

LA.5.1.4.2 Recognize structural analysis

LA.5.1.4.3 Use language structure to read multi-syllabic words in text

LA.5.1.6.7 Use meaning of familiar base words and affixes to determine meanings of unfamiliar complex words

LA.5.1.7.1 Make predictions

. . . and, finally, after much hesitation, a back flip that nearly cost me my life . . .

495

VOCABULARY STRATEGY

Word Structure

TEACH

Read aloud p. 495. Model how to use word parts to figure out the meaning of *hesitation*.

Think Aloud **MODEL** On page 495, I see the word *hesitation*. I'm not sure about that word, so I'll look for familiar word parts. I see the base word *hesitate* and the suffix *-ion*, which I know means "state of." I know *hesitate* means "fail to act promptly." So *hesitation* must mean "in a state of failing to act promptly."

PRACTICE AND ASSESS

Have students use word parts to determine the meaning of *bluish* in the first paragraph on p. 497. (The suffix *-ish* means "somewhat" or "like." *Bluish* means "somewhat blue.")

Page 495

LA.5.1.4.2 Recognize structural analysis

LA.5.1.4.3 Use language structure to read multi-syllabic words in text

LA.5.1.6.7 Use meaning of familiar base words and affixes to determine meanings of unfamiliar complex words

LA.5.1.7.2 Identify how an author's perspective influences text

EXTEND SKILLS

Personal Essay

A personal essay is a brief discussion of a topic, using first-person pronouns and often revealing the personality of the author. It may include humor and usually supports a relaxed tone. The main purpose of a personal essay is to entertain. Although "The Gymnast" is an autobiography, what features in the selection might lead someone to say that this is a personal essay?

Time for SOCIAL STUDIES

Nadia Comaneci

One of the most famous gymnasts of all time is Nadia Comaneci. At the age of fourteen, she was the first gymnast to score a perfect 10 in Olympic competition. This occurred during her first event, the uneven parallel bars, at the 1976 Olympics. She then went on to receive three gold medals, one silver, and one bronze. Four years later, she won two gold medals and two silver medals at the Olympic Games in Moscow. Comaneci retired from competition in 1984.

Guiding Comprehension

8 🔟 **Visualize • Inferential**

What details on p. 497 help you visualize the scene?

Possible responses: Throbbing feet, toes cooling on the summery grass, bluish ankles, chill up the back, piranha-like eating, cartwheels by the dizzy dozen, smoke of a barbecue, orange burst, pinpoints of unfortunate light.

9 **Author's Purpose • Inferential**

Question the Author **What is the author trying to tell you when he says, "I ate a plum and pictured my cousin, who was probably cartwheeling to the audience of one sleeping dog"?**

Possible response: He is saying that he realized at that point that gymnastics might not be great as he first thought it was.

10 **Visualize • Critical**

Text to Text **Does this autobiography remind you of any other nonfiction selections you've read? Think about events, characters, and the point of view from which it's told.**

Students' responses should include a comparison to another autobiography they've read. They may mention the first-person point of view, the challenge the author faces, etc.

Strategy Response Log ✏️

Summarize When students finish reading the selection, provide this prompt: Imagine that a friend has asked you to tell what happens in "The Gymnast." Summarize the selection in four or five sentences.

Use Strategies Meet with students to review their list of the reading strategies they realized they were using as they read.

My toes cooled on the summery grass.

496

🇪🇱🇱

Access Content Reread aloud the sentence "Dinner was a ten-minute affair of piranha-like eating and thirty minutes of washing dishes." Explain that a piranha is a meat-eating fish known for consuming large amounts of food very fast. *A ten-minute affair* means that it took them ten minutes to eat. Ask students to use this information to describe the family dinner.

Page 496
LA.5.1.7.2 Identify author's purpose
LA.5.1.7.7 Compare and contrast elements in multiple texts (characters)
LA.5.1.7.8 Use strategies to repair comprehension when self-monitoring, including summarizing
LA.5.2.1.7 Identify and explain author's use of descriptive language and examine how it is used to describe people, feelings, and objects

I walked to Romain playground where I played Chinese checkers and was asked a dozen times why I was wearing slippers. I'm taking gymnastics, I lied, and these are the kind of shoes you wear. When one kid asked why I had white powder on my hands and in my hair, I gave up on Chinese checkers and returned home, my feet throbbing. But before I went inside, I took off the slippers. My toes cooled on the summery grass. I ran a garden hose on my feet and bluish ankles, and a chill ran up my back.

Dinner was a ten-minute affair of piranha-like eating and thirty minutes of washing dishes. Once finished, I returned to the backyard, where I again stuffed my feet into the slippers and did *cartwheels by the dizzy dozens.* After a while they were easy. I had to move on. I sucked in the summer air, along with the smoke of a faraway barbecue, and tried a back flip. I landed on my neck again, this time I saw an orange burst behind my eyes. I lay on the grass, tired and sweaty, my feet squeezed in the vise of cruel slippers.

8

I watched the dusk settle and the first stars, pinpoints of unfortunate light tangled in telephone wires. I ate a plum and pictured my cousin, who was probably cartwheeling to the audience of one sleeping dog.

9

10

497

Develop Vocabulary

PRACTICE LESSON VOCABULARY

As a class, have students complete the following sentences orally.

1. As he walked in the slippers, Gary's feet were (*throbbing*).
2. Gary's ankles turned (*bluish*) in color.
3. Gary's first (*somersault*) made him feel a little dizzy.
4. Issac loved the (*limelight*), so he looked around for an audience.
5. Gary was nervous, but he finally tried a back flip after much (*hesitation*).

BUILD CONCEPT VOCABULARY

Review previous concept words with students. Ask if students have come across any words today in their reading or elsewhere that they would like to add to the Improving Ourselves Concept Web, such as *tired* and *sweaty*.

STRATEGY SELF-CHECK

Visualize

Remind students that visualizing means using imagery and sensory details to create pictures in your mind as you read. Visualizing can help readers understand what they read and draw conclusions about events and characters. Use Practice Book p. 197.

SELF-CHECK

Students can ask themselves these questions to assess understanding of the selection.

- Can I visualize what the author describes?
- Does visualizing help me draw conclusions about events and characters?
- Can I use the strategy to help me better understand and enjoy what I'm reading?

Monitor Progress	
Draw Conclusions	
If… students have difficulty visualizing and drawing conclusions,	**then…** use the Reteach lesson on p. 503b.

Draw Conclusions

- A **conclusion** is a sensible decision you make after you think about facts or details that you read.
- Drawing conclusions may also be called making inferences.
- Use your prior knowledge to help you draw conclusions.

Directions Read the following passage. Then answer the questions below.

When Lance Armstrong was 20, he made the U.S. Olympic cycling team. Three years later, he won an important cycling race, the Tour Du Pont, a premier U.S. cycling event. In 1996, he made the U.S. Olympic team again. That same year, he was diagnosed with cancer. He suffered terrible pain during his treatments and fought hard to get back to cycling. Five months after his diagnosis, he was training again determined to return to the sport he loved. Even though he was weakened from the disease, he wouldn't give up. In 1998, he finally returned to professional cycling. In 1999 he won the Tour de France. In 2005, he became the first seven-time winner of the Tour de France. Lance Armstrong inspires many people with his courage and abilities.

Possible answers given.
1. What conclusion can you draw about Lance Armstrong's character?
   Lance Armstrong is persistent and dedicated to cycling.

2. What is one detail from the passage that supports your conclusion?
   He was cycling five months after his cancer diagnosis.
3. What is another detail from the passage to support your conclusion?
   He won the Tour de France seven times.
4. What conclusion can you draw about how Lance Armstrong inspired other people?
   Lance Armstrong probably inspires people to work to overcome tragedy.
5. How does visualizing help you understand what you read about Lance Armstrong?
   Visualizing him first as sick, then as a champion makes his accomplishments seem more significant.

School + Home Home Activity Your child read a short passage and draw conclusions based on details in the passage. Read a newspaper or magazine article about a famous athlete with your child. Ask your child to visualize the details. Afterwards, ask your child to draw a conclusion about this sports star.

▲ **Practice Book** p. 197

Page 497

LA.5.1.6.1 Use new vocabulary that is introduced and taught

LA.5.1.7.3 Determine the main idea or essential message through inferring and identifying relevant details

LA.5.1.7.8 Use strategies to repair comprehension when self-monitoring, including questioning

Reader Response

Open for Discussion Personal Response

 MODEL I'd begin by thinking about how the narrator's jealousy made him pretend he was a gymnast too. This will help me think of other similar instances.

Comprehension Check Critical Response

1. Possible responses: "dizzy and itchy with grass"; "skidded to a stop on his bike." Yes. The words describe Gary's experiences and can describe our own. ***Author's Purpose***

2. Possible response: Isaac looks to see if people driving by notice his flips. ***Draw Conclusions***

3. Responses will vary but should include details such as Isaac's shoes were "slim, black, and cool," while Gary's feet looked like "bloated water balloons" in his slippers. ***Visualize***

4. Responses will vary but could include *limelight* and *gymnastics*. ***Vocabulary***

 THINK AND EXPLAIN For test practice, assign a 5 minute time limit. For assessment, see the Scoring Rubric at the right.

Retell

Have students retell "The Gymnast."

Monitor Progress
Check Retelling Rubric 4 3 2 1

If... students have difficulty retelling the selection,	then... use the Retelling Cards and the Scoring Rubric for Retelling on p. 499 to assist fluent retelling.

SUCCESS PREDICTOR

 ELL

Check Retelling Model retelling by talking about the first photograph. Then have students use photos and other text features to guide their retellings. For more ideas on assessing students' retellings, see the ELL and Transition Handbook.

 498 Adapting • Week 5

Reader Response

Open for Discussion The narrator of "The Gymnast" says, "I was jealous and miserable." Why was he jealous? What did his jealousy make him do? Do you know anyone who has had an experience like his? What was the outcome?

1. Gary Soto has taken an incident from his childhood and packed it with sensory details to bring it to life. Find details that tell how things looked and sounded and felt. Do these details bring the incident to life? Explain. Think Like an Author

2. Young Gary draws the conclusion that his cousin Isaac is a showoff. Find details from the selection that support this conclusion. Draw Conclusions

3. Find passages that show how Gary looks in his gymnastics outfit and how his cousin looks. Discuss how the visual details help make them two very different people. Visualize

4. *Somersault* and *cartwheels* are names for gymnastic feats. What other words from the Words to Know list would go into a web with *gymnast* at the center? Vocabulary

 Think and Explain The dog in "The Gymnast" acts as an audience on pages 493 and 497. How does the dog-as-audience change and what does this tell you about the gymnast? Support your answer with details and information.

Meet author **Gary Soto** *on page 763.*

 LA.5.1.6.4 Categorize key vocabulary
LA.5.2.1.7 Identify descriptive language

498

 THINK AND EXPLAIN TWO-POINT SCORING RUBRIC
Top-Score Response A top-score response will contrast the attitude of the dog toward the practicing gymnast on pp. 493–497 and relate it to the narrator's view.

Example of a Top-Score Response The dog watches the gymnast with interest at first, then goes to sleep. This change matches the change in the narrator, who goes from strong interest to lack of interest. Now that he is more realistic, the narrator does not envy his cousin as much.

For additional rubrics, see p. WA10.

 Page 498
LA.5.1.6.4 Categorize key vocabulary
LA.5.2.1.7 Identify descriptive language

Write Now

Descriptive Writing

More FCAT WRITING+
See *The Grammar and Writing Book*, pages 164–169.

Prompt

In *The Gymnast*, a boy learns that he can't be anybody but himself.

Think about an important lesson you have learned.

Now write a description of the lesson and how you learned it.

Writing Trait

Effective **word choice** is using exact nouns, strong verbs, and vivid adjectives and images in your descriptive writing.

Student Model

Paragraphs separate events that take place at two different times. Phrases signal time shifts.

Precise nouns, verbs, and adjectives rather than vague ones show effective word choice.

Last sentence describes lesson that was learned.

Not long ago, my classmate Rena invited me to her birthday party. In the invitation, she included a pink printout with exact directions to her house. When I told Mom about the party, she quizzed me about the directions, and I said, "It's cool, Mom. I have them."

Mom often scolds me about the chaos in my room, so I guess she wasn't surprised when on the day of the party I couldn't find Rena's directions. Together we excavated the piles on my desk and found the printout. I arrived at the party late, but I learned a lesson about why I need to keep my room in better order.

Use the model to help you write your own description.

LA.5.3.2.2 Organize information into a logical sequence
LA.5.3.3.3 Create interest by modifying word choices

499

Write Now

Look at the Prompt Explain that each sentence in the prompt has a purpose.

- Sentence 1 presents a topic.
- Sentence 2 suggests students think about the topic.
- Sentence 3 tells what to write—a description.

Strategies to Develop Word Choice

Have students

- use strong, precise nouns and verbs.

NO: Move things on my desk.

YES: Sort magazines on my desk.

- add vivid adjectives or adverbs to make clearer pictures in readers' minds.

NO: I held the vase.

YES: I held the fragile vase nervously.

For additional suggestions and rubric, see pp. 503g–503h.

Writer's Checklist

☑ **Focus** Do all sentences tell about the lesson?

☑ **Organization** Is the lesson clearly stated?

☑ **Support** Are readers given adequate details?

☑ **Conventions** Are indefinite pronouns used correctly?

Page 499

LA.5.3.2.2 Organize information into a logical sequence
LA.5.3.3.3 Create interest by modifying word choices
LA.5.4.1.1 Write narratives

Scoring Rubric | Expository Retelling

Rubric 4 3 2 1	4	3	2	1
Connections	Makes connections and generalizes beyond the text	Makes connections to other events, texts, or experiences	Makes a limited connection to another event, text, or experience	Makes no connection to another event, text, or experience
Author's Purpose	Elaborates on author's purpose	Tells author's purpose with some clarity	Makes some connection to author's purpose	Makes no connection to author's purpose
Topic	Describes the main topic	Identifies the main topic with some details early in retelling	Identifies the main topic	Retelling has no sense of topic
Important Ideas	Gives accurate information about events, steps, and ideas using details and key vocabulary	Gives accurate information about events, steps, and ideas with some detail and key vocabulary	Gives limited or inaccurate information about events, steps, and ideas	Gives no information about events, steps, and ideas
Conclusions	Draws conclusions and makes inferences to generalize beyond the text	Draws conclusions about the text	Is able to draw few conclusions about the text	Is unable to draw conclusions or make inferences about the text

Retelling Plan

☑ **Week 1** Assess Strategic Intervention students.

☑ **Week 2** Assess Advanced students.

☑ **Week 3** Assess Strategic Intervention students.

☑ **Week 4** Assess On-Level students.

☑ **This week assess any students you have not yet checked during this unit.**

Use the Retelling Chart on p. TR17 to record retelling.

Selection Test To assess with *The Gymnast*, use Selection Tests, pp. 77–80.

Fresh Reads for Differentiated Test Practice For weekly leveled practice, use pp. 115–120.

SUCCES
PREDICTO

DAY 4

Reading Online

OBJECTIVES

- Examine the features of online reference sources.
- Compare and contrast across texts.

PREVIEW/USE TEXT FEATURES

Have students preview "All About Gymnastics." Ask:

- **How does Alice get from the search result screen to the encyclopedia entry for gymnastics?** *(She clicks on the gymnastics encyclopedia link.)*

- **How are the dictionary entries on pp. 502–503 like an entry in a printed dictionary?** *(Each entry word is in bold; there is a pronunciation and definition.)*

If students have trouble understanding how to use online reference sources, use the Technology Tools Box below.

Link to Social Studies

Have students work in pairs or groups to brainstorm topic ideas. Before they begin their searches, have them predict which online sources will be the most useful for their topics.

DAY 4 Grouping Options

Reading

Whole Group Discuss the Question of the Day.

Group Time Differentiated Instruction
Read "All About Gymnastics." See pp. 484f–484g for the small group lesson plan.

Whole Group Use p. 503a.

Language Arts
Use pp. 503e–503k.

Reading Online

New Literacies: **PearsonSuccessNet.com**

All About Gymnastics

Online Reference Sources

Genre

- You can find reference sources, such as almanacs and dictionaries, on Internet Web sites.

- Some Web sites give you several different reference sources all in one place.

Text Features

- These electronic reference sources look a lot like printed sources, and they're organized the same way.

- Instead of turning pages by hand, you click through them with a mouse.

Link to Social Studies

Explore a topic you like. Use an encyclopedia, dictionary, and other reference sources. Write down facts you find.

After reading Gary Soto's "The Gymnast," Alice decides she might want to do gymnastics. So she goes to an online reference Web site.

LA.5.6.4.1 Select and use appropriate technologies

For more practice

Take It to the Net

PearsonSuccessNet.com

500

TECHNOLOGY TOOLS

Online Reference Sources

Search Window The search window is where you type the keyword or phrase you want to find information about. In some search engines, you may need to click on the box before typing. To start the search, click on a word like *Search* or *Go,* or press *Enter.*

Search Results The results of a search are displayed in a list below the search window. This list includes links to Web sites that contain the keywords you typed into the search window. Clicking on a link will bring you to a Web site.

 Instead of turning pages, online researchers use these features. The *Back* arrow takes you to the previous page you saw on the screen. The *Forward* arrow returns you to the page you were on before hitting *Back.*

 The home page of any online reference is the first page users see when accessing the site. Other pages usually have the word *Home* or an icon like this. Clicking on it will return you to the home page.

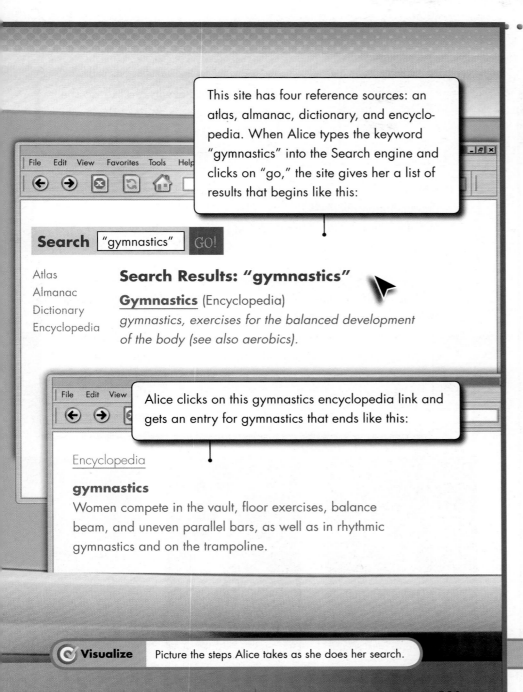

This site has four reference sources: an atlas, almanac, dictionary, and encyclopedia. When Alice types the keyword "gymnastics" into the Search engine and clicks on "go," the site gives her a list of results that begins like this:

Search "gymnastics" GO!

Atlas
Almanac
Dictionary
Encyclopedia

Search Results: "gymnastics"

Gymnastics (Encyclopedia)

gymnastics, exercises for the balanced development of the body (see also aerobics).

File   Edit   View

Alice clicks on this gymnastics encyclopedia link and gets an entry for gymnastics that ends like this:

Encyclopedia

gymnastics

Women compete in the vault, floor exercises, balance beam, and uneven parallel bars, as well as in rhythmic gymnastics and on the trampoline.

Visualize Picture the steps Alice takes as she does her search.

501

WEB-IQUETTE

Online Reference Sources

Tell students that, while online reference sources are a quick and efficient way to find information, there are rules of etiquette they should follow:

- Check to be sure that you've spelled keywords correctly. If words are misspelled, the search engine may not be able to find the information you need.
- Remember that you will need to record the source of any information you use in a report. This usually means printing out a page or cutting and pasting the Web address into a document. If you record the address by hand, be very careful. Every letter and symbol must be exactly the same as it is on your screen.
- Be sure to follow the classroom rules for saving files, printing pages, and bookmarking Web sites.

NEW LITERACIES: ONLINE REFERENCE SOURCES

Use the sidebar on p. 500 to guide discussion.

- Point out that online reference sources are informational sources, such as almanacs, dictionaries, and encyclopedias.
- Tell students that some online resources have their own search engines. Information can be accessed by typing a keyword or phrase in the search window and then clicking a word like *Search* or *Go,* or pressing *Enter.*
- Discuss with students the similarities and differences between online sources and print sources, and the possible benefits and drawbacks of using each.

 **AudioText**

Visualize

Students should visualize the different steps that Alice needs to take in order to use the online reference source. Students should picture her reading text on the screen and using the mouse to click on links.

Pages 500–501

LA.5.1.7.8 Use strategies to repair comprehension when self-monitoring

LA.5.2.2.4 Identify characteristics of types of text (reference)

LA.5.6.2.4 Record basic bibliographic data

LA.5.6.4.1 Select and use appropriate technologies

LA.5.6.4.2 Determine and use appropriate digital tools (web tools)

Access Content Lead a picture walk to reinforce gymnastics-related vocabulary, such as *gymnastics* (p. 500), *vault, floor exercises* (p. 501) and *pommel horse* (p. 502). Point to the dictionary entries and help students use them to confirm the meanings of these words.

Strategies for Navigation

USE GRAPHIC SOURCES Remind students that using graphic sources can help them visualize what they are reading and make information more clear. Graphic sources include maps, pictures, captions, charts, time lines, and video clips.

Use the Strategy

1. The next time you use an online encyclopedia, look for any graphics that may be related to the entry you are reading. Additional information may be supplied by maps, diagrams, pictures, and captions.

2. Try clicking on any graphics-related links that appear. You may be able to enlarge graphics that are shown by positioning your cursor on them and clicking.

3. After you've explored the graphics related to a topic, think about how they enhance the information you've gathered on your topic.

PRACTICE Think about the ways you use graphic sources at home and at school.

Use a printed reference source, such as an encyclopedia, to search for information on a topic. Think about the ways that an online reference source might use graphics to enhance your understanding of the topic.

The next time you access the Internet, try using an online reference source to find out more about your topic.

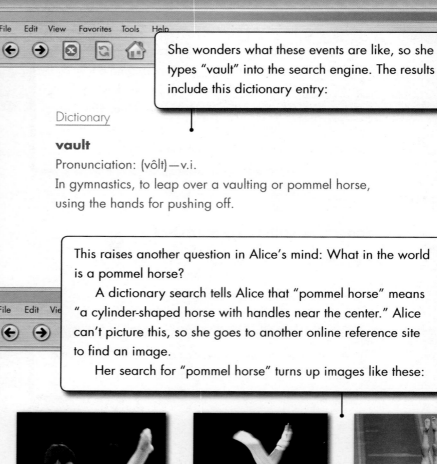

She wonders what these events are like, so she types "vault" into the search engine. The results include this dictionary entry:

Dictionary

vault
Pronunciation: (vôlt)—v.i.
In gymnastics, to leap over a vaulting or pommel horse, using the hands for pushing off.

This raises another question in Alice's mind: What in the world is a pommel horse?

A dictionary search tells Alice that "pommel horse" means "a cylinder-shaped horse with handles near the center." Alice can't picture this, so she goes to another online reference site to find an image.

Her search for "pommel horse" turns up images like these:

502

Guided Practice If there is time, have students log onto the Internet. Show them how to search for information in an online encyclopedia and access its graphic sources. Help students make connections between the steps they are doing and related vocabulary terms.

Page 502
LA.5.1.7.1 Explain purpose of text features (graphics, diagrams, illustrations, charts, and maps)
LA.5.1.7.8 Use strategies to repair comprehension when self-monitoring, including using graphic organizers

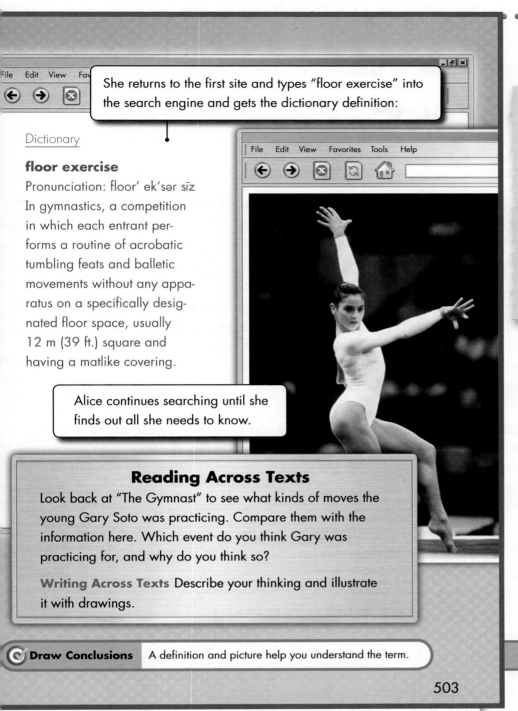

She returns to the first site and types "floor exercise" into the search engine and gets the dictionary definition:

Dictionary

floor exercise

Pronunciation: floor′ ek′sər sīz
In gymnastics, a competition in which each entrant performs a routine of acrobatic tumbling feats and balletic movements without any apparatus on a specifically designated floor space, usually 12 m (39 ft.) square and having a matlike covering.

Alice continues searching until she finds out all she needs to know.

Reading Across Texts

Look back at "The Gymnast" to see what kinds of moves the young Gary Soto was practicing. Compare them with the information here. Which event do you think Gary was practicing for, and why do you think so?

Writing Across Texts Describe your thinking and illustrate it with drawings.

⊘ **Draw Conclusions** A definition and picture help you understand the term.

503

CONNECT TEXT TO TEXT

Reading Across Texts

Locate the descriptions of the different moves that young Gary Soto was practicing in "The Gymnast." Discuss the clues that tell you which event he might have been practicing for.

Writing Across Texts Have students visualize Gary practicing his moves and then make a list of adjectives that describe him as he practices. Students can use the list to describe and illustrate their thinking.

⊘ **Draw Conclusions**

A definition and a photograph provide enough information for a reader to make a sensible decision about the meaning of a term.

Page 503
LA.5.1.7.7 Compare and contrast elements in multiple texts
LA.5.4.2.1 Write in a variety of informational/expository forms
LA.5.4.2.2 Record information (lists) related to a topic

Fluency Assessment Plan

☑ **Week 1** Assess Advanced students.
☑ **Week 2** Assess Strategic Intervention students.
☑ **Week 3** Assess On-Level students.
☑ **Week 4** Assess Strategic Intervention students.
☑ **This week assess any students you have not yet checked during this unit.**

Set individual goals for students to enable them to reach the year-end goal.
• Current Goal: 120–128 wcpm
• Year-End Goal: 140 wcpm

Provide opportunities for English language learners to read aloud to younger children. This allows them to practice their oral reading and improve their fluency.

 Fluency Coach CD To develop fluent readers, use Fluency Coach.

Page 503a
LA.5.1.5.1 Demonstrate the ability to read grade level text
LA.5.1.5.2 Adjust reading rate based on style

DAY 5 Grouping Options

Reading
Whole Group
Revisit the Question of the Week.

Group Time
Differentiated Instruction
Reread this week's Leveled Readers. See pp. 484f–484g for the small group lesson plan.

Whole Group
Use p. 503b–503c.

Language Arts
Use pp. 503d–503l.

PUNCTUATION CLUES
Fluency

DAY 1

Model Reread "The Winning Stroke" on p. 484m. Explain that you will use punctuation as a guide to pause at certain places or raise your voice in excitement. Model for students as you read.

DAY 2

Echo Reading Read aloud the first two paragraphs on p. 493. Have students notice how you pause at commas, dashes, and periods. After you read each sentence, have students repeat after you, doing three echo readings.

DAY 3

Model Read aloud the first paragraph on p. 497. Have students notice how you pause slightly at the commas, and longer at periods. Practice as a class by doing three echo readings.

DAY 4

Partner Reading Partners practice reading aloud paragraph one on p. 497, three times. Students should read using punctuation to pause at appropriate points and offer each other feedback.

Monitor Progress | Check Fluency WCPM

As students reread, monitor their progress toward their individual fluency goals. Current Goal: 120–128 words correct per minute. End-of-Year Goal: 140 WCPM. Have library books or other texts available at a variety of reading levels for students to use to practice fluency. See pp. DI·57–DI·58.

If... students cannot read fluently at a rate of 120–128 words correct per minute, **then...** make sure students practice with text at their independent level. Provide additional fluency practice, pairing nonfluent readers with fluent readers.

If... students already read at 140 words correct per minute, **then...** they do not need to reread three to four times.

 SUCCESS PREDICTOR

DAY 5

Assessment
Individual Reading Rate Use the Fluency Assessment Plan and do a one-minute timed reading of either selection from this week to assess students in Week 5. Pay special attention to this week's skill, punctuation clues. Provide corrective feedback for each student.

RETEACH

Draw Conclusions

TEACH

Review the definition of *draw conclusions* on p. 484. Students can complete Practice Book p. 198 on their own, or you can complete it as a class. Explain to students that they will need to read the passage about gymnastics carefully and answer items 1–5 to complete the graphic organizer.

ASSESS

Have students reread p. 497 and work with partners to draw conclusions about why Gary decides to stop practicing gymnastics. Students should identify the facts that led them to this conclusion. *(Possible response: The back flip scared him and he was afraid of getting really hurt. He saw an orange burst behind his eyes after he landed on his neck trying to do one.)*

For additional instruction on drawing conclusions, see DI·56.

EXTEND SKILLS

Simile

TEACH

A simile is a comparison of two unlike things that are alike in at least one way.
- In a simile, words of comparison such as *like* or *as* are used.
- Simile is a kind of figurative language.

Point out the simile on p. 494, paragraph 1, "...admiring my feet, which looked like bloated water balloons. " Have students write the simile in their notebooks, as well as an explanation of the two things being compared *(feet and water balloons)*.

ASSESS

Have students find another simile in "The Gymnast" on p. 493, paragraph 3. Ask them to write the simile (my hands as white as gloves) and answer these questions.

1. **What comparison word is used in the simile?**

2. **What two things are being compared?**

3. **What other items could have been used to compare the two things?**

Page 503b

LA.5.1.7.3 Determine the main idea or essential message through inferring
LA.5.2.1.7 Identify and explain an author's use of figurative language (similes)

OBJECTIVES

- Draw conclusions.
- Recognize simile.

Skills Trace	
Draw Conclusions	
Introduce/Teach	TE: 5.4 392–393, 484–485; 5.6 634–635
Practice	Practice Book: 153, 157, 158, 186, 193, 197, 198, 253, 257, 258, 286, 296
Reteach/Review	**TE: 5.4 411b, 467, 503b, DI•52, DI•56; 5.6 653b, 683, 687, 735, 745, DI•52**
Test	Selection Test: 61–64, 77–80, 101–104; Benchmark Test: Units 4, 6

ELL

Access Content Reteach the skill by reviewing the Picture It! lesson on author's purpose in the ELL Teaching Guide, pp. 134–135.

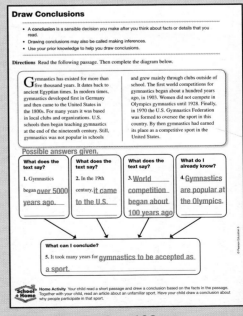

▲ **Practice Book** p. 198

Vocabulary and Word Study

VOCABULARY STRATEGY

⟳ Word Structure

SUFFIXES Remind students that a suffix is a syllable added at the end of a base word that changes its meaning. Common suffixes include *-er, -ment,* and *-ish.* Have students make a list of words with suffixes in "The Gymnast," identify the base words and suffixes, and think of other words with the same suffixes. Make a class list of words and discuss their meanings.

BUILD CONCEPT VOCABULARY

Improving Ourselves

UNIT REVIEW Remind students of the unit theme: Adapting. Discuss the unit focus question, How do people and animals adapt to different situations? Ask students how the Concept Vocabulary from each week of this unit relates to the unit theme and unit focus question. Ask students if they have any words or categories to add. If time permits, create a Unit Concept Web.

Greek and Latin Roots

Explain that the words *gymnastics* and *philosophy* contain the Greek and Latin roots *gym-* and *philo-*. Invite teams of students to come up related words.

gymnastics	philosophy
gym	philosopher

Monitor Progress

Check Vocabulary

If... students suggest words or categories that are not related to the concept,	**then...** review the words and categories on the Concept Web and discuss how they relate to the lesson concept.

SUCCESS PREDICTOR

Speaking and Viewing

SPEAKING

Informational Speech

SET-UP Have students use facts and details from the selection and their research to write an informational speech about a gymnast or gymnastics. Ask them to choose visuals that relate to the information they find.

ORGANIZATION Students should open with an interesting statement or question. Next, they'll explain what they've learned about gymnastics. Students should use visuals to make their speeches more interesting.

MULTIMEDIA PRESENTATION Students should present media images or content (for example, magazine photos, video) to support their spoken information. Share these suggestions:

• Use visual displays that can be seen by the entire audience.

• Organize visuals so that they are easily accessed as needed during the presentation.

Delivery Tips
• Practice your speech often enough so that you can deliver it fluently.
• Use correct grammar and avoid slang.
• Define unfamiliar vocabulary for your audience as you go.
• Explain each visual and how it relates to the information given.

VIEWING

Analyze a Video

Have students view a video or other visual medium that focuses on gymnastics. Then have them answer the following questions, working alone or with a partner.

1. **How is watching gymnastics different from reading about it?**

2. **What are three key facts or details you learned from the video?**

3. **What is the purpose of the video? In what format is gymnastics being shown?**

Have students view the video or other visual medium again. Discuss how viewing the video gives a better understanding of the reading.

Pages 503c–503d

LA.5.1.6.7 Use meaning of familiar base words and affixes to determine meanings of unfamiliar complex words

LA.5.5.2.1 Listen and speak to gain and share information (formal presentations)

LA.5.5.2.2 Make formal oral presentations, demonstrating appropriate language choices, the use of supporting graphics (images), and available technologies

LA.5.6.3.1 Examine how ideas are presented in a variety of print and nonprint media

LA.5.6.4.1 Select and use appropriate available technologies to enhance communication and achieve a purpose (video and presentations)

Support Vocabulary Use the following to review and extend vocabulary and to explore lesson concepts further:
• ELL Poster 20, Days 3–5 instruction
• Vocabulary Activities and Word Cards in ELL Teaching Guide, pp. 136–137

Assessment For information on assessing students' speaking, listening, and viewing, see the ELL and Transition Handbook.

Grammar Using *Who* and *Whom*

OBJECTIVES

- Define and identify pronouns *who* and *whom* as subjects and objects.
- Use *who* and *whom* correctly in writing.
- Become familiar with *who* and *whom* on high-stakes tests.

Monitor Progress

Grammar

If... students have difficulty deciding when it is correct to use *who* and *whom*,	then... provide additional instruction and practice in The Grammar and Writing Book pp. 164–167.

DAILY FIX-IT

This week use Daily Fix-It Transparency 20.

Spiral REVIEW

ELL

Support Grammar See the Grammar Transition lessons in the ELL and Transition Handbook.

▲ **The Grammar and Writing Book** For more instruction and practice, use pp. 164–167.

DAY 1 Teach and Model

DAILY FIX-IT

1. My cousin, whom is two years younger, always copy me. *(who; copies)*

2. Serena is inpatient to grow up but she still acts immature. *(impatient; up, but)*

READING-GRAMMAR CONNECTION

Write this sentence from *The Gymnast* on the board:

People admired an athlete <u>who</u> could somersault without hurting himself.

Explain that the underlined pronoun *who* acts as the subject of a dependent clause *(who could somersault without hurting himself)* in this complex sentence.

Display Grammar Transparency 20. Read aloud the definitions and sample sentences. Work through the items.

Using *Who* and *Whom*

People sometimes confuse the pronouns *who* and *whom* when they write. *Who* is a subject form. It is used as a subject of a sentence or a clause.
 Who made this mess?
 I saw a performer *who* could do four back flips. [*Who* is the subject in the dependent clause *who could do four back flips*.]
Whom is an object form. It is used as the object of a preposition or as a direct object.
 To *whom* did you send a letter?
 Whom will you ask?
In the first example, *whom* is the object of the preposition *to*. In the second example, *whom* is a direct object.
- The subject (*you*) does not come first in a question. Don't be fooled if the subject does not come first.
- To understand why *Whom* is used in the second sentence, change the word order so that the subject comes first. (*Whom will you ask?* becomes *You will ask whom?*) This makes it easier to see that *whom* is a direct object.

Directions How is the underlined word used? Write *subject, object of preposition,* or *direct object.*

1. <u>Who</u> asked for athletic tape? **subject**
2. That is the gymnast with <u>whom</u> I study. **object of preposition**
3. He is an athlete <u>who</u> once tried out for the Olympic team. **subject**
4. <u>Whom</u> have you told? **direct object**
5. I told my cousin, <u>who</u> is only eleven. **subject**

Directions Underline *who* or *whom* to complete each sentence correctly.

6. (<u>Who</u>, Whom) is your favorite athlete?
7. I disagree with Alan, (who, <u>whom</u>) likes basketball players.
8. About (who, <u>whom</u>) is that article written?
9. (<u>Who</u>, Whom) did you choose?
10. I chose Tiger Woods, a golfer for (who, <u>whom</u>) I have great respect.
11. Have you heard of Arthur Ashe, a tennis player (who, whom) died of cancer?
12. He was a tennis champion (who, <u>whom</u>) the public greatly admired for his style.

Unit 4 The Gymnast   Grammar **20**

▲ **Grammar Transparency** 20

DAY 2 Develop the Concept

DAILY FIX-IT

3. Do you has the equipment you need for gymnastics. *(have; gymnastics?)*

4. She runned to the mat and done a back flip. *(ran; did)*

GUIDED PRACTICE

Review the concept of when it is appropriate to use *who* and *whom*.

- The pronoun *who* is used as a subject.
- The pronoun *whom* is used as an object (object of a preposition or direct object).
- In a question that uses *who* or *whom*, change the word order so that the subject comes first. Then see if the pronoun is used as a subject or an object.

HOMEWORK Grammar and Writing Practice Book p. 77. Work through the first two items with the class.

Using *Who* and *Whom*

People sometimes confuse the pronouns *who* and *whom* when they write. *Who* is a subject form. It is used as a subject of a sentence or a clause.
 Who made this mess?
 I saw a performer *who* could do four back flips. [*Who* is the subject in the dependent clause *who could do four back flips*.]
Whom is an object form. It is used as the object of a preposition or as a direct object.
 To *whom* did you send a letter?
 Whom will you ask?
In the first example, *whom* is the object of the preposition *to*. In the second example, *whom* is a direct object.
- To understand why *whom* is used in the second sentence, change the word order so that the subject comes first. (*Whom will you ask?* becomes *You will ask whom?*) This makes it easier to see that *whom* is a direct object.

Directions How is the underlined word used? Write *subject, object of preposition,* or *direct object.*

1. <u>Who</u> wants to learn gymnastics? **subject**
2. She is a person for <u>whom</u> gymnastics is hard. **object of preposition**
3. Matt is the person <u>who</u> did a triple somersault. **subject**
4. <u>Whom</u> did she help the most? **direct object**
5. <u>Who</u> won the Olympic medal last year? **subject**

Directions Underline *who* or *whom* to complete each sentence correctly.

6. (Who, <u>Whom</u>) should we support?
7. Work with Brenda, (<u>who</u>, whom) has taken gymnastics for years.
8. To (who, <u>whom</u>) should we go for advice?
9. (<u>Who</u>, Whom) remembers the order of events?
10. The gymnast (<u>who</u>, whom) stumbled on the dismount still won a medal.

Home Activity Your child learned about using who and whom. Ask your child to write sentences about a sport using whom as an object and who as a subject.

▲ **Grammar and Writing Practice Book** p. 77

CORRECTIVE FEEDBACK

LA.5.3.4.4 Use subjective and objective pronouns

- **Question** Use Whiteboard or Transparency 20b, items 1–3, to ask questions that address this standard in FCAT format. Have students write their answers on a sheet of paper.
- **Check** Scan students' responses by having them hold up their papers.
- **Correct** If necessary, provide corrective feedback and review pp. 164–169 in *The Grammar and Writing Book*.

1 In which sentence is the pronoun *whom* used incorrectly?

- Ⓐ I don't know whom I can write about for my report.
- Ⓑ Whom is your teacher?
- Ⓒ Whom do you want for your writing partner?

◀ **FCAT Whiteboard Activity** 20b/**FCAT Transparency** 20b

DAY 3 Apply to Writing

DAILY FIX-IT

5. Eds somersaults are better than my are. *(Ed's; mine)*

6. I learns how to do a back flip last weak. *(learned; week)*

WHO VERSUS WHOM

By using subordinate clauses, writers add variety and complexity to their sentences. Use *who* and *whom* correctly in subordinate clauses. *Who* is a subject; *whom* is an object.

Subject of clause: Lance Armstrong is a bicyclist <u>who</u> survived cancer.

Direct object in clause: He is the luckiest man <u>whom</u> I know.

- Have students review something they have written to see whether they can improve it by using subordinate clauses with *who* and *whom*.

HOMEWORK Grammar and Writing Practice Book p. 78.

Using Who and Whom

Directions Choose *who* or *whom* to correctly complete each sentence. Then write this sentence and answer or explain it with another sentence or two. **Possible answers:**

1. A person who/whom I admire is _____
   Pronoun: whom
   A person whom I admire is President Kennedy.

2. To who/whom do I go for advice?
   Pronoun: whom
   To whom do I go for advice? I go to my dad for advice.

3. Who/Whom is my good friend?
   Pronoun: who
   Who is my good friend? Leslie is my good friend because she helps me.

4. Who/Whom is a person from history I'd like to meet?
   Pronoun: who
   Who is a person from history I'd like to meet? I would like to meet the astronaut Neil Armstrong.

Directions Write two sentences about a sport you would like to learn and the person whom you would like as a coach. Use *who* or *whom* correctly in each sentence. **Possible answers:**

5. I would like to learn golf from my dad, who is a great player himself.

6. There are other players whom I admire, such as Vijay Singh and Tiger Woods.

Home Activity Your child learned how to use who and whom correctly in writing. Ask him or her to write a fictional news story about sports and use the pronouns who and whom in it.

▲ **Grammar and Writing Practice Book** p. 78

DAY 4 Test Preparation

DAILY FIX-IT

7. The 2004 Olympic Games were holded in greece. *(held; Greece)*

8. Can you learn we how to do a handstand? *(teach us)*

STANDARDIZED TEST PREP

Test Tip

Whom is rarely used in speaking, so we have trouble deciding when it sounds correct. When you find *who* or *whom* in a subordinate clause, make the clause into a separate sentence. Then change *who* or *whom* into a personal pronoun such as *she* or *her*. If *she* sounds correct, use *who*. If *her* sounds correct, use *whom*.

No: You spoke with <u>she</u>.

Yes: You spoke with <u>her</u>.

Yes: You spoke with <u>whom</u>?

HOMEWORK Grammar and Writing Practice Book p. 79.

Using Who and Whom

Directions Mark the letter of the answer that tells how the underlined word is used.

1. That is the teacher <u>whom</u> I like best.
   A subject
   B object of preposition
   Ⓒ direct object
   D noun

2. <u>Whom</u> will you ask to the party?
   Ⓐ direct object
   B verb
   C subject
   D object of preposition

3. Janelle asked, "<u>Who</u> can help me?"
   A object of preposition
   B adjective
   C direct object
   Ⓓ subject

4. She is a gymnast <u>who</u> works hard.
   A verb
   Ⓑ subject
   C direct object
   D object of preposition

5. For <u>whom</u> should we ask?
   A noun
   B subject
   Ⓒ object of preposition
   D direct object

6. Everyone to <u>whom</u> she spoke smiled.
   Ⓐ object of preposition
   B subject
   C direct object
   D verb

Directions Mark the letter of the sentence that is correct.

7. A Whom has finished the assignment?
   Ⓑ By whom was this work done?
   C He is a teacher whom praises students often.
   D Who did he choose?

8. Ⓐ He helped the students who were having trouble.
   B To who can I turn this in?
   C Who did you help?
   D Whom won the gymnastics award this year?

9. A The winner is the one to who a trophy is given.
   B Chele is the partner with who I worked.
   Ⓒ He is the judge who gave high marks.
   D She likes the gymnast whom is short and slim.

10. A I like gymnasts whom take chances.
    B Whom was your favorite performer?
    C I choose someone whom has pluck.
    Ⓓ Whom would you choose?

Home Activity Your child prepared for taking tests on who and whom. Have your child read newspaper articles to highlight uses of who and whom. Then ask him or her to tell whether the words are used correctly, and why.

▲ **Grammar and Writing Practice Book** p. 79

DAY 5 Cumulative Review

DAILY FIX-IT

9. We set with the coach, whom cheered his team loudly. *(sat; who)*

10. Was she the gymnast whom had an inperfect routine? *(who; imperfect)*

ADDITIONAL PRACTICE

Assign pp. 164–167 in The Grammar and Writing Book.

EXTRA PRACTICE Grammar and Writing Practice Book p. 141.

TEST PREPARATION Grammar and Writing Practice Book pp. 155–156.

ASSESSMENT

CUMULATIVE REVIEW Grammar and Writing Practice Book p. 80.

Using Who and Whom

Directions Write *subject, object of preposition,* or *direct object* to identify how the underlined word is used.

1. To <u>whom</u> did Rosa speak? — object of preposition
2. <u>Who</u> likes tumbling? — subject
3. A gymnast is someone <u>who</u> is agile and strong. — subject
4. The girl with <u>whom</u> Jordan practices has real talent. — object of preposition
5. People <u>who</u> are flexible are better at somersaults. — subject
6. <u>Whom</u> did you choose as a partner? — direct object

Directions Underline *who* or *whom* to complete each sentence correctly.

7. (Who, Whom) said that gymnastics is easy?
8. No one (who, whom) has studied gymnastics would say that.
9. Harry, (who, whom) I have coached for three years, shows promise.
10. To (who, whom) shall we give the "Most Improved" award?
11. Marla is the gymnast with (who, whom) most teammates want to work.
12. Our grandfather, (who, whom) is now 65, competed on his college gymnastics team.
13. (Who, Whom) will win Olympic gold this year?
14. (Who, Whom) made the banner congratulating the team?

Directions Cross out mistakes in the use of *who* and *whom* in the paragraph. Write the correct pronoun above the line.

(15) Kids ~~whom~~ **who** live in the same family often compete with each other. (16) They want ~~whom~~ **who** to see the parents like best. (17) Parents, ~~whom~~ **who** love all their children equally, try not to play favorites. (18) Although brothers and sisters like to see ~~whom~~ who is faster or stronger, they love each other, too.

Home Activity Your child reviewed using who and whom. Read a story with your child, then ask him or her to tell about favorite characters, using who and whom correctly.

▲ **Grammar and Writing Practice Book** p. 80

Writing Workshop
Writing for Tests

OBJECTIVES

- Write a description for a test.
- Identify key words in a prompt.
- Focus on word choice.
- Use a rubric.

Genre Descriptive Writing
Writer's Craft Sensory Details
Writing Trait Support/Word Choice

Support/Word Choice Pair an English learner with a proficient English speaker to discuss pictures in books or magazines. Have them list words that appeal to the senses from the discussion to use in writing, such as *feather, exciting, oyster, cherries, spunky, wonderful, tough.*

Writing Traits

FOCUS/IDEAS All details are focused on describing the attempts to mount a horse.

ORGANIZATION/PARAGRAPHS Each paragraph describes a different attempt, telling what the author did and how the horse reacted. Transitions provide flow.

SUPPORT/VOICE The writer speaks to the reader directly, with originality and liveliness.

SUPPORT/WORD CHOICE Details appeal to senses (*velvet muzzle; gigantic frame*); strong, precise verbs communicate action clearly (*snuffed, leap, boosted*).

SUPPORT/SENTENCES Sentences are varied in length and complexity.

CONVENTIONS Spelling, punctuation, grammar, and usage are correct.

DAY 1 — Model the Trait

READING-WRITING CONNECTION

- When you write a response for tests, remember that sensory details and colorful word choice can strengthen your answer.
- Think about the words Soto uses in *The Gymnast* to describe soothing his tortured feet.

MODEL SUPPORT/WORD CHOICE
Discuss Writing Transparency 20A. Point out underlined words in the prompt. Then discuss the model and the writing trait of word choice.

 Think Aloud Soto chooses words that appeal to the senses: "My toes cooled on the summery grass. I ran a garden hose on my feet and bluish ankles, and a chill ran up my back." Details appeal to the senses of touch and sight to help you understand how the boy feels and looks.

Writing for Tests

Most people feel a sense of satisfaction when they achieve a goal. Think about a time when you achieved a goal that was important to you. Now write a description using precise nouns, strong action verbs, and vivid adjectives to tell how you accomplished your goal.

How I Learned to Mount Bareback

Adjectives and precise nouns create a clear picture.

I was determined to ride bareback, like the American Indians I'd seen in drawings. First, I had to find a way to mount our sleepy brown mare, Ladybug. She loomed over me like a mountain.

Details appeal to the senses of touch and sight.

Her velvet muzzle snuffed my hand and her brown eyes questioned, "What's up?" I was going to be up. But how? I leaped up and grabbed her mane, throwing my right leg over her back. As I slid to the ground, Ladybug shot me a look of pity.

Next, I tried pulling myself up by her mane. I grappled at her legs like a mountain climber but couldn't reach the summit. Now she was laughing at me!

Strong, exact verbs make the actions clear.

Then I led her to a stump. It boosted me high enough to throw my leg over her back and haul myself up by her mane. Finally, I was mounted and ready for an adventure.

Unit 4 The Gymnast — Writing Model **20A**

▲ **Writing Transparency** 20A

DAY 2 — Improve Writing

WRITER'S CRAFT
Sensory Details

Display Writing Transparency 20B. Work together to identify senses engaged by writing samples.

Think Aloud **USE SENSORY DETAILS** Tomorrow, we will write a description of an experience that taught us a lesson. I could write about a skating accident that taught me to wear protective gear. I could say, "my shins were on fire." That appeals to the sense of touch. I could say, "they looked like raw hamburger." That appeals to the sense of sight. I'll have to think of other phrases to appeal to senses of smell, taste, and hearing.

GUIDED WRITING Some students may need more help with sensory details. Help them find sensory details in the story and identify senses to which they appeal.

Sensory Details

To bring description to life for readers, include details that appeal to the five senses. Make readers see, hear, feel, smell, and taste what you did.

Directions Write the sense or senses to which each detail appeals: sight, hearing, touch, smell, and taste.

1. My freezing hands plunged gratefully into the soft, warm caves of woolly mittens.
   touch
2. My mouth watered as the yeasty smell of baking bread floated across the room.
   taste, smell
3. An angry squirrel chattered his complaint at me, all the while lashing the air with his tail.
   hearing, sight
4. A few thin clouds drifted in a blue sky, and the sun fell warm on our shoulders.
   sight, touch
5. The baby's eyes opened wide as sweetness flooded its mouth. Honey was an astonishing food!
   sight, taste

Directions Write three to five sentences describing your first experience of a new food. Include details that appeal to each of the five senses. **Possible answers:** The fried pieces of okra looked like fat spears. The hot oil and corn meal smelled like fried fish to me. As I bit into one, first there was a crunch, then a little puff of steam, and a smell like leaves. But as I chewed, the soft, slimy insides made me gag.

Unit 4 The Gymnast — Writer's Craft **20B**

▲ **Writing Transparency** 20B

Pages 503g–503h

LA.5.3.1.1 Generate ideas from multiple sources (graphic organizer) based upon teacher-directed topics and personal interests

LA.5.3.3.3 Create interest by modifying word choices

LA.5.4.1.1 Write narratives that establish a situation and plot with rising action, conflict, and resolution

Trait of the Week

Support/ Word Choice

DAY 3 Prewrite and Draft

READ THE WRITING PROMPT

on page 431 in the Student Edition.

In The Gymnast, *a boy learns that he can't be anybody but himself.*

Think about an important lesson you have learned.

Now write a description of the lesson and how you learned it.

FCAT Writing+ Test Tips

1. **Read the prompt carefully.**
   • Find key words.
   • Consider how the purpose and audience will affect your writing?

2. **Develop a plan.** Think of what you want to say before writing. Fill out a simple graphic organizer. For example, for a story, think of a beginning, middle, and end. For a comparison/ contrast essay, fill out a T-chart or a Venn diagram.

3. **Support your ideas.** Use facts, examples, and details to strengthen your response. Avoid making general statements that are unsupported.

4. **Use a variety of sentence structures.** Include complex and compound sentences, and vary sentence beginnings, lengths, and types.

5. **Check your writing.** If this is a timed test, you may not have time to recopy your work. However, you can neatly add, delete, or change words and make corrections in spelling, punctuation, or grammar. Reread your work before handing it in.

DAY 4 Draft and Revise

EDITING/REVISING CHECKLIST

☑ **Focus** Do sentences stick to the topic of a goal?

☑ **Organization** Is description developed in a logical order with transition words?

☑ **Support** Do descriptive words and sensory details make the writing clear and lively?

☑ **Conventions** Have I used *who* or *whom* correctly as subjects and objects? Are words with negative prefixes il-, in-, and ir- spelled correctly?

See *The Grammar and Writing Book,* pp. 164–169.

Revising Tips

Support/ Word Choice

• Substitute specific nouns for general nouns.

• Use strong verbs to express exactly what happened.

• Involve the five senses as much as possible.

ASSESSMENT Use the scoring rubric to evaluate students' work.

DAY 5 Connect to Unit Writing

Story	
Week 1	E-mail 411g–411h
Week 2	Journal Entry 435g–435h
Week 3	Story About an Animal 457g–457h
Week 4	Advice 483g–483h
Week 5	Describe How You Achieved a Goal 503g–503h

PREVIEW THE UNIT PROMPT

Tell a story about a character who succeeds by adapting to a new situation. Focus on an event that shows this person's resourcefulness. Your story may be real or imagined.

APPLY

• A story has a beginning, middle, and end and focuses on one incident or event.

• A story should contain vivid sensory details to make the action and characters come alive.

Writing Trait Rubric

	6	5	4	3	2	1
Support/ Word Choice	Vivid style created by use of exact nouns, strong verbs, exciting adjectives, and clear figurative language	Style created by use of exact nouns, strong verbs, adjectives, and figurative language	Some style created by strong and precise words	Little style created by strong, precise words; some lack of clarity	No style created by word choice; unclear	Word choice vague or incorrect
	Uses strong, specific words that make description unusually clear and lively	Uses strong, specific words that make description clear and lively	Uses some specific words that make description clear	Needs more precise word choice to create style and clarity in description	Description uninteresting due to dull word choice	Description made dull or unclear by poor word choice

Spelling & Phonics — Negative Prefixes

DAY 1 Pretest and Sort

OBJECTIVE

● Spell words with negative prefixes.

Generalization

Connect to Phonics When adding prefixes *il-, in-, im-,* and *ir-,* make no change in the base word: <u>il</u>legal, <u>in</u>visible, <u>im</u>possible, <u>ir</u>regular. All of the prefixes mean "not." Vowels before double consonants usually have a short sound.

Spelling Words

1. invisible	11. inactive
2. illiterate	12. imperfect
3. irregular	13. impolite
4. irresistible	14. immature
5. impossible	15. illogical
6. informal	16. indefinite
7. illegal	17. inappropriate
8. impatient	18. immobile
9. independent	19. irresponsible
10. incorrect	20. inexpensive

Challenge Words

21. irrelevant	24. indisputable
22. irreparable	25. impersonal
23. intolerant	

ELL

Spelling/Phonics Support See the ELL and Transition Handbook for spelling support.

DAY 1 — Pretest and Sort

PRETEST

Use the Dictation Sentences from Day 5 to administer the pretest. Read the word, read the sentence, and then read the word again. Guide students in self-correcting their pretests and correcting any misspellings.

Monitor Progress

Spelling

If...	then...
If... students misspell more than 5 pre-test words,	**then...** use words 1–10 for Strategic Intervention.
If... students misspell 1–5 pretest words,	**then...** use words 1–20 for On-Level practice.
If... students correctly spell all pretest words,	**then...** use words 1–25 for Advanced Learners.

HOMEWORK Spelling Practice Book, p. 77.

▲ **Spelling Practice Book** p. 77

DAY 2 — Think and Practice

TEACH

Draw four columns on the board labeled *il-, in-, im-,* and, *ir-.* Then say the base of a list word, such as *for-mal,* and ask a volunteer to add the prefix and say the word. Then have the volunteer write the word in the correct column. Continue with all the list words and different volunteers.

in|formal

FIND THE PATTERN Ask students to draw a line between each list word and its prefix. Have them identify words that have double consonants when the prefix is added, such as *irregular.* Remind students that adding these prefixes does not change the spelling.

HOMEWORK Spelling Practice Book, p. 78.

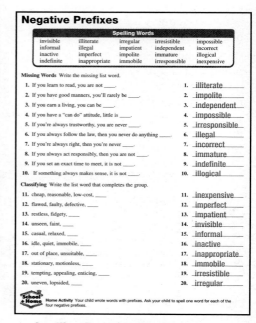

▲ **Spelling Practice Book** p. 78

Pages 503i–503j

LA.5.1.4.1 Understand spelling patterns
LA.5.1.4.2 Recognize structural analysis
LA.5.4.2.1 Write in informational/expository forms

AFTER READING

DAY 3 Connect to Writing

WRITE A DESCRIPTION

Remind students that description gives life to writing. Have students write a paragraph describing a person or thing using at least three list words.

Frequently Misspelled Words

through   always

These words may seem easy to spell, but they are misspelled by fifth-graders a lot. Alert students that *through* has a homonym, *threw,* and *always* is one word, not two words.

HOMEWORK Spelling Practice Book, p. 79.

Negative Prefixes

Proofread a Speech Circle six spelling errors in the toymaker's speech. Write the words correctly. Write the run-on sentence as two sentences.

"I want to create an (irresistable) toy for children. It will make the user (innvisible) I need five independent teams to work on this. As always, I am (impashent) to get this project started! We do not have an (indefinute) amount of time. I'm hoping to have this toy on the market by the end of the year. Does anyone have any questions? Does anyone think this task is (ilogical) or (impossible) to do? Do we all agree this can be done let's get to work!"

Spelling Words
invisible
illiterate
irregular
irresistible
impossible
informal
illegal
impatient
independent
incorrect
inactive
imperfect
impolite
immature
illogical
indefinite
inappropriate
immobile
irresponsible
inexpensive

1. irresistible   2. invisible
3. impatient   4. indefinite
5. illogical   6. impossible
7. Do we all agree this can be done?
   Let's get to work!

Proofread Words Circle the word that is spelled correctly.

8. (irresistible) unresistable   ilresistable
9. ilexpensive   imexpensive   (inexpensive)
10. inmature   (immature)   imature
11. (imperfect)   ilperfect   unperfect
12. independent (independent) ildependent
13. imactive   innactive   (inactive)
14. (impolite)   inpolite   unpolite
15. (illiterate)   iliterate   inliterate
16. imappropriate (inappropriate) inapropriate

Frequently Misspelled Words
through
always

Home Activity Your child identified misspelled list words. Take turns spelling list words that begin with the four prefixes studied.

▲ **Spelling Practice Book** p. 79

DAY 4 Review

REVIEW PREFIXES

Have partners quiz each other on the list words. Have one partner dictate the first ten list words as the other partner writes them. Then have them switch roles. The second partner dictates the last ten spelling words as the first partner writes. Then have them review each other's written work.

Spelling Strategy
Divide and Conquer

It's easier to remember how to spell words if you break them into syllables first. Draw a line between the word and its suffix. Study the word one part at a time.

HOMEWORK Spelling Practice Book, p. 80.

Negative Prefixes

Spelling Words

invisible	illiterate	irregular	irresistible	impossible
informal	illegal	impatient	independent	incorrect
inactive	imperfect	impolite	immature	illogical
indefinite	inappropriate	immobile	irresponsible	inexpensive

Complete the Word Add a prefix to each word to make a list word. Write the word.

1. ___appropriate   1. inappropriate
2. ___correct   2. incorrect
3. ___definite   3. indefinite
4. ___formal   4. informal
5. ___legal   5. illegal
6. ___logical   6. illogical
7. ___mature   7. immature
8. ___patient   8. impatient
9. ___perfect   9. imperfect
10. ___regular   10. irregular

Double Puzzle Unscramble each word. Write one letter in each box. Write the numbered letters to find the answer to the question.

What is the date when the United States celebrates its independence?

11. ALRGIERUR   i r r e g u l a r
12. MALFIRON   i n f o r m a l
13. TOCNRRIEC   i n c o r r e c t
14. CRMEPIFET   i m p e r f e c t
15. PEIMILTO   i m p o l i t e
16. MIEARMTU   i m m a t u r e
17. OCLILGLAI   i l l o g i c a l

F o u r t h   o f   J u l y

Home Activity Your child has learned to read, write, and spell words with prefixes. Take turns using list words in sentences that you say aloud. Ask your child to spell aloud the list word that is used in each sentence.

▲ **Spelling Practice Book** p. 80

DAY 5 Posttest

DICTATION SENTENCES

1. Clear glass is almost invisible.
2. An illiterate person cannot read.
3. The moon's surface is irregular.
4. Delicious food is irresistible.
5. Is that challenge impossible?
6. Pizza is an informal meal.
7. Driving faster than the speed limit is illegal.
8. Waiting makes me impatient.
9. Cats are independent animals.
10. That answer is incorrect.
11. The volcano has been inactive for many years.
12. The diamond was imperfect because of a scratch.
13. It's impolite to talk during a movie.
14. The immature boy is acting silly.
15. He has an illogical fear of the dark.
16. Their plans are still indefinite.
17. They laughed at inappropriate times during the play.
18. The rock was so heavy it was immobile.
19. Leaving the windows open during the storm was irresponsible.
20. That meal was inexpensive.

CHALLENGE

21. Those minor details are irrelevant to the main idea.
22. A broken balloon is irreparable.
23. Some coaches are strict and intolerant.
24. The game's outcome was indisputable.
25. The movie star's attitude was impersonal.

OBJECTIVES

OBJECTIVES

- Formulate an inquiry question that is connected to this week's lesson focus.
- Effectively and efficiently find, evaluate, and communicate information related to an inquiry question using electronic sources.

New Literacies

Day 1	Identify Questions
Day 2	Navigate/Search
Day 3	Analyze
Day 4	Synthesize
Day 5	Communicate

Page 503k

LA.5.6.2.1 Select a topic for inquiry, formulate a search plan, and apply evaluative criteria (usefulness)

LA.5.6.2.2 Read and record information systematically

LA.5.6.4.1 Select and use appropriate available technologies

LA.5.6.4.2 Determine and use appropriate digital tools (word processing) for publishing and presenting a topic

NEW LITERACIES

Internet Inquiry Activity

EXPLORE GYMNASTICS

Use the following 5-day plan to help students conduct this week's Internet inquiry activity about gymnastics. Remind students to follow classroom rules when using the Internet.

DAY 1

Identify Questions Discuss the lesson focus question: *Why do people try to change themselves?* Remind students that Gary wishes to learn gymnastics because his mother is proud of his cousin's involvement in the sport. Brainstorm ideas for inquiry questions about the sport of gymnastics. For example, students might want to learn about specific gymnastic events, such as the balance beam or parallel bars. Have students work individually, in pairs, or in small groups to write inquiry questions they want to answer.

DAY 2

Navigate/Search Tell students to skim the selection for keywords before using a student-friendly search engine for sources to answer their inquiry questions. Remind them to select keywords specific to their topic. Have students scan the blurbs of the "hits" to decide if the site is relevant and a good source of information.

DAY 3

Analyze Have students use the Web sites they identified on Day 2. Tell them to scan each site for information that helps them with their inquiry questions. Students can take notes from the sites or, if appropriate, print out and highlight relevant information.

DAY 4

Synthesize Have students synthesize information from Day 3 by combining the highlighted information or notes they have taken. Ask them to think about the best methods for sharing what they've learned with the class.

DAY 5

Communicate Have students decide how they want to share their inquiry results. They might use a word processing program to create reports, presentation software to create slide shows, or drawing tools to illustrate the key points.

RESEARCH/STUDY SKILLS
Graphs

OBJECTIVES

- Review terms to associated with types of graphs.
- Use graphs to gather information.

TEACH

Explain that graphs are picture representations of information. Ask students to name types of graphs and where they have seen them. Discuss the types of information presented in graphs and the benefits of showing information graphically. Show a graph, perhaps from a math textbook, and define these features.

- **Graphs** present information visually. Graphs compare pieces of information and can show how information changes over time. Graphs are able to show information more concisely than verbal or written explanations can.

- A **bar graph** is used to compare numbers. The bars used to show this data can appear vertically or horizontally. The graphs usually include titles, which explain the type of information being presented. Words below the bars tell what is being compared.

- A **circle graph**, or pie chart, is used to show the relationship of parts to a whole. Circle graphs are split into parts, called sectors, to represent parts of the whole.

- Other types of graphs include line graphs and picture graphs.

Have students work in small groups, and have each group look at a graph in their math text. Students should identify the type of graph, its parts, and the information it presents. Then, discuss these questions:

1. **What is being compared in the graph?** (Responses will vary depending on the graphs.)

2. **Do you think the graph is an effective way to present the information? Why or why not?** (Possible response: Yes, because I can clearly see population changes in the U.S. over the last 200 years.)

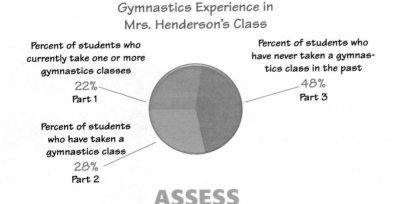

Gymnastics Experience in Mrs. Henderson's Class

Percent of students who currently take one or more gymnastics classes
22%
Part 1

Percent of students who have never taken a gymnastics class in the past
48%
Part 3

Percent of students who have taken a gymnastics class
28%
Part 2

ASSESS

As students examine graphs, check that they can identify the key parts and the information each presents. Make sure that they are able to answer questions about the information being compared in the graphs.

For more practice or to assess students, use Practice Book pp. 199–200.

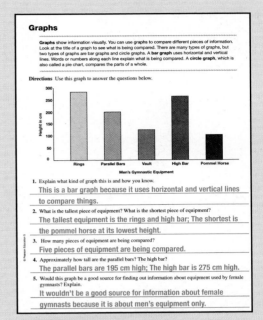

▲ **Practice Book** p. 199

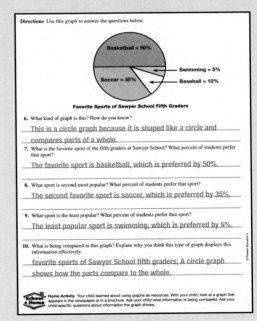

▲ **Practice Book** p. 200

Page 503l

LA.5.1.7.1 Explain the purpose of text features (charts)

LA.5.2.2.1 Locate, explain, and use information from text features (charts and graphs)

Assessment Checkpoints *for the Week*

Selection Assessment

Use pp. 77–80 of Selection Tests **to check:**

 Selection Understanding

 Comprehension Skill *Draw Conclusions*

 Selection Vocabulary

bluish	skidded
cartwheels	somersault
gymnastics	throbbing
hesitation	wincing
limelight	

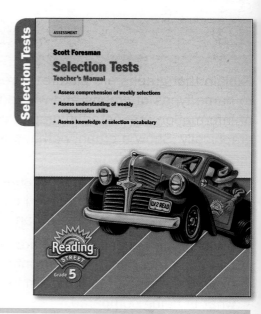

Selection Tests

ASSESSMENT

Scott Foresman
Selection Tests
Teacher's Manual

- Assess comprehension of weekly selections
- Assess understanding of weekly comprehension skills
- Assess knowledge of selection vocabulary

Leveled Assessment

 On-Level

Strategic Intervention

Advanced

Use pp. 115–120 of Fresh Reads for Differentiated Test Practice **to check:**

 Comprehension Skill *Draw Conclusions*

  **Comprehension Skill** *Generalize*

 Fluency *Words Correct Per Minute*

Fresh Reads for Differentiated Test Practice

ASSESSMENT   Teacher's Manual

Scott Foresman
**Fresh Reads
for Differentiated Test Practice**

Leveled passages—strategic intervention, on-level, and advanced—for
- Fluency checks
- Practice and application of weekly comprehension skills
- Answer key for all practice pages

Managing Assessment

Use Assessment Handbook **for:**

 Observation Checklists

 Record-Keeping Forms

 Portfolio Assessment

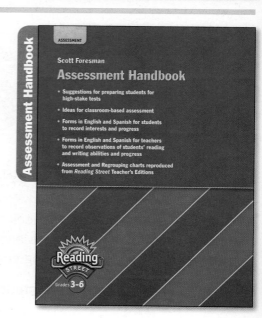

Assessment Handbook

ASSESSMENT

Scott Foresman
Assessment Handbook

- Suggestions for preparing students for high-stake tests
- Ideas for classroom-based assessment
- Forms in English and Spanish for students to record interests and progress
- Forms in English and Spanish for teachers to record observations of students' reading and writing abilities and progress
- Assessment and Regrouping charts reproduced from *Reading Street* Teacher's Editions

Unit 4
Concept Wrap-Up

CONCEPT QUESTION

How do people and animals adapt to different situations?

Students are ready to express their understanding of the unit concept question through discussion and wrap-up activities and to take the Unit 4 Florida Benchmark Test.

Unit Poetry

Use the poetry on pp. 504-507 to help students appreciate poetry and further explore their understanding of the unit theme, Adapting. It is suggested that you

- **read the poems aloud**
- **discuss and interpret the poems with students**
- **have students read the poems for fluency practice**
- **have students write interpretive responses**

Unit Wrap-Up

Use the Unit Wrap-Up on pp. 508-509 to discuss the unit theme, Adapting, and to have students show their understanding of the theme through cross-curricular activities.

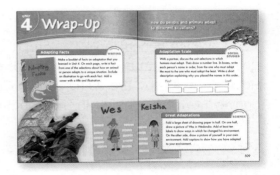

Unit Project

On p. 391, you assigned students a unit-long inquiry project, a graphic organizer that shows how a group of people or animals have adapted to a specific situation. Students have investigated, analyzed, and synthesized information during the course of the unit as they prepared their graphic organizers. Schedule time for students to discuss their organizers. The project rubric can be found to the right.

Unit Inquiry Project Rubric

4	3	2	1
• Research is accurate and very detailed. Sources are reliable and relevant.	• Research is generally accurate and detailed. Most sources are reliable and relevant.	• Research includes inaccuracies, irrelevant information, or little detail. Some sources are unreliable.	• Research is not accurate, detailed, or relevant. Most sources are unreliable.
• Graphic organizer is well chosen. Information on adaptations is clearly and effectively presented.	• Choice of graphic organizer is appropriate. Information is clearly presented.	• Information is presented in a graphic organizer, but some parts are unclear.	• Graphic organizer is incomplete or inappropriate. Information is unclear and confusing.

Unit 4
Reading Poetry

- Listen and respond to poems.
- Identify how meaning is conveyed through word choice.
- Read poetry fluently.
- Connect ideas and themes across texts.

Model Fluent Reading

Read "Which Lunch Table?" aloud. Read the poem slowly, with a dejected tone of voice. Point out how you are using your voice to convey how the speaker in the poem feels.

Discuss the Poem

1 Exaggeration • Critical

Which words suggest that the speaker is exaggerating the seriousness of the situation? Why do you think the speaker uses them?

Possible responses: Words like *fractured*, *lopsided*, and *rearranged* seem like strong words to describe the speaker's world just because he or she has no place to sit at lunchtime. These words show the strength of the speaker's emotional reaction to the situation.

2 Draw Conclusions • Inferential

Why does the speaker say it's going to be a "jigsaw year"?

Possible response: The speaker feels like he or she doesn't fit in, and the school year seems as though it will have to be pieced together like a jigsaw puzzle.

UNIT
4 *Poetry*

Which Lunch Table?
by Kristine O'Connell George

Where do I sit?
All my friends
from last year
have changed;
my world is
   fractured,
   lopsided,
   rearranged. **1**

   Where do I fit?
   Nothing is clear.
   Can already tell
   this will be
   a jigsaw year. **2**

504

Practice Fluent Reading

Have partners take turns reading "Which Lunch Table?" aloud. Tell students to read the poem a number of times, experimenting with different tones of voice. Have students discuss which reading best conveys the speaker's emotions.

AudioText

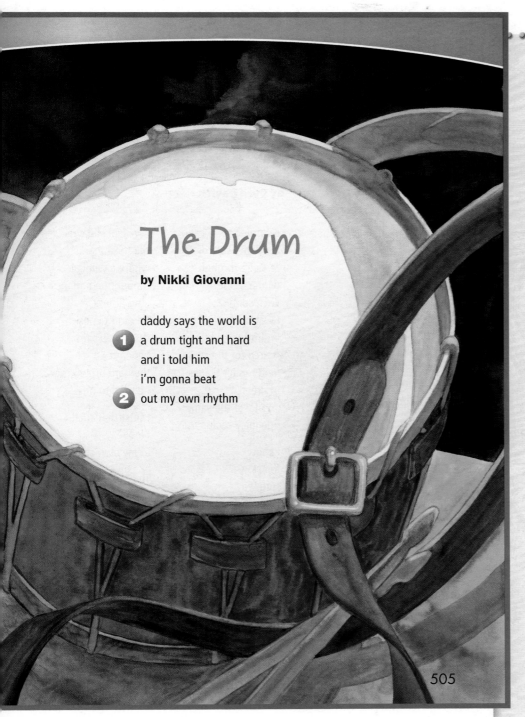

The Drum

by Nikki Giovanni

daddy says the world is
1 a drum tight and hard
and i told him
i'm gonna beat
2 out my own rhythm

505

WRITING POETRY

Have students write their own poems about a time when they felt they didn't fit in.

Model Fluent Reading

Read "The Drum" aloud. Tell students to listen for which words you stress. Point out that by emphasizing key words, the reader can help make the poem more meaningful.

Discuss the Poem

1 Metaphor • Inferential

What metaphor does the father use to describe the world? Why do you think he does so?

Possible response: The father says "the world is a drum tight and hard." Perhaps he has faced hardships in his life, making him feel the need to warn his child about the troubles to come.

2 Character • Inferential

What does this poem tell you about the speaker?

Possible response: The speaker is a child because he or she mentions "daddy." You can also tell that the speaker is strong and independent. He or she plans to face the world described by the father and "beat out my own rhythm."

Pages 504–505

LA.5.1.7.3 Determine the essential message through inferring
LA.5.2.1.3 Demonstrate how descriptive and figurative language help to communicate meaning in a poem
LA.5.2.1.7 Identify and explain an author's use of metaphor
LA.5.4.1.2 Write a variety of expressive forms (poetry)
LA.5.5.2.1 Speak for a variety of purposes, including poetic recitations

Model Fluent Reading

Read "Desert Tortoise" aloud. Tell students to listen to the way you vary your rate, or tempo, to match the meaning of the poem.

Discuss the Poem

1 Compare and Contrast • Inferential

How are the desert tortoise and the other animals in the poem alike? How are they different?

Possible responses: All of the animals live in the desert. The tortoise stays around for a long time, while the other animals "come and go." The tortoise has a better understanding of how the world works.

2 Draw Conclusions • Inferential

Why does the tortoise think that the desert is "a good place for an old tortoise to walk"?

Possible responses: The tortoise seems to enjoy its life. It refers to feeling safe, warm, and well fed.

EXTEND SKILLS

Imagery

Imagery, or sensory language, is the use of words that help the reader experience the way things look, sound, smell, taste, or feel. Metaphors and similes also add to the reader's experience. Explain that there are several sensory images in "Desert Tortoise." The reader can feel the warm sun and taste *the ripe juicy cactus fruit.* Point out that the word *"jigsaw"* is used to illustrate a metaphor in the poem "Which Lunch Table?" on p. 504. Explain that it helps the reader get a better sense of how fitting in at a school is like piecing a puzzle together.

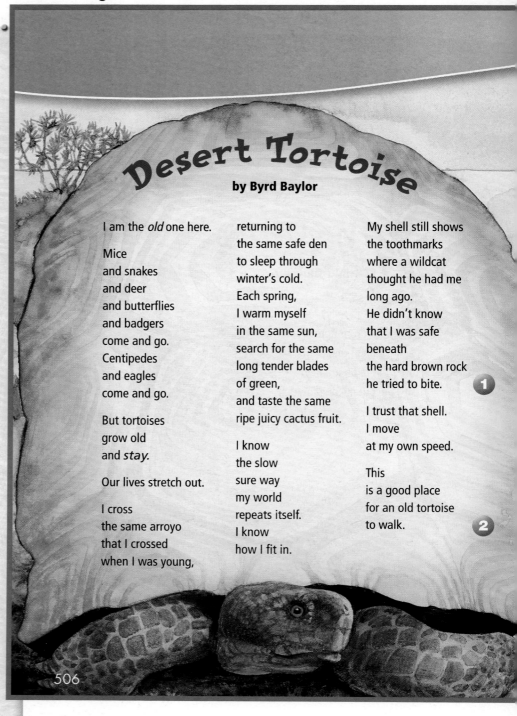

Desert Tortoise
by Byrd Baylor

I am the *old* one here.

Mice
and snakes
and deer
and butterflies
and badgers
come and go.
Centipedes
and eagles
come and go.

But tortoises
grow old
and *stay.*

Our lives stretch out.

I cross
the same arroyo
that I crossed
when I was young,

returning to
the same safe den
to sleep through
winter's cold.
Each spring,
I warm myself
in the same sun,
search for the same
long tender blades
of green,
and taste the same
ripe juicy cactus fruit.

I know
the slow
sure way
my world
repeats itself.
I know
how I fit in.

My shell still shows
the toothmarks
where a wildcat
thought he had me
long ago.
He didn't know
that I was safe
beneath
the hard brown rock
he tried to bite. **1**

I trust that shell.
I move
at my own speed.

This
is a good place
for an old tortoise
to walk. **2**

506

Practice Fluent Reading

Have partners alternate reading sections of "Desert Tortoise" aloud. Tell students to read each section at a rate that matches the meaning. Then ask students to switch parts and read again. Tell them to listen for differences between their readings.

Audio CD AudioText

Camel

by Lillian M. Fisher

A camel is a mammal,
A most extraordinary animal
Whose appearance is a wee bit odd.
His body is lumpy,
Knees calloused and bumpy,
And his feet are naturally shod.
His humps are fantastical,
His manner bombastical,
Due to his proud ancient past.
He feasts upon brambles
And ploddingly ambles.
His gait is not very fast.
But he carries great loads
On long dusty roads
Where many a beast cannot.
He's a tireless walker
And goes without water
In weather increasingly hot. ❶
This strange-looking beast
Who resides in the East
And in far-off places West
Is found at the zoo
Where he's happy, it's true,
But—
Deep inside—desert is best. ❷

507

WRITING POETRY

Have students write a poem about an animal that adapts well to its environment. What physical traits or behaviors help the animal survive?

Pages 506–507

LA.5.1.5.2 Adjust reading rate based on form and style
LA.5.1.7.2 Identify how an author's perspective influences text
LA.5.1.7.3 Determine the essential message through inferring
LA.5.1.7.6 Identify themes or topics across a variety of selections
LA.5.2.1.7 Identify and explain author's use of descriptive and figurative language
LA.5.4.1.2 Write a variety of expressive forms (poetry)

Model Fluent Reading

Read "Camel" aloud. Be sure to pause after punctuation marks, not at line breaks. Point out that it is easy to hear the rhymes in this poem and that it has a steady rhythm pattern.

Discuss the Poem

❶ **Draw Conclusions • Inferential**
Why do you think the speaker thinks the desert is the best place for the camel?
Possible responses: The camel is suited to life in the hot desert. It eats brambles, walks slowly but steadily, and can go without water for long periods of time.

❷ **Tone • Inferential**
What is the tone of the poem? Explain.
The rhymes and the swinging rhythm contribute to a lighthearted tone. The poem is amusing, and the tone reflects that.

Connect Ideas and Themes

Remind students that this unit deals with how people and animals adapt to different situations. Ask students to discuss how each poem relates to this idea. Then have them recall times when they have had to adapt to a new situation.

EXTEND SKILLS

Tone

Tone is the author's attitude toward the subject or the audience. By recognizing tone, the reader can better understand the poem's intended emotional meaning. Students can identify the poem's tone by looking for clue words that illustrate the author's viewpoint, such as those that convey sympathy or humor.

ADAPTING

Discuss the Big Idea

How do people and animals adapt to different situations?

Write the unit theme and Big Idea question on the board. Ask students to think about the selections they have read in the unit. Discuss how each selection and lesson concept can help them answer the Big Idea question from this unit.

Model this for students by choosing a selection and explaining how the selection and lesson concept address the Big Idea.

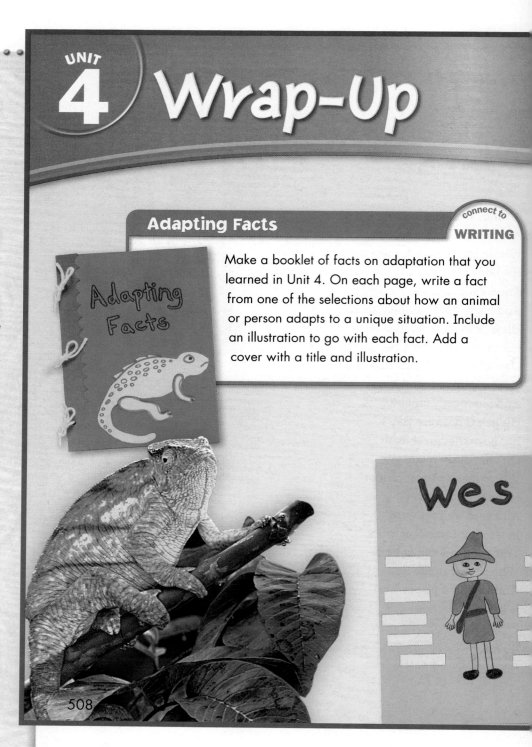

UNIT 4 Wrap-Up

Adapting Facts

connect to WRITING

Make a booklet of facts on adaptation that you learned in Unit 4. On each page, write a fact from one of the selections about how an animal or person adapts to a unique situation. Include an illustration to go with each fact. Add a cover with a title and illustration.

Adapting Facts

Wes

508

How do people and animals adapt to different situations?

Adaptation Scale

connect to **SOCIAL STUDIES**

With a partner, discuss the unit selections in which humans must adapt. Then draw a number line. In boxes, write each person's name in order, from the one who must adapt the most to the one who must adapt the least. Write a short description explaining why you placed the names in this order.

Most   Least

Great Adaptations

connect to **SCIENCE**

Fold a large sheet of drawing paper in half. On one half, draw a picture of Wes in Weslandia. Add at least ten labels to show ways in which he changed his environment. On the other side, draw a picture of yourself in your own environment. Add captions to show how you have adapted to your environment.

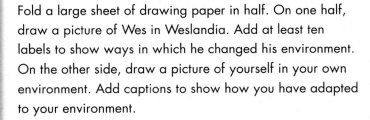

509

ACTIVITIES

Adapting Facts

Make a Booklet Remind students of the difference between a statement of fact and opinion. Tell them to skim the unit selections and list statements of fact about adaptations. Students can review their lists with partners, eliminating any statements of opinion and choosing interesting statements of fact to illustrate for their booklets.

Adaptation Scale

Rate the Adaptations Have partners review the unit selections and list the names of humans who had to adapt to a specific situation. Then have them discuss how they will order the names on their number lines and why. Students should include their reasons for ordering the names the way they did in their written explanations.

Great Adaptations

Make an Illustration Have students make a list of ways Wes changed his environment before adding labels to their illustrations. Before students make labels for their self-portraits, encourage them to think about how their environment affects their choice of clothing, food, shelter, transportation, or entertainment.

 Pages 508–509

LA.5.1.7.6 Identify themes or topics across a variety of fiction and non-fiction selections

LA.5.3.1.1 Generate ideas from multiple sources (text and drawing)

LA.5.4.1.2 Write a variety of expressive forms

Glossary

Glossary

How to Use This Glossary

This glossary can help you understand and pronounce some of the words in this book. The entries in this glossary are in alphabetical order. There are guide words at the top of each page to show you the first and last words on the page. A pronunciation key is at the bottom of every other page. Remember, if you can't find the word you are looking for, ask for help or check a dictionary.

The entry word is in dark type. It shows how the word is spelled and how the word is divided into syllables.

The pronunciation is in parentheses. It also shows which syllables are stressed.

Part-of-speech labels show the function or functions of an entry word and any listed form of that word.

ad·vise (ad vīz′), 1. *V.* to give advice to; offer an opinion to; counsel: *I shall act as you advised.* 2. *V.* to give notice; inform: *We were advised that a storm was approaching, so we didn't go sailing.* ❑ *V.* **ad·vised, ad·vis·ing.**

Sometimes, irregular and other special forms will be shown to help you use the word correctly.

The definition and example sentence show you what the word means and how it is used.

776

abdomen • advise

Aa

ab·do·men (ab′də mən), *N.* the part of the body containing the stomach, the intestines, and other important organs; belly.

ab·o·rig·i·ne (ab′ə rij′ə nē), *N.* one of the earliest known inhabitants of Australia. ❑ *N. PL.* **ab·o·rig·i·nes.**

ab·sence (ab′səns), *N.* condition of being without; lack: *Darkness is the absence of light.*

ac·com·plish·ment (ə kom′plish mənt), *N.* something that has been done with knowledge, skill, or ability; achievement: *The teachers were proud of the pupils' accomplishments.*

a·chieve (ə chēv′), *V.* to carry out to a successful end; accomplish; do: *Have you achieved your purpose?* ❑ *V.* **a·chieved, a·chiev·ing.**

ac·quaint (ə kwānt′), *V.* to make aware; let know; inform: *Let me acquaint you with your new duties.* ❑ *V.* **ac·quain·ted, ac·quain·ting.**

ad·mir·ing·ly (ad mīr′ing lē), *ADV.* With wonder, pleasure, and approval: *We gazed admiringly at the beautiful painting.*

a·dorn (ə dôrn′), *V.* to add beauty to; put ornaments on; decorate: *She adorned her hair with flowers.* ❑ *V.* **a·dorned, a·dorn·ing.**

ad·vice (ad vīs′), *N.* opinion about what should be done; suggestion: *My advice is that you study more.*

ad·vise (ad vīz′), 1. *V.* to give advice to; offer an opinion to; counsel: *I shall act as you advised.* 2. *V.* to give notice; inform: *We were advised that a storm was approaching, so we didn't go sailing.* ❑ *V.* **ad·vised, ad·vis·ing.**

agreement • belfry

a·gree·ment (ə grē′mənt), *N.* harmony in feeling or opinion: *The coaches are in complete agreement that she will be a superb gymnast.*

air·time (âr′tīm), *N.* specific amount of time in a television, radio, or any broadcast media program.

al·gae (al′jē), *N. PL.* group of related living things, mostly living in water.

Alz·heim·er's (älts′hī mərz), *N.* disease of the brain that causes confusion and gradual loss of memory.

a·nat·o·my (ə nat′ə mē), *N.* structure of a living thing: *the anatomy of an earthworm.*

ap·pre·ci·ate (ə prē′shē āt), *V.* to think highly of; recognize the worth or quality of; value; enjoy: *Almost everybody appreciates good food.* ❑ *V.* **ap·pre·ci·at·ed, ap·pre·ci·at·ing.**

ar·chi·tect (är′kə tekt), *N.* person who designs and makes plans for buildings. (*Architect* comes from two Greek words, *archi* meaning "chief" and *tekton* meaning "builder.")

ar·mor (är′mər), *N.* any kind of protective covering. The steel plates of a warship and the bony shell of an armadillo are armor.

armor

ar·ti·fi·cial (är′tə fish′əl), *ADJ.* made by human skill or labor; not natural: *Plastics are artificial substances that do not occur in nature.*

as·cent (ə sent′), *N.* act of going up; upward movement; rising: *The sudden ascent of the elevator made us dizzy.*

as·sign·ment (ə sīn′mənt), *N.* something assigned, especially a piece of work to be done: *Today's assignment in arithmetic consists of ten problems.*

as·ton·ish (ə ston′ish), *V.* to surprise greatly; amaze: *We were astonished by the child's remarkable memory.* ❑ *V.* **as·ton·ished, as·ton·ish·ing.**

au·da·cious (ò dā′shəs), *ADJ.* rudely bold; impudent: *The audacious waiter demanded a larger tip.*

Bb

back·flip (bak′ flip), *N.* backward somersault performed in the air. ❑ *N. PL.* **back·flips.**

back·ground (bak′ ground), *N.* the part of a picture or scene toward the back: *The cottage stands in the foreground with the mountains in the background.*

bar·ber (bär′bər), *N.* person whose business is cutting hair and shaving or trimming beards.

bass[1] (bās), 1. *N.* the lowest male voice in music. 2. *N.* the largest, lowest sounding stringed instrument in an orchestra or band.

bass[2] (bas), 1. *N.* North American freshwater or saltwater fish with spiny fins, used for food.

be·hav·ior (bi hā′vyər), *N.* manner of behaving; way of acting: *Her sullen behavior showed that she was angry.*

bel·fry (bel′frē), *N.* space in a tower in which a bell or bells may be hung.

a	in hat	ō	in open	sh	in she
ā	in age	ò	in all	th	in thin
â	in care	ô	in order	ᴛʜ	in then
ä	in far	oi	in oil	zh	in measure
e	in let	ou	in out	ə	= a in about
ē	in equal	u	in cup	ə	= e in taken
ėr	in term	u̇	in put	ə	= i in pencil
i	in it	ü	in rule	ə	= o in lemon
ī	in ice	ch	in child	ə	= u in circus
o	in hot	ng	in long		

777

benefactor • cavity

ben·e·fac·tor (ben′ə fak′tər), *N.* person who has given money or kindly help. (*Benefactor* comes from two Latin words, *bene* meaning "well" or "good" and *facere* meaning "do.")

be·queath (bi kwēᴛʜ′), *V.* to give or leave by means of a will when a person dies: *He bequeathed his fortune to his children.* ❑ *V.* **be·queathed, be·queath·ing.**

bleach (blēch), *V.* to whiten by exposing to sunlight or by using chemicals: *animal skulls bleached by the desert sun.* ❑ *V.* **bleached, bleach·ing.**

blen·der (blen′dər), *N.* an electric kitchen appliance for grinding, mixing, or beating various foods.

blu·ish (blü′ish), *ADJ.* somewhat blue; somewhat like the color of the clear sky in daylight.

bluish

blun·der (blun′dər), *N.* a stupid mistake: *Misspelling the title of a book is a silly blunder to make in a book report.* ❑ *N. PL.* **blun·ders.**

bound·ar·y (boun′dər ē), *N.* a limiting line or thing; limit; border: *the boundary between Canada and the United States.* ❑ *N. PL.* **bound·aries.**

brack·ish (brak′ish), 1. *ADJ.* slightly salty. Coastal marshes often have brackish waters. 2. *ADJ.* bad-tasting.

brand (brand), 1. *N.* a certain kind, grade, or make: *Do you like this brand of flour?* 2. *V.* to mark by burning the skin with a hot iron: *The cowboys branded the cows.* ❑ *V.* **brand·ed, brand·ing.**

break·fast (brek′fəst), *V.* to eat the first meal of the day. ❑ *V.* **break·fast·ed, break·fast·ing.**

bronze (bronz), *N.* a dark yellow-brown alloy of copper and tin.

Cc

ca·ble (kā′bəl), *N.* a message sent through wires by electric current or electronic signals.

cal·cu·la·tion (kal′kyə lā′shən), *N.* careful thinking; deliberate planning: *The success of the expedition was the result of much calculation.* ❑ *N. PL.* **cal·cu·la·tions.**

cam·e·o (kam′ē ō), *N.* a semiprecious stone carved so that there is a raised design on a background, usually of a different color.

can·non (kan′ən), *N.* a big gun, especially one that is mounted on a base or wheels.

can·tan·ker·ous (kan tang′kər əs), *ADJ.* ready to make trouble; ill-natured; quarrelsome.

car·cass (kär′kəs), *N.* body of a dead animal. ❑ *N. PL.* **car·cass·es.**

cart·wheel (kärt′wēl′), *N.* a sideways handspring with the legs and arms kept straight. ❑ *N. PL.* **cart·wheels.**

cat·er·pil·lar (kat′ər pil′ər), *N.* the wormlike larvae of insects such as butterflies and moths.

cav·i·ty (kav′ə tē), *N.* hollow place; hole. Cavities in teeth are caused by decay. ❑ *N. PL.* **cav·i·ties.**

778

cerebral palsy • cramp

ce·re·bral pal·sy (ser′ə brəl pòl′zē), *N.* paralysis caused by damage to the brain before or at birth. Persons suffering from cerebral palsy have trouble coordinating their muscles.

choir (kwīr), *N.* group of singers who sing together, often in a church service.

cir·cum·stance (sėr′kəm stans), 1. *N.* condition that accompanies an act or event: *Unfavorable circumstances such as fog and rain often delayed us in our trip to the mountains.* 2. *N.* the existing condition or state of affairs: *He was forced by circumstances to resign.* ❑ *N. PL.* **cir·cum·stanc·es.**

civ·i·li·za·tion (siv′ə lə zā′shən), *N.* the ways of living of a people or nation: *The civilizations of ancient Egypt and ancient Greece had many contacts over the centuries.*

clar·i·net (klar′ə net′), *N.* a woodwind instrument, having a mouthpiece with a single reed and played by means of holes and keys.

cleanse (klenz), 1. *V.* to make clean: *cleanse a wound before bandaging it.* 2. *V.* to make pure: *cleanse the soul.* ❑ *V.* **cleansed, cleans·ing.**

close-up (klōs′up′), *N.* picture taken with a camera at close range.

close-up of chimpanzee

cock·le (kok′əl), *N.* any of several kinds of saltwater clams with two-ridged, heart-shaped shells. ❑ *N. PL.* **cock·les.**

co·coon (kə kün′), *N.* case of silky thread spun by the larvae of various insects, to live in while they are developing into adults. Most moth larvae form cocoons.

com·bi·na·tion (kom′bə nā′shən), *N.* series of numbers or letters dialed in opening a certain kind of lock: *Do you know the combination of the safe?*

com·plex (kom′pleks), *ADJ.* hard to understand: *The instructions for building the radio were complex.*

con·ceal (kən sēl′), *V.* to put out of sight; hide: *The murky water concealed the crabs.* ❑ *V.* **con·cealed, con·ceal·ing.**

con·fi·dence (kon′fə dəns), *N.* firm belief in yourself; self-confidence: *Years of experience at her work have given her great confidence.*

con·ser·va·tion (kon′sər vā′shən), *N.* preservation from harm or decay; protection from loss or from being used up: *Conservation of energy saves fuel.*

con·struct (kən strukt′), *V.* to put together; fit together; build: *construct a bridge.* ❑ *V.* **con·struct·ed, con·struct·ing.**

con·tri·bute (kən trib′yüt), *V.* to help bring about: *A poor diet contributed to the child's bad health.* ❑ *V.* **con·tri·but·ed, con·tri·but·ing.**

cove (kōv), *N.* a small, sheltered bay; inlet on the shore.

cramp (kramp), *V.* to shut into a small space; limit: *Living in only three rooms, the family was cramped.* ❑ *V.* **cramped, cramp·ing.**

a	in hat	ō	in open	sh	in she
ā	in age	ò	in all	th	in thin
â	in care	ô	in order	ᴛʜ	in then
ä	in far	oi	in oil	zh	in measure
e	in let	ou	in out	ə	= a in about
ē	in equal	u	in cup	ə	= e in taken
ėr	in term	u̇	in put	ə	= i in pencil
i	in it	ü	in rule	ə	= o in lemon
ī	in ice	ch	in child	ə	= u in circus
o	in hot	ng	in long		

779

Glossary

---

cranny·distribution

cran·ny (kran′ē), *N.* a small, narrow opening; crack; crevice: *She looked in all the nooks and crannies of the house for the misplaced book.* ❑ *N. PL.* **cran·nies.**

crit·i·cal (krit′ə kəl), *ADJ.* being important to the outcome of a situation: *Help arrived at the critical moment.*

crit·i·cize (krit′ə sīz), *V.* to find fault with; disapprove of; blame: *Do not criticize him until you know all the circumstances.* ❑ *V.* **crit·i·cized, crit·i·ciz·ing.**

cruise (krüz), *V.* to travel in a car, airplane, boat, etc. at the speed at which the vehicle operates best. ❑ *V.* **cruised, cruis·ing.**

Dd

dain·ti·ly (dān′tə lē), *ADV.* with delicate beauty; freshly and prettily: *She daintily wiped her mouth with her napkin.*

deaf·en·ing (def′ən ing), *ADJ.* very loud; amazingly noisy.

de·bris (də brē′), *N.* scattered fragments; ruins; rubbish: *The street was covered with broken glass, stone, and other debris from the storm.*

debris in a landfill

de·cay (di kā′), *N.* process of rotting: *The decay in the tree trunk proceeded so rapidly that the tree fell over in a month.*

dem·on·strate (dem′ən strāt), *V.* to show how a thing is done; explain by using examples. ❑ *V.* **dem·on·strates, dem·on·strat·ed, dem·on·strat·ing.**

de·pressed (di prest′), *ADJ.* gloomy; low-spirited; sad. (*Depressed* comes from the Latin word *depressum* meaning "pressed down.")

de·vas·ta·tion (dev′ə stā′shən), *N.* the act of laying waste, destroying.

die-off (dī′ ôf), *N.* to die one after another until all are dead: *The entire herd experienced a die-off during the drought.*

dig·ni·tar·y (dig′nə ter′ē), *N.* person who has a position of honor: *We saw several foreign dignitaries when we visited the United Nations.* ❑ *N. PL.* **dig·ni·tar·ies.**

di·gress (di gres′), *V.* to turn aside from the main subject in talking or writing: *I lost interest in the book because the author digressed too much.* ❑ *V.* **di·gressed, di·gres·sing.**

dip·lo·mat (dip′lə mat), *N.* person whose work is to manage the relations between his or her nation and other nations.

dir·i·gi·ble (dir′ə bəl), *N.* an airship made with a rigid framework. It is filled with gas that is lighter than air.

dis·lodge (dis loj′), *V.* to drive or force out of a place, position, etc.: *She used a crowbar to dislodge a heavy stone.* ❑ *V.* **dis·lodged, dis·lodg·ing.**

dis·re·spect (dis′ri spekt′), *V.* to show a lack of respect; to be rude. ❑ *V.* **dis·re·spect·ed, dis·re·spect·ing.**

dis·tri·bu·tion (dis′trə byü′shən), *N.* the act of giving some of to each, of dividing and giving out in shares.

780

---

drench·explosion

drench (drench), *V.* to wet thoroughly; soak: *A sudden, heavy rain drenched us.* ❑ *V.* **drenched, drench·ing.**

drift·wood (drift′wüd′), *N.* wood carried along by water or washed ashore from the water.

du·o (dü′ō), *N.* pair.

Ee

e·co·nom·ic (ek′ə nom′ik), *ADJ.* of or about the management of the income, supplies, and expenses of a household, government, etc.

eer·ie (ir′ē), *ADJ.* causing fear because of strangeness or weirdness: *a dark and eerie old house.*

el·bow (el′bō), **1.** *N.* joint between the upper and lower arm. **2.** *V.* to push with the elbow; make your way by pushing: *Don't elbow me off the sidewalk.* ❑ *V.* **el·bow·ed, el·bow·ing.**

e·merge (i mėrj′), *V.* to come into view; come out; come up: *The sun emerged from behind a cloud.* ❑ *V.* **e·merged, e·mer·ging.**

em·phat·i·cal·ly (em phat′i cal lē), *ADV.* said or done forcefully; strongly.

en·a·ble (en ā′bəl), *V.* to give ability, power, or means to; make able: *The airplane enables people to travel great distances rapidly.* ❑ *V.* **en·abled, en·a·bling.**

en·case (en kās′), *V.* to cover completely; enclose: *A cocoon encased the caterpillar.* ❑ *V.* **en·cases, en·cased, en·cas·ing.**

en·thu·si·as·tic (en thü′zē as′tik), *ADJ.* full of enthusiasm; eagerly interested: *My little brother is very enthusiastic about going to kindergarten.*

en·vi·ron·ment (en vī′rən ment), *N.* condition of the air, water, soil, etc.: *working for a pollution-free environment.*

en·vy (en′vē), *N.* feeling of discontent, dislike, or desire because another person has what you want: *The children were filled with envy when they saw her new bicycle.*

ep·i·sode (ep′ə sōd), *N.* one part of a story that is published or broadcast in several parts, one at a time.

er·a (ir′ə), *N.* a period of time or history: *We live in the era of space exploration.*

e·rect (i rekt′), *V.* to put up; build: *That house was erected 40 years ago.* ❑ *V.* **e·rec·ted, e·rec·ting.**

es·sen·tial (ə sen′shəl), *ADJ.* absolutely necessary; very important: *Good food and enough rest are essential to good health.*

ex·pand (ek spand′), *V.* to make or grow larger; increase in size; enlarge: *The balloon expanded as it was filled with air.* ❑ *V.* **ex·pan·ded, ex·pan·ding.**

ex·plo·sion (ek splō′zhən), *N.* act of bursting with a loud noise; a blowing up: *The explosions of the bombs shook the whole city.*

a in hat	ò in open	sh in she
ā in age	ô in all	th in thin
â in care	ô in order	℡ in then
ä in far	oi in oil	zh in measure
e in let	ou in out	ə = a in about
ē in equal	u in cup	ə = e in taken
ėr in term	ù in put	ə = i in pencil
i in it	ü in rule	ə = o in lemon
ī in ice	ch in child	ə = u in circus
o in hot	ng in long	

781

---

exquisite·greenhorn

ex·qui·site (ek′skwi zit, ek skwiz′it), *ADJ.* very lovely; delicate: *These violets are exquisite.*

ex·tinct (ek stingkt′), *ADJ.* no longer existing.

ex·tra·ter·res·tri·al (ek′strə tə res′trē al), *N.* a creature from outer space.

an exquisite pattern

Ff

fash·ion (fash′ən), *V.* to make, shape, or form: *He fashioned a whistle out of wood.* ❑ *V.* **fash·ioned, fash·ion·ing.**

fast·ball (fast′bol′), *N.* a pitch thrown at high speed with very little curve.

fate (fāt), *N.* what becomes of someone or something: *The Revolutionary War decided the fate of the United States.*

fear·less (fir′lis), *ADJ.* without fear; afraid of nothing; brave; daring.

fidg·et·y (fij′ə tē), *ADJ.* restless; uneasy: *That fidgety child keeps twisting and moving.*

flee (flē), *V.* to run away; get away by running: *The robbers were fleeing, but the police caught them.* ❑ *V.* **fled, flee·ing.**

fo·cus (fō′kəs), **1.** *N.* the correct adjustment of a lens, the eye, etc., to make a clear image: *If the camera is not brought into focus, the photograph will be blurred.* **2.** *N.* the central point of attraction, attention, activity, etc.: *The new baby was the focus of attention.*

foot·man (fút′mən), *N.* a uniformed male servant who answers the bell, waits on the table, goes with a car or carriage to open the door, etc. ❑ *N. PL.* **foot·men.**

for·get·ful (fər get′fəl), *ADJ.* apt to forget; having a poor memory: *When I get too tired, I become forgetful.*

foun·da·tion (foun dā′shən), *N.* part on which the other parts rest for support; base: *the foundation of a house.* ❑ *N. PL.* **foundations.**

Gg

gait (gāt), *N.* the kind of steps used in moving; manner of walking or running: *A gallop is one of the gaits of a horse.*

ges·ture (jes′chər), *V.* to make a movement to help express an idea or feeling. ❑ *V.* **ges·tured, ges·tur·ing.**

glim·mer (glim′ər), *N.* a faint, unsteady light.

gnaw (nó), *V.* to bite at and wear away: *A mouse has gnawed the cover of this box.* ❑ *V.* **gnawed, gnaw·ing.**

gos·pel (gos′pəl), *N.* religious music with much emotion and enthusiasm, including features of spirituals and jazz.

grat·i·tude (grat′ə tüd), *N.* kindly feeling because of a favor received; desire to do a favor in return; thankfulness. (*Gratitude* comes from the Latin word *gratia* meaning "favor.")

grav·i·ty (grav′ə tē), *N.* the natural force that causes objects to move or tend to move toward the center of the earth. Gravity causes objects to have weight.

green·horn (grēn′hôrn′), *N.* person without training or experience.

782

---

grenadier·ichthyosaurus

gren·a·dier (gren′ə dir′), *N.* a member of a specially chosen unit of foot soldiers. ❑ *N. PL.* **gren·a·diers.**

guar·an·tee (gar′ən tē′), *V.* to make certain that something will happen as a result: *Not studying for a test is a guaranteed way to make a poor grade.* ❑ *V.* **guar·an·teed, guar·an·tee·ing.**

gym·nas·tics (jim nas′tiks), *N.* a sport in which very difficult exercises are performed.

girl doing gymnastics

Hh

ham·mock (ham′ək), *N.* a hanging bed or couch made of canvas, cord, etc. It has cords or ropes at each end for hanging it between two trees or posts. ❑ *N. PL.* **ham·mocks.**

hand·i·capped (han′dē kapt′), *ADJ.* having a physical or mental disability.

Ha·nuk·kah (hä′nə kə), *N.* a yearly Jewish festival that lasts eight days, mostly in December. It celebrates the rededication of the temple in Jerusalem after a victory over the Syrians in 165 B.C. Candles are lighted on each of the eight days of Hanukkah.

head·land (hed′land), *N.* narrow ridge of high land jutting out into water; promontory.

hes·i·ta·tion (hez′ə tā′shən), *N.* act of failing to act promptly; doubt; indecision.

hid·e·ous (hid′ē əs), *ADJ.* very ugly; frightful; horrible: *a hideous monster.*

hu·mane (hyü mān′), *ADJ.* not cruel or brutal; kind; merciful: *We believe in the humane treatment of animals.*

hus·tle (hus′əl), **1.** *V.* to push or shove roughly or hurriedly; jostle rudely: *Guards hustled the demonstrators away from the mayor's office.* **2.** *V.* to hurry along: *He had to hustle to get the lawn mowed before dinner.* **3.** *V.* INFORMAL. get or sell in a hurried or illegal way. ❑ *V.* **hus·tled, hus·tling.**

hy·dro·gen (hī′drə jən), *N.* a colorless, odorless gas that burns easily. Hydrogen is a chemical element that weighs less than any other element. It combines with oxygen to form water and is present in most organic compounds.

Ii

ich·thy·o·sau·rus (ik′thē ə sôr′əs), *N.* large, fishlike reptile, now extinct, that lived in the sea. It had a long beak, paddlelike flippers, and a tail with a large fin.

a in hat	ò in open	sh in she
ā in age	ô in all	th in thin
â in care	ô in order	℡ in then
ä in far	oi in oil	zh in measure
e in let	ou in out	ə = a in about
ē in equal	u in cup	ə = e in taken
ėr in term	ù in put	ə = i in pencil
i in it	ü in rule	ə = o in lemon
ī in ice	ch in child	ə = u in circus
o in hot	ng in long	

783

Glossary **509b**

Glossary

im·mi·grant (im′ə grənt), *N.* someone who comes into a country or region to live there: *Canada has many immigrants from Europe.* □ *N. PL.* **im·mi·grants.**

in·con·ceiv·a·ble (in′kən sē′və bəl), *ADJ.* hard to imagine or believe; incredible: *It is inconceivable that two nations so friendly for centuries should now be at odds.*

in·con·ven·ience (in′kən vē′nyəns), *N.* something inconvenient; cause of trouble, difficulty, or bother.

in·de·pend·ence (in′di pen′dəns), *N.* freedom from the control, influence, support, or help of others: *The American colonies won independence from England.*

in·no·va·tion (in′ə vā′shən), *N.* change made in the established way of doing things: *The principal made many innovations.* □ *N. PL.* **in·no·va·tions.**

in·spire (in spīr′), *V.* to fill with a thought or feeling; influence: *A chance to try again inspired her with hope.* □ *V.* **in·spired, in·spir·ing.**

in·tact (in takt′), *ADJ.* with nothing missing or broken; whole; untouched; uninjured: *The missing money was found and returned to the bank intact.*

in·ter·i·or (in tir′ē ər), *N.* inner surface or part; inside: *The interior of the house was beautifully decorated.*

theater **interior**

in·ter·sec·tion (in′tər sek′shən), *N.* point, line, or place where one thing crosses another: *a dangerous intersection.*

in·ves·ti·ga·tion (in ves′tə gā′shən), *N.* a careful search; detailed or careful examination: *An investigation of the accident by the police put the blame on the drivers of both cars.*

i·ras·ci·ble (i ras′ə bəl), *ADJ.* easily made angry.

is·sue (ish′ü), *V.* to send out; put forth: *The government issues money and stamps.* □ **is·sued, is·su·ing.**

Jj

jam (jam), **1.** *V.* to press or squeeze tightly between two surfaces: *The ship was jammed between two rocks.* **2.** *V.* to make music with other musicians without having practiced (*SLANG*). □ *V.* **jammed, jamm·ing. 3.** *N.* preserve made by boiling fruit with sugar until thick: *strawberry jam.*

Kk

kelp (kelp), *N.* any of various large, tough, brown seaweeds.

Ll

lair (lâr), *N.* den or resting place of a wild animal.

la·ment (lə ment′), **1.** *V.* to feel or show grief for; mourn aloud for: *We lament the dead.* **2.** *V.* to say sadly, with grief: *She lamented his absence.* □ *V.* **la·ment·ed, la·ment·ing.**

land·scape (land′ skāp), *N.* **1** view of scenery on land. **2** picture showing a land scene.

life·less (līf′lis), *ADJ.* without life: *a lifeless statue.*

lime·light (līm′līt′), *N.* center of public attention and interest: *Some people are never happy unless they are in the limelight.*

lin·ger (ling′gər), *V.* to stay on; go slowly, as if unwilling to leave: *He lingers after the others leave.* □ *V.* **ling·ered, ling·er·ing.**

log·ger (lò′gər), *N.* a person whose work is cutting down and removing trees. □ *N. PL.* **log·gers.**

lul·la·by (lul′ə bī), *N.* song for singing to a child in a cradle; soft song to lull a baby to sleep.

lux·ur·y (luk′shər ē), **1.** *N.* use of the best and most costly food, clothes, houses, furniture, and amusements: *The movie star was accustomed to luxury.* **2.** *N.* something pleasant but not necessary: *Candy is a luxury.*

Mm

mag·ni·fy (mag′nə fī), *V.* to cause something to look larger than it actually is; increase the apparent size of an object: *A microscope magnifies bacteria so that they can be seen and studied.* □ *V.* **mag·ni·fied, mag·ni·fy·ing.**

match·mak·er (mach′mā′kər), *N.* person who arranges, or tries to arrange, marriages for others.

mer·can·tile (mėr′kən til), *ADJ.* of merchants or trade; commercial: *a mercantile company.*

midst (midst), *N.* in the middle of.

mi·grant (mī′grənt), *ADJ.* migrating; roving: *a migrant worker.*

min·i·a·ture (min′ē ə chùr, min′ə chər), *ADJ.* a reduced image or likeness: *miniature furniture for a dollhouse.*

mock (mok), *V.* to laugh at; make fun of: *The student was punished for mocking the kindergartner.* □ *V.* **mocked, mock·ing.**

mold¹ (mōld), *N.* a hollow shape in which anything is formed, cast, or solidified, such as the mold into which melted metal is poured to harden into shape, or the mold in which gelatin is left to stiffen.

mold² (mōld), *N.* loose or broken earth.

mon·i·tor (mon′ə tər), **1.** *N.* a television set connected to a computer. □ *N. PL.* **mon·i·tors. 2.** *V.* to listen to and check radio or television transmissions, telephone messages, etc., by using a receiver. □ *V.* **mon·i·tored, mon·i·tor·ing.**

mon·u·men·tal (mon′yə men′tl), *ADJ.* very great: *monumental ignorance.*

mu·cus (myü′kəs), *N.* a slimy substance produced in the nose and throat to moisten and protect them.

Nn

nau·se·at·ing (nò′shē ā ting), *ADJ.* sickening; causing nausea.

Na·zi (nä′tsē *or* nat′sē), *N.* member of the National Socialist Party, a fascist political party in Germany, led by Adolf Hitler. □ *N. PL.* **Nazis.**

new·com·er (nü′kum′ər), *N.* person who has just come or who came not long ago.

news·reel (nüz′rēl′), *N.* a short news story for a movie audience. □ *N. PL.* **news·reels.**

night·time (nīt′tīm′), *N.* time between evening and morning.

nu·tri·tious (nü trish′əs), *ADJ.* valuable as food; nourishing.

a in hat	ò in open	sh in she
ā in age	ò in all	th in thin
â in care	ô in order	ᴛʜ in then
ä in far	oi in oil	zh in measure
e in let	ou in out	ə = a in about
ē in equal	u in cup	ə = e in taken
ėr in term	ù in put	ə = i in pencil
i in it	ü in rule	ə = o in lemon
ī in ice	ch in child	ə = u in circus
o in hot	ng in long	

Oo

oc·ca·sion (ə kā′zhən), *N.* a special event: *The jewels were worn only on great occasions.*

on·stage (on′stāj′), *ADV.* on the part of a stage that the audience can see: *walk onstage.*

ooze (üz), *N.* a soft mud or slime, especially at the bottom of a pond or river or on the ocean bottom.

out·field (out′fēld′), **1.** *N.* the part of a baseball field beyond the diamond or infield. **2.** *N.* the three players in the outfield.

o·ver·run (ō′vər run′), *V.* to spread over: *Vines overran the wall.* □ *V.* **o·ver·ran, o·ver·run·ning.**

Pp

par·a·pet (par′ə pet), *N.* a low wall at the edge of a balcony, roof, or bridge.

par·a·site (par′ə sīt), *N.* any living thing that lives on or in another, from which it gets its food, often harming the other in the process. Lice and tapeworms are parasites. □ *N. PL.* **par·a·sites.**

parapet

pa·vil·ion (pə vil′yən), *N.* a light building, usually somewhat open, used for shelter, pleasure, etc.: *The swimmers took shelter from the sudden storm in the beach pavilion.*

ped·dler (ped′lər), *N.* person who travels about selling things carried in a pack or in a truck, wagon, or cart.

per·mit (pər mit′), **1.** *V.* to let; allow: *My parents will not permit me to stay up late.* □ *V.* **per·mit·ted, per·mit·ting. 2.** *N.* license or written order giving permission to do something: *Do you have a permit to fish in this lake?*

phi·los·o·pher (fə los′ə fər), *N.* a person who attempts to discover and understand the basic nature of knowledge and reality. (*Philosopher* comes from a Greek word *philosophia* meaning "love of wisdom.")

pitch (pich), **1.** *V.* to throw or fling; hurl; toss: *They were pitching horseshoes.* □ *V.* **pitched, pitch·ing. 2.** *N.* thick, black, sticky substance made from tar or turpentine, used to fill the seams of wooden ships, to cover roofs, to make pavements, etc.

ple·si·o·saur·us (plē′sē ə sôr′əs), *N.* any of several large sea reptiles that lived about 200 million years ago. They had long necks and flippers instead of legs.

plesiosaurus

plunge (plunj), *V.* to fall or move suddenly downward or forward: *The sea turtle plunged into the water.* □ *V.* **plunged, plung·ing.**

pon·der (pon′dər), *V.* to consider carefully; think over: *ponder a problem.* □ *V.* **pon·dered, pon·der·ing.** (*Ponder* comes from a Latin word *pondus* meaning "weight.")

post·hu·mous·ly (pos′chə məs lē), *ADV.* happening after death: *The author was honored posthumously.*

pot·hole (pot′hōl′), *N.* a deep hole in the surface of a street or road. □ *N. PL.* **pot·holes.**

pre·cious (presh′əs), *ADJ.* having great value; worth much; valuable. Gold, platinum, and silver are often called the precious metals. Diamonds, rubies, and sapphires are precious stones.

pred·a·tor (pred′ə tər), *N.* animal or person that lives by killing and eating other animals.

pre·his·tor·ic (prē′hi stôr′ik), *ADJ.* Of or belonging to periods before recorded history: *Some prehistoric people lived in caves.*

pro·ce·dure (prə sē′jər), *N.* way of proceeding; method of doing things: *What is your procedure in making bread?* □ *N. PL.* **pro·ce·dures.**

pro·ces·sion (prə sesh′ən), *N.* something that moves forward; persons marching or riding: *The opening procession started at noon.*

pro·file (prō′fil), **1.** *N.* a side view, especially of the human face. **2.** *N.* low profile; moderate attitude or position, deliberately chosen in order to avoid notice (*IDIOMATIC*).

pro·por·tion (prə pôr′shən), *N.* a proper relation among parts: *The dog's short legs were not in proportion to its long body.*

pros·per·i·ty (pro sper′ə tē), *N.* prosperous condition; good fortune; success: *a time of peace and prosperity.*

pro·to·type (prō′tə tīp), *N.* the first or primary type of anything: *A modern ship has its prototype in the hollowed log used by primitive peoples.*

push·cart (pùsh′kärt′), *N.* a light cart pushed by hand. □ *N. PL.* **push·carts.**

Rr

ra·vine (rə vēn′), *N.* a long, deep, narrow valley eroded by running water.

realm (relm), *N.* kingdom.

re·as·sem·ble (rē′ə sem′ bəl), *V.* come or bring together again. □ *V.* **re·as·sem·bled, re·as·sem·bling.**

rec·om·mend (rek′ə mend′), *V.* to speak in favor of; suggest favorably: *The teacher recommended him for the job.* □ *V.* **rec·om·men·ded, rec·om·men·ding.**

ref·u·gee (ref′yə jē′ *or* ref′yə jē′), *N.* person who flees for refuge or safety, especially to a foreign country, in time of persecution, war, or disaster: *Refugees from the war were cared for in neighboring countries.* □ *N. PL.* **refugees.**

re·lease (ri lēs′), *V.* to permit to be published, shown, sold, etc. □ *V.* **re·leased, re·leas·ing.**

re·li·gious (ri lij′əs), *ADJ.* much interested in the belief, study, and worship of God or gods; devoted to religion: *He is very religious and prays often.*

a in hat	ò in open	sh in she
ā in age	ò in all	th in thin
â in care	ô in order	ᴛʜ in then
ä in far	oi in oil	zh in measure
e in let	ou in out	ə = a in about
ē in equal	u in cup	ə = e in taken
ėr in term	ù in put	ə = i in pencil
i in it	ü in rule	ə = o in lemon
ī in ice	ch in child	ə = u in circus
o in hot	ng in long	

Ren·ais·sance (ren′ə säns′ *or* ren′ə säns), *N.* the great revival of art and learning in Europe during the 1300s, 1400s, and 1500s; the period of time when this revival occurred.

rep·re·sent·a·tive (rep′ri zen′tə tiv), *N.* person appointed or elected to act or speak for others: *She is the club's representative at the convention.* ❑ *N. PL.* **rep·re·sent·a·tives.**

re·proach·ful·ly (ri prōch′fəl lē), *ADV.* with disapproval.

rep·u·ta·tion (rep′yə tā′shən), *N.* what people think and say the character of someone or something is; character in the opinion of others; name; repute: *This store has an excellent reputation for fair dealing.*

re·source·ful (ri sôrs′fəl), *ADJ.* good at thinking of ways to do things; quick-witted: *The resourceful children mowed lawns to earn enough money to buy new bicycles.*

ri·val (rī′vəl), *N.* person who wants and tries to get the same thing as another or who tries to equal or do better than another; competitor: *The two girls were rivals for the same class office.*

ro·bo·tic (rō bot′ik), *ADJ.* of or for a machine with moving parts and sensing devices controlled by a computer: *robotic design.*

role (rōl), **1.** *N.* an actor's part in a play, movie, etc.: *She played the leading role in the school play.* **2.** *N.* role model, a person whose patterns of behavior influence someone else's actions and beliefs: *Parents are important role models for children.*

rus·tle (rus′əl), *V.* to make or cause to make a light, soft sound of things gently rubbing together: *The leaves were rustling in the breeze.* ❑ *V.* **rus·tled, rus·tling.**

Ss

sa·cred (sā′krid), **1.** *ADJ.* worthy of reverence: *the sacred memory of a dead hero.* **2.** *ADJ.* not to be violated or disregarded: *a sacred promise.* (*Sacred* comes from a Latin word *sacrare* meaning "holy.")

scarce (skârs), *ADJ.* hard to get; rare: *Water is becoming scarce.*

scin·til·late (sin′tl āt), *V.* to sparkle; flash: *Her brilliant wit scintillates.* ❑ *V.* **scin·til·lat·ed, scin·til·lat·ing.**

scoun·drel (skoun′drəl), *N.* an evil, dishonorable person; villain; rascal: *The scoundrels who set fire to the barn have been caught.*

scrawl (skrȯl), *V.* to write or draw poorly or carelessly. ❑ *V.* **scrawled, scrawl·ing.**

scraw·ny (skrȯ′nē), *ADJ.* having little flesh; lean; thin; skinny: *Turkeys have scrawny necks.*

sea ur·chins (sē′ ėr′chəns), *N.* any of numerous small, round sea animals with spiny shells.

sec·ond·hand (sek′ənd hand′), **1.** *ADJ.* not new; used already by someone else: *secondhand clothes.* **2.** *ADV.* from other than the original source; not firsthand: *The information came to us secondhand.*

sed·i·ment (sed′ə mənt), *N.* material that settles to the bottom of a liquid: *A film of sediment covered the underwater wreck.*

seed·ling (sēd′ling), *N.* a young plant grown from a seed. ❑ *N. PL.* **seed·lings.**

sem·i·pro (sem′ī prō′), *N.* a part-time professional athlete.

ser·pent (sėr′pənt), *N.* snake, especially a big snake.

se·vere (sə vir′), *ADJ.* serious; grave: *a severe illness.*

shell·fish (shel′fish′), *N.* a water animal with a shell. Oysters, clams, crabs, and lobsters are shellfish.

shut·down (shut′doun′), **1.** *N.* act of closing of a factory, or the like, for a time: *The factory had a partial shutdown last week to fix some faulty equipment.* **2.** *N.* a stopping; a checking of (INFORMAL): *His reply was a real shutdown to her negative comment.*

side·track (sīd′trak′), *V.* to draw someone's attention away from something: *Don't sidetrack me with pointless questions.* ❑ *V.* **side·tracked, side·track·ing.**

sin·ew (sin′yü), *N.* tendon.

sketch (skech), *V.* to draw roughly and quickly. ❑ *V.* **sketched, sketch·ing.**

skid (skid), *V.* to slip or slide sideways while moving: *The car skidded on the slippery road.* ❑ *V.* **skid·ded, skid·ding.**

slav·er·y (slā′vər ē), *N.* the condition of being owned by another person and being made to work without wages.

sol·i·tar·y (sol′ə ter′ē), *ADJ.* without companions; away from people; lonely.

som·ber (som′bər), **1.** *ADJ.* having deep shadows; dark; gloomy: *A cloudy winter day is somber.* **2.** *ADJ.* sad; gloomy; dismal: *His losses made him somber.*

a **somber** picture (def. 2)

som·er·sault (sum′ər sȯlt), *V.* to run or jump, turning the heels over the head. ❑ *V.* **som·er·saul·ted, som·er·saul·ting.**

so·nar (sō′när), *N.* device for finding the depth of water or for detecting and locating underwater objects. Sonar sends sound waves into water, and they are reflected back when they strike the bottom or any object.

So·vi·et (sō′vē et), *N.* a person belonging to or fighting for the former Soviet Union. ❑ *N. PL.* **So·vi·ets.**

spe·cial·ize (spesh′ə līz), *V.* to develop in a special way: *Animals and plants are specialized to fit their surroundings.* ❑ *V.* **spe·cial·ized, spe·cial·iz·ing.**

spe·cif·ic (spi sif′ik), *ADJ.* definite; precise; particular: *There was no specific reason for the party.*

spec·ta·cles (spek′tə kəlz), *N. PL.* eyeglasses. (*Spectacles* comes from a Latin word *spectare* meaning "to watch.")

spec·tac·u·lar (spek tak′ yə lər), *ADJ.* making a great display or show; very striking or imposing to the eye: *a spectacular storm.*

spin·dly (spind′lē), *ADJ.* very long and slender; too tall and thin: *a spindly plant.*

spir·i·tu·al (spir′ə chü əl), *N.* a religious song which originated among African Americans of the southern United States. ❑ *N. PL.* **spir·i·tu·als.**

a	in hat	ō	in open	sh	in she
ā	in age	ȯ	in all	th	in thin
â	in care	ô	in order	ᴛʜ	in then
ä	in far	oi	in oil	zh	in measure
e	in let	ou	in out	ə	= a in about
ē	in equal	u	in cup	ə	= e in taken
ėr	in term	ů	in put	ə	= i in pencil
i	in it	ü	in rule	ə	= o in lemon
ī	in ice	ch	in child	ə	= u in circus
o	in hot	ng	in long		

spoon·ful (spün′fůl), *N.* as much as a spoon can hold.

star·va·tion (stär vā′shən), *N.* suffering from extreme hunger; being starved: *Starvation caused his death.*

stealth·y (stel′thē), *ADJ.* done in a secret manner; secret; sly: *The cat crept in a stealthy way toward the bird.*

steed (stēd), *N.* horse, especially a riding horse.

ster·ile (ster′əl), *ADJ.* free from germs: *Bandages should always be kept sterile.*

stern·ly (stėrn′ lē), *ADV.* strictly; firmly: *The teacher frowned sternly.*

strat·e·gy (strat′ə jē), *N.* the skillful planning and management of anything.

strict (strict), *ADJ.* very careful in following a rule or in making others follow it: *The teacher was strict but fair.*

stroke (strōk), *N.* a sudden attack of illness, especially one caused by a blood clot or bleeding in the brain; apoplexy.

sub·ject (sub′jikt), **1.** *N.* something that is thought about, discussed, investigated, etc.; topic: *The subject for our composition was "An Exciting Moment."* **2.** *N.* person under the power, control, or influence of another: *subjects of the king.*

su·per·i·or (sə pir′ē ər), *N.* person who is higher in rank, position, or ability: *A captain is a lieutenant's superior.* ❑ *N. PL.* **su·per·i·ors.**

sus·pend·ers (sə spen′dərz), *N. PL.* straps worn over the shoulders to hold up the trousers.

sus·pi·cion (sə spish′ən), *N.* belief; feeling; thought: *I have a suspicion that the weather will be very hot today.* ❑ *N. PL.* **sus·pi·cions.**

Tt

tape·worm (tāp′wėrm′), *N.* any of the numerous long, flat worms that live during their adult stage as parasites in the intestines of human beings and other animals. ❑ *N. PL.* **tape·worms.**

teen·ag·er (tēn′ā′jər), *N.* person in his or her teens.

ther·a·pist (ther′ə pist), *N.* person who specializes in the treatment of diseases, injuries, or disorders.

thieve (thēv), *V.* to steal. ❑ *V.* **thieved, thiev·ing.**

throb (throb), *V.* to beat rapidly or strongly: *My injured foot throbbed.* ❑ *V.* **throb·bed, throb·bing.**

ti·dy (tī′dē), *V.* to put in order; make neat: *I tidied the room.* ❑ *V.* **ti·died, ti·dy·ing.**

to·ga (tō′gə), *N.* a loose, outer garment worn in public. ❑ *N. PL.* **to·gas.**

tra·di·tion (trə dish′ən), *N.* custom or belief handed down from generation to generation: *According to tradition, Betsy Ross made the first American flag.* ❑ *N. PL.* **tra·di·tions.**

trans·at·lan·tic (tran′sət lan′tik), *ADJ.* crossing the Atlantic: *a transatlantic liner.*

tum·ble·down (tum′bəl doun′), *ADJ.* ready to fall down; not in good condition; dilapidated: *a tumbledown shack in the mountains.*

tun·dra (tun′drə), *N.* a vast, level, treeless plain in the arctic regions. The ground beneath its surface is frozen even in summer.

tweez·ers (twē′zərz), *N.* small pincers for pulling out hairs, picking up small objects, etc.

Uu

u·nique (yü nēk′), *ADJ.* having no like or equal; being the only one of its kind: *a unique specimen of rock, a unique experience.*

un·screw (un skrü′), *V.* to loosen or take off by turning: *Can you help me unscrew this tight lid?* ❑ *V.* **un·screwed, un·screw·ing.**

Vv

va·cant (vā′kənt), *ADJ.* not occupied: *a vacant chair, a vacant house.*

var·mint (vär′mənt), *N.* an objectionable animal or person (*DIALECT*).

vein (vān), *N.* **1.** membranous tubes forming part of the system of vessels that carry blood to the heart. **2.** a small natural channel within the earth through which water trickles or flows. ❑ *N. PL.* **veins.**

vi·bra·phone (vī′brə fōn), *N.* musical instrument similar to the xylophone, with metal bars and artificially increased vibration; vibraharp.

view·port (vyü′pôrt), *N.* small window in a small vessel, such as a space capsule or mini-submarine.

vi·sa (vē′zə), *N.* an official signature or endorsement upon a passport, showing that it has been examined and approved. A visa is granted by the consul or other representative of the country to which a person wishes to travel.

Ww

wai·tress (wā′tris), *N.* woman who serves or brings food to people in a restaurant.

weak·ness (wēk′nis), *N.* a weak point; slight fault: *Putting things off is her weakness.*

weight·less·ness (wāt′lis nis), *N.* the condition of being free from the pull of gravity: *weightless travelers in space.*

wheel·chair (wēl′châr′), *N.* chair on wheels, used especially by people who are sick or unable to walk. It can be moved by the person who is sitting in the chair.

wince (wins), *V.* to draw back suddenly; flinch slightly: *I winced when the dentist's drill touched my tooth.* ❑ *V.* **winced, winc·ing.**

wind·up (wīnd′up′), *N.* (in baseball), a swinging movement of the arms while twisting the body just before pitching the ball.

with·er (wiᴛʜ′ər), *V.* to lose or cause to lose freshness; make or become dry and lifeless; dry up; fade; shrivel: *Age had withered the old woman's face.* ❑ *V.* **with·ered, with·er·ing.**

work·shop (wėrk′shop′), *N.* space or building where work is done.

wor·ship (wėr′ship), *V.* to pay great honor and reverence to: *to worship God.* ❑ *V.* **wor·shipped, wor·ship·ping.**

worth·less (wėrth′lis), *ADJ.* without value; good-for-nothing; useless: *Throw those worthless, broken toys away.*

a	in hat	ō	in open	sh	in she
ā	in age	ȯ	in all	th	in thin
â	in care	ô	in order	ᴛʜ	in then
ä	in far	oi	in oil	zh	in measure
e	in let	ou	in out	ə	= a in about
ē	in equal	u	in cup	ə	= e in taken
ėr	in term	ů	in put	ə	= i in pencil
i	in it	ü	in rule	ə	= o in lemon
ī	in ice	ch	in child	ə	= u in circus
o	in hot	ng	in long		

English/Spanish Selection Vocabulary List

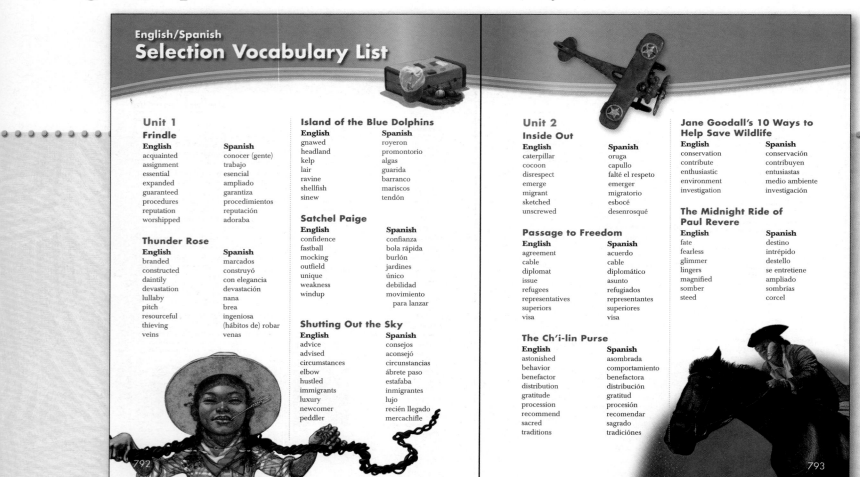

English/Spanish Selection Vocabulary List

Unit 1

Frindle

English	Spanish
acquainted	conocer (gente)
assignment	trabajo
essential	esencial
expanded	ampliado
guaranteed	garantiza
procedures	procedimientos
reputation	reputación
worshipped	adoraba

Thunder Rose

English	Spanish
branded	marcados
constructed	construyó
daintily	con elegancia
devastation	devastación
lullaby	nana
pitch	brea
resourceful	ingeniosa
thieving	(hábitos de) robar
veins	venas

Island of the Blue Dolphins

English	Spanish
gnawed	royeron
headland	promontorio
kelp	algas
lair	guarida
ravine	barranco
shellfish	mariscos
sinew	tendón

Satchel Paige

English	Spanish
confidence	confianza
fastball	bola rápida
mocking	burlón
outfield	jardines
unique	único
weakness	debilidad
windup	movimiento para lanzar

Shutting Out the Sky

English	Spanish
advice	consejos
advised	aconsejó
circumstances	circunstancias
elbow	ábrete paso
hustled	estafaba
immigrants	inmigrantes
luxury	lujo
newcomer	recién llegado
peddler	mercachifle

Unit 2

Inside Out

English	Spanish
caterpillar	oruga
cocoon	capullo
disrespect	falté el respeto
emerge	emerger
migrant	migratorio
sketched	esbocé
unscrewed	desenrosqué

Passage to Freedom

English	Spanish
agreement	acuerdo
cable	cable
diplomat	diplomático
issue	asunto
refugees	refugiados
representatives	representantes
superiors	superiores
visa	visa

The Ch'i-lin Purse

English	Spanish
astonished	asombrada
behavior	comportamiento
benefactor	benefactora
distribution	distribución
gratitude	gratitud
procession	procesión
recommend	recomendar
sacred	sagrado
traditions	tradiciónes

Jane Goodall's 10 Ways to Help Save Wildlife

English	Spanish
conservation	conservación
contribute	contribuyen
enthusiastic	entusiastas
environment	medio ambiente
investigation	investigación

The Midnight Ride of Paul Revere

English	Spanish
fate	destino
fearless	intrépido
glimmer	destello
lingers	se entretiene
magnified	ampliado
somber	sombrías
steed	corcel

792

793

Unit 3

Wings for the King

English	Spanish
admiringly	con admiración
permit	permítame
scoundrel	canalla
subject	súbdita
worthless	inútiles

Leonardo's Horse

English	Spanish
achieved	logrado
architect	arquitecto
bronze	bronce
cannon	cañón
depressed	deprimido
fashioned	elaboró
midst	(en) medio (de)
philosopher	filósofo
rival	rival

The Dinosaurs of Waterhouse Hawkins

English	Spanish
erected	erigió
foundations	cimientos
mold	molde
occasion	ocasión
proportion	proporción
tidied	ordenó
workshop	taller

Mahalia Jackson

English	Spanish
appreciate	apreciar
barber	barbero
choir	coro
released	se publicó
religious	religiosa
slavery	esclavitud
teenager	adolescente

Special Effects in Film and Television

English	Spanish
background	fondo
landscape	paisaje
miniature	miniatura
prehistoric	prehistórico
reassembled	reensamblados

Unit 4

Weslandia

English	Spanish
blunders	tropezones
civilization	civilización
complex	complejo
envy	envidia
fleeing	huir
inspired	inspiró
rustling	susurrando
strategy	estrategia

Stretching Ourselves: Kids with Cerebral Palsy

English	Spanish
abdomen	abdomen
artificial	artificial
gait	manera de caminar
handicapped	discapacitado
therapist	terapeuta
wheelchair	silla de ruedas

Exploding Ants: Amazing Facts About How Animals Adapt

English	Spanish
critical	críticos
enables	permite
mucus	mucus
scarce	escaso
specialize	se especializan
sterile	estériles

The Stormi Giovanni Club

English	Spanish
cavities	caries
combination	combinación
demonstrates	demuestra
episode	episodio
profile	(mantenerse en) segundo plano
strict	estricto

The Gymnast

English	Spanish
bluish	azulados
cartwheels	volteretas laterales
gymnastics	gimnástica
hesitation	duda
limelight	centro de atención
skidded	patinó
somersault	dar saltos mortales
throbbing	latía
wincing	haciendo una mueca de dolor

794

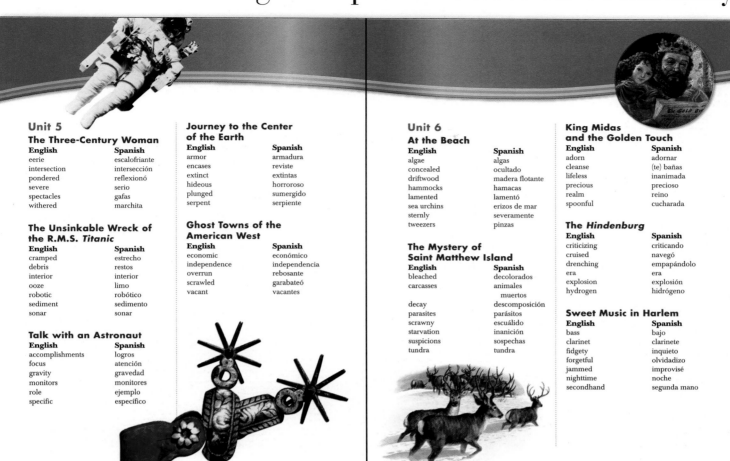

Unit 5

The Three-Century Woman

English	Spanish
eerie	escalofriante
intersection	intersección
pondered	reflexionó
severe	serio
spectacles	gafas
withered	marchita

The Unsinkable Wreck of the R.M.S. *Titanic*

English	Spanish
cramped	estrecho
debris	restos
interior	interior
ooze	limo
robotic	robótico
sediment	sedimento
sonar	sonar

Talk with an Astronaut

English	Spanish
accomplishments	logros
focus	atención
gravity	gravedad
monitors	monitores
role	ejemplo
specific	específico

Journey to the Center of the Earth

English	Spanish
armor	armadura
encases	reviste
extinct	extintas
hideous	horroroso
plunged	sumergido
serpent	serpiente

Ghost Towns of the American West

English	Spanish
economic	económico
independence	independencia
overrun	rebosante
scrawled	garabateó
vacant	vacantes

Unit 6

At the Beach

English	Spanish
algae	algas
concealed	ocultado
driftwood	madera flotante
hammocks	hamacas
lamented	lamentó
sea urchins	erizos de mar
sternly	severamente
tweezers	pinzas

The Mystery of Saint Matthew Island

English	Spanish
bleached	decolorados
carcasses	animales muertos
decay	descomposición
parasites	parásitos
scrawny	escuálido
starvation	inanición
suspicions	sospechas
tundra	tundra

King Midas and the Golden Touch

English	Spanish
adorn	adornar
cleanse	(te) bañas
lifeless	inanimada
precious	precioso
realm	reino
spoonful	cucharada

The *Hindenburg*

English	Spanish
criticizing	criticando
cruised	navegó
drenching	empapándolo
era	era
explosion	explosión
hydrogen	hidrógeno

Sweet Music in Harlem

English	Spanish
bass	bajo
clarinet	clarinete
fidgety	inquieto
forgetful	olvidadizo
jammed	improvisé
nighttime	noche
secondhand	segunda mano

796

797

Acknowledgments

Acknowledgments

Text

22: From *Frindle* by Andrew Clements. Text ©1996 by Andrew Clements. Reprinted by permission of Simon & Schuster Books for Young Readers, an imprint of Simon & Schuster Children's Publishing Division; **36:** *Punctuation Takes a Vacation* by Robin Pulver. Text ©2003 by Robin Pulver. All rights reserved. Reprinted by permission of Holiday House, Inc.; **46:** *Thunder Rose*, text ©2003 by Jerdine Nolen. Illustrations ©2003 by Kadir Nelson. Reprinted by permission of Harcourt, Inc.; **66:** "Measuring Tornadoes" from *Storm Chasers* by Trudi Strain Trueit. ©2002 Franklin Watts, a Division of Scholastic, Inc. Used by permission of Scholastic Library Publishing; **72:** From *Island of the Blue Dolphins*. ©1960, renewed 1988 by Scott O'Dell. Reprinted by permission of Houghton Mifflin Company. All rights reserved; **86:** "7 Survival Questions," by Buck Tilton. Used with permission of Buck Tilton and *Boys' Life*, April 2001. Published by the Boy Scouts of America; **94:** From *Satchel Paige* by Lesa Cline-Ransome, paintings by James E. Ransome. Text ©2000 Lesa Cline-Ransome. Illustrations ©2000 James E. Ransome. Reprinted with the permission of Simon & Schuster Books for Young Readers, an imprint of Simon & Schuster Children's Publishing Division; **110:** From "The Girls of Summer" by Ellen Klages. Adapted with permission, © Exploratorium, www.exploratorium.edu. Used by permission; **116:** From *Shutting Out the Sky* by Deborah Hopkinson. Published by Orchard Books, a division of Scholastic Inc. ©2003 by Deborah Hopkinson. Reprinted by permission of Scholastic Inc.; **130:** "The Immigrant Experience" from *Tenement Tid-Bits*, e-mail newsletter of The Lower East Side Tenement Museum, November 2003. Reprinted by permission of The Lower East Side Tenement Museum at www.tenement.org/immigrantexperience; **134:** "The Microscope" by Maxine W. Kumin. ©1968 by Maxine W. Kumin. Used by permission of The Anderson Literary Agency Inc; **136:** "Full Day" from *Come With Me: Poems For A Journey* by Naomi Shihab Nye. Text ©2000 by Naomi Shihab Nye, Greenwillow Books. Used by permission of HarperCollins Publishers; **146:** From "Inside Out," from *The Circuit* by Francisco Jiménez. ©1997 by Francisco Jiménez. Reprinted by permission of the University of New Mexico Press; **160:** "Random Acts of Kindness" from the Random Acts of Kindness Web site. Reprinted by permission of The Random Acts of Kindness Foundation at www.actsofkindness.org; **166:** *Passage to Freedom: The Sugihara Story*. Text ©1997 by Ken Mochizuki. Illustrations ©1997 by Dom Lee. Afterword ©1997 by Hiroki Sugihara. Permission arranged with Lee & Low Books Inc., New York, NY 10016; **180:** From "I Wanted My Mother," from *Hiding to Survive: Stories of Jewish Children Rescued from the Holocaust*. ©1994 by Maxine B. Rosenberg. Reprinted by permission of Clarion Books/Houghton Mifflin Company. All rights reserved; **190:** "The Ch'i-lin Purse" from *The Ch'i-lin Purse* by Linda Fang. ©1963 by Linda Fang. Reprinted by permission of Farrar, Straus & Giroux, LLC; **206:** "Lion and the Mouse" from *The Fables of Aesop* retold by Ruth Spriggs. ©1975 by Eurobook Limited, Oxfordshire, England. Used by permission; **212:** "Jane Goodall's 10 Ways to Help Save Wildlife," from *National Geographic KIDS*, April 2003. ©2003 National Geographic Society. Reprinted by permission; **226:** "Why Some Animals Are Considered 'Bad' or 'Scary'" from SanDiegoZoo.org. Used by permission of the Zoological Society of San Diego; **234:** Illustrations from *The Midnight Ride of Paul Revere* by Henry Wadsworth Longfellow, graved and painted by Christopher Bing, ©2001 Christopher Bing. Reproduced with permission of the publisher, Handprint Books, Inc.; **250:** "Deborah Sampson" by Michael Zullo from www2.1hric.org. Used by permission of Michael Zullo; **254:** "For Peace Sake" by Cedric McClester ©1990 by Cedric McClester. Used by permission of the author; **256:** "Two People I Want to Be Like" from *If Only I Could Tell You* by Eve Merriam. ©1983 Eve Merriam. Used by permission of Marian Reiner; **257:** "Strangers" from *Good Luck Gold and Other Poems* by Janet S. Wong. ©1994 by Janet S. Wong. Reprinted with the permission of Margaret K. McElderry Books, an imprint of Simon & Schuster Children's Publishing Division. All rights reserved; **266:** From *Wings for the King* by Anne Sroda from *Plays*, November 2000, Vol. 60, No.2. Reproduced with permission of Sterling Partners, Inc./PLAYS, P. O. Box 600160, Newton, MA 02460; **282:** "Becky Schroeder: Enlightened Thinker" from *Brainstorm! The Stories of Twenty American Kid Inventors* by Tom Tucker, illustrated by Richard Loehle. ©1996 by Tom Tucker. Reprinted by permission of Farrar, Straus & Giroux, LLC; **292:** *Leonardo's Horse* by Jean Fritz and illustrated by Hudson Talbott. Text ©Jean Fritz, 2001. Illustrations ©Hudson Talbott, 2001. Published by arrangement with G. P. Putnam's Sons, a division of Penguin Young Readers Group, a member of Penguin Group (USA) Inc. All rights reserved; **312:** "Humans with Wings," from *HumanPower* by Roger Yepsen. ©1992 Roger Yepsen. Reprinted with the permission of Simon & Schuster Books for Young Readers, an imprint of Simon & Schuster Children's Publishing Division; **320:** From *The Dinosaurs of Waterhouse Hawkins* by Barbara Kerley Kelly. Text ©2001 by Barbara Kerley Kelly. Illustrations ©2001 by Brian Selznick. Reprinted by permission of Scholastic, Inc; **340:** "A Model Scientist" adapted from *OWL Magazine*, Oct. 2002. Used by permission of Bayard Canada Inc.; **350:** "Mahalia Jackson" from *The Blues Singers* by Julius Lester. ©2001 Julius Lester. Illustrated by Lisa Cohen. Reprinted by permission of Hyperion Books for Children; **360:** From *Perfect Harmony* by Charles Smith. ©2002 Charles Smith. Reprinted by permission of Hyperion Books For Children; **368:** From *Special Effects in Film and Television* by Jake Hamilton. ©1998 Dorling Kindersley. Reprinted by permission; **380:** Adaptation of "A Trick of the Eye" by Brian Sibley from http://ww.bfi.org.uk. Used by permission of Sheil Land Associates Ltd.; **384:** "Chemistry 101" from *Carver: A Life In Poems* by Marilyn Nelson. ©2001 by Marilyn Nelson. Used by permission of Front Street, a division of Boyds Mill Press, Inc; **385:** "The Bronze Horse" by Beverly McLoughland, *Cricket*, November 1990. Used by permission of the author; **386:** "The Termites" from *Insectlopedia*, ©1998 by Douglas Florian, reprinted by permission of Harcourt, Inc. This material may not be reproduced in any form or by any means without the prior written permission of the publisher; **387:** "Stairs" from *Excuse It Please* by Oliver Herford, J. B. Lippincott Company, 1929; **396:** *Weslandia* by Paul Fleischman. Text ©1999 by Paul Fleischman. Illustrations ©1999 by Kevin Hawkes. Reproduced by the publisher Candlewick Press, Inc., Cambridge, MA; **410:** "Under the Back Porch" by Virginia Hamilton. ©1992, 2004 by Virginia Hamilton. Reprinted by permission of Arnold Adoff, 750 Union St., Yellow Springs, OH 45387; **411:** "Keziah," from *Bronzeville Boys and Girls* by Gwendolyn Brooks. ©1956 by Gwendolyn Brooks Blakely. Used by permission of HarperCollins Publishers; **416:** From *Stretching Ourselves* by Alden R. Carter, Photographs by Carol S. Carter. ©2000 Alden R. Carter. Reprinted by permission of John Hawkins & Associates, Inc.; **434:** "Helpful Tools" from *Do You Remember the Color Blue?* by Sally Hobart Alexander, ©2000 by Sally Hobart Alexander. Used by permission of Viking Children's Books, A Division of Penguin Young Readers Group, A Member of Penguin Group (USA) Inc., 345 Hudson Street, New York, NY 10014, the Author and BookStop Literary Agency. All rights reserved; **440:** From *Exploding Ants* by Joanne Settel, Ph.D. Text ©1999 by Joanne Settel. Reprinted with the permission of Atheneum Books for Young Readers, an imprint of Simon & Schuster Children's Publishing Division; **480:** "Think Dress Codes Are a Drag?" by Emilie Ostrander from the *Chicago Tribune*, April 15, 2003. Copyrighted 4/15/2003, Chicago Tribune Company. All rights reserved. Used with permission; **488:** "The Gymnast" by Gary Soto from *A Summer Life* ©1990 by University Press of New England. Reprinted with permission; **501:** From "Gymnastics" from *The Columbia Electronic Encyclopedia, 6th ed.* ©2003, Columbia University Press. Used by permission; **502:** *Random House Webster's Unabridged Dictionary*. New York: Random House, 1991. **504:** "the drum" from *Spin A Soft Black Song* by Nikki Giovanni. ©1971, 1985 by Nikki Giovanni. Reprinted by permission of Hill and Wang, a division of Farrar, Straus & Giroux, LLC; **505:** "Which Lunch Table?" from *Swimming Upstream: Middle Grade Poems* by Kristine O'Connell George. Text ©2002 by Kristine O'Connell

798

George. Reprinted by permission of Clarion Books, an imprint of Houghton Mifflin Company. All rights reserved; **506:** "Desert Tortoise" from *Desert Voices* by Byrd Baylor. Text ©1981 by Byrd Baylor. Reprinted with the permission of Atheneum Books for Young Readers, an imprint of Simon & Schuster Children's Publishing Division; **507:** "Camel" by Lillian M. Fisher. All other rights reserved, ©Lillian M. Fisher 2004. Used by permission of the author, Lillian M. Fisher; **516:** "The Three-Century Woman" ©1996 by Richard Peck. First published in *Second Sight: Stories for a New Millennium*, Philomel Books. All rights reserved. Used by permission of Sheldon Fogelman Agency, Inc; **540:** "The Unsinkable Wreck of the R.M.S. Titanic" from *Ghost Liners: Exploring the World's Greatest Lost Ships* by Robert D. Ballard and Rick Archbold, illustrations by Ken Marschall. Text ©1998 by Odyssey Corporation and Ken Marschall, from *Ghost Liners*, a Little Brown Madison Press Book. Used by permission; **554:** Excerpt from *Shipwreck Season* by Donna Hill. ©1998 by Donna Hill. Reprinted by permission of Clarion Books, an imprint of Houghton Mifflin Company. All rights reserved; **564:** "Talk with an Astronaut" from "Meet Famous Latinos: Ellen Ochoa" from scholastic.com. ©2004 by Scholastic Inc. Reprinted by permission of Scholastic Inc; **578:** "Crust, Mantle, Core," from Scott Foresman *Science for Texas* by Dr. Timothy Cooney, Michael Anthony DiSpezio, et al. ©2000, Addison-Wesley Educational Publishers, Inc. All Rights Reserved; **608:** Text and Photographs from *Ghost Towns of the American West* by Raymond Bial. ©2001 by Raymond Bial. Reprinted by permission of Houghton Mifflin Company. All rights reserved; **622:** "Dame Shirley Goes to the Gold Rush" from *Journeys in Time: A New Atlas of American History* by Elspeth Leacock and Susan Buckley. Text ©2001 by Elspeth Leacock and Susan Washburn Buckley. Reprinted with permission of Houghton Mifflin Company. All rights reserved; **626:** "Your World" from *The Selected Works of Georgia Douglas Johnson*, by Georgia Douglas Johnson, G. K. Hall ©1997, G. K. Hall. Reprinted by permission of The Gale Group; **627:** "Share the Adventure" ©1993 by Patricia and Fredrick McKissack. First appeared as a National Children's Book Week Poem by The Children's Book Council, Curtis Brown, Ltd., 1993; **628:** "A Path to the Moon," *Giants, Moosequakes and Other Disasters* by bp Nichol, Black Moss Press, 1985. Used by permission of the Estate of bp Nichol; **638:** "At the Beach," from *Salsa Stories* by Lulu Delacre. ©2000 Lulu Delacre. Reprinted by permission of Scholastic, Inc; **652:** "The Eagle and the Bat" from *The Sound of Flutes and Other Indian Legends* by Richard Erdoes and illustrated by Paul Goble, ©1976 by Richard Erdoes. Illustrations ©1976 by Paul Goble. Used by permission of Random House Children's Books, a division of Random House, Inc.; **658:** "The Mystery of Saint Matthew Island" from *The Case of the Mummified Pigs and Other Mysteries in Nature,* written by Susan E. Quinlan, illustrated by Jennifer Owings Dewey. Text ©1995 by Susan E. Quinlan; Illustrations ©1995 by Jennifer Owings Dewey. Published by Caroline House, Boyds Mills Press, Inc. Reprinted by permission; **670:** "Get the Lead Out" from *The Sky's the Limit: Stories of Discovery by Women and Girls* by Catherine Thimmesh, illustrated by Melissa Sweet. Text ©2002 by Catherine Thimmesh. Illustrations ©2002 by Melissa Sweet. Reprinted by permission of Houghton Mifflin Company. All rights reserved; **678:** *King Midas and the Golden Touch* as told by Charlotte Craft, illustrated by K. Y. Craft. Text ©1999 by Charlotte Craft. Illustrations ©1999 Kinuko Y. Craft. Used by permission of HarperCollins Publishers; **698:** "Jimmy Jet and His TV Set" from *Where the Sidewalk Ends* by Shel Silverstein. ©2004 by Evil Eye Music. Used by permission of HarperCollins Publishers; **705:** Adaptation of *The Hindenburg* by Patrick O'Brien, ©2000 by Patrick O'Brien. Reprinted by permission of Henry Holt and Company, LLC; **730:** *Sweet Music in Harlem*. Text ©2004 by Debbie A. Taylor. Illustrations ©2004 by Frank Morrison. Permission arranged with Lee & Low Books, Inc., New York, NY 10016; **754:** "A Sinister Spider Named Ruth" from *Pocketful of Nonsense* by James Marshall, Golden Books, Western Publishing Company, Inc., 1992; **755:** "Sunflakes" from *Country Pie* by Frank Asch, HarperCollins Publishers, 1979; **756:** "Almost Human" from *Earth Lines: Poems for the Green Age* by Pat Moon. ©1993 by Pat Moon. Used by permission of Greenwillow Books and HarperCollins Publishers; **757:** "The Bat", from *The Collected Poems of Theodore Roethke* by Theodore Roethke. ©1938 by Theodore Roethke. Used by permission of Doubleday, a division of Random House, Inc.

Illustrations

Cover: Greg Newbold; **12, 510, 630** Steven Adler; **22-34** James Bernardin; **37-41, 161** Laura Huliska-Beith; **44-45** Jason Wolff; **46-48** Darryl Ligasan; **69-84** E. B. Lewis; **86-88, 317** Maryjo Koch; **110** Charles Pyle; **134-136** Greg Newbold; **146-158** Raul Colon; **160, 206-207** Vladimir Radunsky; **181-185** John Sandford; **190-204** Ed Young; **226-229, 263-265** John Manders; **260, 388** Melissa Sweet; **266-280, 454, 546, 794** Franklin Hammond; **282-286** Leslie Cober-Gentry; **312-315** Dahl Taylor; **317, 340-344** Phil Wilson; **410** Jui Ishida; **437-451, 795** Robert Mancini; **462-478** Gregory Christie; **480-482** Robert Wagt; **504-506, 630** Bob Dacey; **513-530** Matt Faulkner; **532-534** Janan Cain; **554-558** Francis Livingston; **586-598** Marc Sasso; **601** Matt Zang; **622, 625** Rodica Prato; **626-628** Shelly Hehenberger; **637-650** Michael Steirnagle; **652** Amanda Hall; **657-665, 797** Tom McNeely; **666** John Burgoyne; **678-696, 704-720** Patrick O'Brien; **754-756** Laura Ovresat.

Photographs

Every effort has been made to secure permission and provide appropriate credit for photographic material. The publisher deeply regrets any omission and pledges to correct errors called to its attention in subsequent editions.

Unless otherwise acknowledged, all photographs are the property of Scott Foresman, a division of Pearson Education.

Photo locators denoted as follows: **Top (T), Center (C), Bottom (B), Left (L), Right (R), Background (Bkgd).**

4 ©Sean Murphy/Getty Images; **6** ©Gary Braasch/Corbis; **10** ©Gary Braasch/Corbis; **16** ©Sean Murphy/Getty Images; **17** ©Bettmann/Corbis; **19** Getty Images; **20** ©Jutta Klee/Corbis; **21** ©Corbis; **66** International Stock Photography/Taxi/Getty Images; **67** (TL, CL) ©Jim Reed/Corbis; **91** ©Vintage Military; **92** ©Stephen Dunn/Getty Images; **93** Getty Images; **95** Legends Archive; **113** Corbis; **114** Corbis; **115** Corbis; **116** ©Bettmann/Corbis; **118** (TL, CL) Bettmann/Corbis; (TR) Prints & Photographs Division/Library of Congress, (CR) Corbis; **120** ©Bettmann/Corbis; **121** Corbis; **122** Brown Brothers; **123** (TL) Getty Images, (TR) New York Public Library/Art Resource, NY; **124** Museum of the City of New York; **125** Getty Images; **126** Photo Collection Alexander Alland, Sr./Corbis; **127** Corbis; **128** ©Tony Linck/Time Life Pictures/Getty Images; **130** Corbis; **132** Corbis; **133** ©Joseph Sohm/ChromoSohm Inc./Corbis; **138** ©Sean Murphy/Getty Images; **139** (TR) Sports Icons/©Comstock, Inc., (CR) ©Brad Yeo Collection/the i spot; **140** ©Peter Beck/Corbis; **141** ©Michael Nichols/NGS Image Collection; **143** ©Larry Dale Gordon/Getty Images; **144** ©Tony Cordoza/Getty Images; **145** (T) ©Geoff Du Feu/Getty Images, (BR) ©Stephen Dalton/NHPA Limited; **163** Corbis; **164** ©Ken Davies/Masterfile Corporation; **165** Getty Images; **168** (Bkgd) ©Anne Frank House/Getty Images, (C) Courtesy of Joseph Shadur/United States Holocaust Museum; **170** (C) Courtesy of Joseph Shadur/United States Holocaust Museum, (Bkgd) ©Anne Frank House/Getty Images; **171** Bonhams, London, UK/Bridgeman Art Library; **172** (C) Courtesy of Joseph Shadur/United States Holocaust Museum, (Bkgd) Anne Frank House/Getty Images; **174** (C) Courtesy of Joseph Shadur/United States Holocaust Museum, (Bkgd) ©Anne Frank House/Getty Images; **175** ©Jeffrey Coolidge/Getty Images; **176** (C) Courtesy of Joseph Shadur/United States Holocaust Museum, (Bkgd) ©Anne Frank House/Getty Images; **187** Illustration Works, Inc.; **188** ©2000 Kinuko Y. Craft ; **189** ©2000 Kinuko Y. Craft; **209** (BL) ©Anup Shah/Nature Picture Library,

799

(TR) ©Renee Lynn/Corbis; **210** ©Lori Adamski Peek/Getty Images/Stone; **211** (BR) Melanie Acevedo/FoodPix, (BC, CC) ©Photodisc Green/Getty Images; **212** (TC, TL) ©Roger Eritja/Alamy, (C) ©Michael Nichols/NGS Image Collection; **214** (TC) ©JH Pete Carmichael/Getty Images, (R) ©David Fleetham/Mira; **216** (BR) ©Gay Bumgarner/Stone/Getty Images, (R) ©Anup Shah/Nature Picture Library; **218** ©Ariel Skelley/Corbis; **219** (CL, CC) ©Photodisc Green/Getty Images, (BC) ©Melanie Acevedo/FoodPix; **220** (BR) ©Ken J. Howard/Sea Images, (R) ©Michael & Patricia Fogden/Corbis; **222** ©Paco Feria/Peter Arnold, Inc.; **223** ©Bob Hallinen/Anchorage Daily News; **224** ©David Fleetham/Mira; **231** (BR) ©Freelance Photography Guild/Corbis, (BR) ©Comstock Inc.; **232** ©Kevin Fleming/Corbis; **233** ©Kevin Fleming/Corbis; **240** ©Hans Neleman/Getty Images; **241** (TR, BR, BL) ©Hans Neleman/Getty Images; **250** ©Bettmann/Corbis; **252** (TR) The Granger Collection, NY, (B) Corbis; **253** ©Bettmann/Corbis; **254** ©Images/Corbis; **256** ©Images/Corbis; **258** ©Gary Braasch/Corbis; **259** (TR) ©David A. Northcott/Corbis, (CR) Getty Images, (BL) ©Gavin Wickham/Eye Ubiquitous/Corbis; **261** ©Jim Henson's Creature Shop/©DK Images; **289** ©State Museum of Georgia/AKG London Ltd.; **290** ©Marc Moritsch/NGS Image Collection; **310** ©Leonardo da Vinci's Horse, Inc.; **341** ©Kevin Kelly; **345** ©Kevin Kelly; **347** ©Andy Warhol Foundation/Corbis; **348** ©Lewis W. Hine/Getty Images; **361** The Boys Choir of Harlem, Inc.; **363** ©Charles R. Smith, Jr.; **365** ©Tom Wagner/Corbis; **366** ©Richard Cummins/Corbis; **367** ©Mitchell Gerber/Corbis; **368** ©Jim Henson's Creature Shop/©DK Images; **369** ©Millenium FX Ltd/©DK Images; **370** ©Mike Valentine (BSC)/©DK Images; **371** Millenium FX Ltd/©DK Images; **372** ©Millenium FX Ltd/©DK Images; **373** (TL) ©Millenium FX Ltd/©DK Images, (R) ©Turbo Squid, Inc.; **374-376** ©Millenium FX Ltd/©DK Images; **377** ©Paramount/Everett Collection, Inc.; **378** ©Millenium FX Ltd/©DK Images; **381** Getty Images; **382** (CL, TR) ©American Artist, (BL) ©Matthias Kulka/Corbis; **384** (TR) Getty Images, (Bkgd) ©Steve Drake/Veer, Inc.; **385** ©Stuart McClymont/Getty Images; **386** ©Walter Bibikow/Index Stock Imagery; **387** ©Pete Turner/Getty Images; **389** ©Richard T. Nowitz/Corbis; **390** (C) ©Royalty-Free/Corbis, (Bkgd) ©Stephen Frink/Corbis; **393** ©PBNJ Productions/Corbis; **413** ©Tom Stewart/Corbis; **414** ©Tom Stewart/Corbis; **415** ©Royalty-Free/Corbis; **437** ©Hans Neleman/Getty Images; **438** (TL) ©1984 Defense Mechanisms in Social Insects, Hermann. Reproduced with permission of Greenwood Publishing Group, Inc., Westport, CT., (BL, BC) ©BSIP Agency/Index Stock Imagery; **439** ©BSIP Agency/Index Stock Imagery; **442** (BL) ©Steven Hunt/Getty Images, (TR) ©Oliver Strewe/Getty Images; **443** (TL) ©Fred Bavendam/Minden Pictures, (TR) ©Bob Elsdale/Getty Images; **444** (CL) ©Tim Flach/Getty Images, (BL) ©Ant Photo Library/NHPA Limited; **445** ©Studio Carlo Dani/Animals Animals/Earth Scenes; **446** (TL) ©Tim Flach/Getty Images, (TC) ©Premaphotos/Animals Animals/Earth Scenes; **447** (TL) ©Scott Camazine, (TR) ©Mitsuaki Iwago/Minden Pictures; **448** (TL) ©Tim Flach/Getty Images, (BL) ©Art Wolfe/Getty Images, (BR) ©David Tipling/Photographer's Choice/Getty Images; **450** (CL) ©Tim Flach/Getty Images, (T) ©Joe McDonald/Corbis, (BL) ©Michael & Patricia Fogden/Minden Pictures; **451** ©Michael & Patricia Fogden/Corbis; **459-461** ©Illustration Works, Inc.; **485** ©Rubberball Productions; **487** ©Reuters/Jeff J. Mitchell/Corbis; **490** Brand X Pictures; **493** Veer, Inc.; **498** Rubberball Productions; **500** ©Don Mason/Corbis; **502** (BL) Corbis, (BC) ©Jon Feingersh/Corbis, (BR) ©Caron P./Corbis; **503** ©Dave Black/Corbis; **508** Digital Vision; **509** ©Stuart Westmorland/Corbis; **514** ©Paul Barton/Corbis; **515** ©Royalty-Free/Corbis; **537** (B, BC) Getty Images; **538** ©Ralph White/Corbis; **539-542** ©1998 from Ghost Liners/Little Brown Madison Press Books; **543** (CR) The Granger Collection, NY, (BL) ©1998 from Ghost Liners/Little Brown Madison Press Books; **543-546** ©1998 from Ghost Liners/Little Brown Madison Press Books; **546** Woods Hole Oceanographic Institution; **547** Woods Hole Oceanographic Institution; **548-550** ©1998 from Ghost Liners/Little Brown Madison Press Books; **551** (TL, TR) Woods Hole Oceanographic Institution, (Inset) Michael Freeman/Corbis; **552** ©1998 from Ghost Liners/Little Brown Madison Press Books; **562** Corbis; **563** Corbis; **564** ©World Perspectives/Getty Images; **566** Getty Images; **567** ©Mark M. Lawrence/Corbis; **569** Corbis; **570** NASA; **573** NASA; **574** Digital image ©1996 Corbis/Original image courtesy of NASA/Corbis; **576** ©Digital image ©1996 Corbis/Original image courtesy of NASA/Corbis; **578** (C) Getty Images, (CR) Corbis, (T) NASA; **579** ©Premium Stock/Corbis; **580** ©Time Life Pictures/NASA/Getty Images; **581** ©NASA/Roger Ressmeyer/Corbis; **583** ©DK Images; **585** ©Illustration Works, Inc.; **602** (TL) ©DK Images, (CL) Colin Keates/©DK Images, (TC, CC, TR, CR) Harry Taylor/©DK Images; **605** ©Bettmann/Corbis; **606** ©K.D. Swan/Corbis; **607** (T) ©Joseph Sohm/Visions of America/Corbis, (CC) ©Lester Lefkowitz/Corbis; **608** ©James Nazz/Corbis; **609** ©Chris Collins/Corbis; **610** (L) ©DK Images, (C) ©Raymond Bial; **611** ©John Cancalosi/Peter Arnold, Inc.; **612** ©Bettmann/Corbis; **613** ©Western History Department/Denver Public Library, Western History Collection; **614** (T) Museum of History & Industry/Corbis, (BL) ©Raymond Bial; **616** (BL) ©Raymond Bial, (BR) David Stoecklein/Corbis; **617** ©Raymond Bial; **619** (T) ©Lynn Radeka/SuperStock, (BR) ©Western History Department/Denver Public Library/Denver Public Library, Western History Collection; **620** ©Bettmann/Corbis; **630** NASA; **632** ©Jerry Lofaro/Courtesy of Konica Minolta Business Solutions/American Artists Represents; **633** ©Natalie Fobes/Corbis; **635** (TC) Getty Image, (BL) Brand X Pictures/Getty Images; **636** ©Pat O'Hara/Corbis; **637** ©Martin Harvey/Peter Arnold, Inc.; **655** ©Paul Chinn/San Francisco Chronicle/Corbis; **656** ©Simon Battersby/©DK Images; **658** ©Natalie Fobes/Corbis; **663** ©David Klein; **664** (TC) ©Darrell Gulin/Corbis, (TL) ©David Muench/Corbis, (CR) ©Steve Austin/Papilio/Corbis; **667** (TR) ©David Roseneau, (CL) ©David Klein/George Allez; **668** ©David Klein; 670 (CR) ©Kathleen Murray, (TR) ©Royalty-Free/Corbis; **671** ©Royalty-Free/Corbis; **672** (BL) ©Kathleen Murray, (L, TR) ©Royalty-Free/Corbis; **673** Christine M. Douglas/©DK Images; **675** (BL) ©Images/Corbis, (TR) ©Royalty-Free/Corbis; **677** Brand X Pictures; **701** ©Tim Hawkins/Eye Ubiquitous/Corbis; **702** (BL) ©Lake County Museum/Corbis, (BC) ©Bettmann/Corbis; **703** ©Bettmann/Corbis; **722** ©Owen Franken/Corbis; **724** (CR) Corbis, (B) The Granger Collection, NY; **725** (TR, C) Corbis; **727** ©Underwood & Underwood/Corbis; **728** Corbis; **729** ©Bettmann/Corbis; **752** ©Art Kane Archives; **758** (CL) ©Werner Dieterich/Getty Images, (CR) Corbis, (BL) ©Jerry Lofaro/Courtesy of Konica Minolta Business Solutions/American Artists Represents; **762** ©William Philpott/Reuters America, Inc.; **764** (C) ©Linda Fang, (T) ©Charlotte Craft; **765** (T) ©UPP/Topham/The Image Works, Inc., (B) ©Susan Quinlan; **766** ©Sarah Bial; **767** ©Milan Sabatini; **769** AP Images; **770** Lebrecht Collection; **771** ©Michael Nicholson/Corbis; **772** ©Handprint Books; **774** Courtesy, Lee & Low Books; **777** (C) Art Resource, NY, (Bkgd, Insert) SuperStock; **778** Daemmrich Photography; **779** ©Tom McHugh/Photo Researchers, Inc.; **782** Planet Art; **786** SuperStock; **789** ©1996 Grant Wood/VAGA/SuperStock; **794** ©Millenium FX Ltd/©DK Images; **796** (TL) ©Corbis/Corbis, (BR) ©David Stoecklein/Corbis.

Glossary

The contents of this glossary have been adapted from *Thorndike Barnhart Advanced Dictionary*. Copyright ©1997, Pearson Education, Inc.

777 (C) Art Resource, NY, (Bkgd) SuperStock, (Insert) SuperStock; 778 Daemmrich Photography; 779 ©Tom McHugh/Photo Researchers, Inc.; 782 Planet Art; 786 SuperStock; 789 ©1996 Grant Wood/VAGA/SuperStock

800

Writing Workshop

UNIT 4 STORY . . . . WA2—WA9

Goal: A score of 6 on a well-written story with

- well-focused, clear ideas closely related to one event
- logical organization with a clear beginning, middle, and end
- strong support through elaborated details, a distinctive voice, and time-order language
- excellent control of writing conventions, with an attention-grabbing first sentence

EVERY CHILD A 6

HERE'S HOW TO MAKE

READING FCAT PREP

READ THINK EXPLAIN

Writing Workshop

UNIT 4 TEST PREPARATION

The chart below shows how the Writing Traits taught every week of this unit can be applied to a Story. Mastery of these traits and their counterparts in the Florida Writing Elements will assure success in producing any writing product.

	Writing Trait of the Week	Florida Writing Element	Tips for applying Trait of the Week to the Unit 4 Writing Workshop
Week 1 *Weslandia*	Conventions	Conventions	As students **edit** their writing, share with them the *Editing Checklist* found on p. WA6.
Week 2 *Stretching Ourselves*	Focus/Ideas	Focus	As students work on **prewriting**, share with them *Finding a Topic* on p. WA3 to help them generate ideas for their stories.
Week 3 *Exploding Ants*	Support/Word Choice	Support	When students **publish** their writing, share with them the *Self-Evaluation* on p. WA7. Have students focus on their use of lively verbs and precise nouns.
Week 4 *The Stormi Giovanni Club*	Support/Voice	Support	As students **draft** their writing, share with them *Writer's Craft: Moods* on p. WA4. Emphasize that use of strong sensory details and descriptive language can help establish the mood or tone of their stories.
Week 5 *The Gymnast*	Support/Word Choice	Support	As students **revise** their drafts, encourage them to replace common verbs with strong, precise verbs. Share with students the *Writer's Craft: Elaboration* note on p. WA5.

FLORIDA WRITING KIT

Florida Grammar and Writing Book

Florida Writing Rubrics and Anchor Papers

Florida Writing Transparencies

Grammar and Writing Practice Book

Grammar Transparencies

Daily Fix-It Transparencies

FCAT WRITING ✚ Elements

**The elements combine to make a writing task successful.
The six-trait writing in Reading Street correlates to these elements.**

Six Traits

Focus/Ideas
The main purpose for writing and the development of ideas

Organization/Paragraphs
The overall structure of a piece of writing; the connectedness of ideas

Voice
The writer's personality that comes through in the written piece

Word Choice
The use of precise, vivid words to communicate ideas

Sentences
Fluent, skillful sentences that vary in type and length

Conventions
Grammar, usage, spelling, punctuation, and capitalization

Four Elements

- **Focus** refers to how clearly the paper presents and maintains a main idea, theme, or unifying point.
  - Papers receiving high scores maintain a consistent awareness of the topic and include no unrelated or loosely related information.

- **Organization** refers to the structure or plan of development (beginning, middle, and end) and the relationship of one point to another. Organization relies on transitional devices to signal both the relationship of the supporting ideas to the main idea, theme, or unifying point, and the connections between and among sentences.
  - Papers receiving high scores have a logical organizational pattern and use transitional devices to connect ideas.

- **Support** refers to the quality of details used to explain, clarify, or define. The quality of the support depends on word choice, specificity, depth, relevance, and thoroughness.
  - Papers receiving high scores provide elaborated examples, and the relationship between the supporting ideas and the topic is clear. Word choice is precise and vivid, and voice is engaging.

- **Conventions** refer to punctuation, capitalization, spelling, usage, and sentence structure. These conventions are basic writing skills included in Florida's Sunshine State Standards.
  - Papers receiving high scores demonstrate a good control of the conventions of punctuation, capitalization, and spelling, as well as a variety of sentence structures.

Writing Workshop

OBJECTIVES

- Develop an understanding of a story.
- Create a particular mood in your story.
- Use pronouns and antecedents correctly.
- Establish criteria for evaluating a story.

Key Features
Story

In a story, a writer spins a real or imagined tale.
- Has a beginning, middle, and end
- Uses time-order words to show the sequence of events
- Has characters, plot, setting

Connect to Weekly Writing

Week 1	E-mail 411g–411h
Week 2	Journal Entry 435g–435h
Week 3	Story About an Animal 457g–457h
Week 4	Advice 483g–483h
Week 5	Describe How You Achieved a Goal 503g–503h

Strategic Intervention
See Differentiated Instruction p. WA8.

Advanced
See Differentiated Instruction p. WA9.

ELL
See Differentiated Instruction p. WA9.

Additional Resources for Writing
- Writing Rubrics and Anchor Papers, pp. 58–69
- The Grammar and Writing Book TAE, pp. FL1–FL64

WA2 *Story*

Writing Prompt: Adapting

Adapting to a new situation might require resourcefulness. Think about a real or imagined event that shows how a resourceful person succeeds by adapting. Now write a story about how this person succeeds by adapting.

The word *story* in the prompt signals narrative writing. The purpose of such writing is usually to entertain.

READ LIKE A WRITER

Ask students to look back at *Weslandia.* Point out several passages with dialogue, or spoken words between characters. Explain that the author of a story includes dialogue to help bring the story characters to life. Characters' words can also help create mood and humor. Tell students that they will write a **story** using dialogue and other story elements to create a mood.

EXAMINE THE MODEL AND RUBRIC

GUIDED WRITING Read the model aloud. Point out that the writer grabs the reader's attention in the first sentence by asking a question. Discuss how the model reflects traits of good writing.

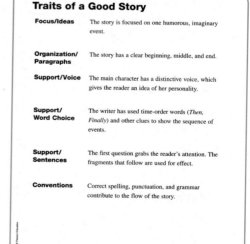

Secret Student Superhero

Was it something I ate? Something I drank? A wish upon a star? You won't believe what happened to me yesterday. I woke up with superpowers.

That's right, superpowers. Don't ask me what caused it. All I know is that I felt different as soon as I put my feet on the floor yesterday morning. Lighter. Smarter. Stronger.

I realized my powers on the playground right before the first bell. Lisa was complaining that she hadn't finished the math homework because it had been too hard. I asked to see her paper and blinked at it. Suddenly the answers were all filled in!

"Awesome! Thank you, Sara," Lisa shouted.

I handed her paper back, feeling totally confused. Then, when I got to my classroom, things turned even weirder. I had X-ray vision—but only for the teacher's edition of our textbook. I didn't participate in the class discussion because it wouldn't have been fair. I could see all the answers! Red words floated right in front of my teacher.

Finally, at lunchtime recess, my superpower secret was revealed. We played our usual basketball game, boys against the girls. I was unstoppable! Usually, I can't score a single basket. But with superpowers I was getting some serious air on my slam dunk.

That's how I learned what happens when you're a superpower showoff. You lose those superpowers. After lunch I returned to my classroom and couldn't see any answers from the teacher's edition. And we had a pop quiz!

It was fun while it lasted, but it sure didn't last long. I had been looking forward to flying home too.

Unit 4 Story • PREWRITE   Writing Process **22**

▲ **Writing Transparency** WP22

Traits of a Good Story

Focus/Ideas	The story is focused on one humorous, imaginary event.
Organization/ Paragraphs	The story has a clear beginning, middle, and end.
Support/Voice	The main character has a distinctive voice, which gives the reader an idea of her personality.
Support/ Word Choice	The writer has used time-order words (*Then, Finally*) and other clues to show the sequence of events.
Support/ Sentences	The first question grabs the reader's attention. The fragments that follow are used for effect.
Conventions	Correct spelling, punctuation, and grammar contribute to the flow of the story.

Unit 4 Story • PREWRITE   Writing Process **23**

▲ **Writing Transparency** WP23

Pages WA2–WA3

LA.5.3.1.1 Generate ideas from multiple sources
LA.5.3.1.2 Determine the purpose and intended audience
LA.5.3.1.3 Organize ideas using graphic organizers

FINDING A TOPIC

- Have students discuss times when they had to adapt to a new situation. Tell them that a real event can be the basis for a fictional story.
- Ask students to think of people they know about, such as historical figures, celebrities, or family members. Tell students that a writer may borrow characteristics from real people to create a believable fictional character.
- Share classic stories. Have students answer the following questions about a few favorites: Who is the story about? What is the problem or conflict? Tell them to consider those same questions when coming up with their own ideas.

NARROW A TOPIC Have students jot down topics and ideas.

Molly bakes a cake What is the problem or conflict?
Transferring to a new school I've never done this, so I lack information.
A boy gets lost on a bike ride I have firsthand knowledge of this.

PREWRITING STRATEGY

GUIDED WRITING Display Writing Transparency WP24. Model how to complete a story chart.

Think Aloud

MODEL This student will write a story about a boy who gets lost on a bike ride with his dad. The main character is also the narrator. The setting is a specific place: country roads. In a short story, be specific with the setting and events and keep characters to a minimum. If you think of a better solution while writing, use it.

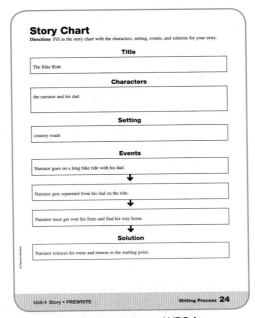

Story Chart
Directions Fill in the story chart with the characters, setting, events, and solution for your story.

Title
The Bike Ride

Characters
the narrator and his dad

Setting
country roads

Events
Narrator goes on a long bike ride with his dad.
↓
Narrator gets separated from his dad on the ride.
↓
Narrator must get over his fears and find his way home.
↓

Solution
Narrator retraces his route and returns to the starting point.

Unit 4 Story • PREWRITE   Writing Process **24**

▲ **Writing Transparency** WP24

PREWRITING ACTIVITIES

- Have students use Grammar and Writing Practice Book p. 172 to map out the characters, setting, events, and solution for their story.
- Students can brainstorm how to adapt to a new situation.

Adapting to something new

Real	**Imagined**
going to a new school	falling into an underground world winning the lottery
getting my first job	
advancing on swim team	being selected for the Olympics

During this Writing Workshop, work with students to strengthen their ability to focus, organize, and support their ideas and to use correct conventions. Use pp. FL1–FL64 in The Grammar and Writing Book TAE for exercises, models, rubrics, and strategies to help them produce a top-score piece of writing.

Monitor Progress

Differentiated Instruction

If... students have trouble deciding on a story idea,	**then...** ask them to tell you a story they've heard about a family member.

Story Chart
Directions Fill in the story chart with the characters, setting, events, and solution for your story.

Title

Characters
Answers should include details on character, setting, plot, and solution.

Setting

Events

Solution

▲ **Grammar and Writing Practice Book** p. 172

Adapting   **WA3**

Writing Workshop

1 PREWRITE · 2 DRAFT · 3 REVISE · 4 EDIT · 5 PUBLISH

Think Like a Writer

Create a Fictional World An engaging story draws the reader in by painting a picture of the setting and providing details. Sensory details show your reader what the setting looks, smells, tastes, sounds, and feels like. Include sensory details, and the reader will fully experience your fictional world.

Support Writing If students include home-language words in their drafts, help them find replacement words in English.
Resources can include
- conversations with you
- other home-language speakers
- bilingual dictionaries, if available
- online translation sources

Good Beginnings

Directions Practice writing sentences that will grab your reader's attention. Using your story idea as the topic, write one sentence for each strategy. You can use one of the sentences to start your first draft.

1. Ask a question.
   Answers should be based on the provided strategies and should be complete sentences
2. Use an exclamation. with correct capitalization and punctuation.
3. Use a sound word.
4. Hint at the ending.
5. Use a simile.
6. Make a list.
7. Set the scene.

▲ **Grammar and Writing Practice Book** p. 173

WRITING THE FIRST DRAFT

GUIDED WRITING Use Writing Transparency WP25 to practice writing good beginnings.

- Discuss why a good beginning is essential to a story. Have students read the strategies for writing a good beginning.
- Read through the sample sentences and have students identify which strategy the writer used in each sentence.

MODEL Read these sentences and think about the strategies for writing a good beginning. How does each beginning sentence really grab the reader's attention? Let's identify the strategy used for each. You will choose one of these when writing your own stories.

Good Beginnings

Every story must have a beginning, middle, and an end, but a good beginning is most important. If your story beginning does not grab the reader, he or she may not continue reading to the middle and the end.

Strategies for Writing a Good Beginning

Ask a question	Use a simile
Use an exclamation	Use a sound word
Make a list	Set the scene
Hint at the ending	

Directions Read the beginning sentences below and identify which strategy the author uses in each sentence.

1. Crack! Sometimes you know it's a home run the moment the bat strikes the ball.
   Use a sound word.
2. Kate's knees felt like water as she walked onstage.
   Use a simile.
3. Did anyone ask me if I wanted to transfer schools?
   Ask a question.
4. Swimsuit, swim cap, goggles, nose clips. Grace checked her bag one last time before leaving for the swim meet.
   Make a list.
5. Hooray! I finally got my first job, a paper route.
   Use an exclamation.
6. Jack always said he wanted a little sister, but he hadn't thought his wish would be doubled.
   Hint at the ending.
7. The sun warmed the back of my neck, and a gentle breeze cooled the sweat on my forehead as I pedaled along the country road.
   Set the scene.

Unit 4 Story • DRAFT   Writing Process **25**

▲ **Writing Transparency** WP25

WRITER'S CRAFT Mood

Here are some ways writers can create mood:
- Include sensory details.
- Use descriptive language.
- Create characters who fit the tone of the story.

DRAFTING STRATEGIES

- Have students review their story chart before they write.
- Students should use one strategy for writing a good beginning.
- Remind students to keep their audience and purpose in mind.
- Students should reread their story to see where they might add sensory details to support the mood.
- Have students use Grammar and Writing Practice Book p. 173 to practice writing good beginnings.

Pages WA4–WA5

LA.5.3.2.1 Use a pre-writing plan to focus the narrative

LA.5.3.2.2 Organize into a logical sequence

LA.5.3.2.3 Create interesting leads

LA.5.3.3.4 Apply appropriate strategies to evaluate and refine the draft

LA.5.3.4.4 Use subjective, objective, and demonstrative pronouns correctly

WRITER'S CRAFT Elaboration

PRONOUNS AND ANTECEDENTS Explain that one way to elaborate is to use pronouns and antecedents correctly. Antecedents, or referents, are the noun each pronoun refers back to. With pronouns, writers can avoid repeating nouns.

Needs a Pronoun
Bill looked for his homework, but he couldn't find <u>his homework</u>.
Bill looked for his homework, but he couldn't find <u>it</u>.

Needs an Antecedent
I looked for <u>them</u> at the park, but I couldn't find them.
I looked for <u>Jessica and Ann</u> at the park, but I couldn't find them.

Use Grammar and Writing Practice Book p. 174 to practice using pronouns and antecedents correctly.

REVISING STRATEGIES

GUIDED WRITING Use Writing Transparency WP26 to model revising. Point out the Revising Marks, which students should use when they revise their work.

Think Aloud

MODEL This is part of the story about a boy who gets separated from his dad on a bike ride. The first sentence has been replaced with a sentence that uses one of the strategies for good beginnings. *It was sunny and breezy* doesn't grab the reader's eye the way setting the scene does. In the second paragraph, the writer has deleted the words *and trains,* which are not necessary to the story. The writer has also taken out a lengthy description about asking his dad to ride and replaced it with a shorter sentence. The writer does not want to give too much information in the first paragraph.

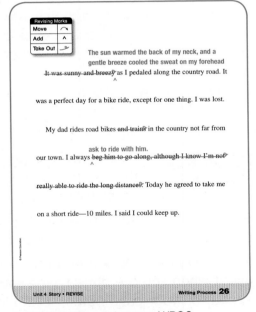

Revising Marks	
Move	⌒
Add	^
Take Out	⤴

The sun warmed the back of my neck, and a gentle breeze cooled the sweat on my forehead
~~It was sunny and breezy~~ as I pedaled along the country road. It
^

was a perfect day for a bike ride, except for one thing. I was lost.

My dad rides road bikes ~~and trains~~ in the country not far from

                                    ask to ride with him.
our town. I always ~~beg him to go along, although I know I'm not~~
^

~~really able to ride the long-distance~~. Today he agreed to take me

on a short ride—10 miles. I said I could keep up.

Unit 4 Story • REVISE   Writing Process **26**

▲ **Writing Transparency** WP26

PEER REVISION Write the Revising Checklist on the board or make copies to distribute. Students can use this checklist to revise their stories. Have partners read each other's first drafts. Remind them to be courteous and specific with suggestions.

Elaboration
Pronouns
Directions The sentences below need a pronoun or an antecedent. Replace the underlined word or words with an appropriate pronoun or antecedent. **Possible answers:**

1. <u>It</u> is so useful. Did you ever wonder who invented it?
   <u>A calculator is so useful. Did you ever wonder who invented it?</u>

2. I've had my skateboard for so long, my <u>skateboard</u> is covered in stickers.
   <u>I've had my skateboard for so long, it is covered in stickers.</u>

3. Beth is such a great singer because <u>Beth</u> has been taking lessons since <u>Beth</u> was five years old.
   <u>Beth is such a great singer because she has been taking lessons since she was five years old.</u>

4. <u>She</u> is the best runner in class. No one can beat her in the 50-yard dash.
   <u>Susie is the best runner in class. No one can beat her in the 50-yard dash.</u>

5. Dan left for school without <u>it</u>, and he had to call home and ask his mom to bring it to him.
   <u>Dan left for school without his backpack, and he had to call home and ask his mom to bring it to him.</u>

6. John asked if <u>John</u> could go to the movies Friday night.
   <u>John asked if he could go to the movies Friday night.</u>

▲ **Grammar and Writing Practice Book** p. 174

Writing Workshop

1 PREWRITE 2 DRAFT 3 REVISE **4 EDIT** 5 PUBLISH

Editing Checklist

Conventions

✔ Did I spell all homophones correctly?

✔ Did I use subject and object pronouns correctly?

✔ Did I check the punctuation and capitalization of every sentence?

✔ Did I check words with suffixes and prefixes?

Support Writing Invite students to read their drafts aloud to you. Observe whether they seem to note any spelling or grammatical errors by stumbling or self-correcting. Return to those errors and explain how to correct them. Use the appropriate Grammar Transition Lessons in the ELL Resource Handbook to explicitly teach the English conventions.

EDITING STRATEGY

READ YOUR WORK ALOUD Suggest that students use an editing strategy. Have them read their stories aloud with a partner. Students should consider the following questions as they listen to the stories: Whose story is it? What is the problem? Is the solution clear?

GUIDED WRITING Use Writing Transparency WP27 to model the process of editing by reading work aloud. Indicate the Proofreading Marks, which students should use when they edit their work. Write the Editing Checklist on the board or make copies to distribute. Students can use this checklist to edit their work.

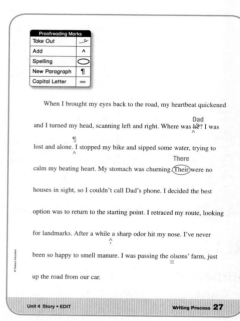

▲ **Writing Transparency** WP27

Think Aloud

MODEL The second sentence says *Where was he?* The writer has used a pronoun without an antecedent, so *he* has been changed to *Dad.* A new paragraph starts with the words *I stopped my bike.* A new paragraph is necessary because this section of the story is when the character thinks about a solution. The word *Their* has been replaced with *There.* The writer had confused these homophones. Finally, the writer needs a comma following the phrase *After a while* and a capital *o* for the proper possessive noun *Olsons'.*

Tech Talk OFFLINE

USING TECHNOLOGY Students who have written or revised their stories on computers should keep these points in mind as they edit:

- Select a special font for your final draft to give your story a professional look. Choose script or a style that matches the mood of your story.

- If your program has a print preview or a page layout feature, you may wish to use it when you are done typing your work. It will show you how the work will appear on your page before it is printed.

- When you have questions about how to do something, check with a friend or use the Help menu.

SELF-EVALUATION

Prepare students to fill out a Self-Evaluation Guide. Display Writing Transparency WP28 to model the self-evaluation process.

Think Aloud

MODEL I would give the story a *6*. This story clearly focuses on how a character gets into a difficult situation and then out of it. The organization is chronological, except for paragraphs 2 and 3, which contain exposition in a kind of flashback. Time words such as *today, when,* and *as* help readers follow the events. The voice is consistently that of its young narrator, and word choice contributes to establishing his character. Variety in sentence structure is created by sentences beginning with dependent clauses and prepositional phrases. Conventions are followed.

EVALUATION Assign the Self-Evaluation Guide on p. vi of Writing Rubrics and Anchor Papers.

The Bike Ride

The sun warmed the back of my neck, and a gentle breeze cooled the sweat on my forehead as I pedaled along the country road. It was a perfect day for a bike ride, except for one thing. I was lost.

My dad rides road bikes in the country not far from our town. I always ask to ride with him. Today he agreed to take me on a short ride—10 miles. I said I could keep up.

My muscles burned as I pumped up hills, right behind my dad. He told me to ride in his "draft." That way he cut the oncoming wind for me. On the wide open road, I didn't need to ride so close. The surface was flat, and I pedaled along slowly as I looked out at fields of grain, horses, a white barn with black trim.

When I brought my eyes back to the road, my heartbeat quickened, and I turned my head, scanning left and right. Where was Dad? I was lost and alone.

I stopped my bike and sipped some water, trying to calm my beating heart. My stomach was churning. There were no houses in sight, so I couldn't call Dad's cell phone. I decided the best option was to return to the starting point. I retraced my route, looking for landmarks. After a while, a sharp odor hit my nose. I've never been so happy to smell manure. I was passing the Olsons' farm, just up the road from our car.

As I turned the final corner, I saw Dad, standing by the car, talking on his cell phone. He threw his arms around me and congratulated me on finding my way back to our starting point. I'm glad Dad gave me a chance to ride with him, but for now, I think I'll stick to neighborhood bike rides.

Unit 4 Story • PUBLISH   Writing Process **28**

▲ **Writing Transparency** WP28

Ideas for Publishing

Class Storybook Bind students' stories into a class book. Have students design a cover that reflects the theme of the unit.

Act It Out Choose a few of the students' stories and have those students act them out for the class, incorporating mood and dialogue.

Self-Evaluation Guide

Name _____ Date _____

Name of Writing Product _____

Directions Review your final draft. Then rate yourself on a scale from 6 to 1 (6 is the highest). After you fill out the chart, answer the questions.

Writing Elements	Description	6	5	4	3	2	1
Focus/Ideas	Focused writing reflects a sense of purpose. A clear main idea is supported with details.						
Organization/ Paragraphs	Ideas progress logically. Transitions connect ideas.						
Support • Word Choice • Voice • Sentences	Support is convincing and specific. Good word choice conveys a strong voice and creates pictures in the reader's mind. Sentences vary in length, type, and structure.						
Conventions	There are few errors in mechanics, spelling, and grammar.						

1. What part do you like best about this piece of writing? Why?

_____

_____

2. What part could you improve? How could you make it better?

_____

_____

_____

vi

▲ **Writing Rubrics and Anchor papers** p.vi

Scoring Rubric — Personal Narrative

	6	5	4	3	2	1
Focus/ Ideas	Story well focused on one event or time period; interesting narrative	Story focused on one event; narrative has some interest	Generally focused on one event; narrative shows some effort	Generally focused narrative; event generic or of little interest	Story sometimes unfocused; narrative goes astray	Unfocused, rambling narrative
Organization/ Paragraphs	Strong beginning; clear sequence of events with time-order words	Coherent beginning, middle, and end; some order words	Beginning, middle, and end easily identifiable	Recognizable beginning, middle, and end; some order words	Little direction from beginning to end; few order words	Lacks beginning, middle, end; incorrect or no order words
Support/ Voice	Voice of character or narrator believable and consistent	Reveals personality of character or narrator	Pleasant voice but generic, not unique	Character or narrator lacking distinct voice	Little development of character or personality	Character or narrator not believable
Support/ Word Choice	Vivid, precise words that show instead of tell	Clear words to bring story to life	Some specific word pictures	Language adequate but lacks color	Generally limited or redundant language	Vague, dull, or misused words
Support/ Sentences	Excellent variety, including use of compound and complex; natural rhythm	Varied lengths, styles; generally smooth	Correct sentences with some variations in style	Correctly constructed sentences; some variety	May have simple, awkward, or wordy sentences; little variety	Short, choppy sentences; many incomplete or run-on
Conventions	Excellent control; few or no errors	No serious errors to affect understanding	General mastery of conventions but some errors	Reasonable control; few distracting errors	Weak control; enough errors to affect understanding	Many errors that prevent understanding

For additional rubrics and scoring information, see pp. WA11–WA14.

Writing Workshop

Story
Differentiated Instruction

WRITING PROMPT: Adapting

Adapting to a new situation might require resourcefulness.

Think about a real or imagined event that shows how a resourceful person succeeds by adapting.

Now write a story about how this person succeeds by adapting.

MODIFY INSTRUCTION

Pick One

ALTERNATIVE PROMPTS

The word *story* in the prompt signals narrative writing. The purpose of such writing is usually to entertain.

ALTERNATIVE PROMPTS: Narrative Writing

Strategic Intervention Think of a familiar tale about a character who changes. Retell this story in your own words. Begin your story with a sentence that shows one of the ideas for a good beginning.

On-Level A resourceful character deals well with problems. Write your story about a main character who finds a particularly clever way to solve his or her problem.

Advanced Your real or imagined story should include at least three characters. How do your characters work together to solve the problem? Develop a clear obstacle that they must overcome.

Strategic Intervention

MODIFY THE PROMPT

Help emerging writers organize their ideas by transferring their story chart into three paragraphs. Write the headings *Beginning, Middle,* and *End.* Have students write several sentences under each heading.

PREWRITING SUPPORT

- Invite a guest speaker or storyteller to come to your class to generate interest in storytelling and demonstrate the power of story.
- Work with your students to narrow their story ideas, focusing on only one event.
- Interview students to get details about their characters, setting, and plot. Make suggestions about any elements they may be missing.

OPTIONS

- Give students the option of writing a group story under your supervision.

CHECK PROGRESS Segment the assignment into manageable pieces. Check work at intervals, such as graphic organizers and first drafts, to make sure writing is on track.

Advanced

MODIFY THE PROMPT

Expect advanced writers to target a problem and solution in their story. Encourage them to incorporate sensory details to create a mood. Their stories should include a larger cast of characters and possibly dialogue.

APPLY SKILLS

- As students revise their work, have them consider some ways to improve it.

  Begin with a question, a sound word, or one of the other strategies for writing a good beginning.

  Use sensory details to enhance your story.

  Look for opportunities to use time-order words.

OPTIONS

- Students can follow these steps to create their own class rubrics.

  1. Read examples of class stories and score them 1–6, with 6 the highest.

  2. Discuss how they arrived at each rank.

  3. Identify the elements of good writing that make this piece strong.

CHECK PROGRESS Discuss students' Self-Evaluation Guides. Work with students to monitor their growth and identify their strengths and weaknesses as writers.

ELL

MODIFY THE PROMPT

Allow beginning speakers to dictate their stories to you or a classmate to record. In the revising step, have students copy the story they have dictated.

BUILD BACKGROUND

- Write the word *Story* on the board. Ask students to think about the earliest stories. How were stories passed down before people had a written language? Ask for examples of early stories and famous oral storytellers. *(Aesop, Homer)* Discuss the list of Key Features of a story that appears in the left column of p. WA2.

OPTIONS

- As students write their stories, guide them toward books, magazines, or Web sites that provide comprehension support through features such as the following.

  strong picture/text correspondence

  text in the home language

  detailed photographs or illustrations

- For more suggestions on scaffolding the Writing Workshop, see the ELL and Transition Handbook.

CHECK PROGRESS You may need to explain certain traits and help students fill out their Self-Evaluation Guides. Downplay conventions and focus more on ideas. Recognize examples of vocabulary growth and efforts to use language in more complex ways.

THINK AND EXPLAIN RUBRICS

THINK AND EXPLAIN TWO-POINT SCORING RUBRIC

2 points   The response indicates that the student has a complete understanding of the reading concept embodied in the task. The response is accurate, complete, and fulfills all the requirements of the task. Necessary support and/or examples are included, and the information given is clearly text-based.

1 point   The response indicates that the student has a partial understanding of the reading concept embodied in the task. The response includes information that is essentially correct and text-based but too general or simplistic. Some of the support and/or examples may be incomplete or omitted.

0 points   The response indicates that the student does not demonstrate an understanding of the reading concept embodied in the task. The student has either failed to respond or has provided a response that is inaccurate or has insufficient information.

THINK AND EXPLAIN FOUR-POINT SCORING RUBRIC

4 points   The response indicates that the student has a thorough understanding of the reading concept embodied in the task. The response is accurate, complete, and fulfills all the requirements of the task. Necessary support and/or examples are included, and the information is clearly text-based.

3 points   The response indicates that the student has an understanding of the reading concept embodied in the task. The response is accurate and fulfills all the requirements of the task, but the required support and/or details are not complete or clearly text-based.

2 points   The response indicates that the student has a partial understanding of the reading concept embodied in the task. The response includes information that is essentially correct and text-based but too general or simplistic. Some support and/or examples may be incomplete or omitted.

1 point   The response indicates that the student has a very limited understanding of the reading concept embodied in the task. The response is incomplete, may exhibit many flaws, and may not address all requirements of the task.

0 points   The response indicates that the student does not demonstrate an understanding of the reading concept embodied in the task. The student has either failed to respond or has provided a response that is inaccurate or has insufficient information.

SCORE POINTS IN RUBRIC

The rubric below provides information about how each score point is determined. Although parts of the rubric reflect writing behaviors of students in fourth grade and above, the rubric can be adapted for scoring the work of younger students.

Scoring Rubric

Writing is focused on the topic and organized into a logical pattern (including a beginning, middle, and conclusion). Transitional devices connect ideas, sentences, and paragraphs. Ideas have clear and sufficient supporting details. The paper gives an impression of completeness or wholeness. The writer displays a skillful command of language, including word choice that is fresh, vivid, and precise. Writing shows a general mastery of grammar, usage, and mechanics, including subject/verb agreement and correct verb and pronoun forms. Sentences are complete, except when fragments are used for effect. Sentence structures and types are varied and sound smooth.

The writing is focused on the topic with adequate development and support. An organizational pattern is evident, although sometimes more transitions could be used to connect ideas more clearly. The paper gives an impression of completeness or wholeness. Word choice is adequate and often vivid. Most sentences are complete, although a few unintentional fragments may occur. There may be occasional errors in subject/verb agreement and in forms of verbs and pronouns, but such errors do not prevent understanding. Conventions of punctuation, capitalization, and spelling are generally followed. Various sentences structure and types are used.

The writing is generally focused on the topic, although it may include unrelated or loosely related information. An organizational pattern is evident with occasional lapses. The paper gives an impression of completeness or wholeness. In parts of the response, the supporting ideas may contain specifics and details, while in other parts, the supporting ideas may lack development. Word choice is generally adequate although at times vague or imprecise. Knowledge of the conventions of punctuation and capitalization is demonstrated, and errors do not prevent understanding. There has been an attempt to use a variety of sentence structures and types, although most are simple constructions and declarative sentences.

Continued

Scoring Rubric

The writing is generally focused on the topic, although parts may seem repetitious, unrelated, or loosely related. Although the writer attempts an organizational pattern and uses some transitional devices, lapses may occur. The paper may seem incomplete. Some of the supporting ideas may not be developed with specifics and details. Word choice is adequate but limited, redundant, and occasionally vague. Knowledge of the conventions of punctuation and capitalization is demonstrated, and commonly used words are usually spelled correctly. Although the writer has attempted to use a variety of sentence structures, most are simple constructions.

The writing may be only slightly related to the topic or may include little relevant information and few supporting details. There is scant evidence of an organizational pattern and few, if any, transitional devices. Development of supporting ideas may be inadequate, confusing, or list-like. Word choice is limited, imprecise, or redundant. Frequent errors in punctuation, capitalization, spelling, and grammar may distract readers. Sentence structure is generally limited to simple constructions.

The writing may only minimally address the topic with little, if any, development of supporting ideas and unrelated information. The writing that is relevant to the topic does not follow an organizational pattern. Writing lacks transitional devices to signal movement and connect ideas. There are few supporting ideas, and they are usually provided through list-like details that lack elaboration. Word choice is vague, limited, or immature. Frequent errors in spelling, capitalization, punctuation, and sentence structure often impede communication. Sentence structure may be limited to simple constructions or fragments.

Unscorable The paper is unscorable for any of the following reasons:

- The response does not address the prompt.
- The response is simply a rewording of the prompt.
- The response has been copied from another source.
- The student has not written anything.
- The response is written in a foreign language.
- The response is illegible.
- The response is incomprehensible.
- The response is too brief to be evaluated.

Scoring Rubric — Narrative Writing

	6	5	4	3	2	1
Focus/Ideas	Excellent, focused narrative; well elaborated with quality details	Good, focused narrative; elaborated with telling details	Narrative focused; adequate elaboration	Generally focused narrative; some supporting details	Sometimes unfocused narrative; needs more supporting details	Rambling narrative; lacks development and detail
Organization/ Paragraphs	Strong beginning, middle, and end; appropriate order words	Coherent beginning, middle, and end; some order words	Beginning, middle, and end easily identifiable	Recognizable beginning, middle, and end; some order words	Little direction from beginning to end; few order words	Lacks beginning, middle, end; incorrect or no order words
Support/Voice	Writer closely involved; engaging personality	Reveals personality	Pleasant but not compelling voice	Sincere voice but not fully engaged	Little writer involvement, personality	Careless writing with no feeling
Support/ Word Choice	Vivid, precise words that bring story to life	Clear words to bring story to life	Some specific word pictures	Language adequate but lacks color	Generally limited or redundant language	Vague, dull, or misused words
Support/ Sentences	Excellent variety of sentences; natural rhythm	Varied lengths, styles; generally smooth	Correct sentences with some variations in style	Correctly constructed sentences; some variety	May have simple, awkward, or wordy sentences; little variety	Choppy; many incomplete or run-on sentences
Conventions	Excellent control; few or no errors	No serious errors to affect understanding	General mastery of conventions but some errors	Reasonable control; few distracting errors	Weak control; enough errors to affect understanding	Many errors that prevent understanding

Scoring Rubric — Descriptive Writing

	6	5	4	3	2	1
Focus/Ideas	Excellent, focused description; well elaborated with quality details	Good, focused description; elaborated with telling details	Description focused; good elaboration	Generally focused description; some supporting details	Sometimes unfocused description; needs more supporting details	Rambling description; lacks development and detail
Organization/ Paragraphs	Compelling ideas enhanced by order, structure, and transitions	Appealing order, structure, and transitions	Structure identifiable and suitable; transitions used	Adequate order, structure, and some transitions to guide reader	Little direction from beginning to end; few transitions	Lacks direction and identifiable structure; no transitions
Support/Voice	Writer closely involved; engaging personality	Reveals personality	Pleasant but not compelling voice	Sincere voice but not fully engaged	Little writer involvement, personality	Careless writing with no feeling
Support/ Word Choice	Vivid, precise words that create memorable pictures	Clear, interesting words to bring description to life	Some specific word pictures	Language adequate; appeals to senses	Generally limited or redundant language	Vague, dull, or misused words
Support/ Sentences	Excellent variety of sentences; natural rhythm	Varied lengths, styles; generally smooth	Correct sentences with variations in style	Correctly constructed sentences; some variety	May have simple, awkward, or wordy sentences; little variety	Choppy; many incomplete or run-on sentences
Conventions	Excellent control; few or no errors	No serious errors to affect understanding	General mastery of conventions but some errors	Reasonable control; few distracting errors	Weak control; enough errors to affect understanding	Many errors that prevent understanding

Scoring Rubric · Persuasive Writing

	6	5	4	3	2	1
Focus/Ideas	Persuasive argument carefully built with quality details	Persuasive argument well supported with details	Persuasive argument focused; good elaboration	Persuasive argument with one or two convincing details	Persuasive piece sometimes unfocused; needs more support	Rambling persuasive argument; lacks development and detail
Organization/ Paragraphs	Information chosen and arranged for maximum effect	Evident progression of persuasive ideas	Progression and structure evident	Information arranged in a logical way with some lapses	Little structure or direction	No identifiable structure
Support/Voice	Writer closely involved; persuasive but not overbearing	Maintains persuasive tone	Persuasive but not compelling voice	Sometimes uses persuasive voice	Little writer involvement, personality	Shows little conviction
Support/ Word Choice	Persuasive words carefully chosen for impact	Argument supported by persuasive language	Uses some persuasive words	Occasional persuasive language	Generally limited or redundant language	Vague, dull, or misused words; no persuasive words
Support/ Sentences	Excellent variety of sentences; natural rhythm	Varied lengths, styles; generally smooth	Correct sentences with variations in style	Carefully constructed sentences; some variety	Simple, awkward, or wordy sentences; little variety	Choppy; many incomplete or run-on sentences
Conventions	Excellent control; few or no errors	No serious errors to affect understanding	General mastery of conventions but some errors	Reasonable control; few distracting errors	Weak control; enough errors to affect understanding	Many errors that prevent understanding

Support (side tab)

Scoring Rubric · Expository Writing

	6	5	4	3	2	1
Focus/Ideas	Insightful, focused exposition; well elaborated with quality details	Informed, focused exposition; elaborated with telling details	Exposition focused, good elaboration	Generally focused exposition; some supporting details	Sometimes unfocused exposition needs more supporting details	Rambling exposition; lacks development and detail
Organization/ Paragraphs	Logical, consistent flow of ideas; good transitions	Logical sequencing of ideas; uses transitions	Ideas sequenced with some transitions	Sequenced ideas with some transitions	Little direction from beginning to end; few order words	Lacks structure and transitions
Support/Voice	Writer closely involved; informative voice well suited to topic	Reveals personality; voice suited to topic	Pleasant but not compelling voice	Sincere voice suited to topic	Little writer involvement, personality	Careless writing with no feeling
Support/ Word Choice	Vivid, precise words to express ideas	Clear words to express ideas	Words correct and adequate	Language adequate but may lack precision	Generally limited or redundant language	Vague, dull, or misused words
Support/ Sentences	Strong topic sentence; fluent, varied structures	Good topic sentence; smooth sentence structure	Correct sentences that are sometimes fluent	Topic sentence correctly constructed; some sentence variety	Topic sentence unclear or missing; wordy, awkward sentences	No topic sentence; many incomplete or run-on sentences
Conventions	Excellent control; few or no errors	No serious errors to affect understanding	General mastery of conventions but some errors	Reasonable control; few distracting errors	Weak control; enough errors to affect understanding	Many errors that prevent understanding

Support (side tab)

Unit 4
Monitoring Fluency

Ongoing assessment of student reading fluency is one of the most valuable measures we have of students' reading skills. One of the most effective ways to assess fluency is taking timed samples of students' oral reading and measuring the number of words correct per minute (WCPM).

How to Measure Words Correct Per Minute—WCPM

Choose a Text
Start by choosing a text for the student to read. The text should be:
- narrative
- unfamiliar
- on grade level

Make a copy of the text for yourself and have one for the student.

Timed Reading of the Text
Tell the student: As you read this aloud, I want you to do your best reading and to read as quickly as you can. That doesn't mean it's a race. Just do your best, fast reading. When I say *begin,* start reading.

As the student reads, follow along in your copy. Mark words that are read incorrectly.

Incorrect
- omissions
- substitutions
- mispronunciations
- reversals

Correct
- self-corrections within 3 seconds
- repeated words

After One Minute
At the end of one minute, draw a line after the last word that was read. Have the student finish reading but don't count any words beyond one minute. Arrive at the words correct per minute—WCPM—by counting the total number of words that the student read correctly in one minute.

Fluency Goals
Grade 5 End-of-Year Goal = 140 WCPM

Target goals by unit

Unit 1 105 to 110 WCPM	**Unit 4** 120 to 128 WCPM
Unit 2 110 to 116 WCPM	**Unit 5** 125 to 134 WCPM
Unit 3 115 to 122 WCPM	**Unit 6** 130 to 140 WCPM

More Frequent Monitoring
You may want to monitor some students more frequently because they are falling far below grade-level benchmarks or they have a result that doesn't seem to align with their previous performance. Follow the same steps above, but choose 2 or 3 additional texts.

Fluency Progress Chart Copy the chart on the next page. Use it to record each student's progress across the year.

· See also Assessment Handbook, p. 174

Fluency Progress Chart, Grade 5

Name —

Timed Reading

	1	2	3	4	5	6	7	8	9	10	11	12	13	14	15	16	17	18	19	20	21	22	23	24	25	26	27	28	29	30
175																														
170																														
165																														
160																														
155																														
150																														
145																														
140																														
135																														
130																														
125																														
120																														
115																														
110																														
105																														
100																														
95																														
90																														
85																														
80																														

Assessment and Regrouping Chart

	Day 3 Retelling Assessment			Day 5 Fluency Assessment			Reteach	Teacher's Comments	Grouping
The assessed group is highlighted for each week.	Benchmark Score	Actual Score	The assessed group is highlighted for each week.	Benchmark WCPM	Actual Score		✓		
WEEK 1 — *Weslandia* Draw Conclusions	Strategic 1–2		Strategic	Less than 120					
	On-Level 3		On-Level	120–128					
	Advanced 4		Advanced*	120–128					
WEEK 2 — *Stretching Ourselves* Generalize	Strategic 1–2		Strategic	Less than 120					
	On-Level 3		On-Level	120–128					
	Advanced 4		Advanced*	120–128					
WEEK 3 — *Exploding Ants* Graphic Sources	Strategic 1–2		Strategic	Less than 120					
	On-Level 3		On-Level	120–128					
	Advanced 4		Advanced*	120–128					
WEEK 4 — *The Stormi Giovanni Club* Generalize	Strategic 1–2		Strategic	Less than 120					
	On-Level 3		On-Level	120–128					
	Advanced 4		Advanced*	120–128					
WEEK 5 — *The Gymnast* Draw Conclusions	Strategic 1–2		Strategic	Less than 120					
	On-Level 3		On-Level	120–128					
	Advanced 4		Advanced*	120–128					
Unit 4 Benchmark Test Score									

* **RECORD SCORES** Use this chart to record scores for the Day 3 Retelling, Day 5 Fluency, and Unit Benchmark Test Assessments.

*Students in the advanced group should read above-grade-level materials.

* **REGROUPING** Compare the student's actual score to the benchmark score for each group level and review the *Questions to Consider*. Students may move to a higher or lower group level, or they may remain in the same group.

* **RETEACH** If a student is unable to complete any part of the assessment process, use the weekly Reteach lessons for additional support. Record the lesson information in the space provided on the chart. After reteaching, you may want to reassess using the Unit Benchmark Test.

See also *Assessment Handbook*, p. 178

May be reproduced for classroom use.

Assess and Regroup

FYI In Grade 5 there are opportunities for regrouping every five weeks—at the end of Units 2, 3, 4, and 5. These options offer sensitivity to each student's progress, although some teachers may prefer to regroup less frequently.

Regroup for Unit 5

To make regrouping decisions at the end of Unit 4, consider student's end-of-unit scores for

- Unit 4 Retelling
- Fluency (wcpm)
- Unit 4 Benchmark Test

Group Time

On-Level	Strategic Intervention	Advanced
To continue On-Level or to move into the On-Level group, students should	**Students would benefit from Strategic Intervention if they**	**To move to the Advanced group, students should**
• score 3 or better on their cumulative unit rubric scores for Retelling	• score 2 or lower on their cumulative unit rubric scores for Retelling	• score 4 on their cumulative unit rubric scores for Retelling and demonstrate expansive vocabulary and ease of language in their retellings
• meet the current benchmark for fluency (120–128 wcpm), reading On-Level text such as Student Edition selections	• do not meet the current benchmark for fluency (120–128 wcpm)	• score 95% on the Unit 4 Benchmark Test
• score 80% or better on the Unit 4 Benchmark Tests	• score below 60% on the Unit 4 Benchmark Tests	• read above-grade-level material fluently (120–128 wcpm)
• be capable of working in the On-Level group based on teacher judgment	• are struggling to keep up with the On-Level group based on teacher judgment	• be capable of handling the problem solving and investigative work of the Advanced group based on teacher judgment

QUESTIONS TO CONSIDER

- What types of test questions did the student miss? Are they specific to a particular skill or strategy?
- Does the student have adequate background knowledge to understand the test passages or selections for retelling?

- Has the student's performance met expectations for daily lessons and assessments with little or no reteaching?
- Is the student performing more like students in another group?
- Does the student read for enjoyment, different purposes, and varied interests?

Benchmark Fluency Scores

Current Goal: **120–128** wcpm

End-of-Year Goal: **140** wcpm

Leveled Readers

Table of Contents

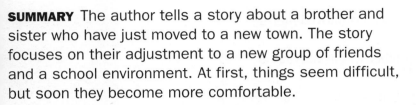

Learning to Play the Game
Social Studies
by Adam McClellan
illustrated by Dan Grant

Learning to Play the Game

 **DRAW CONCLUSIONS**

 **ANSWER QUESTIONS**

LESSON VOCABULARY blunders, civilization, complex, envy, fleeing, inspired, rustling, strategy

SUMMARY The author tells a story about a brother and sister who have just moved to a new town. The story focuses on their adjustment to a new group of friends and a school environment. At first, things seem difficult, but soon they become more comfortable.

INTRODUCE THE BOOK

BUILD BACKGROUND Discuss with students what they know about moving from one place to another. Ask: Have you moved to a new town? What were some of the differences between your new town and your old community? Discuss how it is sometimes difficult at first to make new friends.

PREVIEW Invite students to look at the cover of the book. Discuss what you can tell about the book just from looking at this illustration. Ask: What can you guess about how these children feel? Where are they? Discuss what students might already be able to predict about the story they are about to read.

TEACH/REVIEW VOCABULARY Use one of the vocabulary words in a sentence that shows its meaning in context, such as "I felt *envy* when my best friend got new sneakers before I did." Then invite students to give another sentence that uses the vocabulary word. Repeat this process with each vocabulary word.

TARGET SKILL AND STRATEGY

 **DRAW CONCLUSIONS** Remind students that when we *draw conclusions,* we read with the idea that we will make a decision based on our reading. Suggest that as they go through this book, they try to draw conclusions about how Ella and Pete are going to adjust to their new home.

ANSWER QUESTIONS Remind students that *answering questions* about their reading helps them to remember important information. Suggest that as they read, they think about questions the teacher may ask about their reading and try to take notes about what their answers will be.

READ THE BOOK
Use the following questions to support comprehension.

PAGES 4–5 Look at the illustrations. What are some of the things Ella and Pete will see in their new neighborhood? *(They will see unfinished houses and a park.)*

PAGE 8 Based on the illustration, what conclusions can you draw about what is happening to Pete and Ella? *(They are waiting to be chosen for teams to play a game.)*

PAGE 24 Why do you think the author may have included a page explaining what goes on at festivals in different towns? *(The author is trying to suggest a way to become more comfortable in a new place.)*

TALK ABOUT THE BOOK
READER RESPONSE
1. Possible response: new attitude about their move because they are making friends
2. Possible response: ask Mom, read books, talk to friends
3. Possible response: *simple, easy, basic*
4. Possible response: assembly and lunch routines, location of important places in school

RESPONSE OPTIONS

WRITING Invite students to write a paragraph about the first thing they would do to get comfortable in a new place.

CONTENT CONNECTIONS

SOCIAL STUDIES Suggest that students go to the library to look for books about friendship.

Time for SOCIAL STUDIES

ELL Show students a picture of someone from another culture or country that they are not familiar with. Discuss how it might feel for that person to move to the United States.

Page LR1
LA.5.1.7.3 Determine the main idea or essential message through inferring
LA.5.1.7.8 Use strategies to repair comprehension when self-monitoring, including questioning
LA.5.4.2.1 Write in informational/expository forms

Learning to Play the Game   **LR1**

Draw Conclusions

- When we **draw conclusions**, we make a decision based on what we have read. We use details and facts to help us.

Directions Reread the following excerpt from *Learning to Play the Game* and answer the following questions.

> "Hi," said Ella. The sudden silence made her nervous. "Ummm . . . we just moved in. I'm Ella, and this is my brother Pete. Pete, say hello to everyone."
> "Ummm, hello?" was all Pete could say. Ella could tell that her brother was as nervous as she was!
> A tall girl with blond hair nodded. "OK, Ella and Pete," she said. "I'm Tiffany. We're going to play Two Bases. Want to play?"
> "Sure," Ella nodded. "Is it like baseball?"

1. What conclusion can you draw about how well Pete and Ella know the other children?

_____

2. Which detail helped you reach the conclusion for question #1?

_____

3. What conclusion can you draw about who the leader is among the group of children?

_____

4. Which detail helped you reach the conclusion for question #3?

_____

5. What conclusion can you draw about Ella's knowledge of the game Two Bases?

_____

© Pearson Education 5

74

Vocabulary

Directions Review the meanings of these words.

blunders	mistakes
civilization	society; a group of people who follow rules
complex	complicated; not simple
envy	jealousy
fleeing	running away
inspired	hopeful; interested
rustling	shuffling; moving in a noisy way
strategy	approach

Check the Words You Know

____blunders
____civilization
____complex
____envy
____fleeing
____inspired
____rustling
____strategy

Directions Read the sentence. Then write your own sentence using each vocabulary word.

1. I hope I didn't make too many *blunders* on my spelling test.

_____

2. Our *civilization* may end if we keep polluting.

_____

3. Understanding how budgets work is a *complex* idea.

_____

4. I felt *envy* when I saw their new car.

_____

5. The mouse was *fleeing* as the cat chased it.

_____

6. Hearing your new song, I became *inspired* to write my own song.

_____

7. There was a *rustling* in the leaves as my cat came near.

_____

8. Our team needed a new *strategy* if we were going to win the game.

_____

75

Adventure to the New World

ADVENTURE TO THE NEW WORLD
BY GRETCHEN MCBRIDE
ILLUSTRATED BY PHYLLIS POLLEMA-CAHILL

DRAW CONCLUSIONS

ANSWER QUESTIONS

LESSON VOCABULARY blunders, civilization, complex, envy, fleeing, inspired, rustling, strategy

SUMMARY Jane and her family emigrate to Roanoke, Virginia. They plan to join earlier colonists, but find the colony deserted. Thanks to hard work and a friendly encounter with an Indian girl, Jane and her family hope the colony will survive.

INTRODUCE THE BOOK

BUILD BACKGROUND Ask students what they know about life in the early colonies. Ask: "Was it easy for English settlers to adapt to their new environment? What did they have trouble with? What did they need to learn?"

PREVIEW Have students preview the book by looking at the illustrations. Ask: "How do these text features give an idea of what this book will be about?" Ask what they think they will learn from this book.

TEACH/REVIEW VOCABULARY Invite students to use each vocabulary word in a sentence. Challenge them to write sentences related to the selection.

ELL Invite students to make a dictionary entry or bilingual glossary for each of the vocabulary words. Have them include the sentences they write for each word in their entries or glossaries.

TARGET SKILL AND STRATEGY

DRAW CONCLUSIONS Remind students that *drawing conclusions* means to make sensible decisions or form reasonable opinions after thinking about the facts and details in what you are reading. Challenge students, as they read, to jot down notes for conclusions. Challenge them to test their conclusions after reading. Have them ask: Are there other alternatives? Are the facts accurate?

ANSWER QUESTIONS Remind students that *answering questions* is the ability to provide complete, accurate, and focused responses to questions posed by others. Explain the four kinds of questions: **Right There** (answer in one sentence of text), **Think and Search** (answer in several sentences throughout the text), **Author and You** (reader needs text plus prior knowledge to answer question), and

On My Own (reader needs prior knowledge to answer question). Challenge students to preview the Reader Response on page 32. Discuss the category to which each question belongs. Explain: Answering questions can help you draw conclusions.

READ THE BOOK

Use the following questions to support comprehension.

PAGE 7 What does Jane's dream foreshadow? *(Roanoke Colony may not succeed)*

PAGE 15 What conclusion can you draw about Governor White and his leadership abilities? *(He is a good leader who thinks of practical solutions and tries to remain optimistic.)*

PAGE 25 What did Jane know about raspberries and how did she know this? *(edible; she had seen raspberries but never eaten one because they were too expensive.)*

REVISIT THE BOOK

READER RESPONSE
1. Students might say the soldiers fought with the Indians or joined a group of Indians.
2. Possible response: The Indians were wise and skillful house builders and farmers.
3. Acceptable answers: *civil, civics, civilian, city*
4. Students might say that they would have brought the other settlers back to the ship, and had them return to England.

RESPONSE OPTIONS

WRITING Invite students to write a journal entry from the point of view of one of the characters from the story.

CONTENT CONNECTIONS

SOCIAL STUDIES Students can learn more about Roanoke Colony by going to the library or using the Internet.

Time for SOCIAL STUDIES

Page LR4

LA.5.1.7.3 Determine the main idea or essential message through inferring
LA.5.1.7.8 Use strategies to repair comprehension when self-monitoring, including questioning

Draw Conclusions

- A **conclusion** is a sensible decision you reach after you think about details or facts in what you read.
- **Drawing conclusions** means to make sensible decisions or form reasonable opinions after thinking about the details or facts in what you read.

Directions Read the paragraph below. Then, answer the questions that follow.

> Jane and the other passengers also took comfort from the fact that they would be greeted by a small group of English soldiers when they arrived at Roanoke. During the previous year, a large group of colonists had left Roanoke and returned to England after running low on supplies and encountering difficulties with the local Indians. The leaders of Roanoke wouldn't allow the island to be totally abandoned, so they had a dozen soldiers sent over from England to guard the settlement until Jane's family and everyone else arrived.

1. What conclusion can you draw about the new colonists' expectations about Roanoke?

   _____

2. Give two facts or details to support your conclusion.

   _____

   _____

3. What conclusion can you draw about why the first group of colonists returned to England?

   _____

   _____

4. Give two facts or details to support your conclusion.

   _____

   _____

5. Write a well-supported conclusion about how Jane and her family might have felt differently about their plans if they had known what awaited them.

   _____

   _____

   _____

74

Vocabulary

Directions Read each sentence. Write the word from the Word Box that fits correctly in each sentence. Some words may be used more than once.

Check the Words You Know

____blunders
____civilization
____complex
____envy
____fleeing
____inspired
____rustling
____strategy

1. Jane and her family, like many others, were

_____ economic hardships in England.

2. They were _____ by stories they heard of a new colony in Virginia, where the climate was good and the land was fertile.

3. Queen Elizabeth's _____ for England's future was to build colonies in the New World.

4. The relationship between the early colonists and the local Indians was very

_____.

5. The English believed their own _____ was more advanced than the Indians' way of life.

6. The English colonists hoped to avoid repeating the _____ of the earlier settlers.

7. They did not _____ the fate of the earlier colonists.

8. Instead, they listened to Governor White's passionate speech and were

_____ by it.

9. The colonists' _____ was to first build themselves shelters, and then get some crops planted.

10. As the wind gently blew through the _____ bushes, Jane peeked out at the Indian village.

© Pearson Education 5

75

Cheaper, Faster, Better

DRAW CONCLUSIONS

ANSWER QUESTIONS

LESSON VOCABULARY CD-ROM, Computer Age, computer viruses, e-mail, Industrial Revolution, Internet, search engine, telecommuting, World Wide Web

SUMMARY Technological advances in the past twenty years, such as the creation of the personal computer, the Internet, cell phones and DVD players, have had a huge impact on the way we run our daily lives.

INTRODUCE THE BOOK

BUILD BACKGROUND Ask students to discuss the computerized devices they use every day. Have students share stories about using the World Wide Web to complete daily activities, such as looking up weather reports or checking movie times.

PREVIEW/USE TEXT FEATURES Have students preview the text by looking at the Table of Contents, the photos and captions, the heading/subheadings and the time line.

TEACH/REVIEW VOCABULARY Have students share glossary terms they know; define words they don't.

TARGET SKILL AND STRATEGY

DRAW CONCLUSIONS Remind students that *drawing conclusions* is making sensible decisions. Have students ask questions as they read, like: "What is the author's point?" Conclusions should be logical.

ANSWER QUESTIONS Review the **QAR** (Question-Answer Relationship) strategy with students, including: **Right There**—The answer is in a sentence in the text. **Think and Search**—The answer is in several places in the text. **Author and You**—The answer is not explicitly in the text; students need text and prior knowledge to find it. **On My Own**—The answer is not in the text and students need to do additional research to find it.

READ THE BOOK

Use the following questions to support comprehension.

PAGES 4, 5 What problems did Sally confront? *Research was tedious, overseas mail took a long time, photos had to be processed at a lab, typewriters made it hard to correct errors, etc.*

PAGE 11 How are the Industrial Revolution and Computer Age similar? *Both led to dramatic changes and inventions to simplify tasks.*

PAGES 20–21 What conclusions can you draw about the pros and cons of computer technology? *Pros: speedy access to information; tasks are easier to accomplish. Cons: computer viruses; important hands-on interaction is lost.*

ELL Ask to discuss what the word *revolution* (*revolucion* in Spanish) means to them. Share examples of inventions created during the Industrial Revolution. Ask: How might an industrial revolution differ from a political revolution?

TALK ABOUT THE BOOK

READER RESPONSE

1. **Advantages:** can work from home, don't have to dress up for work, can set own schedule. **Disadvantages:** don't get to interact with colleagues, dependent on computer to get work done, could be lonely or distracting.

2. Questions: "How did you create the idea? When? Why? What is the future of the WWW?"

3. Sample: We lost our Internet connection when the power went out. Then, we couldn't surf the *World Wide Web* to find movie show times.

4. Answers will vary. The computers shown are different in size and appearance than the computers of today.

RESPONSE OPTIONS

WRITING Have students write a short description of a problem for which they'd like to find a high-tech solution and describe the solution. Encourage students to draw a picture of their solution.

CONTENT CONNECTIONS

SOCIAL STUDIES Have students research the history of the Internet or the Industrial Revolution. Have students present their findings to the class.

Time for **SOCIAL STUDIES**

Page LR7
LA.5.1.7.3 Determine the main idea or essential message through inferring
LA.5.2.2.2 Use information from text to answer questions

Cheaper, Faster, Better **LR7**

Draw Conclusions

- A **conclusion** is a sensible decision you reach after you think about the details or the facts in what you read.
- **Drawing conclusions** means to make sensible decisions or form reasonable opinions after thinking about the details or facts in what you read.

Directions Read the paragraph below, then answer the questions that follow.

Completing tasks we now do quickly was not nearly as easy in the 1970s, when Sally was growing up. If Sally wished to do research for a report, she had to ask her parents to drive her to the library. There, she used a large encyclopedia; her parents could not afford to buy her such a set. If Sally needed to type her report, she had to use a manual typewriter. Whenever she made mistakes, she had to use a special white solution to paint over the wrong letters. Then she could retype the correct letters. When Sally didn't remember the spelling for a word, she hauled out a huge dictionary to look it up. Sally was also a movie buff. To figure out which shows she would attend, she had to wait for the newspaper to be delivered. And if she wanted to shop, her only choices were to go to a mall and endure long lines and bustling crowds or to pore over heavy catalogues. If she wanted to shop at midnight, she was out of luck!

1. What conclusion can you draw about what it was like to do homework in the 1970s?

_____

2. Give two facts or details to support your conclusion.

_____

_____

3. What conclusions can you draw about what shopping was like in the 1970s?

_____

4. Give two facts or details to support your conclusion.

_____

_____

5. Write a well-supported conclusion about how technology would have made life easier for Sally.

_____

_____

© Pearson Education 5

74

Name_____

Vocabulary

Directions Choose the word from the box that best matches each definition. Write the word on the line.

_____ **1.** when people work from home using their personal computers

_____ **2.** programs, designed by people, that do damage to computers or data

_____ **3.** system that allows people to review, retrieve, and modify the Web sites found on the Internet

_____ **4.** a compact disc that plays on a computer's CD-ROM drive

_____ **5.** a term describing the changes in technology of the 1800s that changed how people lived

_____ **6.** a program that helps people find data on the Internet

_____ **7.** system of sending messages using computers linked by telephone wires

_____ **8.** worldwide computer network, linked by telephone lines, that is used to send messages, data, and other services

_____ **9.** a term used to describe how computers have transformed modern life

_____ **10.** computer programs that edit, store, and retrieve documents and texts

© Pearson Education 5

75

A New Girl in Class

Unit 4 Week 2

GENERALIZE

PREDICT

LESSON VOCABULARY abdomen, artificial gait, handicapped, therapist, wheelchair

SUMMARY This is a fictional story about two friends who help organize a walk-a-thon to raise money for further research on muscular disorders.

INTRODUCE THE BOOK

BUILD BACKGROUND Ask students if any of them ever volunteered for a fundraiser? If so, what cause did it benefit? What types of activity did they take part in to raise money? Ask them if they know how the money raised helped the cause.

PREVIEW Have students study the illustrations. Ask them what they think is going on in the illustrations. Ask students if any of them have seen a scene similar to the illustration of the girl on the parallel rails on page 10, and if so, do they know what she is doing and why.

ELL Have students discuss in English what they see in the illustrations. Elicit responses specifically referring to crutches, handicaps, and therapy. Have them share equivalent words from their home language regarding handicaps.

TEACH/REVIEW VOCABULARY Review the vocabulary words and definitions with students. Use the illustrations in the book to discuss *handicapped, therapist,* and *abdomen*. Have the students use the rest of the words in sentences.

TARGET SKILL AND STRATEGY

GENERALIZE Remind students that a *generalization* is a broad statement that applies to many examples. Explain that an author's generalizations often sum up information in a story. Stress that there are clue words that can signal generalizations, and offer these words as examples: *often, usually,* and *in general.*

PREDICT Explain to students that to *predict* means to tell what you think might happen in a story based on what has already happened. Explain that students should look for clues in the text and use prior knowledge and logic to make their predictions. As they read, they should monitor their predictions to see if they match the text. If not, they should refine their predictions in light of new information.

READ THE BOOK

Use the following questions to support comprehension.

PAGE 4 What is cerebral palsy? *(a condition that prevents a person from developing motor skills properly)*

PAGE 6 Which sentence is a generalization? *("In general, some scientists believe it's the result of not enough oxygen getting to the brain in the early stages of development.")*

PAGE 12–13 What did the students decide to do to help kids like Lisa? *(Possible responses: to raise money for research; a walk-a-thon)*

TALK ABOUT THE BOOK

READER RESPONSE

1. Possible responses: [Details] Muscular disorders result in trouble with motor skills; they can improve with time; physical therapy can help; [Generalizations] Muscular disorders bring many challenges; these circumstances can often be improved.

2. Possible responses: A large amount of money will go to cerebral palsy research; Lisa may feel good about attending this school.

3. *Abdomen* means *stomach; stomach, belly.*

4. Possible responses: Premature birth may have led to her brain not getting enough oxygen for normal development.

RESPONSE OPTIONS

WRITING Have students pretend that they are organizing a walk-a-thon for someone like Lisa. Ask them to write a poster that encourages other students to participate in the walk-a-thon. Their posters should inform and inspire.

CONTENT CONNECTIONS

SCIENCE Divide students into groups. Have students do further research on the causes of, effects of, and interesting facts about muscular disorders.

Generalize

A **generalization** is made after thinking about a number of examples or facts and identifying what they have in common.

Directions Read this information about cerebral palsy.

> Cerebral Palsy is a condition that a person is sometimes born with. It prevents the person from developing motor skills properly. Babies born with cerebral palsy often have a hard time learning to roll over, sit up, stand, or walk. They can develop these skills, but it takes them much longer than usual—sometimes many years.
>
> They usually need a lot of physical therapy to learn to control and develop their muscles. Sometimes kids with cerebral palsy are helped by wearing braces.

Directions Use the information in the passage to fill out the graphic organizer. You may find several generalizations, but try to identify the main generalization and three of the supporting details.

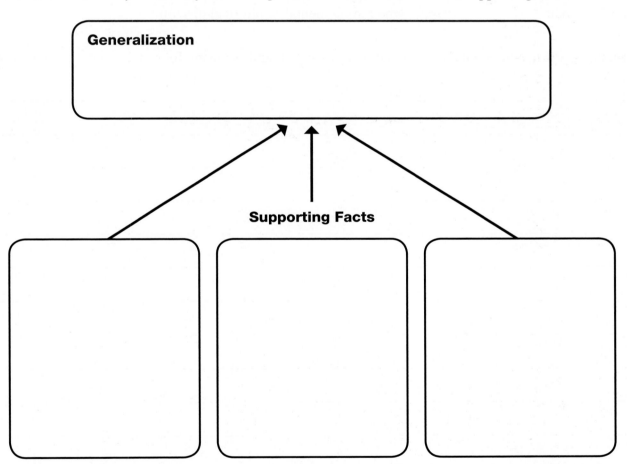

Generalization

Supporting Facts

78

© Pearson Education 5

Vocabulary

Directions Draw a line from each word to its definition.

> ### Check the Words You Know
> ___abdomen   ___artificial   ___gait
> ___handicapped   ___therapist   ___wheelchair

1. abdomen   a particular way of walking, stepping, or running

2. artificial   produced by humans, not nature

3. gait   a specialist who provides treatment or healing of an illness or disability

4. handicapped   a chair equipped with large wheels for the use of a disabled person

5. therapist   the section of the body that holds the intestines and stomach; the belly

6. wheelchair   people who have a mental or physical disability

Directions Write a paragraph about what you learned about Lisa using four of the vocabulary words.

_____

_____

_____

_____

_____

_____

_____

_____

_____

_____

79

© Pearson Education 5

Everybody Wins! The Story of Special Olympics

by Cynthia Swain

Unit 4 Week 2

◉ **GENERALIZE**

◉ **PREDICT**

LESSON VOCABULARY abdomen, artificial, gait, handicapped, therapist, wheelchair

Everybody Wins!

SUMMARY This reader gives information about the Special Olympics. It explains how and when they were started and the events that are included.

INTRODUCE THE BOOK

BUILD BACKGROUND Ask students if anyone knows about the Special Olympics or if anyone knows someone who has competed in the Special Olympics.

PREVIEW/USE TEXT FEATURES Invite students to flip through the book, studying the *photos, captions,* and *heads.* Ask students whether they notice anything different about the sporting events in the photos. Ask, What types of emotions do the people in the photos appear to be experiencing?

ELL Ask students to share home-language words that relate to the Special Olympics and intellectual and physical handicaps. Ask them to look at the photos and use English words to describe the emotions on people's faces or words that relate to being handicapped (for example, *wheelchairs* or *artificial* limbs in the photographs).

TEACH/REVIEW VOCABULARY Review vocabulary words with students. Read the definitions to the students and ask them to write down the correct vocabulary word. Encourage students to use the words in a sentence. You may even ask them to use all or some of the words in a short paragraph.

TARGET SKILL AND STRATEGY

◉ **GENERALIZE** Remind students that a *generalization* is a broad statement or rule that applies to many examples. Explain to students that generalizations should be adequately supported by specific facts and logic. Suggest that, as they read, students write down supported generalizations that they find in the text.

◉ **PREDICT** Remind students that a *prediction* is what you think will happen in a story based on what you have read. Encourage students to anticipate what will come next in the story as they read.

READ THE BOOK

Use the following questions to support comprehension.

PAGES 12–14 Support the generalization: Many people who compete in the Special Olympics overcome obstacles just to get there. *(Possible responses: Five orphans from Afghanistan competed, even though their country was at war; Luis Canel couldn't afford a bike, but eventually won medals for bike racing.)*

PAGE 16 Why did physical educators, physical therapists, and recreation therapists develop the Special Olympics Motor Activities Training Program? *(to help people with physical disabilities)*

TALK ABOUT THE BOOK

READER RESPONSE
1. Responses will vary.
2. Prediction: They thought they wouldn't perform well. Reason for Prediction: They had only one month to train; their government was not supportive of their efforts.
3. Possible responses: Hesitant means Gary is reluctant, he is unsure of what to make of the cheering.
4. Possible responses: They are happy; they get a sense of pride from it.

RESPONSE OPTIONS

WRITING Have students write a letter to the athletes from Afghanistan saying how impressed they are with the athletes' efforts to get to the Special Olympics.

CONTENT CONNECTIONS

SCIENCE Have students research intellectual disabilities and find various diseases or occurrences that can cause them.

Page LR13
LA.5.1.7.1 Use prior knowledge to make and confirm predictions
LA.5.1.7.3 Determine the main idea or essential message through inferring
LA.5.4.2.4 Write a variety of communications (formal letters)

Generalize

A **generalization** is made after thinking about a number of examples or facts and identifying what they have in common.

Directions Reread the following passage from *Everybody Wins!* Use the information from the passage to fill in the graphic organizer.

> The First International Special Olympics Summer Games were held in Chicago in July 1968. One thousand people who are developmentally challenged came to compete. This was the start of something big.
>
> Two years later, another Special Olympics in Chicago attracted more than twice as many athletes.
>
> Then, in 1977, the First International Special Olympics Winter Games were held. Over 500 athletes competed in skiing and skating events.
>
> In 1993, Special Olympics Games went worldwide when the Games were held in Austria. More than 1,600 athletes from more than 50 countries participated.

Generalization
1.

Supporting Facts

2.

3.

4.

Directions Some generalizations are faulty. Describe why this generalization is a faulty generalization.

Intellectually disabled people can't play sports.

5. _____

_____

78

Vocabulary

Directions Match the word to the definition. Write the word on the line.

Check the Words You Know

___abdomen   ___artificial
___gait   ___handicapped
___therapist   ___wheelchair

1. _____ a specialist who provides treatment or healing of an illness or disability

2. _____ people who have a mental or physical disability

3. _____ the section of the body that holds the intestines and stomach; the belly

4. _____ a chair equipped with large wheels for use by a disabled person

5. _____ a particular way of walking, stepping, or running

6. _____ produced by humans, not nature

Directions Write a paragraph that describes how a community can make life easier for a handicapped person. Use at least three of the vocabulary words.

_____

_____

_____

_____

_____

79

Feel, Think, Move

Page LR16

LA.5.1.7.1 Make and confirm predictions

LA.5.4.2.1 Write in informational/expository forms

◉ **GENERALIZE**

◉ **PREDICT**

LESSON VOCABULARY abdomen, cerebral hemispheres, coordination, musculoskeletal, neurons, organ, physical therapists

SUMMARY This is an informational article about how the brain communicates with the musculoskeletal system to enable you to move.

INTRODUCE THE BOOK

INTRODUCE THE TITLE AND AUTHOR Discuss with students the title and the author of *Feel, Think, Move.* Based on the title, ask students what kind of information they think this book will provide. Ask: "What do the words *feel, think,* and *move* have to do with the action in the photograph?"

PREVIEW/USE TEXT FEATURES Have students scan the book and look at the illustrations. Ask: "What do you think you are about to learn from reading this book?" From the illustration on page 6, ask: "What do you already know about the brain from this illustration?"

TEACH/REVIEW VOCABULARY Review vocabulary words. Have students turn to page 20 and describe the events in the photo using the vocabulary words.

TARGET SKILL AND STRATEGY

◉ **GENERALIZE** A *generalization* is a broad statement or rule that applies to many examples. Ask students to identify the faulty generalization in these two statements: "Men are always better athletes than women," and "In general, men are taller than women." Then, have students explain why the first statement is faulty (Mia Hamm is a better soccer player than most men) and why the second statement is valid (average heights of men and women prove that this is true).

ELL Explain the term *generalization* to students. Point out clue words, such as *always, in general,* and *usually* to students and have them give the equivalent word in their home language. Then, have them state faulty and valid generalizations and support or discredit those generalizations using their new clue words in English.

◉ **PREDICT** To *predict* means to tell what you think might happen next in a story or article based on what has already happened. Scan the book, looking at the

chapter heads and illustrations. Ask: "How does learning about the brain help you understand and predict how the musculoskeletal system works?"

READ THE BOOK

Use the following questions to support comprehension.

PAGE 13 What does it mean that muscles work in opposing pairs? *(It means that one muscle contracts to bend a joint, and the other contracts to straighten it.)*

PAGES 16–17 Support this generalization: On average, women are shorter than men. *(Possible responses: because boys grow for longer than girls; because boys grow more per year during their growth spurt)*

PAGE 18 Why does practice make Lisa Leslie a great athlete? *(Possible response: Practice improves her motor skills.)*

TALK ABOUT THE BOOK

READER RESPONSE
1. Boys' growth spurts are on average six years longer than those of girls.
2. Occipital–You see the ball with your eyes, Temporal–You recall how to kick the ball, Frontal–The brain tells your legs to move.
3. *Cardiac* means having to do with the heart. Cardiovascular, Cardiology, Electrocardiogram
4. An athlete's treatment might focus on ankle sprains or pulled tendons, while an older person's therapy might center on recovery from joint replacement surgery.

RESPONSE OPTIONS

WRITING Have students write a description of a day at a physical therapist's appointment.

CONTENT CONNECTIONS

SCIENCE Have students research diseases that affect people's motor skills. They should identify the cause, effects, and the cure or treatment of the disease.

Generalize

A **generalization** is made after thinking about a number of examples or facts and identifying what they have in common.

Directions Reread the following passage from *Feel, Think, Move.*

> Physical therapists use a wide range of treatments, and they treat all types of people—old, young, fit, inactive. Sometimes they have patients exercise to increase flexibility or strength. Other times they use heat or cold to reduce pain. And sometimes they massage muscles to increase blood circulation.

1–4. Use the information in the passage to complete the graphic organizer.

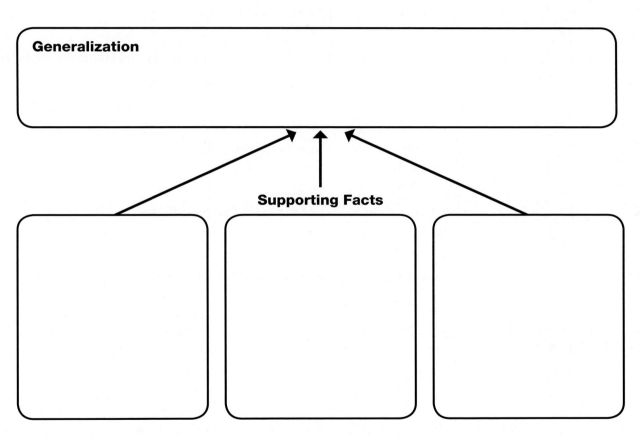

Generalization

Supporting Facts

5. Now write a different generalization you can make from reading *Feel, Think, Move.*

_____

_____

78

Vocabulary

Directions Write the vocabulary word that matches the definition.

Check the Words You Know

____abdomen   ____cerebral hemispheres
____coordination   ____musculoskeletal
____neurons   ____organ
____therapists

1. _____ muscles working together smoothly for efficient movement

2. _____ main cells of the nervous system

3. _____ the section of the body that holds the intestines and stomach; the belly

4. _____ an internal part of the body that perfoms a specific function

5. _____ having to do with the system that includes the muscles and the skeleton

6. _____ left and right halves of the brain that control the opposite sides of the body

7. _____ specialists who provide treatment or healing of an illness or disability

Directions Write a short paragraph about how the body works to make itself move. Use at least three vocabulary words.

_____
_____
_____
_____
_____

79

Surviving the Weather

Surviving the Weather: Animals in Their Environments
by Joe Adair

 **GRAPHIC SOURCES**

 **MONITOR AND FIX UP**

LESSON VOCABULARY critical, enables, mucus, scarce, specialize, sterile

SUMMARY This book presents information about various world habitats, from the Antarctic to tropical forests, and the animals that live in these areas.

INTRODUCE THE BOOK

BUILD BACKGROUND Ask students to share information about any animals they are interested in. Do they know where these animals live?

ELL Invite students to talk about parts of the world they may have visited. Perhaps they can name some animals in their home languages. You may wish to introduce the terms, *environment, migrate,* and *adapt.*

PREVIEW/USE TEXT FEATURES Have students look at the Table of Contents on page 3. Ask how this book is organized. Have students look at the photos and the maps.

TEACH/REVIEW VOCABULARY Have students locate the vocabulary words in the text. Have them define each word using context clues, the glossary, and a dictionary. Then invite students to list for each word as many words as possible that have similar meanings or are related in some way.

TARGET SKILL AND STRATEGY

GRAPHIC SOURCES Remind students that *graphic sources* are graphs, maps, pictures, photographs, and diagrams that help strengthen their understanding of the text. Have students read the text and look at the map on page 15. Discuss how the map helps deepen their understanding of the text. Encourage students to keep in mind the connection between graphic sources and the text as they read.

MONITOR AND FIX UP Have students read pages 8 and 9. Encourage them to ask questions as they read (*"Do I understand this?"*) and use fix-up strategies when their comprehension falters.

READ THE BOOK

Use the following questions to support comprehension.

PAGES 16–17 What animals do you see in the photos? What did you learn about these animals in the text? Find the African grasslands on the map on page 15. *(Elephants, lions. Elephants get water from Boabab trees, Lions live in prides to hunt together.)*

PAGE 19 How has the black-tailed Jack Rabbit adapted to life in the desert? *(Spends most of day in shade to conserve water and stay cool)*

PAGE 21 Why do you think so many different types of plants and animals live in tropical rain forests? *(Possible response: Plentiful food and water, trees offer protection from predators)*

TALK ABOUT THE BOOK

READER RESPONSE
1. Student responses will vary but should mention one of the habitats from the book.
2. Possible response: Tundra: Average winter temperature is −30°, Permafrost is frozen all year; musk ox, polar bear, brown bear. Temperate Forests: Four seasons; squirrels, raccoon
3. Possible response: Animal would have to change its coat to live in a cold environment.
4. Student responses will vary.

RESPONSE OPTION

WRITING Encourage students to pick a favorite animal from the book. Have them write a poem about the animal. They should include facts they learned from the book in their poems.

CONTENT CONNECTIONS

SCIENCE Have students research an endangered animal. They should include information about that animal's habitat and how that habitat may be changing.

TIME FOR Science

Graphic Sources

Graphic sources are graphs, maps, pictures, photographs, and diagrams that help strengthen one's understanding of text.

Directions On the map below, mark where the world's different habitats are found, including the Arctic, temperate areas, grasslands, deserts, and tropical rain forests. Show the animals that live in each area. Remember to include a title for your map and a key.

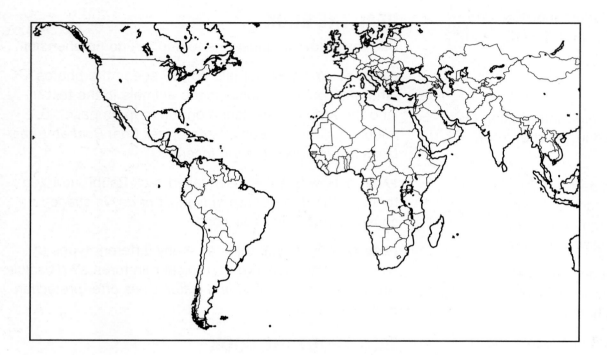

82

Vocabulary

Directions Choose the word from the box that best matches each clue. Write the word on the line.

<table>
<tr><td></td><td></td></tr>
</table>

_____   **1.** If a person does this, he or she helps make something possible.

_____   **2.** This is something slippery that comes from the body of an animal.

_____   **3.** This means you are referring to something that is very important.

_____   **4.** This refers to a place that cannot sustain life.

_____   **5.** This is when there aren't very many of a certain thing.

_____   **6.** When an animal does this, it changes to suit its habitat.

> **Check the Words You Know**
> ___critical
> ___enables
> ___mucus
> ___scarce
> ___specialize
> ___sterile

Directions Write a brief paragraph about *Surviving the Weather: Animals in Their Environments* using each of the words in the box above.

_____

_____

_____

_____

_____

_____

Changing to Survive

Page LR22
LA.5.1.7.1 Explain purpose of text features (illustrations and maps)

👁 **GRAPHIC SOURCES**
👁 **MONITOR AND FIX UP**
LESSON VOCABULARY critical, enable, mucus, scarce, specialize, sterile

SUMMARY This book surveys various birds from around the world. It identifies and describes different bird groups, including sea birds, shore birds, birds of prey, and songbirds. It describes their habitats, eating habits, behavior, and physical make-up.

INTRODUCE THE BOOK

BUILD BACKGROUND Invite students to share what they know about birds. Ask if anyone has owned a bird. What sorts of bird behaviors have students observed?

ELL Encourage ELL students to share names of birds in their home languages.

PREVIEW/USE TEXT FEATURES Have the students look at the photographs, captions, maps, and headings in the book. Ask students what they notice about the way this book is organized. What other text features do students see?

TEACH/REVIEW VOCABULARY Have students locate the vocabulary words in the text. Have them define each word using context clues, the glossary, and a dictionary. Then invite students to list for each word as many words as possible that have similar meanings or are related in some way.

TARGET SKILL AND STRATEGY

👁 **GRAPHIC SOURCES** Remind students that *graphic sources* are graphs, maps, pictures, photographs, and diagrams that help strengthen their understanding of the text. Have students create a KWL chart. They should list what they already know about birds and what they want to know.

👁 **MONITOR AND FIX UP** Remind students that good readers constantly *monitor,* or check, comprehension as they read. If the text isn't making sense, they can use *fix-up* strategies, such as adjusting reading rate, reading on, or rereading and reviewing. Have students read page 3. Encourage them to practice one of the fix-up strategies mentioned. Discuss which strategy worked best and why.

READ THE BOOK

Use the following questions to support comprehension.

PAGES 4–5 How have birds evolved into "flying machines"? *(Wings and bodies covered with feathers, lightweight bodies, eat a lot for energy)*

PAGES 6 AND 7 What do these photos show you? *(Possible responses: Birds live in many different areas. There are many types of birds.)*

PAGE 22 What are some challenges that birds face? *(Possible responses: Growing cities, pollution, cutting down forests, destroyed habitat)*

TALK ABOUT THE BOOK

READER RESPONSE
1. The author uses them as headings for pages that follow.
2. Possible response: Shore birds and water birds have both similarities and differences: Shore birds like shallow water, while water birds are good swimmers. Both types of birds use their beaks or bills to obtain food and both types live in many different regions of the world.
3. Thick, sticky liquid; makes insects stick to the bird's tongue.
4. Responses will vary.

RESPONSE OPTION

WRITING Encourage students to pick a favorite bird from *Changing to Survive*. Have them write a poem about the bird. They should include facts they learned from the book in their poems.

CONTENT CONNECTIONS

SCIENCE How have other animals adapted to their environments? Have students choose an animal to research. Encourage them to pay special attention to how the animal has adapted to its habitat.

TIME FOR Science

Name_____

Graphic Sources

Graphic sources are graphs, maps, pictures, photographs, and diagrams that help strengthen understanding of text.

Directions On the map below, show the ranges of the birds you learned about in the book. Include a title and a key.

Vocabulary

Directions Fill in the missing spaces in each sentence below with the correct word from the "Words to Know" box and an appropriate word from the "Birds to Know" box. You may refer to your reader for information about the birds.

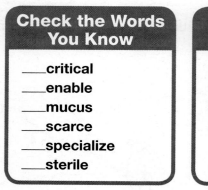

Check the Words You Know

___critical
___enable
___mucus
___scarce
___specialize
___sterile

Birds to Know

penguins
pelican
woodpeckers
ostriches

1. _____ have a special _____ on their tongues for snatching up insects to eat.

2. _____ live in an environment where food is _____.
They have to walk a long way in search of food.

3. _____ have adapted flippers in place of wings that _____ them to swim underwater.

4. The _____ has the longest beak of any bird. It allows it to _____ in fishing by scooping fish from the water.

5. Scientists who work with baby birds keep them in a _____ environment so they stay healthy.

6. When birds are endangered, bird conservationists feel it is _____ to help save them.

83

Unit 4 Week 3

GRAPHIC SOURCES

MONITOR AND FIX UP

LESSON VOCABULARY asteroids, astronomically, contend, cycle, deflect, extraterrestrial, vegetation

A Home for Humans...

SUMMARY This book presents information about research on deep-space travel and the adaptations humans would have to make to sustain long voyages.

INTRODUCE THE BOOK

BUILD BACKGROUND Ask students to share what interests them about space and space travel. Ask what they think it would be like to live in outer space.

ELL Build background for English language learners by using a map of the solar system to introduce and talk about space and space travel.

PREVIEW/USE TEXT FEATURES Have students look at the photos, captions, and headings. How do these text features help them know how this book is organized?

TEACH/REVIEW VOCABULARY Have students locate the vocabulary words in the text. Have them define each word using context clues, the glossary, and a dictionary. Then invite students to list for each word as many words as possible that have similar meanings or are related in some way.

TARGET SKILL AND STRATEGY

GRAPHIC SOURCES Remind students that *graphic sources* are graphs, maps, photographs, and diagrams that help strengthen their understanding of the text. Students may also use graphic sources before reading to predict and preview information. Have students read page 18 and then look at the chart. Ask: What information is in the chart? How does the chart add to what they read in the text?

MONITOR AND FIX UP Remind students that good readers constantly *monitor,* or check, comprehension as they read. If the text isn't making sense, they can use *fix-up* strategies, such as adjusting reading rate, reading on, or rereading and reviewing. Have students read pages 6–7. Encourage them check their comprehension by working with a partner to ask each other questions and review the text.

READ THE BOOK

Use the following questions to support comprehension.

PAGE 8 Why do scientists think Mars is the most likely planet to support life? *(A meteorite that fell to Earth from Mars 13,000 years ago appeared to have bacteria in it. Mars has, or once had, water.)*

PAGES 10–11 Why is zero gravity a problem for humans? *(People lose muscle and bone strength, heart becomes inefficient)*

PAGE 14 Name some benefits of a space colony. *(Helpful to have experiments done in zero gravity; develop vaccines; conversion of solar power)*

TALK ABOUT THE BOOK

READER RESPONSE

1. Oil
2. Responses will very but should show an understanding of centripetal force and use common examples such as spinning a bucket of water in a circle.
3. Possible response: *performed*
4. Student questions will vary. Possible response: Possible source could include International Energy Agency.

RESPONSE OPTIONS

WRITING Ask students what their opinions are about space travel. Have students write a persuasive paper about whether we should or shouldn't pursue space travel. Be sure students include facts they learned from the book to support their main idea.

CONTENT CONNECTIONS

SCIENCE Have students explore space by looking on the internet.

 Page LR25

LA.5.1.7.1 Explain purpose of text features (diagrams, illustrations, and charts)

LA.5.1.7.8 Use strategies to repair comprehension when self-monitoring, including rereading and questioning

LA.5.4.3.1 Write persuasive text that establishes and develops a controlling idea and supporting arguments

Graphic Sources

Graphic sources are graphs, maps, pictures, photographs, and diagrams that help strengthen understanding of text.

Directions Using information you learned from the book, show the distance between Earth and the moon and Earth and Mars. On the lines provided below the diagram write what scientists are learning about life in space and questions they still have. Add questions that you have.

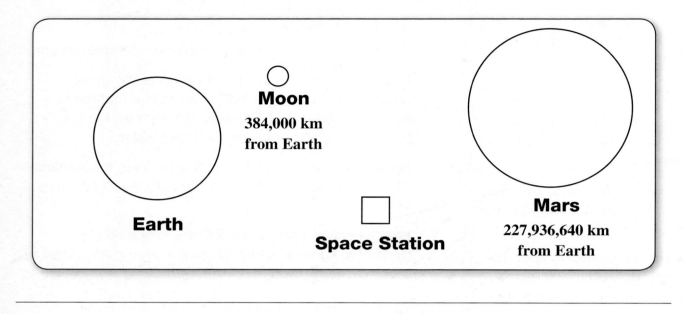

_____

_____

_____

_____

_____

_____

_____

_____

© Pearson Education 5

82

Vocabulary

Directions Fill in the blanks in the sentences below with the correct word from the box.

> ### Check the Words You Know
>
> ___asteroids   ___astronomically
> ___contend   ___cycle
> ___deflect   ___extraterrestrial
> ___vegetation

1. Scientists are studying ways to _____ debris from space before it hits Earth.

2. Astronauts must _____ with many challenges presented by space travel.

3. There are about 100,000 _____ orbiting the sun.

4. The amount of money required to build a space colony is

   _____ large.

5. The moon is on a twenty-nine day _____ as it circles around the earth.

6. Some people support space travel as a way to search for

   _____ life.

7. Human beings depend on _____ as a source of oxygen and food.

83

Vocabulary

Directions Complete each sentence with a word from the box.

> ### Check the Words You Know
>
> ___ cavities   ___ combination
> ___ demonstrates   ___ episode
> ___ profile   ___ strict

1. Joey's new teacher in Toronto was very _____ .

2. Each time they moved, Joey felt a _____ of excitement and fear.

3. When Joey visited the dentist in London, he found he had two _____ .

4. At the street fair in London, an artist _____ her talent and skill.

5. Joey hurried home to watch the next _____ of his favorite TV program.

6. When you looked at his _____ , you could see that Joey had his mother's nose.

Directions Write a brief paragraph discussing Marcus's first day at school, using as many vocabulary words as possible.

_____

_____

_____

_____

_____

_____

_____

_____

_____

_____

_____

87

The New Kid at School

The New Kid at School
by Lisa Oram

◎ **GENERALIZE**

◎ **STORY STRUCTURE**

LESSON VOCABULARY cavities, combination, demonstrates, episode, profile, strict

---

SUMMARY This story is about what it is like to be the new student at school. It provides a lot of good suggestions of what new students can do to make the transition to a new school less difficult. It also talks about what other students can do to welcome the new student.

INTRODUCE THE BOOK

BUILD BACKGROUND Ask students if they have ever been the new kid at school. If not, have they ever helped a new kid trying to fit in at a new school. Discuss some of the things they did as a new student to make friends and fit in. Also discuss things they did to make a new student feel more at home.

PREVIEW/USE TEXT FEATURES Have students look through the book at all the illustrations and the captions. Ask students how the illustrations give clues to what is going to happen in the story.

ELL Ask your ELL students what it felt like for them on the first day at a new school. What did they do to try to make friends?

TEACH/REVIEW VOCABULARY Review the vocabulary words. Then play "Vocabulary Master" with students. Give students three different definitions for each vocabulary word, including one that is fantastical or silly, and have them select the correct definition and then use the word in a sentence.

TARGET SKILL AND STRATEGY

◎ **GENERALIZE** Because this reader presents a number of examples of ways to deal with difficult transitions regarding school, students will need to organize these facts in order to *generalize* them.

◎ **STORY STRUCTURE** Tell students that most fiction stories are told in time order. Events are usually presented from first to last. Ask students to discuss the story structure of this story.

Page LR31

LA.5.1.7.3 Determine the main idea or essential message though inferring and identifying relevant details

LA.5.1.7.5 Identify text structure (sequence of events) and explain how it impacts meaning

READ THE BOOK

Use the following questions to support comprehension.

PAGE 6 What are some simple things you can do to make a new student feel at home? *(Responses may vary: say hello, strike up a conversation.)*

PAGE 6 What are some different feelings that might be a reaction to change? *(Responses may vary: excited, nervous)*

PAGE 15 What are some of the ways you can say goodbye? *(Responses may vary, but may include: say goodbye to friends and teachers, take photos and mementos with you.)*

TALK ABOUT THE BOOK

READER RESPONSE

1. Responses will vary, but may include: A new student may feel nervous and alone. She/he might not know where things are in the new school. The new student might want to find out how to continue activities he/she did at the old school or might want to use the opportunity to try completely new things.

2. Responses will vary but may include: What he or she can do: pursue a favorite activity, be yourself, expect ups and downs; What we can do: introduce yourself, start a conversation, be a mentor, share information.

3. Responses will vary.

4. Responses will vary, but may include: Pursue activities you enjoy, expect ups and downs, be yourself.

RESPONSE OPTION

WRITING Have the students write a brief essay about a new kid at their school. What might each student do to help a new student feel more at home? What kinds of questions would be good to ask?

CONTENT CONNECTION

SOCIAL STUDIES Have the class create a welcome kit like the one on page 10. Give it to the next new student who joins the class.

Time for SOCIAL STUDIES

Generalize

- A **generalization** is a broad statement or rule that applies to many examples. A generalization is made after thinking about a number of examples or facts and what they have in common.

Directions Reread the following passage from *The New Kid at School*.

> About his first day, Marcus says, "I was worried about a lot of things. The new school was much bigger than my old one, and I was scared of getting lost.
>
> I wondered if my new teacher would be strict or nice. I was afraid I would never make new friends or that other kids might be mean to me."

Directions Answer the questions below.

1. When we are afraid, we often make generalizations about the future. What generalizations does Marcus make about the other students at his new school?

_____

2. List another fear Marcus has about his new school.

_____

3. List another fear Marcus has about his new school.

_____

4. List another fear Marcus has about his new school.

_____

5. What if Marcus could turn these negative expectations around? What would be a more positive generalization he could make about his fellow students?

_____

6. How might you turn around the fear you listed in question 2?

_____

7. How might you turn around the fear you listed in question 3?

_____

8. How might you turn around the fear listed in question 4?

_____

© Pearson Education 5

86

Name_____

Vocabulary

Directions Complete each sentence with a word from the box.

Check the Words You Know
___ cavities   ___ combination
___ demonstrates ___ episode
___ profile   ___ strict

1. Marcus was afraid that his teacher would be _____ .

2. The teacher told them to watch tonight's _____ of *Star Trek*.

3. Marcus's new school was a _____ of old and new.

4. The bulletin board in art class _____ the students' artistic talents.

5. Marcus had not had _____ for three years.

6. The art teacher traced his _____ on a piece of paper.

Directions Write a brief paragraph discussing Marcus's first day at school, using as many vocabulary words as possible.

_____

_____

_____

_____

_____

_____

_____

_____

_____

_____

87

Nathaniel Comes to Town

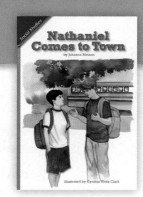

🔊 **GENERALIZE**

🔊 **STORY SEQUENCE**

LESSON VOCABULARY annoyingly, foreboding, gallantly, humiliation, jostling, skeptically

SUMMARY Drew hates school and has very few friends. Then Nathaniel, a boy he met at the beach the summer before, moves to town. Drew and Nathaniel become friends, although there are some bumps in their relationship. By the end of the story, their friendship is patched and Drew feels better about school.

INTRODUCE THE BOOK

BUILD BACKGROUND Ask students if any of them have ever had trouble finding friends in school. What did they do to make new friends?

PREVIEW/USE TEXT FEATURES Encourage students to look at the chapter headings and illustrations to guess what happens in this book.

ELL Give ELL students a list of vocabulary definitions and have them match the definition with the correct vocabulary word.

TEACH/PREVIEW VOCABULARY Go over the vocabulary words with students. Have them note that all the words have one or more endings. Have students tell the base word, the definition, and how the ending affects the word's meaning.

TARGET SKILL AND STRATEGY

🔊 **GENERALIZE** Remind students that a *generalization* is a broad statement or rule that applies to many examples. There are several different examples of friendship in the story. Have the students try to generalize what friendship means based on the examples in the story.

🔊 **STORY SEQUENCE** Tell students that authors sometimes write stories that trace a character's change of heart through the story. Have students look at the story in this light.

READ THE BOOK

Use the following questions to support comprehension.

PAGES 4–6 List all of the reasons you can find in the first chapter that Drew doesn't like school. *(no friends, former friends, feeling sick)*

PAGE 8 What did Drew think of Nathaniel after spending time with him at the beach? *(He thought he was annoyingly smart.)*

PAGES 24–27 What happens between Drew and Nathaniel while they are playing basketball? *(They become friends again.)*

TALK ABOUT THE BOOK

READER RESPONSE
1. Possible response: Moving to a new school can be difficult.
2. Responses will vary.
3. Responses will vary.
4. Possible responses: Nathaniel makes friends by actively trying and not being easily defeated. Drew takes longer to make friends.

RESPONSE OPTIONS

WRITING Have students think back to their first day in grammar school. Have them write about how they felt and if they made any new friends that day.

CONTENT CONNECTIONS

SOCIAL STUDIES Have students read about the Three Famous Failures on p. 32. Have them choose one of the three and research that person on the Internet or in the library.

Page LR34
LA.5.1.7.3 Determine the main idea or essential message through inferring
LA.5.4.1.1 Write narratives

LR34 Nathaniel Comes to Town • Week 4

Generalize

- A **generalization** is a broad statement or rule that applies to many examples. A generalization is made after thinking about a number of examples or facts and what they have in common.

Directions What are some of the difficulties faced by Nathaniel as a new student? What can you generalize about the difficulties that all new students face?

1-5.

_____

_____

_____

_____

_____

Directions Based on Drew's experiences, what can you generalize about how difficult it is to help a new student find his way?

6-10.

_____

_____

_____

_____

_____

_____

© Pearson Education 5

86

Vocabulary

Directions Fill in the blank with the word from the box that fits best.

Check the Words You Know
___ annoyingly   ___ foreboding
___ gallantly   ___ humiliation
___ jostling   ___ skeptically

1. Drew viewed going to school with _____ and dread.

2. Nathaniel _____ tried to make friends at his new school.

3. The color of Drew's basketball caused him _____ .

4. In gym class, Nathaniel tried _____ for the ball.

5. Drew's sister liked to tease him _____ .

6. Drew reacted _____ to his teacher's cheerful greeting.

Directions Write a brief paragraph discussing Nathaniel's first day at school, using as many vocabulary words as possible.

_____

_____

_____

_____

_____

_____

_____

_____

_____

_____

87

Let the Games Begin

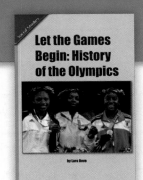

Let the Games Begin: History of the Olympics
by Lara Bove

Unit 4 Week 5

DRAW CONCLUSIONS

VISUALIZE

LESSON VOCABULARY bluish, cartwheels, gymnastics, hesitation, limelight, skidded, somersault, throbbing, wincing

---

SUMMARY This book describes the history of the Olympic Games and how the games have changed through the years. It focuses on the historic 1904 Olympics and its memorable athletes like Felix Carvajal.

INTRODUCE THE BOOK

BUILD BACKGROUND Discuss what students know about the Olympics. If they have watched the Olympic Games, ask them to describe the events. Prompt them to discuss which event they would most like to try.

PREVIEW/USE TEXT FEATURES As students preview the book, have them look at the photographs and read the captions. Ask them to point to specific photographs that give them clues about what the book will teach them. Have them explain their choices.

TEACH/REVIEW VOCABULARY Have students write each vocabulary word on a sheet of paper and look for words with suffixes. Have them circle the suffixes and write a new word containing each suffix.

ELL Have students write each vocabulary word on a sheet of paper and look for words with suffixes. Have them circle the suffixes. Then have them look up the meaning of each suffix in a dictionary and write their answers on a sheet of paper. If time permits, ask students to write a new word using each suffix.

TARGET SKILL AND STRATEGY

DRAW CONCLUSIONS Remind students that a *conclusion* is a sensible decision reached after thinking about details or facts in what is read. As they read, have them ask themselves this question: What facts tell me that Felix Carvajal was a strong-minded man? Have them write the facts on a sheet of paper as they read.

VISUALIZE Remind students that to *visualize* is to create a picture in the mind. As students read, suggest that they visualize what it was like to compete in the early Olympics.

READ THE BOOK

Use the following questions to support comprehension.

PAGES 11 AND 13 What conclusions can you draw about Felix Carvajal? *(He didn't give up on reaching his goal.)*

PAGES 14 AND 15 What made the 1904 marathon difficult? *(Roads were unpaved, runners had no water.)*

PAGE 18 Why was it amazing that Ray Ewry competed in the Olympics? *(He had polio as a child and the doctors said he would never walk again.)*

TALK ABOUT THE BOOK

TALK ABOUT IT
1. Responses will vary.
2. dirt road, no water, hot weather, dust in their eyes
3. Responses will vary.
4. Possible response: He had a wooden leg and yet medaled in these events.

RESPONSE OPTIONS

WRITING Suggest that students write about one of the sports in this book and what it would be like to play it in the Olympics.

CONTENT CONNECTIONS

SOCIAL STUDIES Students can learn more about these and other interesting sports through Internet and library research.

Time for SOCIAL STUDIES

Page LR37

LA.5.1.7.3 Determine main idea or essential message through inferring
LA.5.1.7.8 Use strategies to repair comprehension when self-monitoring
LA.5.4.2.1 Write in a variety of informational/expository forms

Name_____

Draw Conclusions

A **conclusion** is a sensible decision reached after thinking about details or facts in what is read.

Directions Read the following paragraph and answer the questions.

The most amazing athlete of the 1904 Olympics was Ray Ewry. He was a track athlete from America. He had polio when he was a child and the doctors said he would never walk again. The young boy wanted to make his legs stronger, so he began jumping. Ewry's legs got so strong that when he went to the 1900 Games in Paris, he won first place three times! His medals were for the standing long jump, the standing high jump, and the standing triple jump. He won gold medals in the same events in the 1904 Olympics. The crowds loved him and cheered for him. He must have enjoyed being in the limelight.

1-5. What conclusions can you draw about the kind of person Ray Ewry was?

_____

_____

_____

_____

6-10.   What details about him helped you come to these conclusions?

_____

_____

_____

_____

© Pearson Education 5

90

Name_____

Vocabulary

Directions Write the word from the box that best matches each definition.

Check the Words You Know

____bluish   ____cartwheels
____gymnastics   ____hesitation
____limelight   ____skidded
____somersault   ____throbbing
____wincing

---

1. the focus of attention _____

2. having a blue tint _____

3. exercises that use strength, agility, and coordination _____

4. shrinking one's face or body in pain or disgust _____

5. slid _____

6. rolling over by turning heels over head _____

7. a pause _____

8. sideways handsprings _____

9. pulsating or beating strongly _____

10. Write a sentence using any vocabulary word from the box.

_____

_____

91

Strange Sports with Weird Gear

DRAW CONCLUSIONS

VISUALIZE

LESSON VOCABULARY bluish, cartwheels, gymnastics, hesitation, limelight, skidded, somersault, throbbing, wincing

---

SUMMARY This book describes strange sports that use unusual gear. It describes the sports of curling, rhythmic gymnastics, and jai alai.

INTRODUCE THE BOOK

BUILD BACKGROUND Discuss students' favorite sports. Ask them to name some unusual sports they know and describe why they think they are unusual.

ELL Ask students to describe a favorite sport that is popular in their culture. Ask them to describe how the sport is played and tell if there is anything unusual about it.

PREVIEW/USE TEXT FEATURES As students preview the book, action shots of sports will probably immediately attract their interest. Have students look at the photographs and read the captions. Ask them how the photographs help them visualize what the author is describing.

TEACH/REVIEW VOCABULARY Divide students into small groups. Have each group write a funny sentence using each vocabulary word correctly. Then have each group read their sentences leaving out the vocabulary word. Have other groups race to find which vocabulary word fits into the sentence.

TARGET SKILL AND STRATEGY

DRAW CONCLUSIONS Remind students that a *conclusion* is a sensible decision reached after thinking about details or facts in what is read. As they read, have students write down important details about each sport. Ask them to draw conclusions about each sport based on the facts.

VISUALIZE Remind students that to *visualize* is to create a picture in the mind. As students read, suggest that they visualize what it would be like to play each sport.

READ THE BOOK

Use the following questions to support comprehension.

PAGE 11 What conclusions can you draw about why changes in curling were made? *(Changes were made because the curling stone used to be very heavy and hard to get down the ice. It was hard on the players.)*

PAGE 12 What are the two main parts of rhythmic gymnastics? *(Dancing and gymnastics)*

PAGE 23 What gear do jai alai players wear? *(Wooden basket, gloves, and a helmet)*

TALK ABOUT THE BOOK

READER RESPONSE
1. Jai-alai, curling, rhythmic gymnastics
2. Jai-alai because of the crack of the ball against the wall and baskets
3. The suffix changes the meaning of each word by converting an action verb to an adjective.
4. Responses will vary.

RESPONSE OPTIONS

WRITING Suggest that students choose one of the sports in this book and imagine what it would be like to play it. Have them write a brief description of the experience using vivid details.

CONTENT CONNECTIONS

SOCIAL STUDIES Students can learn more about these or other sports that interest them by researching them on the Internet or at the library.

Time for SOCIAL STUDIES

Page LR40
LA.5.1.7.3 Determine the main idea or essential message through inferring
LA.5.1.7.8 Use strategies to repair comprehension when self-monitoring
LA.5.4.2.1 Write in a variety of informational/expository forms
LA.5.4.2.2 Record information related to a topic

LR40 Strange Sports with Weird Gear • Week 5

Draw Conclusions

A **conclusion** is a sensible decision reached after thinking about details or facts in what is read.

Directions Based on the equipment used in each sport, answer the following questions.

1. Does curling take a lot of strength?

_____

_____

2. Are rhythmic gymnasts hurt easily?

_____

_____

3. Can jai alai be dangerous?

_____

_____

4. Why are the ropes used by rhythmic gymnasts often made to look like snakes?

_____

_____

5. Which of the three sports would you like to try? Why?

_____

_____

Vocabulary

Directions Write the word from the box that best matches each definition.

> ### Check the Words You Know
> ___bluish   ___cartwheels
> ___gymnastics   ___hesitation
> ___limelight   ___skidded
> ___somersault   ___throbbing
> ___wincing

1. the focus of attention _____

2. a touch of blue _____

3. exercises that use strength, agility, and coordination _____

4. shrinking one's face or body in pain or disgust _____

5. slid _____

6. rolling over by turning heels over head _____

7. a pause _____

8. sideways handsprings _____

9. pulsating or beating strongly _____

10. Write a sentence using any vocabulary word from the box.

_____

_____

91

What Makes Great Athletes

WHAT MAKES GREAT ATHLETES?

BY C.A. BARNHART

➲ **DRAW CONCLUSIONS**

➲ **VISUALIZE**

LESSON VOCABULARY archaeologists, artifacts, Colosseum, coordination, endurance, esteem, mastery, persistence, rigorous

SUMMARY This book discusses what it takes to be a great athlete. It tells about the demands of training and competing that athletes have to endure to prepare for a major competition. It also highlights various notable athletes, such as Jim Thorpe and Babe Didrikson Zaharias.

INTRODUCE THE BOOK

BUILD BACKGROUND Ask students what sports they like to play or if they are on a sports team. Generate a discussion about what they think makes a good athlete. Prompt them to think of qualities like practice and determination.

PREVIEW/USE TEXT FEATURES Ask students to read the captions that go with the photographs. Have them look at the photographs on page 7 and ask them how they think these images will help them better understand the text.

TEACH/REVIEW VOCABULARY Divide students into small groups. Have each group race to make new words from the vocabulary words by removing the suffixes or adding new ones. Have groups add up their new words and share their words with the class.

ELL Have students write each vocabulary word on a separate index card. Then, have them sort words into words with suffixes. Finally, ask them to write the root word of each word, using a dictionary, if necessary.

TARGET SKILL AND STRATEGY

➲ **DRAW CONCLUSIONS** Remind students that a conclusion is a sensible decision reached after thinking about details or facts in what is read. As they read, have students *draw conclusions* about what qualities a good athlete possesses using a graphic organizer.

➲ **VISUALIZE** Remind students that to *visualize* is to create a picture in the mind. As students read, suggest that they visualize what it would be like to be a great athlete in their favorite sport.

READ THE BOOK

Use the following questions to support comprehension.

PAGE 6 What conclusion can you draw about what the Ancient Greeks thought about athletes? *(They valued them.)*

PAGE 8 What details helped you come to your conclusion in the question above? *(They gave winning athletes large amounts of money, free meals, decorated jars, and even built statues of them.)*

PAGE 15 What made Babe Didrikson Zaharias such a good athlete? *(She focused on her dream and she was strong mentally and physically.)*

TALK ABOUT THE BOOK

READER RESPONSE
1. Responses will vary.
2. Responses will vary.
3. spectacular; energy; hesitating; hesitate; marvel; accurate; honorable
4. Responses will vary but may include references to how athletes were treated then and now, the emphasis on running in ancient times, and on team sports in modern times.

RESPONSE OPTIONS

WRITING Ask students to imagine they have to prepare for a major competition. Have them make a daily training and meal schedule to help them train for the event.

CONTENT CONNECTIONS

Time for SOCIAL STUDIES

SOCIAL STUDIES Students can learn more about how athletes train by researching them on the Internet or at the library.

Page LR43

LA.5.1.7.3 Determine the main idea or essential message through inferring
LA.5.1.7.8 Use strategies to repair comprehension when self-monitoring
LA.5.4.2.2 Record information related to a topic

Draw Conclusions

A **conclusion** is a sensible decision reached after thinking about details as facts in what is read.

Directions Read the following paragraph. Then answer the questions.

Much of our interest in sports and athletes comes from our knowledge of sporting events in ancient Greece. The first Olympics were held at least 2,800 years ago, and scholars believe that such games were probably held before then. The games were held at Olympia, a center of religious ceremonies, in honor of Zeus, the most powerful of the Greek gods. Those early games were festivals that combined races with religious observances.

1. Why did the early Olympics combine races with religious observances?

_____

_____

2. Why did the Greeks think the Olympics would honor Zeus?

_____

_____

3. Why does our interest today come from sporting events in ancient Greece?

_____

_____

4. Do you believe that the first Olympics were held before 2,800 years ago?

_____

_____

5. Do you wish that you could have ran in the first Olympics? Why?

_____

_____

90

Vocabulary

Directions Write the vocabulary word that best matches each definition from the box.

> ### Check the Words You Know
>
> ___archaeologists   ___artifacts
> ___Colosseum   ___coordination
> ___endurance   ___esteem
> ___mastery   ___persistence
> ___rigorous

1. large building where people watched events in ancient Rome _____

2. not giving up _____

3. great knowledge of something _____

4. items made for a special use _____

5. the strength to withstand hard work _____

6. to regard favorably or admirably _____

7. those who study ancient people and civilizations _____

8. working together _____

9. demanding _____

Answer Key for Below-Level Reader Practice

Learning to Play the Game LR1

🎯 Draw Conclusions, LR2

Possible responses given. **1.** They don't know them at all. **2.** Ella introduces herself and her brother. **3.** Tiffany seems to be the leader. **4.** Tiffany talks to the children and invites them to play the game. **5.** She doesn't know how to play the game.

Vocabulary, LR3

Possible responses given. **1.** Her blunders cost us the game. **2.** The president made a great contribution to civilization. **3.** Some people find geometry to be very complex. **4.** We should not feel any envy toward others. **5.** As the school bell rang, the students started fleeing the building. **6.** Your good grades have inspired me to study harder. **7.** The rustling of the blankets told me the puppy was in my bed. **8.** The strategy I use with homework is to do it when I get home.

A New Girl in Class LR10

🎯 Generalize, LR11

Generalization: Possible responses: Cerebral palsy makes it difficult for a person to develop motor skills. Supporting Facts: Support: Babies born with it often have a hard time learning to roll over, sit up, stand, or walk. Support: Physical therapy is usually required for muscle control and development. Support: People with cerebral palsy can't participate normally in regular sports.

Vocabulary, LR12

1. abdomen—the section of the body that holds the intestines and stomach; the belly **2.** artificial—produced by humans, not nature **3.** gait—a particular way of walking, stepping, or running **4.** handicapped—people who have a mental or physical disability **5.** therapist—a specialist who provides treatment or healing of an illness or disability **6.** wheelchair—a chair equipped with large wheels for the use of a disabled person. Responses will vary.

Surviving the Weather LR19

🎯 Graphic Sources, LR20

Responses will vary.

Vocabulary, LR21

1. enables **2.** mucus **3.** critical **4.** sterile **5.** scarce **6.** specialize. Responses will vary.

Moving LR28

🎯 Generalize, LR29

Responses will vary. Supporting Details: Several were on the coast. Joey went to school in each city. Joey made new friends in each city. Supporting Details: He learned to be less shy. He got involved in sports. He listened to his mother's advice.

Vocabulary, LR30

1. strict **2.** combination **3.** cavities **4.** demonstrates **5.** episode **6.** profile **7–10.** Responses will vary.

Let the Games Begin LR37

🎯 Draw Conclusions, LR38

Possible responses given. **1–5.** He was determined, worked hard to reach his goals, never gave up, didn't let obstacles get in his way. **6–10.** He had polio, but was determined to be in the Olympics. He practiced jumping. He didn't listen to people who said he couldn't do it.

Vocabulary, LR39

1. limelight **2.** bluish **3.** gymnastics **4.** wincing **5.** skidded **6.** somersault **7.** hesitation **8.** cartwheels **9.** throbbing **10.** Responses will vary.

Adventure to the New World   LR4

⟳ Draw Conclusions, LR5

Possible responses given. **1.** They expected to find the colony guarded by soldiers. **2.** English soldiers had been sent to guard the settlement. Roanoke leaders wouldn't allow the island to be totally abandoned. **3.** They had trouble growing food and were not able to make friends with the local inhabitants. **4.** They ran low on supplies and they encountered difficulties with local Indians. **5.** Jane and her family might likely have decided not to go to the New World if they had known that they would find the soldiers vanished and the fort in ruins.

Vocabulary, LR6

1. fleeing **2.** inspired **3.** strategy **4.** complex **5.** civilization **6.** blunders **7.** envy **8.** inspired **9.** strategy **10.** rustling

Everybody Wins! The Story of Special Olympics   LR13

⟳ Generalize, LR14

Generalize/The Special Olympics have grown considerably. Supporting Facts/In the first year, 1,000 people competed. Two years later, more than twice as many athletes competed. The first winter games attracted 500 athletes; in 1993, more than 1,600 athletes competed. **5.** Possible response: The success of the Special Olympics proves that intellectually disabled people can play sports.

Vocabulary, LR15

1. therapist **2.** handicapped **3.** abdomen **4.** wheelchair **5.** gait **6.** artificial **7–10.** Responses will vary.

Changing to Survive: Bird Adaptations   LR22

⟳ Graphic Sources, LR23

Responses may vary.

Vocabulary, LR24

1. Woodpeckers, mucus **2.** Ostriches, scarce **3.** Penguins, enable **4.** Pelican, specialize **5.** Sterile **6.** critical

The New Kid at School   LR31

⟳ Generalize, LR32

Possible answers given. **1.** that they will be mean to him **2.** that he will never make new friends **3.** He's afraid of getting lost. **4.** He's afraid his teacher may be strict. **5.** that they will be nice to him **6.** that he will easily make new friends **7.** That he won't get lost, or if he does, he can ask for directions. **8.** That his teacher may be nice

Vocabulary, LR33

1. strict **2.** episode **3.** combination **4.** demonstrates **5.** cavities **6.** profile **7–10.** Responses will vary.

Strange Sports with Weird Gear   LR40

⟳ Draw Conclusions, LR41

Possible responses given. **1.** Yes, because the equipment is heavy and difficult to move **2.** No, because they don't need to wear protective gear **3.** Yes, because the players wear protective head and hand gear **4.** to make their routine more exciting **5.** rhythmic gymnastics because I like to dance

Vocabulary, LR42

1. limelight **2.** bluish **3.** gymnastics **4.** wincing **5.** skidded **6.** somersault **7.** hesitation **8.** cartwheels **9.** throbbing **10.** Responses will vary.

Answer Key for Advanced-Level Reader Practice

Cheaper, Faster, Better: Recent Technological Innovations   LR7

Draw Conclusions, LR8

Possible responses given. **1.** Resources could be hard to get and time-consuming. **2.** Students had to go to libraries to use reference books and had to use manual typewriters. **3.** Shopping took more time and work too. **4.** People went to malls or shopping centers or poured over catalogues. **5.** Technology would have made shopping, studying, and selecting movies more convenient and less expensive activities.

Vocabulary, LR9

1. telecommuting **2.** computer viruses **3.** World Wide Web **4.** CD-ROM **5.** Industrial Revolution **6.** search engine **7.** e-mail **8.** Internet **9.** Computer Age **10.** word processors

Feel, Think, Move   LR16

Generalize, LR17

1–4. Possible responses given. Generalization: Physical therapists use a wide range of treatments. Supporting Facts: They exercise patients to increase flexibility or strength. They use heat or cold to reduce pain. They massage muscles to increase blood circulation. **5.** If you exercise and eat healthily, you can improve the strength of your bones and muscles.

Vocabulary, LR18

1. coordination **2.** neurons **3.** abdomen **4.** organ **5.** musculo-skeletal **6.** cerebral hemispheres **7.** therapists
Paragraphs will vary.

A Home for Humans in Outer Space   LR25

Graphic Sources, LR26

Possible response: Must learn to live in zero gravity; on long space flights, would need to spend a lot of time exercising to decrease effects of zero gravity; could possibly use centripetal force instead of gravity on space station; could have orbiting space colony with vegetation to supply oxygen and food; could create solar power plants in space; space travel is expensive.

Vocabulary, LR27

1. deflect **2.** contend **3.** asteroids **4.** astronomically **5.** cycle **6.** extraterrestrial **7.** vegetation

Nathaniel Comes to Town   LR34

Generalize, LR35

1–5. Nathaniel needs to make new friends, he needs to find his way in his new class, and he needs to make Drew be his best friend. In general, all new students have to make new friends at a new school and fit in with the other students. **6–10.** Drew has trouble because Nathaniel is younger than him and he's afraid that other students will make fun of him for having a younger friend. He gets jealous when Nathaniel sits down with one of his friends for lunch, and later that day he snaps at him. In general, it's very hard to fit a new person into an existing group of friends at school. But many of Drew's problems were overcome by the end of the story.

Vocabulary, LR36

1. foreboding **2.** gallantly **3.** humiliation **4.** jostling **5.** annoyingly **6.** skeptically **7–10.** Possible responses will vary.

What Makes Great Athletes   LR43

Draw Conclusions, LR44

Possible responses given. **1.** because they took place at a center for religious ceremonies **2.** because he is powerful and it takes a lot of strength to be in the Olympics **3.** that is where our knowledge came from; that is how we learned about many sports **4.** yes, because scholars think so **5.** no, because I don't like to run

Vocabulary, LR45

1. Colosseum **2.** persistence **3.** mastery **4.** artifacts **5.** endurance **6.** esteem **7.** archaeologists **8.** coordination **9.** rigorous

Differentiated Instruction

Table of Contents

Daily Group Time Lessons

Routine Cards

Routine Card

Multisyllabic Word Routine

Teach students this Routine to read long words with meaningful parts.

1 Teach Tell students to look for meaningful parts and to think about the meaning of each part. They should use the parts to read the word and determine meaning.

2 Model Think aloud to analyze a long word for the base word, ending, prefix, and/or suffix and to identify the word and determine its meaning.

3 Guide Practice Provide examples of long words with endings (-ing, -ed, -s), prefixes (un-, re-, dis-, mis-, non-), and/or suffixes (-ly, -ness, -less, -ful, and so on). Help students analyze base words and parts.

4 Provide Feedback Encourage students to circle parts of the words to help identify parts and determine meaning.

Routine Card

Picture Walk Routine

To build concepts and vocabulary, conduct a structured picture walk before reading.

1 Prepare Preview the selection and list key concepts and vocabulary you wish to develop.

2 Discuss As students look at the pages, discuss illustrations, have students point to pictured items, and/or ask questions that target key concepts and vocabulary.

3 Elaborate Elaborate on students' responses to reinforce correct use of the vocabulary and to provide additional exposure to key concepts.

4 Practice For more practice with key concepts, have each student turn to a partner and do the picture walk using the key concept vocabulary.

Routine Card

Multisyllabic Word Routine

Teach students this Routine to chunk words with no recognizable parts.

1 Teach Tell students to look for chunks in words with no meaningful parts. They should say each chunk slowly and then say the chunks fast to make a whole word.

2 Model Think aloud to demonstrate breaking a word into chunks, saying each chunk slowly, and then saying the chunks fast to make a word.

3 Guide Practice Provide examples of long words with no meaningful parts. Help students chunk the words.

4 Provide Feedback If necessary, reteach by modeling how to break words into chunks.

Routine Card

Concept Vocabulary

Use this Routine to teach concept vocabulary.

1 Introduce the Word Relate the word to the week's concept. Supply a student-friendly definition.

2 Demonstrate Provide several familiar examples to demonstrate meaning.

3 Apply Have students demonstrate understanding with a simple activity.

4 Display the Word Relate the word to the concept by displaying it on a concept web. Have students identify word parts and practice reading the word.

5 Use the Word Often Encourage students to use the word often in their writing and speaking. Ask questions that require students to use the word.

Weslandia
Group Time

DAY 1

ONLINE

PearsonSuccessNet.com

Monitor Progress

Selection Reading and Comprehension

If... students have difficulty reading the selection with a partner,	**then...** have them follow along as they listen to the Online Leveled Reader Audio.
If... students have trouble understanding ways Ella and Pete adapted to the new game,	**then...** reread pp. 20–23 and discuss these pages together.

Strategic Intervention

ROUTINE

1 Build Background

REINFORCE CONCEPTS Display the People Adapting Concept Web. This week's concept is *people adapting*. People adapt by changing to fit different conditions and situations. Discuss the meaning of each word on the web, using the definitions on p. 392l and the Concept Vocabulary Routine on p. DI·1.

CONNECT TO READING This week you will read about ways people adapt in difficult situations. Using what you know can help you adapt to a different situation. In "The Black Stallion," Alec used what he knew from biology class to survive on the island by eating carragheen.

2 Read Leveled Reader *Learning to Play the Game*

BEFORE READING Using the Picture Walk Routine on p. DI·1, guide students through the text focusing on key concepts and vocabulary. Ask questions such as:

pp. 4–5 What do Ella and Pete see in their new neighborhood? *(a park, an unfinished house)* How do you think they feel?

pp. 14–15 How do you think Ella and Pete feel in these pictures? *(possibly sad, frustrated)*

DURING READING Read pp. 3–5 aloud, while students track the print. Do a choral reading of pp. 6–9. If students are capable, have them read and discuss the remainder of the book with a partner. Ask: How did Ella and Pete adapt to their new neighborhood? What did Ella and Pete do when they played with the other kids in the park?

AFTER READING Have pairs of students discuss the ways to adapt to a new neighborhood. We read *Learning to Play the Game* to learn about how Ella and Pete adapted to their new neighborhood. Understanding how people adapt will help us as we read *Weslandia*.

Pages DI•2–DI•3

🌴 LA.5.1.6.3 Use context clues to determine meanings of unfamiliar words

LA.5.1.6.10 Determine meanings of words by using a dictionary

LA.5.1.7.3 Determine the main idea or essential message through inferring

For alternate Leveled Reader lesson plans that teach
🔄 **Draw Conclusions,** 🔄 **Answer Questions,**
and **Lesson Vocabulary,** see pp. LR1–LR9.

On-Level

ROUTINE

1 Build Background

DEVELOP VOCABULARY Write the word *island* and ask students to define it in their own words. *(a small piece of land, land surrounded by water)* Have you ever been on an island? How did you get there? Repeat this activity with the word *wharf* and other words from the Leveled Reader *Adventure to the New World.* Use the Concept Vocabulary Routine on p. DI•1 as needed.

2 Read Leveled Reader
Adventure to the New World

BEFORE READING Have students create a web with the label *Starting a New Settlement.* This book tells about the adventure that Jane and her family had as they moved to Virginia. As you read, look for key words that relate to Jane's new home. Record them in your web.

DURING READING Have students follow along as you read pp. 4–10. Then let them complete the book on their own. Remind students to add words to their web as they read.

AFTER READING Have students compare the words on their web. Point out the words that describe doing something in a new situation that will help them as they read tomorrow's story *Weslandia.*

Advanced

ROUTINE

1 Read Leveled Reader
Cheaper, Faster, Better

BEFORE READING Recall the Read Aloud "The Black Stallion." How did Alec adapt to his surroundings? *(He remembered what he learned in biology class and ate carrageen.)* Today you will read about how people adapted to changes in technology.

CRITICAL THINKING Have students read the Leveled Reader independently. Encourage them to think critically. For example, ask:

• What does the word *adapt* mean, and how can you apply that to technology?

• How did your parents adapt to changes in technology? Do they think their lives are better or worse for it?

AFTER READING Have students review the selection to find five or more unfamiliar words and determine their meanings by using context clues or by consulting a dictionary. Then ask them to write statements or questions that both include the words and convey their meanings. Have students meet with you to discuss the selection and the statements or questions they wrote.

2 Independent Extension Activity

NOW TRY THIS Assign "Now Try This" on pp. 22–23 of *Cheaper, Faster, Better* for students to work on throughout the week.

Weslandia
Group Time

Weslandia

Audio CD   AudioText

Strategic Intervention

ROUTINE

1 Word Study/Phonics

LESSON VOCABULARY Use p. 394b to review the meanings of *blunders, civilization, complex, envy, fleeing, inspired, rustling,* and *strategy.* Have individuals practice reading the words from word cards.

DECODING MULTISYLLABIC WORDS Write *outcast,* saying the word as you write it. Then model how to use meaningful parts to read longer words. First I ask myself if I see any parts that I know. I see *out* at the beginning of the word, and *cast* at the end. I know that the *out* is "away" and that *cast* is "throw." So I think an *outcast* is "something that is thrown away." Use the multisyllabic Word Routine on p. DI·1 to help students read these other words from *Weslandia: miserable, disliked, alarming, tormentors, snapping, mumbled, almighty.* Be sure students understand the meanings of words such as *tormentors* and *almighty.*

Use *Strategies for Word Analysis,* Lesson 16, with students who have difficulty mastering word analysis and need practice with decodable text.

2 Read *Weslandia,* pp. 396–403

BEFORE READING *Learning to Play the Game* explained how Ella and Pete adapted to their new neighborhood. Think about this as you read *Weslandia.*

Using the Picture Walk Routine on p. DI·1, guide students through the text asking questions such as those listed below. Read the question on p. 396. Together, set a purpose for reading.

pp. 398–399 What do the illustrations show Wesley doing? *(In one picture he is standing on a pogo stick in a room full of things, and in the other picture, he seems to be running away from young people with odd haircuts.)*

pp. 402–403 Why do you think the two boys are spying on Wesley?

DURING READING Follow the Guiding Comprehension routine on pp. 398–403. Have students read along with you while tracking the print or do a choral reading. Stop every two pages to ask what has happened so far. Prompt as necessary.

- What was the idea Wes came up with for his summer project?
- Why did Wes decide to wear a robe?

AFTER READING What has happened in the selection so far? What do you think will happen next? Reread passages with students for comprehension as needed.

Monitor Progress

Word and Story Reading

If... students have difficulty reading multisyllabic words in the selection,	**then...** have them look for and read meaningful parts in the words or have them chunk words with no recognizable parts.
If... students need practice reading words fluently,	**then...** use the Fluent Word Reading Routine on the DI tab.
If... students have difficulty reading along with the group,	**then...** have them follow along as they listen to the AudioText.

Pages DI•4–DI•5

LA.5.1.4.2 Recognize structural analysis

LA.5.1.6.7 Use meaning of familiar base words and affixes to determine meanings of unfamiliar words

LA.5.2.1.5 Demonstrate understanding of a literary selection

Advanced

ROUTINE

1 Extend Vocabulary

WORD STRUCTURE Choose a word, such as the word *engaging* from p. 10 of *Cheaper, Faster, Better:* "Whether you're checking movie times, looking for blouses, doing literary research, or engaging in any other activity..." What does the word *engaging* mean? *(Engaging is participating.)* How did you determine the word's meaning? *(I checked to see if an ending has been added to the base word. Then I determined how the ending changed the meaning of the word.)* Discuss why word structure is helpful, and remind students to use the strategy as they read *Weslandia*.

2 Read *Weslandia*, pp. 396–403

BEFORE READING Today you will read a fiction story about a boy who creates his own world to adapt to his surroundings. As you read, think about other selections you have read in which people adapted to new situations.

For their Strategy Response Log (p. 396), have students make a list of questions they have about the selection based on the artwork. Encourage students to review and answer their questions as they read.

PROBLEM SOLVING Have students read pp. 398–403 independently. Have them list difficult situations that people their age can face, such as having an argument with a friend, not getting invited to a party, or not having anyone to be with at recess, and think about ways to meet or adapt to those situations.

AFTER READING Have partners discuss the selection and share their Strategy Response Log entries. Have students select three or four difficult situations that they wrote about previously. Then have the students write a short paragraph providing someone with advice to help deal with each situation.

DAY 2

Audio CD   AudioText

Weslandia
Group Time

AudioText

Monitor Progress

Word and Story Reading

If... students have difficulty reading multisyllabic words in the selection,	then... have them look for and read meaningful parts in the words or have them chunk words with no recognizable parts.
If... students have difficulty reading along with the group,	then... have them follow along as they listen to the AudioText.

Strategic Intervention

ROUTINE

1 Reinforce Comprehension

🎯 **SKILL DRAW CONCLUSIONS** Have students tell what drawing conclusions is *(a decision you make after thinking about the details in a story).* If necessary, review the meaning and provide a model. Conclusions are decisions you make after thinking about the details in a story. One example of drawing a conclusion is deciding that Wes sticks out from other boys, as his mother says. Using the details in the story, that he dislikes pizza, soda, and football, doesn't shave his head, and is good at fleeing, or running away, helps me draw that conclusion.

Ask students what they can conclude about Wes when he doesn't plant vegetables but is thrilled about the plant seeds that blow into his garden. *(He likes surprises.)*

2 Read *Weslandia,* pp. 404–407

BEFORE READING Have students retell what happened in the story so far. Ask: What was the idea that Wes came up with for his summer project? Reread p. 400 and model how to answer the question. As I read I use the answer to the question to help me draw a conclusion. Wesley turned over a plot of ground so I think Wes is going to grow his own crop. Remind them to think about their own experiences and the answers to questions that were raised about the rest of *Weslandia.* 🎯 **STRATEGY Answer Questions**

DURING READING Follow the Guiding Comprehension routine on pp. 404–407. Have students read along with you while tracking print or do a choral reading. Stop every two pages to ask students what has happened so far. Prompt as necessary.

- Why did Wesley's schoolmates become curious about what he was doing?
- What did Wesley call his plant?

AFTER READING How does Wesley adapt his environment when he doesn't have friends? Reread with students for comprehension as needed. Tell them that tomorrow they will read two poems, "Under the Back Porch" and "Keziah," that explain how children adapt in their own way.

Pages DI•6–DI•7

LA.5.1.5.1 Demonstrate the ability to read grade level text
LA.5.1.7.3 Determine main idea or essential message through inferring

DAY 3   Weslandia

Advanced

ROUTINE

1 Extend Comprehension

SKILL DRAW CONCLUSIONS Have the students draw a conclusion about a friend they think might have characteristics similar to Wesley. Tell the students to give several reasons for their conclusion.

STRATEGY ANSWER QUESTIONS Have students write questions about Wesley that are not in the story. They should give their questions to a partner and answer each other's questions. Ask questions such as:

- What kind of student do you think Wesley is?
- What would Wesley be like as an adult?

2 Read *Weslandia*, pp. 404–407

BEFORE READING Have students recall what has happened in the selection so far. Remind them to draw conclusions and to answer questions they have as they read the remainder of the story.

CRITICAL THINKING Have students read pp. 404–407 independently. Encourage them to think critically. For example, ask:

- Were Wesley's ways of dealing with his situation good ways? Are there better ways he could have handled it?

AFTER READING Have students complete the Strategy Response Log activity (p. 406). Then have the students review the story to find descriptions of an unfamiliar setting. Tell students to make a list of words or phrases the author uses that help them imagine this setting. Students can circle the images on their list that best help them picture what the author is describing.

DAY 3

Audio CD   AudioText

Weslandia

Group Time

Audio CD · AudioText

1 Practice Retelling

REVIEW STORY ELEMENTS Help students identify the main character, minor characters, and the setting of *Weslandia*. Then guide them in using the Retelling Cards to list story events in sequence. Prompt students to include important details.

RETELL Using the Retelling Cards, have students work in pairs to retell *Weslandia*. Monitor retelling and prompt students as needed. For example, ask:

- Tell me what this story is about in a few sentences.
- What is the main character in this story like?
- Why do you think the author wrote this story?

If students struggle, model a fluent retelling.

Grade 5
Retelling
Cards
PEARSON
Scott Foresman

2 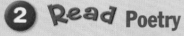 Read Poetry

BEFORE READING Read the genre information on p. 410. Have students share what they know about poetry. Then explain that "Under the Back Porch" and "Keziah" are written in the first person, but *Weslandia* is not. This means that a speaker is saying the poems, using the word *I*, whereas in *Weslandia* a storyteller or narrator told the story.

DURING READING Have students read along with you while tracking the print or do a choral reading of the poems. Stop to discuss imagery, pointing out that images in the lines are used to express thoughts and feelings. As you read, think about the image in this sentence about the speaker's house: *There is a yard stretched around it and in back.*

AFTER READING Have students share their reactions to the poems. Then guide them through the Reading Across Texts and Writing Across Texts activities, prompting if necessary.

- How would you describe Weslandia?
- Which details about Weslandia do you find interesting?
- How could you put them into a poem?

Monitor Progress

Word and Poem Reading

If... students have difficulty reading multisyllabic words in the selection,	**then...** have them look for and read meaningful parts in the words or have them chunk words with no recognizable parts.
If... students have difficulty reading along with the group,	**then...** have them follow along as they listen to the AudioText.

LA.5.1.5.1 Demonstrate the ability to read grade level text
LA.5.1.7.7 Compare and contrast elements in multiple texts
LA.5.2.1.1 Demonstrate knowledge of characteristics of various genres (poetry)

Advanced

ROUTINE

DAY 4

1 Read Poetry

CREATIVE THINKING Have students make a list of different literary genres, such as fantasy, fiction, biography, poetry, expository nonfiction, and so on. Tell students to pick one literary genre, identify its genre, and choose a passage to rewrite in a different genre. Students can share their writing with a partner.

AFTER READING Discuss Reading Across Texts. Have students do Writing Across Texts independently.

2 Extend Genre Study

RESEARCH Have students research other forms of poetry. Have them make a list of different forms of poetry, such as haiku, limericks, and acrostics.

WRITE Have students rewrite either "Under the Back Porch" or "Keziah" in different forms of poetry. Have students share their poems in small groups.

AudioText

Group Time

DAY 5

ONLINE

PearsonSuccessNet.com

① Reread for Fluency

MODEL Read aloud pp. 4–5 of the Leveled Reader *Learning to Play the Game,* emphasizing observing punctuation marks. Have students notice how you pause at commas and raise your voice slightly to indicate a question. Then read pp. 6–7 word-by-word without pausing in sentences. Have students tell you which model sounded better. Discuss how reading and observing punctuation with the tone of voice creates expression.

PRACTICE Have students reread passages from *Learning to Play the Game* with a partner or individually. For optimal fluency, they should reread three or four times. As students read, monitor fluency and provide corrective feedback. Students in this group are assessed in Weeks 2 and 4.

② Retell Leveled Reader *Learning to Play the Game*

Model how to skim the book, retelling as you skim. Then ask students to retell the book, using the pictures to help them retell each event. Prompt them as needed.

- When and where does this story take place?
- What happened next in the story?

Monitor Progress

Fluency

If... students have difficulty reading fluently,	**then...** provide additional fluency practice by pairing nonfluent readers with fluent ones.

For alternate Leveled Reader lesson plans that teach
🔄 **Draw Conclusions,** 🔄 **Answer Questions,**
and **Lesson Vocabulary,** see pp. LR1–LR9.

On-Level

1 Reread for Fluency ROUTINE

MODEL Read aloud p. 4 of the Leveled Reader *Adventure to the New World,* emphasizing observing punctuation marks. Have students note that you pause at commas and you raise your voice slightly to indicate a question. Discuss how observing punctuation by the tone of voice creates better expression.

PRACTICE Have students reread passages from *Adventure to the New World* with a partner or individually. For optimal fluency, they should reread three or four times. As students read, monitor fluency and provide corrective feedback. Students in this group are assessed in Week 3.

2 Retell Leveled Reader *Adventure to the New World*

Have students use chapter titles and illustrations as a guide to retell the story. Prompt as needed.

- Tell me what this story is about in a few sentences.
- What is Jane like in the story?
- How does this story remind you of other stories?

Advanced

1 Reread for Fluency ROUTINE

PRACTICE Have students reread passages from the Leveled Reader *Cheaper, Faster, Better* with a partner or individually. As students read, monitor fluency and provide corrective feedback. If students read fluently on the first reading, they do not need to reread three to four times. Assess the fluency of students in this group using p. 411a.

2 Revisit Leveled Reader *Cheaper, Faster, Better*

RETELL Have students retell the Leveled Reader *Cheaper, Faster, Better.*

NOW TRY THIS Have students complete their projects. You may wish to explore with them their ideas of life without familiar technology.

Stretching Ourselves
Group Time

Leveled Reader Database ONLINE

PearsonSuccessNet.com

DAY 1

Monitor Progress

Selection Reading and Comprehension

If... students have difficulty reading the selection with a partner,	**then...** have them follow along as they listen to the Online Leveled Reader Audio.
If... students have trouble understanding the causes of cerebral palsy,	**then...** reread pp. 6, 8, and 9 and discuss the importance of getting oxygen to the brain.

Strategic Intervention

ROUTINE

1 Build Background

REINFORCE CONCEPTS Display the Overcoming Physical Limitations Concept Web. This week's concept is *overcoming physical limitations.* Overcoming physical limitations is one way of adapting. Discuss the meaning of each word on the web, using the definitions on p. 412l and the Concept Vocabulary Routine on p. DI·1.

CONNECT TO READING This week you will read about ways people with cerebral palsy have met challenges and overcome their physical limitations. You will learn how their lives are like and unlike your own. What did Wilma Rudolph in "Wilma Unlimited" have to do to overcome her physical limitations and finally represent the United States in the Olympic Games? *(She was dedicated, worked hard, and didn't give up.)*

2 Read Leveled Reader *A New Girl in Class*

BEFORE READING Using the Picture Walk Routine on p. DI·1, guide students through the text focusing on key concepts and vocabulary. Ask questions such as:

pp. 4–5 This selection is about a new class member who has cerebral palsy and about how the class reacts to her arrival. How do the students prepare for her? *(They look as if they're researching cerebral palsy.)* Research is one way to learn new information.

p. 10 This picture shows Lisa, the new student, and her physical therapist. What do you think a physical therapist does? *(helps physically handicapped people move)* What objects help Lisa walk? *(leg braces and bars)*

DURING READING Read pp. 3–5 aloud, while students track the print. Do a choral reading of pp. 6–9. If students are capable, have them read and discuss the remainder of the book with a partner. Ask: What do some scientists believe causes cerebral palsy? What does the class decide to do to support research on cerebral palsy?

AFTER READING Encourage pairs of students to discuss what they have learned about cerebral palsy. We read *A New Girl in Class* to learn about the causes of cerebral palsy and how people can work to overcome this physical limitation. Understanding cerebral palsy will help us as we read *Stretching Ourselves.*

LA.5.1.6.1   Use new vocabulary
LA.5.2.2.1   Use information from text features (glossary)
LA.5.6.1.1   Read informational text and organize information (timelines)

For alternate Leveled Reader lesson plans that teach ↻**Generalize,** ↻**Predict,** and **Lesson Vocabulary,** see pp. LR10–LR18.

On-Level

ROUTINE

1 Build Background

DEVELOP VOCABULARY Write the word *dedication* and ask students to define it in their own words. *(When you feel dedication to something, you feel loyalty or devotion to it.)* Where or when would you expect to find dedication? *(anytime someone is committed or devoted to something or somebody)* Whom do you know who has shown dedication? Repeat this activity with the word *therapist* and other words from the Leveled Reader *Everybody Wins!* Use the Concept Vocabulary Routine on p. DI•1 as needed.

2 Read Leveled Reader *Everybody Wins!*

BEFORE READING Have students create a time line starting with the 1960s and continuing to the present. This book tells about people who have overcome physical limitations to become participants in the Special Olympics. We will learn how the Special Olympics began and how it expanded to the present. As you read, look for important dates. Record these dates, along with labels of what happened, on your time line.

DURING READING Have students follow along as you read pp. 3–9. Then let them complete the book on their own. Remind students to add facts to their time lines as they read.

AFTER READING Have students compare the facts on their time lines. Point out that knowing about overcoming physical limitations will help them as they read tomorrow's story *Stretching Ourselves.*

Advanced

ROUTINE

1 Read Leveled Reader *Feel, Think, Move*

BEFORE READING Recall the Read Aloud selection "Wilma Unlimited." Why do you think athletes and people who have physical limitations may need physical therapists? *(to help strengthen and mend damaged bones and muscles)* Today you will read about how the brain communicates with muscles and bones to enable the human body to move.

CREATIVE THINKING Have students read the Leveled Reader independently. Encourage them to think creatively. For example, ask:

- How would you explain a growth spurt to a teenager who is afraid of growing too fast?
- Imagine you are writing a job description for a therapist. What qualities are important for this line of work?

AFTER READING Have students review the meanings of the following words in the Glossary on p. 22: *cerebral hemispheres, coordination, musculoskeletal, neurons, therapists.* Then ask them to write a summary of *Feel, Think, Move* that includes the words and uses context to convey their meanings. Encourage students to meet with you and discuss the summaries they wrote.

2 Independent Extension Activity

NOW TRY THIS Assign "Now Try This" on pp. 20–21 of *Feel, Think, Move* for students to work on throughout the week.

Stretching Ourselves
Group Time

Strategic Intervention

DAY 2

AudioText

1 Word Study/Phonics

LESSON VOCABULARY Use p. 414b to review the meanings of *abdomen, artificial, gait, handicapped, therapist,* and *wheelchair.* Have individuals practice reading the words from word cards.

DECODING MULTISYLLABIC WORDS Write *abdomen,* saying the word as you write it. Then model how to use chunking to read longer words. I see a chunk at the beginning of the word: *ab.* I see a part in the middle: *do,* and another part: *men.* I say each chunk slowly: *ab do men.* I say the chunks fast to make a whole word: *abdomen.* Is it a real word? Yes, I know the word *abdomen.*

Use the Multisyllabic Word Routine on p. DI·1 to help students read these other words from *Stretching Ourselves: medicine, cerebral, tendons, muscles, oxygen, impatiently, especially,* and *particularly.* Make sure students understand the meanings of words such as *tendons* and *impatient.*

Use *Strategies for Word Analysis,* Lesson 17, with students who have difficulty mastering word analysis and need practice with decodable text.

2 Read *Stretching Ourselves,* pp. 416–423

BEFORE READING *A New Girl in Class* explained what causes cerebral palsy and how a girl with CP learned to overcome her physical limitations. Remember what you have learned as you read *Stretching Ourselves.*

Using the Picture Walk Routine on p. DI·1, guide students through the text asking questions such as those listed below. Read the question on p. 417. Together, set a purpose for reading.

pp. 416–419 How is the girl stretching in each picture?

pp. 420–423 What are these children doing? *(looking into a machine, playing with dogs, painting, using a computer)* Do they seem interested in these activities? Do they seem handicapped?

DURING READING Follow the Guiding Comprehension Routine on pp. 418–423. Have students read along with you while tracking the print or do a choral reading. Stop every two pages to ask what has happened so far. Prompt as necessary.

- What did you learn about cerebral palsy?
- What do you learn about Nic on p. 422?

AFTER READING What have you learned in the selection so far? What do you think you will learn about tomorrow? Reread passages with students for comprehension as needed.

Monitor Progress

Word and Selection Reading

If... students have difficulty reading multisyllabic words in the selection,	then... have them look for and read meaningful parts in the words or have them chunk words with no recognizable parts.
If... students need practice reading words fluently,	then... use the Fluent Word Reading Routine on the DI tab.
If... students have difficulty reading along with the group,	then... have them follow along as they listen to the AudioText.

Pages DI•14–DI•15

LA.5.1.5.1 Demonstrate the ability to read grade level text
LA.5.1.6.3 Use context clues to determine meanings of unfamiliar words

Advanced

ROUTINE

1 Extend Vocabulary

CONTEXT CLUES Choose and read a sentence or passage containing a difficult word, such as this passage from p. 3 of *Feel, Think, Move:* "Your muscles and bones make up an amazing system known as the musculoskeletal system. Working together, muscles and bones enable the body to move." What does the word *musculo-skeletal* mean? *(a system of muscles and bones that enables the body to move)* How did you determine the word's meaning? *(I used the context clues system, muscles and bones, enable the body to move.)* Discuss why context clues are helpful, and remind students to use the strategy as they read *Stretching Ourselves.*

2 Read *Stretching Ourselves,* pp. 416–423

BEFORE READING Today you will read a selection about people with cerebral palsy and how they work with family and therapists to overcome their physical limitations. As you read, think about what causes cerebral palsy and how it affects muscles.

Have students continue to ask questions for their Strategy Response Log (p. 416). Encourage them to write answers to their questions as they read.

CREATIVE THINKING Have students read pp. 416–423 independently. Encourage them to think critically and creatively. For example, ask:

• On p. 421, it says that Emily calms herself down when she's upset by mothering her dolls and caring for her dogs. What are some other things Emily could do to relax when she is upset or tired?

AFTER READING Have partners discuss the selection and share their Strategy Response Log entries. Encourage them to discuss how computers can be used to help students with disabilities. Have students research ways computers can help these students.

DAY 2

Stretching Ourselves
Kids with Cerebral Palsy

Audio CD **AudioText**

Stretching Ourselves
Group Time

DAY 3

Audio CD AudioText

Strategic Intervention

ROUTINE

1 Reinforce Comprehension

SKILL GENERALIZE Have students tell what a generalization is *(a broad statement or rule that applies to many examples)* and list clue words that often signal generalizations *(all, most, always, usually, never, everyone).* If necessary, review the meaning and provide a model. A generalization is a broad statement or rule that applies to many examples. *All people with cerebral palsy have to work hard to do ordinary activities* is a generalization. It is a statement that refers to all people with cerebral palsy. The word *all* helps me identify it as a generalization.

Ask students to make generalizations about Emily or Nic or have them choose a generalization from a group of statements. For example, ask: Which of the following is a generalization? *(Nick always rides home on the handicapped bus.)* What clue word helped you? *(always)*

> **Emily enjoys skating.**
> **I know someone who has cerebral palsy.**
> **Nick always rides home on the handicapped bus.**

2 Read *Stretching Ourselves*, pp. 424–431

BEFORE READING Have students retell what happened in the selection so far. Ask:

Do you think Emily will continue to make progress overcoming her physical challenges? Reread the first three paragraphs on p. 421 and model how to make predictions about Emily. Yes, she will make progress. She is having tests and works with a therapist. She has had operations that have helped her, and she will probably have more operations. Remind students to make predictions as they read the rest of *Stretching Ourselves.* **STRATEGY Predicting**

DURING READING Follow the Guiding Comprehension routine on pp. 424–431. Have students read along with you while tracking print or do a choral reading. Stop every two pages to ask students what has happened so far. Prompt as necessary.

• Tanner has milder CP than Nic or Emily. What does he like to do?
• What does Nic's pump do? Why does he need it?

AFTER READING How does *Stretching Ourselves* show that people can overcome physical limitations? Reread with students for comprehension as needed. Tell them that tomorrow they will read "Helpful Tools," an article about inventions that help blind people.

Monitor Progress

Word and Selection Reading

If... students have difficulty reading multisyllabic words in the selection,	**then...** have them look for and read meaningful parts in the words or have them chunk words with no recognizable parts.
If... students have difficulty reading along with the group,	**then...** have them follow along as they listen to the AudioText.

Pages DI•16–DI•17

LA.5.1.5.1 Demonstrate the ability to read grade level text
LA.5.1.7.1 Make and confirm predictions
LA.5.1.7.3 Determine the main idea or essential message through summarizing

Advanced

ROUTINE

1 Extend Comprehension

SKILL GENERALIZE Have students imagine an invention that would be helpful for people with cerebral palsy. Have them suggest a generalization about what this invention could do to make their lives easier or more productive.

STRATEGY PREDICT Have a volunteer reread paragraphs 3–6 on p. 421. Ask students what they learn about Emily's emotional reactions to her physical condition. Then ask questions such as:

• As we read about other children facing physical challenges, what emotions might they exhibit?

2 Read *Stretching Ourselves*, pp. 424–431

BEFORE READING Have students recall what has happened in the selection so far. Remind them to look for generalizations and to make predictions as they read the remainder of the selection.

CRITICAL THINKING Have students read pp. 424–431 independently. Encourage them to think critically. For example, ask:

• What are the advantages of Nic's medicine pump over medication taken orally?
• What is the author's point of view toward his subjects? How does he want readers to feel about the people he describes? What evidence is in the text to support your answer?

AFTER READING Have students complete the Strategy Response Log activity (p. 430). Then have them research someone who has overcome physical limitations to accomplish an important goal. Have students present a report to the class.

DAY **3**

Audio CD AudioText

Group Time

Audio CD   **AudioText**

Strategic Intervention

ROUTINE

1 Practice Retelling

REVIEW MAIN IDEAS Help students identify the main ideas in *Stretching Ourselves*. List the ideas students mention. Then ask questions to help students differentiate between essential and nonessential information.

RETELL Using the Retelling Cards, have students work with partners to retell the important ideas. Show partners how to summarize in as few words as possible. Monitor retelling and prompt students as needed. For example, ask:

- What was this selection mostly about?
- Why do you think the author wrote this selection?
- What was the author trying to tell us or teach us?

If students struggle, model a fluent retelling.

Grade 5 Retelling Cards PEARSON Scott Foresman

2 Read "Helpful Tools"

BEFORE READING Read the genre information on p. 434. Expository nonfiction provides information or an explanation. *Stretching Ourselves* is expository nonfiction. You find this kind of writing everywhere, including encyclopedias and magazines. It is often divided into sections with headings to make it easier to read. As we read "Helpful Tools," think about what it explains.

Read the rest of the panel on p. 434. Then have students scan the pages looking for headings and illustrations.

DURING READING Have students read along with you while tracking the print or do a choral reading of the selection. Reread the last sentence of paragraph one to make sure that students understand that Braille helps blind people read through the sense of touch—with a system of raised dots that stand for letters and numbers.

AFTER READING Have students share their reactions to the selection. Then guide them through the Reading Across Texts and Writing Across Texts activities, prompting if necessary.

- What are three inventions or devices that help people with physical limitations?
- How does each tool help these people?

Advanced

ROUTINE

1 Read "Helpful Tools"

CREATIVE THINKING Have students read pp. 434–435 independently. Encourage them to think creatively. For example, ask:

• This article mentions Braille clothing tags. What kinds of tags would be useful in the kitchen or bathroom of someone without sight?

• Imagine someone who cannot talk or someone who cannot hear. Think of one invention that would make his or her life easier.

AFTER READING Discuss Reading Across Texts. Have students do Writing Across Texts independently.

2 Extend Genre Study

RESEARCH Have students use online or print resources to find other expository nonfiction articles about new inventions. Have them make a list of inventions they find interesting.

WRITE Have students choose one of the inventions on their lists and write an article explaining the invention to a second grader. Add labels and pictures to help break up text and explain it.

DAY
4

AudioText

DAY 5

ONLINE

PearsonSuccessNet.com

Strategic Intervention

ROUTINE

1 Reread for Fluency

MODEL Read aloud p. 15 of the Leveled Reader *A New Girl in Class* using your voice to show the emotion in the characters' speeches. Have students notice how you read the first paragraph to indicate Mr. Forgle's friendly, welcoming tone. Read the speeches of Karen and Dave in tones that show their interest and respect. Read the final paragraph to show Mr. Forgle's enthusiastic support of the students' idea. Then read p. 17 in an unemotional monotone voice. Have students tell you which model sounded better. Discuss how reading aloud with emotion can make the characters seem alive.

PRACTICE Have students reread passages from *A New Girl in Class* with a partner or individually. For optimal fluency, they should reread three or four times. As students read, monitor fluency and provide corrective feedback. Assess the fluency of students in this group using p. 435a.

2 Retell Leveled Reader *A New Girl in Class*

Model how to skim the book, retelling as you skim. Then ask students to retell the book, one incident at a time, using the pictures to help them retell. Prompt them as needed.

- What are these pages mostly about?
- What did the characters do?
- What else happened in this story?

Monitor Progress

Fluency

If... students have difficulty reading fluently,	then... provide additional fluency practice by pairing nonfluent readers with fluent ones.

Pages DI•20–DI•21

LA.5.1.5.2 Adjust reading rate based on purpose, form, and style

For alternate Leveled Reader lesson plans that teach ↻ **Generalize,** ↻ **Predict,** and **Lesson Vocabulary,** see pp. LR10–LR18.

On-Level

1 Reread for Fluency   ROUTINE

MODEL Read aloud p. 15 of the Leveled Reader *Everybody Wins!* Have students note the rhythmic patterns in Liinah's quote and the determination in your voice as you read the quote. Have them note the rise of your voice in the exclamatory sentences. Discuss how reading people's direct quotes should communicate their feelings, and illustrate further by reading aloud quotes on pp. 12, 17, and 18.

PRACTICE Have students reread passages from *Everybody Wins!* with a partner or individually. For optimal fluency, they should reread three or four times. As students read, monitor fluency and provide corrective feedback. Students in this group are assessed in Week 3.

2 Retell Leveled Reader *Everybody Wins!*

Have students use section heads and illustrations as a guide to summarize the important facts they learned from each section of the book. Prompt as needed.

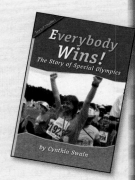

- What did you learn from reading this selection?
- Why do you think the author wrote this selection?
- What was the author trying to teach us?

Advanced

1 Reread for Fluency   ROUTINE

PRACTICE Have students reread passages from the Leveled Reader *Feel, Think, Move* with a partner or individually. As students read, monitor fluency and provide corrective feedback. If students read fluently on the first reading, they do not need to reread three to four times. Students in this group were assessed in Week 1.

2 Revisit Leveled Reader *Feel, Think, Move*

RETELL Have students retell the Leveled Reader *Feel, Think, Move.*

NOW TRY THIS Have students complete their projects. You may wish to review their sources and see whether they need any additional diagrams, information, or resources. Have them present their projects.

Exploding Ants

Group Time

DAY 1

Leveled Reader
Database
ONLINE
PearsonSuccessNet.com

Monitor Progress

Selection Reading and Comprehension

If... students have difficulty reading the selection with a partner,	then... have them follow along as they listen to the Online Leveled Reader Audio.
If... students have trouble understanding how animals specialize,	then... reread p. 16 and discuss how elephants are specialists in getting water from baobab trees.

Strategic Intervention

ROUTINE

1 Build Background

REINFORCE CONCEPTS Display the Animal Adaptations Concept Web. This week's concept is *animal adaptations.* Animals, people—even plants—have to adapt, or change, in order to survive in their environments. **Discuss the meaning of each word on the web, using the definitions on p. 436l and the Concept Vocabulary Routine on p. DI·1.**

CONNECT TO READING This week you will read about many different kinds of animals that have adapted to their environments in order to survive. For instance, you already learned that snakes have learned to "hear" by sensing vibrations through their jawbones. Can you think of other ways animals have adapted in order to survive? *(Answers will vary.)*

2 Read Leveled Reader *Surviving the Weather*

BEFORE READING Using the Picture Walk Routine on p. DI·1, guide students through the text, focusing on key concepts and vocabulary. Ask questions such as:

pp. 4–5 This selection describes how animals have adapted to many different environments. Which of these photographs shows an animal using a special physical trait in order to survive? *(the giraffe)*

pp. 8–9 The images on pp. 8–9 show a harsh habitat, the Arctic tundra. The Arctic tundra has a layer of permafrost. *Permafrost* is ground that stays frozen all year. How do these animals look as if they have adapted to permafrost and very cold weather?

DURING READING Read pp. 4–5 aloud, while students track the print. Do a choral reading of pp. 6–14. If students are capable, have them read and discuss the remainder of the book with a partner. Ask: In what ways have animals adapted to survive in the Arctic tundra? (Possible responses: *The polar bear and musk ox have thick coats. The brown bear hibernates.*) How have animals adapted to survive in savannas? (Possible response: *Elephants get water from the baobab tree, and lions live in prides.*) How have animals adapted to survive in rain forests? *(Animals such as monkeys live in trees to protect themselves from animals that would eat them.)*

AFTER READING Have pairs of students discuss the different ways animals have adapted in order to survive. We read *Surviving the Weather* to learn about how animals adapt to their environments to survive. Understanding animal adaptation will help us as we read *Exploding Ants.*

Pages DI•22–DI•23

LA.5.1.6.1 Use new vocabulary
LA.5.1.6.4 Categorize key vocabulary and identify salient features
LA.5.3.1.3 Organize ideas using strategies and tools (KWL chart)

For alternate Leveled Reader lesson plans that teach
⟳ **Graphic Sources,** ⟳ **Monitor and Fix Up,**
and **Lesson Vocabulary,** see pp. LR19–LR27.

On-Level

DAY 1

1 Build Background

DEVELOP VOCABULARY Write the word *reptiles* and ask students to define the word and list all the reptiles they can think of. *(cold-blooded animals with backbone and lungs, usually covered with horny plates or scales; alligators, caimans, crocodiles, lizards, snakes, turtles)* Then have students define and discuss *flamingo* and other bird names from the Leveled Reader *Changing to Survive.* Use the Concept Vocabulary Routine on p. DI•1 as needed.

2 ℞ℯad Leveled Reader *Changing to Survive*

BEFORE READING Have students create a KWL chart with the topic head *Birds.* Have them fill out the columns for What I **K**now and What I **W**ant to Know. This book tells about different types of birds. As you read, look for facts you can add to the third column of your chart.

DURING READING Have students follow along as you read pp. 3–9. Then let them complete the book on their own. Remind students to add facts to the What I **L**earned column as they read.

AFTER READING Have students compare information from columns 2 and 3 of their KWL charts. Point out that understanding how different animals adapt to survive will help them as they read tomorrow's selection, *Exploding Ants.*

Advanced

DAY 1

1 ℞ℯad Leveled Reader *A Home for Humans in Outer Space*

BEFORE READING Recall the Read Aloud "Snake Scientist." How can you tell that snakes adapted to their surroundings better than their cousins, the dinosaurs? *(Snakes have survived, whereas dinosaurs are extinct.)* Today you will read a selection that describes how humans may have to adapt themselves right off the planet in order to survive.

PROBLEM SOLVING Have students read the Leveled Reader independently. Encourage them to think analytically. For example, ask:

- What are some other ways scientists could try to prevent an asteroid from crashing into Earth?
- Do you think space colonization will be possible in your lifetime? Why or why not?

AFTER READING Have students review the selection to find words that relate to the idea of adaptation. They can use a web or other graphic organizer to categorize the words and show how they are related. Students can put a star next to the words they like best and explain why the words appeal to them. Have students meet as a group or with you to discuss the selection and the word web.

2 Independent Extension Activity

NOW TRY THIS Assign "Now Try This" on pp. 18–19 of *A Home for Humans in Outer Space* for students to work on throughout the week.

Exploding Ants
Group Time

ROUTINE

DAY 2

1 Word Study/Phonics

LESSON VOCABULARY Use p. 438b to review the meanings of *critical, enables, mucus, scarce, specialize,* and *sterile.* Have individuals practice reading the words from word cards.

DECODING MULTISYLLABIC WORDS Write *similarly,* saying the word as you write it. Then model how to use meaningful parts to read longer words. This is a four-syllable word formed from the base word *similar* and the suffix *-ly.* First I cover the suffix and sound out the base word: *sim-ə-lər, similar,* which means "alike" or "much the same." I already know that the suffix *-ly* means "in a _____ way." So *similarly* must mean "in an alike way" or "in much the same way."

Use the Multisyllabic Word Routine on p. DI·1 to help students read these other words from *Exploding Ants: aborigines, nectar, nutrients, nutritious, opponents, predators, predigested,* and *regurgitated.* Be sure students understand words such as *nutrients* and *predators.*

Use *Strategies for Word Analysis,* Lesson 18, with students who have difficulty mastering word analysis and need practice with decodable text.

2 Read *Exploding Ants,* pp. 440–447

BEFORE READING *Surviving the Weather* described how animals adapt to a wide range of habitats. The selection you are going to read today also shows how animals adapt—in rather unusual ways.

Using the Picture Walk Routine on p. DI·1, guide students through the text, asking questions such as those listed below. Read the question on p. 441. Together, set a purpose for reading.

pp. 444–445 Look at the images on these two pages. What do you think this part of the selection will be about? *(ants that live in a very dry climate and how they adapt to survive)*

pp. 446–447 What is happening in this drawing? *(Ants and a scorpion seem to be fighting each other.)* Which do you think would be the winner?

DURING READING Follow the Guiding Comprehension routine on pp. 442–447. Have students read along with you while tracking the print, or do a choral reading. Stop every two pages to ask what has happened so far. Prompt as necessary.

• What did you learn about honey ants?
• What did you learn that you didn't already know about how animals specialize in order to survive?

AFTER READING What have you learned so far? What do you think you will learn about tomorrow? **Reread passages as needed.**

Monitor Progress

Word and Selection Reading

If... students have difficulty reading multisyllabic words in the selection,	then... have them look for and read meaningful parts in the words or have them chunk words with no recognizable parts.
If... students need practice reading words fluently,	then... use the Fluent Word Reading Routine on the DI tab.
If... students have difficulty reading along with the group,	then... have them follow along as they listen to the AudioText.

Pages DI•24–DI•25

LA.5.1.5.1 Demonstrate the ability to read grade level text
LA.5.1.6.3 Use context clues to determine meanings of unfamiliar words
LA.5.1.6.7 Use meaning of familiar base words and affixes to determine meanings of unfamiliar words

Advanced

ROUTINE

1 Extend Vocabulary

CONTEXT CLUES Choose and read a sentence or passage containing a difficult word, such as this passage from p. 10 of *A Home for Humans in Outer Space:* "One of the most critical issues scientists are investigating is how people can survive for long periods in zero gravity." In this context, what does the word *critical* mean? *(of a crisis; important)* How did you determine the word's meaning? (Possible response: *The selection is about making homes for people in outer space. The heading for this section is "Space and the Human Body." Therefore, investigating how people can survive in zero gravity sounds as if it would be a very important issue.)* Discuss why context clues are helpful, and remind students to use the strategy as they read *Exploding Ants.*

2 Read *Exploding Ants,* pp. 440–447

BEFORE READING Recall the Read Aloud selection "Snake Scientist" and how the author marvels at how fascinating snakes are in the ways they have adapted. Today you will read a selection that describes some other unusual ways animals have adapted in order to survive.

Have students write some animal adaptation facts for their Strategy Response Logs (p. 440).

CRITICAL THINKING Have students read pp. 442–447 independently. Have them think critically. For example, ask:

• How would your understanding have been different if there were no art or photographs on these pages?

AFTER READING Have partners discuss the selection, add information about animal adaptation to their Strategy Response Logs, and share their Strategy Response Log entries. Then have students draw pictures illustrating one or more of their adaptation facts.

DAY 2

Audio CD **AudioText**

Exploding Ants
Group Time

ROUTINE

DAY 3

Audio CD — AudioText

Monitor Progress

Word and Selection Reading

If... students have difficulty reading multisyllabic words in the selection,	then... have them look for and read meaningful parts in the words or have them chunk words with no recognizable parts.
If... students have difficulty reading along with the group,	then... have them follow along as they listen to the AudioText.

1 Reinforce Comprehension

SKILL GRAPHIC SOURCES Have students explain what graphic sources are *(charts, diagrams, pictures and photographs with captions, graphs, and maps, among other things, that can help strengthen students' understanding of what they read).* If necessary, review the meaning and provide a model. Graphic sources are ways of showing information visually. The drawings and photographs in *Exploding Ants* are all examples of graphic sources. They help increase your understanding of what you read in the selection.

If students have trouble explaining how a graphic source clarifies or adds to the text, have them identify each graphic source on pp. 442–443. Then, working in pairs, have students tell what each picture shows and explain how it relates to the text. Help students as needed.

2 Read *Exploding Ants*, pp. 448–451

BEFORE READING Have students retell what they have learned in the selection so far. Then ask: What could you do if you didn't understand how the replete ants provide food for the honey ant colony? Reread the second paragraph on p. 445 and model the monitor and fix-up strategy. I read on page 445 that the *repletes regurgitate big drops of golden honey*. I'm not sure what *regurgitate* means, but I remember seeing a similar word earlier in the selection, so I'm going to reread a few paragraphs to see if I can figure it out. Read the third paragraph on p. 444. Here it says that the replete *receives regurgitated, or spit up, food*, so it sounds as if the replete "spits up" food to feed the other ants. The author is right: that *is* gross. **STRATEGY Monitor and Fix Up**

DURING READING Follow the Guiding Comprehension routine on pp. 448–451. Have students read along with you while tracking the print, or do a choral reading. Stop every two pages to ask what has happened so far. Prompt as necessary.

- What did you learn about owls' eating habits that you didn't already know?
- What was the last paragraph on page 451 about?

AFTER READING What did reading *Exploding Ants* help you learn about how animals have to adapt in order to survive? Reread passages with students for comprehension as needed. Tell them that tomorrow they will read "The Creature from the Adapting Lagoon," a science experiment that will further help them understand the concept of how animals adapt to survive.

LA.5.1.7.8 Use strategies to repair comprehension when self-monitoring, including rereading, checking context clues, questioning, and clarifying

LA.5.2.2.1 Locate, explain, and use information from text features (graphs and illustrations)

Advanced

ROUTINE

1 Extend Comprehension

SKILL GRAPHIC SOURCES Have students choose at least three images from *Exploding Ants* and write captions for them. They should glean information from the selection, as well as from print or online resources, to provide information that will enhance and strengthen readers' understanding of the selection.

STRATEGY MONITOR AND FIX UP Read or have a volunteer read the second paragraph on p. 446. Ask:

- What could you do if you didn't understand some of the words in this paragraph?
- What could you do if some of the information is confusing?

2 Read *Exploding Ants,* pp. 448–451

BEFORE READING Have students recall what they have learned from the selection so far. Remind them to use graphic sources and monitor and fix-up strategies as they read the rest of the selection.

CREATIVE THINKING Have students read pp. 448–451 independently. Have them think creatively. For example, ask:

- What would you do if you were a scientist studying the animals on these pages?

AFTER READING Have students complete the Strategy Response Log activity on p. 450. Then have students use online or print resources to find information about some careers available in a zoo or another facility or in conservation that focuses on working with animals. Tell students to write down a few details about each career on the list. Students can note which careers, if any, appeal to them and why.

DAY 3

AudioText

Group Time

Audio CD AudioText

Monitor Progress

Word and Selection Reading

If... students have difficulty reading multisyllabic words in the selection,	then... have them look for and read meaningful parts in the words or have them chunk words with no recognizable parts.
If... students have difficulty reading along with the group,	then... have them follow along as they listen to the AudioText.

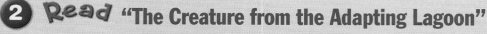

Strategic Intervention

ROUTINE

1 Practice Retelling

REVIEW MAIN IDEAS Help students identify the main ideas in *Exploding Ants*. List the ideas students mention. Then ask questions to help students differentiate between essential and nonessential information.

RETELL Using the Retelling Cards, have students work with partners to retell the important ideas. Show partners how to summarize in as few words as possible. Monitor retelling and prompt students as needed. For example, ask:

• What was the selection mostly about?
• What was the author trying to teach us?

If students struggle, model a fluent retelling.

Grade 5
Retelling Cards
PEARSON
Scott Foresman

2 Read "The Creature from the Adapting Lagoon"

BEFORE READING Read the genre information on p. 454. Recall the Leveled Reader *Surviving the Weather*, rereading portions of the selection as needed. We have read several selections this week about how animals adapt in order to survive. What did *Surviving the Weather* explain about how the environment affects animals' characteristics? *(Animals specialize in order to survive in their various habitats.)* Now you will be able to use what you learned about animals adapting to conduct an experiment.

Read the rest of the panel on p. 454. Then have students scan the steps to familiarize themselves with the experiment.

DURING READING Have students read along with you while tracking the print, or do a choral reading of the selection. Stop to discuss difficult language, such as *appendage* and *criteria*. Help students understand all the steps in the experiment and the items in the criteria list before moving forward with the experiment.

AFTER READING Have students share their reactions to the selection. Then guide them through the Reading Across Texts and Writing Across Texts activities, prompting if necessary.

• What facts from *Exploding Ants* will help you create your criteria list for the animal you have chosen?
• How many criteria can you develop based on facts from the selection and what you already know?

Pages DI•28–DI•29

LA.5.1.5.1 Demonstrate the ability to read grade level text

LA.5.2.2.2 Use information from the text to answer questions related to explicitly stated main ideas

LA.5.2.2.3 Represent main ideas within text by summarizing

Advanced

ROUTINE

DAY 4

1 Read "The Creature from the Adapting Lagoon"

CREATIVE THINKING Have students read pp. 454–457 independently. Encourage them to think creatively. For example, ask:

• How can an animal from one living environment survive in another?

AFTER READING Discuss Reading Across Texts. Have students do Writing Across Texts independently.

2 Extend Genre Study

RESEARCH Have students use online or print resources to find other experiments involving animals in nature. Suggestions include finding research on the migratory patterns of geese, experiments about bears' hibernating cycles, or experiments on insect behavior.

WRITE Using some of the research they uncovered, have students design their own experiment. It should include a purpose (what the student is trying to find out), materials needed to conduct the experiment, and a list of procedures to follow.

 AudioText

Exploding Ants

Group Time

ONLINE
PearsonSuccessNet.com

Strategic Intervention

ROUTINE

1 Reread for Fluency

MODEL Read aloud pp. 4–5 of the Leveled Reader *Surviving the Weather*, emphasizing your tempo and rate. Read the selection slowly and carefully, paying special attention to scientific words such as *specialize* and *habitats*. Then read pp. 6–7 in a fast-paced, clipped rate. Have students tell you which model sounded better. Discuss how reading at a tempo appropriate to the material will help the listener to understand what is being read more easily. Point out that the reader is also less likely to make mistakes.

PRACTICE Have students reread passages from *Surviving the Weather* with a partner or individually. For optimal fluency, they should reread three or four times. As students read, monitor fluency and provide corrective feedback. Students in this group are assessed in Weeks 2 and 4.

2 Retell Leveled Reader *Surviving the Weather*

Model how to skim the book, retelling as you skim. Then ask students to retell the book, one chapter at a time. Prompt them as needed.

- What is this chapter mostly about?
- What did you learn from reading this chapter?

Monitor Progress

Fluency

If... students have difficulty reading fluently,	then... provide additional fluency practice by pairing nonfluent readers with fluent ones.

For alternate Leveled Reader lesson plans that teach **Graphic Sources, Monitor and Fix Up,** and **Lesson Vocabulary,** see pp. LR19–LR27.

On-Level

1 Reread for Fluency   ROUTINE

MODEL Read aloud pp. 4–5 of the Leveled Reader *Changing to Survive,* emphasizing your tempo and rate. Read the selection slowly and carefully, paying special attention to scientific words such as *Archaeopteryx.* Discuss how reading at a tempo appropriate to the material will help the listener to understand what is being read more easily. Point out that the reader is also less likely to make mistakes.

PRACTICE Have students reread passages from *Changing to Survive* with a partner or individually. For optimal fluency, they should reread three or four times. As students read, monitor fluency and provide corrective feedback. Assess the fluency of students in this group using p. 457a.

2 Retell Leveled Reader *Changing to Survive*

Have students use subheads and photographs as a guide to summarize the important facts they learned from each section of the book. Prompt as needed.

- What is this book mostly about?
- What did you learn from reading this book?

Advanced

1 Reread for Fluency   ROUTINE

PRACTICE Have students reread passages from the Leveled Reader *A Home for Humans in Outer Space* with a partner or individually. As students read, monitor fluency and provide corrective feedback. If students read fluently on the first reading, they do not need to reread three to four times. Students in this group were assessed on Week 1.

2 Revisit Leveled Reader *A Home for Humans in Outer Space*

NOW TRY THIS Have students complete their projects. You may wish to review their ideas and drawings to see whether they need any additional suggestions. Have them present their projects.

Group Time

ONLINE

PearsonSuccessNet.com

1 Build Background

REINFORCE CONCEPTS Display the Adapting to a New Place Concept Web. This week's concept is *adapting to a new place*. Adapting is changing in order to fit into a different or new situation. Adapting takes time. Even though it can be hard at first, it can also be a good experience. Discuss the meaning of each word on the web, using the definitions on p. 458l and the Concept Vocabulary Routine on p. DI·1.

CONNECT TO READING This week you will read about ways people adapt to new places. You will read about what makes changing hard and what makes it exciting. You will also read about how even though places can be different, they can share similarities too. Adapting then can be a more pleasant experience. Do you think excerpts from "Only Fiona" showed both sides of adapting to a new place? *(Yes, because Fiona says that giving up friends she's counted on is hard, but she realizes she can count on her family. Her parents also remind Fiona that she's already making friends and that once she gets used to her new town, she's going to like it a lot.)*

2 Read Leveled Reader *Moving*

BEFORE READING Using the Picture Walk Routine on p. DI·1, guide students through the text focusing on key concepts and vocabulary. Ask questions such as:

pp. 6–7 Do the map and the photograph show what is difficult and what is nice about moving? *(Yes. The map shows that places can be far. Moving to faraway places can be tough. The photograph shows that seeing new places can be good travel experiences.)*

pp. 10–12 These images show life in London, England. The photograph on pp. 10–11 shows the London Underground. The image on p. 12 shows schoolchildren in England. What do you know about life in England? What do these pictures tell you? How is life in England similar to and different from life in the United States?

DURING READING Read pp. 3–7 aloud, while students track the print. Do a choral reading of pp. 8–11. Have students read and discuss the remainder of the book with a partner. Ask: What makes moving to a new place hard? What things make moving to another country hard? What are some good things about moving to new places?

AFTER READING Encourage students in groups of two or three to discuss ways people adapt to new places. We read *Moving* to learn about the pluses and minuses of adapting to a new place. Understanding both sides will help us as we read the play *The Stormi Giovanni Club*.

Monitor Progress

Selection Reading and Comprehension

If... students have difficulty reading the selection with a partner,	**then...** have them follow along as they listen to the Online Leveled Reader Audio.
If... students have trouble understanding the positive and negative aspects of moving,	**then...** reread pp. 4–7 and discuss the aspects along with the differences and similarities between places.

For alternate Leveled Reader lesson plans that teach **Generalize, Story Structure,** and **Lesson Vocabulary,** see pp. LR28–LR36.

On-Level

1 Build Background

DEVELOP VOCABULARY Write the phrase *count on* and ask students to define it in their own words. *(to expect or depend on for help)* Tell about people or things you count on. *(parents, teachers, friends, school)* Repeat this activity with the phrase *fit in* and other words from the Leveled Reader *The New Kid at School*. Use the Concept Vocabulary Routine on p. DI·1 as needed.

2 Read Leveled Reader *The New Kid at School*

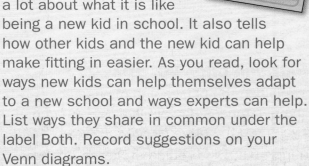

BEFORE READING Have students create Venn diagrams with the labels The New Kid, Both, and The Expert. This book tells a lot about what it is like being a new kid in school. It also tells how other kids and the new kid can help make fitting in easier. As you read, look for ways new kids can help themselves adapt to a new school and ways experts can help. List ways they share in common under the label Both. Record suggestions on your Venn diagrams.

DURING READING Have students follow along as you read pp. 3–10. Then let them complete the book on their own. Remind students to add information to their Venn diagrams as they read.

AFTER READING Have students compare the suggestions they have written on their Venn diagrams. Point out that the information about fitting into a new school will help them as they read tomorrow's play *The Stormi Giovanni Club.*

Advanced

1 Read Leveled Reader *Nathaniel Comes to Town*

BEFORE READING Recall the Read Aloud "Only Fiona." Fiona thought that the hardest thing about leaving a place was giving up friends she's counted on for so long. Do you think making new friends is one of the hardest things about adapting to a new place? *(Answers will vary.)* Today you will read about how adapting takes place in friendships both old and new.

CRITICAL THINKING Have students read the Leveled Reader independently. Encourage them to think critically. For example, ask:
- How does the author show Drew's thoughts and feelings about friendships? Nathaniel's?
- In what way or ways does Drew have to adapt? Nathaniel?

AFTER READING Have students review the selection to find ten words having to do with emotions. Students should organize the words from most negative to most positive. Have students meet with each other and you to discuss how Drew's negative attitude about school and Nathaniel's positive attitude about school affected their abilities to make and keep friends.

2 Independent Extension Activity

INDEPENDENT INVESTIGATIVE WORK Have students use online or print resources to find out more about Marian Anderson, Albert Einstein, or Amy Van Dyken. Throughout the week, have students work on biographies that tell how their subject had to adapt in order to overcome something or to succeed.

Group Time

AudioText

DAY 2

ROUTINE

1 Word Study/Phonics

LESSON VOCABULARY Use p. 460b to review the meanings of *cavities, combination, demonstrates, episode, profile,* and *strict.* Have individuals practice reading the words from word cards.

DECODING MULTISYLLABIC WORDS Write *guaranteed,* saying the word as you write it. Then model how to use meaningful parts to read longer words. First I ask myself if I see any parts I know. If I see a part I know, like *-ed,* I look at the base word. The base word is long, so I will read the chunks. I see *-an* and *-tee.* The *u* in *guar-* is confusing, but I try reading the chunks several ways and realize the *u* is silent. I add the *-ed* and say the chunks fast to read the whole word: *guar an teed.* I read the word again faster: *guaranteed.* It means "promised or made certain."

Use the multisyllabic word routine on p. DI·1 to help students read these words from *The Stormi Giovanni Club: professors, philosophers, distressed, digressed, gestures, examining, promises, scintillating,* and *designing.* Be sure students understand the meanings of words such as *distressed, digressed,* and *scintillating.*

Use *Strategies for Word Analysis,* Lesson 19, with students who have difficulty mastering word analysis and need practice with decodable text.

2 Read *The Stormi Giovanni Club,* pp. 462–469

BEFORE READING *Moving* explained the pluses and minuses of moving to new places and the differences and similarities between places. Think about this as you read the play *The Stormi Giovanni Club.*

Using the Picture Walk Routine on p. DI·1, guide students through the text asking questions such as those listed below. Read the question on p. 463. Together, set a purpose for reading.

pp. 464–465 What do these illustrations show? How do you know?

pp. 466–468 What kinds of situations do you see? How are these pictures related?

DURING READING Follow the Guiding Comprehension routine on pp. 464–469. Have students read along with you while tracking the print or do a choral reading. Stop every two pages to ask what has happened so far. Prompt as necessary.

• Why does Stormi decide to form the Stormi Giovanni Club?
• How does Stormi feel about making new friends? How do you know?

AFTER READING What has happened in the play so far? What do you think will happen next? Reread passages as needed.

Monitor Progress

Word and Play Reading

If... students have difficulty reading multisyllabic words in the selection,	then... have them look for and read meaningful parts in the words or have them chunk words with no recognizable parts.
If... students need practice reading words fluently,	then... use the Fluent Word Reading Routine on the DI tab.
If... students have difficulty reading along with the group,	then... have them follow along as they listen to the AudioText.

Pages DI•34–DI•35

LA.5.1.5.1 Demonstrate the ability to read grade level text
LA.5.1.6.1 Use new vocabulary
LA.5.1.6.3 Use context clues to determine meanings of unfamiliar words

Advanced

ROUTINE

1 Extend Vocabulary

CONTEXT CLUES Choose and read a sentence or passage containing a difficult word, such as this sentence from p. 23 of *Nathaniel Comes to Town*: "My dad's voice reverberates from inside the oven, where he's scraping at something from Julie's cooking mishap." What does the word *reverberates* mean? *(echoes)* How did you determine the word's meaning? *(I used the context clues* voice, inside, *and* oven *and imagined sound bouncing around inside the oven.)* Discuss why context clues are helpful, and remind students to use the strategy as they read the *The Stormi Giovanni Club.*

2 Read *The Stormi Giovanni Club,* pp. 462–469

BEFORE READING Today you will read a play called *The Stormi Giovanni Club.* It tells the experience of a girl who has to adapt to a new city and school and make new friends. As you read, think about other ways people adapt to new cities or schools that you have read about.

Have students write predictions in their Strategy Response Log (p. 462). Encourage students to revise predictions as they read.

PROBLEM SOLVING Have students read pp. 464–469 independently. Encourage them to use problem-solving skills and strategies. For example, ask:

- When have you had to adapt to a new place? How did you feel about it?
- What advice can you give to others who are experiencing the same situation?

AFTER READING Have partners discuss the selection and share their Strategy Response Log predictions and how accurate they were. Then have students write about a time when they had to adapt to a new place, such as a new town or new school or new classroom, perhaps even an entirely different country. Tell students to include what it was like to leave old friends and make new ones and how they had to adjust in order to fit in. Have students meet with you to discuss the selection and their writings.

DAY 2

The
Stormi
Giovanni
Club
by Lydia R. Diamond
Illustrated by R. Gregory Christie

How will Stormi do
in her new school?

Audio
CD   AudioText

The Stormi Giovanni Club

Group Time

ROUTINE

DAY 3

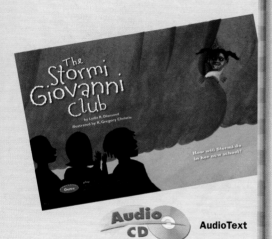

Audio CD   AudioText

1 Reinforce Comprehension

SKILL GENERALIZE Have students tell what a generalization is *(a broad statement or rule that applies to many examples)* and list clue words that often signal generalizations *(all, none, most, many, always, usually, never, generally, everyone)*. If necessary, review the meaning and provide a model. A generalization is a broad statement or rule that applies to many examples. *Most people need time to adapt to new situations* is a generalization. It is a statement that refers to most people. The word *most* helps me identify it as a generalization.

Ask students to make generalizations about adapting to a new place or have them choose a generalization from a group of statements. For example, ask: Which of the following is a generalization? *(Some children have a hard time fitting into a new school.)*

In one year, 14% of the population moved within the U.S. Stormi is having a hard time in her new school. Some children have a hard time fitting into a new school.

2 Read *The Stormi Giovanni Club,* pp. 470–477

BEFORE READING Have students retell what happened in the selection so far. Remind students that most stories begin with a conflict, or problem, that the characters have to solve. Discuss the conflict or problem in the play. Reread the dialogue on pp. 468–469 to identify the rising action. Model the story structure so far. As I read I know that Stormi moves to a new school and is unhappy about it. When Penelope, her old friend, asks about Stormi's new friends, Stormi e-mails back that she won't be making any. Remind students to pay attention to how the play is organized. Students should be able to identify the conflict, rising action, climax, and resolution as they finish reading the play. **STRATEGY Story Structure**

DURING READING Follow the Guiding Comprehension routines on pp. 470–477. Have students read along with you while tracking print or do a choral reading. Stop every two pages to ask students what has happened so far. Prompt as necessary.

- Describe Stormi's feelings about lunch at her new school.
- How does Stormi finally describe the experience of moving?

AFTER READING How does this play explain the pluses and minuses of adapting to new places? Reread with students for comprehension as needed. Tell them that tomorrow they will read a newspaper article entitled "Think Dress Codes Are a Drag?" which will discuss adapting in a different way.

Monitor Progress

Word and Play Reading

If... students have difficulty reading multisyllabic words in the selection,	**then...** have them look for and read meaningful parts in the words or have them chunk words with no recognizable parts.
If... students have difficulty reading along with the group,	**then...** have them follow along as they listen to the AudioText.

Pages DI•36–DI•37

LA.5.1.5.1 Demonstrate the ability to read grade level text

LA.5.1.7.3 Determine the main idea or essential message through summarizing

LA.5.2.1.2 Locate and analyze character development, setting, and plot structure, including rising/falling action and problem/resolution

Advanced

ROUTINE

1 Extend Comprehension

SKILL GENERALIZE Based on generalizations students have made about Stormi, allow them to write another scene between her and Hannah e-mailing each other after reading pp. 468–469. Remind students to include speech tags to indicate when each character is speaking and stage directions to explain what characters are doing and how they are feeling. Allow students to share their scenes if they choose.

STRATEGY STORY STRUCTURE Have students begin a story elements chart to summarize the setting, characters, and plot so far. Encourage students to add to the chart as they read the rest of the play.

2 Read *The Stormi Giovanni Club*, pp. 470–477

BEFORE READING Have students recall what has happened in the play so far. Remind them to look for generalizations and to keep track of the story structure in order to identify the climax and resolution as they read the remainder of the play.

CRITICAL THINKING Have students read pp. 470–477 independently. Encourage them to think critically. For example, ask:

• What is a theme for the play?

AFTER READING Have students complete the Strategy Response Log activity (p. 476). Then have them pretend to be Stormi as an advice columnist for her school newspaper. Have her write an advice column about moving and adapting to a new place or about making new friends at a new school. Have students meet with you to discuss the selection and the columns they wrote.

DAY 3

AudioText

The Stormi Giovanni Club

Group Time

ROUTINE

DAY
4

Audio CD   AudioText

Monitor Progress

Word and Selection Reading

If... students have difficulty reading multisyllabic words in the selection,	then... have them look for and read meaningful parts in the words or have them chunk words with no recognizable parts.
If... students have difficulty reading along with the group,	then... have them follow along as they listen to the AudioText.

1 Practice Retelling

REVIEW STORY ELEMENTS Have students identify the main characters and the setting of *The Stormi Giovanni Club*. Then guide them in using the Retelling Cards to list the play's events in sequence. Prompt students to include important details.

RETELL Using the Retelling Cards, have students work in pairs to retell *The Stormi Giovanni Club*. Monitor retelling and prompt students as needed. For example, ask:

- What is the problem in the play?
- How was the problem solved?
- Has anything like this happened to you?

2 Read "Think Dress Codes Are a Drag?"

BEFORE READING Read the genre information on p. 480. Discuss the features of newspaper articles such as datelines, headlines, bylines, lead paragraphs, and bodies. Help with students' understanding by identifying the features of newspaper articles using a sample article from a newspaper that contains all of these features. Emphasize to students the purposes of newspaper articles. As we read "Think Dress Codes Are a Drag?" think about the features of the article as well as what information or issue it presents.

Read the rest of the panel on p. 480. Then have students scan the pages, identifying the features of the newspaper article and the pictures used to support the ideas.

DURING READING Have students read along with you while tracking the print or do a choral reading of the selection. Stop to discuss difficult vocabulary. Also, discuss words related to clothing styles or types of clothing mentioned in the selection.

AFTER READING Have students share their reactions to the selection. Then guide them through the Reading Across Texts and Writing Across Texts activities, prompting if necessary.

- What problems did the students in *The Stormi Giovanni Club* and the newspaper article have?
- How did the students handle their problems?
- How would you have handled these problems?

Pages DI•38–DI•39

LA.5.1.5.1 Demonstrate the ability to read grade level text
LA.5.2.1.2 Locate and analyze plot structure
LA.5.5.2.1 Listen and speak to gain and share information (personal interviews)

Advanced

ROUTINE

1 Read "Think Dress Codes Are a Drag?"

CRITICAL THINKING Have students read pp. 480–483 independently. Encourage them to think critically. For example, ask:

- What views do the three students and two adults mentioned in the article have about dress codes?
- What is your school dress code? How do you feel about it?
- What are the benefits and pitfalls of having dress codes at school?

AFTER READING Discuss the selection and Reading Across Texts with students. Have student do Writing Across Texts independently.

DAY 4

Audio CD   AudioText

2 Extend Genre Study

RESEARCH Have students use the local newspaper to find other newspaper articles that tell readers about current events, issues, people, and places of interest. Have students clip three articles and highlight and label the datelines, headlines, bylines, and lead paragraphs. Have students read the articles in order to answer Who? What? When? Where? Why? and How? in their own words for the three articles.

WRITE Have students plan to interview an adult family member. Have students formulate five to six questions related to the topic of schools and dress codes, either related to the adult's own childhood or about policies held for students today. Encourage students to use the 5W's and How when devising questions. Meet with students individually to review questions. Students should conduct their interviews and write down the interviewee's responses after each question asked. At least one response should be a direct quote, preferably one that conveys the interviewee's overall opinion on the issue. Display interviews on a bulletin board for the entire class to read.

The Gymnast
Group Time

DAY

DAY
1

ONLINE

PearsonSuccessNet.com

Strategic Intervention

ROUTINE

1 Build Background

REINFORCE CONCEPTS Display the Improving Ourselves Concept Web. This week's concept is *improving ourselves.* People often adapt to new situations by improving themselves in some way. Discuss the meaning of each word on the web, using the definitions on p. 484l and the Concept Vocabulary Routine on p. DI·1.

CONNECT TO READING This week you will read about how athletes improve themselves to become better at sports. How was Jerry trying to improve his swimming in "The Winning Stroke"? *(He was practicing his turns and dives.)*

2 Read Leveled Reader *Let the Games Begin*

BEFORE READING Using the Picture Walk Routine on p. DI·1, guide students through the text focusing on key concepts and vocabulary. Ask questions such as:

pp. 4–5 These pictures show the opening ceremony for the Olympic Games. Look at all the athletes. How do you think they feel? How much work do you think it took to get there?

pp. 6–7 This picture is of the 1904 World's Fair in St. Louis, Missouri. How can you tell this was an important event? *(Many people attended the fair.)*

DURING READING Read pp. 3–7 aloud, while students track the print. Do a choral reading of pp. 8–13. If students are capable, have them read and discuss the remainder of the book with a partner. Ask: What problems did some athletes face in the 1904 Olympics?

AFTER READING Encourage pairs of students to discuss how athletes improve themselves to compete in the Olympics. We read *Let the Games Begin* to learn how athletes adapt to new situations to compete in the Olympics. Understanding how people adapt to improve themselves will help us as we read *The Gymnast.*

Monitor Progress

Selection Reading and Comprehension

If... students have difficulty reading the selection with a partner,	then... have them follow along as they listen to the Online Leveled Reader Audio.
If... students have trouble understanding how athletes adapt to new situations,	then... reread pp. 11–13 and discuss Felix Carvajal together.

Pages DI•42–DI•43

LA.5.1.6.1 Use new vocabulary
LA.5.6.1.1 Read and interpret informational text and organize the information

For alternate Leveled Reader lesson plans that teach **Draw Conclusions, Visualize,** and **Lesson Vocabulary,** see pp. LR37–LR45.

On-Level

DAY 1

1 Build Background

DEVELOP VOCABULARY Write the word *competitive* and ask students to define it in their own words. *(trying to win something)* When might you be competitive? *(during a race, playing basketball or some other game)* Repeat this activity with the word *accuracy* and other words from the Leveled Reader *Strange Sports with Weird Gear.* Use the Concept Vocabulary Routine on p. DI•1 as needed.

2 Read Leveled Reader *Strange Sports with Weird Gear*

BEFORE READING Have students create three-column charts with the labels Sport, Gear, and Physical Traits. This book tells about sports and what it takes to play them. As you read, look for facts about each sport, the gear needed to play it, and the physical traits players should have. Record them in your three-column chart.

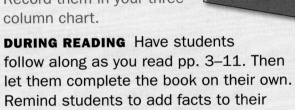

DURING READING Have students follow along as you read pp. 3–11. Then let them complete the book on their own. Remind students to add facts to their three-column charts as they read.

AFTER READING Have students compare the facts on their three-column charts. Point out that facts about what it takes to be an athlete will help them as they read tomorrow's story *The Gymnast.*

Advanced

DAY 1

1 Read Leveled Reader *What Makes Great Athletes?*

BEFORE READING Recall the Read Aloud "The Winning Stroke." What did Jerry do to improve his swimming? *(He practiced his strokes until he got them right.)* Today you will read about what it takes to be a great athlete.

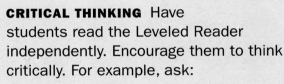

CRITICAL THINKING Have students read the Leveled Reader independently. Encourage them to think critically. For example, ask:

- How can athletes encourage us to make changes in ourselves?
- How can people prepare to compete in challenging sports?

AFTER READING Have students review the selection to find words that describe great athletes. Then ask them to use these words to write sentences that describe athletes. Have students meet with you or as a group and discuss the selection and the sentences they wrote.

2 Independent Extension Activity

NOW TRY THIS Assign "Now Try This" on pp. 18–19 of *What Makes Great Athletes?* for students to work on throughout the week.

Group Time

DAY 2

Audio CD — AudioText

Strategic Intervention

ROUTINE

1 Word Study/Phonics

LESSON VOCABULARY Use p. 486b to review the meanings of *bluish, cartwheels, gymnastics, hesitation, limelight, skidded, somersault, throbbing,* and *wincing.* Have individuals practice reading the words from word cards.

DECODING MULTISYLLABIC WORDS Write *solitary,* saying the word as you write it. Then model how to use chunking to read longer words. *I see a chunk at the beginning of the word, sol. I see a chunk in the middle, i, and another chunk, tar. I see a chunk at the end, y. I say each chunk slowly, sol i tar y. I say the chunks fast to make a whole word: solitary. Is it a real word? Yes, I know the word solitary.*

Use the Multisyllabic Word Routine on p. DI·1 to help students read these other words from *The Gymnast: aluminum, instructed, dully, appreciative, disdain,* and *nutrients.* Be sure students understand the meanings of words such as *disdain* and *nutrients.*

Use *Strategies for Word Analysis,* Lesson 20, with students who have difficulty mastering word analysis and need practice with decodable text.

2 Read *The Gymnast,* pp. 488–493

BEFORE READING *Let the Games Begin* explained how athletes improved themselves to compete in the Olympics. Think about these athletes as you read *The Gymnast.*

Using the Picture Walk Routine on p. DI·1, guide students through the text asking questions such as those listed below. Read the question on p. 489. Together, set a purpose for reading.

pp. 488–489 What is this boy doing? Why do you think he's doing this? *(a cartwheel; he wants to improve his gymnastics)*

pp. 490–493 What do you see on these pages? *(someone's legs, someone doing a cartwheel)* Why do you think there are pictures of cartwheels? *(The boy needs more practice to do cartwheels correctly.)*

DURING READING Follow the Guiding Comprehension routine on pp. 490–493. Have students read along with you while tracking the print or do a choral reading. Stop every two pages to ask what has happened so far. Prompt as necessary.

- What is Gary's problem?
- Who is Isaac? What does Gary think of Isaac?

AFTER READING What has happened in the selection so far? What do you think will happen next? Reread passages with students for comprehension as needed.

Advanced

ROUTINE

1 Extend Vocabulary

WORD STRUCTURE Read this sentence from p. 3 of *What Makes Great Athletes:* "We can smile with admiration at the height, grace, and form of a ballplayer's jump as he makes a catch." What does the word admiration mean? *(a feeling of wonder, pleasure, and approval)* How could you use word structure to determine the word's meaning? *(I recognize the base word admire, even though the final e is dropped. I know what admire means, and I know the suffix -tion means the state of being, so I determined the meaning.)* Discuss why suffixes are helpful, and remind students to use the strategy as they read *The Gymnast.*

2 Read *The Gymnast,* pp. 488–493

Audio CD   **AudioText**

BEFORE READING Today you will read about a boy who wants to become a great athlete. As you read, think about what you have read about great athletes.

Have students create a T-chart for their Strategy Response Log (p. 488). Students should add to it as they read.

CRITICAL THINKING Have students read pp. 490–493 independently. Encourage them to think critically and creatively. For example, ask:

• Which sport do you think is the most challenging? How can athletes prepare for it?

AFTER READING Have partners discuss the selection and share their Strategy Response Log entries and the images they have visualized. Have students write sentences in the right column of their charts explaining their images. Then have students choose the one image that best describes the selection so far.

The Gymnast
Group Time

DAY
3

Audio CD   AudioText

Monitor Progress

Word and Selection Reading

If... students have difficulty reading multisyllabic words in the selection,	then... have them look for and read meaningful parts in the words or have them chunk words with no recognizable parts.
If... students have difficulty reading along with the group,	then... have them follow along as they listen to the AudioText.

Strategic Intervention

① Reinforce Comprehension

SKILL DRAW CONCLUSIONS Have students explain what a conclusion is *(a sensible decision you make after you think about facts or details that you read).* If necessary, review the meaning and provide a model.

Drawing a conclusion means making a sensible decision after you have the facts or details about something. For example, if the sky suddenly turned dark, that probably means it's going to rain. I can draw this conclusion based on my prior knowledge of this happening.

Ask students to draw conclusions using the following examples.

I did well on my last math test because I studied for it. I have another test tomorrow. *(I should study for tomorrow's test.)*

Ralph always has everything he needs when it's time to start class. He has all of his assignments completed on time. *(Ralph is a very organized student.)*

② Read *The Gymnast,* pp. 494–497

BEFORE READING Have students retell what happened in the selection so far. Ask: What seems to interest Gary the most about gymnastics? Reread the last paragraph on p. 493 and model how to draw a conclusion. As I read I try to picture what Gary looks like. He is wearing his cousin's shoes and has tape wrapped around his wrists. Gary must really like the gymnastics gear. Remind students to visualize as they read the rest of *The Gymnast.* **STRATEGY Visualize**

DURING READING Follow the Guiding Comprehension routine on pp. 494–497. Have students read along with you while tracking the print or do a choral reading. Stop every two pages to ask what has happened so far. Prompt as necessary.

• What does Gary do the next day to improve his gymnastics?
• How does Gary feel about gymnastics at the end of the selection?

AFTER READING How does Gary try to improve himself? Reread with students for comprehension as needed. Tell them that tomorrow they will read "All About Gymnastics," a selection about using online reference sources to find information about doing gymnastics.

ROUTINE

Pages DI•46–DI•47

LA.5.1.7.3 Determine the main idea or essential message through inferring

LA.5.2.2.2 Use information from text to answer questions

Advanced

ROUTINE

1 Extend Comprehension

SKILL DRAW CONCLUSIONS Have students discuss Gary and Isaac. Have students draw conclusions about the motives and characteristics behind the cousins' actions.

STRATEGY VISUALIZE Have a volunteer reread p. 493 while others close their eyes. Ask students which words or phrases help them visualize Gary and Isaac. Ask questions such as:

- What does Gary look like compared to his cousin?
- Why does Gary want to try on the gymnastic gear?

2 Read *The Gymnast,* pp. 494–497

BEFORE READING Have students recall what has happened in the selection so far. Remind them to draw conclusions and to visualize as they read the remainder of the selection.

CRITICAL THINKING Have students read pp. 494–497 independently. Encourage them to think critically. For example, ask:

- Why is Gary pushing himself so hard?

AFTER READING Have students complete the Strategy Response Log activity (p. 496). Then have them list other sports and visualize the movements or plays associated with those sports. Tell students to write descriptive sentences about the sports. Have students read their sentences aloud to the group while the others close their eyes and visualize.

Audio CD   AudioText

The Gymnast

Group Time

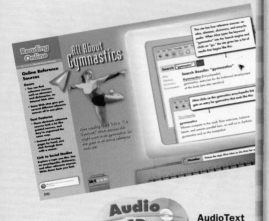

Audio CD AudioText

Monitor Progress

Word and Selection Reading

If... students have difficulty reading multisyllabic words in the selection,	then... have them look for and read meaningful parts in the words or have them chunk words with no recognizable parts.
If... students have difficulty reading along with the group,	then... have them follow along as they listen to the AudioText.

ROUTINE

1 Practice Retelling

REVIEW MAIN IDEAS Help students identify the main ideas in *The Gymnast*. List the main events in this selection from the autobiography. Then ask questions to help students differentiate between essential and nonessential information.

RETELL Using the Retelling Cards, have students work with partners to retell the important ideas from *The Gymnast*. Monitor retelling and prompt students as needed. For example, ask:

Grade 5
Retelling Cards
PEARSON
Scott Foresman

- What was the selection mostly about?
- Why do you think the author wrote this selection?

If students struggle, model a fluent retelling.

2 Read "All About Gymnastics"

BEFORE READING Read the genre information on p. 500. Recall the Read Aloud "The Winning Stroke," rereading portions of the text as needed. We have read several selections about how athletes improve themselves for their sports. What did Jerry do to improve his swimming in "The Winning Stroke"? *(He practiced his swimming strokes until he got them right.)* As we read "All About Gymnastics," think about what other information about gymnastics you could find by using online reference sources.

Read the rest of the panel on p. 500. Then have students scan the pages looking for images of online resources.

DURING READING Have students read along with you while tracking the print or do a choral reading of the selection. Stop to discuss the search windows and the search results. Make sure students understand the difference between the window and the results.

AFTER READING Have students share their reactions to the selection. Then guide them through the Reading Across Texts and Writing Across Texts activities, prompting if necessary.

- What gymnastic moves was Gary practicing?
- What would Gary look like while doing these moves?
- Which gymnastic event would he most likely be practicing for?

Pages DI•48–DI•49

LA.5.1.5.1 Demonstrate the ability to read grade level text
LA.5.2.2.1 Locate, explain, and use information from text features

Advanced

ROUTINE

1 Read "All About Gymnastics"

CRITICAL THINKING Have students read pp. 500–503 independently. Encourage them to think critically. For example, ask:

- Are there any other possible online reference sources not listed here?
- What other key words might you use to find information about gymnastics?

AFTER READING Discuss the selection and Reading Across Texts with students. Have students do Writing Across Texts independently.

DAY 4

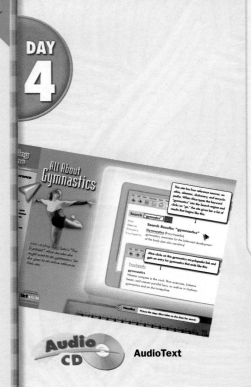

Audio CD   AudioText

2 Extend Genre Study

RESEARCH Have students locate print sources for information about gymnastics. Have them compare the information found in these sources to the information that would be found using online sources. Discuss which sources provide the best or most reliable information.

WRITING Have students write online dictionary entries for plays or moves from other sports. Have them list key words that would link online search engines to their entries.

The Gymnast

Group Time

DAY 5

ONLINE

PearsonSuccessNet.com

① Reread for Fluency

MODEL Read aloud pp. 3–4 of the Leveled Reader *Let the Games Begin,* emphasizing how you use punctuation clues. Have students note the changes in your intonation for question marks and exclamation marks. Also point out how you pause after commas and periods. Then reread pp. 3–4 in a monotone voice. Do not pause for commas or stop for periods. Have students tell you which model made more sense. Discuss how using punctuation clues helps you understand what you are reading.

PRACTICE Have students reread passages from *Let the Games Begin* with a partner or individually. For optimal fluency, they should reread three or four times. As students read, monitor fluency and provide corrective feedback. Assess any students you have not yet checked during this unit.

② Retell Leveled Reader *Let the Games Begin*

Model how to use heads and photographs to retell. Then ask students to retell the book, one section at a time. Prompt them as needed.

- What are these pages mostly about?
- What did you learn from reading these pages?

Monitor Progress

Fluency

If... students have difficulty reading fluently,	then... provide additional fluency practice by pairing nonfluent readers with fluent ones.

Pages DI•50–DI•51

LA.5.1.5.2 Adjust reading rate
LA.5.1.7.3 Determine the main idea or essential message through summarizing
LA.5.2.2.1 Locate, explain, and use information from text features

For alternate Leveled Reader lesson plans that teach 🔊 **Draw Conclusions,** 🔊 **Visualize,** and **Lesson Vocabulary,** see pp. LR37–LR45.

On-Level

1 Reread for Fluency   ROUTINE

MODEL Read aloud p. 3 of the Leveled Reader *Strange Sports with Weird Gear,* emphasizing how you use punctuation clues. Have students note the rise of your voice for questions and how you pause a little longer for the dash. Discuss how changing your intonation helps listeners understand better what you are reading.

PRACTICE Have students reread passages from *Strange Sports with Weird Gear* with a partner or individually. For optimal fluency, they should reread three or four times. As students read, monitor fluency and provide corrective feedback. Assess any students you have not yet checked during this unit.

2 Retell Leveled Reader *Strange Sports with Weird Gear*

Have students use heads and photographs as a guide to summarize the important facts they learned from each section of the book. Prompt as needed.

- What is this book mostly about?
- What did you learn from reading this book?
- Why do you think the author wrote this book?

Advanced

1 Reread for Fluency   ROUTINE

PRACTICE Have students reread passages from the Leveled Reader *What Makes Great Athletes?* with a partner or individually. As students read, monitor fluency and provide corrective feedback. If students read fluently on the first reading, they do not need to reread three or four times. Assess any students you have not yet checked during this unit.

2 Revisit Leveled Reader *What Makes Great Athletes?*

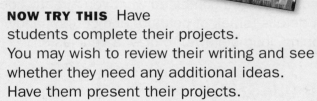

RETELL Have students retell the Leveled Reader *What Makes Great Athletes?*

NOW TRY THIS Have students complete their projects. You may wish to review their writing and see whether they need any additional ideas. Have them present their projects.

Draw Conclusions

When students move beyond the literal meaning of a text to draw conclusions, they get more ideas from what they read and understand better the points an author is trying to make. Use the following routine to guide students in drawing conclusions.

1 DISCUSS DRAWING CONCLUSIONS

Tell students a conclusion is a sensible decision they reach based on details or facts in a story or an article. Explain when they draw conclusions, they think about information in the text and what they already know.

2 MODEL DRAWING A CONCLUSION

Model using your own experiences to draw a conclusion.

MODEL The smell of peanuts and cotton candy filled the air. I heard clapping, I even heard loud bellows that sounded like elephants. I knew a circus was going on.

Discuss how you combined what you already knew with details (smell of peanuts and cotton candy, clapping, loud bellows) to draw a conclusion.

3 ASK QUESTIONS

Read aloud a passage and ask questions that foster drawing conclusions. For example: *What kind of person is the main character? How can you tell? Why do you think the character acts this way?*

4 USE A GRAPHIC ORGANIZER

Have partners read both fiction and nonfiction passages. Students can ask each other questions that lead to drawing conclusions. Suggest that they use webs or charts to show the facts or details that support their conclusions.

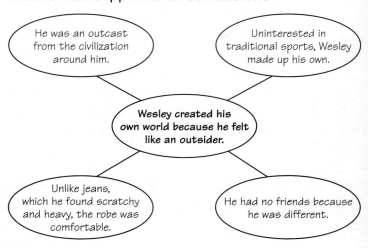

He was an outcast from the civilization around him.

Uninterested in traditional sports, Wesley made up his own.

Wesley created his own world because he felt like an outsider.

Unlike jeans, which he found scratchy and heavy, the robe was comfortable.

He had no friends because he was different.

▲ **Graphic Organizer** 15

Research on Drawing Conclusions

"Inference is a mosaic, a dazzling constellation of thinking processes, but the tiles available to form each mosaic are limited, circumscribed. There must be a fusion of words on a page—and constraints of meaning they impose—and the experience and knowledge of the reader."

Ellin Oliver Keene and Susan Zimmerman,
Mosaic of Thought

Keen, Ellin Oliver, and Susan Zimmermann. *Mosaic of Thought: Teaching Comprehension in a Reader's Workshop.* Heinemann, 1997, p. 154; 1992, p. 238.

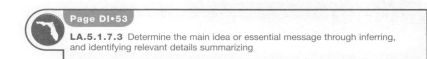

Generalize

Recognizing generalizations helps students judge the validity of an argument. Making their own generalizations helps students understand and summarize texts. Use this routine to teach generalizing.

1 DEFINE GENERALIZATION

Explain that a *generalization* is a broad statement or rule that applies to many examples. A *valid generalization* is well supported by facts and logic. A *faulty* one is not well supported.

2 DISCUSS CLUE WORDS

Students should look for clue words that signal generalizations as they read. List words on the board:

all	none
most	few
always	never
generally	in general

3 MODEL GENERALIZING

Explain that when readers generalize, they think about a number of examples and decide what they have in common. After reading a passage containing several facts, model how to generalize.

4 SCAFFOLD GENERALIZING

Before students write their own generalizations, have them choose from several the one most valid for a paragraph. You may also ask them to complete stems, such as: *The climate in the Arctic is generally _____ .*

5 PRACTICE GENERALIZING

Have students record a generalization and examples in a web.

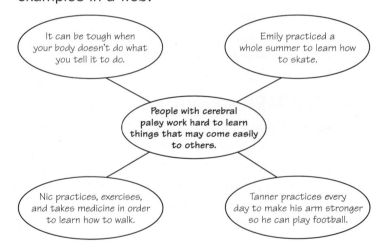

▲ **Graphic Organizer** 15

Research on Generalizing

"To be able to create a summary of what one has just read, one must discern the most central and important ideas in the text. One also must be able to generalize from examples or from things that are repeated. In addition, one has to ignore irrelevant details."

National Reading Panel,
Teaching Children to Read

National Reading Panel. *Teaching Children to Read: Reports of the Subgroups.* National Institute of Child Health & Human Development, National Institutes of Health, 2000, p. 4-92.

Page DI•54

LA.5.1.7.8 Use strategies to repair comprehension when self-monitoring, including using graphic and semantic organizers
LA.5.2.2.1 Use information from text features (charts, graphs, and illustrations)
LA.5.2.2.3 Organize information (charting and mapping)
LA.5.3.1.3 Organize ideas using graphic organizers

Graphic Sources

Graphic sources can be a valuable aid to readers in previewing and comprehending text. When students interpret and create graphics as they read, they often strengthen their understanding of the text. Use this routine to teach graphic sources.

1 DISCUSS GRAPHIC SOURCES

Explain that a graphic is a way of showing information visually. Graphics can include pictures, charts, graphs, maps, diagrams, schedules, and so on. Graphics often show information from the text in a visual way. They can organize many facts or ideas.

2 USE GRAPHICS TO PREVIEW

Remind students to look for graphics when they preview. Graphics are often a good way to discover what the story or article is about.

3 COMPARE GRAPHICS TO TEXT

Have students compare a selection with graphics and discuss the author's purpose for including graphics. Captions, charts, diagrams, and maps may present information that is not found elsewhere in the article. They may also help the reader better understand text information.

4 CREATE GRAPHICS

Give students opportunities to create their own pictures, charts, and other graphics to help them organize and understand text information.

5 USE A GRAPHIC ORGANIZER

Have students create a chart from information in a selection. Depending on the content, they may use a two-, three-, four-, or five-column chart.

Ways Animals Adapt to Find Food	Ways Animals Adapt to Find Shelter	Ways Animals Adapt to Find Safety
• When food is scarce, worker ants called "repletes" feed honey stored in their bodies to their fellow ants. • Large pythons can swallow big prey, like a pig, and go for more than a year without any other food.	• Holes and organs inside the body of a bigger animal can provide a warm, safe home for a smaller animal like an insect.	• When other insects invade their colony, soldier ants explode, spraying a deadly chemical at their enemies.

▲ **Graphic Organizer** 26

Research on Graphic Sources

"Teaching students to organize the ideas that they are reading about in a systematic, visual graph benefits the ability of the students to remember what they read and may transfer, in general, to better comprehension and achievement in Social Studies and Science content areas."

National Reading Panel,
Teaching Children to Read

National Reading Panel. *Teaching Children to Read: Reports of the Subgroups.* National Institute of Child Health & Human Development, National Institutes of Health, 2000, p. 4-45.

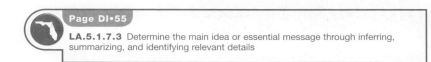

Page DI•55
LA.5.1.7.3 Determine the main idea or essential message through inferring, summarizing, and identifying relevant details

Generalize

Recognizing generalizations helps students judge the validity of an argument. Making their own generalizations helps students understand and summarize texts. Use this routine to teach generalizing.

1 DEFINE GENERALIZATION

Explain that a *generalization* is a broad statement or rule that applies to many examples. A *valid* generalization is well supported by facts and logic. A *faulty* one is not well supported.

2 DISCUSS CLUE WORDS

Students should look for clue words that signal generalizations as they read. List words on the board:

all	none
most	few
always	never
generally	in general

3 MODEL GENERALIZING

Explain that when readers generalize, they think about a number of examples and decide what they have in common. After reading a passage containing several facts, model how to generalize.

4 SCAFFOLD GENERALIZING

Before students write their own generalizations, have them choose from several the one most valid for a paragraph. You may also ask them to complete stems, such as: *The climate in the Arctic is generally _____ .*

5 PRACTICE GENERALIZING

Have students record a generalization and examples in a web.

Stormi misses her old friends in Chicago.

She says she'd rather not go to school at all.

Starting at a new school is difficult.

Stormi loses her locker combination.

She reads a book at lunchtime because she has no one to sit with.

▲ **Graphic Organizer** 15

Research on Generalizing

FOCUS ON RESEARCH

"To be able to create a summary of what one has just read, one must discern the most central and important ideas in the text. One also must be able to generalize from examples or from things that are repeated. In addition, one has to ignore irrelevant details."

National Reading Panel,
Teaching Children to Read

National Reading Panel. *Teaching Children to Read: Reports of the Subgroups.* National Institute of Child Health & Human Development, National Institutes of Health, 2000, p. 4-92.

Draw Conclusions

When students move beyond the literal meaning of a text to draw conclusions, they get more ideas from what they read and understand better the points an author is trying to make. Use the following routine to guide students in drawing conclusions.

1 DISCUSS DRAWING CONCLUSIONS

Tell students a conclusion is a sensible decision they reach based on details or facts in a story or an article. Explain when they draw conclusions, they think about information in the text and what they already know.

2 MODEL DRAWING A CONCLUSION

Model using your own experiences to draw a conclusion.

 MODEL The smell of peanuts and cotton candy filled the air. I heard clapping, I even heard loud bellows that sounded like elephants. I knew a circus was going on.

Discuss how you combined what you already knew with details (smell of peanuts and cotton candy, clapping, loud bellows) to draw a conclusion.

3 ASK QUESTIONS

Read aloud a passage and ask questions that foster drawing conclusions. For example: *What kind of person is the main character? How can you tell? Why do you think the character acts this way?*

4 USE A GRAPHIC ORGANIZER

Have partners read both fiction and nonfiction passages. Students can ask each other questions that lead to drawing conclusions. Suggest that they use webs or charts to show the facts or details that support their conclusions.

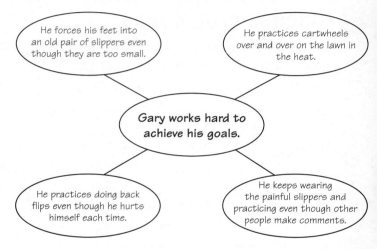

He forces his feet into an old pair of slippers even though they are too small.

He practices cartwheels over and over on the lawn in the heat.

Gary works hard to achieve his goals.

He practices doing back flips even though he hurts himself each time.

He keeps wearing the painful slippers and practicing even though other people make comments.

▲ **Graphic Organizer** 15

Research on Drawing Conclusions

"Inference is a mosaic, a dazzling constellation of thinking processes, but the tiles available to form each mosaic are limited, circumscribed. There must be a fusion of words on a page—and constraints of meaning they impose—and the experience and knowledge of the reader."

Ellin Oliver Keene and Susan Zimmerman,
Mosaic of Thought

Keen, Ellin Oliver, and Susan Zimmermann. *Mosaic of Thought: Teaching Comprehension in a Reader's Workshop.* Heinemann, 1997, p. 154; 1992, p. 238.

Providing students with reading materials they can and want to read is an important step toward developing fluent readers. A running record allows you to determine each student's instructional and independent reading level. Information on how to take a running record is provided on pp. DI•59–DI•60.

Instructional Reading Level

Only approximately 1 in 10 words will be difficult when reading a selection from the Student Edition for students who are at grade level. (A typical fifth-grader reads approximately 120–140 words correct per minute.)

- Students reading at grade level should read regularly from the Student Edition and On-Level Leveled Readers, with teacher support as suggested in the Teacher's Editions.
- Students reading below grade level can read the Strategic Intervention Leveled Readers. Instructional plans can be found in the Teacher's Edition and the Leveled Reader Teaching Guide.
- Students who are reading above grade level can read the Advanced Leveled Readers. Instructional plans can be found in the Teacher's Edition and the Leveled Reader Teaching Guide.

Independent Reading Level

Students should read regularly in independent-level texts in which no more than approximately 1 in 20 words is difficult for the reader. Other factors that make a book easy to read include the student's interest in the topic, the amount of text on a page, how well illustrations support meaning, and the complexity and familiarity of the concepts. Suggested books for self-selected reading are provided with each lesson on pp. TR14–TR15 in this Teacher's Edition.

Guide students in learning how to self-select books at their independent reading level. As you talk about a book with students, discuss the challenging concepts in it, list new words students find in sampling the book, and ask students about their familiarity with the topic. A blackline master to help students evaluate books for independent reading is provided on p. DI•58.

Self-Selected/Independent Reading

While oral reading allows you to assess students' reading level and fluency, independent reading is of crucial importance to students' futures as readers and learners. Students need to develop their ability to read independently for increasing amounts of time.

- Schedule a regular time for sustained independent reading in your classroom. During the year, gradually increase the amount of time devoted to independent reading.
- Encourage students to track the amount of time they read independently and the number of pages they read in a given amount of time. Tracking will help motivate them to gradually increase their duration and speed. A blackline master for tracking independent reading is provided on p. DI•58.

Choosing a Book for Independent Reading

When choosing a book, story, or article for independent reading, consider these questions:

_____ 1. Do I know something about this topic?

_____ 2. Am I interested in this topic?

_____ 3. Do I like reading this kind of book (fiction, fantasy, biography, or whatever)?

_____ 4. Have I read other things by this author? Do I like this author?

If you say "yes" to at least one of the questions above, continue:

_____ 5. In reading the first page, was only about 1 of every 20 words hard?

If you say "yes," continue:

_____ 6. Does the number of words on a page look about right to me?

If you say "yes," the book or article is probably at the right level for you.

Silent Reading

Record the date, the title of the book or article you read, the amount of time you spent reading, and the number of pages you read during that time.

Date	Title	Minutes	Pages

Taking a Running Record

A running record is an assessment of a student's oral reading accuracy and oral reading fluency. Reading accuracy is based on the number of words read correctly. Reading fluency is based on the reading rate (the number of words correct per minute) and the degree to which a student reads with a "natural flow."

How to Measure Reading Accuracy

1. Choose a grade-level text of about 80 to 120 words that is unfamiliar to the student.
2. Make a copy of the text for yourself. Make a copy for the student or have the student read aloud from a book.
3. Give the student the text and have the student read aloud. (You may wish to record the student's reading for later evaluation.)
4. On your copy of the text, mark any miscues or errors the student makes while reading. See the running record sample on page DI·60, which shows how to identify and mark miscues.
5. Count the total number of words in the text and the total number of errors made by the student. Note: If a student makes the same error more than once, such as mispronouncing the same word multiple times, count it as one error. Self-corrections do not count as actual errors. Use the following formula to calculate the percentage score, or accuracy rate:

$$\frac{\text{Total Number of Words} - \text{Total Number of Errors}}{\text{Total Number of Words}} \times 100 = \text{percentage score}$$

Interpreting the Results

- A student who reads **95–100%** of the words correctly is reading at an **independent level** and may need more challenging text.
- A student who reads **90–94%** of the words correctly is reading at an **instructional level** and will likely benefit from guided instruction.
- A student who reads **89%** or fewer of the words correctly is reading at a **frustrational level** and may benefit most from targeted instruction with lower-level texts and intervention.

How to Measure Reading Rate (wcpm)

1. Follow Steps 1–3 above.
2. Note the exact times when the student begins and finishes reading.
3. Use the following formula to calculate the number of words correct per minute (wcpm):

$$\frac{\text{Total Number of Words Read Correctly}}{\text{Total Number of Seconds}} \times 60 = \text{words correct per minute}$$

Interpreting the Results

An appropriate reading rate for a fifth-grader is 120–140 (wcpm).

Running Record Sample

Running Record Sample

Symbols

> Did you know that every day in cities across the United States, students like you are helping others?
>
> Each year in Louisiana, a young student and her younger brother have gone around collecting stuffed animals for the children who live in a homeless shelter.
>
> In New York City, seventy-six students from Harlem teamed up with four Olympic athletes to transform a run-down park into a playground featuring a daffodil garden.
>
> And each year in Indiana, a young student has gone around collecting hundreds of bundles of baby clothes and other baby items. In the fall she delivers them to a home for mothers who are having tough times.

—From *Using Special Talents*
On-Level Reader 5.2.1

Accurate Reading
The student reads a word correctly.

Hesitation
The student hesitates over a word, and the teacher provides the word. Wait several seconds before telling the student what the word is.

Insertion
The student inserts words or parts of words that are not in the text.

Omission
The student omits words or word parts.

Substitution
The student substitutes words or parts of words for the words in the text.

Self-Correction
The student reads a word incorrectly but then corrects the error. Do not count self-corrections as actual errors. However, noting self-corrections will help you identify words the student finds difficult.

Mispronunciation/Misreading
The student pronounces or reads a word incorrectly.

Running Record Results	▶	Reading Accuracy	▶	Reading Rate—WCPM
Total Number of Words: **107**		$\frac{107 - 5}{107}$ x 100 = 95.327 = 95%		$\frac{102}{51}$ x 60 = 120 = 120 words correct per minute
Number of Errors: **5**				
Reading Time: **51 seconds**		Accuracy Percentage Score: **95%**		Reading Rate: **120** WCPM

Teacher Resources

Table of Contents

Unit 1   Vocabulary Words   Spelling Words

Frindle

Vocabulary Words	
acquainted	guaranteed
assignment	procedures
essential	reputation
expanded	worshipped

Short vowel VCCV, VCV

distance	enjoy	husband	regular
method	perhaps	tissue	denim
anger	figure	mustard	
problem	channel	shuttle	
butter	admire	advance	
petals	comedy	drummer	

Thunder Rose

Vocabulary Words	
branded	pitch
constructed	resourceful
daintily	thieving
devastation	veins
lullaby	

Long vowel VCV

fever	native	agent	legal
broken	silent	motive	solo
climate	labor	vital	
hotel	spider	acorn	
basic	label	item	
vocal	icon	aroma	

Island of the Blue Dolphins

Vocabulary Words	
gnawed	ravine
headland	shellfish
kelp	sinew
lair	

Long vowel digraphs

coast	arrow	crease	complain
feast	needle	groan	sneeze
speech	charcoal	breeze	
wheat	praise	willow	
Spain	faint	appeal	
paint	maintain	bowling	

Satchel Paige

Vocabulary Words	
confidence	unique
fastball	weakness
mocking	windup
outfield	

Adding -ed, -ing

supplied	included	qualified	satisfied
supplying	including	qualifying	satisfying
denied	admitted	identified	
denying	admitting	identifying	
decided	occurred	delayed	
deciding	occurring	delaying	

Shutting Out the Sky

Vocabulary Words	
advice	immigrants
advised	luxury
circumstanc-es	newcomer
elbow	peddler
hustled	

Contractions

they're	what'll	wouldn't
you've	doesn't	who've
weren't	hadn't	shouldn't
needn't	could've	who'd
there'd	would've	this'll
they've	should've	couldn't
mustn't	might've	

Unit 2 | Vocabulary Words | Spelling Words

Inside Out

Vocabulary Words: caterpillar, cocoon, disrespect, emerge, migrant, sketched, unscrewed

Spelling Words — Digraphs th, sh, ch, ph

shovel	establish	shatter	attach
southern	although	ethnic	ostrich
northern	challenge	shiver	
chapter	approach	pharmacy	
hyphen	astonish	charity	
chosen	python	china	

Passage to Freedom

Vocabulary Words: agreement, cable, diplomat, issue, refugees, representatives, superiors, visa

Spelling Words — Irregular plurals

staffs	chiefs	quizzes	chefs
ourselves	buffaloes	sheriffs	pianos
pants	flamingos	dominoes	
scissors	beliefs	thieves	
loaves	echoes	measles	
volcanoes	shelves	avocados	

The Ch'i-lin Purse

Vocabulary Words: astonished, behavior, benefactor, distribution, gratitude, procession, recommend, sacred, traditions

Spelling Words — Vowel sounds with r

snore	report	repair	volunteer
tornado	prepare	sword	declare
spare	pioneer	ignore	
appear	chair	order	
career	beware	engineer	
square	smear	resort	

Jane Goodall's 10 Ways to Help Save Wildlife

Vocabulary Words: conservation, contribute, enthusiastic, environment, investigation

Spelling Words — Final Syllables -en, -an, -el, -le, -il

example	oxygen	fossil	sudden
level	wooden	toboggan	beagle
human	double	veteran	
quarrel	travel	chisel	
scramble	cancel	suburban	
evil	chuckle	single	

The Midnight Ride of Paul Revere

Vocabulary Words: fate, fearless, glimmer, lingers, magnified, somber, steed

Spelling Words — Final Syllables -er, -ar, -or

danger	surrender	caterpillar
wander	solar	rumor
tractor	sticker	glimmer
dollar	locker	linger
harbor	helicopter	sensor
eager	pillar	alligator
eraser	refrigerator	

Unit 3	Vocabulary Words		Spelling Words

Wings for the King

Vocabulary Words:
admiringly, permit, scoundrel, subject, worthless

Schwas

jewel	pajamas	carnival	operate
kingdom	estimate	illustrate	celery
gasoline	tomorrow	elegant	
factory	humidity	census	
garage	Chicago	terrific	
tropical	bulletin	celebrate	

Leonardo's Horse

Vocabulary Words:
achieved, architect, bronze, cannon, depressed, fashioned, midst, philosopher, rival

Compound words

waterproof	earthquake	spotlight	postcard
teaspoon	rowboat	blindfold	humming-bird
grasshopper	scrapbook	whirlpool	thumbtack
homesick	countryside	tablespoon	
barefoot	lightweight	greenhouse	
courthouse	fishhook		

The Dinosaurs of Waterhouse Hawkins

Vocabulary Words:
erected, foundations, mold, occasion, proportion, tidied, workshop

Consonant sounds /j/, /ks/, /sk/, and /s/

excuse	science	exclaim	smudge
scene	schedule	fascinate	schooner
muscle	gigantic	ginger	
explore	scheme	scholar	
pledge	Japan	scent	
journal	excellent	dodge	

Mahalia Jackson

Vocabulary Words:
appreciate, barber, choir, released, religious, slavery, teenager

One consonant or two

address	Mississippi	Tennessee	allowance
college	immediate	gallop	zucchini
mirror	command	opponent	
recess	appreciate	barricade	
committee	announce	broccoli	
collect	possess	accomplish	

Special Effects in Film and Television

Vocabulary Words:
background, landscape, miniature, prehistoric, reassembled

Prefixes un-, de-, dis

uncover	disability	unpredict-able	disqualify
defrost	discomfort		undecided
uncomfortable	deodorant	disapprove	
discourage	unemployed	disappoint	
disadvantage	deflate	unpleasant	
unfortunate	disbelief	dehydrated	
unfamiliar			

Unit 4 — Vocabulary Words — Spelling Words

Weslandia
Vocabulary Words: blunders, civilization, complex, envy, fleeing, inspired, rustling, strategy

Words from many cultures

khaki	vanilla	cobra	karate
hula	canyon	koala	kiosk
banana	yogurt	barbecue	
ballet	banquet	safari	
waltz	macaroni	buffet	
tomato	polka	stampede	

Stretching Ourselves: Kids with Cerebral Palsy
Vocabulary Words: abdomen, artificial, gait, handicapped, therapist, wheelchair

Prefixes over-, under-, sub-, super-, out-

overlook	underground	submarine	subdivision
underline	overboard	undercover	subhead
subway	undercurrent	overcast	
subset	superstar	outfield	
supermarket	overtime	output	
outlet	supersonic	supernatural	

Exploding Ants: Amazing Facts About How Animals Adapt
Vocabulary Words: critical, enables, mucus, scarce, specialize, sterile

Homophones

cent	whether	tide	course
sent	their	tied	coarse
scent	there	pale	
threw	they're	pail	
through	chili	aloud	
weather	chilly	allowed	

The Stormi Giovanni Club
Vocabulary Words: cavities, combination, demonstrates, episode, profile, strict

Suffixes -ible, -able

sensible	flexible	laughable	responsible
washable	reasonable	sociable	tolerable
available	favorable	allowable	
agreeable	breakable	divisible	
fashionable	convertible	hospitable	
valuable	forgettable	reversible	

The Gymnast
Vocabulary Words: bluish, cartwheels, gymnastics, hesitation, limelight, skidded, somersault, throbbing, wincing

Negative prefixes

invisible	impatient	illogical
illiterate	independent	indefinite
irregular	incorrect	imperfect
irresistible	inactive	immobile
impossible	imperfect	irresponsible
informal	impolite	inexpensive
illegal	immature	

Unit 5   Vocabulary Words   Spelling Words

The Three-Century Woman	eerie intersection pondered severe spectacles withered	

Multisyllabic words

elementary	variety	mosaic	centennial
vehicle	literature	tuxedo	curiosity
miniature	elevator	meteorite	
probability	Pennsylvania	fascination	
definition	ravioli	cylinder	
substitute	cafeteria	intermediate	

The Unsinkable Wreck of the R.M.S. *Titanic*	cramped debris interior ooze	robotic sediment sonar

Unusual spellings

league	blood	intrigue	subtle
sergeant	vague	villain	disguise
yacht	anxious	cantaloupe	
doubt	foreign	flood	
fatigue	bargain	depot	
debt	condemn	cordial	

Talk with an Astronaut	accomplish- ments focus gravity	monitors role specific

Greek word parts

geology	disaster	biosphere	ecology
thermometer	meteorology	thermos	mythology
astronaut	technology	asterisk	
atmosphere	hemisphere	thermostat	
biology	zoology	astronomy	
thermal	sociology	spherical	

Journey to the Center of the Earth	armor encases extinct	hideous plunged serpent

Latin roots

project	decimal	audit	dejected
audience	injection	decimeter	terrain
decade	December	audition	
territory	reject	audible	
auditorium	eject	decathlon	
terrier	terrace	terrarium	

Ghost Towns of the American West	economic independence overrun	scrawled vacant

Related words

politics	signature	clean
political	arrive	cleanse
major	arrival	resign
majority	inspire	resignation
equal	inspiration	unite
equation	human	unity
sign	humanity	

Unit 6

Unit 6	Vocabulary Words		Spelling Words

At the Beach

Vocabulary Words:
algae, concealed, driftwood, hammocks, lamented, sea urchins, sternly, tweezers

Suffixes -ous, -sion, -ion, -ation

famous	nervous	tension	occupation
invention	explanation	humorous	destination
election	various	exhibition	
furious	decision	attraction	
imagination	relaxation	invasion	
education	conversation	creation	

The Mystery of Saint Matthew Island

Vocabulary Words:
bleached, carcasses, decay, parasites, scrawny, starvation, suspicions, tundra

Final Syllable -ant, -ent, -ance, -ence

important	absence	confidence	excellence
experience	appearance	conference	persistent
ignorant	intelligent	insurance	
entrance	evidence	ambulance	
difference	pollutant	hesitant	
instance	clearance	consistent	

King Midas and the Golden Touch

Vocabulary Words:
adorn, cleanse, lifeless, precious, realm, spoonful

Words with ei and ie

brief	seize	yield	shield
believe	ceiling	deceive	conceited
receive	field	achieve	
leisure	neither	grief	
piece	apiece	niece	
relief	receipt	protein	

The Hindenburg

Vocabulary Words:
criticizing, cruised, drenching, era, explosion, hydrogen

Compound words

ice cream	textbook	dead end	cartwheel
a lot	guidelines	password	root beer
keyboard	newspaper	teenager	fingerprint
fairy tale	space shuttle	skateboard	
horseshoe	hay fever	everything	
piggy bank		barbed wire	

Sweet Music in Harlem

Vocabulary Words:
bass, clarinet, fidgety, forgetful, jammed, nighttime, secondhand

Easily confused words

quiet	than	from	medal
quite	then	form	metal
finely	since	later	
finally	sense	latter	
except	affect	adapt	
accept	effect	adopt	

Grade 4 Vocabulary

Use this list of fourth grade tested vocabulary words for review and leveled activities.

A

aboard
affords
amazed
amphibians
ancestors
ancient
anticipation
appeared
aquarium
astronauts
atlas
aviator
avoided
awkward

B

bargain
bawling
bewildered
biologist
bluff
boarding school
bow
brilliant
brisk
bustling

C

canopy
capable
capsule
cargo
celestial
chant
chorus
cockpit
colonel
conducted
Constitution
continent
convergence
cord

coward
coyote
cradle
crime
crumbled
curiosity

D

dangle
dappled
daring
depart
destruction
dignified
dismay
docks
dolphins
dormitory
draft
drag
dudes
duke
dungeon

E

elegant
enchanted
endurance
escape
etched
exhibit
expected

F

fascinated
favor
flex
flexible
forbidding
forecasts
fouled
fragrant

frost
furiously

G

generations
genius
glacier
gleamed
glider
glimpses
glint
glorious
grand
granite
grizzly

H

hangars
hatch
heaves
homeland
hoop
horizon
howling
humble

I

icebergs
immense
impressive
inland

J

jersey

L

lagoon
lassoed
link
lizard
longed
loomed

lunar
lurking

M

magician
majesty
manual
marveled
massive
mechanical
memorial
migrating
minister
miracle
module
monument

N

naturalist
navigation
noble
numerous

O

offended
outspoken

P

palettes
parlor
payroll
peasant
peculiar
politics
pollen
pollinate
porridge
positive
prairie
preserve
prideful
pulpit
pulses

Q

quaint
quarantine
quivered

R

recalls
reference
reptiles
reseats
resemblance
reservation
responsibility
rille
rim
riverbed
roundup
rudder
ruins
rumbling
runt

S

salamander
scan
scent
scholars
sculptures
seeker
selecting
shatter
shielding
shimmering
shrieked
slithered
slopes
society
solemnly
solo
species
speechless
spurs

staggered
stalled
stern
still
stumped
summoning
surface
surge
swatted

T

taunted
temple
terraced
terror
thickets
timid
torrent
towering
trench
triumph
tropical
trudged

U

unbelievable
uncover

V

vain
vanished
vehicle

W

wharf
wilderness
wondrous

Y

yearned

Grade 6 Vocabulary

Use this list of sixth grade tested vocabulary words for leveled activities.

A

absurd
abundant
access
accustomed
aggressive
aliens
apparently
application
architecture
artifacts
astronomers
authority

B

barge
basin
beacon
behalf
benefits
bondage
burden

C

campaigns
candidate
captive
caravans
characteristic
charities
collapse
collide
combustion
commissioned
compact
companionship
comrades
confidently
conformed
conquer
converts
corridors
corrode

counselor
customary

D

dean
decline
decrees
delirious
democracy
densest
destination
destiny
detect
devise
dingy
diploma
disgraced
dismounted
distressed
dramatic
dubiously

E

earthen
eaves
efficiency
emphasized
empire
encounter
engulfed
enraged
enrich
equator
erosion
eternity
evaporates
existence
expanse
expedition
exploit
exported
extract

F

fixtures
flimsy
flourish
foreigners
formal
former
fragile
frantic
frustration
fulfill

G

galaxy
generated
groping

H

hatchet
hoard
homesteaders
hospitable
hovers

I

ideal
identity
ignite
immortal
imprinted
incident
industrial
insulated
invaders
isolation

L

lance
legacy
leisure
lunging
lush

M

maintenance
manuscripts
materialize
medieval
menacing
migration
misfortune
moisture
molten
momentous
mongrel
mythology

N

navigator
negotiate
nub

O

obedient
observatory
obstacle
opera
ordeal
ore

P

painstaking
particles
patron
percentage
permission
persisted
physical
pleas
poisonous
prejudice
presence
prey
primitive
privileged
proclaimed

progress
promoted
provisions

Q

quests
quill

R

receded
recital
recycled
refrain
registered
reigned
reject
relish
renewed
renowned
repay
reproduce
resound
retreat
revolting
romping
rowdy
rural

S

sanctuaries
secretive
settlement
sluggish
slung
smoldered
specimens
speckled
squire
stiffened
stimulating
stunned
subscribe
sufficient

surplus
survive

T

technology
tolerated
toll
torment
transmitted
traversed
treacherous
treaded
tropics

U

unaccompanied
unison
universal
urban

V

ventured
verify
version
vigorously
volcanic

W

waft
waning
wilt

Legibility

When handwriting is legible, letters, words, and numbers can be read easily. Handwriting that is not legible can cause problems for the reader and make communication difficult. Legibility can be improved if students are able to identify what is causing legibility problems in their handwriting. Focus instruction on the following five elements of legible handwriting.

Size

Letters need to be a consistent size. Students should focus on three things related to size: letters that reach to the top line, letters that reach halfway between the top and bottom line, and letters that extend below the bottom line. Writing letters the correct size can improve legibility. Often the letters that sit halfway between the top and bottom line cause the most problems. When students are writing on notebook paper, there is no middle line to help them size letters such as *m, a, i,* and *r* correctly. If students are having trouble, have them draw middle lines on their notebook paper.

Shape

Some of the most common handwriting problems are caused by forming letters incorrectly. These are the most common types of handwriting problems:

- Round letters such as *a, o,* and *g* are not closed.
- Looped letters such as *l, e,* and *b* have no loops.
- Letters such as *i, t,* and *d* have loops that shouldn't be there.

Have students examine one another's writing to indicate which words are hard to read, and then discuss which letters aren't formed correctly. They can then practice those particular letters.

Spacing

Letters within words should be evenly spaced. Too much or too little space can make writing difficult to read. A consistent amount of space should also be used between words in a sentence and between sentences. Suggest that students use the tip of their pencil to check the spacing between words and the width of their pencil to check the spacing between sentences.

Slant

Correct writing slant can be to the right or to the left, or there may be no slant at all. Slant becomes a legibility problem when letters are slanted in different directions. Suggest that students use a ruler to draw lines to determine if their slant is consistent.

Smoothness

Written letters should be produced with a line weight that is not too dark and not too light. The line should be smooth without any shaky or jagged edges. If students' writing is too dark, they are pressing too hard. If the writing is too light, they are not pressing hard enough. Usually shaky or jagged lines occur if students are unsure of how to form letters or if they are trying to draw letters rather than using a flowing motion.

D'Nealian™ Cursive Alphabet

© Pearson Education

D'Nealian™ Alphabet

a b c d e f g h i

j k l m n o p q r s t

u v w x y z

A B C D E F G

H I J K L M N O

P Q R S T U V

W X Y Z . , ' ?

1 2 3 4 5 6

7 8 9 10

Manuscript Alphabet

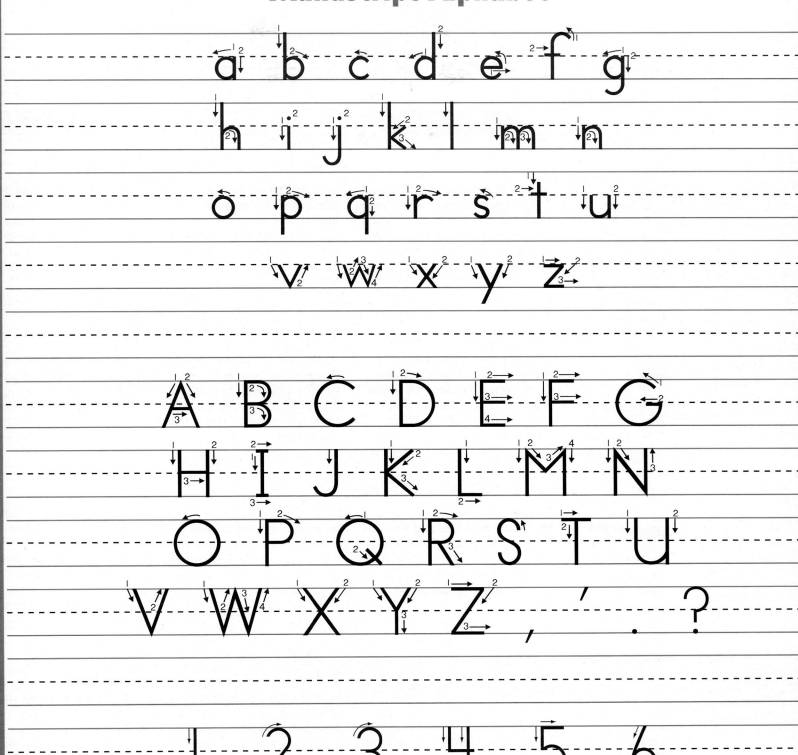

Unit 4 *Adapting*

Page TR14

LA.5.2.1.9 Use interest and recommendations to select appropriate fiction materials to read

LA.5.2.2.5 Use interest and recommendations to select appropriate non-fiction materials to read

Below-Level	**On-Level**	**Advanced**

Weslandia

To Read Aloud!
The Magic of the Glits
by Carole Adler (MacMillan, 1979) A summer becomes enchanted and unforgettable when Jeremy creates a world of magical beach creatures to comfort a young orphan girl.

Martin's Mice
by Dick King-Smith (Knopf, 1988) A farm cat does not want to catch mice and decides to keep them as pets instead in this delightful tale about difference and self-esteem.

Loser
by Jerry Spinelli (HarperCollins, 2002) An exuberant, eccentric boy, labeled a loser by his classmates, eventually shows the power of the human spirit and that anyone can become a hero.

Seedfolks
by Paul Fleischman (HarperCollins, 1997) In this story of a girl planting a garden in a trash-filled vacant lot, the author shows us a community born and nurtured in an urban environment.

Stretching Ourselves

To Read Aloud!
Teens with Physical Disabilities
by Glen Alan Cheney (Enslow; 1995) Eight teenagers tell of the challenges they face in their everyday lives.

What's Wrong with Timmy?
by Maria Shriver (Warner, 2001) As Kate and Timmy, a boy with Down Syndrome, become friends, Kate realizes that they have a lot in common, despite their differences.

Sparks
By Graham McNamee (Yearling, 2003) When Todd is moved from Special Education to a regular fifth grade class, he struggles to keep up, but eventually finds his own special gift.

Petey
by Ben Mikaelsen (Hyperion, 1998) Petey, an elderly man with cerebral palsy, befriends a boy and shares with him the joy of life.

Exploding Ants: Amazing Facts About How Animals Adapt

To Read Aloud!
Hiding Out: Camouflage in the Wild
by James Martin and Art Wolfe (Random House, 1993) Text and photographs explore why and how animals use camouflage for adaptation.

Animals in Motion
by Pamela Hickman and Pat Stephens (Kids Can Press, 2000) This book contains facts, activities and easy experiments that show kids the amazing ways animals move.

One Day in the Desert
by Jean Craighead George (HarperCollins, 1983) The animals and people of the Sonoran Desert in Arizona adapt to cruel living conditions.

The Case of the Monkeys That Fell From the Trees: And Other Mysteries in Tropical Nature
by Susan Quinlan (Boyd Mills, 2003) Eleven scientific investigations reveal the interdependence between plants, animals and insects.

The Stormi Giovanni Club

To Read Aloud!
Dear Mr. Henshaw
by Beverly Cleary (HarperCollins, 1994) In letters to his favorite author, ten-year-old Leigh reveals his problems with his parents' divorce, being the new boy in school and finding his place in the world.

Alexander, Who's Not (Do You Hear Me! I Mean It!) Going to Move
by Judith Viorst (Atheneum, 1995) Alexander is horrified at the prospect of moving 1,000 miles away in this raucous picture book.

P.S. Longer Letter Later
by Paula Danziger and A.M. Martin (Scholastic, 1998) When Tara Starr moves away she and her best friend work hard to continue their friendship through letters.

The Ballad of Lucy Whipple
by Karen Cushman (Houghton Mifflin, 1996) When California Morning Whipple moves with her family to a rugged California mining town, she is unhappy until she begins to feel at home.

The Gymnast

To Read Aloud!
Pool Party
by Gary Soto (Yearling Books, 1995) Rudy is worried when he's invited to a pool party hosted by the most popular girl at school.

The Skirt
by Gary Soto (Doubleday, 1992) Miata leaves her precious folkorico skirt on the bus and she and her friend Ana must figure out how to get it back.

Fearless Fernie: Hanging Out with Fernie and Me
by Gary Soto (Putnam, 2002) These poems tell about the lives of two best friends and will speak to any child who has ever faced embarrassing moments at school.

Baseball in April and Other Stories
by Gary Soto (Harcourt, 1990) These stories feature young people whose joys and pain are brought to life through daily events that reveal love, friendship, growing up, success and failure.

See also *Assessment Handbook*, p. 119

Unit 4 Reading Log

Name _____

Dates Read	Title and Author	What is it about?	How would you rate it?	Explain your rating.
From ___ to ___			Great Awful 5 4 3 2 1	
From ___ to ___			Great Awful 5 4 3 2 1	
From ___ to ___			Great Awful 5 4 3 2 1	
From ___ to ___			Great Awful 5 4 3 2 1	
From ___ to ___			Great Awful 5 4 3 2 1	

Unit 4 Narrative Retelling Chart

Selection Title _____

Name _____   Date _____

Retelling Criteria/Teacher Prompt	Teacher-Aided Response	Student-Generated Response	Rubric Score (Circle one.)
Connections Has anything like this happened to you? How does this story remind you of other stories?			4 3 2 1
Author's Purpose Why do you think the author wrote this story? What was the author trying to tell us?			4 3 2 1
Characters Describe _____ (character's name) at the beginning and end of the story.			4 3 2 1
Setting Where and when did the story happen?			4 3 2 1
Plot Tell me what the story was about in a few sentences.			4 3 2 1

Summative Retelling Score   4   3   2   1   _____

Comments _____

See also Assessment Handbook, p. 112

Unit 4 Expository Retelling Chart

Name _____

Date _____

Selection Title _____

Retelling Criteria/Teacher Prompt	Teacher-Aided Response	Student-Generated Response	Rubric Score (Circle one.)
Connections Did this selection make you think about something else you have read? What did you learn about as you read this selection?			4 3 2 1
Author's Purpose Why do you think the author wrote this selection?			4 3 2 1
Topic What was the selection mostly about?			4 3 2 1
Important Ideas What is important for me to know about _____ (topic)?			4 3 2 1
Conclusions What did you learn from reading this selection?			4 3 2 1

Summative Retelling Score   4   3   2   1

Comments _____

_____

Reading

Concepts of Print and Print Awareness	Pre-K	K	1	2	3	4	5	6
Develop awareness that print represents spoken language and conveys and preserves meaning	•	•	•					
Recognize familiar books by their covers; hold book right side up	•	•						
Identify parts of a book and their functions (front cover, title page/title, back cover, page numbers)	•	•	•					
Understand the concepts of letter, word, sentence, paragraph, and story	•	•	•					
Track print (front to back of book, top to bottom of page, left to right on line, sweep back left for next line)	•	•	•					
Match spoken to printed words	•	•	•					
Know capital and lowercase letter names and match them	•	• T	•					
Know the order of the alphabet	•	•	•					
Recognize first name in print	•	•	•					
Recognize the uses of capitalization and punctuation		•	•					
Value print as a means of gaining information	•	•	•					

Phonological and Phonemic Awareness	Pre-K	K	1	2	3	4	5	6
Phonological Awareness								
Recognize and produce rhyming words	•	•	•					
Track and count each word in a spoken sentence and each syllable in a spoken word	•	•	•					
Segment and blend syllables in spoken words			•					
Segment and blend onset and rime in one-syllable words		•	•					
Recognize and produce words beginning with the same sound	•	•	•					
Identify beginning, middle, and/or ending sounds that are the same or different	•	•	•					
Understand that spoken words are made of sequences of sounds	•	•	•					
Phonemic Awareness								
Identify the position of sounds in words		•	•					
Identify and isolate initial, final, and medial sounds in spoken words	•	•	•					
Blend sounds orally to make words or syllables		•	•					
Segment a word or syllable into sounds; count phonemes in spoken words or syllables		•	•					
Manipulate sounds in words (add, delete, and/or substitute phonemes)	•	•	•					

Phonics and Decoding	Pre-K	K	1	2	3	4	5	6
Phonics								
Understand and apply the **alphabetic principle** that spoken words are composed of sounds that are represented by letters	•	•	•					
Know letter-sound relationships		• T	• T	• T				
Blend sounds of letters to decode		•	• T	• T	• T			
Consonants, consonant blends, and consonant digraphs		•	• T	• T	• T			
Short, long, and r-controlled vowels; vowel digraphs; diphthongs; common vowel patterns			• T	• T	• T			
Phonograms/word families		•	•	•	•			
Word Structure								
Decode words with common word parts		•	• T	• T	• T	•	•	•
Base words and inflected endings			• T	• T	•	•	•	•
Contractions and compound words			• T	• T	• T	•	•	•
Suffixes and prefixes			• T	• T	• T	•	•	•
Greek and Latin roots						•	•	•
Blend syllables to decode words			• T	• T	• T	•	•	•
Decoding Strategies								
Blending strategy: Apply knowledge of letter-sound relationships to decode unfamiliar words		•	•	•	•			
Apply knowledge of word structure to decode unfamiliar words		•	•	•	•	•	•	•
Use context and syntax along with letter-sound relationships and word structure to decode		•	•	•	•	•	•	•
Self-correct			•	•	•	•	•	•

Fluency	Pre-K	K	1	2	3	4	5	6
Read aloud fluently with accuracy, comprehension, appropriate pace/rate; with expression/intonation (prosody); with attention to punctuation and appropriate phrasing			• T	• T	• T	• T	• T	• T
Practice fluency in a variety of ways, including choral reading, partner/paired reading, readers' theater, repeated oral reading, and tape-assisted reading		•	•	•	•	•	•	•

• instructional opportunity   **T** tested in standardized test for

	Pre-K	K	1	2	3	4	5	6
...rk toward appropriate fluency goals by the end of each grade			•T	•T	•T	•T	•T	•T
...ad regularly in independent-level material			•	•	•	•	•	•
...ad silently for increasing periods of time			•	•	•	•	•	•

Vocabulary (Oral and Written)

	Pre-K	K	1	2	3	4	5	6
...ord Recognition								
...cognize regular and irregular high-frequency words	•	•	•T	•T				
...cognize and understand selection vocabulary		•	•	•T	•	•	•	•
...derstand content-area vocabulary and specialized, technical, or topical words			•	•	•	•	•	•
...ord Learning Strategies								
...velop vocabulary through direct instruction, concrete experiences, reading, listening to text read aloud	•	•	•	•	•	•	•	•
...e knowledge of word structure to figure out meanings of words			•	•T	•T	•T	•T	•T
...e context clues for meanings of unfamiliar words, multiple-meaning words, homonyms, homographs			•	•T	•T	•T	•T	•T
...e grade-appropriate reference sources to learn word meanings	•	•	•	•	•T	•T	•T	•T
...e picture clues to help determine word meanings	•	•	•	•	•			
...e new words in a variety of contexts	•	•	•	•		•	•	•
...mine word usage and effectiveness		•	•	•	•	•	•	•
...ate and use graphic organizers to group, study, and retain vocabulary			•	•	•	•	•	•
...tend Concepts and Word Knowledge								
...ademic language	•	•	•	•	•	•	•	•
...ssify and categorize	•	•	•	•	•	•	•	•
...onyms and synonyms			•	•T	•T	•T	•T	•T
...mographs, homonyms, and homophones				•	•T	•T	•T	•T
...ltiple-meaning words			•	•	•T	•T	•T	•T
...ated words and derivations					•	•	•	•
...alogies						•		•
...nnotation/denotation						•	•	•
...urative language and idioms			•	•	•	•	•	•
...scriptive words (location, size, color, shape, number, ideas, feelings)	•	•	•	•	•	•	•	•
...h-utility words (shapes, colors, question words, position/directional words, and so on)	•	•	•	•				
...e and order words	•	•	•	•	•	•	•	•
...nsition words						•	•	•
...rd origins: Etymologies/word histories; words from other languages, regions, or cultures						•	•	•
...ortened forms: abbreviations, acronyms, clipped words			•	•	•	•	•T	

...xt Comprehension

	Pre-K	K	1	2	3	4	5	6
...omprehension Strategies								
...view the text and formulate questions	•	•	•	•	•	•	•	•
...t and monitor purpose for reading and listening	•	•	•	•	•	•	•	•
...tivate and use prior knowledge	•	•	•	•	•	•	•	•
...ke predictions	•	•	•	•	•	•	•	•
...nitor comprehension and use fix-up strategies to resolve difficulties in meaning: adjust reading rate, ...ead and read on, seek help from reference sources and/or other people, skim and scan, summarize, ...e text features			•	•	•	•	•	•
...eate and use graphic and semantic organizers		•	•	•	•	•	•	•
...swer questions (text explicit, text implicit, scriptal), including *who, what, when, where, why, what if, how*	•	•	•	•	•	•	•	•
...Look back in text for answers			•	•	•	•	•	•
...Answer test-like questions			•	•	•	•	•	•
...nerate clarifying questions, including *who, what, where, when, how, why,* and *what if*	•	•	•	•	•	•	•	•
...cognize text structure: story and informational (cause/effect, chronological, compare/contrast, ...scription, problem/solution, proposition/support)	•	•	•	•	•	•	•	•
...mmarize text		•	•	•	•	•	•	•
...Recall and retell stories	•	•	•	•	•	•	•	•
...dentify and retell important/main ideas (nonfiction)	•	•	•	•	•	•	•	•
...dentify and retell new information			•	•	•	•	•	•
...sualize; use mental imagery		•	•	•	•	•	•	•
...e strategies flexibly and in combination			•	•	•	•	•	•

Comprehension Skills

	Pre-K	K	1	2	3	4	5	6
Author's purpose			• T	• T	• T	• T	• T	•
Author's viewpoint/bias/perspective					•	•	•	•
Categorize and classify	•	•	•	•				
Cause and effect		•	• T	• T	• T	• T	• T	
Compare and contrast	•	•	• T	• T	• T	• T	• T	•
Details and facts		•	•	•	•	•	•	•
Draw conclusions		•	• T	• T	• T	• T	• T	
Fact and opinion				• T	• T	• T	• T	
Follow directions/steps in a process	•	•	•	•	•	•	•	
Generalize					• T	• T	• T	•
Graphic sources		•	•	•	•	• T	• T	
Main idea and supporting details		• T	• T	• T	• T	• T	• T	
Paraphrase				•	•	•	•	
Persuasive devices and propaganda				•	•	•	•	•
Realism/fantasy	•	•	• T	• T	• T	•	•	
Sequence of events	•	• T	• T	• T	• T	• T	• T	

Higher Order Thinking Skills

	Pre-K	K	1	2	3	4	5	6
Analyze				•	•	•	•	•
Describe and connect the essential ideas, arguments, and perspectives of a text				•	•	•	•	•
Draw inferences, conclusions, or generalizations, support them with textual evidence and prior knowledge	•			•	•	•	•	•
Evaluate and critique ideas and text				•	•	•	•	•
Hypothesize						•	•	•
Make judgments about ideas and text				•	•	•	•	•
Organize and synthesize ideas and information				•		•	•	•

Literary Analysis, Response, & Appreciation

	Pre-K	K	1	2	3	4	5	6
Genre and Its Characteristics								
Recognize characteristics of a variety of genre	•	•	•	•	•	•	•	
Distinguish fiction from nonfiction	•	•	•	•	•	•	•	
Identify characteristics of literary texts, including drama, fantasy, traditional tales			•	•	•	•	•	
Identify characteristics of nonfiction texts, including biography, interviews, newspaper articles			•	•	•	•	•	
Identify characteristics of poetry and song, including nursery rhymes, limericks, blank verse	•	•	•	•	•	•	•	
Literary Elements and Story Structure								
Character	•	• T	• T	• T	• T	• T	• T	
Recognize and describe traits, actions, feelings, and motives of characters			•	•	•	•	•	
Analyze characters' relationships, changes, and points of view			•	•	•	•	•	
Analyze characters' conflicts					•	•	•	
Plot and plot structure	•	• T	• T	• T	• T	• T	• T	
Beginning, middle, end	•	•	•	•	•			
Goal and outcome or problem and solution/resolution			•	•	•	•	•	
Rising action, climax, and falling action/denouement; setbacks						•	•	
Setting	•	• T	• T	• T	• T	• T		
Relate setting to problem/solution						•	•	
Explain ways setting contributes to mood						•	•	
Theme		•	• T	• T	•	•	•	
Use Literary Elements and Story Structure	•	•	•	•	•	•	•	
Analyze and evaluate author's use of setting, plot, character					•	•	•	
Identify similarities and differences of characters, events, and settings within or across selections/cultures		•	•	•	•	•	•	
Literary Devices								
Allusion								
Dialect						•	•	•
Dialogue and narration	•	•	•	•	•	•	•	
Exaggeration/hyperbole						•	•	•
Figurative language: idiom, jargon, metaphor, simile, slang			•	•	•	•	•	

• instructional opportunity   **T** tested in standardized test fo

	Pre-K	K	1	2	3	4	5	6
hback						•	•	•
shadowing							•	•
nal and informal language				•	•	•	•	•
nor						•	•	•
gery and sensory words				•	•	•	•	•
•d				•	•	•	•	•
sonification				•	•	•	•	•
t of view (first person, third person, omniscient)					•	•	•	•
s and word play				•	•	•	•	•
nd devices and poetic elements	•	•	•	•	•	•	•	•
literation, assonance, onomatopoeia	•	•	•	•	•	•	•	•
ayme, rhythm, repetition, and cadence	•	•		•	•	•	•	•
ord choice				•	•	•	•	•
bolism				•	•	•	•	•
e							•	•

thor's and Illustrator's Craft

	Pre-K	K	1	2	3	4	5	6
inguish the roles of author and illustrator	•	•	•	•				
ognize/analyze author's and illustrator's craft or style			•	•	•	•	•	•

erary Response

	Pre-K	K	1	2	3	4	5	6
ollect, talk, and write about books	•	•	•	•	•	•	•	•
ect on reading and respond (through talk, movement, art, and so on)	•	•	•	•	•	•	•	•
sk and answer questions about text	•	•	•	•	•	•	•	•
rite about what is read	•	•	•	•	•	•	•	•
se evidence from the text to support opinions, interpretations, or conclusions		•	•	•	•	•	•	•
upport ideas through reference to other texts and personal knowledge				•	•	•	•	•
cate materials on related topic, theme, or idea				•	•	•	•	•
enerate alternative endings to plots and identify the reason for, and the impact of, the alternatives	•	•	•	•	•	•	•	•
chesize and extend the literary experience through creative responses	•	•	•	•	•	•	•	•
e connections: text to self, text to text, text to world	•	•	•	•	•	•	•	•
uate and critique the quality of the literary experience				•	•	•	•	•
r observations, react, speculate in response to text				•	•	•	•	•

erary Appreciation/Motivation

	Pre-K	K	1	2	3	4	5	6
w an interest in books and reading; engage voluntarily in social interaction about books	•	•	•	•	•	•	•	•
ose text by drawing on personal interests, relying on knowledge of authors and genres, estimating text culty, and using recommendations of others	•	•	•	•	•	•	•	•
d a variety of grade-level appropriate narrative and expository texts		•	•	•	•	•	•	•
d from a wide variety of genres for a variety of purposes	•	•	•	•	•	•	•	•
d independently			•	•	•	•	•	•
ablish familiarity with a topic			•	•	•	•	•	•

ltural Awareness

	Pre-K	K	1	2	3	4	5	6
elop attitudes and abilities to interact with diverse groups and cultures	•	•	•	•	•	•	•	•
nect experiences and ideas with those from a variety of languages, cultures, customs, perspectives	•	•	•	•	•	•	•	•
erstand how attitudes and values in a culture or during a period in time affect the writing from that ure or time period						•	•	•
pare language and oral traditions (family stories) that reflect customs, regions, and cultures		•	•	•	•	•	•	•
ognize themes that cross cultures and bind them together in their common humanness						•	•	•

nguage Arts

ting	Pre-K	K	1	2	3	4	5	6
ncepts of Print for Writing								
elop gross and fine motor skills and hand/eye coordination	•	•	•					
t own name and other important words	•	•	•					
e using pictures, some letters, and transitional spelling to convey meaning	•	•	•					
ate messages or stories for others to write	•	•	•					

	Pre-K	K	1	2	3	4	5	6
Create own written texts for others to read; write left to right on a line and top to bottom on a page	•	•	•					
Participate in shared and interactive writing	•	•	•					

Traits of Writing

Focus/Ideas

	Pre-K	K	1	2	3	4	5	6
Maintain focus and sharpen ideas		•	•	•	•	•	•	
Use sensory details and concrete examples; elaborate		•	•	•	•	•	•	
Delete extraneous information			•	•	•	•	•	
Rearrange words and sentences to improve meaning and focus				•	•	•	•	
Use strategies, such as tone, style, consistent point of view, to achieve a sense of completeness						•	•	

Organization/Paragraphs

	Pre-K	K	1	2	3	4	5	6
Use graphic organizers to group ideas		•	•	•	•	•	•	
Write coherent paragraphs that develop a central idea			•	•	•	•	•	
Use transitions to connect sentences and paragraphs			•	•	•	•	•	
Select an organizational structure based on purpose, audience, length						•	•	
Organize ideas in a logical progression, such as chronological order or by order of importance		•	•	•	•	•	•	
Write introductory, supporting, and concluding paragraphs					•	•	•	
Write a multi-paragraph paper				•	•	•	•	

Support/Voice

	Pre-K	K	1	2	3	4	5	6
Develop personal, identifiable voice and an individual tone/style			•	•	•	•	•	
Maintain consistent voice and point of view						•	•	
Use voice appropriate to audience, message, and purpose						•	•	

Support/Word Choice

	Pre-K	K	1	2	3	4	5	6
Use clear, precise, appropriate language		•	•	•	•	•	•	
Use figurative language and vivid words			•	•	•	•	•	
Select effective vocabulary using word walls, dictionary, or thesaurus		•	•	•	•	•	•	

Support/Sentences

	Pre-K	K	1	2	3	4	5	6
Combine, elaborate, and vary sentences		•	•	•	•	•	•	
Write topic sentence, supporting sentences with facts and details, and concluding sentence			•	•	•	•	•	
Use correct word order			•	•	•	•	•	
Use parallel structure in a sentence						•	•	

Conventions

	Pre-K	K	1	2	3	4	5	6
Use correct spelling and grammar; capitalize and punctuate correctly		•	•	•	•	•	•	
Correct sentence fragments and run-ons				•	•	•	•	
Use correct paragraph indention			•	•	•	•	•	

The Writing Process

	Pre-K	K	1	2	3	4	5	6
Prewrite using various strategies	•	•	•	•	•	•	•	
Develop first drafts of single- and multiple-paragraph compositions		•	•	•	•	•	•	
Revise drafts for varied purposes, including to clarify and to achieve purpose, sense of audience, precise word choice, vivid images, and elaboration		•	•	•	•	•	•	
Edit and proofread for correct spelling, grammar, usage, and mechanics		•	•	•	•	•	•	
Publish own work	•	•	•	•	•	•	•	

Types of Writing

	Pre-K	K	1	2	3	4	5	6
Narrative writing (such as personal narratives, stories, biographies, autobiographies)	•	•	• T	• T	• T	• T	• T	•
Expository writing (such as essays, directions, explanations, news stories, research reports, summaries)		•	• T	• T	• T	• T	• T	•
Descriptive writing (such as labels, captions, lists, plays, poems, response logs, songs)	•	•	• T	• T	• T	• T	• T	•
Persuasive writing (such as ads, editorials, essays, letters to the editor, opinions, posters)		•	• T	• T	• T	• T	• T	•

Writing Habits and Practices

	Pre-K	K	1	2	3	4	5	6
Write on a daily basis	•	•	•	•	•	•	•	
Use writing as a tool for learning and self-discovery					•	•	•	
Write independently for extended periods of time			•	•	•	•	•	

ENGLISH LANGUAGE CONVENTIONS in WRITING and SPEAKING

	Pre-K	K	1	2	3	4	5	6

Grammar and Usage in Speaking and Writing

Sentences

	Pre-K	K	1	2	3	4	5	6
Types (declarative, interrogative, exclamatory, imperative)	•	•	• T	• T	• T	• T	• T	
Structure (simple, compound, complex, compound-complex)	•	•	•	•	•	• T	• T	

• instructional opportunity   **T** tested in standardized test fo

	Pre-K	K	1	2	3	4	5	6
...arts (subjects/predicates: complete, simple, compound; phrases; clauses)				• T	•	• T	• T	• T
...agments and run-on sentences		•	•	•	•	•	•	•
...ombine sentences, elaborate			•	•	•	•	•	•
...ts of speech: nouns, verbs and verb tenses, adjectives, adverbs, pronouns and antecedents, ...junctions, prepositions, interjections		•	• T	• T	• T	• T	• T	• T
...ge								
...ubject-verb agreement		•	• T	•	•	• T	• T	• T
...ronoun agreement/referents			• T	•	•	• T	• T	• T
...isplaced modifiers						•	• T	• T
...isused words					•	•	•	• T
...egatives; avoid double negatives					•	•	•	•

...echanics in Writing

	Pre-K	K	1	2	3	4	5	6
...italization (first word in sentence, proper nouns and adjectives, pronoun *I*, titles, and so on)	•	•	• T	• T	• T	• T	• T	• T
...ctuation (apostrophe, comma, period, question mark, exclamation mark, quotation marks, and so on)		•	• T	• T	• T	• T	• T	• T

...elling

	Pre-K	K	1	2	3	4	5	6
...ll independently by using pre-phonetic knowledge, knowledge of letter names, sound-letter knowledge	•	•	•	•	•	•	•	•
...sound-letter knowledge to spell	•	•	•	•	•	•	•	•
...onsonants: single, double, blends, digraphs, silent letters, and unusual consonant spellings		•	•	•	•	•	•	•
...owels: short, long, *r*-controlled, digraphs, diphthongs, less common vowel patterns, schwa		•	•	•	•	•	•	•
...knowledge of word structure to spell		•	•	•	•	•	•	•
...ase words and affixes (inflections, prefixes, suffixes), possessives, contractions and compound words		•	•	•	•	•	•	•
...reek and Latin roots, syllable patterns, multisyllabic words			•	•	•	•	•	•
...ll high-frequency, irregular words		•	•	•	•	•	•	•
...ll frequently misspelled words correctly, including homophones or homonyms		•	•	•	•	•	•	•
...meaning relationships to spell					•	•	•	•

...ndwriting

	Pre-K	K	1	2	3	4	5	6
...n increasing control of penmanship, including pencil grip, paper position, posture, stroke	•	•	•	•				
...e legibly, with control over letter size and form; letter slant; and letter, word, and sentence spacing		•	•	•	•	•	•	•
...e lowercase and capital letters	•	•	•	•				
...anuscript	•	•	•	•	•	•	•	•
...ursive				•	•	•	•	•
...e numerals	•	•	•					

...stening and Speaking

	Pre-K	K	1	2	3	4	5	6

...tening Skills and Strategies

	Pre-K	K	1	2	3	4	5	6
...en to a variety of presentations attentively and politely	•	•	•	•	•	•	•	•
...-monitor comprehension while listening, using a variety of skills and strategies	•	•	•	•	•	•	•	•
...en for a purpose								
...or enjoyment and appreciation	•	•	•	•	•	•	•	•
...o expand vocabulary and concepts	•	•	•	•	•	•	•	•
...o obtain information and ideas	•	•	•	•	•	•	•	•
...o follow oral directions	•	•	•	•	•	•	•	•
...o answer questions and solve problems	•	•	•	•	•	•	•	•
...o participate in group discussions	•	•	•	•	•	•	•	•
...o identify and analyze the musical elements of literary language	•	•	•	•	•	•	•	•
...o gain knowledge of one's own culture, the culture of others, and the common elements of cultures	•	•	•	•	•	•	•	•
...ognize formal and informal language			•	•	•	•	•	•
...en critically to distinguish fact from opinion and to analyze and evaluate ideas, information, experiences		•		•	•	•	•	•
...luate a speaker's delivery				•	•	•	•	•
...rpret a speaker's purpose, perspective, persuasive techniques, verbal and nonverbal messages, and ...of rhetorical devices						•	•	•

...eaking Skills and Strategies

	Pre-K	K	1	2	3	4	5	6
...ak clearly, accurately, and fluently, using appropriate delivery for a variety of audiences, and purposes	•	•	•	•	•	•	•	•
...e proper intonation, volume, pitch, modulation, and phrasing		•	•	•	•	•	•	•
...ak with a command of standard English conventions	•	•	•	•	•	•	•	•
...e appropriate language for formal and informal settings	•	•	•	•	•	•	•	•

	Pre-K	K	1	2	3	4	5
Speak for a purpose							
To ask and answer questions	•	•	•	•	•	•	•
To give directions and instructions	•	•	•	•	•	•	•
To retell, paraphrase, or explain information		•	•	•	•	•	•
To communicate needs and share ideas and experiences	•	•	•	•	•	•	•
To participate in conversations and discussions	•	•	•	•	•	•	•
To express an opinion	•	•	•		•	•	•
To deliver dramatic recitations, interpretations, or performances	•	•	•	•	•	•	•
To deliver presentations or oral reports (narrative, descriptive, persuasive, and informational)	•	•	•	•	•	•	•
Stay on topic	•	•	•		•	•	•
Use appropriate verbal and nonverbal elements (such as facial expression, gestures, eye contact, posture)	•	•	•	•	•		•
Identify and/or demonstrate methods to manage or overcome communication anxiety						•	•

Viewing/Media	Pre-K	K	1	2	3	4	5
Interact with and respond to a variety of print and non-print media for a range of purposes	•	•	•	•	•	•	•
Compare and contrast print, visual, and electronic media					•	•	•
Analyze and evaluate media			•	•	•	•	•
Recognize purpose, bias, propaganda, and persuasive techniques in media messages			•	•	•	•	•

Research and Study Skills

Understand and Use Graphic Sources	Pre-K	K	1	2	3	4	5	6
Advertisement			•	•	•	•	•	
Chart/table	•	•	•	•	•	•	•	
Diagram/scale drawing				•	•	•	•	
Graph (bar, circle, line, picture)			•		•	•	•	
Illustration, photograph, caption, label	•	•	•	•	•	•	•	
Map/globe	•	•	•	•	•	•	•	
Order form/application						•	•	
Poster/announcement	•	•	•	•	•	•	•	
Schedule						•	•	
Sign	•	•	•	•		•		
Time line			•	•	•	•	•	

Understand and Use Reference Sources	Pre-K	K	1	2	3	4	5	6
Know and use parts of a book to locate information	•	•	•	•	•	•	•	
Use alphabetical order			•	•	•	•		
Understand purpose, structure, and organization of reference sources (print, electronic, media, Internet)	•	•	•	•	•	•	•	
Almanac						•	•	
Atlas		•		•	•	•	•	
Card catalog/library database				•	•	•	•	
Dictionary/glossary		•	•	•	• T	• T	• T	•
Encyclopedia			•	•	•	•	•	
Magazine/periodical				•	•	•	•	
Newspaper and newsletter			•	•	•	•	•	
Readers' Guide to Periodical Literature						•	•	
Technology (computer and non-computer electronic media)		•	•	•	•	•	•	
Thesaurus				•	•	•	•	

Study Skills and Strategies	Pre-K	K	1	2	3	4	5	6
Adjust reading rate			•	•	•	•	•	
Clarify directions	•	•	•	•	•	•	•	
Outline				•	•	•	•	
Skim and scan			•	•	•	•	•	
SQP3R						•	•	
Summarize		•	•	•	•	•	•	
Take notes, paraphrase, and synthesize			•	•	•	•	•	
Use graphic and semantic organizers to organize information		•	•	•	•	•	•	

• instructional opportunity   **T** tested in standardized test fo

st-Taking Skills and Strategies	Pre-K	K	1	2	3	4	5	6
erstand the question, the vocabulary of tests, and key words			•	•	•	•	•	•
wer the question; use information from the text (stated or inferred)		•	•	•	•	•	•	•
e across texts				•	•	•	•	•
mplete the sentence				•	•	•	•	•

chnology/New Literacies	Pre-K	K	1	2	3	4	5	6
n-Computer Electronic Media								
o tapes/CDs, video tapes/DVDs	•	•	•	•	•	•	•	
, television, and radio		•	•	•	•	•	•	•
mputer Programs and Services: Basic Operations and Concepts								
accurate computer terminology	•	•	•	•	•	•	•	•
ate, name, locate, open, save, delete, and organize files		•	•	•	•	•	•	•
input and output devices (such as mouse, keyboard, monitor, printer, touch screen)	•	•	•	•	•	•	•	•
basic keyboarding skills		•	•	•	•			
ponsible Use of Technology Systems and Software								
k cooperatively and collaboratively with others; follow acceptable use policies	•	•	•	•	•	•	•	•
ognize hazards of Internet searches		•	•	•	•	•	•	•
pect intellectual property					•	•	•	•
ormation and Communication Technologies: Information Acquisition								
electronic web (non-linear) navigation, online resources, databases, keyword searches			•	•	•	•	•	•
visual and non-textual features of online resources	•	•	•	•	•	•	•	•
rnet inquiry			•	•	•	•	•	•
entify questions			•	•	•	•	•	•
cate, select, and collect information			•	•	•	•	•	•
alyze information			•	•	•	•	•	•
Evaluate electronic information sources for accuracy, relevance, bias				•	•	•	•	•
Understand bias/subjectivity of electronic content (about this site, author search, date created)					•	•	•	•
nthesize information					•	•	•	•
mmunicate findings				•	•	•	•	•
fix-up strategies (such as clicking *Back, Forward,* or *Undo;* redoing a search; trimming the URL)			•	•	•	•	•	•
mmunication								
aborate, publish, present, and interact with others		•	•	•	•	•	•	•
online resources (e-mail, bulletin boards, newsgroups)			•	•	•	•	•	•
a variety of multimedia formats			•	•	•	•	•	•
blem Solving								
ect the appropriate software for the task	•	•	•	•	•	•	•	•
technology resources for solving problems and making informed decisions			•	•	•	•	•	•
ermine when technology is useful				•	•	•	•	•

e Research Process	Pre-K	K	1	2	3	4	5	6
ose and narrow the topic; frame and revise questions for inquiry		•	•	•	•	•	•	•
ose and evaluate appropriate reference sources				•	•	•	•	•
ate and collect information	•	•	•	•	•	•	•	•
e notes/record findings				•	•	•	•	•
bine and compare information				•	•	•	•	•
uate, interpret, and draw conclusions about key information		•	•	•	•	•	•	•
marize information		•	•	•	•	•	•	•
e an outline				•	•	•	•	•
anize content systematically		•	•	•	•	•	•	•
municate information		•	•	•	•	•	•	•
rite and present a report				•	•	•	•	•
Include citations						•	•	•
Respect intellectual property/plagiarism						•	•	•
elect and organize visual aids		•	•	•	•	•	•	•

ACKNOWLEDGMENTS

Teacher's Edition

Text

KWL Strategy: The KWL Interactive Reading Strategy was developed and is used by permission of Donna Ogle, National-Louis University, Evanston, Illinois, co-author of *Reading Today and Tomorrow*, Holt, Rinehart & Winston Publishers, 1988. (See also *The Reading Teacher*, February 1986, pp. 564–570.)

Page 392m: From "At the Water's Edge" from *The Black Stallion* by Walter Farley. © 1941 by Walter Farley. Copyright renewed 1969 by Walter Farley. Used by permission of Random House Children's Books, a division of Random House, Inc.

Page 412m: Excerpt from *Wilma Unlimited: How Wilma Rudolph Became the World's Fastest Woman*. Text © 1996 by Kathleen Krull. Reprinted by permission of Harcourt, Inc.

Page 436m: Text excerpt from "Reptile Superheroes" from *The Snake Scientist* by Cy Montgomery. Text © 1999 by Cy Montgomery. Reprinted by permission of Houghton Mifflin Company. All rights reserved.

Page 458m: From "Count on Fiona" from *Only Fiona* by Beverly Keller. Reprinted by permission of Beverly Keller.

Page 484m: From "Jerry Takes Off" from *The Winning Stroke* by Matt Christopher. © 1994 by Matt Christopher (Text); © 1994 by Karen Lidbeck (Illustration). Used by permission of Little, Brown and Co., Inc.

Artists

Greg Newbold: cover, page i

Photographs

Every effort has been made to secure permission and provide appropriate credit for photographic material. The publisher deeply regrets any omission and pledges to correct errors called to its attention in subsequent editions.

Unless otherwise acknowledged, all photographs are the property of Scott Foresman, a division of Pearson Education.

Photo locators denoted as follows: Top (T), Center (C), Bottom (B), Left (L), Right (R), Background (Bkgd)

18M Getty Images;

42M (Bkgd) (TR) Getty Images; (TC) Hemera Technologies;

87L (BL) ©Royalty-Free/Corbis, (BR) Comstock Images/Getty Images;

88M (T) Getty Images; (BR) Digital Vision;

111L Brand X Pictures/Getty Images;

112M Brand X Pictures;

137N Getty Images;

146M Getty Images;

148J NASA;

160J Digital Wisdom, Inc.;

220M Brand X Pictures;

223N Getty Images;

228I Getty Images;

240J Getty Images;

288M Getty Images;

315L Getty Images;

316M Getty Images;

322M Getty Images;

346M Getty Images;

388K Brand X Pictures;

392M Getty Images;

408M Getty Images;

412M (T) ©Comstock Inc, (Bkgd) Getty Images;

430M Getty Images;

436M ©Dover Publications;

456M Getty Images;

457L Getty Images;

476K Getty Images;

484M ©Image Source Limited;

512M Getty Images;

535L ©Royalty-Free/Corbis;

536M Hemera Technologies;

560M Getty Images;

582M Getty Images;

600M ©Dover Publications;

634M Brand X Pictures;

643M (TC) Brand X Pictures, (Bkgd) Getty Images;

654M Getty Images;

674M ©Dover Publications;

700M (C) ©Dover Publications; (Bkgd) Getty Images;

724M ©Dover Publications;

762M Brand X Pictures.

TEACHER NOTES

TEACHER NOTES